angles on applied psychology

KT-380-086

WITHDRAWN
FROM
STOCKPORT COLLEGE
LEARNING CENTRE

130833

dedications

To my mum and dad, thanks for your unceasing support,
with love   *JR*

To Sam and Clare   MJ

angles on applied psychology

Julia Russell   Matt Jarvis

Text © Julia Russell and Matt Jarvis 2003
Original illustrations © Nelson Thornes Ltd 2003

The right of Julia Russell and Matt Jarvis to be identified as authors of this work has
been asserted by them in accordance with the Copyright, Designs and Patents Act
1988.

All rights reserved. No part of this publication may be reproduced or transmitted in
any form or by any means, electronic or mechanical, including photocopy, recording
or any information storage and retrieval system, without permission in writing from the
publisher or under licence from the Copyright Licensing Agency Limited, of Saffron House,
6-10 Kirby Street, London, EC1N 8TS

Any person who commits any unauthorised act in relation to this publication may be
liable to criminal prosecution and civil claims for damages.

Published in 2003 by:
Nelson Thornes Ltd
Delta Place
27 Bath Road
CHELTENHAM
GL53 7TH
United Kingdom

07 / 10 9 8 7 6 5 4

STOCKPORT COLLEGE
LIBRARY+

I976235 | 16/5/08
11580
4WK | 150
130833 | RUS

A catalogue record for this book is available from the British Library

ISBN 978 0 7487 7259 9

Page make-up by Northern Phototypesetting Co. Ltd.

Printed and bound in Slovenia by Korotan-Ljubljana

contents

Child psychology

Health psychology

Environmental psychology

acknowledgements

We would like to thank everyone who has worked with us on this book, including Rick, Eve and Helen at Nelson Thornes, Carol Franklin and, of course, those authors who have contributed to the Angles series, Craig, Di and Dave – we couldn't have done it without you!

JR/MJ

I'd like to express my particular gratitude to Craig whose determined search for up-to-date research and imagination on activities has helped me through some of the difficult bits! Thanks.

JR

The authors and publishers are grateful to the following for permission to reproduce material:

American Psychiatric Association pp 3, 4, 58, 71, 72, 81, 82; Company magazine pp. 381, 406; CNN pp. 106, 118; Daily Express pp. 249, 291; Daily Telegraph pp. 190, 266; Eve magazine p. 366; Friends of the Earth p. 370; The Guardian pp. 6, 14, 56, 115, 130, 298; The Independent pp. 114, 202, 244, 307, 383; New York Times p. 112; News of the World p. 19; The Observer pp. 38, 215, 265, 301; Sunday Telegraph p. 148; Sunday Times pp. 122, 180; University of Leicester p. 368.

Every effort has been made to contact copyright holders and we apologise if any have been overlooked. Should copyright have been unwittingly infringed in this book, the owners should contact the publishers, who will make corrections at reprint.

Photo credits:
The Advertising Archive p. 412; Alan Gibson & The Wing Chun Federation p. 183; Andes Press Agency pp. 310, 331; Art Directors & Trip Photo Library p. 317; Associated Press p. 83; British Psychological Society p. 200; Capilano Suspension Bridge and Park p. 413; Corbis pp. 20, 53, 107, 274, 284, 298, 351, 381, 435; Corel 423 (NT) pp. 169, 191; Corel (NT) p. 46; Empics pp. 175, 180, 190; Family Life Picture Library/Angela Frampton p. 232; Family Planning Association p. 299; Format Photographers p. 68; Gasp p. 300; Getty p. 189; Impact Photos p. 161; John Birdsall Photography p. 380; John Walmsley p. 328; Julia Russell pp. 330, 332; Kobal Collection pp. 139, 181, 374; Oscar Newman/Defensible Space p. 323; Photodisc 71 (NT) p. 175; Photofusion p. 141; Photofusion/Mark Campbell p. 352; Photofusion/Ray Roberts p. 361; Press Association p. 121; Robert Harding Picture Library p. 8; Rex Photo Library pp. 38; Rex Features/Laurence Kiely p. 221; Sally & Richard Greenhill Photo Library p. 84; Science and Society Picture Library pp. 39, 51; Science Photo Library p. 23; Science Photo Library/David Gifford p. 12; Terrence Higgins Trust p. 303; The Wellcome Foundation p. 18.

introduction

Psychology, as the study of people's thinking and behaviour, has many useful applications to everyday life. Some of these, such as ways to reduce stress, attempt to help us to overcome everyday hurdles that can become problematic. Others, such as understanding mental disorders, aim to help individuals with specific problems. In each area of applied psychology that we explore, we will be looking at the background to the topics, up-to-date research and theories that help us to understand the key issues. These chapters will prepare you for the applied psychology questions in unit 4 and unit 5 examinations for Edexcel A2. The chapters on research methods will complete the knowledge you will need for unit 5 part b. In the last section of this book we consider how all the ideas that you have met at AS and A2 can help you to answer questions on the Edexcel synoptic examination paper, unit 6.

If you used *Angles on Psychology* at AS, you will be familiar with many of the features you will find in *Angles on Applied Psychology*. The *interactive angles* and *media watch* boxes will help you to consolidate your learning and will provide you with practice at source-based examination style questions. Remember that, compared to AS, your thinking and writing at A2 needs to be more evaluative. The strengths and criticisms identified in the *for and against* boxes are summaries, you will need to use the material in each chapter to support your arguments. The *interactive angles* and *media watch* questions will help you with this too, as will the *what do you know* sections which have examination style questions for you to use for practice. You will also find a glossary at the back to help you with the new ideas you will meet in each chapter.

1 Defining and classifying psychological abnormality

what's ahead?

In this chapter we look at the various ways in which we can define human behaviour, emotion and thinking as 'abnormal' and examine systems by which we can classify the range of psychological abnormalities into categories of mental disorder. We look in detail at the Diagnostic & Statistical Manual of Mental Disorder, produced by the American Psychiatric Association. We consider research into how reliable and valid this system is, and what the implications are of receiving a psychiatric diagnosis. Finally, we examine a range of cultural issues in the classification and diagnosis of mental disorder, including the importance of different cultural attitudes to mental disorder and the existence of race discrimination in the diagnostic process.

Who is abnormal?

Perhaps the most fundamental question we can consider in a discussion of clinical psychology is what precisely makes us think of a particular pattern of thinking, behaviour or emotion as abnormal. We can look here at three particularly important ways by which we might classify people as abnormal. As we shall see, none of these consistently distinguishes psychologically 'normal' and 'abnormal' people, although all are used in the diagnostic process.

Statistically unusual people

The most literal way of defining something as abnormal is according to how often it occurs. According to this definition anything that occurs relatively rarely can be thought of as 'abnormal'. This approach is most useful when dealing with human characteristics that can be reliably measured, for example, intelligence, anxiety and depression. We know that in any measurable human characteristic, the majority of people's scores will cluster around the average, and that as we move away from this average fewer and fewer people will attain that score. This is called the *normal distribution*. We can look at the normal distribution of IQ (intelligence quotient) in figure 1.1.

The average IQ according to tests on a cross-section of the population is set at 100. The 85 and 115 scores are set as those between which 65 per cent of people will fall, and the 70 and 130 scores are set as those between which 95 per cent of people will fall. If someone scores below 70 they fall in the bottom 2.5 per cent of the population. This means that they meet one of the three criteria for diagnosis of *mental retardation* (the other two being onset of the low IQ before 18 years of age and the inability of the individual to meet the standards of their cultural group in communication, self-care, social skills, work, health or safety).

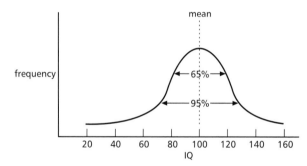

Figure 1.1 The normal distribution of IQ scores

The limitations of the statistical infrequency approach to defining atypicality are as obvious as they are serious. IQ scores of 130+ are just as infrequent as those of below 70, but we wouldn't consider calling someone abnormal or giving them a diagnosis just because they were very bright! Neither would there be any advantage to giving someone a diagnosis of retardation based on their IQ score if they were living a happy and fulfilled life. Statistical infrequency on its own is thus not a sufficient criterion for defining behaviour as abnormal, although statistical measures, for example, of IQ, depression or anxiety may form part of the process of diagnosis.

People whose behaviour deviates from social norms

Most of us tend to be at least a little wary of those whose behaviour does not conform to social norms. In some cases we might choose to define behaviour as abnormal just because it offends our sense of what is 'normal' or 'right' or 'moral'. There are behaviours that virtually all of us would agree to be abnormal on moral grounds, and this is reflected in the diagnosis of *anti-social personality disorder*, commonly called *psychopathy*. The psychopath is impulsive, aggressive and irresponsible. According to the DSM-IV-TR, one important symptom of anti-social personality disorder is 'failure to conform to social norms with respect to lawful behaviours as indicated by repeatedly performing acts that are grounds for arrest'.

Although we would generally agree that psychopaths are abnormal on the basis that they defy what we think of as important social norms, too much reliance on deviation from norms to define someone as abnormal can lead to the abuse of people's rights. Some particularly 'tragicomic' examples of mental disorders were defined purely according to social convention in the nineteenth century (Gomm, 1996; Masson, 1992). Examples are shown in table 1.1.

Table 1.1 Examples of socially constructed nineteenth-century 'mental disorders'

Classification	Symptoms
Drapetomania	Slaves experienced an irrational desire to run away
Nymphomania	Middle class women were sexually attracted to working class men
Moral insanity	Women who inherited money spent it on themselves rather than male relatives

Looking at the three examples given in table 1.1 it is clear that one reason for defining behaviour as abnormal (and hence unacceptable) is to maintain social control over a group (such as women or a minority ethnic group). Thus, by being able to get women diagnosed with nymphomania or moral insanity (with the co-operation of male doctors), nineteenth-century men were able strictly to control women's economic and sexual lives, in line with their own interests.

The classifications of drapetomania, nymphomania and moral insanity all appear quite ludicrous nowadays – *but only because social conventions have changed.* Whenever we define someone as abnormal because they breach a social norm, we place restrictions on people's personal freedom. As well as raising these important ethical issues, defining atypicality by social deviation has important practical limitations. Social norms are culturally specific, thus they can differ significantly from one generation to the next, and between different ethnic, regional and socio-economic groups. Imagine the response of people in Britain as recently as the early twentieth century to the idea of a modern rave or punk concert as entertainment, and you start to see just how much social conventions change from one generation to another.

Figure 1.2 Cultural attitudes to what is normal change over time

People whose behaviour is maladaptive or dangerous

The terms *adaptive* and *maladaptive* come originally from evolutionary biology and refer to behaviours and characteristics that increase and decrease respectively the chances of an individual surviving or reproducing. One way of defining a person as abnormal is when their behaviour, thinking or emotional state reduces their chances of survival. Using the term 'maladaptive' a little more broadly, we can also apply it to people whose behaviour, thinking or emotional state prevents them living a happy, fulfilling life. This can include any symptom that prevents people holding down a job or having successful relationships.

Maladaptiveness in this broader sense forms an important part of diagnosis. For example, diagnosis of depression, anxiety disorders and schizophrenia usually requires that the everyday life of the individual be significantly affected by their symptoms. This is important as it gives us a relatively fair and objective way of identifying the point at which a person's individual characteristics become abnormal – whenever they start to interfere with their life. There may be cases, however, when someone's behaviour may appear maladaptive to others, but is seen by the individual in terms of expressing themselves or making a political statement. People who take part in high-risk sports or political protest are technically behaving maladaptively as they are decreasing their chances of survival. However, as a society we generally do not class these behaviours as abnormal, although we may think of them as irresponsible. If we were to class any behaviour that carried personal risk as abnormal we would significantly interfere with people's civil liberties. Thus boxing remains legal, although it is against the opinion of most doctors.

Maladaptiveness in the narrower sense of decreasing one's chances of survival becomes especially important when we start to consider the issue of whether to force someone to accept treatment against their will. Under the 1983 Mental Health Act, people can only be detained against their will for a mental health problem when their condition presents a significant risk to their own safety or that of others.

Conclusions: what is abnormality?

Although all three criteria discussed above play a significant role in diagnosis of mental disorder, none of them on their own stand up very well as sufficient to define people's behaviour or experience as abnormal. In practice we use a mixture of criteria to decide who will benefit from being classified as abnormal; thus mental retardation, for example, is diagnosed when an individual's IQ is statistically unusually low **and** their behaviour is maladaptive.

interactive angles

Consider the three following case examples of potential abnormality. Match the case examples (1 to 3) to the criteria for defining them as abnormal (A to C).

1   A young woman cuts her arms following a family argument.

2   A psychologist is concerned about a schoolboy because his IQ is 64.

3   A man complaining about his late housing benefit gestures at staff with a stuffed lobster.

A   Deviation from social norms.
B   Maladaptive behaviour.
C   Statistically unusual.

Systems for the classification and diagnosis of abnormality

There are a number of systems by which we can classify abnormal patterns of thinking, behaviour and emotion into mental disorders. These systems not only classify abnormality into mental disorders but also give guidelines on how to diagnose them. The two most widely used systems of classification and diagnosis are the Diagnostic & Statistical Manual of Mental Disorder (DSM), produced by the American Psychiatric Association, and the International Classification of the Causes of Disease & Death (ICD), produced by the World Health Organisation. We can consider the DSM system in detail.

The DSM system

The American Psychiatric Association published the original DSM system in 1952. The current version of the DSM system is the fourth edition with *text revisions* (ie changes to the structure of the classification system rather than to the classifications themselves). The DSM-IV (ie the fourth edition) was published in 1994, and the DSM-IV-TR (the fourth edition with text revisions) was published in 2000. DSM-IV contains over two hundred distinct mental disorders. Each successive version of the DSM has tightened up the criteria for diagnosing disorders. Newer versions, for example, tend to specify how long symptoms are required to last for diagnosis. There have also been some changes in the nature of disorders identified by the DSM in line with changing social norms. Prior to the publication of DSM-III in 1980, homosexuality was classified as a mental disorder, but this has now been dropped. New disorders have also been identified since the earlier versions of DSM. For example, since DSM-III the category of eating disorders has included bulimia as well as anorexia and since DSM-IV it has included binge-eating disorder. The major categories of the DSM are shown in box 1.1.

Clinical syndromes:
1   Disorders usually first diagnosed in infancy, childhood, or adolescence
2   Delirium, dementia, amnestic and other cognitive disorders
3   Substance-related disorders
4   Schizophrenia and other psychotic disorders
5   Mood disorders
6   Anxiety disorders
7   Somatoform disorders
8   Factitious disorder
9   Dissociative disorders
10 Sexual and gender identity disorders
11 Eating disorders
12 Sleep disorders
13 Impulse control disorders not elsewhere classified
14 Adjustment disorders

Box 1.1 The major categories of DSM-IV-TR

Since the publication of DSM-III-R in 1987, diagnosis takes place on five different bases or *axes*. This approach is called *multiaxial diagnosis*. Although clinicians are not obliged to use all five axes when making a diagnosis, it is widely agreed that it is helpful to do so. The five axes of DSM-IV-TR are shown in box 1.2.

Axis I: **clinical disorder**; the disorder or disorders from which the patient is suffering. In addition, other circumstances that may require intervention are noted here, including stress-related physical symptoms and a history of sexual abuse.

Axis II: **personality disorders and retardation**; because these chronic conditions often go alongside axis I disorders they are looked at separately.

Axis III: **general medical conditions**; medical problems that are of relevance to the condition or its treatment.

Axis IV: **Psychosocial and environmental problems**; life problems that influence the psychological well-being of the individual, eg homelessness, unemployment.

Axis V: **Global assessment of functioning (GAF)**; a score from 0–100 given to the individual to classify their overall functioning.

Box 1.2 The five axes of the DSM-IV-TR

Davison and Neale (1994) have provided a case example of a multiaxial diagnosis. A 45-year-old American construction worker named Alex was assessed, having been arrested for sexually assaulting a woman when drunk. He had been almost continually drunk since his daughter had been killed in an accident four years before, and he was now suffering liver damage. On investigation it turned out that Alex had a history of gang and domestic violence. He showed no concern or remorse. The multiaxial diagnosis was as follows:

- Axis I: alcohol dependence;
- Axis II: antisocial personality disorder;
- Axis III: liver damage;
- Axis IV: arrest, death of child;
- Axis V: 42.

You can see the advantages of multiaxial diagnosis from this case. Alex's current clinical condition of alcohol dependency is not sufficient to explain the complexity of his situation. From his history of violence and lack of remorse or concern at his current situation it appears that Alex also suffers from a long-standing personality problem. It is important to be aware of his liver damage as this may influence what treatments are safe for him. We would certainly also wish to take account of the death of Alex's daughter in planning any psychological treatment. The GAF score gives an idea of how urgent is Alex's need for treatment.

Evaluation of diagnostic systems

For a system like DSM to work effectively it must satisfy two important criteria, reliability and validity. A system is *reliable* if those using it consistently make the same diagnoses. It is *valid* if the diagnoses identify something 'real' in the sense of being a distinct condition that has different symptoms from other conditions and that is likely to progress in a certain way and respond to one treatment rather than another.

Reliability

The major way of assessing reliability of psychiatric diagnosis is by assessing the agreement with which different clinicians diagnose conditions in the same patients (this is known as *inter-rater reliability*). Studies of inter-rater reliability reveal that some diagnostic categories are much more reliable than others, and that procedures are more reliable for some types of patient than others. A recent study by Nicholls et al (2000) shows that neither ICD-10 nor DSM-IV demonstrates good inter-rater reliability for the diagnosis of eating disorders in children. Eighty-one patients aged 7–16 years with some eating problem were classified using ICD-10, DSM-IV and a system developed especially for children by Great Ormond Street Hospital. Over 50 per cent of the children could not be diagnosed according to DSM criteria. Reliability was 0.64 (ie. 64 per cent agreement between raters), but this figure was inflated by the fact that most raters agreed that they couldn't make a diagnosis. Using ICD-10 criteria there was 0.36 reliability (36 per cent agreement between raters). The Great Ormond Street system emerged as far superior, having a reliability of 0.88 (88 per cent agreement between raters).

Validity

Judging the validity of a system like DSM or ICD is rather more complex than judging reliability. A classic study by Rosenhan (1973) demonstrated how diagnosis could have good reliability but poor validity, as doctors consistently but wrongly diagnosed pseudopatients whose symptoms were faked.

classic
research

situation affects clinical judgement

Rosenhan D.L. (1973) On being sane in insane places. *Science* **179: 250–8**

aim: Rosenhan was interested in how good diagnostic procedures were under DSM-II, specifically whether the diagnosis was really tied to the patient's symptoms or whether it is also affected by the environment in which the diagnosis takes place. The rationale for the procedure was that clinicians should be able to tell the difference between a patient suffering from a real mental disorder and a healthy 'pseudopatient' who, having reported a single symptom, then acts normally.

procedure: Rosenhan himself and seven volunteers, five of whom were doctors or psychologists (a total of three women and five men), arrived at a range of hospitals reporting a single symptom, hearing voices saying 'empty', 'hollow' and 'thud'. Once admitted they then acted the role of model patients, co-operating with staff and seeking to be released as soon as possible. They recorded the responses of doctors and nurses when they spoke to them.

findings: all eight pseudopatients were admitted to hospitals. The average stay was 19 days (the range being 7–52 days). In every case they were released with a diagnosis of schizophrenia in remission. In a number of the cases, real patients made comments to the effect that the pseudopatients had nothing wrong with them. However, in no case did doctors or nurses notice that there was nothing wrong with them. This is unsurprising given their lack of responsiveness to patients. In response to questions psychiatrists (71 per cent of occasions) and nurses (88 per cent of occasions) looked away and walked on without responding. Only on 4 per cent of occasions did psychiatrists stop to talk to the pseudopatients, and the figure was even lower (0.5 per cent) for nurses.

conclusions: the study revealed two major weaknesses in the psychiatric system of the time. First, the environment has a major impact on the process of diagnosis, and in the hospital environment staff could not tell the mentally disordered from the mentally healthy. Secondly, once labelled with a condition like schizophrenia, patients find it very difficult to escape the label and be judged as 'normal'.

It is important to remember that Rosenhan's study took place 20 years ago, and that diagnostic procedures have improved in response. There have been major changes since the DSM-II, under which Rosenhan and his participants were diagnosed. The study should thus not be seen as an indictment of the current mental health system. Remember as well that the study showed extremely good reliability for the diagnosis of schizophrenia (100 per cent agreement between psychiatrists seeing the same symptoms), and that in real life doctors are not normally confronted with people wishing to be admitted to psychiatric hospitals. The British novelist Ian McEwan recently used a different method to 'fake' a mental disorder and so test the validity of psychiatric classification.

Few people, on the face of it, would seem so well acquainted with the strange place where imagination meets reality as the readers of the Royal College of Psychiatrists' *Psychiatric Bulletin.* As expert navigators of the wilder shores of delusion and hallucination, surely they of all people can be relied on to spot the difference between fact and fiction – to tell for example when they're being had? Well no, actually, as it turns out. Ian McEwan, the best-selling novelist, comes clean in this month's edition of the *Bulletin* about a literary sleight of hand perpetrated on the world of psychiatry that seems to have had several of its respected members comprehensively fooled.

The saga began in 1997 with the publication of McEwan's acclaimed novel *Enduring Love,* the story of a science journalist, Joe Rose, obsessively and violently stalked by a religious loner called Jed Parry. Joe diagnoses Jed's condition as a homoerotic manifestation of De Clerambault's Syndrome, an nightmarish state of erotomania named after the turn of the century French psychiatrist who first identified it. It's a compelling, deeply disturbing tale – and one rendered even more haunting by the presence in the book's appendix of a case report reprinted from the *British Review of Psychiatry.* Only it isn't. The *British Review of Psychiatry* doesn't exist. McEwan decided to take the hoax a step further and submitted the appendix to the *British Journal of Psychiatry.*

It never made it into print but the novel was admiringly reviewed in the *Psychiatric Bulletin* by Ronan McIvor, a consultant psychiatrist. McIvor swallowed McEwan's jest whole, in a review which began with the fateful words: 'Based on a published case report ...'

From an article by Oliver Burkeman, *Guardian*, 16 August 1999

1 What does McEwan's hoax suggest about psychiatric diagnosis?

2 What ethical issues are raised by hoaxes of this sort?

Another way of assessing the validity of diagnosis using the DSM system is to diagnose people using DSM and ICD and see to what extent the two diagnoses agree. This approach is known as *criterion validity.* Of course this only tells us if DSM is valid provided that ICD is also valid and vice versa; nonetheless it is useful in itself to be able to tell when the two systems agree and when they differ. Andrews et al (1999) assessed 1500 people using DSM-IV and ICD-10 and found very good agreement on diagnoses of depression, substance dependence and generalised anxiety. Moderate agreement was found for other anxiety disorders. However there was agreement only 35 per cent of the time on post-traumatic stress, with ICD-10 identifying twice as many cases as DSM-IV. Overall, the agreement between the systems was 68 per cent. Generally people were more likely to receive a diagnosis according to ICD-10 than according to DSM-IV. We would expect this because the criteria for diagnosis are tighter in DSM-IV, and it suggests that either they are too narrow in DSM-IV or too broad in ICD-10.

for and against

reliability and validity of the DSM system

+ the reliability and validity of DSM systems have increased with each new version. DSM-IV-TR is more reliable and valid than previous versions

+ the inter-rater and test-retest reliability of some disorders are now very good

− the reliability of some diagnoses is much lower

− inter-rater reliability for diagnosing childhood conditions using DSM-IV is poor

+ agreement on diagnosis using DSM-IV is quite good for most conditions

The implications of receiving a diagnosis

Although clinicians are aware of the limited reliability and validity of diagnosis, there is a sound pragmatic reason why it remains standard practice. This is that in practice a diagnosis increases the likelihood of the patient accessing the most effective treatment. For example, if a patient receives a diagnosis of schizophrenia, even if it is an unusual case, the chances are that they will respond better to anti-psychotic drugs rather than anti-depressants.

An important downside, however, to receiving a psychiatric diagnosis is the risk of *social stigmatisation*. Stigmatisation occurs when we have an identifiable characteristic that predisposes people against us. People suffering from mental disorders attract considerable prejudice, and this can add significantly to the distress they already experience. To some commentators the social stigma of mental disorder constitutes sufficient reason not to diagnose mental disorder at all.

The media have been widely blamed for portraying negative stereotypes of people with mental disorders. This was investigated in a study by Philo et al (1994), in which the content of local and national media in Scotland was analysed for coverage of mental health issues during the month of April 1993. The results showed strong support for the role of media in perpetuating negative stereotypes of people with mental disorders.

Sixty-six per cent of all incidents (including factual and fictional cases) covering mental health issues involved accounts of violence. A further 13 per cent showed people with mental health problems harming themselves. Overall, only 18 per cent of fictional and factual incidents were judged to give sympathetic coverage of mental health issues. The researchers then used questionnaire and interviews to try to get at viewers' responses to the coverage of mental health issues. With the exception of those who had personal experience of people with mental health problems, for example, through family or work, viewers reported negative stereotyped views of the sufferers of mental disorder.

One of the saddest aspects of the stigma attached to mental disorder is the tendency of people with mental health problems to contribute to their own isolation by refusing to disclose personal and emotional experiences for fear of others' reactions. This phenomenon was investigated in a recent study conducted by MacDonald and Morley (2001).

research
now

patients are afraid to tell people how they feel

MacDonald J. & Morley I. (2001) Shame and non-disclosure: a study of the emotional isolation of people referred for psychotherapy. *British Journal of Medical Psychology* 74: 1–22

aim: it is now well documented that there is a social stigma surrounding the experience of psychological problems and in particular having a psychiatric diagnosis. However, there has been relatively little research into how sufferers of psychological problems respond to this stigma. The aim of this study was to find out whether outpatients would be reluctant to discuss their feelings with other people for fear of their response.

procedure: 34 outpatients attending a clinic for psychotherapy were asked to complete an emotion diary for one week. In the diary participants noted any experiences that caused them to react with strong emotion, and whether they had disclosed their feelings to anyone. After a week the diaries were collected and participants were interviewed.

findings: it emerged that in general the participants tended not to disclose their feelings. In 68 per cent of cases incidents that aroused strong emotional responses were not disclosed to anyone. This contrasts with the results of studies using emotion diaries in the general population, which reveal that usually only about 10 per cent of such incidents are not disclosed. Interviews revealed that the major reason for the reluctance of patients to disclose was fear of negative responses from others.

conclusion: patients receiving psychotherapy for a psychological problem are reluctant to disclose their emotional responses to everyday events for fear of being judged. This adds to the distress and isolation that frequently accompany mental health problems.

The following is a good source of further information concerning psychiatric diagnosis.

▶ **Davison G.C. & Neale J.M. (2001)** *Abnormal psychology*. **New York: Wiley.** Contains excellent sections on the criteria for defining behaviour as abnormal and the development of the DSM system.

Cultural issues in diagnosis

Culture is of great importance to psychiatric diagnosis in a number of ways. Culture is a set of beliefs, values and practices that characterises a group of people. Culture varies between people from different parts of the world, between different ethnic and religious groups living in the same region, between socio-economic groups, between men and women, and even between families. Most research has focused on differences between different national and ethnic groups.

Cultural attitudes to mental disorder

Different cultural groups have different attitudes to psychological distress and mental disorder, and these attitudes can impact on the processes of reporting symptoms and receiving a diagnosis. Particular disorders may have particular meanings to cultures. Kim and Berrios (2001) have identified the problems caused by the fact that in some Asian languages the terms for schizophrenia literally translate as 'the disease of the disorganised mind'. In Japan, the idea of a disorganised mind is so stigmatising that psychiatrists are reluctant to tell patients of their condition, and as a result only around 20 per cent of people with schizophrenia in that country are aware of it.

A recent study in Britain (Cinnerella & Loewenthal, 1999) examined the influence of religious and cultural influences on mental disorder, with particular regard to the symptoms and causes of depression and schizophrenia, and the most effective strategies for tackling symptoms. A total of 52 participants (including white Catholics, Indian Hindus, black Christians, Muslim Pakistanis and Orthodox Jews) were given in-depth interviews in their own homes. Some important cultural

attitudes emerged. Although all groups saw depression as the result of life events and other environmental factors, there was a wide range of beliefs about the origins of schizophrenia. Across all groups except the white Catholics there was a fear of being misunderstood by health professionals. Among the black Christian and Muslim Pakistani groups there was also a sense that depression and schizophrenia carried a social stigma. These two groups in particular believed in the power of prayer to relieve symptoms. Clearly these findings have important implications, as they suggest that certain communities in Britain are more reluctant than others to seek help for mental health problems than others.

Culture and vulnerability to mental disorder

In a number of cases it seems that some cultural and ethnic groups are affected more by particular disorders than others. Levav et al (1997) compared the incidence of depression and alcoholism among American Jews, Catholics and Protestants. Overall the Jewish population had a higher rate of depression and a lower rate of alcohol abuse than the other groups. Interestingly, males accounted for the differences alone; Jewish men, but not women were twice as likely to suffer depression and only half as likely to abuse alcohol as Catholics and Protestants. While these differences could conceivably be explained by genetic predispositions in the Jewish and Christian populations, the most likely explanation for these findings is that some aspect of Jewish culture makes men more likely to respond to adversity with depression rather than alcohol abuse. In Britain, black and Irish people are significantly more likely than other groups to receive a diagnosis of schizophrenia. In these cases it seems likely that cultural bias in diagnosis rather than genuine greater frequency of schizophrenia is the problem.

Figure 1.3 In many societies including Britain it is common for men to abuse alcohol in response to stress or adversity

Race discrimination in diagnosis and assessment

Littlewood and Lipsedge (1997) have suggested that the reason why black and Irish people in Britain are more likely than others to receive a diagnosis of serious mental disorder has more to do with bias in the system than a genuine greater vulnerability in those groups. They describe a case of Calvin, a Jamaican man arrested following an argument with the police when a post office clerk believed he was cashing a stolen postal order. We look at an extract from the psychiatrist's report on Calvin below.

interactive angles

Read the following description from a British prison psychiatrist of a Jamaican patient on remand, having been arrested for arguing with the police who wrongly accused him of stealing a postal order.

> 'This man belongs to Rastafarian – a mystical Jamaican cult, the members of which think they are God-like. The man has ringlet hair, a straggly goatee beard and a type of turban. He appears eccentric in his appearance and very vague in answering questions. He is an irritable character and has got arrogant behaviour.'

1 *What cultural misunderstanding can you see in the psychiatrist's view of Calvin's religion?*

2 *In what other way does the psychiatrist describe Calvin in unflattering terms that relate to his ethnic or cultural group.*

As always in psychology, we need to be aware of the limitations of case studies – we don't know how representative Calvin's case is of the treatment of minority groups in the mental health system. However, there is further evidence to suggest that mental health professionals perceive different ethnic and cultural groups rather differently. Stowell-Smith and McKeown (1999) performed a discourse analysis on the psychiatrists' reports on 18 black and 18 white male psychopaths from a range of maximum-security institutions. Discourse analysis is associated with the social constructionist approach to psychology (discussed on page 52), and involves the *deconstruction* of written or verbal narrative

in order to reveal the hidden assumptions in people's use of language. In this case discourse analysis revealed that the psychiatrists were much more likely to look at white patients' experiences of trauma and at their emotional state. Reports of black patients placed much more emphasis on the danger posed by the patients. This contrast suggests that the doctors saw white psychopaths more sympathetically.

The following is a good source of further information about cultural issues in diagnosis.

> **Littlewood R. & Lipsedge M. (1997) *Aliens and alienists. Ethnic minorities and psychiatry.* London: Routledge.** A highly critical look at current mental health practices in Britain with regard to the treatment of different cultural groups.

Conclusions

Drawing the line between normal and abnormal behaviour is a tricky business. Statistical rarity, social deviance and maladaptiveness are all important criteria for defining behaviour as abnormal in systems of diagnosis, but there is no single criterion for abnormality that reliably distinguishes between people whom we would and would not diagnose with a mental disorder. There are two particularly popular and sophisticated systems for the classification and diagnosis of mental disorder, the DSM-IV-TR and the ICD-10. Despite the sophistication of these systems there have been challenges to their reliability and validity. Moreover, having a psychiatric diagnosis carries a serious social stigma and we need to balance the costs and benefits of diagnosis. It is also important to consider issues of culture when thinking about diagnosis of mental disorder. Different cultural groups have different attitudes to mental disorder and certain groups appear to be more vulnerable to certain disorders.

what do you know ?

1 Compare two or more criteria used for identifying psychological abnormality. How important is each criterion in the process of diagnosis?

2 (a) Describe the DSM system of classification.

(b) To what extent can we consider systems like DSM reliable and valid?

3 How much of a problem is the social stigma of mental disorder?

4 In what ways do we have to consider issues of culture in the diagnosis of mental disorder?

2 The biomedical model of abnormality

what's ahead?

In this chapter we consider a model that explains mental disorders in the same terms as physical illness are explained; as being caused by the disruption or malfunction of biological processes. We consider the evidence for the role of genes and the biochemistry of the nervous system in mental disorder. Having looked at the role of biology in explaining the origin of mental disorder, we will then focus on some of the treatments such an approach offers. The rather controversial therapies of drugs and electroconvulsive therapy (ECT) will be considered, together with the considerable changes that have occurred in the application of such treatments since they were first introduced. Finally, in 'what's new?', we will discuss a promising new alternative to ECT, transcranial magnetic brain stimulation.

Assumptions of the approach

The biomedical model (or *disease* model) of psychopathology views psychological disorders as being caused by biological malfunction or disruption. Biomedical approaches to treatment are based on the idea that we can correct or at least reduce the effects of these malfunctions or disruption.

- Mental disorder can be understood as illness in the same way as can physical conditions. It can thus be classified, diagnosed and treated by medical personnel in the same way as physical disease.

- The emphasis of the explanations is on the physiological aspects of mental disorder rather than its behavioural, thinking or emotional aspects. For example, the physiological approach would explain depression in terms of an imbalance of biochemical substances in the brain, such as serotonin, rather than in terms of low self-esteem, feelings of helplessness, irrational thinking and so on. This emphasis on physiology is of course on a theoretical level and is not to suggest that medical practitioners are not concerned with cognitive and emotional aspects of mental disorder.

- The symptoms of mental disorder can be understood in terms of malfunction of or disruption to biological systems. This may, for example, involve the abnormal development of part of the nervous system or too high or low levels of neurotransmitters. The underlying causes of these symptoms are also biological in origin, for example, faulty genes or brain damage.

- Mental disorder can be treated by physiologically based approaches, including drugs, surgery and the application of electric shocks, magnetic fields and bright light.

The biomedical position is one with a very long history – indeed, the very language of psychopathology is grounded in the medical model, the most obvious example being that such conditions are often called mental *illnesses*. At one time all mental disorders were seen by some as being caused entirely by biological factors, but this position is now seen by most as untenable and it is recognised that most, if not all, psychological conditions (and some physical illnesses) are the result of a complex interaction of physiology and environment.

The role of genes

Behaviour genetics is the study of individual differences in psychological characteristics that are attributable in part to differences in genetic makeup. Before we consider the effects that genes may have on abnormal behaviour, it is useful briefly to consider how genes are inherited and the way in which they exert an effect.

Human beings have 46 chromosomes (23 pairs) in the cells of their bodies except in the ova (eggs) and sperm in which there are 23, one of each pair. Via the egg and sperm, a child randomly inherits half its chromosomes from the mother and half from the father. Each chromosome is made up of thousands of *genes,* which are the carriers of the genetic information (DNA) that is passed from parent to child. The total genetic makeup of an individual is known as the *genotype*. Genes contain the instruction for producing a physical body, which in turn have an effect on psychological characteristics. The observable physical and behavioural characteristics of an individual are known collectively as their *phenotype*. The phenotype is the result of both genetic and environmental influences. For example, two children may be born with a similarly high predisposition to suffer anxiety. If one then experiences a very stressful environment, he may become a very anxious adult and perhaps be prone to anxiety disorders such as phobias. The other may, in contrast, have a supportive and benign upbringing that results in a well-adjusted adult capable of coping well with anxiety-provoking situations. Their genotypes are similar, but their phenotypes are very different. The role of genes in the development of schizophrenia, depression, eating disorders and anxiety conditions is considered in the relevant chapters.

The biochemistry of the nervous system

The human nervous system is the most important system for the control of behaviour and the experience of mental events. At the centre of the nervous system is the brain, which manages all human capacities including learning, feeling emotions, relating to other people and perceiving

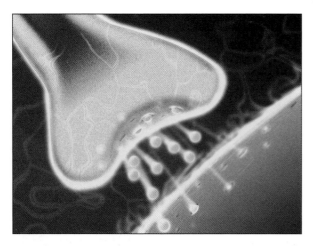

Figure 2.1 A nerve cell and synapse

the world. The nervous system is composed of billions of neurons, highly specialised nerve cells 'woven into a complex tapestry of connections and interconnections' (Dwyer & Scampion, 1996, page 176).

Neurons are specially adapted to receive, process and/or transmit information to other cells. They communicate with each other (and with muscles and glands), both electrically and chemically. When a neuron is stimulated, a wave of electrical voltage, called a nerve impulse, passes down the axon (see figure 2.1) to the terminal ending. Between the nerve ending and the next cell there is a small gap called a *synapse* across which electricity cannot pass. The impulse then passes to the next neuron by

means of chemicals called *neurotransmitters*. These neurotransmitters are chemical messengers, which travel the small distance across the synaptic gap and excite or inhibit the next neuron. When a neurotransmitter is released, some of it remains in the synapse and needs to be removed so that the synapse can return to its normal state. Some of it is broken down by enzymes while some of it is pumped back into the neuron ending from which it came, a process known as *reuptake*. If this process is faulty, then problems arise. As we shall see later in this chapter, and in chapter 9, some therapeutic drugs operate by inhibiting the reuptake of certain neurotransmitters, thus preventing further uptake.

Neurotransmitters play a crucial role in many psychological processes including mood and emotion. It is now clear that abnormalities in the production of neurotransmitters can contribute to psychopathological conditions. *Noradrenaline* (called *norepinephrine* in American texts) has been implicated in anxiety disorders; serotonin may be involved in some types of depression and eating disorders and dopamine appears to be implicated in schizophrenia.

Evaluation of biomedical explanations for mental disorder

A large and impressive body of research that demonstrates a link between biology and psychopathology has supported the biomedical model. This in turn has led to the development of drug therapies and other biological therapies (discussed in the next section), many of which have offered significant help in coping with abnormal psychological functioning.

However, there are several criticisms and limitations to the approach. First, the biomedical model is essentially a *reductionist* model because it reduces the explanation of psychopathology down to its most basic element, in this case, to simple biology. Such a reductionist stance can result in the neglect of some of the most important psychological causes of behaviour and we may fail to see an individual as a whole person, regarding them rather as a body in which some part is malfunctioning. We may be able to explain a headache in terms of brain chemistry, but that tells us little or nothing about the possible life stresses that may have given rise to that biological condition. Secondly, although biological processes certainly do affect our behaviour, thoughts and emotions, it is not a one-way process. We are increasingly coming to recognise that our behaviour, thoughts and emotions affect our biology.

Thirdly, much of the research into the biological causes of abnormality have been conducted on animals in whom various conditions such as anxiety and helplessness have been induced in these unfortunate creatures by drugs, surgery or the way they have been conditioned. These procedures provide very little information about human functioning. Biological explanations based on such research are often incomplete or simply irrelevant to understanding human behaviour.

Fourthly, evidence from family, twin and adoption studies indicating a link between genetics and clinical syndromes are open to other interpretations. The closer the genetic link, the more similar the environment is likely to be. Siblings not only have certain genes in common, but it is quite likely that they have also shared any potentially

for and against

biomedical explanations

+ there is a large amount of empirical research to support biological explanations of mental disorders

– the biomedical approach tends to neglect the role of psychological factors in the aetiology (cause) of atypical behaviour

– our behaviour may affect our biology; therefore even when malfunctions of the brain or hormone imbalances occur they may be the consequence not the cause of abnormal behaviour

where to now?

▶ **Murray R., Hill P. & McGuffin P. (1996)** *The essentials of postgraduate psychiatry.* **Cambridge: Cambridge University Press.** Although a large and detailed book, this is not as intimidating as its name suggests, and has lots of good information on biomedical approaches to mental disorder.

▶ **Davison G.C. & Neale J.M. (2001)** *Abnormal psychology,* **8th edn. New York: Wiley.** A standard undergraduate level text with good general information on biomedical and other approaches to explaining mental disorder.

damaging experiences. We cannot therefore conclude that genes rather than environment were responsible for the abnormality. As mentioned earlier, there is a doubtless a complex interaction of environment and biology, and concentration on one at the expense of the other is liable to lead us up blind alleys.

Therapies based on the biomedical approach

The brain is an amazingly complex and delicate structure and has thus been difficult to study. Because the study of the brain has been limited by lack of technology until modern imaging techniques such as PET and MRI scanning were developed, the development of biological treatments has lagged behind that of the psychological therapies. Often, when drugs and other biological therapies have been introduced, it has been as the result of an accidental discovery rather than the result of systematic research into a particular condition. Nowadays, thorough research is conducted into biological therapies, which are very commonly used. In this section we will look at the two main biological therapies: drugs and ECT.

Drug therapies

The use of drugs to treat psychological disorders has a relatively short but controversial history. It started in the 1950s with the discovery of *psychotropic* drugs, drugs that act mainly on the brain and seem to alleviate the symptoms of various mental disorders. These were seen by some as a magic cure and were possibly over-prescribed without due appreciation of their side-effects, both physical and psychological. Over the years, research has led to a broadening of the range of available medication. Many new drugs have been introduced that do not have the same problems but controversy in many areas still rages.

There are four main classes of psychotropic drugs. *Antianxiety drugs* (also known as minor tranquillisers) help people relax and reduce tension. An often-prescribed group of antianxiety drugs are the *benzodiazepines*, the trade names of two of which, namely Valium and Librium, have become universally known. Although these drugs do reduce anxiety, they also induce both physical and psychological dependence, and this produced serious problems for those people, mainly women, who, in the 1960s, were prescribed these drugs for years on end. They experienced such enormous problems with withdrawal symptoms that some people have literally continued taking them for a lifetime. Nowadays they tend to be prescribed for very short periods, perhaps for 'one-off' anxiety provoking situations.

Antidepressant drugs help elevate mood and lift depression.

One of the most recent of these drugs is fluoxetine hydrochloride, more commonly known by its trade name of *Prozac*. Along with *Seroxat*, Prozac is one of a group of drugs in the SSRI (selective serotonin reuptake inhibitor) class, which was hailed as being entirely safe because people could not get dependent on them or even overdose. However, recently concerns have been expressed that the use of such drugs may actually increase suicide risk in the first few weeks of treatment (Harriman, 2001). There is also concern that such drugs are being marketed for a ever-widening range of complaints, including premenstrual tension, and are far more often prescribed by GPs than by psychiatrists. Prozac is now so widely used and the prescribing of it so contentious that it has been the subject of several books and numerous newspaper articles.

Antibipolar drugs are used to stabilise the mood of those people suffering from bipolar disorder (discussed in chapter 9), in which moods swing between depression and mania. The most commonly used of these is lithium carbonate, which is estimated to help in 70 to 80 per cent of cases. The doses, however, have to be carefully monitored or they may threaten a person's life (Jefferson & Geist, 1989). Despite this, lithium is often regarded as one of the success stories of drug therapy since, as Comer (1992) comments, 'Administered properly ... this and related drugs represent a true medical miracle for people who previously would have spent their lives on an emotional roller coaster' (1992, page 165).

Antipsychotic drugs are used in the treatment of psychotic conditions such as schizophrenia. The older class of drugs

media watch

A group of psychiatrists has made a formal protest to the president of the profession's royal college against a drug company's sponsorship of a conference opening today.

They complain that the industry's marketing distorts the mental health agenda to the point where pills are seen as the answer to all ills.

In a letter to John Cox, president of the Royal College of Psychiatrists, the group says that money widely available for sponsoring meetings and of doctors is an attempt to persuade psychiatry to go down the biomedical route and to ignore social circumstances that might be the true cause of the illness.

Two consultant psychiatrists, Pat Bracken and Phillip Thomas from the University of Bradford, members of the group that calls itself the Critical Psychiatry Network, will join mental health service users in demonstrating their concerns.

The group claims that 'biomedical frameworks' – the focus on drugs – increasingly dominate research and education in psychiatry, in spite of limited evidence as to how or whether the drugs work. Dr Bracken points to a paper in the journal *Ethical Human Sciences and Services* last year on the efficacy of SSRI (selective serotonin reuptake inhibitor) class of antidepressant, which includes Prozac, which concluded that the drugs worked little better than dummy pills – 'there is a less than 10% difference in the antidepressant effect of drug versus placebo'.

Dr Bracken and colleagues feel the drive to find a medical cause of all mental illness ignores issues such as poverty, family breakdown, or other social or cultural problems. They call for the college to pull back from the increasingly close relationship with the pharmaceutical industry.

Taken from an article by Sarah Boseley, *Guardian*, 9 July 2001

1 What are the implications of drug companies funding research into therapies for certain disorders?

2 What factors are likely to be ignored if a biomedical approach is taken?

3 Why may it be tempting for state health services to concentrate on biomedical rather than psychological therapies?

4 What ethical concerns are expressed in this article?

were the *phenothiazines*. A major problem with these drugs is the side-effects of movement disorders such as severe shaking, muscle tremors and spasms of involuntary jerky movements. An irreversible condition known as tardive dyskinesia affects about 10 to 20 per cent of all patients treated over a long period of time (Sweet et al, 1995).

As with other classes of drugs, those first introduced in the 1950s have been superseded by more effective ones with fewer side-effects, for example *clozapine*. This can be effective in patients who do not respond to traditional antipsychotics (Kane et al, 1998) and is actually more effective overall (Rosenhack et al, 1999). It can, however, impair the immune system in a very small percentage of patients. Even more recently, two new antipsychotics have been introduced, olanzapine and risperidone, both with fewer side-effects and equally if not more effective than the traditional antipsychotics. The search for ever-more effective drugs with fewer side-effects is ongoing.

Although they are more effective than any other single form of treatment for schizophrenia, drugs alone are not sufficient treatment for most sufferers. Nevertheless, combined with psychotherapy, they can help many patients with schizophrenia lead a normal life. Unfortunately, however, some patients do not respond to any antipsychotic drugs.

interactive angles

There has been considerable media coverage of the alleged side-effects of SSRIs, and about the allegations of dodgy practices on the part of drug companies. Carry out an Internet search, using a search engine like Alta Vista or Google and key words like Prozac, Seroxat, drug companies etc. Compile a list of arguments for and against the use of these drugs.

Electroconvulsive therapy (ECT)

ECT is a procedure in which a very brief application of electricity is used to induce a seizure. It has a fearful reputation dating back to a time when it was applied without anaesthetic or muscle relaxant and was almost certainly used to subdue troublesome patients. Nowadays its application is very different. The patient is anaesthetised with a fast-acting barbiturate and given a muscle relaxant to temporarily paralyse the muscles so they do not contract during the seizure and cause broken bones. Electrodes are fitted to the head and a small electric current is passed through the brain for one second or less. The resulting

seizure, monitored by an EEG machine, lasts from about 30 seconds to a minute and the patient regains consciousness about 15 minutes later. He or she usually experiences confusion, a headache and sometimes nausea and has no memory for events surrounding the treatment. These symptoms usually disappear within a few hours.

ECT is usually given two to three times a week for between one and four weeks, until the patient appears recovered, then two more treatments are administered to prevent relapse. No one knows how or why ECT works or what the electrically stimulated seizure does to the brain. It is thought that it acts by temporarily altering some of the brain's electrochemical processes (see page 12 for a further discussion). ECT is still a very widely used form of treatment, mainly for those whose depression is so severe that they cannot wait three weeks or so for antidepressants to take effect (due to absolute desperation and suicide risk) or for those for whom these drugs are ineffective. It is also used for acute mania and certain forms of schizophrenia.

The use of ECT is still highly controversial. Much of this controversy surrounds its effectiveness, the severity and extent of the side-effects and the lack of knowledge of how it works. There is also concern that its use is viewed as a quick and easy solution to a problem better tackled by long-term psychotherapy. It is very difficult to be objective about the use of ECT because opinions about it are so extreme. Recent studies have tended to show good effectiveness, but some side-effects. Ng et al (2000) administered ECT to the right hemisphere of 32 patients suffering from major depression (see page 70 for a discussion of major depression). Depression scores decreased by around 50 per cent following treatment, but memory was found to be seriously affected when tested immediately after six weeks of treatment (over 30 per cent of personal memories were lost). Most of this memory loss was made up though within the next month, thus overall the study was supportive of the value of ECT.

Papolos (1997) claims that ECT has a higher success rate for severe depression than any other form of treatment and that suicide attempts are relatively rare after ECT. In a recent follow-up of 58 depressed patients by Gagne et al (2000) it was found that 93 per cent of patients who continued to have ECT and antidepressants following an episode of major depression remained free of symptoms two years later as opposed to 52 per cent of those who continued to take antidepressants alone. This suggests that ECT is helpful in preventing recurrence of depression. On the other hand, Youssef and Youssef (1999), in an article entitled 'Time to abandon electroconvulsion as a treatment in modern psychiatry', claim that ECT is not superior to drugs, and that much of the improvement attributed to ECT is an effect of placebo or possibly anaesthesia. They argue that the treatment only shortens the duration of an illness rather than improves the outcome. The controversy is ongoing. However, there is now a new and exciting alternative to ECT that is painless and safe. This is called transcranial magnetic brain stimulation.

what's **new?**

Transcranial magnetic brain stimulation (TMS)

Transcranial brain stimulation (TMS) is a non-invasive and painless method of brain stimulation, which may offer an alternative to ECT. The method involves the production of a magnetic field produced by a wire coil held outside the head. The magnetic field then induces an electric current in nearby regions of the brain. Unlike electricity, which is diffused by bone, high intensity magnetic pulses pass readily through it. Therefore, when a magnetic current is passed through the skull, it is possible to focus on a more specific area of the brain than is possible with ECT. Perhaps the most crucial difference between ECT and TSM is that the latter does not produce major motor seizures. It is therefore possible to avoid side-effects such as transient memory loss; neither is it necessary to use an anaesthetic. The treatment is usually administered daily for at least a week and is referred to as rTMS (repetitive TMS).

Research on rTMS gives cause for cautious optimism. George et al (1995) conducted a pilot study of the effect of rTMS on six long-term depressed patients who had previously not responded to treatment. Two of them showed considerable improvement. One of the responders, a middle-aged woman, reported feeling well for the first time in three years. Pridmore et al (2000) compared the effect of rTMS and ECT in patients suffering from major depression who had failed to respond to at least one course of medication. Although ECT was slightly better overall, the difference was not great. The researchers therefore concluded that rTMS has antidepressant effects of sufficiently useful proportions to make further research worth while. Klein (2000) similarly comments that preliminary evidence from studies of depressed individuals suggest that it might, in some cases, offer an alternative to ECT.

Figure 2.2 The TMS apparatus

for and against

biomedical treatments

+ there is substantial evidence for the effectiveness of biomedical treatments in relieving the symptoms of mental disorder

− biomedical treatments sometimes have serious side-effects

− there are concerns in some quarters that drugs may be over-used because of the importance of sponsorship by drug companies

+ biomedical treatments are becoming increasingly safe and effective, and there are innovative new treatments such as TMR

where to now?

▶ **Kramer P. (1997) *Listening to Prozac*. London: Penguin.** Puts the case in favour of Prozac use.

▶ **Glenmullen J. (2001) *Prozac backlash*. California: Touchstone Books.** Argues the case against Prozac.

▶ **Healy D. (1993) *Psychiatric drugs explained*. Kings Lynn: Mosby.** A well-written guide to the use of psychotropic drugs.

▶ **Fancher R.T. (1995) *Cultures of healing*. New York: Freeman.** Takes a very critical look at the biomedical model in general.

Conclusions

It is important to note that even those people who recognise that biology may be the cause of a mental problem do not necessarily advocate biological intervention, but feel that psychological methods are appropriate in some cases. Indeed, rarely are biological therapies advocated as the only means of treatment. Sometimes such interven-

tions are advocated to put the patient in a frame of mind in which they are receptive to psychological therapy. For example, in some cases of anxiety disorders and depression, drugs may be deemed necessary to bring the individual to a state in which they can then benefit from psychological treatments. In the case of other conditions, such as bipolar disorder and schizophrenia, it may be necessary for the patient to receive medication for life but these medications are only likely to be fully effective when used alongside psychological therapies.

The use of biological therapies implies that there is a direct relationship between biological dysfunction and mental dysfunction, but this is by no means always the case. For example, stress causes the release of adrenaline and noradrenaline in the bloodstream, which can then have an adverse effect on behaviour. Rather than taking medication to reduce the levels of these particular hormones, it is better to help the individual to reduce the level of stress, or to help them find ways of coping with situations so that they are no longer stressful .

To sum up, biological therapies provide an invaluable and sometimes life-saving tool in the treatment of mental disorder. Improvements in the existing methods and better alternatives are constantly being researched. However, it is unlikely and probably undesirable that biological treatments should ever be the only help that sufferers are given. A combination of appropriate somatic and psychological therapies is always likely to provide the most favourable outcomes to the alleviation of mental distress.

what do you know?

1 Discuss ways in the role of genetic factors in abnormal behaviour can be investigated.

2 What role may be played by the biochemical factors in causing abnormal behaviour?

3 Discuss arguments or and against the biomedical approach to explaining atypical behaviour.

4 Describe and evaluate the use of two biomedical therapies for abnormal behaviour.

5 Evaluate the use of biological therapies in treating abnormal behaviour.

3 The behavioural model of abnormality

what's  ahead?

In this chapter we look at how the processes involved in learning have been used to explain the origins of mental disorders. We consider how classical conditioning can lead to the association of fear and anxiety with everyday events or objects. In addition, we consider how operant conditioning can result in maladaptive behaviours being, often unwittingly, reinforced and therefore encouraged. Having considered ways in which learning theory explains the origins of mental disorders, we then focus on the therapies that this theoretical approach offers. This will include the traditional approaches such as systematic desensitisation and token economies and, in 'what's new?', the more recently developed virtual reality exposure therapy.

Assumptions of the approach

The learning or *behavioural* approach views abnormal behaviour as having developed in the same way as all other behaviour; as the result of learning processes. In essence, the symptoms of psychological disorders arise because an individual has learned self-defeating or ineffective ways of behaving.

- Mental disorders can be understood as patterns of learned maladaptive behaviour.

- The emphasis of the approach is on observable behaviour as opposed to physiology, emotion or thinking.

- The learning of maladaptive behaviour takes place by processes including classical and operant conditioning.

- Mental disorder can be treated by behavioural therapies, in which maladaptive behaviours can be unlearned and replaced with new and more adaptive behaviours.

Classical conditioning

Classical conditioning was originally demonstrated by Pavlov (see *Angles on psychology*).

In the case of Pavlov's dogs the emotional response was a pleasant one, but any emotional response, including anx-

Figure 3.1 Pavlov's dogs

iety and fear, can become associated through learning with any neutral stimulus. This is important in the development of anxiety disorders (discussed in chapter 11). Over time, if a stimulus is regularly coupled with an unpleasant experience, then this stimulus will elicit fear and dread, possibly throughout a lifetime. In the case of a very intense emotion it may require only one coupling for the fear to become well established. If, for example, a person was brutally assaulted in a certain street, then entering that street may produce the same emotional response that was associated with the assault. Likewise, the smell of an aftershave used by a rapist may trigger dreadful feelings in a victim after the event.

interactive angles

Complete the following classical conditioning table to show how being assaulted in a street can lead to a fear of that street. Insert the following terms in the spaces provided: street (x 2), fear (x 3), assault (x 2).

UCS————————————————>UCR

....

NS + UCS————————————————>UCR

....

CS————————————————>CR

....

Another area where classical conditioning is important in explaining mental health problems is in the *paraphilias* (or sexual fetishes). Studies have demonstrated that we can condition animals to respond sexually to neutral stimuli. Kippin (2000) classically conditioned ejaculation in rats to the smell of lemon or almond. The male rats were allowed to copulate with females bearing one of the two odours. Although the males initially showed no preference for copulating with a female bearing a particular smell, they subsequently displayed a preference to mate again with those bearing the smell that they had come to associate with ejaculation. It is believed that humans can acquire sexual fetishes by similar processes. A harmless example of such a conditioned response is shown in 'media watch'.

media watch

Question: My boyfriend and I tried an experiment which I'd like to tell you about. For two months we made love every night with Barry White on continuous play on our CD player. Now whenever either of us hears that music we become sexually aroused.

Answer: A long-dead foreigner called Pavlov did much the same sort of experiment but used dogs, bells and food. Your research project sounds far more interesting and I suggest you apply for a grant to help you continue your studies.

Taken from a letter to the problems page in the *News of the World*, January 2000

1 Explain this couple's experience in terms of classical conditioning.

2 Give an example of how a more serious sexual fetish might be acquired by classical conditioning.

While this is a harmless and even amusing account of a conditioned sexual response it is believed that similar processes can be involved in the development of more serious sexual fetishes including paedophilia.

Operant conditioning

In *operant conditioning* animals and humans learn by the consequences of their actions. If a behaviour is reinforced it is more likely to be repeated. If it is punished it is less likely to be repeated (see *Angles on psychology* for a more detailed account). Operant conditioning may be involved in the development of certain symptoms. For example, if someone shops to make themselves feel better (we all feel a high at spending money and acquiring nice new possessions), then shopping may be reinforced until it takes on the characteristics of an addiction. This is called *self-reinforcement*. Depressed individuals, who enjoy relatively few activities, may be particularly vulnerable to such patterns of self-reinforcement.

Figure 3.2 Shopping is self-reinforcing, hence can be addictive

Evaluating the learning approach to explaining mental disorders

On the positive side, the learning approach has been heralded as a precise and objective way of regarding human behaviour. It has also been very useful in drawing our attention to the effects of conditioning (and hence certain experience) on behaviour. By using carefully controlled experimental procedures, it has offered a wealth of empirical evidence in support of the underlying theories. The research has also demonstrated the effectiveness of the application of these theories to changing behaviour.

However, the approach is not without shortcomings. First, although therapies based on the learning approach have been fairly successful in changing certain types of behaviour, this does not necessarily mean that faulty learning *caused* the problems in the first place. Davison and Neale (2001) use a commonsense example, provided by Rimland (1964) to illustrate this argument. The mood of a depressed person may well be improved by providing positive reinforcement every time they increase their activity level, but this is not evidence that their depression and apathy was originally caused by absence of rewards.

Secondly, one of the major problems with the behavioural account of humans is that it underestimates the complexity and flexibility of the human mind. A fundamental characteristic of humans is their ability to think and reason – we are not simply puppets with no free will

or ability to critically consider our own behaviour. Some recognition of this has been made by the *cognitive behavioural* theorists (see chapter 4) who have moved away from the very strict traditional behaviourist approach and now take account of the fact that people's behaviour is influenced by their own interpretation of a situation, by their hopes and expectations, and by their capacity to take some control over their lives.

for and against

the learning model as an explanation for abnormal behaviour

+ the basic concepts of the learning approach can easily be empirically tested, and have largely been supported by research

+ clinicians have successfully used behavioural techniques to help change some problem behaviour

— there is no strong evidence to suggest that most mental disorders are acquired as the result of faulty conditioning

— the fact that clinical symptoms can be simulated under laboratory conditions does not necessarily mean that these symptoms are acquired in this way in ordinary life

— the learning approach underestimates the complexity of humans and sees them as being entirely at the mercy of environmental influences; there is little consideration for free will, consciousness or personality

where to now?

▶ **Jarvis M., Russell J., Flanagan C. & Dolan L. (2000)** *Angles on psychology*. **Cheltenham: Nelson Thornes.** Gives a good general account of the learning approach to psychology.

▶ **Davison G.C. & Neale J.M. (2001)** *Abnormal psychology*, **8th edn. New York: Wiley.** Good coverage of all the major theoretical approaches to explaining mental disorder.

Behavioural therapies

Therapies based on the learning approach are collectively known as *behavioural* therapies. The principle underlying such therapies is that since maladaptive behaviour is the product of unfortunate earlier conditioning then it can be modified through relearning. We can look here at three therapies based on classical conditioning: systematic desensitisation, flooding and implosion; and also one based on operant conditioning, namely token economy.

Systematic desensitisation, flooding and implosion therapy

We discussed earlier the concept of extinction – if, after conditioning, Pavlov's dogs heard a bell ring but were given no food, the conditioned response of salivation would

classic research

experimental desensitisation of a phobia

Lang P.J. & Lazovik D.A. (1963) Experimental desensitisation of a phobia. *Journal of Abnormal and Social Psychology* 66: 519–25

aim: the main aim of the study was to test the effectiveness of desensitisation in treating phobia of snakes. A secondary aim was to assess the validity of the criticism made of desensitisation by psychodynamic therapists – that because symptoms ultimately come from unconscious conflicts, one phobia, when removed, is likely to be replaced by another.

procedure: the participants, all college students, were chosen from a group who all rated themselves on a questionnaire as having a fear of snakes that was 'intense'. The assignment of participants to the control or experimental group was essentially random although there was some attempt to balance participants roughly in terms of intensity of fear and motivation to participate in the study. There were 24 participants in all, with the experimental group consisting of 4 males and 9 females, and the control group comprising 3 males and 8 females.

Participants in the experimental condition were trained in deep muscle relaxation over a number of sessions. They also drew up a fear hierarchy, which was different for everyone but typically consisted of 'writing the word snake', 'seeing a caged snake in a zoo', 'accidentally treading on a dead snake'. They were given 11 45-minute sessions of systematic desensitisation during which they were hypnotised, instructed to relax deeply and then asked to imagine each step of the hierarchy in turn. Only when totally relaxed did they move up the hierarchy.

To assess the success of the treatment each participant was told that there was a non-poisonous snake in a glass case in a nearby laboratory. He or she was encouraged to enter and describe their reactions. The experimenter then walked to the case and removed the wire grid covering it. The participant was asked to come to the cage and see what the experimenter was doing. If they came to the cage they were asked to touch the snake. If this was successful, the participant was invited to hold the snake. The participant was asked to rate their anxiety on a 10-point scale and the experimenter also estimated it on a 3-point scale.

findings: the treatment programme successfully reduced phobic behaviour in the experimental group, as shown by reduction in avoidance behaviour and subjective ratings of fear. However, this programme was not successful with the entire experimental group. None of the control group showed any change. The improvements were maintained six months later and no new phobias had appeared.

conclusion: these findings are consistent with the learning theory of phobias. There was no evidence at all that other symptoms had appeared to replace the phobic behaviour.

eventually disappear. However, in the case of some abnormal behaviours, especially phobias, extinction has no opportunity to occur. Consider a woman who is phobic of cats. She will do everything possible to avoid them. On seeing a cat, her anxiety level rises sharply and when she escapes from it, it drops. In the language of learning theory, she has developed a *conditioned avoidance response* to all cats. Such a response is highly resistant to extinction because the avoidance response is *negatively reinforced* – the cat has led to escape from an extremely unpleasant feeling. So, in theoretical terms, classical conditioning has caused the problem (association of cats with fear), while operant conditioning maintains it by negative reinforcement. Behavioural therapies for phobias therefore concentrate on providing *exposure* to the phobic object or situation and thus providing an environment in which extinction can occur. Systematic desensitisation does this gradually and provides an alterative, incompatible response, while flooding, implosion therapy and virtual reality therapy do it rather more abruptly.

Systematic desensitisation

Based on the work of Mary Jones (1924), who recognised that one way to treat a phobia was to introduce an individual to the phobic object very gradually while inducing responses that are incompatible with fear, Wolpe (1958) devised a systematic programme for reducing anxiety before exposure. The procedure is composed of three stages:

> 1 The individual is given training in deep relaxation. This may occasionally involve the use of hypnosis or drugs.
>
> 2 He or she is asked to imagine situations that provoke anxiety and build up a hierarchy from least to most fear provoking. These situations create a scale of increasing levels of anxiety known as subjective units of discomfort (SUD) scale.
>
> 3 The client is then asked to imagine the anxiety provoking situations starting with the least disturbing and moving gradually up the scale to the most disturbing. At all stages, the person is encouraged to relax and no advancement is made to the next stage until relaxation is achieved. Because it is impossible to be relaxed and anxious at the same time, the individual becomes gradually (systematically) desensitised to the frightening situation.

Box 3.1 The three stages of systematic desensitisation

An early example of the use of systematic desensitisation for a simple phobia is provided in 'classic research'.

Flooding and implosion

In flooding, the client is exposed to the feared stimulus in a highly disturbing form for a prolonged period of time. Implosion therapy is similar except that the individual is asked to imagine and relive anxiety-provoking scenes. These therapies differ from systematic desensitisation in that, rather than trying to prevent fear occurring, they deliberately elicit a massive amount of anxiety. Both flooding and implosion therapy are based on the idea that a high level of autonomic arousal is impossible to sustain and eventually the feelings of fear and panic subside. After many sessions in a safe therapeutic environment the maladaptive responses are extinguished.

A classic example of the use of flooding for phobias was that of an adolescent girl with a phobia of travelling in cars who was driven around for four hours until her initial hysterical response subsided and her fear disappeared (Wolpe, 1973). A typical way in which it would be used for obsessive-compulsive disorders would be to oblige an individual with hand-washing obsession to touch something they regarded as 'dirty', such as a newspaper, and then not wash their hands for several hours afterwards until the anxiety had extinguished.

Marks (1976) maintains that in vivo (real life) exposure is more effective than in vitro (imagined) exposure no matter what the therapy. (As mentioned earlier, some therapists believe that systematic desensitisation is only really effective if carried out in vivo.) Foa and Tillmanas (1980) also argue that real life exposure plus imagined exposure is better than real life exposure alone. Marks (1987) argues that flooding overall is more effective than systematic desensitisation.

From an ethical point of view, the main problems with flooding and implosion therapies, especially the former, is that they are very traumatic. If the client decides to discontinue treatment then they can even do more harm than good since escape from the fearful stimulus has been reinforced. A new form of exposure therapy is that of virtual reality, as documented below in 'what's new?'.

what's new?

virtual reality exposure therapy

One of the most recent developments in behaviour therapies is the use of a virtual reality environment in order to expose a participant to a realistic simulation of a particular situation. Virtual reality offers a realistic environment in which participants becomes active within a computer-generated three-dimensional virtual world. This gives the user a sense of *presence* or *immersion* in the virtual environment (Rothbaum et al, 2000). The most usual way to create a virtual reality environment is to use a head-mounted display consisting of a separate screen for each eye with optics, stereo earphones and a head-tracking device. Users then interact with a virtual world that changes in a natural way as they move their head and body (see figure 3.3).

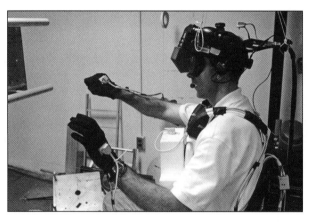

Figure 3.3 A virtual reality apparatus

Rothbaum (1995) was the first researcher to conduct a controlled study using VR. She treated acrophobia (fear of heights) by exposing phobics to virtual footbridges of various heights and stability; outdoor balconies and a glass elevator that ascended 50 floors. The participants reported physical symptoms of anxiety such as sweating, 'butterflies', loss of balance and heart palpitations. All of the 10 people treated showed a significant reduction in fear of heights and seven of them actually exposed themselves to heights in real life even though this was not part of the treatment. No member of an untreated control showed improvement.

The fear of flying is a phobia particularly suited to VR exposure therapy because of the difficulty and expense of using real aircraft and flights. Moreover, it is a common fear, estimated to affect between 10 to 25 per cent of the population. Rothbaum et al (2000) used VR exposure and standard exposure (SE) to treat fear of flying using eight sessions over six weeks. The study was very well controlled with participants being randomly assigned to the treatment groups and standard measure being used so that replication was possible. DSM classification was used to ensure that participants were genuinely suffering from fear of flying and the same therapist delivered both treatments, thus eliminating potential therapist effects. After treatment participants were given a flight and their willingness to fly and anxiety during the flight was used as a measure of success. The VR exposure was very effective, with 93 per cent of participants agreeing to fly, the same as the SE group. Both treatment groups were better than the controls and gains were maintained at a six-month follow-up.

Other studies of VR therapy include its use for spider phobia (Gilroy et al, 2000), fear of driving (Weiderhold & Weiderhold, 1999) and claustrophobia (Botella et al, 1999). Of particular significance is the finding that spider phobics are more inclined to seek treatment if it involves VR exposure than if they have to face real spiders. Thus, VR exposure may prove valuable in increasing the number of phobics who seek therapy (Garcia-Palacios et al, 2001). Although it is a little premature to assess the effectiveness of VR exposure therapy, the signs are that it is very effective and that improvements are maintained.

for and against

use of virtual reality exposure therapy

+ it is less time consuming than traditional methods such as systematic desensitisation

+ it creates a more realistic environment than using imagination or computer graphics

+ it is often more convenient, practical and inexpensive than in vivo exposure.

− its use is limited; it is unsuitable for use with some conditions. For example, it is not really suitable for coping with some social phobias such as eating in public

− some people have suffered cybersickness after wearing the head-mounted displays for some time

− the equipment required is complex, expensive and cumbersome (Rizzo et al, 1998)

Token economies

Token economies are based on the basic principles of operant conditioning, that behaviour that is reinforced is likely to be strengthened. When using a token economy the participant is rewarded for appropriate behaviour by the secondary reinforcers, namely tokens, which can be exchanged later for desirable items such as luxury food, television watching or additional recreational time. In institutions, they may even be used for weekend passes. It has been used with problem school children, juvenile delinquents and people suffering from developmental disability and schizophrenia.

Allyon and Azrin (1968) used this system with female long-stay patients with schizophrenia in a psychiatric hospital, reinforcing behaviours such as neat appearance, hair brushing, bed making and performing other chores. It not only led to a marked improvement in behaviour but an important additional benefit was an increase in staff morale. One of the problems in many institutions (and in families for that matter) is that inappropriate behaviour is often unwittingly reinforced by the attention it receives. A token economy system focuses staff attention on rewarding appropriate behaviour while ignoring inappropriate actions (Menditto et al, 1994). Recently the token economy system has been elaborated and extended for use with patients with schizophrenia. It is not claimed that such programmes will cure their condition but does lead to a marked improvement in their quality of life by resocialising such patients and teaching basic self-care.

Token economy programmes have been very successful in a variety of settings but work best in institutions where there can be careful control over the reinforcement programme. However, there are both practical and ethical problems involved. Sometimes the improvements in behaviour do not extend outside the setting in which they were implemented. Another problem is that this system is impractical as a means of encouraging some complex behaviours such as language. With regard to ethics, some people have criticised the token economy system as manipulative and inhumane, treating people as performing animals. However, others argue that in real life most people work for 'tokens' in that they earn money and it is part of everyday life to have our behaviour shaped by reinforcers. Moreover, as Carson and Butcher (1992) remark, the view of some lay people that token economy systems are the equivalent to expecting people in institutions to 'perform' for simple amenities is highly misjudged. Leaving them without the normal systems of rewards and punishments that operate in everyday life is liable to result in chronic social disability.

Modified use of token economy systems, all based on providing reinforcement but sometimes combined with punishment for unwanted or inappropriate behaviour, are common in many therapeutic settings. An example of the use of operant conditioning in therapy for alcohol abuse is related in 'research now'.

Petry N.M., Martin B., Cooney J.L. & Kranzler H.R. (2000) Give them prizes, and they will come: contingency management for treatment of alcohol dependence. *Journal of Counselling and Clinical Psychology* 68(5): 250–7

give them prizes, and they will come: contingency management for treatment of alcohol dependence

aim: to evaluate the effectiveness of a contingency management (operant conditioning) procedure that involved giving the opportunity to win prizes as reinforcers.

procedure: 42 alcohol-dependent males, diagnosed using DSM-1V, were randomly assigned to receive standard treatment or standard treatment plus contingency management.

Standard treatment consisted of four weeks of an intensive outpatient day programme followed by aftercare. The intensive day programme consisted of five-hour sessions, five days a week, focusing on factors such as life skills training, relapse prevention and coping skills training. During this time, participants were required to provide breath alcohol samples daily. In addition, once a week they were interviewed about any alcohol or drug use in the past week and provided a urine sample. During the four weeks aftercare, participants provided a breath and urine sample weekly.

Those in the *contingency management* group received this standard treatment but in addition every time they provided a negative breath test they earned a draw from a bowl. If they provided five consecutive negative breath tests, they were given five bonus draws. Seventy-five per cent of the slips were 'winning' ones with prizes that were either small, medium or large. The majority (90 per cent) were small prizes of $1 tokens (for use in certain shops); 9 per cent were medium prizes of objects worth $20 and there was a single large prize of a handheld TV, a boom box or a choice of five medium prizes.

Participants in this group also earned draws for completing other steps in their treatment programmes, such as becoming active in Alcoholics Anonomous. In keeping with the principles of a behavioural programme, the precise behaviours that would constitute these steps were clearly laid down and specific verification obtained.

findings: the reinforcement system was very effective in retaining the participants in treatment and in reducing the number who relapsed. Eighty-four per cent of the CM participants were retained in treatment for the eight-week period, compared with 22 per cent of the standard treatment ($p<0.001$). By the end of this period 69 per cent of the CM and only 39 per cent of the ST group were still abstinent. ($p<0.05$).

conclusion: the contingency management programme was demonstrated to be effective in the treatment of alcohol abuse. It can be used in addition to standard treatment procedures in order to increase the success of such a treatment programme.

► Paul G.L. & Menditto A.A. (1992) **Effectiveness of inpatient treatment programs for mentally ill adults in public facilities.** *Applied and Preventative Psychology Current Scientific Perspectives* **1: 41–63.** This is a useful discussion of the use of token economy and other related techniques for the treatment of people in institutional care.

for and against

behavioural therapies

+ there is a large body of evidence to suggest that behavioural therapies are successful in tackling the symptoms of mental disorder

+ there is no doubt that behavioural therapies can improve patients' quality of life

– there is a question of whether altering someone's behaviour is really a cure, and there may be cases where doing this may simply mask the underlying problem

– there are serious ethical issues to be considered in the use of behavioural therapies

where to now ?

► **Roth A., Fonagy P., Parry G. & Target M. (1996)** *What works for whom: a critical review of psychotherapy research.* **New York: Guilford Press.** This book provides a fairly recent report on the effectiveness and appropriateness of therapies, including behavioural ones.

► **Davey G.C.L. (ed) (1997)** *Phobias: a handbook of therapy research and treatment.* **Chichester, Wiley.**

► **Davison G.C. & Neale J.M. (2001)** *Abnormal psychology*, **8th edn. New York: Wiley.** Offer an in-depth discussion of several issues mentioned in this chapter, including the use of virtual reality as a therapeutic tool (page 47); the use of modelling and role play in assertiveness training (page 50); and the use of behaviour therapy for hospitalised patients with schizophrenia (page 306).

Conclusions

Behavioural therapies are very popular methods of treatment that have several advantages. They have a widely accepted theoretical underpinning: the principles of learning on which it is based have been demonstrated in many studies to have scientific validity. At the beginning of therapy, a list is drawn up of the precise behavioural changes that are required, making it possible to measure the therapy's effectiveness precisely. It is also a very economical method of treatment since most programmes require only a short period of treatment.

Like all therapeutic methods, behaviour therapy works better with some conditions than others. Since these therapies operate by defining what precise behaviours need to be changed, the more vague and ill defined the symptoms that the patient presents, the less appropriate behaviour therapy is likely to be. On the other hand, as we have seen, it has been shown to be effective in treating anxiety-based disorders such as simple phobias, obsessive-compulsive disorders and post-traumatic stress disorder (Smith et al, 1980; DeRubies et al, 1998). Operant techniques based on systematically rewarding desirable behaviours and extinguishing undesirable ones have been particularly successful in the treatment of a wide range of childhood problems including bed-wetting, extreme social withdrawal and severely disruptive behaviour (Kazdin & Weisz, 1998).

Some critics of behavioural therapy point to the fact, by treating specific behaviours, it provides clients with little insight into the causes of their symptoms or the associated psychological disorder from which they are suffering. Psychodynamic therapists maintain that in some cases behaviour therapy may treat the symptoms rather than the causes of mental disorder and is therefore of limited value. However, as Costello et al (1995) point out, the therapist invariably offers more than simply a means of specific behaviour change but offers encouragement and counselling as an integral part of the treatment. Indeed, this may be the very reason for the effectiveness of behaviour therapy, that it involves discovering the source of the anxiety underlying a patient's problems (Goldfried & Davison, 1994). This introduces a rather different criticism – that the success of behaviour therapy may depend at least partly on the attention and interest of the therapist rather than on the strict application of learning principles. Nevertheless, it is fair to say that therapies based on learning principles, while they can never be a 'cure-all', do offer a practical and effective treatment for a wide variety of conditions and, for this reason, are here to stay.

what do you know ?

1 Describe and evaluate classical conditioning as an explanation of mental disorders.

2 Outline two psychological therapies based on the learning approach.

3 Discuss the effectiveness and appropriateness of behavioural therapies.

4 The cognitive model of abnormality

what's ahead ?

The cognitive approach has been the dominant force in academic psychology since the early 1970s. The essence of this approach is to study internal mental processes such as perception, attention, memory and problem solving. Although these processes cannot be directly observed (ie we cannot open up someone's brain and 'see' their memory), they can be inferred from experimental tasks (eg we can work out what is going on in memory, from how well participants remember things). In this chapter we take a look at how the cognitive approach has been applied in the study of psychopathology, to explain the development of mental disorders such as depression and also how the link between cognition and brain function. The latter is known as the *cognitive-neuropsychological approach*. The later part of the chapter looks at how the cognitive approach has been used to develop therapeutic techniques for mental disorders and the effectiveness of these cognitive and cognitive-behavioural therapies.

Assumptions of the cognitive approach

The cognitive approach to the study of mental disorders developed in the late 1960s and early 1970s following the so-called 'cognitive revolution' in psychology. Dissatisfied with the limitations of learning approaches (see chapter 3), psychologists began to study internal mental processes such as perception, attention, memory and problem solving using the experimental method. The cognitive paradigm has now become the dominant approach in psychology (Richards, 1996) and as a direct consequence cognitive explanations and treatments for mental disorders have become dominant over other psychological approaches. The cognitive approach makes a number of implicit assumptions about the study of mental disorders:

- Rather than aiming to provide complete explanations for mental disorders, the cognitive approach focuses on explaining specific symptoms. For example, cognitive theories of schizophrenia focus on explaining symptoms such as thought insertion (see page 64) rather than the totality of the disorder.

- The emphasis in the cognitive approach is on the role of cognitive processes, for example, memory and thinking, in mental disorder. In certain disorders these cognitive factors are believed to play a direct causal role in mental disorder. Thus irrational beliefs about personal vulnerability are believed to put people at risk of anxiety. In other disorders such as schizophrenia, cognitive factors may not be the cause of the disorder in themselves, but are themselves the results of neurological factors (remember that brain function will affect cognitive function and vice versa).

- If symptoms of mental disorders are linked to cognitive factors, then it should be possible to treat these symptoms by targeting these cognitive factors. This is the basis behind the cognitive therapies developed by Aaron Beck and Albert Ellis.

Beck's cognitive theory of emotional disorders

Beck (1976) proposed a cognitive theory to explain mental disorders characterised by cognitive content, including depression, anxiety disorders and eating disorders. The starting point of Beck's theory is that people react differently to unpleasant or *aversive* situations. For example, some people might develop depression following an unrelenting succession of tragedies, but this is not necessarily true of all of us. Beck argued that it is necessary to consider internal mental processes in order to explain why some people might develop this or that disorder and why others do not. As figure 4.1 shows, when aversive life events are combined with a certain set of cognitive processes, then they might interact to produce an emotional disorder. Essentially, Beck's view is that cognition precedes an emotional response, so that a disorder characterised by emotional content is caused (in part) by cognitive processes.

Early experience
↓
Formation of dysfunctional beliefs
↓
Critical life incidents
↓
Assumptions activated
↓
Biased information processing
↓ ↑
Symptoms of emotional disorders;
behavioural, motivational, affective, cognitive,
somatic

Figure 4.1 Beck's cognitive theory of emotional disorders (Beck, 1976)

Beck believed that dysfunctional beliefs are formed early in childhood through the acquisition of certain types of *schemas* (ie packets of information about different aspects of the world), and that different disorders are characterised by different types of schemes. For example, depression is characterised by what Beck calls a *cognitive triad* of negative schemas; a negative view of one's self, one's personal world and one's future (see page 76 for a fuller account). In contrast, anxiety is characterised by *vulnerability schemas*; a perceived physical and psychological threat to oneself. A key point in Beck's theory is that an individual who has acquired these schemas will not necessarily develop an emotional disorder. Some kind of critical life event is required to activate these schemas. For example, someone who has acquired a cognitive triad will not necessarily develop depression, if they experience a situation similar to the one in which the negative schemas were initially acquired they are likely to be activated, leading to a negative world-view that in turn predisposes the individual to depression.

Once schemas are activated they influence information processing so that only information consistent with that schema is processed and other information tends to be disregarded. For example, once a cognitive triad is activated the individual will only process information consistent with their negative view of their self, their world and their future It is this biased information processing that gives rise to the symptoms of the emotional disorder. Because the individual is only processing information consistent with their dysfunctional beliefs, it reinforces their distorted view of the world and confirms their belief that they were right all along.

There is no doubt that Beck's theory has been enormously influential in establishing the cognitive approach as the dominant approach in clinical psychology and his

ideas were eagerly taken up by the clinical psychology profession in the UK as they attempted to forge a separate identity from psychiatric profession (Parker et al, 1995). However, evidence for Beck's therapy is mixed and there are a number of important criticisms to be made of his theory. The key to finding evidence for Beck's theory is by showing that cognitive processes are causing the emotional disturbance. This can be difficult in practice, as when somebody with an emotional disorder meets a clinical psychologist, they already have the disorder and it is not possible to measure their cognitive processes before the onset of the disorder. None the less there are two potential routes to take. One is utilise experimental tasks to try and measure differences in cognitive processes between participants with and without an emotional disorder. Another approach to testing Beck's approach is to evaluate his therapy, ie to tell whether an emotional disorder can be treated by changing cognition.

Research has also supported Beck's notion of biased information processing in depression, at least in cases of major depression (see page 76). It is also well documented that childhood life events are associated with adult depression (Brown & Harris, 1978; Eley & Stevenson, 2000). This is consistent with Beck's ideas (as it is with other explanations, such as that of Freud, see page 75), but this does not directly support cognitive theory unless it can be demonstrated that the early experience actually leads to the formation of dysfunctional beliefs, which then put an individual at risk of developing an emotional disorder later in life. Research into this issue is discussed on page 76).

The effectiveness of Beck's cognitive therapy as a treatment is well documented, but does not in itself demonstrate the validity of Beck's theory (Oie & Free, 1995). That is, just because Beck's therapy may work, it does not necessarily mean his theory is correct. Eysenck (1997) is highly critical of the way schematic processing is used in Beck's theory. It is not well defined and may account to little more than a belief. More importantly though, the existence of schemas in Beck's theory is established through the use of circular reasoning. The existence of schemas is inferred from certain responses (on experimental tasks for example), and then that schema is used to explain the information processing biases producing that response. Such an approach is not scientific and there is no way of independently verifying the existence of such hypothetical cognitive structures. For social constructionists the cognitive approach is overly reductionist and mechanistic, having difficulty in explaining people who hold contradictory beliefs, or who think dynamically rather than rationally (Parker et al, 1995).

for and
against

Beck's theory

+ research has supported Beck's view that depressed participants show biases in information processing

+ research has supported Beck's view that in depression at least, cognitive factors do appear to play a causal role

– Beck's cognitive therapy is effective in treating a wide range of emotional disorders, but this in itself does not necessarily mean that Beck's theory is correct

– concepts like schemas are not well defined and are established through circular reasoning

where to now?

▶ **Beck A.T. (1976)** *Cognitive therapy and the emotional disorders*. **New York: International Universities Press.** This classic text outlining Beck's cognitive theory and therapy for emotional disorders is still available, reprinted by Penguin.

The cognitive neuropsychological approach

The cognitive neuropsychological approach is based on the relationship between cognitive function and brain function. Brain function has a profound affect on cognitive function and any changes in brain function often manifest as changes in cognitive function. In fact, the use of patients with brain damage has become one of the key methods in advancing knowledge about cognitive function (Eysenck & Keane, 2000). For example, in the area of memory, the famous case study of H.M. (Blakemore, 1988), who had difficulty forming new long-term memories following surgery to remove his hippocampus, has been cited as the single strongest piece of evidence for the distinction between a short-term and long-term memory.

In psychological disorders, there remains the possibility that cognitive symptoms might be manifestations of an underlying change in brain function. This will not be the case for all psychological disorders. For example, Beck's theory outlined above is probably a 'pure' cognitive theory in that disorders such as depression and phobias are (partly) caused by cognitive factors themselves. In other

disorders such as schizophrenia and post-traumatic stress disorder (PTSD) it seems likely that cognitive symptoms are themselves caused by changes in brain function. Therefore a cognitive theory for some disorders (eg depression) may be causal, and for other disorders (eg schizophrenia) may be more explanatory than causal. Frith (1992) makes the point strongly, that even though a cognitive theory of schizophrenia may not be causal, it may still represent the best theory of schizophrenia. This is partly because of cognitive theories tend to work with symptoms rather than disorders, and therefore avoids problems of changing diagnostic criteria, and partly because cognition can be mapped on to brain function.

An influential cognitive theory of post-traumatic stress disorder (PTSD) was proposed by Brewin et al (1996) based on the theory of cue-dependent forgetting (see *Angles on psychology*). The main feature that distinguishes PTSD from other anxiety disorders such as phobias, is the force by which the person re-experiences the traumatic event, complete with the full sensory and emotional range present at the original event. It is almost as if the person is back in the original traumatic event. Often these experiences are triggered by seemingly insignificant sights, sounds or smells related to the traumatic event. For example, someone with PTSD following a particularly traumatic car crash may experience a 'flashback' triggered by the smell of petrol. Brewin et al (1996) argue that these flashbacks are types of cue-dependent memories, where stimuli similar to the original traumatic event may trigger sensory and emotional aspects of the memory. These cue-dependent memories operate on two levels; verbally accessible memories such as the ability to recount the traumatic experience and situationally accessible memories. These are the non-verbal, sensory and emotional memories, associated with flashbacks.

for and
against

the cognitive neuropsychological approach

+ neuropsychological evidence about brain function can be used to test cognitive theories of mental disorders

– cognitive neuropsychological theories of mental disorders can somewhat speculative as they involve mapping one type of explanation (neuropsychological) on to another (cognitive)

– neuropsychological evidence is often of a very complex nature, with many contradictory findings

where to
now?

▶ **Frith C.D. (1992)** *The cognitive neuropsychology of schizophrenia*. **Hove: Psychology Press.** A landmark text tracing the history of neurological research into schizophrenia, and how such a body of findings can be incorporated with the cognitive approach.

▶ **Scott M.J. & Stradling S.G. (2001)** *Counselling for post-traumatic stress disorder*. **London: Sage.** This extremely accessible text outlines both cognitive and neurological correlates for PTSD, going on to suggest how a synthesis of the two approaches can be used in cognitive therapy for PTSD.

Cognitive and cognitive-behavioural therapies

Cognitive therapy refers to those therapeutic techniques aiming to change or modify a person's thoughts or beliefs. This is in part based on the belief in *cognitive primacy*, the idea that thinking occurs before and leads to emotion and behaviour. For example, in Beck's theory outlined above certain negative schema (the cognitive triad) can result in depression. Based on this therefore the way to treat depression is to target these negative schemas and dysfunctional beliefs. Sometimes cognitive therapists will set clients behavioural tasks (sometimes referred to as *homework*) in order to dispute dysfunctional beliefs. For example, a therapist might ask a depressed client to plan an evening out to the cinema to counter their belief that the life is always dull. For reason, these therapies are sometimes referred to as cognitive-behavioural therapies. The two terms are used interchangeably and do not refer to different techniques or therapies. There are a number of variations on the cognitive-behavioural therapies. We can look here at one approach in particular – Ellis's rational emotive behaviour therapy.

Rational-emotive behaviour therapy (REBT)

Ellis (1962) proposed that we have two basic goals; to feel relatively happy and to be free of pain. These are, however, preferences and not necessities. In Ellis's view,

rationality consists of thinking in ways that contribute to the attainment of these goals, irrationality consists of thinking in ways that block their attainment. Thus a rational outlook to life consists of striking a balance between short-term and long-term goals. Ellis (1991) proposed three key ideas behind rational emotive behaviour therapy – REBT (see box 4.1).

---

1 Thought and emotion are closely related.

2 Thought and emotion are so closely related that they usually accompany each other in a circular cause and effect relationship, and in certain respects are the same thing, so that one's thinking becomes one's emotion and one's emotion becomes one's thinking.

3 Thought and emotion take the form of self-talk, sentences that we keep saying to ourselves eventually become thoughts and emotions, thus a person's self-statements are capable of both generating and modifying their emotions.

Box 4.1 The key ideas behind REBT

REBT is not a theory of no emotions, but one of appropriate emotions. It may be appropriate for someone in an alien and difficult world to be fearful, cautious and vigilant so that they make take steps necessary for realistic protection. Anxiety, however, is seen as an inappropriate emotion based on irrational thinking and may block appropriate behaviour. Thus emotions are appropriate when they are accompanied by rational beliefs, which are functional in the sense that they do not block the possibility of effective action and attainment of goals.

Ellis's emphasis is much more on how people sustain their irrationality than on how they develop it. He considers that psychology has focused on how people originally become illogical, but this by no means indicates how people maintain their illogical behaviour or what they should do to change it. REBT operates within an ABC framework:

● A is the activating event, a fact or event or the behaviour or attitude of another person.

● B is the beliefs we hold about A.

● C is the cognitive, emotional or behavioural consequence resulting from A.

Ellis considers that humans largely control their own emotional destinies through the beliefs held at B. Thus the emotional and behavioural consequences of the various activating events in our lives are controlled by our belief systems and we are capable of learning to control and modify our belief systems and hence their consequences. The following example shows the ABC model applied to understanding the effects of failing an exam (from Palmer & Dryden, 1995).

Table 4.1 Example of the ABC model

A	activating event	failing exam
B	beliefs	'I should have passed.'
		'I am a failure.'
		'I can't bear not passing.'
C	consequences	depression

The existence of this type of irrational belief prevents people exhibiting *stoicism*. Stoicism is the ability to withstand the effects of adverse events. Ellis proposed that the most efficient way of helping someone to feel better was to change their irrational beliefs and make them more stoical. Abrams and Ellis (1996) identify two types of irrational belief that cause particular problems when we encounter adversity. *Musturbation* is the tendency to think that we *must* be perfect and successful at all times. *I-can't-stand-it-itis* is the belief that it is a disaster whenever something does not go smoothly. Musturbation makes us too sensitive to failure and I-can't-stand-it-itis makes even minor problems seem disastrous.

interactive angles

Jot down as many examples of musturbation and I-can't-stand-it-itis as you can. To what extent do you think these are irrational and how effective do you think therapy might be in changing them?

Changing to rational beliefs

The major objective of REBT is to substitute rational and functional beliefs for irrational and dysfunctional beliefs at stage B. This can be cognitive through helping the client to identify their 'shoulds' and 'musts' or behavioural through homework assignments (similar to Beck) and self-reinforcement. The ABC model is expanded here:

● D is disputing irrational beliefs;

● E is the effects of successfully disputing irrational beliefs. These can be cognitive (rational beliefs), emotional (appropriate feelings) and behavioural (desirable behaviour).

The effectiveness of REBT

A meta-analysis of 31 outcome studies was conducted by Engels et al (1993), finding that REBT was more effective for treating anxiety based disorders than systematic desensitisation or combination therapies where REBT was combined with some form of behavioural therapy. The effect sizes shown in table 4.2 show all forms of therapy to be effective (remember, an effect size of 0.8+ is a highly effective treatment), in particular REBT. For a brief outline of measuring the effectiveness of therapy using effect size, see the discussion of Beck's cognitive therapy above.

Table 4.2 The effectiveness of REBT (Engels et al, 1993)

Therapy	Mean effect size
REBT	1.62
Combination therapy	1.42
Systematic desensitisation	1.35

Further evidence for the effectiveness of REBT comes from a review of 89 outcome studies by Silverman et al (1992). REBT was shown to be either more effective or equal to other types of therapy (such as systematic desensitisation) for a wide range of disorders including depression, anxiety disorders, sexual dysfunction, type A behaviour, anger, self-esteem, stress and alcohol abuse. REBT was also shown to be equal to person-centred therapy for clients with a variety of symptoms not specific to any particular disorder:

● 49 studies showed REBT to be the most effective treatment;

● 40 studies showed no difference between REBT and other therapies;

● 0 studies showed any treatment to be more effective than REBT.

While these reviews seem to be leading to the conclusion than REBT is without doubt a highly effective treatment, Solomon and Haaga (1995) discuss whether results of these kinds of studies can be generalised to routine clinical practice (this is an issue for all therapy outcome research – see the discussion of Beck's cognitive therapy above). Due to various methodological difficulties in outcome studies, such as the lack of an equivalent control group and only using short-term follow-ups, the effectiveness of REBT may have been seriously underestimated. This problem however is offset by another, which is that REBT outcome studies tended to be conducted by highly trained therapists who are proponents of REBT. These therapists are likely to be better at delivering REBT than the non-specialist. Solomon and Haaga argue that these factors will probably balance each other out in a meta-analysis, but more research is required.

Discussion of the effectiveness of cognitive-behavioural therapy

Most contemporary CBT practitioners freely mix techniques from Beck's cognitive therapy, Ellis's REBT and other more recently developed approaches. Thus most studies have evaluated the success of this 'mixed CBT'. A very large number of studies now support the effectiveness of CBT. An exciting recent development has been in the application of CBT to treat schizophrenia and related conditions. Until recently it was widely believed that this type of disorder was not treatable by psychological therapies, but there is now research to show that in some patients symptoms can be alleviated by CBT. We can examine one such study in detail.

research now

CBT can help some patients with schizophrenia

Chadwick P., Sambrooke S., Rasch S. & Davies E. (2000) Challenging the omnipotence of voices: group cognitive behaviour therapy for voices. *Behaviour Research & Therapy* 38: 993–1003

aim: until recently it has been widely believed that schizophrenia does not respond to psychological therapies and can only be treated by biomedical means such as drugs. The aim of the study was to test the relatively new idea that CBT can be helpful in tackling the symptoms of schizophrenia. More specifically the effectiveness of CBT conducted in groups was examined.

procedure: 22 participants with a diagnosis of schizophrenia, characterised by the symptom of hearing voices, were assessed with regard to their cognitive and emotional symptoms. Depression and anxiety were measured, as were beliefs in the power and control of voices. They took part in eight sessions of group CBT, in which therapists focused on challenging patients' beliefs about their voices. At the end of the course of treatment patients were reassessed.

findings: the major finding was that participants experienced a significant reduction in negative beliefs about the power of their voices, and the extent to which they were controlled by them. No reduction in anxiety or depression was reported, however patients reported benefiting from the groups and in some cases their behaviour was visibly less affected by their schizophrenia.

conclusion: CBT is effective in tackling the cognitive aspects of schizophrenia, and it appears that improvements in this area have a positive effect on patients' general functioning and quality of life.

Despite the positive findings of most research, and the exciting range of conditions to which CBT can be applied, some researchers have reservations about the zeal with which clinical psychology has embraced the approach. Harrington et al (1998) have pointed out that some key published reviews of CBT effectiveness have ignored studies that have shown CBT in a less positive light. There are also a minority of instances where CBT has been found to be distinctly inferior to alternative therapeutic approaches. In a study of alcohol dependency Sandahl et al (1998) found that at 15-month follow-up significantly more patients were abstaining from alcohol after psychodynamic therapy (see chapter 5 for a discussion) than following CBT. Concerns have also been raised about the kind of research on which our understanding of CBT effectiveness is based. Most studies have focused on the short-term benefits on *monosymptomatic* patients, ie those only showing symptoms of one condition. We thus know relatively little about long-term effects of CBT or its effects on patients with a broad range of symptoms.

what's
new

eye movement desensitisation and reprocessing (EMDR)

EMDR is a controversial treatment, originally designed as a therapy for PTSD by Shapiro (1989). The therapy involves exposure to the traumatic stimuli while the client follows an object moving horizontally back and forth. This can be done by the therapist moving their hand back and forth (does this sound similar to hypnosis?) or by a more sophisticated device with a light moving back and forth. The use of EMDR has produced heated debate, partially because Shapiro claims it is so effective and partially due to a lack of understanding about how it might work.

Shapiro has suggested a cognitive-neuropsychological basis for EMDR where eye movements trigger a physiological mechanism promoting an information processing system to restructure memory. Hence traumatic memories of the sort experienced in a PTSD flashback can be successfully reintegrated into its original time and place. Shapiro (1995) has gone on to suggest that EMDR could be used to treat pain control, delusions, ritual abuse, phobias, generalised anxiety, schizophrenia and eating disorders and many more disorders beside, a grand claim indeed, and one that is not always supported.

Renfrey and Spates (1994) compared PTSD patients in groups with and without eye movements and found that both groups were equally effective in symptom reduction. In a review of several EMDR outcome studies, Lohr et al (1998) concludes that eye movements are not necessary for a reduction of PTSD symptoms. In fact finger tapping has been shown to have the same therapeutic effect as eye movements (Wilson et al, 1996). If as these studies suggest, therapeutic effectiveness of EMDR is not due to eye movement, then it seems the crucial component of this therapy is the exposure to traumatic memories in a safe environment. As such, Senior (2001) makes the point that really the treatment should be renamed.

Conclusions

The cognitive approach was taken up enthusiastically by clinical psychologists in the UK in the 1970s as they attempted to forge a separate identity from psychiatry (Parker et al, 1995). The cognitive approach has now become the dominant force in clinical psychology, resulting in an enormous amount of research into cognitive factors and mental disorders. There are now cognitive theories for virtually every disorder, more than this chapter has the scope to deal with, and has also formed the basis of many treatment programmes for offenders. The growth of cognitive psychology in clinical psychology has resulted in a dramatic increase in the use of cognitive based therapies for mental disorders. Cognitive therapies have shown themselves to be extremely effective in reducing symptoms for a wide range of disorders, and for many therapists and clinical psychologists cognitive based approaches are now the therapy of choice.

**what
do you
know ?**

1 Describe the cognitive approach to the study of mental disorders. Include both assumptions and cognitive theories in your answer.

2 Evaluate the cognitive approach to the study of mental disorders. You could consider the advantages of taking a cognitive approach compared to other approaches, or evidence to support cognitive theories.

3 Are cognitive therapies effective? Support your answer with evidence from outcome studies.

5 The psychodynamic model of abnormality

what's ahead?

The psychodynamic approach is one of the older psychological models still used to understand and treat mental disorder. You should already have studied the work of Sigmund Freud, who developed the psychodynamic approach in the late nineteenth and early twentieth century. In this chapter, having looked the general assumptions of the psychodynamic approach, we take a look at some of Freud's ideas on mental health and examine them in the light of contemporary research. The remainder of this chapter will be spent looking at psychodynamic therapies and evaluating their usefulness in tackling mental disorder.

Assumptions of the approach

General assumptions of the psychodynamic approach to psychology can be found in Jarvis et al (2000) *Angles on psychology*. Here, we are interested more specifically in the assumptions made when taking a psychodynamic approach to understanding psychological distress and mental health problems.

- The quality of our early relationships, particularly those with parents, is of critical importance for our mental health in later childhood and adulthood.

- Early traumatic experiences, in particular those that cause disruption to our early relationships, are associated with later mental health problems.

- Our early experiences are retained in the *unconscious mind* and affect our later feelings, motives and relationships. By 'the unconscious mind' we mean those aspects of mental functioning of which we are not normally aware.

- Whereas the biomedical model treats mental disorder as physical illness, and learning and cognitive models see it in terms of acquired patterns of maladaptive behaviour and thinking, the psychodynamic model views mental disorder as emotional responses to trauma, unmet needs or unsatisfied instincts.

When considering the psychodynamic approach to mental health, it is important to make a distinction between these broad principles and specific psychodynamic theories. Psychodynamic theories, for example, that of Freud, are attempts to explain the reasons why these broad psychodynamic principles appear to hold true. The distinction is important because it is quite possible to work in mental health taking a psychodynamic approach without accepting the details of any particular theory. In this chapter we will explore both general psychodynamic principles and Freudian theory.

Early experience and later mental disorder

Before looking in some detail at Freudian and attachment perspectives on mental disorder it is worth first considering whether the broad psychodynamic assumptions about the impact of early relationships and trauma hold true – if not then there is little point in taking the theory seriously! To understand the ways in which early trauma can affect our adult functioning, let us begin with a case study from Lemma-Wright (1995), shown in box 5.1.

Alex was the older of two young adult sisters. One weekend Alex organised a sea boat-trip to celebrate her sister's birthday. The trip went well, but Alex suffered a panic attack on the boat. Alex had always loved her sister dearly, but she had also resented her a little, believing that her family had always doted on her while ignoring Alex. On one occasion as a child, Alex had become so angry with her sister for being the centre of attention that she dragged her into the sea, frightening her badly. As an adult, Alex frequently felt obliged to organise her sister's life and to help her out of financial difficulties. She had no idea why she suffered the panic attack until a few days later when she had a dream in which she had a fight with a friend (who reminded her of her sister) and wished her dead. It then became apparent to Alex that the boat-trip, in which Alex had once again taken her sister into the sea, had stirred up guilty memories of the time she had dragged her into the sea.

Box 5.1 The case of Alex (adapted from Lemma-Wright, 1995)

We can understand Alex's problem by referring to the psychodynamic assumptions about the origins of mental disorder. Her difficulties began with her poor relationship with her parents, which in turn resulted in the traumatic experience of dragging her sister into the sea. The guilt resulting from this experience remained in Alex's unconscious mind, influencing her to look after her sister as an adult. When Alex organised the boat trip for her sister, this triggered the memory of the traumatic event in their childhood and the resulting flood of anxiety led her to have a panic attack. In this case Alex's condition, which might be diagnosed as *panic disorder* (see chapter 10, which deals with anxiety disorders), can be explained as an emotional response to early trauma.

Research firmly supports the association between early trauma and poor early relationships and the incidence of

classic
research

The case of Anna O

Breuer J. & Freud S. (1896) *Studies on hysteria.* **The complete works of Sigmund Freud, volume II. London: Hogarth**

---

aim: the aim of the case was primarily the treatment of Anna's symptoms. However, the case also served as a valuable demonstration of the usefulness of Freud's theory and therapy, which was just becoming well known.

case history: Anna O was a 21-year-old, highly intellectual woman. Her symptoms developed when she was nursing her father through a long illness. During the first five months of his illness Anna devoted herself to caring for her father. Her own health deteriorated and she suffered weakness, anaemia and lack of interest in food. She became bed-ridden, meaning that she was unable to continue to nurse her father. It was at this point that her hysterical symptoms manifested themselves. She suffered a range of symptoms, including headaches, a narrowing of the visual field, deafness, paralysis of the neck and lack of sensation in the limbs. Towards the end of the period before her father died in April 1881 she also suffered speech-related symptoms, forgetting words, then becoming mute for two weeks.

Anna's father's death and the shock of it worsened her symptoms. She began to suffer new symptoms including prosopagnosia (inability to recognise faces). During this period Anna also had symptoms of dissociation, displaying two personalities. One personality was anxious and depressed but fully aware of what was happening. The second was irrational and aggressive, throwing pillows and tearing buttons from her nightdress. Breuer had Anna removed to a country sanatorium, where she began what she called her 'talking cure'. This is the first recorded reference to the term and marks the birth of psychodynamic therapy. Breuer noted that when allowed to speak unchecked Anna tended to speak of events prior to the development of her symptoms, and that she would frequently link events to her symptoms. For example, she made an association between her deafness and a childhood incident where Anna's brother had caught her listening at her parents' door one night. During this process the symptoms would often worsen, however following the focus on each symptom it would disappear.

interpretation: Freud explained Anna's symptoms and treatment in terms of his hydraulic model. Her frustrated intellectual abilities had led to a build up of psychic energy. The trauma of her father's illness had triggered a process where this energy was converted into symptoms. The process of catharsis that resulted when Anna talked to Breuer released the psychic energy and so lessened her symptoms.

later mental health problems. In chapters 8 to 11, which deal with specific mental disorders, we can examine in detail the links between childhood events and relationships and each of these conditions. For example, early loss experiences are associated with depression (see page 75).

Freudian theory and psychopathology

For a more detailed general account of Freudian theory, see Jarvis et al (2000) *Angles on psychology*. In this book we are just concerned with how Freud explained mental disorder. Freud's more specific ideas about particular disorders are examined in the relevant chapters. The aim of this section is to examine in more general terms how Freud's understanding of the mind helped him explain mental disorder. We can look in particular at Freud's hydraulic model of the mind and the controversial idea of psychosexuality. For further useful details of Freudian theory of mental disorder, see in particular page 75 where the role of early loss experiences in depression is discussed and page 90 where we look at Freud's view of anxiety.

Freud's hydraulic model of the mind

Freud got the idea of the hydraulic model from literature, where phrases like 'to cry oneself out' and 'to blow off steam' were commonly used to describe emotional responses. These phrases suggest that the mind is a system in which psychic (mental) energy behaves in much the same way as physical energy. Freud believed that, like other forms of energy, psychic energy could be discharged or transformed but not destroyed. Trauma and the inability to express instincts resulted in a build up of psychic energy that led to the symptoms of mental disorder. One of the aims of psychodynamic therapy is *catharsis*, the release of accumulated psychic energy. Breuer and Freud (1896) explained the classic case study of Anna O in terms of dammed energy and her treatment in terms of catharsis. This case is discussed in 'classic research'.

interactive angles

How credible do you think Freud's interpretation is of Anna O's symptoms and recovery?

Some psychologists find the hydraulic model a useful metaphor for explaining why the effects of early events can be experienced in the form of symptoms some time later. However, it is simply a metaphor, and modern studies of the brain have revealed that there is no actual build up and discharge of any form of energy (Miller, 1999). Thus the hydraulic model describes effectively how people experience psychological distress but not literally what is happening to them. Psychologists are divided on the issue of whether metaphors like this are useful. From a psychodynamic point of view it is most important to understand how people experience psychological distress, and metaphors are a useful tool for this. However, more hard-nosed scientists say that the hydraulic model is unsupported and outdated, and would suggest that metaphors like this are misleading rather than helpful.

Psychosexuality

Freud's view of psychosexuality is the most socially sensitive and controversial aspect of his theory. In his early work Freud proposed *seduction theory*, in which he emphasised the role of childhood sexual abuse in causing psychological problems. He famously put it thus; 'whatever case and whatever symptom we take as our starting point, in the end we infallibly come to the realm of sexual experience' (underscore added) (Freud, 1896, page 193). The term 'sexual experience' is quite broad and describes a range of sexual traumas. Recall the case of Anna O (opposite), whose deafness in early adulthood was linked to her listening at her parents' bedroom door as a child. However, Freud identified sexual abuse as the major cause of psychopathology.

Contemporary research supports Freud's early view that childhood sexual abuse (CSA) is common and very harmful. In a review of studies Finkelhor (1994) found that reported rates of CSA ranged from 7–36 per cent in women and 3–29 per cent in men. Of the mental disorders examined in detail in this book, sexual abuse is associated with increased risk of anxiety disorders (Christo, 1997), depression (Stoppard, 2000), eating disorders (Schmidt et al, 1997) and multiple personality disorder (Kluft, 1993). Some of these associations are extremely strong. Although this whole area is surrounded by controversy and no statistics can be taken as fact, some research has suggested that up to half of those suffering from eating disorders have been sexually abused as have the majority of sufferers of multiple personality disorder (Crowe, 1997).

Connolly on the couch

When Connolly's father returned from the [Second World] war to live in the overcrowded flat, he came home drunk most nights to share a sofabed with his son. For a period of about five years, Connolly says, his father, a fierce Catholic, 'interfered with him' – a secret he did not share with anyone until the day of his father's death, when he broke down and told his wife.

Billy Connolly has never told jokes; he has just let off steam and has enjoyed fabulously the process of doing it. Talking about the source of his humour, he says: 'I don't know why I'm funny. But there are reasons for my attitudes. People ask why I'm still angry when I'm loaded? And I don't know. But I like my anger. I find it comforting.'

Taken from an interview with the comedian Billy Connolly, *The Observer Magazine*, 23 September 2001

1 What lasting consequences of sexual abuse can you pick out of these extracts?

2 Explain Connolly's humour using Freud's hydraulic model.

Figure 5.1 Comedian Billy Connolly

Unfortunately, Freud shifted the emphasis of his work on psychosexuality away from sexual abuse towards the role of sexual fantasy. Freud believed that some of children's reports of CSA were actually sexual fantasies of their own, and that symptoms resulted from the repression of the sexual instinct, and in some cases the shameful memories of these fantasies. This has been interpreted by some writers, for example Masson (1984), as the deliberate abandonment of sexually abused children in order to escape the controversy his seduction theory had generated. Whatever Freud's motives, it is generally agreed that his shift away from seduction theory was a serious error.

Freud believed that one fantasy shared by all children took place in the *Oedipus complex*. This is a three-way family dynamic in which children in their phallic stage (3–6 years) develop a powerful attachment to the opposite sex parent and see the same-sex parent as a rival. On an unconscious level they want to kill the same sex parent and have sex with the opposite sex parent (although they do not have an adult understanding of either death or sex). A classic case study of the Oedipus complex,

Little Hans (Freud, 1909) is discussed on page 90, in our later discussion of phobias.

Discussion of Freud's contributions

Although Freud is one of the most heavily (and unreasonably) criticised of all psychologists (Masling & Bornstein, 1996; Mollon, 2000), some of his ideas remain useful in understanding the links between childhood experience and later psychopathology. Freud's observations that depression often followed an early experience of loss (page 76), and that a variety of problems typically follow sexual abuse are well supported by contemporary research. His development of the 'talking cure', which underlies modern psychological therapies, is one of the greatest ever contributions to psychology.

Brilliant as Freud was, we should not lose sight of the limitations of his theory. He was operating at a time when we knew almost nothing about the workings of the brain, and modern neuroscience has found no evidence of any biological process that might be related to 'dammed psychic energy' or its release. Freud's notion of psychosexuality (with the exception of seduction theory) now seems dated and irrelevant, and there is firm evidence that, even if the Oedipus complex exists, it is not a key determinant of mental health. If it were we would expect children of single and gay parents (who presumably do not have the opportunity to develop an Oedipus complex) to suffer serious mental health problems but this is not the case (see Jarvis & Russell, 2002, for a detailed discussion of gay parenting).

for and against

Freudian theory

 some aspects of Freudian theory, for example, seduction theory and the importance of early loss experiences are supported by contemporary research

— Freud's later emphasis on sexual fantasy is not supported by research, and it is widely agreed that his theoretical move away from seduction theory has been very unhelpful in understanding the effects of CSA

+ Freud developed the 'talking cure,' which still underlies modern psychological therapies

— Freud's hydraulic model of the mind is not supported by contemporary research

where to now?

The following are good sources of further information about Freud's theory of psychopathology.

▶ **Bateman A. & Holmes J. (1995)** *Introduction to psychoanalysis*. **London: Routledge.** An excellent account of a range of psychodynamic theories, including explanations of mental disorder.

▶ **Jarvis M. (2003)** *Psychodynamic psychology: classical theory and contemporary research*. **London: Thomson Learning.** A state-of-the-art account of psychodynamic ideas, with a particular emphasis on up-to-date studies.

Psychodynamic approaches to therapy

The psychodynamic approach to psychological therapy originated with the case of Anna O (page 36). Initially, in line with Freud's hydraulic model of the mind, the aim of the therapy was catharsis. Catharsis remains an important part of therapy. We can isolate catharsis from other therapeutic factors in order to test its importance by asking patients to write about traumatic or unhappy experiences (this is called *scriptotherapy*). In a recent review of studies of scriptotherapy, Smyth and Greenberg (2000) concluded that scriptotherapy reliably reduced psychological and physiological symptoms, supporting its usefulness in therapy.

Freud and later psychodynamic therapists added further *interpretive* techniques that aim to give patients *insight* into the origins of their symptoms. Psychodynamic therapies thus focus on the personal history of the patient, viewing their current emotional state, behaviour and relationships as products of their earlier experiences. For this reason, there is an emphasis in therapy sessions on discussion of the patient's past, and the therapist may make connections between present and past events or direct the patient to introspect further on childhood issues. However, a basic principle of psychodynamic therapy is that if allowed to *free-associate*, ie to speak without direction patients frequently return to childhood events and relationships. This means that psychodynamic therapists frequently do not need to direct patients to think about these things.

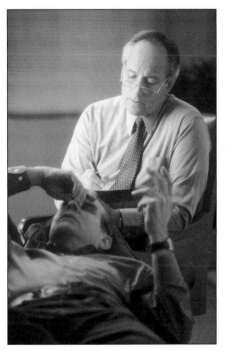

Figure 5.2 Traditionally, patients in psychodynamic therapy lie on a couch, while the therapist sits behind

Interpretation and insight

A distinguishing feature of the psychodynamic therapies is the use of interpretation. The aim of interpretation is to give the patient insight into their origins of their feelings and behaviour. The most important way in which insight can be achieved is by the interpretation of *transference*. Transference occurs when the patient relates to the therapist as if they were a significant figure from their past. For example, someone who has childhood memories of harsh parents may become very angry towards the therapist, transferring on to them the anger that they have carried towards their parents since childhood. By feeding back an interpretation of this transference of anger to the patient, the therapist can give them insight into how their past relationships affect their current relationships, for example becoming unreasonably angry with people. One way in which therapists aid the development of transference is to minimise the details of their own lives and personality that are available to patients. This means that they maintain a 'blank screen' to patients, showing little emotion and not normally disclosing details of their own lives or their feelings towards the patient.

Resistance can also be interpreted. Freud (1912) placed great emphasis on the resistance of the patient to change, and described therapy as a battle to overcome resistance. According to Freud, resistance can manifest itself in a number of ways, including the use of psychological defences and establishing a negative transference towards the therapist. Resistance may also manifest as

research
now

does insight really help?

Kivlighan D.M., Multon K.D. & Patton M.J. (2000) Insight and symptom reduction in time-limited psycho-analytic counselling. *Journal of Counselling Psychology* 47: 50–8

aim: the major aim of all varieties of psychodynamic therapy is to give patients insight into their feelings, interpersonal behaviour and, when possible, their origins. However, there has been very little research to test the assumption that these insights actually make patients feel better. The aim of this study was to see whether new insights are followed by a reduction in symptoms.

procedure: the participants were 12 psychodynamic counsellors and their patients. Patients and counsellors rated the severity of patients' symptoms before and after each of 20 sessions. Patients also completed a questionnaire called the important events questionnaire (IEQ) to assess their insight after each session. Three independent judges rated patient insight from the IEQ. Changes in insight and symptom severity were tracked across the 20 sessions.

findings: over the course of the 20 sessions there was a steady increase in insight and a steady reduction in the severity of symptoms, showing that psychodynamic counselling is associated with both increased insight and a reduction in symptoms. By looking at the sessions where key insights were gained and the points where symptoms declined it was possible to see whether the two variables seemed to have a cause and effect relationship. Immediately after each major new insight as measured on the IEQ, the severity of symptoms declined significantly, suggesting that the insight led to the decline in symptoms.

conclusion: psychodynamic counselling 'works' in that it is associated with increased insight and reduced symptom severity. Results also suggest that the insight actually led to the symptom reduction. This finding provides very strong support for the rationale underlying psychodynamic therapy, that insight into psychological problems helps reduce their impact.

silence and missing sessions. These are thus all open to interpretation. A good question to ask at this point might be whether insight really helps patients. This has been addressed in a study by Kivlighan et al (2000), shown in 'research now'.

We can see then that insight as well as catharsis is implicated in the benefits of psychodynamic therapies. One way of assessing what factors are helpful is to survey patients. Mahon and Kempler (1995) asked patients who had just completed group psychoanalytic psychotherapy what factors they had found most helpful. Insight came out top, with catharsis second. More general factors like encouragement were reported as least helpful.

So what of transference? Remember that transference has traditionally been regarded as the single most important therapeutic factor in the psychodynamic approach to therapy. Research into transference has found rather mixed results. In a review of research, Henry (1994) reports that, in general, research has found a negative rather than positive relationship between frequency of transference interpretations and the outcome of the therapy. However, Crits-Christoph et al (1988) found a positive correlation between outcome and patients' agreement with transference interpretation. The lesson from these studies is clear; use transference interpretation sparingly and get it right!

Varieties of psychodynamic therapy

Psychology texts often speak of *psychoanalysis* when discussing psychodynamic therapies. Actually this is a little misleading as classical psychoanalysis is relatively rare and in decline, while other forms of psychodynamic therapy are increasing in popularity. A range of psychodynamic therapies is shown on box 5.2.

Being long term and intensive, psychoanalysis and psychoanalytic psychotherapy are expensive and disruptive to the lives of patients. In some cases this expense and disruption may be unnecessary. Some of Freud's cases showed very rapid improvement, for example, the composer Gustav Mahler, who was treated successfully in only four sessions in 1908. However, for some decades virtually all psychodynamic treatment was long term. Recently, some psychodynamic therapists have returned to the idea of brief dynamic therapy (BDT), and this is growing in popularity. Molnos (1995) has suggested that some features of long-term psychodynamic therapies, for example, the use of free association and the therapist's 'blank screen' artificially lengthen the process. By focusing the therapy on particular issues, directing patients to introspect on particular events and educating them about their interpersonal behaviour rather than waiting for a transference relationship to develop, the processes of catharsis and insight in psychodynamic therapy can be greatly speeded up.

Classical psychoanalysis; a very intensive and long-term therapy. Takes place five times per week and typically lasts for several years. Sessions are particularly tightly boundaried and normally last exactly 50 minutes. Analytic technique is normally limited to the traditional use of free association and interpretation, particularly of the transference relationship. The patient often lies on a couch as opposed to sitting facing the therapist.

Psychoanalytic (or psychodynamic) psychotherapy; a slightly less intensive but still usually long-term therapy. Sessions take place one to three times per week and therapy typically lasts one to five years. Analytic technique approximates that of classical psychoanalysis, but adherence to orthodox technique is often less strict and may occasionally include humour and information giving.

Group psychoanalytic therapy; applies the principles of psychodynamic therapy to working with groups, typically of 6 to 12 patients. There are most commonly two therapists, often paired as a male–female dyad to enact maternal and paternal transference. Technique depends on theoretical model. In *group analysis*, insight comes mainly from interaction with other group members (analysis by the group), while in the Bion model of group therapy the group is seen as adopting the behaviour of a single individual and is collectively interpreted by the therapists (analysis of the group).

Brief dynamic therapy; there are a variety of subtly differing brief approaches to psychodynamic therapy. As in long-term therapies there is an emphasis on the interpersonal functioning and affective state of the patient, however, in order to speed up the process therapy is typically more confrontational and patients are explicitly educated about their relationships as opposed to waiting for the development of a transference relationship.

Box 5.2 Varieties of psychodynamic therapy (adapted from Jarvis, 2003)

The effectiveness of psychodynamic therapies

Early psychodynamic therapists did not systematically evaluate the effectiveness of their work, but psychologists became interested in outcome research. An early review by Eysenck (1952) brought attention to what he termed the 'outcome problem'.

The Eysenck review

Hans Eysenck (1952) published a review of early outcome studies into psychodynamic approaches to therapy. Eysenck concluded that, based on this early research, there was no evidence that psychodynamic psychotherapy increased the probability of a reduction in symptoms. Patients in both no treatment and therapy conditions both had on average a rate of improvement of around 66 per cent. Although Eysenck's review is still sometimes talked about uncritically in psychology texts, it has some fairly serious flaws in its methodology (Bergin & Garfield, 1978). Eysenck included flawed studies that showed poor outcomes for therapy conditions while discounting the results of better studies that found better outcomes. He also used much tougher criteria for improvement in therapy conditions than in no treatment conditions and did not take account of the time taken for symptoms to disappear. This means that a lack of symptoms two years later in a no treatment condition were counted as the same outcome as the disappearance of symptoms in therapy after a few weeks. Bergin and Garfield (1978) reanalysed Eysenck's data and concluded that the real rate of improvement without treatment was 30–43 per cent, compared with an 83 per cent success rate for psychodynamic therapies.

Contemporary outcome research

The backdrop to modern outcome research has changed considerably since Eysenck's original work. Nowadays, public health care organisations such as the National Health Service are expected to provide psychological therapies that are supported by outcome research. The development of this new ethos since the early 1990s has stimulated a new wave of psychodynamic outcome research. The findings of this new wave of research are very positive, and the latest findings suggest that psychodynamic therapies are at least as effective as other psychological treatments.

Psychoanalysis and psychoanalytic psychotherapy

These are distinguished by their long duration and intensiveness. A major research issue is the extent of differences between classical psychoanalysis and the slightly less intensive and long-term psychoanalytic psychotherapy. This, as well as the general effectiveness of psychoanalytic treatments, has been addressed in a recent series of Swedish studies. Sandell (1999) studied outcomes for 756 patients receiving state-funded psychoanalysis or psychoanalytic psychotherapy and found

strong support for the effectiveness of long-term psychodynamic therapies and for the difference between the two therapies. Psychoanalysis was defined by having four to five sessions per week, in contrast to psychotherapy, which took place once or twice a week. Therapy continued for up to three years. At the end of treatment there were substantial gains in both the psychotherapy and psychoanalysis conditions, but no difference between the two groups. However, at three-year follow-up the psychoanalysis group were rated as having significantly fewer symptoms. It seems that, unlike the psychotherapy group, the psychoanalysis group continued to improve after the end of the treatment. This is a highly significant study, being the first to demonstrate that classical psychoanalysis really is different from psychoanalytic psychotherapy.

Brief dynamic therapy

Because of its brevity, BDT lends itself to outcome research and there is a large body of evidence to support its effectiveness. In one recent study Guthrie et al (2001) tested the effect of four sessions of BDT with 119 patients following attempted suicide by poisoning. A control group received standard treatment, ie a referral back to their GP. Six months later the BDT group had significantly lower suicidal thinking than the controls and they were significantly less likely to have made further suicide attempts. In another recent study by de Jonghe et al (2001) patients suffering depression were allocated to either standard treatment with antidepressants or an experimental condition of antidepressants plus BDT. The experimental group reported the combined treatment to be more acceptable than medication alone, drop out was significantly lower and symptoms were further reduced.

for and against

the effectiveness of psychodynamic therapies

— early studies found no evidence that psychodynamic treatments had any effect on patients

+ recent studies have found much more positive results, showing that psychodynamic therapies are at least as effective as other psychological treatments

The following are good sources of further information about psychodynamic therapies.

▶ **Jarvis M. (2003)** *Psychodynamic psychology: classical theory and contemporary research.* **London: Thomson Learning.** Contains detailed chapters on both the process and outcome of psychodynamic therapies.

▶ **Malan D. (1995)** *Individual psychotherapy and the science of psychodynamics.* **London: Butterworth-Heinemann.** An excellent guide to psychodynamic therapy, illustrated throughout with extremely useful case examples.

Conclusions

Broadly, research has supported the general assumptions of the psychodynamic approach to understanding mental disorder. Factors such as early trauma and poor early relationships increase the probability of suffering a variety of psychological problems. There are a number of psychodynamic theories that aim to explain these findings. Some of Freud's ideas still have some support and others remain useful metaphors to help understand the experience of

psychological distress. However, others now appear outdated, and Freud has been extensively criticised for his theoretical shift away from the effects of sexual abuse towards an emphasis on sexual fantasy.

Psychodynamic approaches to therapy include long-term intensive treatment such as psychoanalysis and briefer and less intensive brief dynamic therapy. These all work on broadly similar principles, aiming to achieve catharsis and insight, although the ways in which these aims are achieved vary between short-term and long-term therapies. There is now a substantial body of evidence to support the effectiveness of both short-term and long-term psychodynamic therapies in treating a variety of psychological problems.

what do you know ?

1 Compare and contrast Freudian and attachment theories of mental disorder. Which is better supported by research?

2 What factors make psychodynamic therapy helpful?

3 Discuss Eysenck's conclusion that there is no evidence for the effectiveness of psychodynamic therapies in the light of contemporary research.

6 The humanistic model of abnormality

what's ahead

Humanistic psychology is deliberately constructed so as to be able to understand human nature using simple principles and a minimum of theory. This is therefore the shortest chapter in the book! Humanistic psychologists reject both psychiatric diagnosis and complex theories like those favoured by psychodynamic and cognitive therapists, relying instead on a number of basic assumptions about human nature. In this chapter we look at these assumptions underlying the humanistic approach and look in some detail at the theory of Carl Rogers. We then consider the most popular humanistic approaches to psychological therapy, Rogers' person-centred approach.

Assumptions of the approach

Humanistic psychology emerged in the 1930s and 1940s. It aimed to be a 'third force' in psychology, the field at the time being dominated by learning theory and Freudian psychoanalysis. The assumptions of humanistic psychology concerning the origins of mental disorder are not dissimilar to those of the psychodynamic approach, however, humanistic psychologists adopt a rather different view of human nature.

- People have a basic tendency to grow and fulfil their potential. Psychological problems result when external forces prevent us achieving this growth.

- Diagnosis of mental disorder is unhelpful, and the symptoms a person displays can be better understood as their individual response to the blockage of their growth.

- There is a strong association between mental health and a healthy self-image. Our self-image is affected by our treatment by others.

- Like the psychodynamic approach, humanistic psychology is primarily concerned with emotion rather than cognition or behaviour.

- People can make their own life choices, and under the right circumstances will make the best choices for them. The aim of humanistic therapies is to help people make the right life choices and so fulfil their human potential.

In contrast to the psychodynamic approach, which emphasises the potential for things to go wrong in children's development – in particular what parents can do wrong, the humanistic model puts its emphasis on the potential of the individual to achieve and become the best person they can. This is a highly optimistic (some would say naive)

view of human nature. The divergence of humanistic psychologists from other psychological perspectives is actually more philosophical than psychological. Self-image is considered important in both Freudian and cognitive theory, and the humanistic emphasis on emotion is shared by the psychodynamic model. In one sense, therefore, the humanistic model is not a theoretical perspective in the same way as behavioural, psychodynamic and cognitive models are, but rather a philosophical position.

Carl Rogers' theory

In the field of mental health Carl Rogers has been the most influential of the humanistic psychologists. He proposed that understanding healthy psychological development depends on two ideas, the actualising tendency and the self-concept.

The actualising tendency

Rogers (1959) believed that humans are primarily motivated by the need to *actualise*, ie to fulfil their potential and achieve the best level of 'human-beingness' they can. The relationship between the environment and the ability to actualise can be understood using the analogy of a flower, which will only grow to its full potential if the conditions are right. Just as a flower is constrained by the availability of environmental variables, such as light, water and nutrients, so people flourish and reach their potential only if their environment is good enough. An unconscious process of *valuing* guides us towards choosing behaviours that will help us fulfil our potential. This valuing process can, however, be prevented from operating by the use of strict social rules and by a poor self-concept. Rogers believed that people are inherently good and creative. They can, however, become destructive when their valuing process is interfered with.

The self-concept

Rogers noticed that in therapy patients would often make reference to themselves, saying things like 'I'm not being my real self' or 'I wonder who I really am'. Rogers began to place great importance on this emphasis on the 'self' and how people thought of themselves. Rogers (1961) proposed that the most important aspect of the self-concept is *self-esteem*. Self-esteem means essentially how much we like ourselves. Rogers believed that we hold in our mind an image of our self as we currently are and an image of our ideal-self, what we would like to be. If these two self-images are *congruent* (the same), we will experience a good level of self-esteem.

The development of congruence and the resulting healthy self-esteem depends on receiving *unconditional positive regard* from others in the form of acceptance, love and affection. Without unconditional positive regard we cannot self-actualise. Some children lack unconditional positive regard from their families in childhood. Harsh, inattentive parenting or parenting that involves *conditional love*, ie love that is only available if the child conforms to certain conditions, is likely to lead to low self-esteem in adulthood, and such individuals are thus vulnerable to mental disorder, especially depression.

There is considerable support for the central ideas of Rogers' theory, ie that self-esteem is crucial to our well-

classic
research

it's important to like ourselves!

Coopersmith S. (1967) *The antecedents of self-esteem.* **San Francisco: Freeman**

aim: Coopersmith was interested in the importance of self-esteem in child development. He aimed to learn about both what effects having high or low self-esteem might have on a child and about what factors might determined a child's individual level of self-esteem.

procedure: Coopersmith studied several hundred 9–10-year-old white, middle-class boys. He used four measures to establish the self-esteem of each boy. These were a psychometric test called the self-esteem inventory, teachers' estimates of how well the boys reacted to failure, a test called the thematic apperception test (in which pictures are presented and participants say what they think is happening) and assessment of their confidence in an unfamiliar situation. On the basis of these measures, Coopersmith divided the boys into groups of high, middle and low self-esteem. He then looked at the characteristics of the boys in each group, including their confidence, ability to take criticism, popularity and academic success. Coopersmith also went on to investigate the types of upbringing the children had had, using questionnaires and in-depth interviews with both the boys and their mothers.

findings: distinct differences emerged between the groups. High self-esteem boys were most expressive and active. They were the most successful and confident group, both academically and socially. The middle group were the most conforming. The low self-esteem children were the lowest achievers and tended to under-rate themselves. They were the most socially isolated group, self-conscious and sensitive to criticism. Coopersmith found that parenting style was very significant. High self-esteem children had plenty of positive regard from parents, but they also had firm boundaries on acceptable behaviour. Low self-esteem appeared to follow harsh or unloving parenting or lack of behavioural restrictions. Coopersmith followed up the boys into adulthood and found that the high-esteem group remained more successful in terms of work and relationships.

conclusion: the Coopersmith study clearly supports Rogers's ideas, both that self-esteem is important for healthy psychological development and that positive regard from parents is a major factor in the development of self-esteem. However, Coopersmith also found that firm boundaries in behaviour laid down by parents predicted high self-esteem and this is perhaps less in keeping with Rogers's ideas.

Figure 6.1 Some humanistic therapists compare human development to that of a flower

being and that unconditional positive regard in parenting is important for the development of high self-esteem. In a classic study Coopersmith (1967) demonstrated both the importance of self-esteem for development and the importance of unconditional positive regard in development of self-esteem.

Figure 6.2 Children's self-esteem can be powerfully affected by positive comments from teachers

Numerous studies have supported the link between parenting style, self-esteem and mental health. Lau and Pun (1999) looked at the relationship between parents' evaluations of children in 974 families and the self-esteem of the children, who were aged 8–13 years. Where parents had positive views of their children, the children tended to have higher self-esteem. This was especially the case where the positive parental attitude was shared by both parents. In another study Burnett (1999) collected information from 269 Australian primary school children regarding their self-concept, and the frequency of positive and negative comments from teachers. It was found that positive comments from teachers were associated with improved self-concept, which was in turn associated with greater achievement. This supports the view that achievement (actualisation) is dependent on self-esteem, which is in turn dependent on positive regard from others.

You can see how Rogers' emphasis is not on what goes wrong in human development to cause psychopathology, but rather what are the necessary ingredients of healthy development. In the main Rogers did not explore in detail the mechanisms by which failure to meet the optimum conditions for psychological growth actually led to mental disorder, but emphasised the broad humanistic principles instead.

for and against

Rogers's explanation of mental health

+ there is ample support for the link between parenting style and self-esteem, and for the importance of self-esteem in mental health

– other theories can explain these links as neatly as can Rogers

+ Rogers's emphasis on the causes of mental health complements the emphasis in other theories on the origins of mental disorder

– Rogers did not explain in the same detail as alternative theories exactly how parenting, self-esteem and mental health are linked

where to now?

The following are good sources of further information about humanistic psychology, and in particular the ideas of Carl Rogers.

▶ **Merry T. (1995) *Invitation to person-centred psychology*. London: Whurr.** An interesting introduction to humanistic psychology, answering key questions about human nature from a humanistic perspective.

▶ **Thorne B. (1992) *Carl Rogers*. London: Sage.** A general introduction to the ideas and techniques of Carl Rogers.

Humanistic approaches to therapy

Although humanistic therapies are broadly informed by the assumptions of humanistic psychology, they are quite distinct from one another in their techniques – much more so than are different psychodynamic or cognitive therapies. We look here at person-centred therapy, the most popular of the humanistic therapies.

Person-centred therapy

A patient whom Rogers saw at the Rochester Society for the Prevention of Cruelty to Children may have particularly influenced his ideas about therapy. She was the mother of a delinquent boy whom Rogers was seeing for therapy. Rogers made interpretations about her behaviour towards her son based on psychodynamic theory. However, the woman consistently rejected all interpretations. She asked if Rogers took on adults for counselling. When he said that he did she began to tell him (for the first time) about her problems and how these had affected her son. Rogers became convinced by this incident of the importance of allowing patients to talk freely, and this was the idea behind his person-centred therapy (or *counselling* – unlike practitioners of other models Rogerians do not distinguish between the two).

One major difference between humanistic counsellors and other therapists is that they refer to those in therapy as 'clients' as opposed 'patients'. This reflects the fact that they see the therapist and client as equal partners rather than as an expert treating a patient. Humanistic counsellors do encourage clients to focus on and explore feelings, but, unlike psychodynamic therapists, they are completely non-directive, refraining from asking clients to focus on or explain things they have said. Rogerians do not offer interpretations but merely encourage the client to keep on talking in the belief that they would eventually find their own answers. One reason why Rogers rejected interpretation was that he believed that, although symptoms did arise from past experience, it was more useful for the client to focus on the present and future than on the past.

The core conditions for personal growth

Rogers worked towards personal fulfilment in his clients. Rather than just liberating them from the effects of their past experience, as psychodynamic therapists do, Rogerians try to help their clients to achieve personal growth and eventually to self-actualise. Rogers (1961) suggested three *core-conditions*, which facilitate clients in their personal growth:

● **Empathy**; the ability to understand what the client is feeling. An important part of the task of the person-centred counsellor is to follow precisely what the client is feeling and to communicate to them that the therapist understands what they are feeling.

● **Congruence**; also called genuineness. This means that, unlike the psychodynamic therapist who generally maintains a 'blank screen' and reveals little of their own personality in therapy, the Rogerian is keen to allow the client to experience them as they really are.

● **Unconditional positive regard**; Rogers believed that for people to grow and fulfil their potential it is important that they are valued as themselves. The person-centred counsellor is thus careful to always maintain a positive attitude to the client, even if they are disgusted by their actions.

As Mearns and Thorne (1988) point out, we cannot understand person-centred counselling by its techniques alone. As humanistic psychology is primarily a philosophical system the person-centred counsellor is distinguished by their positive and optimistic view of human nature. The philosophy that people are essentially good, and that ultimately the individual knows what is right for them, are the essential ingredients of successful person-centred work. Mearns and Thorne sum up person-centred therapy as 'all about loving'. Because person-centred counsellors place so much emphasis on genuineness and on being led by the client, it is not possible to have the same strict boundaries of time and technique as practised in psychodynamic therapy. If they judged it appropriate, a person-centred counsellor might diverge considerably from orthodox counselling techniques.

interactive angles

Match the three scenarios (A to C) to the therapeutic technique being employed (1 to 3).

Techniques
1 empathy
2 congruence
3 unconditional positive regard

Scenario
A The therapist looks unfazed when a client tells them they are cutting themselves.
B The therapist tells a bereaved client that they too have lost a loved one.
C The therapist smiles when the client recalls a happy event and frowns when they recall an unhappy one.

Spirituality

The person-centred tradition is unique in psychology in that, with its emphasis on 'growth', it is easily compatible with the idea of *spirituality*. Although not all person-centred therapists are religious, and although you certainly do not have to be religious to practise or benefit from person-centred therapy, there has been a long association between this style of therapy and the Church. One of the main factors in deciding what you think of person-centred therapy may be how comfortable you are with ideas like *personal growth* and *spirituality*. To some people these will be essential aspects of life; to others they will be meaningless. One effect humanistic psychology has had on the field of psychopathology in general is to have recognised the spiritual dimension. This reflected in the publication of the DSM-IV in 1994, when for the first time, the category *Religious or spiritual problem* was included as a diagnostic category (Lukoff, 1998).

Discussion of person-centred therapy

The commonsense ideas behind person-centred counselling are immensely appealing to many people, and this approach now dominates the counselling field. One reason for the popularity of the person-centred approach is its simplicity. Rogerian ideas are relatively easy to understand (though not to practise), so much less academic study is needed for trainees than is the case for those studying cognitive or psychodynamic therapy. Rogers and his followers have also brought home to psychologists the importance of truly listening to clients. Myers (2000) performed a qualitative study on the impact of being listened to on five female clients in person-centred therapy. Each client's experience was quite distinct, but in each case it could be seen that the experience of counselling in some gave them an experience they had not had in previous relationships.

Person-centred counselling is undoubtedly helpful for many clients. Greenberg et al (1994) reviewed the results of 37 outcome studies looking at the effectiveness of person-centred therapy in a variety of situations and conditions. They concluded that person-centred counselling is as effective as other approaches to therapy, and more successful than no treatment. There are published case studies that appear to show that for some people, adopting a humanistic approach to therapy is the most effective intervention. Siebert (2000) describes the case of an 18-year-old girl diagnosed with severe paranoid schizophrenia and expected to remain institutionalised for life who had all her symptoms disappear following person-centred counselling. Of course this is a one-off case and actually few psychologists would recommend a humanistic approach to schizophrenia. In general person-centred therapy is employed for working with less severe cases.

There is rather less research published concerning the effectiveness of person-centred therapy with specific disorders than is the case for the other major psychological therapies. McLeod (1996) has suggested that this is why person-centred therapy currently has less of a foothold in the NHS than other therapies. The research that is available paints a fairly optimistic picture. Beutler (1991) assessed the effectiveness of person-centred therapy on 20 clients treated for depression and found moderate improvement, maintained at 10-month follow-up. More dramatic improvement was found in a study by Borkovec (1991), who found large improvements in 14 clients suffering from generalised anxiety.

for and against

person-centred therapy

+ research has supported the usefulness of person-centred therapy

− the body of research supporting person-centred therapy is very small compared to that for other psychological therapies

+ person-centred therapy may be particularly helpful to patients to whom spirituality is important

The following are good sources of further information on person-centred therapy.

▶ **Mayhew J. (1996)** *Psychological change: a practical introduction*. **Basingstoke: Macmillan.** A very user-friendly book comparing the humanistic, learning and psychodynamic approaches to therapy.

▶ **Mearns D. & Thorne B. (1988)** *Person-centred counselling in action*. **London: Sage.** A detailed account of person-centred therapy including some useful case material.

Conclusions

The humanistic approach is more of a philosophical position than a distinct theoretical approach to psychology. Humanistic psychologists see people as fundamentally good and emphasise their capacity to change and to choose their own destiny. Like psychodynamic psychologists they see the roots of psychological problems in relationships. The most influential humanistic ideas of mental health come from Carl Rogers, who emphasised the human need to actualise and the requirement for unconditional positive regard to achieve this.

The two most important humanistic therapies are Rogers's person-centred approach and Perls's Gestalt approach. Despite sharing the basic humanistic assumptions these models of therapy are very different. Person-centred therapy uses a minimum of intervention on the assumption that if a therapist can create the correct conditions then clients will work things out for themselves. By contrast, Gestalt therapy involves a range of powerful techniques designed to prod clients into greater awareness and honesty. There is a relatively small body of research into the humanistic therapies, but the research that does exist is supportive of their effectiveness.

what
do you
know ?

---

1 Outline the ideas that distinguish the humanistic approach from other psychological models of mental health and therapy.

2 To what extent is humanistic theory and therapy supported by empirical evidence?

3 Compare and contrast person-centred and Gestalt therapies.

---

7 The social model of abnormality

what's

In this chapter we consider the alternatives to traditional psychological and biomedical models of abnormality. We begin by taking a look at three theoretical positions on abnormality, which are critical of traditional approaches for ignoring social aspects of abnormality; social psychiatry, labelling theory and social constructionism. We then take a brief look at the role of demographic variables – in particular socio-economic status and gender in mental disorder. The final part of this chapter takes a look at *care in the community*, a social programme of treatment used as an alternative to long-term hospitalisation for patients with chronic psychiatric conditions.

Assumptions of the social approach

The social approach to understanding and treating mental disorder has developed out of two main strands; first, theoretical approaches to the study of psychopathology and mental health and, secondly, practical approaches based on therapies and interventions, which are social in their outlook. Theoretical approaches include social constructionism and labelling theory, both of which are critical of mainstream psychological and biological approaches to mental health. Social therapies and interventions include psychiatric social work, community mental health support and drop-in centres provided by charities such as Mind. Therefore, the social approach should not be considered as a unified approach in the same way that learning theory unifies the behavioural approaches to explaining and treating mental disorder. Instead it can be seen as a collection of different theoretical and therapeutic approaches, which all had one thing in common; they all emphasise the existence of a social dimension in describing and explaining abnormality (Putwain et al, 2000). Some of these assumptions include the following:

- The development of diagnostic categories (such as schizophrenia) and the actual process of diagnosis by a clinician (such as a psychiatrist or a clinical psychologist) is rooted in social processes, for example making judgements about what is and what is not abnormal.

- Social factors may partially cause or trigger a predisposition to a mental disorder. For example, depression is linked to poor relationships and social networks.

- Some disorders can be explained in social, rather than individual-psychological or biological terms. For example, feminist approaches emphasise the role of the relative social power of men and women in the development of mental disorder in women.

- Patients suffering mental disorder can be aided by social as well as medical and psychological interventions. For example, those released from hospital into the community require social support such as social skills training and help with day-to-day living.

Social perspectives on abnormality

Social psychiatry

The social-psychiatry movement in the UK (also referred to as the anti-psychiatry movement) tends to be associated with the radical psychiatrist R.D. Laing. Although trained as a psychiatrist, Laing rejected the medical model of mental disorders, which he saw as treating the symptoms first and the patient second. Laing advocated a more humane model of treatment, where first and foremost the patient was treated as a human being. He rejected the idea that psychotic disorders such as schizophrenia were 'illnesses', and that symptoms of such disorders were meaningless. In *Sanity, madness and the family*, Laing and Esterson (1964) presented a series of case studies, showing how the symptoms of patients diagnosed as schizophrenic could be seen to make sense in the context of their family relationships.

In *The divided self*, Laing (1965), inspired by the existential writings of the French philosopher Jean-Paul Sartre, argued that psychosis was an understandable reaction to living in an intolerable situation. Faced for a search for meaning, the person goes on a journey 'into themselves' where they experience a loss of identity, and become insightful into the contradictions and hypocrisies of a world gone mad. Laing's solution was to provide a space, a retreat, where people could complete their journey in a safe environment – notably not a psychiatric hospital. A community was set up in 1965 at Kingsley Hall in London with this aim. Several of the members became well-known figures, including the nurse turned artist, Mary Barnes, whose 'journey' is recorded in the book *Two accounts of a journey through madness*.

Laing's writings and practice came under sustained criticism from the medical profession, both personal and professional. From one side, it was argued that his methods of treatment (which they referred to as the 'psychedelic' model) did not work and few if any of his patients emerged from their 'journey' as better people. As a result Laing was accused of lacking responsibility for the safety of his patients. From another angle, it was argued that Laing's writings only described a brief psychotic episode and thus did not apply to the more serious psychotic disorders. Laing's personal beliefs in mysticism, in particular his belief in the 're-birthing' technique (where a patient regresses to the womb and is metaphorically re-born), were heavily criticised as lacking any scientific credibility. Detractors pointed to his illicit lifestyle, and his abuse of alcohol and drugs, as evidence for his unsuitability as a practising clinician.

Despite these criticisms, Laing's work has been enormously influential. His books were popular with both mental health professionals (and radicals) and patients, who found in his writings an advocate who would not dismiss their experiences out of hand without a second thought. The radical element to Laing's work highlighted the power invested in the psychiatric profession, providing a voice to those who believed that the medical treatments (such as forcefully medicating patients against their wishes) employed by psychiatrists were barbaric and abusive. Even if Laing's ideas about schizophrenia were rejected, there is no doubt that his campaign for the humane treatment of psychiatric patients was instrumental in raising awareness of the issues faced by users of mental health services. His legacy can still be seen today in, among others, Psychology Politics Resistance (who campaign against the oppressive and abusive uses of psychology), the magazine for democratic psychiatry *Asylum*,

for and against

social psychiatry

+ Laing's work drew attention to the power invested in psychiatry and the use of barbaric treatments, and led to psychiatric patients being treated in a humane manner

– from a medical perspective, the psychedelic model was not effective (ie it did not reduce psychotic symptoms)

– some of Laing's therapeutic techniques (eg the 're-birthing technique') were criticised for lacking scientific credibility

where to now?

▶ **Mullan B. (1995)** *Mad to be normal: conversations with R.D. Laing.* **London: Free Association Books.** A biography of sorts, covering Laing's writings, Kingsley Hall and the social/anti-psychiatry movement.

Figure 7.1 Laing's ideas helped to reduce the use of traditional psychiatric practices, for example, restraining patients

and the academic journal *Changes* (which places emphasis on humanitarian values rather than psychological therapy or professional boundaries).

Social constructionism

Social constructionism presents a serious challenge to the mainstream medical and psychological (learning, cognitive and psychodynamic) approaches to abnormality, by viewing the way in which knowledge is produced as a social process. Just as the cognitive approach does not refer to a single theory, but a group of approaches that are unified by several key assumptions (such as information processing), so the social constructionist approach does not refer to a single theory but is also unified by a set of common assumptions (Putwain et al, 2000), as follows.

---

1 Doubt in the objective basis of knowledge: the claims made by scientific knowledge to provide an objective truth are rejected and instead the *production* of scientific knowledge becomes a topic of research.

2 Emphasis on historical and cultural context: psychological knowledge is specific to a particular time and a particular culture and so generalising findings beyond a particular time and culture is pointless.

3 An understanding of language is of central importance: our understanding of the world is constructed through language and so an analysis of language (eg discourse analysis) can reveal how certain versions of the world are constructed and function.

Adapted from Gergen (1985)

Box 7.1 Assumptions of the social constructionist approach

Parker et al (1995) examined how different accounts (medical, cognitive etc) of psychopathology *position* those people who have been diagnosed with a mental disorder, eg what rights, responsibilities, attributes and so forth, do these people have. The traditional medical and psychological models of abnormality *individualise* mental disorders. That is, once a social judgement about whether someone is abnormal has been made, that abnormality is then believed to exist inside somebody (eg biochemical imbalances, cognitive biases etc). Traditional models of abnormality also *pathologise* people with mental disorders. That is, once somebody is deemed to have a mental illness, they are seen as different from other people, and are subsequently stigmatised (see page 7 for a discussion of stigmatisation). Finally, traditional models of abnormality silence the 'voices' of people diagnosed with a mental disorder by treating their

experiences as irrational or meaningless. The accounts of mental disorders given by psychologists and psychiatrists (eg in terms of learning or cognitive processes) become dominant and privileged over the accounts of people who have to live with these disorders. This raises an ethical and moral dilemma, where the patient is encouraged to accept the knowledge and value system of the mental health professional as the correct or true version of events. Thus the person diagnosed with anorexia, for example, comes to experience themselves as having 'faulty' or 'biased' thinking patterns.

for and against

the social constructionist approach

+ the focus on language can highlight how traditional models of abnormality position people diagnosed with mental disorders in negative ways

− the approach does not provide much of an alternative theory, although it does provide commentary on the traditional models of mental disorder (medical, cognitive, learning etc)

where to now?

The following are good sources of further information about social constructionism.

▶ **Parker I., Georgaca E., Harper D., McLaughlin T. & Stowell-Smith M. (1995)** *Deconstructing psychopathology***. London: Sage.** A super text tracing the history and social practices that have led to psychology and psychiatry as it exists today. The hidden assumptions of mainstream models of abnormality are peeled away, revealing the contradictions and regulating practices that lie beneath. A thoroughly recommended read.

▶ **Putwain D.W., Gray M. & Emiljanowicz C.M. (2000) Psychopathology: the social approach.** *Psychology Review* **7**(2): 8–11. Includes a short review of the social constructionist approach.

Social explanations of mental disorders

A variety of social factors have been linked to mental disorders. Although there is considerable overlap between social and psychological factors it is possible to make a distinction between the two on the following basis. Psychological explanations of mental disorders such as cognitive, behavioural or psychodynamic factors provide *intra-psychic* (within the mind) explanations. That is, they all locate the cause of mental disorders within the individual. Social explanations on the other hand take a broader view, looking at how mental disorders are influenced by factors beyond the individual. These social factors tend to come in one of two types.

The first type of social explanation can bee seen in feminist explanations of eating disorders (see chapter 10). Feminist explanations of eating disorders are highly critical of mainstream psychological and biological models of mental disorder precisely because they are individual explanations. They argue that *individualising* a disorder such as anorexia ignores the political dimension associated with control of the female body and images of femininity. This approach deliberately sets out to look beyond individual explanations of eating disorders by looking at how such disorders are represented in discourse, and what positions these discourses offer for women. Such a move enables resistance by those who feel marginalised by mainstream psychology.

interactive angles

Make a list of the major role models to which you have been exposed. Think about entertainers, media personalities, athletes and popular politicians (if you can come up with any of those). Classify each person by sex and body type. How prevalent are thin role models? Are they more likely to be women than men?

The second type of social explanation looks at how social factors may put an individual at risk from a particular disorder. For example, people who live in deprived inner city areas are more at risk from schizophrenia (see chapter 8) and people with weak social support are at risk from depression. These types of explanations are most likely to be incorporated into a stress-diathesis model, where no single factor is seen as entirely responsible for causing a disorder, but a combination of social, psychological and biological factors. For example, the cultural ideals about body size have been suggested as a possible cause of anorexia (see chapter 10) and certain sections of the media have been heavily criticised for their role in presenting these images. However, not everyone who is subject to these images will develop anorexia. Therefore, it has been suggested that cultural ideals about body size may be an additional factor for those already at risk from developing the disorder, perhaps through biological (eg a genetic predisposition) or psychological means (eg a cognitive vulnerability).

Figure 7.2 Some psychologists believe that media images of thin, glamorous women marginalise women of other body types and may even lead to eating problems

for and against

social explanations

+ social explanations provide a contrast with the individual explanations offered by the other biological and psychological perspectives

− often social explanations are merely seen as adjuncts to individual explanations and incorporated into a stress-diathesis framework

where to now?

The following is a good source of further information about the social approach to mental disorder.

▶ **Parker I., Georgaca E., Harper D., McLaughlin T. & Stowell-Smith M. (1995)** *Deconstructing psychopathology*. **London: Sage.** For a social account of psychopathology, look no further than this.

Recent developments in the social approach: care in the community

In the 1950s and 1960s traditional care of chronic psychiatric patients in mental hospitals came under sustained criticism. It was claimed that in general conditions were poor, and that the emphasis was on containment, rather than rehabilitation of patients. As a result patients became *institutionalised*, unable to function outside of hospital, where their condition continued to deteriorate. A graphic illustration of these conditions is shown in the novel and subsequent film, *One flew over the cuckoo's nest*.

Figure 7.3 A traditional psychiatric hospital or *asylum*

The 1970s and 1980s witnessed a move towards treating chronic mental disorders (such as schizophrenia) in the community. Old Victorian mental asylums were shut down and a variety of community based care programmes established. The extent of this shift in health care policy can be seen in the number of in-patients receiving psychiatric care. In the 1950s there were

approximately 150,000 patients on long-term psychiatric wards. In 1998 that figure had dropped below 30,000. There is still the same number of psychiatric patients today as in the 1950s, but the type of care they receive has changed dramatically (Shepherd, 1998). The emphasis of these programmes is on rehabilitation of patients through providing a variety of social and health care services. The NHS aims to provide a 'Spectrum of Care' (Department of Health, 1997) involving the following elements:

---

1 Sheltered accommodation with 24-hour care.

2 Work and employment opportunities in sheltered social firms and co-operative businesses.

3 Specialist mental health outreach teams to provide long-term social support and care.

4 In-patient hospital care when required.box ends:

Box 7.2 Elements of community care

Patients living in the community may still require hospitalisation if their condition worsens. In a *revolving door policy*, patients requiring hospitalisation are admitted to a psychiatric ward on a short-term basis, until their condition stabilises. Sheltered accommodation is provided for patients who cannot live by themselves or with their family, when released from hospital, in *halfway houses*. These are communities of up to approximately 20 people with care staff who provide emotional support and help with day-to-day living. Residents are encouraged to be independent and responsible, setting their own rules and maintaining the community house themselves.

Does care in the community work?

Outcome research has shown that care in the community has undoubted potential, but only when services are properly coordinated and funded. Leshner (1992) found that all too often communication between different agencies was poor with no overall strategy for coordinating patient care. For example, patients were given differing advice by care staff, and community care services would not be informed when a patient was released from hospital. In addition, patients on community programmes were not given the opportunity to develop lasting trusting relationships with care workers, essential to their progress.

Another problem is that community care is severely under-funded. The government saved £2000 million by closing psychiatric hospitals between 1985 and 1991 alone, yet none of this money was reinvested in community care (Shepherd, 1998). The result is an insufficient number of community based programmes and halfway houses to provide adequate care and supervision. Patients are housed in low cost private accommodation supported by welfare with no care staff to provide emotional support and help rehabilitate patients. Essentially these patients are 'dumped' in the community rather than cared for; their condition worsens and they are readmitted into hospital (Geller, 1992). Sadly, a large number of these patients end up homeless (Opler et al, 1994).

research
now

how successful is care in the community?

Trauer T., Farhall J., Newton R. & Cheung P. (2001) From long-stay psychiatric hospital to Community Care Unit: evaluation at 1 year. *Social Psychiatry and Psychiatric Epidemiology* **36: 416–19**

aim: to assess the effects of community care, one year after patients were released from hospital.

procedure: community care units (similar to halfway houses in the UK) were established to provide accommodation, clinical care and rehabilitation for patients discharged from long-term hospital care. Based in suburban settings, these units could house up to 20 patients each, providing 24-hour care from a multi-disciplinary clinical team. One hundred and twenty-five patients were assessed one month before leaving hospital, one month after leaving hospital and one year after leaving hospital on measures of symptom severity, personal functioning, quality of life and residential preferences, as well as the preferences and attitudes of care staff and relatives.

findings: after one year symptom levels and personal functioning had changed little, however, the quality of life for patients had significantly improved. The community care units were much less regimented and restricted than hospital environments, giving a greater sense of autonomy and responsibility to the patients. Care staff and relatives also preferred the community care units to hospitalisation.

conclusion: a well-organised and resourced community care programme can improve the quality of life for patients released from long-term hospital care.

When community care services are properly funded and coordinated they show a range of potential benefits for patients (see 'research now'). One study by Leff (1997) showed that patients suffering from schizophrenia cared for in the community, housed in long-term sheltered accommodation, showed much lower levels of symptom severity (especially negative symptoms) than hospitalised patients. In a similar vein, Shepherd et al (1996) showed a 40 per cent improvement in social functioning for patients in sheltered accommodation compared to those receiving hospital care. The Shepherd study also highlighted how community care could improve the patients' quality of life. The most important factor determining patient quality of life was choice, for example, over meals, mealtimes, access to bedroom, access to personal possessions and so forth. Although these factors may seem relatively insignificant, they are often difficult to provide in a hospital.

Shepherd (1998) highlights a number of methodological problems in trying to assess the effectiveness of community care. The major problem is that there is not enough longitudinal research, especially in the UK. Living with a chronic psychiatric illness is a long-term problem and outcome research needs to reflect this by looking at long-term effects of community care. The other problem with research is a poor definition of services and lack of consistency in the way that different types of community care are defined. Simply referring to a service as community care gives no information about hours of care available or how many patients a community team has to look after, for example. These are exactly the type of factors that may affect the success of community care and they need to be highlighted and researched.

media watch

Mentally ill face enforced treatment

Thousands of people with mental illness face compulsory treatment in the community under radical plans set out yesterday by the government. Alan Milburn, the health secretary, said the proposals would give 'proper protection to the public and to patients', but mental health groups warned they were too sweeping. As it became clear that the government had rejected advice on balancing new controls with strengthened patient rights, campaigners promised ministers a tough battle over the legislative blueprint. Judi Clements, chief executive of the mental health charity Mind, said: 'They are creating the illusion that this will make a huge difference to public safety, when it is more likely to backfire.'

Reform of the 1983 Mental Health Act is widely advocated, as the focus of care for people with mental health problems has shifted from hospital to the community. Under the Act, a patient can only be forced to have treatment in a hospital. Some inquiries into killings by people with severe mental illness have found that they had defaulted on prescribed medication and lost contact with mental health services. Mr Milburn said: 'For too many people, care in the community has become "couldn't care less in the community" sometimes with the most tragic consequences.' The plans for a new Act, outlined in a green paper, foreshadowed the biggest shake-up in mental health services for 40 years, he said, announcing an extra £53m for services next year.

The green paper, Reform of the Mental Health Act 1983, was published simultaneously with the recommendations of a government appointed expert group led by Genevra Richardson, professor of law at Queen Mary and Westfield college, London university. The group, which had been mandated to recommend compulsory treatment in the community, said that where patients were capable of giving consent, compulsion should be authorised only if they posed a 'substantial risk of serious harm' to themselves or others. But the green paper says the degree of risk must be paramount and proposes compulsion 'for the protection of others from serious harm' or 'for the protection of the patient from serious exploitation'.

The Richardson group also said that until suitable alternative facilities were available, patients in the community should be taken to hospital for any compulsory treatment. The green paper does not specify where treatment should take place, although ministers have given assurances that it would not be 'on the kitchen table'. Cliff Prior, chief executive of the charity the National Schizophrenia Fellowship, said the green paper 'fails to take the chance to give people a right to decent care and treatment' a right demanded in a 20,000-signature petition delivered yesterday to Mr Milburn.

The Liberal Democrats branded the proposals 'illiberal and inadequate', and Julia Neuberger, chief executive of the King's Fund, an independent health policy think tank, said: 'Community care should help people with mental illnesses to live ordinary lives, not contain and control them.' But Michael Howlett, director of the Zito trust, set up by Jayne Zito whose husband was killed by a mental patient, welcomed the plans. Consultation on the green paper is open until March 31 next year. Mr Howlett said: 'We hope it goes ahead as stated and there isn't any kind of watering down over the next few months.'

Guardian, 17 November 1999

1 What limitations of the current care in the community system are highlighted in the article?

2 What issues are raised by attempts to 'tighten up' on care in the community?

for and
against

care in the community

+ patients on community care programmes are happier and make better progress than long-term hospitalised patients

— often community care is not well funded, resulting in patients receiving inadequate care and ending up back in hospital or homeless

— sometimes community care services are not well coordinated, with no overall strategy for providing patient care

where to now?

The following books are good sources of further information about care in the community.

▶ **Comer R.J. (1995)** *Abnormal psychology*. **New York: Freeman.** Contains an excellent section on the community care of schizophrenic patients in the United States.

▶ **Shepherd G. (1998) Models of community care.** *Journal of Mental Health* **7**: **165–77.** A 'state of the art' overview of community care.

Conclusions

Those psychologists and psychiatrists working within the mainstream medical and psychological approaches have largely rejected the criticisms of theoretical social approaches. Some argue that these social approaches are simply trying to wish away the suffering experienced by people with mental disorders, who are 'ill' and require help. Such a humanitarian argument is commendable, but ignores the large number of psychiatric patients who feel that medical treatments are crude and abusive (eg a patient who refuses medication and is pinned down by psychiatric nurses and forcibly injected). Perhaps these social approaches are too radical and those working within mainstream models feel threatened. Social interventions with their emphasis on rehabilitation, such as care in the community, have generally been welcomed by those working within mainstream psychology and psychiatry. However, community care has not always been a success story, with under-funded programmes leaving patients without the appropriate level of care.

what do you know?

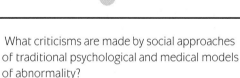

1 What criticisms are made by social approaches of traditional psychological and medical models of abnormality?

2 What is the 'revolving door' policy?

3 Does care in the community work?

8 Schizophrenia

what's **ahead**?

This chapter begins with a description of the clinical characteristics of schizophrenia. The remainder of the chapter will deal with the causes of schizophrenia. There are important biomedical, psychological and social aspects to schizophrenia, and it therefore has a range of theoretical explanations, each focusing on one such aspect. Biomedical approaches emphasise the biological aspects of schizophrenia, including raised levels of a neurotransmitter called dopamine, and the role of genes in individual vulnerability to the condition. Psychological theories include the cognitive approach, which focuses on the abnormal ways in which patients with schizophrenia process information, and the psychodynamic approach, that looks instead at the possible role of family dynamics. Social factors, including urban living, also appear to impact on schizophrenia.

Symptoms and phenomenology

This condition refers to a group of '*psychotic*' disorders characterised by major disturbances of thought, emotion and behaviour. The patient often withdraws from people and reality, often into a fantasy life of delusions and hallucinations. This debilitating disorder affects approximately one person in every hundred and is equally common in men and women. For men the disorder usually begins in their mid-20s and for women, in their early 30s.

The condition was first termed 'dementia praecox' (youthful insanity) by Kraepelin (1896). Since then there has been some dispute over the diagnosis of schizophrenia, with different diagnostic systems (eg DSM-I, DSM-II) proposing different symptoms and different ways of diagnosing the disorder. This had led to widespread criticism of the concept of the disorder called 'schizophrenia' and led some radical 1960s thinkers (known as social-psychiatrists or anti-psychiatrists) to reject the medical approach, proposing that schizophrenia does not exist as a disease (cf Laing, 1967). These historical changes in diagnostic criteria for schizophrenia highlight how such diagnostic categories are not set in stone, but are socially constructed (Putwain et al, 2000). The two diagnostic systems used in UK today, DSM and ICD, are largely in agreement over the diagnosis.

Although the cause of schizophrenia is not known, most psychologists and other mental health professionals believe that it has a biological basis, some kind of brain dysfunction that is triggered by psychosocial factors. Consequently, a large proportion of psychiatrists and biologically oriented psychologists refer to schizophrenia as a disease. Strictly speaking in medical terms, schizophrenia is not a disease. For a disorder to be called a disease it must have a set of core symptoms with an established cause and schizophrenia has neither. A more accurate term for schizophrenia in medical terminology is a '*syndrome*', a set of signs and symptoms, which appear to occur together and which probably have the same cause (see box 8.1).

A) two characteristic symptoms for at least one month

Characteristic symptoms must include:
(1) delusions
(2) hallucinations
(3) disorganised speech
(4) grossly disorganised or catatonic behaviour
(5) negative symptoms (eg affective flattening)

OR one characteristic symptom if delusions are bizarre or hallucination consist of a voice keeping up a running commentary on the person's behaviour or thoughts, or two or more voices conversing with each other.

B) social/occupational functioning below levels prior to onset
C) continuous signs of the disturbance for at least six months
D) no major changes in mood (depression or elation)
E) no evidence of organic factors (eg drugs) or medical conditions
F) if there is history of a developmental disorder (eg autism), prominent delusions or hallucinations must be present for a month.

Source: American Psychiatric Association (2000)

Box 8.1 Signs and symptoms of schizophrenia

One of the key problems with establishing a diagnostic class called schizophrenia and in diagnosing schizophrenia in practice is that, compared to other disorders, schizophrenia has a very large number of signs and symptoms. A DSM-IV-TR diagnosis of schizophrenia only requires a very small number of these signs and symptoms to be present, hence it is rare to find two schizophrenic individuals who present the same symptoms. This wide array of signs and symptoms has made the search for causes all the more difficult, however a major breakthrough by Crowe (1980) was to distinguish between positive and negative symptoms. *Positive symptoms* refer to the bizarre experiences and beliefs that the patient tells the clinician about and are diagnosed by their presence. *Negative symptoms* (or more accurately signs) refer to abnormalities in behaviour, diagnosed by their absence. Table 8.1 below gives some examples.

Positive symptoms	
Hallucinations	Patients hear voices talking to them or commenting on what they are doing
Delusions of control	Patients experience their actions as being controlled by outside forces
Thought insertion	Patients experience thoughts coming into their mind from an external source
Negative symptoms	
Poverty of speech	Patients respond using the minimum number of words possible
Social withdrawal	Patients withdraw from family and friends and refuse company
Flattening of affect	Lack of expression in face and voice

Table 8.1 Positive and negative symptoms in schizophrenia

Biomedical theories of schizophrenia

Biomedical theories of schizophrenia view schizophrenia as being caused by physiological processes. This is the kind of view taken up by many psychiatrists (who after all are medically trained doctors) and biologically oriented psychologists. We can consider here four broad biological influences on schizophrenia. *Genetic factors* involve the link between schizophrenia and inherited genetic material. *Biochemical factors* involve the unusual brain chemistry associated with schizophrenia. *Neurological factors* involve the role of brain structure, which may be damaged in the womb or during birth.

Genetic factors

Adoption studies

Since the 1920s there have been many studies attempting to establish the role of genetics in schizophrenia using methods developed by behavioural geneticists (family, twin and adoptee studies). The first firm evidence for a role for genes in the development of schizophrenia came from an adoption study by Heston (1966), who compared the rates of schizophrenia in children adopted at birth from mothers suffering the condition to adoptees with mentally healthy parents (a control group). Around 10 per cent of the children with a parent suffering from schizophrenia also developed the condition, as opposed to none of the control group. This suggested that it was the genes inherited from the mother that led to the development of schizophrenia in the adopted children. Heston's results were dramatic, suggesting that schizophrenia may be entirely genetic in origin, and that environmental factors may play little or no role in its development. As we shall see, later research suggests a role for both genes and environment. On page 66 we examine a much larger and more sophisticated adoption study that provides joint support for genetic and psychodynamic factors.

Family studies

The simplest way of studying genetic factors in schizophrenia looks at the instances of schizophrenia in families. These studies, called *family studies*, ask the following question: if one person has been diagnosed with schizophrenia, how many other members of their family have also been diagnosed with schizophrenia? If schizophrenia has a genetic component, then the chance of developing the disorder will increase, the closer our genetic link to that individual. Twin studies compare the rates of diagnosis between identical (MZ) and non-identical (DZ) twins. MZ twins are 100 per cent genetically identical, whereas DZ twins are only 50 per cent identical. If schizophrenia has a genetic component, MZ twins should show a higher rate of concordance than DZ twins. One very large-scale family study was carried out by Gottesman (1991). He pooled the data from 40 European studies published between 1920 and 1987, in a meta-analysis of the genetic influences on schizophrenia (see table 8.2). Some of the older studies can be hard to interpret as the diagnostic criteria for schizophrenia has changed over the years. However, in this analysis Gottesman only used data compatible with the diagnostic criteria used today.

Relative	% Risk
General population	1%
Uncles/aunts	2%
Nephews/nieces	4%
Grandchildren	5%
Half-siblings	6%
Children	13%
Siblings	9%
DZ Twins	17%
MZ Twins	48%

Table 8.2 The risk of developing schizophrenia. From Gottesman (1991)

Superficially Gottesman's results seem to support the genetic hypothesis. In general the data show that the more genetic material individuals share, the greater the chance of developing schizophrenia. For instance, there is a much higher risk of developing schizophrenia for the MZ twin of a schizophrenic than for a DZ twin. However, before such an interpretation is uncritically accepted, several comments must be made and problems highlighted.

- First, these data show that schizophrenia can only be in part genetic. If the disorder were entirely genetic then MZ twins would show a 100 per cent risk, as they are 100 per cent genetically identical. The 48 per cent risk shows that other factors must be involved. Therefore genetic factors probably do not cause schizophrenia, but provide a *predisposition* to developing it.

- Secondly, family studies have been criticised, as they do not remove environmental influences. Members of the same family share a similar environment and so the higher risk for close family members could reflect elements of a common environment such as pychosocial stress or social learning rather than genetic factors.

Molecular genetics

Recent research has focused on identifying the individual genes associated with developing schizophrenia. Several genes have been studied, and appear to be associated with schizophrenia. In the 1980s it appeared for a while that the HLA gene, a major gene important in the body's immune response, was associated with schizophrenia (McGuffin & Sturt, 1986), but more recent and sophisticated studies have not confirmed this. However, there is currently a more promising line of research involving a variation in the *TPH* gene (so called because we know that it is involved with production of an enzyme called tryptophan hydroxylase). In one recent study,

Hong et al (2001) found that this variation in the TPH gene was significantly more common in Chinese patients with schizophrenia than in Chinese controls.

Despite the strong support from family and adoption studies that genes are involved; there are only very moderate associations between variations in particular genes and schizophrenia. This suggests that there are actually a number of genes involved. Kelly and Murray (2000) suggest that each of these genes identified by molecular genetics researchers is innocent in itself, however people who inherit a number of them are at high risk of developing schizophrenia.

Discussion of genetic factors

Many abnormal psychology textbooks take this and other similar kinds of genetic data to indicate strong evidence for a heritable component in schizophrenia. Although there is no doubt these studies show that genetics does play some role in schizophrenia, it possible that some biologically oriented authors are overstating the case for genetics. Genetics is only part of the picture and other factors must also be involved. One way of accounting for these findings is a *stress-diathesis* model of schizophrenia, where certain individuals may have a genetic predisposition to the disorder, but it is not certain that they will definitely develop the disorder. Environmental factors are required to trigger off this predisposition and this is where social-psychological factors, such as urban living and expressed emotion, may come into play.

for and against

a genetic basis to schizophrenia

- **+** there is support from family and adoption studies to suggest that genes play a significant role in individual vulnerability to schizophrenia

- **−** evidence from family and adoption studies does not suggest that schizophrenia is entirely genetic in origin, but that environmental factors are at least as important

- **+** molecular studies have found that variations in certain genes are more common in patients with schizophrenia than in controls

- **−** no single gene or cluster of genes has been found to be very strongly associated with schizophrenia

Biochemical factors: the dopamine hypothesis

A number of biochemical processes appear to work somewhat differently in the brains of people with schizophrenia. Research has focused in particular on the role of a neurotransmitter called *dopamine* or DA. Our understanding of the link between dopamine and schizophrenia has been developed from several sources (see box 8.2).

- *Amphetamine psychosis*, which closely resembles some forms of schizophrenia, is caused by an excess of DA, suggesting that perhaps schizophrenia might be caused by an excess of DA (Angrist et al, 1974).

- When amphetamines are given to schizophrenics their symptoms worsen.

- Drugs used to treat schizophrenia such as chlorpromazine are *DA antagonists*. This means that they reduce activity in dopaminergic systems and are effective at treating some forms of schizophrenia (Jonstone et al, 1978).

Box 8.2 Origins of the dopamine hypothesis

Evidence concerning the dopamine hypothesis is very mixed. For ethical reasons we cannot directly measure how much DA there is in the brains of live patients, but methods have been developed to suggest indirectly whether levels are higher than usual. Lindstroem et al (1999) performed a PET scan study on 10 untreated patients with schizophrenia and 10 healthy controls. They labelled a chemical called I-DOPA, which is used in the production of DA, with radioactivity and, using the PET scan, traced what happened to the radioactive I-DOPA. It was found that the I-DOPA was taken up more quickly in the patients with schizophrenia, suggesting that more dopamine was being produced.

Another way to test the hypothesis that schizophrenia is caused by excess levels of DA is to examine the DA metabolite, *homovanillic acid*. Neurotransmitters are broken down into metabolites and passed out of the body like any other waste product. So if schizophrenia were linked to an excess of DA, then we would expect to find an excess of homovanillic acid in the urine or cerebrospinal fluid of schizophrenic patients. Studies (eg Donnelly et al, 1996) consistently show that schizophrenic patients show levels of homovanillic acid that are significantly higher than those in control patients, suggesting patients have higher levels of DA in their brain.

However, other lines of research have cast doubt on the dopamine hypothesis. A drug called *apomorphine*, which

acts as a *DA agonist* (ie it increases the effects of dopamine) does not induce schizophrenic symptoms (Depatie & Lal, 2001). Both these findings are difficult to reconcile with the dopamine hypothesis. Another problem with the dopamine hypothesis relates to the effectiveness of anti-psychotic medication. Chlorpromazine only effectively treats about of patients (those with positive symptoms), partially treats another one-third of patients (those with mixed positive and negative symptoms) and has no effect whatsoever on the remaining third of patients (those with negative symptoms). This finding suggests that there might be different forms of schizophrenia and it is only the form of schizophrenia with positive symptoms that is linked to overactive dopaminergic systems.

for and against

the dopamine hypothesis

+ much indirect evidence, for example, reduced levels of the products of broken-down DA in patients' urine, supports the idea that schizophrenia is associated with very high levels of dopamine in the brain

− there are ethical difficulties in directly testing the dopamine hypothesis, as this would involve extracting it from live brains

+ anti-psychotic drugs appear to work by reducing the activity of dopamine

− some lines of research, for example, using dopamine agonists, have not found evidence for the dopamine hypothesis

Neurological factors

The idea that schizophrenia is linked to structural changes in the brain dates back to the early 1900s. It was not until new technology was developed in the 1970s, allowing for detailed brain scans, that researchers identified a consistent pattern.

Several studies using computerised axial tomography (CAT) scans in the 1970s have shown that approximately 25 per cent of schizophrenic patients have enlarged ventricles in the brain. The ventricles in the brain are fluid-filled cavities that supply oxygen and blood to the densely packed neurons and remove waste product. Enlarged ventricles are usually caused by the death of brain tissue surrounding the ventricles and the fluid expands to fill the space. More sophisticated studies have since shown more details about where there are deficits in brain tissue.

An MRI study by Crow et al (1989) has revealed that one area where tissue has been lost is an area of the temporal lobe, the hippocampus, particularly on the left-hand side of the brain. A more recent MRI study by Goldstein et al (1999) demonstrated that the greatest reductions of brain matter are in an area called the paralimbic cortex. This region is shown in figure 8.1, and the Goldstein et al study is described in 'research now'.

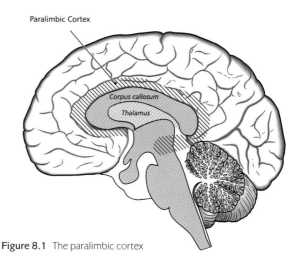

Figure 8.1 The paralimbic cortex

research
now

what parts of the brain are reduced in schizophrenia?

Goldstein J.M. et al (1999) Cortical abnormalities in schizophrenia identified by structural magnetic resonance imaging. *Archives of General Psychiatry* **56: 537–47**

aim: it has been established by previous studies that schizophrenia is associated with reduced brain mass and larger ventricles. However, most published studies have focused on small regions. The aim of this study is to scan the whole of the brain cortex in a sample of patients with schizophrenia and compare the size of each region to that in a control group of healthy volunteers.

procedure: participants were 29 patients diagnosed with schizophrenia according the DSMIIIR system and a control group of healthy adults. A matched pairs design was used, in which the two groups were matched for sex, age, ethnicity, socio-economic status, handedness and catchment area. The brain of each participant was scanned using a MRI scanner, and the average sizes of 48 areas of brain were compared in the patients and the controls, controlling for head-size.

findings: in several areas of the cortex, the patients with schizophrenia were significantly smaller than the control group. The greatest differences in size were in the paralimbic cortex and a related area called the middle frontal gyrus. Smaller differences were noted in a number of regions of the cortex that connected to the paralimbic cortex and fontal gyrus.

conclusions: the finding that schizophrenia is associated with reduced brain mass is confirmed by this study. In addition, it demonstrates the particular importance of reduced mass in the paralimbic region and frontal gyrus.

Further research has confirmed the findings of Crow et al (1989) that the left side of the brain is more implicated in schizophrenia than the right. A simple neurological technique for testing general left and right brain function is to compare the motor skills of the left side of the body (controlled by the right brain), and the right side of the body (controlled by the left brain). Purdon et al (2001) compared the persistent application of force using the right and left hand in 21 healthy controls matched for relevant variables. Ten of the treatment group were then given anti-psychotic medication and tested again. The untreated patient group were significantly weaker in the right hand, though not the left. This deficit disappeared after treatment. This suggests that schizophrenia involves a dysfunction of the left brain, and that anti-psychotic drugs rectify this dysfunction.

A general problem with identifying neurological differences in patients with schizophrenia is that these physical changes in the brain are not unique to schizophrenia. Patients with organic brain disease, such as Parkinson's disease, also show similar kinds of structural changes in the brain. However, three factors suggest that this is not the same. First, in schizophrenia, there is no gliosis (a type of scar tissue) left in the brain from tissue death. Secondly, unlike organic brain disease, the ventricles do not continue to get larger, indicating that schizophrenia is not a progressive disease. Finally, a small number of cases have shown that schizophrenic patients had enlarged ventricles before the onset of the disorder (Weinberger, 1988).

where to now?

▶ **Gottesman I.I. (1991)** *Schizophrenia genesis: the origins of madness.* **New York: Freeman.** Although best known for its analysis of family studies, this is an excellent general text on schizophrenia.

▶ **Lavender T. (2000) Schizophrenia. In Champion L. & Power M. (eds)** *Adult psychological problems.* **Hove: Psychology Press.** Contains a good, critical account of the genetic, biochemical and neurological models of schizophrenia.

for and against

a neurological basis to schizophrenia

+ a consistent finding has been that brains of patients with schizophrenia have lower mass than those of healthy controls

+ there is evidence of neurological dysfunction in the left brain of people with schizophrenia

– findings are inconsistent and we do not have a good idea of what might lead to abnormal neurological functioning

– there are also psychological and social factors not accounted for by a purely neurological model of schizophrenia

interactive angles

The dominant biomedical model of schizophrenia views it as a physical illness with psychological symptoms. Having now read the evidence for a biological basis to schizophrenia, what do you think? To what extent can the syndrome be accounted for by biological factors?

Psychological theories of schizophrenia

Of the major psychological models of mental disorder, only two are of real importance when considering the causes of schizophrenia. The *cognitive* approach explains the symptoms of schizophrenia in terms of the ways in which people with schizophrenia process information. Of the psychological approaches to schizophrenia, the cognitive approach is currently the most popular in Britain and the USA. The psychodynamic approach, based on the fundamental psychodynamic assumption that mental disorder has its roots in early relationships, is rather less popular in Britain and the USA, but is extensively used and researched in Northern Europe.

The cognitive approach

A comprehensive cognitive theory of schizophrenia was presented by Frith (1992). The aim of this cognitive approach is to explain the specific signs (behaviours) and symptoms (subjective experiences) of schizophrenia in terms of information processing difficulties in a cognitive system referred to as the 'metarepresentation' system. *Metarepresentation* is a higher cognitive process referring to the ability to reflect upon thoughts, behaviour and experience. It is one of the most important features of conscious experience, affording us self-awareness of our own intentions and goals, and allowing us to interpret the intentions of others. Information processing difficulties in metarepresentation would seriously disrupt self-awareness, resulting in difficulties in self-initiated actions and the ability to recognise one's own actions and thoughts as being carried out by 'me', rather than someone else.

Negative symptoms

According to Shallice (1988), we have two potential types of action. The first type are self-initiated or self-willed actions such as starting a conversation or planning a surprise party for a friend. The second type of action is stimulus-driven. These behaviours are responses to different types of environmental stimuli, such as responding to someone else's questions. Shallice proposes that patients with negative symptoms have a deficit in the 'supervisory attention system', which is the cognitive process responsible for generating self-initiated actions. Such deficits can be seen as underlying negative symptoms, such as lack of volition, poverty of speech and thought, social withdrawal and flattening of affect.

Evidence for this theory comes in the form of experimental fluency tasks where patients are asked to generate certain types of self-initiated actions and their responses are measured. In a verbal fluency task, participants were asked to generate as many responses as possible to a verbal prompt by the experimenter (eg 'Name as many types of fruit as you can'). Compared to controls participants, schizophrenic patients with negative symptoms produced very few words (Frith & Done, 1986). Such patients either did nothing, repeated their previous response or responded to some irrelevant environmental stimulus.

In a design fluency task, participants were asked to generate as many designs as possible. Again, compared to a control group, schizophrenic patients with negative symptoms had great difficulty in producing spontaneous responses (Frith & Done, 1983). This evidence strongly supports the notion of a deficit in the ability to produce self-initiated actions underlying negative symptoms. This single cognitive deficit will produce different types of behaviour depending on what responses are acceptable: poverty of action (including speech and thought); stereotyped action (repeating the same response); or inappropriate stimulus-driven behaviour.

Positive symptoms

Frith (1992) proposes that a deficit in the 'central-monitoring system' underlies positive symptoms such as hallucinations and delusions. The central-monitoring system is the cognitive process responsible for labelling actions and thoughts as 'being done by me' or 'as mine'. Hallucinations refer to unusual experiences such as hearing voices. Frith (1987) proposes that such experiences are caused when inner speech (the articulatory loop of working memory, see Jarvis et al, 2000) is not recognised as self-generated. Hallucinating patients misattribute self-generated inner speech to an external source and experience the speech as voices belonging to others. Even some pre-lingually deaf schizophrenic patients report they 'hear' voices (Critchley et al, 1981).

Such a theory would predict that people with hallucinations would be worse at remembering whether they had said something or not. This hypothesis was tested by Bentall et al (1991), in a study where participants were asked either to generate category items themselves (eg animals beginning with the letter B) or read out category items. One week later, participants were given a list of words and were asked to decide whether they had generated the words themselves, read them or whether the words were new. Results showed that schizophrenic patients with hallucinations performed worse than schizophrenic patients without hallucinations. Both of these groups performed worse than a control group of non-schizophrenic patients. Although such results might indicate that hallucinating patients have a problem with memory, Frith (1992) suggests that at least provisionally there is some basis for the idea that hallucinations are a consequence of misattributing inner speech to external sources.

Delusions include *thought insertion* (experiencing thoughts being implanted into one's mind) and *delusions of control* (experiencing one's actions as being caused by others). Once again, such experiences suggest a deficit in self-monitoring. Thoughts and intentions are not labelled as 'mine', so are experienced as being controlled from external

for and against

the cognitive approach

+ the approach does not attempt to explain schizophrenia as a whole, but specific symptoms. Such a position avoids the problems of changing diagnostic criteria

+ cognitive mechanisms not only give rise to cognitive deficits but also behaviours. Therefore hypotheses can be formed about patients' responses and measured using experimental tasks. This enables a degree of objectivity to be added to patients' subjective descriptions of their experiences (Frith, 1992)

− schizophrenic patients have often been treated with anti-psychotic medication for a number of years. It is difficult (probably impossible) to find a comparable group of control group patients to use in experiments who have also been treated with medication. This can make interpretation of results difficult and may not always be possible to distinguish whether results are due to cognitive deficits or the effects of anti-psychotic medication

sources. Such a theory was tested by Frith and Done (1989). Participants were asked to follow a target on a videogame using a joystick. The task was deliberately designed to be difficult and induce errors. When participants could watch their responses on the screen, there were little differences between schizophrenic patients with delusions and control participants. However, when participants had no visual feedback for their errors, schizophrenic patients with delusions performed significantly worse than control group participants. Such patients had difficulty in monitoring their intended actions without visual feedback.

Psychodynamic approaches

There are a number of theories from the psychoanalytic tradition that seek to explain the development of schizophrenia. They share the assumption that disruption to early family relationships can in some way drastically affect the way the developing child perceives reality and interacts with the world. Klein (1946) and Bion (1967) proposed that all children go through stages of development in which they are dominated by feelings of persecution and omnipotence. A poor relationship with the primary carer in infancy can prevent the child outgrowing these beliefs, rendering the individual very vulnerable to later developing schizophrenia. Bion (1967) suggested that when a child develops a 'schizophrenic core of personality' due to poor early social relations, they are likely as an adult to regress in response to stress to an early mental state characterised by feelings of persecution and omnipotence – classic symptoms of schizophrenia. Another psychodynamic approach came from Fromm-Reichmann (1948). Based on her patients' accounts of their childhoods, she proposed the existence of a *schizophrenogenic mother*. The term 'schizophrenogenic' refers to a factor that causes schizophrenia. Fromm-Reichmann proposed that where families were characterised by high emotional tension and secrecy, and where the mother was cold and domineering in her attitude, children were at high risk of developing schizophrenia.

Evidence for the role of the family in developing schizophrenia

There is some evidence that certain types of family interactions are associated with schizophrenia. This idea was tested in a classic study by Schofield and Balian (1959).

classic
research

a family basis to schizophrenia?

Schofield W. & Balian L. (1959) A comparative study of the personal histories of schizophrenic and nonpsychiatric patients. *Journal of Abnormal and Social Psychology* 59: 216–25

aim: psychodynamic writers had for some time suggested that schizophrenia was the result of poor or disrupted early family relationships. However, evidence for this was largely limited to case studies in which patients with schizophrenia who reported unhappy childhoods. The aim of this study was to compare the childhood experiences of people with and without schizophrenia to see whether the patients really had more difficult childhood relationships.

procedure: 178 patients with schizophrenia who were being treated at an American teaching hospital were given in-depth interviews regarding childhood traumas, maternal characteristics and the quality of relationships between parents. A control of group of 150 non-psychiatric participants matched for education, socio-economic status and marital status received the same interviews. The two groups were compared.

findings: with regard to the quality of relationships between parents, no differences emerged between the two groups. As regards childhood trauma, patients with schizophrenia were significantly less likely to report poverty or an invalid parent. There was no difference in the frequency of parental divorce, death or alcohol abuse. There were, however, significant differences in the reported quality of mothering. Mothers of patients were less likely to have been affectionate and more likely to be domineering and over-protective.

conclusion: results were consistent with Fromm-Reichmann theory of the schizophrenogenic mother. The only childhood circumstances that appeared to increase the risk of schizophrenia in adulthood were related to the quality of the maternal relationship.

In another early study, Lidz et al (1965) looked at the cases of 50 schizophrenic patients and investigated their family backgrounds. Forty-five of the 50 (90 per cent) were found to have seriously disturbed families. Sixty per cent of the patients had one or both parents with serious personality disorders. Parental marriages were typically characterised by either constant discord or one dominant and one submissive parent. Parents frequently made considerable emotional demands on children. Fathers of male schizophrenics were typically very passive, while mothers of female schizophrenics were typically cold and dominant.

The studies carried out by Lidz et al and Schofield and Balian both have the serious limitation that they were carried out *retrospectively*, ie the researchers gathered data about families after the patient had developed schizophrenia. It is quite possible that the pre-schizophrenic child caused the unusual patterns of family interaction. For example, parents might wish to be unusually protective of a child who appeared to be a very vulnerable child because of the early symptoms of schizophrenia.

Traditionally it has been widely believed that adopting a psychodynamic approach to treating schizophrenia is at best ineffective and potentially harmful. This belief has in turn damaged the credibility of the approach as an explanation. However, recent studies are more supportive of the usefulness to sufferers of schizophrenia of exploring their early family dynamics.

Alanen's integrated psychodynamic-genetic theory

Until the work of Heston (1966) (see page 59), psychologists tended to believe that schizophrenia was entirely psychodynamic in origin. Since then there has been something of a backlash, and many psychologists now believe that schizophrenia is principally biological in origin. However, given the accumulated evidence for both biomedical and family factors, it is difficult to take an entirely biomedical or psychodynamic stance. Alanen (1994) has attempted to resolve this by producing an integrative model that explains the role of both genes and family dynamics.

Unlike early psychodynamic theories, Alanen's theory is based on large-scale studies of families of people with schizophrenia as well as clinical case studies. He proposed a five-point theory of how the family social environment can lead to schizophrenia.

● Vulnerability to schizophrenia is largely determined by the quality of relationships within the family. The whole family is important, not just the primary carer.

● Parental personalities and their impact on their relationship with the child are critically important in the development of schizophrenia.

● Families in which feelings of persecution or omnipotence are fostered encourage the development of schizophrenia.

● Family relationships that encourage dependence rather than independence are associated with the development of schizophrenia.

● Genes play an important role because they determine the *temperament* of the child (ie the child's inborn personality characteristics), which is important in determining the role the child plays in family interactions.

To summarise these five points, Alanen is proposing that genes determine the ability of a child to cope with difficult family dynamics. A child who is genetically vulnerable but who has a happy childhood with a supportive family will thus not go on to develop schizophrenia. Nor will a child who has a difficult family life but is resilient to its effects because of their genes. However, a genetically vulnerable child who then experiences poor family relationships is vulnerable to developing schizophrenia.

Alanen's theory differs from the early psychodynamic viewpoint by taking into account research into the behaviour of the whole family as well as the relationship with parents. Alanen has also updated psychodynamic thinking by acknowledging the importance of genes and the active role the child takes in affecting family dynamics.

Perhaps the best evidence for Alanen's theory of schizophrenia comes from the Finnish adoption study, a longitudinal study running since the 1960s of children born to Finnish mothers with schizophrenia and adopted at or shortly after birth. Tienari (1992) followed up 200 children in this position. It was found that around 10 per cent went on to develop schizophrenia – the same percentage as we would expect were schizophrenia entirely genetic in origin. However, the most significant finding of this study was which children made up the 10 per cent. Those children who developed schizophrenia were almost all from families that had been previously assessed by the researchers as in some way dysfunctional.

A more recent analysis of results of the Finnish adoption study comes from Wahlberg et al (1997). They compared 56 adoptees from mothers with schizophrenia with a control group of 96 children adopted from parents without mental health problems, looking at communication patterns in the adoptive families. In direct support of Alanen's theory it emerged that neither a parent with schizophrenia nor deviant communication in the adoptive family alone were associated with schizophrenia. However, there was a massive interaction between genes and environment, ie where a child had both a mother suffering from schizophrenia and an adoptive family with deviant communication, they were at greatly increased risk of schizophrenia.

for and against

psychodynamic explanations

+ there is considerable evidence to suggest that poor family dynamics increase the risk of schizophrenia in individuals already vulnerable because of their genes

– however, there is little or no sound evidence to suggest that family dynamics alone can lead to the development of schizophrenia. Early studies that implicated family dynamics were methodologically flawed. In contrast, there is a large body of sound evidence to support the biological aspects of schizophrenia

– by attributing responsibility for schizophrenia to families, when some individuals are highly genetically vulnerable or have suffered biological insults like maternal flu or birth complications, psychodynamic psychologists risk adding to the misery of families with a schizophrenic member by blaming them

+ Alanen has successfully integrated psychodynamic and genetic explanations and has shown how psychodynamics is an important, though incomplete model of schizophrenia

Social theories of schizophrenia

Biological and psychological theories of schizophrenia both provide individual explanations of schizophrenia. Social theories provide a contrast, in that they look beyond the individual for causes of schizophrenia. One line of social research examines the relationship between urban living and schizophrenia. In the clinical psychology literature, these factors are not presented as direct causes of schizophrenia. Rather, they are thought of as factors that may trigger schizophrenia (see the stress-diathesis model). Some writers (eg Parker et al, 1995) are sceptical of such a position, believing that it diverts attention away from the social nature of schizophrenia and back to the individual.

Schizophrenia and urban living: social drift and social causation

A consistent finding in Western industrialised nations for the past 40 years is that the incidence of schizophrenia is much higher in urban than rural areas. For example, studies in Stockholm, Mannheim, Chicago, London, Nottingham and Salford have all shown an above average incidence of schizophrenia in comparison to the incidence of schizophrenia in the normal population (Freeman, 1994). Some psychologists have framed this relationship in terms of social class, as in most cases the individuals who live in deprived inner city areas tend to belong to the lowest social classes. There are two traditional explanations for the relationship between schizophrenia and urban living.

- According to the 'social causation' hypothesis, living in an urban area may be a cause of schizophrenia in itself. Several characteristics associated with urban living; social deprivation, unemployment, high population density, poor housing and low social status may provide a high level of psychological stress leading to a schizophrenic breakdown in those who are vulnerable.

- The alternative explanation, referred to as the 'social selection' hypothesis, is that higher rates of schizophrenia in cities are a result of migration (Freeman, 1984). Individuals who develop schizophrenia may drift into inner city areas where they can obtain cheap, single-person accommodation, casual, low-paid work and have few social and emotional demands. The other side of the coin is that

Figure 8.2 Schizophrenia is more common in urban areas

mentally healthy people migrate away from undesirable inner city areas, leaving such areas with a high rate of schizophrenia. According to this hypothesis, living in an urban area is not a cause of schizophrenia, but a consequence.

Comparing the two explanations

A number of studies have attempted to establish which explanation can provide the best account of the relationship between schizophrenia and social class. One such study by Castle et al (1993) tested the social selection hypothesis by comparing the birthplace of schizophrenic individuals in Camberwell (an area of South London) with a control group of non-schizophrenic patients. The results did not support the social selection hypothesis. They showed that most schizophrenic individuals were born into deprived, urban areas and had not 'drifted' into such areas following the onset of the disorder. The results of this and a range of other studies suggest that although migration (usually of mentally healthy people out of inner city areas) does occur, it is only in small numbers and is not enough to account for the high incidence of schizophrenia in inner city areas (Freeman, 1994).

It would therefore seem plausible to say that, as the social causation hypothesis suggests, some aspect of urban life is responsible for causing schizophrenia. However, the development of schizophrenia does not tend to reflect the characteristics of a stress-related breakdown, making it unlikely that the *social* aspect of urban life is responsible for causing schizophrenia (Jablensky, 1988). The alternative is that some *non-social* aspect of urban life could be the cause. One clue provided by the Castle et al study is that schizophrenic individuals tend to be born into deprived inner city areas. Such areas are well known for high rates of birth complications and infectious diseases (Jablensky, 1988). When combined with the finding that maternal influenza and maternal dietary deficiency are risk factors for schizophrenia (O'Callaghan et al, 1991), it possible to see how a link could be established between environmental factors and the development of schizophrenia.

Although the social causation hypothesis in its pure form is not supported, social factors such as overcrowded housing and unemployment may contribute to poor health leading to maternal influenza infection. Maternal influenza in turn may provide the neuro-developmental basis for schizophrenia, as seen in the neurological changes in the brains of schizophrenic individuals.

Conclusions

The evidence from the different theories considered here suggests that schizophrenia should be seen as a developmental disorder, ie it develops through childhood due to a combination of biological and psychological factors. On a biological level, the disorder is linked to the neurotransmitter dopamine and to abnormalities in brain structure. On a cognitive level, changes in brain function may appear as certain deficits in information processing. Genetic factors, family dynamics, urban living and maternal influenza all constitute risk factors. Remember, however, that the whole idea of schizophrenia as a single condition is controversial. There is, for example, a definite possibility that two distinct forms of schizophrenia exist, based on positive and negative symptoms, each of which has different causes, course and outcome.

what do you know?

1 Describe the clinical characteristics of schizophrenia (eg diagnostic criteria or different types of symptoms).

2 Describe one biological factor (eg genetics, biochemistry or neurology) that may be linked to the development of schizophrenia. What is the evidence for that biological factor?

3 Describe one psychological factor (eg cognitive processing) that may be linked to the development of schizophrenia. What is the evidence for that psychological factor? How strong is the evidence for that factor?

4 Discuss one social factor (eg urban living) that may be linked to the development of schizophrenia.

9 Depression

what's ahead? This chapter opens with a description of the clinical characteristics of depressive, seasonal and bipolar disorders, including details of diagnosis using the DSM system. The bulk of the chapter is devoted to theories of the origins of depression. Like schizophrenia, depression has important biological, psychological and social aspects, and there have been various theoretical attempts to explain it from the biomedical perspective, and using cognitive and psychodynamic approaches. Social factors also appear to be important in depression, and we shall examine in particular social explanations of why depression affects women more commonly than men, and lower rather than higher socio-economic groups.

Symptoms and phenomenology

We have almost certainly all described ourselves at some point as depressed. We might for example feel sad, dejected or lonely. These feelings are a perfectly normal part of human existence, often in a response to losses and disappointments that we all encounter. Depression as a mental disorder is defined by a particular set of symptoms. Most professionals, particularly those writing from a medical perspective, tend to see *clinical depression* – depression that meets the criteria for psychiatric diagnosis – as a distinct condition, quite different to our everyday life experience of sadness.

Categories of clinical depression

To receive a diagnosis of clinical depression, one must have a certain number of symptoms for a certain period of time. Both the ICD10 and the DSMIV make a distinction between *major depressive episode* or *major depressive disorder* and *dysthymia* or *dysthymic disorder*. Both also recognise an additional condition, bipolar depression, what is commonly called 'manic depression'.

Major depressive disorder

The symptoms of major depression come and go in cycles. During a depressive episode, symptoms can be extremely severe. The majority of people who experience a major depressive episode go on to experience further episodes. Usually depressive episodes last from four to six months, but there are exceptions and some episodes last over a year. Thornicroft and Sartorius (1993) calculated that the average patient with major depression is depressed 27.5 per cent of the time. The criteria for diagnosis of a major depressive episode according to the DSM-IV-TR are shown in box 9.1.

Dysthymia

In contrast to major depression, which is characterised by periods with no symptoms, followed by episodes of often severe depression, dysthymia involves constant but generally less severe symptoms. Depression must last for longer than two years for dysthymia to be diagnosed. Of course, treatment of the symptoms can begin earlier. Dysthymia tends to be most severe in those in which it begins before age 21. Diagnostic criteria for dysthymia according to the DSM-IV-TR are shown in box 9.2.

Bipolar disorder

Bipolar disorder, more commonly known as manic depression, is diagnosed when patients suffer from episodes of *mania*, ie states of high arousal and irritability or excitement; the opposite of depressive symptoms. Goodwin and Jamison (1990) calculated that 72 per cent of those diagnosed as having a manic episode also suffered depression. Periods of depression are not however necessary for a person to receive a diagnosis of bipolar disorder. Patients typically feel full of energy and they may feel elated or irritable. There is a reduced need for sleep and there may be an increased sexual appetite. Manic patients are often extremely impulsive and their judgement is impaired, for example, leading to spending sprees and bizarre business schemes. Bipolar disorder is much less common than unipolar depression, occurring in 0.7–1.6 per cent of the population. Box 9.3 shows the criteria according to DSM-IV-TR for a manic episode.

A   Five (or more) of the following symptoms have been present during the same two-week period and represent a change from previous functioning; at least one of the symptoms is either (1) depressed mood or (2) loss of interest or pleasure.

Note: Do not include symptoms that are clearly due to a general medical condition, or mood-incongruent delusions or hallucinations.

(1) Depressed mood most of the day, nearly every day, as indicated by either subjective report (eg feels sad or empty) or observation made by others (eg appears tearful). **Note:** In children and adolescents, can be irritable mood.

(2) Markedly diminished interest or pleasure in all, or almost all, activities most of the day, nearly every day (as indicated by either subjective account or observation made by others).

(3) Significant weight loss when not dieting or weight gain (eg a change of more than 5% of body weight in a month), or decrease or increase in appetite nearly every day. **Note:** In children, consider failure to make expected weight gains.

(4) Insomnia or hypersomnia nearly every day.

(5) Psychomotor agitation or retardation nearly every day (observable by others, not merely subjective feelings of restlessness or being slowed down).

(6) Fatigue or loss of energy nearly every day.

(7) Feelings of worthlessness or excessive or inappropriate guilt (which may be delusional) nearly every day (not merely self-reproach or guilt about being sick).

(8) Diminished ability to think or concentrate, or indecisiveness, nearly every day (either by subjective account or as observed by others).

(9) Recurrent thoughts of death (not just fear of dying), recurrent suicidal ideation without a specific plan, or a suicide attempt or a specific plan for committing suicide.

B   The symptoms do not meet criteria for a mixed episode.

C   The symptoms cause clinically significant distress or impairment in social, occupational, or other important areas of functioning.

D   The symptoms are not due to the direct physiological effects of a substance (eg a drug of abuse, a medication), or a general medical condition (eg hypothyroidism).

E   The symptoms are not better accounted for by bereavement, ie after the loss of a loved one, the symptoms persist for longer than 2 months or are characterised by marked functional impairment, morbid preoccupation with worthlessness, suicidal ideation, psychotic symptoms, or psychomotor retardation.

Box 9.1 Diagnostic criteria for a major depressive episode

A   Depressed mood for most of the day, for more days than not, as indicated either by subjective account or observation by others, for at least 2 years.

Note: In children and adolescents, mood can be irritable and duration must be at least 1 year.

B   Presence, while depressed, of two (or more) of the following:

(1) Poor appetite or overeating
(2) Insomnia or hypersomnia
(3) Low energy or fatigue
(4) Low self-esteem
(5) Poor concentration or difficulty making decisions
(6) Feelings of hopelessness.

C   During the 2-year period of the disturbance (1 year for children or adolescents), the person has never been without the symptoms in Criteria A and B for more than 2 months at a time.

D   No major depressive episode has been present during the first 2 years of the disturbance (1 year for children and adolescents), ie the disturbance is not better accounted for by chronic major depressive disorder, or major depressive disorder, in partial remission.

Note: There may have been a previous major depressive episode provided there was a full remission (no significant signs or symptoms for 2 months) before development of the dysthymic disorder. In addition, after the initial 2 years (1 year in children or adolescents) of dysthymic disorder, there may be superimposed episodes of major depressive disorder, in which case both diagnoses may be given when the criteria are met for a major depressive episode.

E   There has never been a manic episode, a mixed episode, or a hypomanic episode and criteria have never been met for cyclothymic disorder.

F   The disturbance does not occur exclusively during the course of a chronic psychotic disorder, such as schizophrenia or delusional disorder.

G   The symptoms are not due to the direct physiological effects of a substance (eg a drug of abuse, a medication) or a general medical condition (eg hypothyroidism).

Box 9.2 Diagnostic criteria for dysthymic disorder

> **A** Presence of only one manic episode and no past major depressive episodes.
>
> **Note:** Recurrence is defined as either a change in polarity from depression or an interval of at least 2 months without manic symptoms.
>
> **B** The manic episode is not better accounted for by schizoaffective disorder and is not superimposed on schizophrenia, schizophreniform disorder, delusional disorder, or psychotic disorder not otherwise specified.
>
> Specify if:
>
> **Mixed:** if symptoms meet criteria for a mixed episode.
>
> If the full criteria are currently met for a manic, mixed, or major depressive episode, *specify* its current clinical status and/or features:
>
> - **Mild, moderate, severe without psychotic features/severe with psychotic features.**
> - **With catatonic features.**
> - **With postpartum onset.**
>
> If the full criteria are not currently met for a manic, mixed, or major depressive episode, *specify* the current clinical status of the bipolar I disorder or features of the most recent episode.

Box 9.3 Diagnostic criteria for a manic episode

Biomedical theories of depression

In medical circles depression is widely regarded as a physical illness. Hammen (1997) suggests four types of circumstantial evidence why we might believe that depression is a biological condition:

- Some symptoms of depression are physical, for example, disruption to sleep and appetite;
- Depression runs in families;
- Antidepressant medication reduces the symptoms of depression;
- We know that certain medical conditions and certain drugs induce depression.

At first glance these might seem pretty convincing. However, as Hammen points out, none of these facts is in itself particularly strong evidence for the biological nature of depression. It is well known that psychological factors can lead to physical symptoms; patterns of family interaction and the modelling of depressed behaviour can cause patterns of behaviour, thinking and feelings to be passed on through families. Just because depression can be induced and treated biologically, this does not mean that that is how depression naturally occurs.

Evidence for a genetic element to depression

We have long known that the children of depressed parents are more vulnerable to depression than comparable children without depressed parents. The strongest evidence for a genetic element to depression comes from twin studies. McGuffin et al (1996) obtained a sample of 214 pairs of twins, at least one of whom was being treated for major depression. They found that 46 per cent of monozygotic (identical) twins and 20 per cent of dizygotic (fraternal) twins of the patients had also suffered major depression, suggesting moderate genetic influence. Of course, identical twins may be reared more similarly to fraternal twins; therefore once again genes may not be the only factor affecting this finding. Silberg et al (1999) examined both the role of genes and life events in a twin study, discussed in 'research now'.

The findings of the Silberg et al study are particularly interesting because they suggest that there is not a gene for depression as such, but rather that some people are predisposed to be particularly likely to respond with depression when unpleasant things happen to them. Because there appear to be a number of neurochemical and neurological factors associated with depression, it seems likely that more than one gene may be involved. It also appears that the more severe the depression the greater the extent to which genes are involved. Kendler et al (1992) carried out a twin study on sufferers of relatively mild major depressive disorder, and found little difference between the probability of identical and fraternal twins sharing depression (49 per cent and 42 per cent respectively). Compared to the wider disparity between identical and fraternal twins in the more severe cases looked at in the McGuffin et al (1996) study, this suggests that milder depression may have little genetic influence, whereas severe cases have a substantial genetic component.

Interestingly, although major depressive disorder and dysthymia are distinct disorders, the genetic influences on them may be the same. Klein et al (1995) examined depression in the families of 100 patients suffering from dysthymia or major depression. They found that both dysthymia and major depression were more common in the families of both groups of patients than in the general population. Slightly different results are found in the case of bipolar disorder; the families of patients of unipolar disorder are at no increased risk from bipolar disorder than the rest of the population, however, relatives of patients with bipolar disorder are at greater risk from unipolar disorder (Weissman, 1984). This suggests that

research
now

depression; genes, environment or both?

Silberg J. et al (1999) The influence of genetic factors and life stress on depression among adolescent girls. *Archives of General Psychiatry* 56: 225–32

aim: previous twin studies have suggested a moderate role for genetic factors in the development of depression, but most have revealed little about the environmental factors that appear to be rather more important. Other lines of research have suggested that depression is a response to life events. The aim of this study was to assess both the role of genes and recent life events.

procedure: 902 pairs of twins took part in the study; 182 of pre-puberty girls, 314 of pubertal girls, 237 of pre-puberty boys and 171 of pubertal boys. The participants were taken from an ongoing project called the *Virginia Twin Study of Adolescent Behavioural Development*. Each adolescent completed a standard psychiatric interview to assess depression. Life events were measured both by a questionnaire given to the young people and an interview with their parents. Using this data it was possible to see the importance of genes and recent life events, to see whether their importance differed between boys and girls, and to see how genes and life events worked together to cause depression.

findings: overall, girls suffered more depression than boys. On average they were more susceptible to depression in response to recent life events. Interestingly however, there were wider individual differences among girls in their response to life events, and girls who suffered depression after a negative life event were often those whose twin also suffered depression. This suggested an important role for genes in determining individual differences in vulnerability to depression in response to life events.

conclusions: the study supported a role for both genes and environment in the form of life events in the development of depression. Importantly, it also tells us something about the way genes operate. It seems that rather than causing depression directly, genetic factors make us particularly susceptible to the depressing effects of life events.

bipolar disorder may be a particularly severe form of major depression rather than a distinct disorder. Eighty per cent of identical twins and only 16 per cent of fraternal twins share bipolar disorder. Bipolar disorder thus appears to be rather more influenced by genes than unipolar depression.

Biochemical factors

The *monoamine* neurotransmitters, noradrenaline, dopamine and serotonin, appear to be present in lower levels in depressed patients than in the rest of the population. The main evidence for this comes from the action of antidepressant drugs, which are known to increase monoamine levels and to relieve the symptoms of depression. Monoamine oxidase inhibitors prevent the deactivation of the monoamines in the synapse, thus increasing their effectiveness. Serotonin re-uptake inhibitors (such as Prozac) prevent the synaptic re-uptake of serotonin, thus increasing the effectiveness of serotonin alone. Furthermore, Reserpine, a drug which is

for and against

a genetic basis to depression

+ twin studies have shown that depression is more likely to be shared by identical twins than fraternal twins

– twin studies suggest only a moderate genetic component to unipolar depression, especially in milder cases

– studies of gene-environment interaction suggest that rather than causing depression, genes influence how susceptible we are to the effects of life events

+ it appears that bipolar disorder has a larger genetic component than unipolar depression

used for the treatment of hypertension, but which also lowers levels of serotonin and noradrenaline, induces the symptoms of depression (Lemieux et al, 1965).

The role of 5-HT in depression has been strongly supported by metabolite studies. Depressed patients show lower levels of the serotonin metabolite, 5-H1AA, in cerebrospinal fluid (CSF) compared to controls, strongly suggesting that they have lowered levels of serotonin (McNeal & Cimbolic, 1986). It appears that although serotonin is associated with mood this is not a direct effect, but rather occurs because of the role of serotonin in regulating the other monoamines (Barlow & Durand, 1999).

Recent research has focused on the role of noradrenaline, which may directly affect mood. Some new antidepressant drugs (eg reboxetine) work by increasing the action of noradrenaline, thus supporting the importance of noradrenaline (Moffaert & Dierick, 1999). Further evidence for the importance of noradrenaline in depression comes from a post-mortem study by Klimek et al (1997). They compared an area of the brain called the locus coeruleus, which produces noradrenaline, in 15 sufferers of major depression with that in 15 control participants, and found significant differences in structure. This suggests that normal production of noradrenaline may be impaired in depression.

Although research has firmly established that depression is associated with biochemical abnormalities, and although our understanding of the role of particular chemicals is growing, this does not necessarily mean that depression is a direct result of biochemical abnormality. A strict biomedical explanation for depression might be that genetic factors directly lead to abnormal production of monoamines. However, we know from twin studies that genes are less important than environmental factors in depression. It is thus safer to think of biochemical factors as being involved in depression and contributing to its symptoms rather than being its general cause.

for and **against**

biochemical and neurological models of depression

+ there is substantial evidence from drug trials and from autopsies that depression is associated with biochemical abnormalities

− there is little direct evidence to suggest that biochemical abnormalities are causes rather than features of depression

where to now?

▶ **Plomin R. et al (1997)** *Behavioural genetics*. **New York: Freeman.** Contains an excellent discussion of the role of genes in depression.

▶ **Hammen C. (1997)** *Depression*. **Hove: Psychology Press.** A very clearly written book containing good sections on the genetic, biochemical and neurological aspects of depression.

▶ **Barlow D.H. & Durand V.M. (1999)** *Abnormal psychology*. **Pacific Grove: Brooks/Cole.** A very good general text on atypical psychology with a useful chapter on depression, discussing genetic, biochemical and neurological models.

Psychological theories of depression

As for schizophrenia, the cognitive and psychodynamic models are probably the most helpful psychological approaches to understanding depression. Interestingly, although there are differences in emphasis, cognitive and psychodynamic models of depression are similar in that they both see depression as a result of early negative experiences. Cognitive theories are concerned with the way depressed patients think, which is characterised by a highly negative outlook and a sense of hopelessness. Psychodynamic theories are more concerned with the emotional impact of early relationship-based experiences, for example, significant losses and insecure attachment.

The psychodynamic approach

From the psychodynamic perspective, the most important determinants of later mental health are the quality of parent–child relationships and the patterns of family interaction. Freud (1917) proposed that many cases of depression were due to biological factors. However, Freud also believed that some cases of depression could be linked to experiences of loss of or rejection by a parent. Freud drew a parallel between the feelings we have as adults when in mourning for a lost loved one and the experience of depression years after a childhood loss experience. An important part of adult mourning is anger, and Freud proposed that the same anger is important in children's responses to loss. The child's anger at being 'abandoned' through separation or rejection cannot be expressed because of love for the object of the anger, and instead is repressed, turning inwards and causing guilt and low self-esteem as the ego 'rages against itself' (1917: page 257).

Freud's theory of depression provides an alternative to the biomedical model in explaining depressive symptoms. Whereas the biomedical model might explain disruption to appetite in terms of the effects of monoamine disruption, Freud suggested that it is the result of regression to early childhood where nurturance is associated with the primary carer and, following their loss, is not present. The lack of energy associated with depression can be explained according to Freud's *hydraulic model* of the mind (see page 36 for a discussion), as energy is expended maintaining the repression of the rage against the abandoning loved one.

Although in some ways Freud's account appears dated, for example, in his use of the hydraulic model, Champion and Power (2000) suggest that the theory of depression is still helpful in contemporary psychology in two ways. First, it draws our attention to the links between loss and depression and, secondly, it links depression and anger. We can examine research into both these ideas. There is a substantial body of research into the relationship between early loss experiences and later depression, and in general results have supported Freud's view that early loss predicts later depression. In one recent study Maier and Lachman (2000) surveyed 2998 adults aged 30–60 by questionnaire and telephone interview. They found that symptoms of depression were more common in those who had lost a parent in childhood by divorce or death. Particularly interesting in view of Freudian theory was the finding that self-acceptance was sharply lower in those who reported an early loss experience.

Research into the link between anger and depression has produced partial support for Freud. Swaffer and Hollin (2001) gave 100 young offenders questionnaires to assess anger and health. Depression, along with general health was associated with levels of anger, those who suppressed their anger having a greater tendency for depression. This association between depression and anger has also been found in different types of study. In a study of the psychological factors underlying headaches Venable et al (2001) found that headaches were associated with both suppressed anger and depression. Both these studies suggest that Freud was correct to propose a link between depression and anger, however, they do not provide direct support for the idea that loss causes anger, which is turned inwards, leading to depression.

for and against

the psychodynamic model of depression

- depression is associated with early trauma and disruption to early relationships

- in keeping with Freudian theory, early experiences of loss predict depression in adulthood

- although depression is associated with suppressed anger, it is difficult to directly test Freud's idea that anger at early loss becomes turned inward against the self

- it is unclear to what extent the effects of early loss are emotional in nature as opposed to cognitive and behavioural

The cognitive approach

Psychologists adopting a cognitive approach to depression would generally not quibble with Freud's idea that early loss predisposes us to later depression. However, cognitive theory differs in rejecting the Freudian emphasis on emotion and focusing instead on the effects on the developing child's thinking. Cognitive-behavioural therapy differs as well from psychodynamic therapy in ignoring the developmental history of the individual and focusing instead on altering the types of cognition that characterise depression. The rationale is that by making people think in more positive ways we can make them feel better.

Beck's theory

Aaron Beck (1976) described in detail the irrational thinking that characterises depression in his cognitive theory. Beck proposed three factors that contribute to a person's *cognitive vulnerability* to depression. Cognitive vulnerability refers to the ways in which our individual style of thinking and responding to information makes us more or less vulnerable to depression. These three factors are the cognitive triad of negative automatic thinking, faulty information processing and negative self-schemas.

The cognitive triad

Beck identified three types of very negative thoughts that appeared to be automatic in depressed patients, These are a negative view of self, negative view of the world and negative view of the future. The cognitive triad is shown below in figure 9.1.

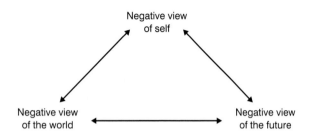

Figure 9.1 Beck's cognitive triad of automatic thoughts

Beck called these *automatic* thoughts because they occur spontaneously. You can imagine that it would be at best discouraging and at worst disabling to be plagued with hopeless and self-critical thoughts.

Faulty information processing

Beck proposed that depressed people tend to selectively attend to the negative aspects of a situation and ignore the positive aspects. This leads to a tendency to overestimate the 'downside' of any situation. We are all illogical in that we attend to some stimuli and not others, and in that we jump to conclusions. The illogic of depression is of a particularly unfortunate kind – the depressive attends to the negative and jumps to the most negative possible conclusions.

Negative self-schemas

Schemas are packets of information in which our knowledge of each aspect of the world is contained. The self-schema contains all our information, beliefs etc. concerning ourselves. Beck suggested that in childhood we acquire a negative set of beliefs about ourselves through experiences of negative or critical parents. We interpret new information relevant to our beliefs about ourselves in the light of our existing self-beliefs. Any situation, which requires us to examine information relevant to ourselves, will activate the self-schema and bring to mind those negative beliefs. Once we have a negative self-schema, it becomes difficult for us to interpret any new information about ourselves positively.

Research into Beck's theory

It is a simple matter to demonstrate that depressed people display faulty information processing and negative thinking. However, this is only of limited use to us as these may be symptoms of depression rather than causes. One way of testing Beck's theory is to examine the incidence of depression in people with different levels of cognitive vulnerability. In one recent study Grazioli and Terry (2000) assessed cognitive vulnerability in 65 women in the third trimester of their pregnancy and found that those with high levels of cognitive vulnerability were more likely to suffer post-natal depression.

Research has also supported Beck's notion of faulty information processing in depression, at least in major depression. Perez et al (1999) compared sufferers of major depression with non-depressed participants in whom a sad mood had been induced by playing sad music and recalling unhappy memories on a Stroop task (see chapter 10) involving unhappy stimuli. The major depressive group but not the sad-mood participants paid significantly more attention to unhappy words in the Stroop task. This phenomenon, where depressed people pay more attention to unhappy stimuli, is called *negative attentional bias*.

Beck's idea that early experience leads to the formation of negative schemas is further supported. In a recent study by Parker et al (2000), 96 depressed patients whose self-reports of their symptoms included the idea of a negative schema being activated under certain circumstances were interviewed about their early experiences. There were significant associations between reports of early experiences and the existence of maladaptive schemas that were in turn associated with the experience of depression. This suggests that early experiences do induce cognitive

for and against
the cognitive approach

+ there is strong support for the idea that depression is associated with negative thinking

+ there is also strong support for the idea that early experience can lead to the negative cognitive style that predisposes people to depression

– cognitive theories fail to neatly explain the link between depression and anger. They thus probably give an incomplete understanding of depression

what's new?

the hopelessness model of depression

There have been newer cognitive models of depression since the pioneering work of Beck. Abramson et al (1989) put forward the *hopelessness model*, in which hopelessness is seen as the main negative cognition underlying depression. Hopelessness consists of two elements; negative expectations of the likelihood of positive events and negative beliefs about the ability of the individual to influence events (helplessness). When the vulnerable individual experiences a negative life event they feel helpless to respond to it, and this helplessness leads to the sense of hopelessness that directly causes depression. Once they are in the pattern of experiencing negative events and not being able to respond positively to them, a general sense of hopelessness results. Note that Abramson et al were not aiming to explain all depression by this model, but rather to identify a particular group of people who are particularly vulnerable.

Following up the idea that there is a subset of people who suffer from a lack of hope, Rose et al (1994) investigated the characteristics of people who displayed hopelessness. They found that hopeless people were particularly likely to have a diagnosis of personality disorder, have suffered sexual abuse and a highly controlling family. These last two are critical as they are both circumstances in which the person will have experienced profound helplessness in childhood. It thus appears that childhood experiences in which the child experiences long-term helplessness in the face of negative events leads to their learning a helpless and hopeless cognitive style.

In general, research has supported the role of hopelessness in depression. Kapci (1998) tested the idea that depressive symptoms follow a helpless response to life events. Thirty-four depressed and 36 non-depressed participants completed the Beck Depression Inventory, a standard test for depression, and a 'hopelessness scale' on two occasions, three months apart. On the second occasion they also completed a questionnaire to assess their recent life events. It was found that worsened depression was associated with negative life events, in particular in those who scored high on helplessness and hopelessness, suggesting that the helpless response to the life events led to an increase in depression. Joiner (2000) tested the same idea in 9–17-year-old children in psychiatric care. Once again, both negative life events and a sense of hopelessness preceded worsening in symptoms.

where to now?

The following are good sources of further information on psychological approaches to depression.

▶ **Champion L. & Power M. (2000)** *Adult psychological problems*. **Hove: Taylor & Francis.** An excellent general text on psychopathology, particularly strong on psychological models.

▶ **Comer R.J. (1995)** *Abnormal psychology*. **Freeman: New York.** Again, a good general text on atypical psychology, with some useful material on psychological models of depression.

vulnerability, however, remember that psychodynamic theories can explain the link between early experience and later depression in other ways, and certainly account more easily for the link between early experience, depression and anger. Beck's theory may therefore not be a complete explanation of the experience-depression link.

Social factors in depression

The distinction between social and psychological factors in depression is a tricky one. In this chapter we have classified social factors as those that involve social interaction, whether this takes place on an individual or societal level. A classic study by Brown and Harris (1978) demonstrates the impact of social factors on

classic
research

life experiences, social support and depression

Brown G.W. & Harris T.O. (1978) *The social origins of depression: a study of psychiatric disorder in women*. London: Tavistock

aim: Brown and Harris (1978) aimed to investigate the link between depression and both current and past life events in the lives of sufferers. They focused on working-class women, as women tend to experience more depression than men, and because working-class people tend to experience more stress than the middle classes.

procedure: a complex structured interview called the life events and difficulties scale (LEDS) was developed. Interviewers were trained in the use of the LEDS. A group of 539 women in Camberwell, London were inter-viewed using the LEDS. Interviewers obtained details of what stressful events had occurred in the previous year, along with the background circumstances in which they occurred. The LEDS also aimed to uncover stressful childhood events. Interviewers had to prepare a written account of each event of source of stress, which could be rated by a panel of researchers for how stressful it would be for a typical person. To avoid bias, these raters had no knowledge of whether the person they were looking at had suffered depression. It was later ascertained which interviewees suffered from depression. Researchers then looked for associations between who suffered depression and who had recently had a stressful life and who had had stressful events in their childhood.

findings: it emerged that both recent high levels of stress and having suffered a stressful childhood event left people particularly vulnerable to depression. Eighty per cent of the women who suffered depression had had a major stressful life event in the previous year, as opposed to 40 per cent of those who did not suffer depres-sion. Three of the four factors that had the strongest associations with depression involved recent levels of stress. These were the lack of an intimate relationship, lack of paid employment and the presence of three or more children in the home. However, childhood events were also important, especially the death of the woman's mother before she reached the age of 11.

conclusions: it was concluded that there was a link between recent negative life events and the onset of depres-sion. It was also concluded that loss in childhood, especially of the mother, also made women more vulnerable to depression. Lack of social support and family discord made women more vulnerable to depression.

the individual. We can look at this study in 'classic research'.

Brown, Harris and colleagues continued to research social factors in depression, and Brown (1996) has sum-marised their overall conclusions. Depression is strongly associated with negative life events. Some individuals are particularly vulnerable to depression following life events as a result of both psychological factors such as cognitive vulnerability, low self-esteem and a history of loss experi-ences (discussed earlier in the chapter). *Social factors* such as lack of social support, low socioeconomic status, unemployment and family discord also lead some people to be especially vulnerable.

Socioeconomic status and depression

Most mental disorders are found more frequently in lower socioeconomic groups, and this is certainly true of depression. In chapter 7, which deals with social models of psychopathology, we talked about social drift and social causation as explanations for this relationship. To briefly recap, social causation is the idea that low socio-economic status (SES) causes psychopathology, whereas social drift is the idea that individuals and families with mental disorders tend to drift into lower socioeconomic groups. Ritsher et al (2001) tested for social causation and drift effects in a study of 756 participants across two generations. It was found that low parental educational level was associated with increased rates of depression in the following generation even when there was previously no depression in the family history. Parental depression did not predict lower SES in offspring. The study thus supports the role of causation and fails to support a role for social drift in depression.

There have been a number of explanations proposed for why depression should be associated with low SES. A study by Lupien et al (2000) suggests that high levels of stress in parents affect children's development by affecting their own levels of stress. One hundred and thirty-nine mothers were regularly assessed for stress and depression by telephone interview. Their children (217 in total) were assessed for salivary cortisol levels (a measure of stress) and for cognitive functioning. Low SES mothers reported more stress, which in turn was reflected in the cortisol levels and cognitive functioning of their children. It seems that the stressed low SES mothers in some way transmitted this stress to their children, and it seems likely that this early stress contributes to later depression. So how might this transmission of stress from one generation to the next take place? One explanation might lie in parenting styles. Radziszewska et al (1996) compared rates of depression in 15 year olds whose parents had adopted different parenting styles. The lowest rates of depression were found in *authoritative* parents (who adopted firm but kind strategies with a degree of democracy) and the highest rates in *unengaged* parents who took little interest in their children's behaviour. Authoritarian (strict and harsh) and permissive (few rules or boundaries) parents had children with intermediate levels of depression. Authoritative parenting was most frequent in the higher socio-economic groups, perhaps because this is the most time-consuming and demanding style of parenting and is very difficult to maintain in the face of the high levels of stress experienced by low SES parents.

Gender and depression: feminist perspectives

A consistent finding is that depression is more common in women than in men (Culbertson, 1997; Weissman & Olfson, 1995). Precise figures are difficult to come by but it seems that depression is two to three times more common in women. This could be explained from a biological perspective, in which depression rates are attributed to genetic and hormonal sex differences. However, feminist psychologists have generally adopted a more social approach, emphasising a number of ways in which women are socially disadvantaged as compared to men.

We have already looked at the work of Brown, Harris and colleagues, who have extensively researched depression in women, and found links with early loss, recent life events and current social support. From a feminist perspective, Stoppard (2000) has attacked the Brown and Harris approach for tackling depression only at the level of the individual and for neglecting the reasons why women experience so many negative life events and have inadequate social support. These factors are undoubtedly linked, at least in part, to discrimination against women.

Discrimination against women begins early in their lives. Women are around twice as likely as men to suffer sexual abuse in childhood and this pattern of victimisation is maintained in adulthood, where women make up the overwhelming majority of victims of physical assault (Koss et al, 1994). Recall from chapter 5, which deals with psychodynamic approaches to mental disorder, that sexual abuse is associated with a range of psychological problems including depression. The lower average earnings of women further contribute to a sense of helplessness and practical difficulties in leaving violent relationships (Stoppard, 2000).

A further factor that appears to be implicated in the higher rates of depression in women is the manner in which men and women respond to the experience of psychological distress. Cochrane (1995) has pointed out that in European and American societies, where women suffer more depression than men, it is also the case that it is the socially norm for women to respond passively to distress. By contrast, it is more socially acceptable for men to respond actively to distress, for example, by alcohol abuse and physical aggression. It seems likely that the passive responses that our culture encourages in women increase the likelihood of depression. Support for this explanation of depression comes from statistics showing that the lower rates of depression in men are matched by higher rates of drug abuse and violent crime in men (Rogers & Pilgrim, 1996).

Conclusions

There are a number of categories of mood disorder. While these are probably influenced by both genes and environment, in appears that genes are more important in the origins of bipolar disorder and more severe cases of major depression. Both brain chemistry and structure appear to be involved in depression, and depression can be treated with drugs, which compensate for the biochemical abnormalities. However, it is not clear to what extent these biological factors are underlying causes of depression and to what extent they are symptoms.

where to now?

The following are good sources of further information about social factors and depression.

▶ **Stoppard J.M. (2000)** *Understanding depression: feminist social constructionist approaches*. **London: Routledge.** An advanced and detailed account of the possible factors influencing the higher incidence of depression in women.

▶ **Brown R. (1996) Life events, loss and depressive disorders. In Heller T. et al (eds)** *Mental health matters*. **Basingstoke: Macmillan.** A review of the Brown & Harris tradition of research.

It seems that in most cases of depression the environment is more critical than genes. Experiences of early loss are particularly associated with later depression – a finding compatible with both the major psychological models of depression, the psychodynamic and cognitive approaches. These models differ, however, in their interpretation of how early experience leads to depression. Social factors are also important in depression. At the individual level, lack of social support and negative life events influence depression. At the societal level low socio-economic status is associated with depression, perhaps because it generates stress in parents, which in turn affects parenting style and so children's development. Women suffer depression more frequently than men. From a feminist perspective this is at least partially a result of social inequalities, which lead women to have more stressful lives, less opportunity to change them and fewer opportunities to respond actively to distress.

what do you know?

1   Discuss the importance of biological factors (eg genes, biochemistry and neurology) in the origins of depression.

2   Compare the evidence to support cognitive and psychodynamic models of depression.

3   How important are social factors in the origin of depression?

10 Anxiety

what's  ahead?

Like depression (see chapter 9), we have all experienced the sensation of anxiety at some point our lives. However, like depression, anxiety can take the form of recognisable mental disorder. In this chapter we focus on five anxiety disorders recognised by DSMIV and ICD10: generalised anxiety disorder; panic disorder; phobias; obsessive-compulsive disorder; and post-traumatic stress. Anxiety disorders can be explained in biological or psychological terms, and we look here at some depth at biomedical, learning and psychodynamic explanations. We also examine briefly the newer cognitive perspective on anxiety in the form of *attentional bias*.

Symptoms and phenomenology of anxiety disorders

Generalised anxiety disorder

This is characterised by unusually high levels of anxiety and worry related to normal everyday events such as performance at work. Diagnosis requires that the person is anxious on most days for a period of six months, and that this is accompanied by restlessness, irritability, fatigue, concentration problems, muscle tension or sleep disturbance.

Panic disorder

This is characterised by recurrent panic attacks (a single panic attack does not warrant a diagnosis). The DSM criteria for a panic attack are shown in box 10.1.

Diagnosis under DSM-IV-TR also requires that at least one attack has been accompanied by a month of worry about having further attacks, concern over the significance of panic attacks (eg are they heart attacks?) or major changes in behaviour as a result of the attack.

Phobic disorders

Specific phobias

Specific phobias involve fear of a single, simple stimulus, such as spiders, snakes or heights. About 13 per cent of people experience a specific phobia at some time in their lives, more than half of sufferers being women. The mean age for the appearance of specific phobias is four years. The intensity of most specific phobias declines through-

Note: A panic attack is not a codable disorder. Code the specific diagnosis in which the panic attack occurs (eg 300.21 Panic disorder with agoraphobia).

A discrete period of intense fear or discomfort, in which four (or more) of the following symptoms developed abruptly and reached a peak within 10 minutes:

1 palpitations, pounding heart, or accelerated heart rate
2 sweating
3 trembling or shaking
4 sensations of shortness of breath or smothering
5 feeling of choking
6 chest pain or discomfort
7 nausea or abdominal distress
8 feeling dizzy, unsteady, light headed, or faint
9 derealisation (feelings of unreality) or depersonalisation (being detached from oneself)
10 fear of losing control or going crazy
11 fear of dying
12 paraesthesias (numbness or tingling sensations)
13 chills or hot flushes.

Box 10.1 Diagnostic criteria for a panic attack

out the lifespan. Interestingly, fear of snakes differs from other specific phobias in that it does not appear to decline with age. Some of the common specific phobias are shown overleaf in table 10.1, and the criteria for diagnosis under DSM-IV-TR are shown in box 10.2.

Table 10.1 Examples of simple phobias

Name	Feared stimulus
Arachnophobia	spiders
Ophidiphobia	snakes
Ornithophobia	birds
Hydrophobia	water
Brontophobia	thunder
Taphenophobia	being buried alive

300.29 Specific phobia (formerly Simple phobia)

A Marked and persistent fear that is excessive or unreasonable, cued by the presence or anticipation of a specific object or situation (eg flying, heights, animals, receiving an injection, seeing blood).

B Exposure to the phobic stimulus almost invariably provokes an immediate anxiety response, which may take the form of a situationally bound or situationally predisposed panic attack. **Note:** In children, the anxiety may be expressed by crying, tantrums, freezing, or clinging.

C The person recognises that the fear is excessive or unreasonable. **Note:** In children, this feature may be absent.

D The phobic situation(s) is avoided or else is endured with intense anxiety or distress.

E The avoidance, anxious anticipation, or distress in the feared situation(s) interferes significantly with the person's normal routine, occupational (or academic) functioning, or social activities or relationships, or there is marked distress about having the phobia.

F In individuals under age 18 years, the duration is at least 6 months.

G The anxiety, panic attacks or phobic avoidance associated with the specific object or situation are not better accounted for by another mental disorder, such as obsessive–compulsive disorder (eg fear of dirt in someone with an obsession about contamination), post-traumatic stress disorder (eg avoidance of stimuli associated with a severe stressor), separation anxiety disorder (eg avoidance of school), social phobia (eg avoidance of social situations because of fear of embarrassment), panic disorder with agoraphobia, or agoraphobia without history of panic disorder.

Box 10.2 Diagnostic criteria for specific phobia

Social phobias

Social phobias are those that relate to other people. Common examples of situations that social phobics find difficult can include public speaking, eating and drinking in front of others and using public toilets. A degree of anxiety prior to social situations is quite normal, reported by about 40 per cent of the population, but it becomes a clinical condition when it interferes with the work and social life of the person. About 2 per cent of the population suffer from social phobias, which affect men and women equally. Social phobias most commonly appear between 15 and 20 years of age.

Agoraphobia

Agoraphobia is often described as fear of open spaces. Actually this is rather misleading. Agoraphobics actually fear public places, sometimes particularly crowded and difficult to escape situations. The dominant anxiety experienced in agoraphobia is of being unable to escape. Public transport is thus particularly difficult for agoraphobics. Agoraphobia occurs in 2–3 per cent of the population. Two-thirds of sufferers are women. The mean age for onset is 24 years, older than the other phobic disorders.

Post-traumatic stress

Post-traumatic stress disorder (PTSD) follows psychological trauma, defined as an extreme stressor that is beyond the range of ordinary human experience. Hunt (1997) suggests five categories of trauma:

- subjecting or being subjected to attack or torture in war;
- acts of terrorism;
- personal attacks, such as rape, sexual abuse and physical assault, within families or on the street;
- natural disasters, such as earthquakes;
- man-made catastrophes.

Symptoms include dreams and waking *flashbacks*, in which the experience is relived, avoidance of circumstances that remind the patient of the traumatic event, increased arousal and partial amnesia for the traumatic event. Other problems often occur alongside the clinical symptoms of PTSD. Sufferers may be prone to guilt or anger, and there is a tendency for serious relationship problems and substance abuse, as patients *self-medicate* with alcohol or illegal drugs in order to ease their distress.

The prevalence of PTSD in the population is thought to be 1–2 per cent. Most people who experience a traumatic event do not go on to suffer PTSD. In one survey in Detroit, USA, Breslau et al (1991) found that 39 per cent of people reported having suffered a psychological

media watch

What are you afraid of?

So what links Dennis Bergkamp with Hans Christian Andersen? Or Kim Basinger with Sir Isaac Newton? Success in very different careers, obviously, but also some extreme, irrational fears. Fears of travelling for the first pair, and for the second agoraphobia, which is a fear of public places.

Footballer Bergkamp is so afraid of flying that he has a clause written into his contract ensuring that his club cannot insist on it. If he can't get to a match by car, coach or train he can't play. Storyteller Andersen would not leave home without a rope, so that he could escape through a window in the case of fire. The rope is now in a museum in Denmark, proof that the fires were only in Andersen's mind.

Newton was housebound with agoraphobia for years after a period of severe stress. Basinger had a similar experience after the birth of her daughter. It's much harder to imagine an agoraphobic actress: academics can succeed with limited socialising, whereas actresses are subject to intense public scrutiny. But in both cases phobia severely impinged on their lives.

Taken from an article by health journalist Helen Saul, published in the magazine *Hotline*, summer 2001

1 Why are phobias so disabling? Give examples.

2 Suggest how people may cope with severe phobias. How effective are these strategies?

---

trauma. Of these, about a quarter went on to develop PTSD. Pynoos (1993) found higher incidence in high-risk groups. Sixty per cent of children who had been exposed to sniper attack and the majority of children surviving the Armenian earthquake suffered PTSD.

Figure 10.1 People exposed to natural disasters such as earthquakes frequently suffer PTSD

Obsessive-compulsive disorder

Obsessive-compulsive disorder (or OCD) is characterised by persistent and intrusive thoughts that can take one or both of two forms:

- Obsessions; these are thoughts that can take the form of doubts, fears, images or chains of future events. These 'invade' the consciousness of the sufferer and dominate their waking life;
- Compulsions; these are desires to carry out a repetitive task, most commonly washing or cleaning.

We are virtually all prone to minor obsessions and compulsions. You will all have had the experience of not being able to get a song out of your head, even though it may be one you hate! Only the bravest of us walk on cracks in the pavement or under ladders, even though we are aware of how irrational these superstitions are. Some of our rituals are helpful, even therapeutic. Comer (1995) suggests that religious rituals, such as fingering rosary beads, are beneficial in helping us deal with stress. However, when obsessions or compulsions either cause distress or significantly interfere with the patient's everyday life, we classify them as a mental disorder. About 1.5 per cent of the population suffers from OCD. The mean age of onset is 20–25 years. Most cases are preceded by stressful life events. Diagnosis of obsessive-compulsive disorder under DSM-IV-TR system requires that either obsessions or compulsions (or both) are present for more than one hour per day or that they interfere with the routine of the sufferer.

Figure 10.2 The tradition of fingering rosary beads can be a helpful ritual to deal with stress

Biomedical explanations of anxiety disorders

There is no doubt that some of the symptoms of anxiety reactions, such as increased heart rate and blood pressure, are biological. What is more controversial is whether biological factors are part of the underlying cause of anxiety. We can look here at an early theory of biological susceptibility to anxiety, contemporary studies of genetic influence and studies of brain functioning in anxiety patients.

Emotional lability theory

Eysenck (1967) suggested that the biological basis of indi-

vidual differences in anxiety lies in the reactivity of the autonomic nervous system. The autonomic nervous system controls the body's arousal. Eysenck described individuals with high autonomic reactivity as *emotionally labile*. Such people are very easily aroused by fear-provoking stimuli. As you can imagine, people who are more easily frightened are more likely to acquire phobias. Eysenck (1967) proposed that emotional lability, which underlies the development of phobias, is determined by genetic factors. Although current research supports the link between anxiety and the autonomic nervous system, we know that different anxiety disorders are associated with distinctive patterns of autonomic activity. In one recent study Friedman and Thayer (1998) compared the responses of 16 patients suffering from panic attacks, 15 blood phobics and 15 control patients without an anxiety condition to laboratory stressors such as electric shocks. The panic group displayed the fastest heart rate but the least variation between stressed and non-stressed states. The blood phobic group displayed the largest variation between physiological states when relaxed and when stressed. This suggests that the autonomic nervous systems of patients with different anxiety disorder function differently, thus Eysenck's idea of emotional lability is over-simple.

Evidence for a genetic predisposition to anxiety

It seems likely that some people are more vulnerable to acquiring phobias than others because of the inherited characteristics of their nervous system. Skre et al (2000) looked at the contributions of genes and environment in phobias by comparing the concordance rates in 23 pairs of identical twins and 38 pairs of same-sex fraternal twins. Identical twins were significantly more likely to share phobic conditions than fraternal twins and this effect was greater for specific phobias than for agoraphobia. This suggests that some people are more likely to acquire phobias (particularly specific phobias) than others as a result of their genetic make-up.

There is also some evidence for a genetic factor in other anxiety disorders. True et al (1993) studied the twins of patients who had developed PTSD following the Vietnam War. Identical twins were more likely than fraternal twins of the soldiers to share PTSD, suggesting that their genetic make-up influenced their susceptibility. Studies of genetic susceptibility to OCD have produced conflicting results. McKeon and Murray (1987) found that relatives of OCD sufferers were more likely than the rest of the population to suffer from anxiety disorders in general, but no more likely to suffer specifically from OCD. However, in a large family study, Black et al (1992) found that relatives of OCD sufferers were likely to suffer a variety of mental disorders, but no more likely than the general population to suffer OCD.

In a recent attempt to isolate just how great are genetic influences on different anxiety disorders, Hetterna et al (2001) reviewed the results of many twin and family studies concerned with generalised anxiety, panic disorder, phobias and obsessive-compulsive disorder. Results of studies of panic disorder and generalised anxiety disorder were meta-analysed and revealed inheritabilities of 0.43 for panic disorder and 0.32 for generalised anxiety disorder. Overall, family members of a patient with an anxiety disorder were four to six times as likely as others to develop an anxiety condition themselves. For all anxiety disorders it was concluded that there is an element of genetic susceptibility, but in all cases this was less important than environmental factors.

for and against

a genetic basis to anxiety

+ twin studies have shown that identical twins are more likely to share anxiety disorders than fraternal twins

+ family studies have shown that family members of a patient with an anxiety disorder are several times more likely than non family members to suffer an anxiety disorder themselves

– in all anxiety disorders the environment has emerged as more important than genetic make-up

Biochemical and neurological factors

We have already looked at Eysenck's lability theory and concluded that anxiety disorders are associated with distinctive patterns of functioning in the autonomic nervous system. In a recent study of autonomic function in Vietnam veterans Muraoka et al (1998) monitored the blood pressure and heart rate of 11 patients with PTSD and a control group of 7 veterans without a diagnosis. The PTSD patients had significantly higher heart rate and blood pressure throughout the 24-hour cycle, including when asleep. Findings like this have been explained by Krystal et al (1989) in terms of the trauma physically damaging the brain, leading to higher output of the neurotransmitter norepinephrine. However, although we know that trauma is associated with physiological changes, there is a lack of direct evidence to suggest that the trauma directly causes the physiological change. It may well be that the psychological symptoms of PTSD – flashbacks, amnesia etc – are sufficiently stressful to result in high arousal.

Neurochemical abnormalities have been found in OCD patients, particularly associated with the neurotransmitter serotonin. Hollander et al (1992) found that the drug M-CCP, which reduces levels of serotonin, made OCD symptoms worse. Pigott et al (1990) found that antidepressant drugs, which increase serotonin levels, can reduce symptoms. Generally, it is not believed, however, that low serotonin levels alone can explain OCD. Some studies have pointed to malfunction of an area of the brain called the *caudate nucleus*. Baxter et al (1992) used PET scanning to observe the differences in brain function in patients before and after successful treatment. They found that the main difference following treatment was that the right caudate nucleus became more active. Johanson et al (1998) carried out a study on 16 women suffering from arachnophobia. By radioactive labelling of oxygen and PET scanning they were able to track what areas of the brain were active when responding to images of spiders. All the participants displayed changes in blood flow to the right frontal lobe. Eight participants who responded with severe panic to the sight of spiders

for and against

biochemical and neurological factors

+ there is evidence from drug studies that serotonin is implicated in anxiety

+ there is evidence that anxiety disorders are associated with particular patterns of autonomic function

– there is an important question of cause and effect. We do not know whether the biological differences found in people with anxiety disorders are causes or results of their condition

where to now?

The following is a good source of further information about biomedical theories of anxiety.

▶ **Comer R.J. (1995) *Abnormal psychology*. New York: Freeman.** The chapter on anxiety disorders explores some different biological approaches to those we have covered here.

showed reduced blood flow to the right frontal lobe, whereas the other eight, who showed some fear but controlled it successfully, showed an increase in blood flow to the same area. This suggests that the right frontal lobe plays a role in the regulation of fear responses and that severe phobias are linked to lack of activity in that region.

Learning theory and anxiety disorders

Learning theory can be used to explain all the anxiety disorders. Actually, learning theory remains more important in explaining anxiety disorders than it does nowadays in

most other conditions. Classical conditioning, operant conditioning and social learning are all implicated in the development of anxiety disorders.

Avoidance conditioning

The simplest account of how people acquire anxiety disorders is the *avoidance-conditioning model,* based on classical conditioning. This involves the pairing of the phobic-stimulus-to-be with another object or event that already provokes fear. The sufferer comes to associate the new stimulus with the fear caused by the already-feared stimulus. This approach explains well how some specific phobias are acquired. For example, if you have been involved in a serious car crash, you might become afraid

classic
research

the case of Little Albert

Watson J.B. & Rayner R. (1920) Conditioned emotional responses. *Journal of Experimental Psychology* **3: 1–14**

aim: at this time the early learning theorists like J.B. Watson were emphasising the importance of classical conditioning in learning human behaviour. The aim of this study was to demonstrate that a fear response to a non-threatening stimulus could be created by classical conditioning.

procedure: the design was an n=1 experiment, ie an experimental procedure carried out on a single participant. The participant was an emotionally stable male infant called Albert, aged nine months at the start of the study. Albert was assessed on his responses to a number of objects, including a white rat, and he displayed no fear. Two months later Little Albert was again shown the white rat. This time, when he reached for it, the researchers struck a four-foot metal bar behind his ear, making a loud noise and frightening the baby. This procedure was repeated 5 times a week later and twice more 17 days later. Albert's responses to the rat and to other white fluffy objects were recorded.

findings: in the first trial when the metal bar was struck, Albert displayed some distress, sticking his face into a mattress. The second time he was a little suspicious of the rat, and by the third session he leaned away from the rat as soon as it was shown to him. When a rabbit was placed next to Albert, he cried. Seven weeks later Albert cried in response to the rat and a variety of other white furry objects.

conclusion: the researchers had succeeded in creating a phobic response to a previously non-threatening stimulus. This demonstrates that phobias can be learnt by classical conditioning.

of driving. In an early and now classic study of avoidance learning, Watson and Rayner (1920) used classical conditioning to create a phobia in a baby. This is described in detail in 'classic research'.

The avoidance-conditioning model can also be applied to social phobias. The former prime minister (PM)

Harold Macmillan suffered severe social phobia prior to Prime Minister's Question Time in Parliament. Now that this event is televised, you can see that it is characterised by highly aggressive confrontation, which would naturally cause anxiety to the PM. It would be impossible now to find out whether Macmillan had a social phobia before becoming PM, or whether he acquired it when he began the job. However, it does seem likely that it was the anxiety regarding confrontation in public that triggered the bouts of anxiety before Question Time.

It seems likely that avoidance conditioning plays a part in the development of agoraphobia. After the first attack of anxiety in a public place, agoraphobics typically display a *fear-of-fear*. This means that one of the reasons why they avoid going out is the fear of becoming afraid once they are out. It seems that going out becomes associated with becoming afraid, causing further fear. Of course, this model of agoraphobia does not explain how the first bout of anxiety occurred, but it might explain the ongoing development of agoraphobia.

Avoidance learning is also the simplest explanation of PTSD. For example, the victim of a mugging may come to associate going out with being attacked. Going out then causes a fear-reaction, which in turn reinforces the avoidance of going out. Ferguson and Cassaday (1999) have suggested that a similar process can explain Gulf War syndrome (GWS). *Gulf War syndrome* is a set of symptoms including memory, sexual and sleep problems, nausea, headaches, depression, rashes and increased sensitivity to pain. Typically, each individual suffers only some of these symptoms. Ferguson and Cassaday have proposed a classical conditioning model that suggests that a sickness response has been acquired by association with a range of stimuli including oil fire fumes (present throughout the fighting) and stressful events such as witnessing injuries during the war. The symptoms of GWS can be explained as the body's conditioned responses to these stimuli. Following the war, exposure to any of these conditioned stimuli would produce the conditioned sickness response.

Classical conditioning can be used to treat anxiety conditions through the processes of behaviour therapy. This might involve systematic desensitisation, implosion or flooding (see chapter 3 for a discussion). The fact that we can treat specific phobias so easily by classical conditioning techniques suggests that this is how they were acquired in the first place. However, while there is nothing controversial about the existence of avoidance learning, we are unsure about just how many cases it can account for. When Menzies (1996) surveyed phobic patients on the origins of their fears, the majority either reported either that they had 'always' had the phobia or that other types of experience accounted for it. We can acquire phobias of things we have never encountered (perhaps most commonly snakes), and with which we could have no conditioning experiences. Moreover, as Lovibond (2001) points out, when we have a 'near miss' experience (eg a near car crash) that does not have a negative outcome, we can still acquire a phobia. According to simple classical conditioning this should not be possible, and it suggests that at least some of the time we use more advanced cognitive processes to acquire phobias.

for and against

learning theory as an explanation of anxiety disorders

+ there is clear evidence that classical conditioning can account for some cases of specific phobias and for some symptoms of PTSD

+ other phobias are probably acquired by social learning

– there are some aspects of anxiety disorders that cannot be explained by learning theory, for example, individual differences in susceptibility to acquiring disorders

– learning theory cannot explain how we can acquire anxiety disorders following near-miss experiences

Other learning mechanisms

Although classic conditioning remains the most common learning explanation for acquiring anxiety, operant conditioning and social learning have also been implicated in some cases. For example, OCD can be explained in terms of operant conditioning, symptoms being seen as learned rituals for reducing anxiety. Thus compulsive hand washing has been explained by Meyer and Chesser (1970) as being learnt as a way of reducing the anxiety from an obsessional fear of dirt or germs. The obsession thus comes before the compulsion. There is empirical support for this view of how compulsions develop. Hodgson and Rachman (1972) placed OCD sufferers with washing compulsions in the presence of 'contaminated' objects. Researchers found that anxiety levels increased. They were then allowed to wash, whereupon anxiety levels decreased again. This demonstrated that compulsive rituals reduce anxiety. However, although learning explanations like this explain well how obsession leads to compulsion, they find it much harder to explain where the obsession came from in the first place.

Social learning theory can also explain the development of phobias. Mineka et al (1984) performed a classic study on the social learning of fear of snakes in rhesus monkeys. Monkeys were reared with parents who had an intense fear of snakes. During sessions of observational learning, adolescent monkeys saw their parents react fearfully to snakes. After only six sessions of observation, the adolescent monkeys exhibited the same reactions as their parents. In humans, this process can account for cases where children develop the same phobias as their parents.

Psychodynamic approaches

Freudian theory

Psychodynamic approaches emphasise the unconscious influence of early events and the family context in which

these events take place. In his early work Freud (1909) emphasised the role of Oedipal conflict (see page 38 for a discussion), exemplified by his classic case of Little Hans who, Freud suggested, displaced anxiety from his father on to horses, leading to a phobia of horses (see 'classic research').

Neglect, abuse or other trauma, and the conflict between the child's desires to act as it wishes and fear of parental disapproval, leads to *free floating anxiety*, which can then be projected on to specific stimuli, leading to a phobia. This is what Freud was getting at in the case of Little Hans, and this idea of displacement of anxiety remains interesting to contemporary psychologists even if we reject the importance of the Oedipus complex.

what's new?

cognitive bias and anxiety disorders

One of the limitations of learning theory in explaining the development of anxiety disorders is that it fails to explain why some people are more vulnerable to acquiring conditions than others. A further problem is in understanding instances where it appears that simple conditioning does not account for the condition, for example, in the cases of near misses. These problems have been addressed by recent research from the cognitive perspective. Various cognitive processes seem to operate somewhat differently in phobic patients, in particular attention. Eysenck M.W. (1992) has suggested that anxiety disorders are caused or at least maintained by *attentional bias*, ie the tendency to attend more than most people to threatening stimuli. Bradley et al (1999) tested this idea. Fourteen patients suffering generalised anxiety disorder and 33 control participants were exposed to slides of happy or threatening faces. The anxious group showed responded with greater vigilance to all the faces than did the control group, providing partial support for Eysenck's theory. In another recent study Friedman et al (2000) asked generalised anxiety patients and non-anxious control participants to silently read words, some of which were intended as neutral and some as threatening. They were then asked to recall as many words as possible. The anxiety patients recalled a disproportionate number of threatening words.

A different approach to investigating cognitive bias has been employed in The Netherlands. In a series of studies Kindt and Brosschot (1997) have used the Stroop task to test processing of spider-relevant information in arachnophobics. In the Stroop task participants are asked to name the ink colour of each word in a multicoloured word list. There are a number of variations in the task, including substituting pictures for words. The task is difficult because participants find themselves attending to the meaning of the words or pictures rather than to the ink colour. Kindt and Brosschot compared arachnophobic and non-phobic participants on Stroop tasks involving spider words or images. The arachnophobics took significantly longer to name the ink colours for spider-related items whether presented as words or pictures, suggesting that phobias involve an automatic process of selectively attending to the phobic stimulus.

Cognitive bias may be important in explaining individual differences in susceptibility to anxiety disorders. It is adaptive to attend to threatening stimuli in our environment, but if some people are born with or develop a particularly strong attentional bias towards threatening stimuli, then those individuals may be particularly likely to become conditioned to respond to threatening stimuli and so acquire anxiety disorders.

Figure 10.3 Public speaking can be an extremely anxiety-provoking experience

where to
now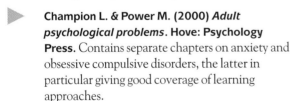

The following is a good source of further information about learning theory and anxiety disorders.

▶ **Champion L. & Power M. (2000)** *Adult psychological problems*. **Hove: Psychology Press.** Contains separate chapters on anxiety and obsessive compulsive disorders, the latter in particular giving good coverage of learning approaches.

In his later work, Freud (1926) suggested that a degree of anxiety is a positive thing as it activates psychological defence mechanisms (see *Angles on psychology* for a discussion of defence mechanisms), which protect the individual from the distress of a situation. However, when a current event triggers the memory of a childhood trauma the resulting anxiety can be too powerful to be contained by psychological defences, and the resulting internal conflict becomes expressed in symptoms. Thus someone who experienced a traumatic separation from parents in early childhood and then faces a situation in adulthood that re-enacts this trauma (such as being left by a partner) is particularly vulnerable to being overcome by a flood of anxiety. The psychological defences that would normally help with this anxiety are overwhelmed because the anxiety released is the sum of that produced by both the current and early experiences.

Contemporary research

In a study of attachment and psychopathology Fonagy (1996) found that in anxiety, as in other mental disorders, the majority of patients were classified as having type D attachments. This suggests that anxiety conditions in general have some association with early family experiences. This is not to say that simpler processes such as conditioning are not important. Contemporary psychodynamic writers, Brown and Pedder (1991), while maintaining the emphasis on the family environment in which phobias develop, have conceded that in the case of specific phobias, learning theories such as avoidance conditioning can

classic
research

a case of the Oedipus complex?

Freud S. (1909) Analysis of a phobia in a five-year old boy. *Collected papers* **vol III, 149–295**

aim: Little Hans, a 5-year-old boy, was taken to Freud suffering from a phobia of horses. As in all clinical case studies, Freud's most important aim was to treat the phobia. However, Freud's therapeutic input in this case was extremely minimal, and a secondary aim of the study was to explore what factors might have led to the phobia in the first place, and what factors led to its remission. By 1909 Freud's ideas about the Oedipus complex were well established and Freud interpreted this case in line with his theory.

case history: Freud's information about the course of Hans's condition was derived partially from observation of Hans himself, but mostly from Hans's father, who was familiar with Freud's work, and who gave him weekly reports. Hans's father reported that from the age of three, Hans had developed considerable interest in his own penis or 'widdler' and that at the age of five his mother had threatened to cut it off if he didn't stop playing with it. At about the same time Hans developed a morbid fear that a white horse would bite him. Hans's father reported that his fear seemed to be related to the horse's large penis. At the time Hans's phobia developed his father began to object to Hans's habit of getting into bed with his parents in the morning. Over a period of weeks Hans's phobia got worse and he feared going out of the house in case he encountered a horse. He also suffered attacks of more generalised anxiety.

Over the next few weeks Hans's phobia gradually began to improve. His fear became limited to horses with black harnesses over their noses. Hans's father interpreted this as related to his own black moustache. The end of Hans's phobia of horses was accompanied by two significant fantasies, which he told to his father. In the first, Hans had several imaginary children. When asked who their mother was, Hans replied 'Why, mummy, and you're their Grandaddy' (page 238). In the second fantasy, which occurred the next day, Hans imagined that a plumber had come and fitted him with a bigger widdler. These fantasies marked the end of Hans's phobia.

interpretation: Freud saw Hans's phobia as an expression of the Oedipus complex. Horses, particularly horses with black harnesses, symbolised his father. Horses were particularly appropriate father-symbols because of their large penises. The fear began as an Oedipal conflict was developing around Hans being allowed in the parents' bed. Freud saw the Oedipus complex happily resolved as Hans fantasised himself with a big penis like his father's and married to his mother with his father present in the role of grandfather.

discussion: the case of Little Hans does appear to provide support for Freud's theory of the Oedipus complex. However, there are difficulties with this type of evidence. Hans's father, who provided Freud with most of his evidence, was already familiar with the Oedipus complex and interpreted the case in the light of this. It is also possible therefore that he supplied Hans with clues that led to his fantasies of marriage to his mother and his new large widdler. There are also other explanations for Hans's fear of horses. It has been reported for example that he saw a horse die in pain and was frightened by it. This might have been sufficient to trigger a fear of horses. Of course, even if Hans did have a fully-fledged Oedipus complex, this shows that the Oedipus complex exists but not how common it is. Freud believed it to be universal.

provide a simpler and neater explanation. However, Brown and Pedder point out that social phobias and agoraphobia are more complex and cannot be explained by simple learning approaches. Actually, research suggests that early family relationships have an impact on vulnerability to all types of phobia. Magee (1999) looked at the history of

patients developing specific phobias, agoraphobia and social phobia, and concluded that long-term childhood trauma in the form of physical aggression, sexual abuse (women only) and verbal aggression between parents were all risk factors for developing phobias. Looking at social phobia in particular, Chartier et al (2001) looked for risk factors in the history of 8116 Canadians taken from the National Risk Survey. A number of psychodynamic risk factors for social phobia emerged, including the lack of a close relationship in childhood, parental discord and sexual abuse. The psychodynamic emphasis on family environment thus remains an important part of understanding vulnerability to phobias.

Psychodynamic approaches have proved useful both in explaining the symptoms of PTSD and in offering an explanation for why some people are more susceptible than others to PTSD. Horowitz (1990) suggested that the flashbacks and dreams associated with PTSD resulted from the attempts of the unconscious mind to integrate the traumatic event into the person's beliefs about themselves and the world. Avoidance behaviour could be seen as an unconscious attempt to suppress memory of the trauma by avoiding memory-cues. Repression may also be associated with more serious symptoms. Joseph et al (1997) assessed the expression of emotion in survivors of the *Herald of Free Enterprise* disaster and found that those who did not freely express emotions had worse symptoms. Breslau et al (1991) found that individuals whose parents had divorced when they were children were more vulnerable to PTSD than those from intact families. Davidson et al (1991) also demonstrated a link between physical abuse in childhood and vulnerability to PTSD as an adult. Studies like this are important because they demonstrate that the quality of early relationships is one factor in the development of anxiety conditions, and hence that PTSD has a psychodynamic component (Callanan, 2000).

The contemporary psychodynamic model sees obsessive and compulsive behaviour as the result of an extreme emotional response to trauma. This trauma can take place in childhood or adulthood. Salzman (1995) suggests that obsessional thoughts represent the memories of trauma breaking through to the conscious mind, while compulsive behaviour represents the mind's attempts to reduce the anxiety that results from this. There is some case-study evidence for links in some people between childhood trauma and later OCD. There is little empirical support for the importance of childhood trauma in cases of OCD, other than clinical case studies, which are not representative of OCD patients as a whole. However, as Lemma-Wright (1996) reports, about 66 per cent of cases of OCD follow shortly after a significant stressful event in adulthood or adolescence. This does suggest that OCD is at least in part an emotional response to trauma.

Conclusions

There are a number of anxiety disorders recognised by DSM-IV and ICD-10. On a biological level these have been explained by emotional lability, the genetic tendency for a highly autonomic nervous system. Research has partially supported the notion of lability, and there appear to be some genetic influences on susceptibility to anxiety. Learning theory provides a simple explanation of and highly effective therapies to tackle anxiety conditions, in particular specific phobias. There are, however, limitations to learning theory in its classic form, and these have been addressed by the newer cognitive perspective. The psychodynamic perspective takes a different and complementary approach, emphasising unconscious influences on anxiety, and seeing susceptibility as the result of factors like poor childhood relationships, insecure attachment and sexual abuse.

for and against

psychodynamic explanations for anxiety disorders

+ research clearly shows that psychodynamic factors including sexual abuse and poor family relationships increase vulnerability to anxiety disorders

+ insecure attachment, in particular type D, predisposes people to anxiety disorders

− some ideas, such as explaining avoidance behaviour as a strategy to suppress anxiety into the unconscious mind, are speculative and untestable

what do you know ?

1 Compare and contrast the cases of Little Hans and Little Albert.

2 What does learning theory explain and fail to explain about anxiety disorders?

3 To what extent are biological factors involved in anxiety disorders?

4 Do we still need a psychodynamic perspective on anxiety disorders?

11 Eating disorders

what's ahead?

This chapter will explore two of the more common eating disorders, anorexia and bulimia. The chapter begins with a description of the symptoms and clinical characteristics for anorexia and bulimia before moving on to consider a diverse range of factors, which may cause these disorders. The section on social perspectives deals with the influence of body image in Western culture with a particular emphasis on the feminist position. The section on psychological perspectives looks at two mainstream approaches, psychodynamic and cognitive. Finally, we examine the role of genetic and biochemical factors in the development of eating disorders.

Symptoms and phenomenology

Anorexia nervosa is a condition in which individuals have an intense preoccupation with body size and a distorted body image. Even those individuals who are emaciated feel fat. The incidence of anorexia rose markedly in late twentieth century Western society, leading some researchers to believe that the disorder is a cultural product of this historical period, but not everyone agrees with this view. Colman (1993) argues that contrary to popular belief, anorexia is not a new disorder. He points to historical medical records showing disorders characterised by extreme weight loss and a refusal to eat were diagnosed as long ago as the eleventh century. However, such a view ignores the possibility that people's experiences and actions had different meanings in different historical periods (Putwain et al, 2000). In the late twentieth century, anorexia is bound up with cultural standards of beauty, but this does not mean that similar disorders in the eleventh century were also.

The term anorexia nervosa was first used in the medical literature in 1874 by Sir William Gull of Guy's Hospital London. *Anorexia* comes from a Greek term meaning severe loss of weight, and *nervosa*, meaning for emotional reasons. There are no universally accepted diagnostic criteria for anorexia and, according to Colman (1993), most doctors diagnose on the basis of intuition rather than by applying rigorous diagnostic criteria. According to DSM-IV-TR, anorexia is diagnosed when an individual has lost 15 per cent of body weight and refuses to eat (see box 11.1). These individuals are obsessed with food and some will engage in frantic exercise to shed imaginary fat. They fear a loss of control, show a lack of inner resources and self-esteem, a fear of sexuality and of being controlled by others. In addition to abnormal eating attitudes and behaviour, there are other outward signs of anorexia, many of which are the physical consequences of starvation. These include a loss of menstruation, low blood pressure and insomnia.

A Refusal to maintain body weight at or above a minimal normal weight for age and height (eg weight loss leading to maintenance of body weight less than 85% of that expected; or failure to make expected weight gain during period of growth, leading to body weight less than 85% of that expected).

B Intense fear of gaining weight, or becoming fat, even though underweight.

C Disturbance in the way in which one's body weight or shape is experienced, undue influence of body weight or shape on self-evaluation, or denial of the seriousness of the current low body weight.

D Amenhorroea, the absence of at least three consecutive menstrual cycles.

Box 11.1 DSM-IV-TR criteria for anorexia. Source: American Psychiatric Association (2000)

According to Colman (1993) two factors make it difficult to establish the prevalence of anorexia. First it is difficult to draw a line between excessive dieting (which is very popular) and mild cases of anorexia. Secondly, most anorexic individuals deny their symptoms and claim there is nothing wrong with them other than being too fat. Between 90–95 per cent of cases are female, the disorder is more common in adolescents than other age groups and two-thirds of reported cases belong to the top two social classes (professional and managerial), even though they only make up one-fifth of the population. Anorexia seems to take a prolonged course, although the outcome is mixed (see table 11.1).

Table 11.1 Results of a 10-year follow up of individuals diagnosed with anorexia. From Herpertz-Dahlmann et al (2001)

69%	Fully recovered
3%	Met full criteria for anorexia
5%	Met full criteria for bulimia
0%	Died

During the 1970s reports began to appear of an eating disorder related to anorexia, which had not been previously described. This was termed *bulimia nervosa* by Russell (1979). Individuals with bulimia are also concerned with body image, with a morbid fear of becoming fat, although unlike anorexics, the bulimic individual does not necessarily have a low weight. Originally bulimia nervosa was considered as an attachment to anorexia, but under DSM-IV-TR the disorder is considered as separate (see box 11.2). Such individuals feel intense anxiety after eating and induce vomiting or use laxatives to avoid weight gain, which is followed by feelings of shame, guilt, depression and a lack of control.

Estimating the prevalence of bulimia is even more difficult than for anorexia as, first, bulimic individuals may have normal body weight and size and, secondly, because the bulimic individual may be very secretive about their bizarre eating habits. A 1980 survey by *Cosmopolitan* magazine invited letters from readers who used vomiting as a means of weight control. An analysis revealed that 83 per cent of respondents met diagnostic criteria for bulimia (Fairburn, 1982). Another study of visitors to a family planning clinic revealed a 1.9 per cent incidence of bulimia, a figure that tallies with American studies of college students. This evidence suggests that bulimia is more common than anorexia. Ninety-nine per cent of reported cases are female (see 'media watch'), most belong to social classes one and two (managerial and professional) and most cases tend to develop in people aged in their early twenties.

what's new?

binge eating disorder

As we have already said, anorexia appears to have been around for many years, but bulimia has only been recognised as a separate disorder since the 1970s. In the last decade, much of the attention of eating disorders researchers has shifted to the phenomenon of binge eating in the absence of bulimia. Currently binge eating without other bulimic symptoms is not classified as an eating disorder in ICD10, however, it does appear in the DSM-IV-TR.

According to a large community survey by Spitzer et al (1993), up to 30 per cent of overweight Americans and 2 per cent of the whole population indulge in binge eating behaviour. In a minority of cases, binge eating disorder or BED also occurs in normal weight individuals. If we were to accept binge eating as an eating disorder, it would be more common than anorexia and bulimia put together.

Proper procedures for recognising and treating binge eating disorder have the potential to save a large number of lives. Currently in Britain BED is not widely recognised by doctors or dieticians. This is a serious problem because conventional treatments for obesity, such as dieting, appear to make BED worse. This means that sufferers, being overweight, frequently receive the worst possible medical advice (Romano & Quinn, 1995). Binge eating can be distinguished from over-eating by the consumption of large volumes of food in short periods, accompanied by a sense of being out of control and feelings of shame or guilt.

Binge eating presents psychologists with something of a problem. Behavioural therapies have been found to be ineffective and in fact may worsen the problem. It seems likely that psychodynamic and cognitive-behavioural therapies may be more successful, however, there is currently a lack of evidence for this.

Frequent vomiting or laxative abuse can also lead to physical problems including severe tooth decay, and stomach rupture. The loss of body fluids can cause cardiac problems, epileptic seizures and kidney damage. Fifty per cent of individuals with anorexia also show the features of bulimia and are referred to as bulimarexics. Initially it was believed that eating disorders had a purely psychological cause, but since the 1950s it has been generally accepted that the disorder stems from an interaction of psychological, physical and social roots.

---

1 Recurrent episodes of binge eating (rapid consumption of a large amount of food in a discrete period of time, usually less than two hours).

2 At least three of the following:
   i consumption of high-calorie, easily ingested food during a binge
   ii inconspicuous eating during a binge
   iii termination of such eating by abdominal pain, sleep or self-induced vomiting
   iv repeated attempts to lose weight by severely restricting diets, self-induced vomiting, or the use of cathartics or diuretics
   v frequent weight fluctuations greater than 10 pounds due to alternating binges and fasts.

3 Awareness that the eating pattern is abnormal and fear of not being able to stop eating voluntarily.

4 Depressed mood and self-depreciating thoughts following eating binges.

5 The bulimic episodes are not due to anorexia nervosa or any known physical disorder.

Box 11.2 DSM-IV-TR criteria for bulimia. Source: American Psychiatric Association (2000)

Theories of eating disorders

Although anorexia and bulimia are considered as separate disorders under DSM-IV-TR, and have separate diagnostic criteria, this distinction has not really been matched in the academic literature. Anorexia and bulimia are almost treated as if they were different manifestations of the same disorder. Therefore the theories outlined below can be considered as explanations of both anorexia and bulimia, unless specified otherwise. The section on social perspectives will consider the role of contemporary culture in providing idealised images of beauty and a radical perspective offered by feminist psychotherapist Colleen Heenan. The section on psychological perspectives will consider the

more individualistic explanations offered by the more mainstream cognitive and psychodynamic approaches. Finally, the section on physiological perspectives will consider the role of genetic and neurological factors in the development of eating disorders.

Social perspectives

The two social perspectives explored here are closely linked by the assumption that eating disorders originate not in the mind or body of the individual but in social processes. The socio-cultural approach focuses on the impact of changing cultural ideas of beauty and the role of the media in bringing these ideas to the individual. Feminist theory takes this a logical stage further and shows how cultural ideas of beauty have been used to oppress women.

The socio-cultural approach

According to socio-cultural theory, anorexia and bulimia are caused by pressure in Western society to conform to an idealised notion of beauty. For women, there is an ideal shape presented by models and film stars, which has become more and more thin over the past 30 years. For example, Owen and Laurel-Seller (2000) examined the vital statistics of *Playboy* centrefolds from 1985 to 1997 and found that 53.2 per cent of the models were underweight, 46 per cent severely underweight and 30.5 per cent reached the weight criteria for anorexia. The average bust and hip measurement did not change much over this period, but as the models were becoming taller, they were becoming more underweight.

A previous study showed that in 1959 the average model weighed 9 per cent less than the average weight for their height (Garner et al, 1980) and by 1997 they weighed 17 per cent less than the average for their height. In conclusion, the centrefolds of today are thinner and weigh less than the centrefolds of the 1960s and 1970s. This is in contrast to the average weight of the female population, which has increased in the same period. The social pressure to become and stay slim has increased as the average woman has drifted further away from the cultural ideal.

The theory is supported by research showing that anorexia and bulimia are more common in Western industrialised countries, compared to non-industrialised countries where a more rounded body shape is preferred (Hsu, 1990). Furthermore, Arab and Asian women are more likely to develop eating disorders if they move to the West (Mumford et al, 1991). Similarly, the rate of anorexia is increasing for Chinese residents in Hong Kong, coinciding with a culture slowly becoming more Westernised (Lai, 2000).

Within Western society, socio-cultural theory predicts a higher incidence of eating disorders for groups where a premium is placed on thinness and evidence tends to support this prediction. Crisp (1976) surveyed 16–18-year-old London schoolgirls, and found that dancers and fashion models were more likely to develop the disorder. This theory can also potentially explain the gradual increase in the incidence of anorexia and bulimia in men as idealised notions of male beauty become more commonplace in the media.

Although the evidence seems to suggest that exposure to an idealised body image is linked to an increase in eating disorders, only a fraction of the people in Western culture exposed to these idealised media images go on to develop eating disorders. These images might prompt some excessive dieting, but as mentioned earlier, this is not necessarily the same as an eating disorder. As a result most researchers conclude that this theory can only be a contributory factor in the development of anorexia and bulimia.

for and against

socio-cultural theory

+ in the West, idealised notions of body shape presented in the media have become more and more thin over the past 30 years

+ anorexia and bulimia are more common in Western countries and individuals who live in the East are more likely to develop an eating disorder if they move to the West

– only a fraction of the people exposed to these images develop eating disorders, so idealised notions of body image can only be a contributory factor to eating disorders

media watch

Are eating disorders a female disorder?

In 1991, 5% of sufferers with eating disorders were men, by 1999 that figure has doubled to 10%, which has prompted the question over why more men are developing the disorder. One suggestion is that in the last decade there has been a decline over societal double standards over body size, now men are under pressure to have an ideal body image. There are differences in how the disorder manifests though. Boys tend to develop the disorder at a younger age than boys and although like girls, boys are more likely to develop bulimia rather than anorexia, they are more likely to exercise obsessively whereas girls are more likely to use laxatives. One alternative explanation is that men have always suffered from eating disorders but that in the past ten years have become more likely to report it.

From *Psychology Today*, July/August, 1999

1 What theories of eating disorders might best explain the greater incidence of eating problems in girls?

2 What reasons can you think of to explain the increasing incidence of eating problems in boys?

The feminist approach

The majority of people with eating disorders are female, yet traditional social, psychological and physiological models fail to contextualise eating disorders in terms of gender, or how culture or history may contribute to the gendered nature of eating disorders (Heenan, 1996a). What makes the feminist approach different from other models is that it attends to the dynamics of gender and power in culture and society. From a feminist position, there must be more to anorexia and bulimia than simply conforming to social pressure to be thin.

Heenan (1996a) argues that the size and shape of a woman's body reflects changing historical and economic trends. Eating disorders are a physical expression of the contradictions facing women in attempting to meet their emotional needs, symbolised through food and body image. Orbach (1986) argues that cultural representations of femininity involve instances of self-denial. In order to be feminine, a woman must ignore her own emotional needs and attend to the needs of others. Women therefore become 'starved' of affection.

The cultural representations of thinness replicates self-denial as seen in phrases such as 'naughty but nice', 'tempting but I shouldn't' and so forth. Our culture markets food for consumption, but simultaneously denies its consumption. Eating disorders arise out of this social context and removing eating disorders from this context functions to 'problematise' women. From a feminist perspective, the symptoms of eating disorders are interpreted as expressions of living in a society that promotes this self-denial.

'Women who starve themselves, binge and vomit or eat compulsively can be understood not simply as "victims" of media hype but as challenging social norms by being very, very good at dieting to extremes; by defying the sanction against women having an appetite, or by being more than "little women". (Heenan, 1996b, page 60).

Through being disordered women are expressing problems of a societal nature by saying 'no' to what is expected of them. Rather than positioning some women as 'normal' and others as 'abnormal' it makes more sense to have a continuum (Burstow, 1992). At one end are women who occasionally worry about food and at the other, those with troubled eating (Burstow's term for eating disorders).

for and against

the feminist approach

+ provides a contrast with mainstream psychological and biological approaches by looking at how eating disorders are bound up with the way that femininity is constructed in society

− focusing on the social and cultural context of the disorder could be seen as ignoring the severity of individual distress experienced by women with eating disorders

+ women with eating disorders are not seen as 'abnormal'. Instead, eating disorders are seen as a physical manifestation of the contradictions and self-denial facing women living in Western culture

− the feminist approach cannot account for different manifestations of eating disorders. That is, why some women develop anorexia and others bulimia

where to now?

The following are good sources of further information about social approaches to eating disorders.

▶ **Petkova B. (1997) Understanding eating disorders: a perspective from feminist psychology.** *Psychology Review* **4(1): 2–7.** A straightforward and simple introduction to what can be a complex theoretical position.

▶ **Hepworth J. (1999)** *The social construction of anorexia nervosa.* **London, Sage.** More advanced and more complex, but very well written. Addresses socio-cultural and feminist perspectives.

Psychological perspectives

There are two major psychological models of eating disorders, the psychodynamic approach and the cognitive approach. The psychodynamic approach focuses on the role of patterns of interaction in the family, while the cognitive approach focuses on the atypical ways in which sufferers of eating disorders think about food.

The psychodynamic approach

One psychodynamic theory put forward by Hilde Bruch (1982) claims that the origins of anorexia can be found in childhood. She distinguishes between different types of parenting based on how parents respond to the needs of their children:

● The *effective parent* is able to correctly distinguish between a child's biological and emotional needs. For example, giving food when child is crying from hunger and comfort when the child is crying from fear;

● The *ineffective parent* does not respond to the child's needs, but imposes their own definitions of needs on their children. These types of parents arbitrarily decide whether children are tired, hungry or cold without correctly interpreting the child's actual condition. They may feed the child when it is anxious and comfort the hungry child.

According to Bruch, the children of these different types of parent(s) will follow different developmental patterns. Children of effective parent(s) are able to distinguish between their own internal emotional and physiological states (this is called *introceptive awareness*). They follow a 'normal' developmental pattern, acquiring control and autonomy as they move into adolescence. In contrast, children of ineffective parent(s) cannot differentiate between their own internal needs. As a result they do not experience themselves as being in control of their own behaviour, needs and impulses. They feel like they do not own their bodies and do not develop a coherent sense of self. The child does not develop as an autonomous individual, but according to the wishes and expectations of their parent(s). During adolescence, the child becomes desperate to overcome their sense of helplessness and exert control over some aspect of their lives. In an attempt to defy the demands of others, the child attempts a form of extreme control over their body and eating habits. Those that are successful at redirecting their need for control go on to develop anorexia and those that are less successful end up in a binge–purge cycle (bulimia).

Although the theory was developed out of Bruch's clinical observations during therapy, subsequent research has begun to systematically test different aspects of the theory. Several studies have analysed interactions between individuals diagnosed with anorexia and bulimia with other family members. Results of such studies have shown that the families of anorexic and bulimic individuals communicate in complicated ways, providing support for various aspects of Bruch's theory.

Within the families of anorexics, parental messages often contain a 'double bind' showing both affection and a disregard for any attempted autonomy (Humphrey, 1989). Anorexic patients have described their own mothers as being excessively dominant, intrusive and overbearing (Dare & Eisher, 1997). Parents of anorexics tend to define the needs of their child themselves, rather than allowing the child to develop their own needs (Steiner et al, 1991). Individuals with eating disorders tend to be conformist, approval seeking and tend to perceive themselves as having little control over their lives (Vitousek & Manke, 1994).

One problem with these kinds of studies, is that while they show that families of individuals with eating disorders show certain types of communications patterns, it is unclear whether these are causing the disorder or simply a response to living with an anorexic or bulimic individual. In a different kind of study, Leon et al (1993) found that anorexic individuals showed a lack of introceptive awareness (awareness of internal cues such as hunger and emotional states), compared to individuals without an eating disorder and that a low level of introceptive awareness could predict the onset of anorexia, two years in the future. These results, therefore, suggest that such factors do play a causal role.

for and against

Bruch's theory

+ a range of studies have found support for different parts of the theory by examining communication patterns in the families of patients with eating disorders

– it is not clear whether these factors are a cause of the disorder or represent a response to living with a family member with an eating disorder

The cognitive approach

One of the defining features of eating disorders is a distorted body image, where individuals perceive themselves as being overweight when they are not. This suggests some kind of bias in the way that visual information about the body is processed. Early research supported this view, finding that anorexic patients tended to overestimate their body size by 25–55 per cent, compared to a control group of non-anorexic participants who made roughly accurate estimates (Slade & Russell, 1973). At the time this discovery was held as a breakthrough, because it seemed to show that body image disturbance lies at the heart of anorexia, and this view has persisted to the present day.

However, this view has been seriously challenged by research showing that body image disturbance may not be unique anorexia. Crisp and Kalucy (1974), using the same body size estimation technique as Slade and Russell, found that while anorexic patients overestimated their body size after eating a fattening meal, so did a group of normal patients. Shortly after these results were published it was found that ordinary people tend to estimate their body sizes more accurately as they grow older. As it happened, the control group patients in Slade and Russell's study were significantly older than the anorexic patients, which may help to explain why the group of patients overestimated their body size more than the control group.

Another problem for the body disturbance hypothesis is that recovery from eating disorders is unrelated to patients' estimation of their body size. Fernandez et al (1999) compared estimated body image in groups of anorexic and bulimic patients before and after a course of cognitive-behavioural therapy. Results showed that estimation of body size did not change during the course of therapy and, crucially, patients who recovered from their eating disorder still overestimated their body size.

The evidence from these two studies suggest that, contrary to popular belief, distorted body size is not a causal factor in eating disorders. Fernandez et al suggest that eating disorders are not caused by a cognitive bias in the way that patients with eating disorders see their body, but about the way they feel about their body. That is, a disturbance in the emotional aspects of body image, not the visual aspects. These emotional aspects of distorted body image will be expressed in negative attitudes and beliefs about one's body.

Cooper and Turner (2000) examined these emotional aspects of body perception in anorexic patients using the *'Eating Disorder Belief Questionnaire'*. Compared to a group of dieters and a control group, the anorexic patients held more negative beliefs about themselves, believed that acceptance from others depended on body shape and size, perceived themselves as having little control over their eating and judged self-esteem on body shape and size.

These negative beliefs may play an important role in the development of eating disorders, however, at this early stage, it is not clear whether these negative beliefs are a cause of eating disorders or whether they simply reflect the cognitive biases of patients with eating disorders. Negative beliefs have been shown to play a causal role in other emotional disorders such as depression and anxiety disorders, and so it is possible that this is also the case with eating disorders. Some evidence has come from outcome studies of cognitive-behavioural therapy. One such study by Newman et al (2000) showed that cognitive-behavioural therapy, which aimed to reduce negative beliefs relating to eating, size and shape, was an effective treatment for bulimia. These results suggest that negative beliefs do indeed play a causal role in the development of eating disorders, but further research is required before such a conclusion uncritically accepted.

for and against

the cognitive model

➕ the symptoms of eating disorders suggest an obvious source of cognitive bias; that individuals with anorexia and bulimia have a distorted body image. They overestimate their body shape and size

➖ research does not support this view. Anorexic patients are do not overestimate their body

shape and size any more than non-anorexic people

➕ another line of research has shown that anorexic patients hold negative beliefs about themselves, food and eating leading to a distorted emotional component of body image

➖ t is not clear at this stage whether these negative beliefs are a cause of eating disorders, or whether they reflect the type of thinking shown by patients with eating disorders

where to now?

The following are good sources of further information about psychological theories of eating disorders.

▶ **Szmukler G., Dare C. & Treasure J. (1995)** *Handbook of eating disorders*. **Chichester: Wiley.** Contains chapters on psychodynamic and cognitive perspectives by leading experts in those approaches.

▶ **Champion L. & Power M. (2000)** *Adult psychological problems*. **Hove: Psychology Press.** Contains a good chapter on eating problems focusing on psychological models.

Biological perspectives

Biological approaches to understanding eating disorders have included examinations of the role of genetic factors and biochemistry. Regardless of our theoretical views on the origins of eating problems, a sound medical understanding of eating disorders is essential for anyone working with patients, as sufferers of eating problems experience serious physical symptoms, sometimes to a life-threatening degree.

Genetic factors

Biological theories of anorexia have suggested that eating disorders may be in part genetic as there is an increased risk of developing an eating disorder for first-degree relatives (parents, siblings etc). Twin studies have provided more direct evidence for a role of genes – see 'research now'.

research now

twins and eating problems

Kortegaard L.S., Hoerder K., Joergensen J., Gillberg C. & Kyvik K.O. (2001) A preliminary population based twin study of self-reported eating disorder. *Psychological Medicine* 31: 361–5

aim: to establish whether anorexia and bulimia have a genetic component by comparing the rates of co-occurrence of eating disorders in identical and fraternal twins. If the identical twins are more likely to share an eating problem than the fraternal twins, then this suggests that it has a genetic component.

procedure: a questionnaire was sent to all 34,076 members of the Danish Twin Register asking three simple questions:

Q1 Have you ever experienced anorexia?

Q2 Has anyone else ever described you as anorexic?

Q3 Have you ever experienced bulimia?

Questionnaires would only be included for analysis if both twins had responded. A narrow definition of anorexia was used if respondents answered yes to question 1 and a broad definition of anorexia was used if respondents answered yes to question 1 and 2.

findings: 29,424 questionnaires were returned (86.2 per cent of register), revealing a group of 1270 individuals who replied yes to one of the above questions. Concordance rates are as follows:

	MZ	DZ
Anorexia (narrow definition)	0.18	0.07
Anorexia (broad definition)	0.25	0.13
Bulimia	0.26	0.11

conclusion: the results show that MZ (identical) twins have a higher chance of developing both anorexia and bulimia than DZ (non-identical twins), suggesting that genes might play some role in the development of eating disorders.

Superficially, the evidence from this study suggests that genetic factors contribute to the development of eating disorders (see chapter 8 for a more thorough discussion of the different types of studies used in behavioural genetics). If eating disorders were 100 per cent genetic, then the concordance rate would be 1.00 for MZ twins. As the concordance rates for MZ twins were so low in this study (0.18 for anorexia [narrow definition] and 0.26 for bulimia), genetic factors can only play a small role at best in eating disorders. Using the stress-diathesis model, genetic factors could be seen as providing a slight predisposition to eating disorders, which could be triggered by other variables psychological variables (such as family background) or socio-cultural variables (such as pressure to be thin). The self-report method used in this study has the advantage of using many more participants than could be included in a clinical trial. However, as participants had not received a formal diagnosis, there is no consistent standard against which participants are judged as having an eating disorder other than their own subjective views.

for and against

a genetic element

+ evidence from twin studies such as that of Kortegaard et al suggest that genetic factors may play a small role in the development of eating disorders

+ genetic factors could provide a predisposition to the development of eating disorders, which is triggered by psychological or socio-cultural variables

— twin studies may not remove the influence of environmental factors and so it is possible they overestimate the influence of genetic factors

Biochemical factors

One biochemical theory of bulimia comes from the basic premise that the disorder is linked to a lack of the monoamine neurotransmitters and in particular serotonin (5-HT). This theory has been developed from two main sources: the drugs used to treat eating disorders, such as Prozac; and diet – see box 11.3.

---

1 Eating disorders tend to co-occur with other disorders linked to low levels of 5-HT (eg depression and obsessive-compulsive disorder), suggesting that eating disorders might also be linked to low levels of 5-HT.

2 Prozac (a selective serotonin re-uptake inhibitor) is effective at treating bulimia, the symptoms of bulimia reduce in severity with increased dosage (Fluoxetine Group, 1992). Prozac works by preventing the re-uptake of 5-HT (therefore increasing 5-HT activity), suggesting that eating disorders might result from a lack of 5-HT.

3 Patients with eating disorders, who have a low tryptophan diet (an essential component of 5-HT) and therefore lower levels of 5-HT, experience more severe symptoms than patients with a high tryptophan diet (Weltzin et al, 1995). This finding suggests that severity of symptoms is linked to levels of 5-HT.

Box 11.3 Origins of the serotonin hypothesis

A neurotransmitter is broken down into a metabolite to pass out of the body like any other waste product. One way to test the serotonin hypothesis would be to test levels of the serotonin metabolite 5-H1AA in cerebrospinal fluid (CSF) and urine to give an indication of levels of neurotransmitter in the brain. If eating disorders are linked to low levels of 5-HT, low levels of 5-H1AA should be found in CSF and urine. Jimerson et al (1992) measured levels of CSF 5-H1AA in bulimic patients classified into high bingers (average 23 binges/week), medium bingers (average 10 binges/week) and a control group of individuals with no history of eating disorders. Results supported the serotonin hypothesis; both groups of bulimic patients showed lower levels of 5-H1AA over a one-week period than the control group. Furthermore, high frequency bingers showed lower levels of 5-H1AA than the medium frequency bingers, supporting the finding that symptom severity is linked to levels of 5-HT.

Measuring neurotransmitter metabolites in urine and CSF is not always an accurate index of neurotransmitter levels in the brain. However, the metabolite studies and Prozac treatment studies lead to the same conclusion, that eating disorders are linked to low levels of 5-HT. One problem is in establishing the direction of causality; do low levels of 5-HT cause eating disorders or vice versa? Psychiatrists and biologically orientated psychologists tend to assume that low levels of 5-HT cause the eating disorder because of their reductionist belief that psychological phenomena are caused by biological phenomena. It would be a mistake uncritically to accept such an interpretation without further evidence.

for and against

the serotonin hypothesis

+ a range of factors suggest that low levels of 5-HT are linked to bulimia

+ drugs used to treat bulimia (eg Prozac) work by raising levels of 5-HT

+ high levels of the 5-HT metabolite (5-H1AA) are found in CSF of bulimic patients

— it is unclear whether low levels of 5-HT are a cause or effect of bulimia

Serotonin is not the only biochemical associated with eating disorders. A number of hormone levels are disrupted in eating disorders, and it has long been a subject of debate whether these may be implicated in the origins of eating pathology. A classic study by Fichter and Pirke (see 'classic research') suggests that, on the contrary, hormone levels are disrupted by not eating and thus they are probably not a causal factor in eating disorders.

classic
research

starvation vs anorexia

Fichter M.M. & Pirke K.M. (1986) Effects of experimental and pathological weight loss on the hypo-thalamo-pituitary-adrenal axis. *Psychoneuroendocrinology* 11: 295–305

aim: the aim of the study was to induce starvation in participants and measure the resulting changes in hormone levels. The idea was to see whether the hormonal changes resulting from starvation were the same as those in anorexia. If they were the same then we could take it that the hormone disruption seen in eating disorders, particularly anorexia, is the result of not eating rather than a cause of the condition.

procedure: 5 healthy male volunteers were selected and studied over four phases. In the first phase, body weight mass maintained and the concentrations of several hormones in the blood were measured every 30 minutes over a 24-hour period in order to establish the normal hormone levels for the five individuals. The hormones measured included growth hormone, cortisol and thyroid-stimulating hormone. In the second phase participants were deprived completely of food for three weeks, and the concentrations of hormone levels measured, again over a 24-hour period. In a third phase, the weight of the volunteers was restored to normal and hormone levels measured. In the final phase, participants were monitored for a time as normal body weight was maintained.

findings: in the starvation phase, there were significant changes to hormone levels. For example, growth hormone levels increased, cortisol levels increased and thyroid-stimulating hormone levels decreased. When weight was restored to normal, the hormone levels returned to normal. The changes in hormone levels were compared to those recorded in eating disorders during previous studies. The hormonal changes in starvation and eating disorders were found to be the same.

conclusion: the hormonal changes induced by starvation were the same as those measured in patients with eating disorders. This implies strongly that the abnormal hormone levels in patients with eating disorders are symptoms of the disruption to eating patterns rather than the underlying cause of eating disorders.

where to now ?

▶ **Chowdhury U. & Lask B. (2001) Clinical implications of brain imaging in eating disorders. *The Psychiatric Clinics of North America* 24: 227–34.** A highly accessible review of the literature on neurological correlates of eating disorders.

▶ **Fichter M.M. & Pirke K.M. (1995) Starvation models and eating disorders. In Szmukler G., Dare C. & Treasure J. (eds) (1995) *Handbook of eating disorders*. Chichester: Wiley.** A good chapter on the relationship between the symptoms of eating problems and the effects of not eating.

Conclusions

A familiar theme begins to emerge when viewing the literature on the causes of eating disorders. There seems to be evidence that each factor seems to play some role in the development of eating disorders, but it is often difficult to establish whether it is a *casual* factor. The common-sense interpretation of these findings would be to suggest that eating disorders are multicausal; an interaction of social, psychological and psychological factors, however, be aware that feminists warn us against such a straightforward explanation. An alternative interpretation would be view each factor as providing an explanation of the disorder at a different level of analysis. For example, rather than biochemical explanation competing against psychodynamic explanation for the 'true' cause of eating disorders, the disorder can be seen as simultaneously psychodynamic and biochemical, with one explanation operating at the biological level and another operating at the psychological level. No one particular explanation can be seen as superior to any other. There is no straightforward resolution to this debate, but one can rest assured that over the coming decades the debate will continue.

what do you know ?

1 Describe the clinical characteristics of anorexia (eg diagnostic criteria).

2 Describe one biological factor (eg genetic factors) that may be linked to the development of anorexia. What is the evidence for that biological factor?

3 Describe one psychological factor (eg psychodynamics) that may be linked to the development of anorexia. How strong is the evidence for that factor?

4 Discuss one social factor (eg media images of the body) that may be linked to the development of anorexia. How strong is the evidence for that factor?

12 The legal aspects of crime

what's ahead?

In this chapter we consider the ways in which psychology has helped us to understand several aspects of the legal process. We begin by exploring factors affecting eye-witness testimony. We describe and evaluate research into the accuracy of eye witnesses including the effects of arousal and the weapon focus effect. We then discuss how recall is affected by attribution biases such as the fundamental attribution error and hedonistic relevance. We also consider whether the use of hypnosis is advisable in criminal investigations. In the second section we discuss offender profiling, comparing and evaluating the British and American approaches. The final section of the chapter provides an exploration of jury decision making. We look at the methods social psychologists use to conduct research in this area, and consider the influence of defendant characteristics, including attractiveness and race, on jury decisions. The importance of the 'just world hypothesis' on juror decision making is considered, and finally we focus on interpersonal factors such as the election of a foreperson by the jury and the effects of conformity and minority influence on the decisions made by juries.

Eye-witness testimony

When someone is a witness to a crime they may be required to do a considerable amount of testifying. They will probably be asked to describe what happened, they may be asked to identify a suspect from an identikit picture and/or an identity parade and, if a criminal trial takes place, they may be called to the stand to recount events that they have witnessed. The evidence they present at the trial is crucial for the judge and/or jury in reaching a verdict on the guilt or innocence of the defendant. Obviously if the testimony these witnesses provide is inaccurate then verdicts are unlikely to be fair; the guilty may go free and the innocent may be prosecuted. Accurate witness testimony is essential to the criminal justice system.

The accuracy of witness testimony

When someone who has witnessed a crime recounts what they have seen 'with their own eyes' they tend to be believed. A leading researcher in this area, Elizabeth Loftus, reported that jury members tend to trust eye-witness reports more than they do fingerprint experts. However, there is a considerable body of evidence which indicates that eye witnesses are disconcertingly unreliable, and it is likely that there are many wrongful convictions every year as a result of faulty eye-witness testimony (Loftus, 1986). In the USA some of the cases

of people convicted of serious crimes before the advent of DNA testing, introduced in 1990, have been reanalysed using this new forensic technique. By March 1994, 40 people were found to have been wrongfully convicted, some of them having been sentenced to death. In 36 of these cases, mistaken eye-witness testimony was the major evidence presented against them (Wells & Bradfield, 1998).

In experimental studies simulating crimes, participants have demonstrated similarly poor recall. Henderson et al (2001) used a poor quality video sequence (similar to that of CCTV used in banks) of a mock bank raid involving two robbers. When given images taken from the video to compare to eight still images of faces, participants frequently confused similar looking people. When the matching task sometimes did not include one of the robbers, correct matching was achieved on average in only 64 per cent of trials and the error rate worsened if one robber's external features (such as hairstyle) were hidden by a hat. When asked to match single individuals on video and in stills, participants were still highly prone to error, making 28 per cent incorrect matches and 45 per cent rejections of correct matches. These findings suggest that evidence from people identified from CCTV alone is unreliable, a conclusion supported by Bruce et al (2001) who, again using CCTV images, found that familiar faces are recognised more reliably than those that are unfamiliar.

General errors in memory

One of the reasons why eye-witness testimony may be inexact is because memory under any circumstances is subject to inaccuracy. In everyday life we often remember things differently from what was experienced. We organise material to make it meaningful, we add details to make sense of events, we change it in the light of subsequent information. Memory does not provide an accurate record of an event but an interpretation of it. There are many reasons why memory may be unreliable; we will concentrate on those that apply particularly to eye-witness testimony.

interactive angles

Think back to your AS course. When you studied the cognitive approach you will have looked at theories of both memory and forgetting – probably two of each. Explain how each of these theories could account for the failure of an individual who witnesses a gang taking over a bank to recall details of the crime accurately when they are asked to make a statement or to identify the muggers. Some factors you might consider are:

- whether the witness was paying attention at the time of the crime;
- how quickly events happened;
- the extent of their involvement (were they hostages or simply observers);
- if they had to wait before recording their observations;
- whether they were taken back to the scene of the crime by investigating officers;
- the emotions they felt at the time;
- how they felt afterwards, such as in court;
- how much they talked to others about the events;
- the nature of questions they were subsequently asked.

If you had been that witness, what would you try to do to maximise your chances of accurate recall?

Estimator and system variables in eye-witness testimony

Wells (1978) distinguishes two types of errors that are liable to occur in eye-witness testimony:

- *Estimator variables* are factors that affect the accuracy of witness testimony over which the justice system has no control, for example, how much attention the witness was paying at the time of the incident or how much stress the witness experienced. Wells labelled them estimator variables because they cannot be controlled in real life criminal situations so their effect can only be guessed (*estimated*) after the event.
- *System variables* are those that affect the accuracy of witness testimony and over which the justice *system* has some control (hence system variables), such as the way in which questions asked of the witness are worded or the way in which a line-up is constructed and conducted.

There are many variables in each of these categories; we will consider a few of the most important ones.

Estimator variables

The amount of stress and arousal

Witnessing a criminal event, especially a serious one, can put witnesses under considerable stress. The *Yerkes-Dodson law* (see page 195) expresses the relationship between arousal levels and performance. We perform poorly when our arousal level is either high or low (when we are very relaxed or extremely nervous) and perform best at medium levels of arousal. If this law is applied when people are witnesses to crime, we may expect their recall of events to be poor since it involves high levels of arousal. Any attempt to conduct simulated research into the effect of such stress on eye-witness testimony is extremely difficult for obvious practical and ethical reasons. However, field studies of witness accuracy in real-life incidents indicate that the Yerkes-Dodson law does not necessarily apply. Nevertheless, some studies do support its predictions.

Stanny and Johnson (2000) conducted two police training exercises during one of which a shooting occurred. The observers (also police officers) recalled significantly fewer details, including those about the perpetrator, in the high-arousal (shooting) scenario than in the low-arousal simulation. Similarly, in a test of face recognition of same and other-race faces, MacLin et al (2001) found that accuracy of recognition decreased in conditions of high arousal.

However, MacLeod and Shepherd (1986) studied 379 reports of eye witnesses to assaults and compared the accuracy of those in which no physical injury occurred with those in which people were hurt. There were no overall differences in the degree of accuracy. A different finding, but one that also contradicts the Yerkes-Dodson law, was demonstrated by Yuille and Cutshall (1986) who found that the greater the reported level of arousal, the more accurate the testimony. The findings of Gendron (2001), who investigated the source of arousal in simulated situations, may account for some of the diversity in experimental outcomes.

research now

remembering scary stories and boring backgrounds

Gendron M.J. (2001) The effects of arousal on memorial accuracy: a comparison of arousal as part of content material and as part of contextual environment. *Dissertation Abstracts International, Section B: The Sciences and Engineering* 61(12-B): 6728

aim: to investigate the effects of the source of arousal on memory.

procedure: 104 volunteers saw an 11-slide show. Participants saw the slides and either heard a neutral or arousing story to accompany them (*content source*). In addition, they were exposed either to arousing or neutral background sounds (*context source*). Memory was tested using a free-recall task and a multiple choice recognition task either immediately or after a one-week delay.

findings: participants exposed to the arousing story demonstrated better memory on the free-recall task for both gist and background detail, particularly in the delayed recall condition. Although they recalled more, they also made many mistakes. In contrast, exposure to an arousing background impaired memory compared to exposure to neutral background sounds.

conclusion: the findings have implications for the study of eye-witness testimony as, for real witnesses, both the content (the event) and context are likely to be arousing. In contrast, in most simulations the content may be arousing but the context, which appears to have the more significant detrimental effect on memory, may not be.

One problem with trying to ascertain the relationship between stress and memory is that many witnesses to really dramatic events believe that they will never forget them because they are so deeply ingrained in their memory. Brown and Kulik (1977) use the term *flashbulb memory* to describe what they believe happens when we witness something that has a huge emotional impact on us – it is as if our mind has taken a flashbulb photograph. These researchers believe that this type of memory is qualitatively different from ordinary memories and leaves an unusually clear, long-lasting, detailed and accurate memory trace. However, various studies have challenged the idea that flashbulb memories are more accurate than other types of memory. Neisser and Harsch (1992) asked a group of Americans to complete a questionnaire concerning the circumstances under which they heard about the Challenger space shuttle disaster the day after it occurred and then repeated the experiment three years later. The findings indicated that the accounts of different individuals differed greatly in terms of accuracy and many had changed considerably since the event. The real problem in such cases is that people sincerely believe that intense emotional experiences cannot be forgotten and that they remember it 'as if it were yesterday'. In other words, people think they recall things very well in such circumstances and therefore may be especially convincing. But, as Neisser and Harsch (1992) found, confidence

is not related to correctness. As Wells et al (1999) observes: 'It might be more appropriate to conclude that significant events leave an impression of indelibility but not an indelible impression' (page 65).

So, the relationship between stress and accuracy of testimony is a complex one. The fact that stress interacts with many other factors means that there is no simple effect, but it is a factor that cannot be ignored, especially when people witness very serious crimes.

Weapon focus effect

Many experimental and field studies indicate that if a witness to a crime sees the perpetrator wielding a weapon, such as a gun or a knife, they will tend to remember details of the weapon but be less accurate on other aspects of the scene, including the perpetrator's face (eg Loftus et al, 1987; Kramer et al, 1990; Stanny & Johnson, 2000, see page 106). This tendency to notice the weapon is known as the *weapon focus effect*.

Loftus et al (1987) suggest that the weapon focus effect occurs because the presence of a weapon focuses attention away from less dramatic visual images, such as the face of the perpetrator. Support for this hypothesis was demonstrated by Loftus et al who found that witnesses looked longer and more often at a gun in a slide sequence than at a neutral object.

One reason why weapons attract attention may be that the threat they pose causes emotional arousal. This then causes the witness to process and remember central information (the weapon itself) more accurately, while being less able to encode other visual information such as the perpetrator's face. Although this is supported by the findings of Stanny and Johnson (2000), Pickel (1998) questions the validity of such a suggestion, arguing that this effect has been found in simulated situations in which participants looked at pictures or videotapes of a scenario in which there is little if any threat. Furthermore, Kramer et al (1990) found that the weapon focus effect can occur even when witnesses' self-reported arousal is low.

Pickel argues that it is *unusualness* rather than the degree of threat that is the key variable producing the weapon focus effect; this is supported by two experiments he conducted (Pickel, 1999). In the first, undergraduates who watched a videotape showing an armed man provided less accurate descriptions of him if the setting was one in which a gun would not be expected (such as at a baseball game) than if it was quite usual (such as at a shooting range). The second study showed that witnesses gave poorer descriptions of an individual if they were carrying an object that did not fit with their occupation (such as a Catholic priest carrying a gun) and better if the object carried was not unexpected (such as a police officer carrying a gun). These results indicate that weapon focus occurs not because of the presence of weapons per se but because weapons are surprising and unexpected in many situations. The explanation of salience rather than threat accounting for the weapon focus effect is supported by Shaw and Skolnick (1999) who used a classroom simulation in which an angry student barged in carrying a book, gun or unusual object.

media watch

This is extracted from an article that appeared on the American news network CNN website on 2 March 2001.

Witness for Puffy's co-defendant says he saw gun, can't ID holder

Defense testimony began Friday for rapper Jamal 'Shyne' Barrow, one of two men standing trial with rap star Sean 'Puffy' Combs for a 1999 incident in which three people were injured.

Barrow is charged with attempted murder in the case. Combs and a bodyguard, Anthony 'Wolf' Jones, are charged with gun possession and bribery.

David Cubilette, who was inside the packed club in the early hours of December 27, 1999, said he 'saw Shyne with a gun in his hands' just after shots rang out.

Cubilette testified he was standing at a bar in the club when he heard an argument. He turned and saw a man gesturing and then throw a wad of money at Combs. Shortly after that, he said, he heard 'one ... two or three shots.'

Looking toward the sound, Cubilette testified, he saw an arm sticking above the crowd with a gun in the hand. He said he was not able to see the face of the person holding the gun.

Under questioning from Barrow's attorney Cubilette said he saw Barrow with a gun shortly afterward in the same area where he had seen the first person.

Combs had disputed prosecution witness testimony that someone had thrown a wad of money at him, sparking the scuffle that led to the shooting.

Combs was hustled out of the club by bodyguards and drove off. After they were stopped, police found a gun in the car. Combs and Jones were charged with bribery for trying to get the car's driver to claim the gun was his.

Having read the article above, write a summary document explaining why the witness is likely to have remembered some details of the incident and not others.

Figure 12.1 Where would your attention be?

How is witness recall affected by attribution biases?

While factors such as arousal and focusing on a weapon can disrupt the attention and recall of a witness, another significant factor affecting the accuracy of witness statements is their belief about why the person they witnessed behaved the way they did. This has a crucial effect on the way witnesses interpret the events that they have seen.

Attribution theory is concerned with how people explain the reasons for behaviour, specifically, how they attribute the causes of behaviour. Although people use different explanations to account for human behaviour, Heider (1958) (the founding father of attribution theory) found it useful to group such explanations into two categories: either dispositional (personal) or situational. If we consider that a person who was driving too fast has a reckless and irresponsible attitude we are making a *dispositional attribution*, an attribution based on that individual's personality (or disposition); whereas if we believe they were hurrying to an urgent appointment, we are making a *situational attribution*. It is not difficult to appreciate that the way in which witnesses attribute causes to people's behaviour is absolutely crucial to the conclusions they draw as to

the guilt or innocence of the accused and to the mitigating circumstances that might be taken into account.

When considering the way witnesses make attributions for the causes of criminal behaviour, we need to pay particular attention to the mistaken assumptions they may make. When we make attributions, we are often limited in our ability to process all relevant facts and, indeed, we may only have incomplete information at our disposal. This inevitably means that our attributions are sometimes incorrect. Attributional biases are those ways in which short cuts in attribution may lead us to false conclusions. We will now take a look at some of the most relevant of these.

The fundamental attribution error

As a general rule, when people explain the behaviour of others, they tend to overestimate the role of personal factors and underestimate the impact of the situation. This is such a pervasive bias that it is known as the *fundamental attribution error* (Ross, 1977). In the courtroom this means that the defendant is likely to be held personally responsible for the alleged crime, even if the events were in fact caused by factors beyond their control.

Many studies have demonstrated that even when the causes of people's behaviour are very obviously situational, people still attribute it to their personality. For example, Jones and Harris (1967) asked students to read out an essay either favouring or opposing Fidel Castro's regime in Cuba. Although it was made quite clear to the audience that the essays had been allocated to the students by their teacher and were not their own work, the narrators were still considered to hold the opinions expressed in the essay they had read.

You will recall the work of Stanley Milgram from your AS. He used an experimental situation that required participants to give a 'learner' an increasingly severe electric shock (never actually administered) every time he made an error on a simple memory task (Milgram, 1963, see *Angles on Psychology*). The results of this study were profoundly disturbing: 65 per cent of people were prepared to administer lethal level shocks, despite the victim's screams, complaints about a serious heart condition and eventual silence. When people hear of such behaviour, their usual conclusion is that any individual capable of performing such acts is a sadist. Psychiatrists, psychologists and members of the general public interviewed by Milgram prior to the study estimated that fewer than one in a thousand people would give the highest level of shock. The behaviour of the participants during the study showed that they were not being deliberately cruel. Most participants were distraught, continually questioned the procedure and argued to be released from the study. They were not sadistic – they hated the experience – but felt locked into a situation from which they could not escape. It was the situation, not the disposition of these individuals, that was responsible for their potentially cruel behaviour. The assumption that cruel actions are motivated by an 'evil personality' is an example of the fundamental attribution error.

So, witnesses may make biased judgements. Not only can memory be distorted after the event by the use of misleading questions or when witnesses hear other people's account of what happened, but the witnesses' attributions may distort the memory as it is formed. The way in which a witness interprets why the event has occurred – whether, for example, a person who swings a punch at someone has been provoked, is drunk or is simply an aggressive person – can distort the way memories are encoded and lead to unreliable recall of events. They are more likely to assume drunkenness or an aggressive personality (that is, dispositional factors) than provocation, a situational cause. Glaser et al (2001) studied 51 juvenile offenders receiving probation services from the juvenile justice system. They compared the views of each adolescent (aged between 13 and 16 years) and of the parents. In general, the parents scored their children's behaviour more negatively than did the children themselves, suggesting that the parents were demonstrating an attribution bias; they were making dispositional judgements so overestimating the children's responsibility for their problem behaviours.

Hedonistic relevance

Piaget (1932), writing about the moral development of children, reported that young children tend to judge right or wrong on the basis of how much harm a person has done. Hence, if a child spills a large amount of ink on a new carpet, even though they may be trying to do dad a favour and fill up his inkwell (remember, this is 1932!), then he or she is deemed to be much naughtier and to deserve a harsher punishment than a child who spills ink on a blotter when he or she has been specifically instructed not to go near the inkwell. Older children are more likely to consider the motivation behind the deed and judge the disobedient child as naughtier.

However, there are instances in which adults judge on the basis of consequences – particularly if these impact upon the perceiver. The principle of *hedonistic relevance* (also called hedonic relevance) states that the more directly the behaviour of another person affects us (be it rewarding or costly) the more likely we are to attribute responsibility to them. So, we tend to make dispositional attributions when there are unpleasant consequences for the perceiver and, as a result, are more likely to judge the act to be deliberate. Thus victims who are negatively affected – and witnesses who may suffer stress or fear – would be more likely to infer intention from an act. In the

case of a crime this means that the cost incurred for us as a victim or witness makes us more likely to place blame on an individual rather than the situation.

To illustrate the point, imagine being told the following scenario by a colleague at work. A man is driving home along a main road after a long day's work. He's been in a meeting all afternoon in a stuffy office and is a little tired. He has not been drinking. He is not driving particularly fast, is within the legal speed limit and is in the inside lane. For a fraction of a second he 'nods off' and his car veers on to the verge where it hits a parked, empty vehicle. Before reading on, think what, in this situation, you would consider to be a fair penalty. Most people opt for a caution, maybe a small fine and points on his licence. Few would find a harsher penalty appropriate.

Now consider an alternative scenario. The circumstances are identical, except the extent to which the action affects you. On this occasion, the parked vehicle is your car. Now what should the penalty be? In this instance, people would tend to say that the driver should receive a more severe punishment, perhaps a large fine or a term of imprisonment. They tend to focus on the ways in which the driver can be blamed – he shouldn't drive when tired. But none of us can pretend that this is as bad as drinking and driving, or that the driver's crime is particularly heinous. The consequences, however, are personal so we tend to focus on the individual (a dispositional attribution) rather than the circumstances (a situational attribution).

So, hedonistic relevance causes us to make dispositional attributions and to judge others more harshly when we feel personally aggrieved but, more leniently, because of situational attributions, when we are not directly affected

interactive angles

Consider the following scenarios. How would the fundamental attribution error and hedonistic relevance cause each individual to respond to the crime?

Nick arrives at the supermarket and parks his car in the first space he sees, in which there is already a trolley, which he hits. Will Nick, and his passenger Chris, blame the accident on Nick himself or the person who failed to return the trolley to the trolley park?

Dave shares a flat with Pete and James. When everyone else is out, Dave and his friend Sam borrow Pete's DVD player and wreck it. How are Pete and James likely to view the behaviour of Dave and Sam?

research
now

hedonistic relevance and retaliation

DeRidder R., Schruijer S.G.L. & Rijsman J.B. (1999) Retaliation to personalistic attack. *Aggressive Behaviour* 25(2): 91–6

aim: to examine whether hedonistic relevance can explain retaliation behaviours after an 'attack'.

procedure: it was hypothesised that:

● if one person is attacked by another person, the victim will react more negatively than when no attack occurs;

● if a person is singled out for attack, they will react more negatively than a victim of an undistinctive attack (when the attacker behaves similarly toward the victim and a third person);

There were therefore two independent variables; 'victim of attack' (attack or no attack) and 'behaviour towards a third person' (attack or no attack). The dependent variable was the number of retaliatory attacks perpetrated by the victim (participant) towards the attacker (an actor). Thirty-two participants were the 'victim'.

findings: victims who were attacked retaliated more than those who were not attacked and victims of a 'personal' attack retaliated more than those who suffered an undistinctive attack.

conclusions: both hypotheses were supported. This suggests that retaliation is more than just behavioural reciprocity – we don't attack just because we are attacked – victims appear to judge the need for retaliation on the basis of dispositional attributions. When their perception is of a deliberate attack directed at themselves alone the event has greater hedonistic relevance so they are more likely to respond negatively.

---

by the consequences of a crime. Since victims will always be directly affected by the crime and witnesses may often be scared or stressed, they are more likely to perceive the perpetrator as responsible for their actions and make more severe judgements.

System variables

The effects of leading questions

A real-life example of the inaccuracy of eye witnesses was graphically demonstrated by Crombag et al (1996). They studied people's memory of an accident in which a Boeing 747 crashed into a high-rise apartment in Amsterdam in October 1992, news of which was extensively reported over two days on Dutch television with scenes of the fire brigade rescuing people from the burning, collapsing building. Despite the fact that no scenes were shown of the actual crash, two-thirds of the 93 students who participated in the study answered 'yes' to the question, 'Did you see the television film of the moment the plane hit the apartment building?'. Many of them felt able to elaborate on what they had supposedly seen; for example, 14 students 'remembered' seeing that the plane was already

on fire when it crashed into the building. When witnesses are interviewed by the police, it is possible that even subtle differences in the wording of questions can affect the witnesses' responses. You may recall a study from your AS course (Loftus, Miller & Burns, 1978), in which a question about a non-existent stop sign caused participants to mistakenly 'recall' having seen one in the film they were shown (see *Angles on Psychology*). The study below demonstrates another way in which leading questions can affect eye witnesses' recall of a scene.

The classic study is one of a series of such studies conducted by Loftus and her colleagues. For example, Loftus and Zanni (1975) asked some of the witnesses 'Did you see a broken headlight?', and asked other witnesses 'Did you see the broken headlight?'. Just 7 per cent of those asked about **a** broken headlight reported seeing one (there wasn't one in the film), compared to 17 per cent of those people asked about **the** broken headlight. These studies show how post-event experience can result in information being added to an earlier memory. Loftus believed such material is incorporated into the original memory, so once such questions have been posed there is no going back.

classic
research

does the wording of questions influence recall?

Loftus E.F. & Palmer J.C. (1974) Reconstruction of auto-mobile destruction: An example of the inter-action between language and memory. *Journal of Verbal Learning and Verbal Behaviour* **13: 585–589**

aim: to see if the wording of questions influences recall. The particular questions used are leading questions, that is questions which, because of their content or the way they are expressed, suggest to witnesses what answer should be given.

procedure: there were two studies which both used the experimental method with an independent groups design.

Study 1: 45 student participants were shown seven film clips of traffic accidents and after each one were asked to write an account of what they had seen. They were then asked specific questions, identical for all participants except one about the speed of the vehicles involved in a collision. This key question was: 'About how fast were the cars going when they … each other?'

There were five groups; each group of nine participants was given a different word or phrase to describe the impact. These were:

collided   smashed   bumped   hit   contacted

The independent variable was the verb used to describe the collision. The dependent variable was the estimated speed.

Study 2: 150 student participants were shown a one-minute film in which there was a four-second scene of a multiple car accident.

The procedure was similar to the previous one: there were two experimental conditions in which the wording of a key question was varied and a control condition in which the participants were not asked a question about the speed of the cars. There were 50 participants in each condition. The questions asked in the two experimental conditions were:

● How fast were the cars going when they *hit* each other?

● How fast were the cars going when they *smashed into* each other?

A week later all the participants, without seeing the film clips again, were asked further questions about the car accident, including the key question, 'Did you see any broken glass?'. There was no broken glass in the film.

findings:
Study 1: the estimated speed varied depending on the wording of the question. The mean speed in each con-dition (rounded to whole numbers) was as follows:

Verb used	Estimated speed
smashed	41 mph
collided	39 mph
bumped	38 mph
hit	34 mph
contacted	32 mph

Thus there was a full 9 miles per hour difference between the 'smashed' and 'contacted' groups.

Study 2: the table below summarises the main findings:

Condition	Percentage of 'yes' responses
smashed	32
hit	14
control	12

It can be seen from the table that the wording of the question had a significant effect on whether participants mis-perceived broken glass.

conclusion: study 1 shows that the wording of a question can have a significant effect on people's memory of events. This may be because the participant, being unsure of the speed, adjusts it to suit what the questioner wants and is therefore influenced by *demand characteristics*. Alternatively, the memory may have been affected by the way in which the crash was labelled. Study 2 shows that the change of a single word a week earlier had had a dramatic effect on memory.

There are likely to be some important differences between the way we respond in a contrived experimental situation and our reaction to witnessing a real event. In the former we are fairly detached and have no vested interest in the estimation of speed. In contrast, when we actually see an accident we inevitably become personally involved in it and that may change our perception. In addition to this, watching a video or film clip of an emotionally disturbing situation does not equate to the real-life situation in terms of the fear and stress that are experienced. Loftus's research has therefore been criticised for its lack of ecological validity. However, given the ethical and practical constraints under which psychologists work, it would be difficult to make it more realistic. Although we need to be aware of the limitations of such studies, the findings are of considerable value.

The use of hypnosis in criminal investigations

Several years ago a woman in the US disappeared without trace and when no one had heard from her for several weeks the police hypnotised her son in order to try to ascertain whether he could shed light on her fate. Under hypnosis the son reported that he had seen his father murder his mother and chop up her body. Although there was no other evidence, the father was sentenced to life imprisonment for her murder. Some months after the conviction the women turned up in another state (reported by Kalat, 1993). Little wonder that psychologists are dubious about the use of hypnosis to supposedly uncover lost memories.

In the US, the Federal Bureau of Investigation (FBI) has been using hypnosis since 1968 and although few other countries are known to use it, interest has been expressed by other police forces including those in Britain (Gibson, 1982). In his 1982 paper, Gibson criticises the use of hypnosis in criminal investigations. The main points he makes are as follows:

● **Increased recall but more errors:** during interrogation, hypnotised witnesses are assured that they can remember details of certain events and this leads to recall of false memories. In a classic study, Stalnaker and Riddle (1932) asked participants to remember various pieces of prose and poetry. A year later they were tested for recall in the normal and the hypnotised state. In comparison to their recall in the normal state, they produced more accurate but also more confabulated information. Similarly, Dwyman and Bowers (1983) showed people photos and asked them to recall as much detail as possible, first in a normal state, then under hypnosis. More items were recalled under hypnosis but most of the additional items were incorrect. The increased error rate may be due to the tendency of hypnotised people to guess or to mistake vividly imagined possibilities for actual memories. What is a cause of concern is that participants are just as convinced of their accuracy on the wrong items as on additional correct ones. Witnesses in court who have been previously hypnotised will innocently but confidently recall confabulated events as if they are real ones.

This is extracted from an article that appeared on the *New York Times* website on 19 March 1999.

A clemency case puts a governor on the spot

Shirley Christian

Little more than a month after bowing to a plea from the Pope and commuting the death sentence of a confessed triple killer, the Governor of Missouri faces the clemency petition of a condemned man who has submitted to a lie detector test to buttress his claim of innocence.

The test, given to Roy Roberts, who is to be executed for the fatal stabbing of a prison guard, showed no deception in his denial of involvement. It was administered by a former officer on the police force who was described by Bruce D. Livingston as a 'reputable, well-respected polygrapher not known as defense-oriented.'

The killing for which Mr. Roberts was sentenced to death occurred during a riot in 1983. Mr. Roberts, who was then serving an 18-year sentence for an armed robbery four years earlier, was charged with holding the guard, Thomas Jackson, while other prisoners killed him.

Mr. Roberts contends that he could not have had a role in the slaying because he was brawling with another guard when it occurred. At the trial, this guard confirmed that he and Mr. Roberts fought during the melee, involving 25 to 30 prisoners. But three other guards identified Mr. Roberts as the man who had held Mr. Jackson. Mr. Livingston says these three guards failed to identify Mr. Roberts when the state initially investigated the riot. They did so, he says, only after undergoing hypnosis in an intense pretrial effort by prosecutors. 'Such "evolving" testimony is inherently suspect,' Mr. Livingston said.

In the Roberts case, Mr. Livingston argues, the outcome of the lie detector test and conflicting witness accounts justify clemency.

His argument has received strong support in recent days. Bill McClellan reported that it was possible that Mr. Roberts was innocent not only of the prison killing but also of the robbery for which he had been sent to prison in the first place. Mr. McClellan quoted an acquaintance of Mr. Roberts as having said in an interview that he himself had committed that robbery.

Mr. Livingston said Mr. Roberts had insisted on taking the lie detector test. 'I was nervous about his doing it,' Mr. Livingston said. 'I told him, "If you fail, it's all over." I also told him we had to have it done by someone whose reputation will mean something to the Governor. Roy said: "I don't care. I didn't do this."'

The man who administered the test was Donald I. Dunlap. Mr. Dunlap's written report says that Mr. Roberts showed 'no deception' in his answers denying involvement in the killing and that he specifically denied holding the victim during the stabbing.

Mr. Roberts was one of three prisoners charged with the killing of Mr. Jackson. All the defendants' lawyers won changes of venue out of the town of Moberly, where the prison is situated, and each of the trials was held in a venue different from the others. In one case, Rodney Carr, identified by guards as having stabbed Mr. Jackson, was sentenced to life in prison. In another, Robert Driscoll was sentenced to death, but his conviction was overturned after it was discovered that there was no blood on the knife he carried during the uprising; he awaits a new trial.

Mr. Roberts, who was not armed, was charged with grabbing the victim, pulling his hair and forcing him against a window as the stabbing ensued.

'Thus Roberts is the only person who was sentenced to death for the crime, even though he is the least culpable, even under the state's version of the evidence,' Mr. Livingston's petition said. 'This disproportionality pales in comparison, however, to that which arises if, as we contend, Roberts is indeed innocent of the crime.'

Having read the excerpt above, prepare two statements; one defending the use of hypnosis in such instances, the other identifying the problems with its use.

- **Alteration of existing true memories:** hypnotised people are highly suggestible and incorporate fantasies into their memories. Witnesses who have undergone hypnosis become unable to differentiate between real and imagined events, and, moreover, neither can anyone else, however expert. Diamond (1980) suggests that hypnotising witnesses amounts to destroying or fabricating evidence.

- **Implanting of false information:** it is quite possible for a hypnotist to implant false memories into a hypnotised person's mind, even if unwittingly. Some psychoanalytic psychiatrists, hypnotists and members of the police force tend to think of memory in terms of an 'exact copy' of what actually occurred, an indelible engram that cannot be altered by leading questions or other suggestions. Memory does not operate in such a way and however detached a hypnotist may try to be, he or she will invariably provide clues to the hypnotised person and influence their recall. Indeed, an attitude of complete detachment is likely to yield no useful material from hypnosis.

- **The facility to lie:** there are occasions when witnesses, victims and suspects wish to lie. Hypnosis offers them an ideal opportunity to do this. If evidence is later found to be false, the individual can then plead ignorance of information that was supposedly produced in good faith under hypnosis.

Vingoe (1991) argues that if hypnosis is used in police investigations, we need to consider carefully who does the hypnotising. Even well-trained senior police officers should not operate without psychological or medical training. A major problem is that investigators are not trained in mental health and mental health professionals are not trained in investigative procedures.

Orne (1979) argues that if hypnosis is used in criminal investigations, the following guidelines should be followed:

- hypnosis should only be carried out by an appropriately trained psychologist or psychiatrist;

- the whole procedure should be videotaped;

- no one other than the hypnotist and the person to be hypnotised should be present;

- interrogations conducted prior to hypnosis should be tape-recorded so that it is possible to ascertain which of the information produced under hypnosis is new.

research now

hypnotic suggestion and uncorroborated memories

Lock T.G. (2000) Implanting or unplanting memories? The role of recall enhancement, anxiety, and psychological symptom interpretation in the creation of false memories. *Dissertation Abstracts International: Section B: The Sciences and Engineering* 61(5B): 2769

aim: to investigate the incidence of false autobiographical memories 'recalled' through hypnosis.

procedure: participants were asked to report childhood memories following the use of a suggestive technique (hypnotic suggestion). Family members were then contacted in order to corroborate the 'recollections'.

findings: the incidence of 'unplanted' (that is, corroborated) memories reported by participants varied between 0 and 17 per cent. The incidence of 'implanted' (or uncorroborated) memories reported was between 3 and 25 per cent. Higher recall was reported by participants who reported that they were highly responsive to the hypnotic protocol. The recall of non-corroborated memories was associated with the participants experiencing pressure to report memories.

conclusions: while participants did recall accurate facts following the hypnotic procedure, particularly if they were highly responsive, the incidence of uncorroborated memories was higher still. Since it would always be critical for a witness to recall they would tend to be 'under pressure' and thus likely to produce inaccurate reports.

The caution with which hypnotically induced memories should be treated given the experimental findings of Lock (2000) appears to translate to the courtroom situation. Coleman et al (2001) studied mock jurors in two scenarios, both involving the intervention of a therapist using various techniques with an alleged victim of childhood abuse. In the first, the therapist was described as using hypnosis, suggestion or symptom management. In this case the evidence from the victim obtained through hypnosis was deemed to be accurate and credible. In the second scenario the therapist had been sued for allegedly influencing a clients' false recall of abuse. In this instance, the use of hypnosis caused jurors to attribute the victims' memories to a creation of the therapist.

Many official bodies have been less than positive about the use of hypnosis in criminal investigations. In 1979 the International Society of Hypnosis condemned the training of police officers by non-psychologists in the techniques of inducing hypnosis for use in interrogations. The American Medical Association (1986) advised that testimony elicited under hypnosis should not be used in courts of law. In Britain the Home Office has produced several circulars (see 'where to now?') on the use of forensic hypnosis, all of which urge extreme caution in its use and some of which suggest that hypnosis risks causing actual harm to the individual (Home Office Circular No 66, 1988).

This is extracted from an article on the *Independent* newspaper website on 8 October 2002.

Murder conviction for handicapped man 'a miscarriage'

A mentally handicapped man who has served 16 years in prison for murdering an elderly pools collector was the victim of a 'miscarriage of justice', the Court of Appeal was told.

Geoffrey Foster was jailed for life partly on the basis of confessions he made that were 'unreliable' and should have never been admitted at his trial, the court was told.

Police had recorded that Foster was 'sub-normal', but he was given no legal or social services support until the 10th interview. He was only offered a solicitor after he had admitted the killing in the penultimate interview.

While he was giving evidence at his trial for the murder of Harold Cheetham at Chester Crown Court, Foster denied that he had killed the 74-year-old and said he admitted it in an interview because police were pressuring him.

Foster, of Knutsford, Cheshire, claimed that one police officer had 'clouted' him across the head and others had tried to put an electric flex around his neck.

During cross-examination, however, he admitted that he had strangled Mr Cheetham, but then retracted the statement later. The jury found him guilty and he was sentenced to life imprisonment in April 1986.

Foster's case was referred back to the Court of Appeal by the Criminal Cases Review Commission, an organisation that investigates possible miscarriages of justice, in November 2000.

Mr Fitzgerald [acting on behalf of Foster] said that Foster had a 'significant impairment of intelligence and a significant impairment of social functioning' and that he had been the victim of a 'miscarriage of justice'.

He said the case against Foster was based largely on the confessions but also relied on a woman, Margaret Patten, who had given a statement saying that she had seen Foster at the gate of Mr Cheetham's house on the night of the killing.

She repeated the statement under hypnosis, but later gave a second statement saying it had been Foster's brother Derek that she had seen, and identified him at the trial.

How could you account for the change in Margaret Patten's statement described in the article above?

Perhaps the safest way forward, as suggested by several researchers (eg Gibson, 1989; Smith, 1983), is to increase research into non-hypnotic ways to facilitate witness memory, such as contextual reinstatement and repeated testing.

where to now?

The following are good sources of further information on hypnosis, both providing accessible and useful insight into its use in criminal investigations:

▶ **Gibson H.B. (1982) The use of hypnosis in police investigations.** *Bulletin of the British Psychological Society* **35: 138–142.**

▶ **Vingoe F.J. (1991). The truth and nothing but the truth about forensic hypnosis.** *The Psychologist* **14(9): 395–397.**

The Home Office has also produced several papers on the use of forensic hypnosis (for example, Gibson, 1989; Orne et al, 1989). These can be obtained from the Home Office website (Circular No. 66 1988). For the No 66/1988 paper mentioned in the text see the *British Journal of Experimental and Clinical Hypnosis*, 1989, vol 6.

what do you know?

1 Describe and evaluate research into the effect of leading questions on the accuracy of eye-witness testimony.

2 'Police investigating the Omagh atrocity failed to interview potential witnesses who might have seen the bombers just before the explosion and could provide vital evidence against them... Police had a list of 150 people who used automatic cash dispensers in the Market Street area of the Co Tyrone town in the hours before the blast...'

   Guardian, 2 February 2002

   Use evidence about the accuracy of eye-witness testimony to critically examine whether the police had lost access to significant useful information by failing to interview the cash dispenser users.

3 Discuss how eye-witness recall is affected by attribution biases.

4 Outline and critically evaluate research into the effects of hypnosis on the accuracy of witness testimony.

Eye-witness testimony: conclusions

In conclusion, psychological research into the accuracy of testimony provided by witnesses to crimes has been valuable in providing an insight into the many factors that affect its accuracy such as the use of leading questions, hypnosis and attribution biases. We must, however, acknowledge the limitations of generalising evidence from simulations to real-life situations.

Offender profiling

The concept of offender profiling currently attracts a great deal of attention, but this fascination is not new; long ago fictional detectives such as Sherlock Holmes and Charlie Chan established its popularity. What is relatively recent is that police forces world wide have begun to recognise its potential. In this section we will look at what

is meant by profiling and at two very different approaches to it – the American and British methods. A real-life case study of the profiling of a serial rapist and murderer in London will be outlined before we go on to consider the important issue of the extent to which profiling actually works – is it a misleading fiction or an indispensable tool in the apprehension of serious criminals? Or, indeed, is it neither, but simply one of many useful police tools?

What is offender profiling?

Offender profiling, a term coined by the FBI, has been defined in many ways, but the underlying concept is the same: profiling entails providing a description of the offender based on an analysis of the crime scene, the victim and any other available evidence.

Offender profiling is one of the most controversial and misunderstood areas of criminal detection. As Davies (1997) comments:

The public perception of the profiler, fuelled no doubt by public portrayals in television series like *Cracker* and films such as *The Silence of the Lambs*, is of the brilliant loner, the gifted psychologist, whose unique insights into the criminal mind lead the police unerringly to the most likely suspect. There is a wealth of anecdote which seems to support this view. One thinks of the fascinating case of the American psychiatrist James Brussel, who pinpointed the 'mad bomber of New York' after a decade of fruitless police work, or the insights of David Canter into the likely background of the 'railway rapist', which brought an end to the criminal career of John Duffy and introduced profiling to the British police in 1986. However … every individual triumph can be balanced with another investigative disaster, where police resources have been wasted pursuing a mythical fugitive who, it subsequently emerges, bears little or no resemblance to the true perpetrator. (page xi)

This last point is brought home by Holmes (1989) who cites FBI data from 1981 indicating that in 192 cases of profiling, arrests were made in 88 but the profile only contributed to 17 per cent of the arrests. These reservations aside, offender profiling is an area of criminology in which psychologists have contributed to the detection of offenders, mainly those who committed serious crimes such as serial rape or serial murder.

The goals of profiling

According to Holmes and Holmes (1996) there are three major goals of profiling:

- **Social and psychological assessments:** the profile should contain basic information about the offender's personality, age, race, type of employment (if any), religion, marital status and level of education. The personality aspects of the profile may help the police to predict possible future attacks.

- **Psychological evaluation of belongings:** once a main suspect has been identified, the profile should provide suggestions as to any possessions the offender may have that would associate him with the crime scene. These may include scene souvenirs, photos or items of pornography. Such physical evidence could be listed on a search warrant so the police take particular care to look for them.

- **Interviewing suggestions and strategies:** even when people have committed similar crimes, they do not respond to questioning in the same way because their motives are different. A good profile can provide the police with strategies that may be effective for a

particular offender. An example cited by Holmes and Holmes (1996) was the murder of a young girl and her boyfriend in which the stepfather was the main suspect but there was no forensic evidence against him. When questioned in a conventional way, he denied any involvement. The profiler suggested that he was a man with a need for control, so a good tactic would be to appear to solicit his help in solving the crime. Under this guise, the suspect was surrounded by photographs of the crime scene and, believing himself in control of the investigation, became so engrossed in talking about the case that he revealed more and more his familiarity with the crime, until he eventually broke down and confessed.

The obvious starting point of any investigation of a crime is the analysis of 'hard' evidence such as blood stains and fibre samples but *behavioural information* from the crime scene may offer additional information that aids the investigation. Such information may be gleaned from various sources. In the case of rape of a woman by a man, for example, it may include how the perpetrator talked to his victim, how he treated her and whether or not he showed remorse. This behavioural information then provides insights into the thinking patterns and personal habits of the offender, which may offer clues as to how they behave in their everyday life: their lifestyle, motivations, personal needs and past history. Offender profiles do not solve crimes, they simply provide a way of narrowing down the range of potential suspects by providing information about the possible personal characteristics of the perpetrator of the crime.

There is no single established method by which profiling is conducted; the approach used by the FBI is rather more systematic than that used in Britain. We will take a look at two different techniques, one practised in America and the other in Britain.

interactive angles

Have a look at some news reports of a crime such as a murder. Try looking through several newspapers for reports of the same incident or use a website such as www.guardian.co.uk, which has a search facility. Read through looking for indicators that could have been used in an attempt to build a profile of the perpetrator.

The American method – a 'top-down' approach

The initial approach adopted by the FBI was two-pronged. One was a series of in-depth interviews with 36 convicted sexually orientated murderers, including Ted Bundy and Charles Manson. The second was the collection of detailed information from members of their Behavioural Science Unit who were experienced in the area of sexual crime and homicide. They then combined this information with detailed examination of the crime scene, the nature of the attacks, forensic evidence and any information relating to the victim to develop models that would result in a profile of the offender. As a consequence, this approach is sometimes called 'crime scene analysis'.

Using this evidence, the FBI developed a classification system for several serious crimes, including murder and rape. Murderers were classified as 'organised' or 'disorganised' and the two types were believed to demonstrate quite different characteristics (see table 12.1). By use of this classification system, an analysis of the crime scene has obvious implications in suggesting possible characteristics of offenders.

organised murderers	disorganised murderers
self control is shown by the murderer at the crime scene	actions are unplanned and haphazard
tracks are covered, few clues are left	more clues are left
victim is likely to be a deliberately targeted stranger	likely to know the victim and be familiar with the scene of the crime
likely to be intelligent and in a skilled occupation	likely to be in an unskilled occupation
socially and sexually competent	socially inadequate, sexual problems
married or cohabiting	live alone, likely to be a first or last-born child
angry or depressed at the time of the murder	confused at the time of the murder
follow reports of the crime in the media	

Table 12.1 Characteristics of 'organised' and 'disorganised' murderers

Having established a classification system, the FBI then detailed what should happen when a very serious crime occurred. Jackson and Bekerian (1997) describe the

series of stages the FBI has developed in their crime analysis as follows.

- Stage 1: *data assimilation* – the collection of all available information from as many sources as possible, such as photographs of the crime scene and autopsy of the victim.

- Stage 2: *crime classification* – putting the crime into a particular category based on the data collected.

- Stage 3: *crime reconstruction* – the development of hypotheses about the behaviour of victims and the modus operandi of the criminal based on reconstruction of the crime.

- Stage 4: *profile generation* – the development of a profile, which includes suggestions about the perpetrator's physical appearance, their demographic characteristics (for example, age range, race, socio-economic status), habits and personality.

This type of profiling is best suited to crime scenes that reveal important details about the suspect, those such as rape, arson and cult killings that involve such macabre practices as sadistic torture, dissection of the body and acting out of fantasy. According to the FBI, crimes such as murder or assault in the course of a robbery and destruction of property do not lend themselves to profiling because the crime scene reveals little about the offender.

The FBI approach has been subject to criticism on several fronts. First, the samples of serious offenders interviewed in order to draw up the classification system were quite small. Secondly, the crime classifications for murderers and rapists were crude and not very helpful in terms of detection. Thirdly, details of the development and efficiency of the methods were not published.

The British method – a 'bottom-up' approach

Whereas the FBI had put the use of offender profiling on to a fairly systematic footing by the late 1970s, profiling in Britain was later in its inception and also has never been uniform. After a fairly reluctant start, profiling in Britain was given a kick start in the mid 1980s by the work of Canter when he produced an astonishingly accurate profile of John Duffy, an account of which is provided in the next section (Canter, 1994). Bearing in mind that the British approach is essentially idiosyncratic, we will consider the techniques used by Canter since this probably best typifies the British approach.

Canter's approach to profiling is more scientific than that of the FBI because it is based more on psychological theories and methodologies. It attempts to formulate psychological theories that will show how and why varia-

media watch

This is extracted from an article that appeared on the CNN website on 9 October 2002.

Hunting the hunter: profiling the sniper

As the hunt for the sniper who has terrorized residents in the Washington, D.C., area enters a second week, the role of the profiler in helping investigators put a face on the killer has received more attention.

Media headlines blare that the profilers are baffled by the failure of the killer to conform to known patterns. But this assertion comes from a misunderstanding of the role, function and method of the profiler, said Clint Van Zandt, a former FBI profiler.

'A profile is an investigative tool. It is not science, it is not DNA, it is not latent fingerprints. … It is just one more tool investigators have. But a profile does not tell you who did the crime,' Van Zandt said.

Profilers are engaged in building a 'constantly evolving' document that is available to investigators to focus their search, Van Zandt said.

Van Zandt disputed the popular notion that research into previous multiple killings has provided clearly defined 'profiles' of killers that can be used to fit each case that comes along.

'There is a skeletal structure of certain individuals, but the clothes that we hang on that skeleton come from investigation. And that's what starts to form the profile,' Van Zandt said.

And sometimes a killer may not fall within even very general categories.

'So far it appears we have a kind of a hybrid. We have what we call a spree killer, in essence someone who kills one person after another without an emotional cooling off period in between,' Van Zandt said.

'And yet, because of the period of time that has lapsed, now it is starting to take on some of the traits of a serial killer, someone who kills with that emotional cooling off period, which can be days, weeks, even months, depending on the serial killer himself or herself.'

What profilers may well be able to offer investigators, depending on the evidence authorities have discovered at each crime scene, is a series of statistical probabilities – the shooter's age, his race, his academic or professional background, perhaps even his motive, Van Zandt said.

This enables those in charge of the investigation to 'take the population group and shrink it until it becomes manageable' he says.

'Hypothetically, we know, it's a statistical probability that a sniper in a situation like this is likely to be a male as opposed to a female. Well, then, we have eliminated 50 percent of the population. Now does that rule out a woman from doing this? No, but we'll say it is a very small chance.

'But if a witness says, "I saw a car with smoke coming out of a window after a shot was fired and I saw a red-haired woman in the passenger seat," profile be damned, you have to go with the evidence that you have,' Van Zandt said.

So what are the types of questions profilers will be asking?

'You start out with very generic profiles, like, Is the offender organized or disorganized? An organized person has transportation, brings the weapon with him, has the ability to get in and out from a crime scene without being detected,' Van Zandt said.

'Or, a disorganized person may walk or take public transportation. He may use a weapon of opportunity. You may see overkill on the part of the victim. He may just escape because he's lucky, not because he's calculating.'

'So you start with an organized-disorganized offender. Then you say: A serial killer is this, a spree killer is that.'

Which approach, 'top-down' or 'bottom-up', has been used to generate the offender profile discussed above?

tions in criminal behaviour occur. Central to this theory building is the need to demonstrate consistencies within the actions of offenders and identifiable differences between them, that is, they are based on the 'criminal consistency hypothesis'.

Canter (1989) has outlined several aspects of criminal behaviour that may provide clues to other facets of the criminal's everyday life and that may reflect the sub-group to which he belongs. (In Canter's 1989 paper, he uses the masculine pronoun with a footnote explaining that this is because most criminals are male and that the material on which his paper is based has not included women criminals. This pronoun, therefore, is not generic – it applies only to men.) Some salient factors are discussed below.

Interpersonal coherence

The degree of violence and control used in serious crimes, especially rape, varies widely between perpetrators but any single individual will tend to be consistent in his treatment of the victim. For example, with respect to rape, some offenders will be very abusive and controlling, maximising their humiliation of the victim; others may be far less violent, even apologetic. This may reflect the way the criminal treats other women in his non-criminal life.

The type of victim may also reflect the sub-group to which the criminal belongs. Canter gives the example of Theodore Bundy who killed over 30 students when he himself was a student. On a psychologically deeper level, the choice of victims, if they are a homogeneous group, may reflect the group against which the offender has a particular grudge. Knowledge of the victims may therefore make it possible to ascertain something about the assailant, his sub-class or his associates.

Significance of time and place

When and where a crime takes place may also furnish clues about the offender. Both the precise location and the map of the relationship between the places in which a series of offences took place may relate to where the offender is living and to his previous experience.

Forensic awareness

If criminals have previously been questioned by the police their subsequent crimes may leave indications of this. Some rapists, for example, make their victims bathe in order to remove significant evidence. In such cases, a check of people who are on police records may well be worth while.

Comparing the two approaches

As you can see, the British approach to profiling is rather different from the American one (although it draws on practices originated by the FBI). Boon and Davies (1992) refer to the British style as 'bottom-up' and the American one as 'top-down'. In general terms a 'bottom-up' approach is one in which a person starts with all the raw data and works their way up to a conclusion that makes sense of this data. In terms of a criminal investigation, you collect all the different pieces of evidence and then piece them together to try and infer the state of mind of the perpetrator (if it was a murder, were there signs of loss of temper or was it cold and calculated?) and from that, their personality, whether or not they had committed such a crime before and so on. A top-down approach looks at the evidence, or data, in light of certain theories or general principles and uses these theories to make sense of the data. In terms of a murder, a theory might state that only people with a particular sexual deviance commit certain crimes, so when such a crime occurs, the investigators look for a person with this particular depravity.

The British approach starts from all the available evidence and then looks for links and associations between them (such as consistency in the treatment of victims or choice of location). It then tries to draw up a profile based on these relationships. The American approach looked originally at the experience of a group of convicted criminals (such as serial killers like Charles Manson) and the knowledge gained by experienced investigators in the field. This was used to devise a classification system into which subsequent crimes could be placed in order to ascertain the type of person who would have committed a crime in that particular fashion. In this way, they distinguished between organised and disorganised crimes, and the characteristics of an individual who is likely to operate in this way. These two styles of profiling, therefore, are quite distinct.

Recent evidence supports the idea that some types of offenders have particular, stable, characteristics in common. Hunter et al (2003) compared juvenile, male sex offenders whose victims had been either prepubescent or pubescent/post-pubescent females. They found clear differences between the groups; the former offenders were less aggressive towards their victims, were more likely to target relatives and had lower psychosocial functioning than the latter group. Predictable patterns have also been demonstrated with adult male sex offenders. Fernandez and Marshall (2003) found that, compared to incarcerated non-sexual offenders, rapists, surprisingly, showed more empathy towards women in general and were equally empathetic to female victims of crimes perpetrated by other males. This led Fernandez and Marshall to conclude that 'rapists may suppress empathy primarily toward their own victim rather than suffer from a generalized empathy deficit' (page 11). These findings may provide groundwork for predicting the social functioning of male sexual offenders.

119

interactive angles

Using a selection of the following websites, try to find articles that describe offender profiling conducted in each of the two ways described on page 117. You will find it easier if you use the search facilities on the sites and look through their archive material. Try the following:

www.guardian.co.uk , www.independent.co.uk , www.bbc.co.uk , www.nytimes.com , www.washingtonpost.com , www.cnn.com

Write a commentary indicating how you have decided which approach is being used. Indicate how the approaches are similar and how they are different.

The bottom-up approach applied: a case study of profiling (Canter, 1994)

The following case study is based on the account by Canter (1994) of the profiling of the so-called 'railway rapist'. Canter first became involved in this case when he bought a newspaper on 9 January 1986, whose front page contained details of a series of 24 sexual assaults in London over the previous four years. All the assaults were assumed to be by the same man, sometimes working alone, sometimes with another person. Canter drew up a table and attempted to see if there was any obvious pattern to the rapes.

Canter made two assumptions based on psychological principles: first, that people influence each other's actions and that any differences between the attacks involving one man and those in which they were both involved might offer clues; secondly, that people's behaviour changes over time and that looking at the changes that took place over the four-year period could provide clues to the offenders.

In December 1985 and spring 1986 two murders took place. Information linking the two murders was discovered by accident when a police officer investigating one saw a *Crimewatch* programme about the second one and realised that they had certain features in common. On analysing the details of these murders, it became appar-

ent that they had been perpetrated by the man responsible for the rapes and a major manhunt was begun in the hope of apprehending him before he murdered again.

Although the police had gathered a wealth of evidence, with every detail of every rape carefully documented, there was so little co-ordination that despite enormous dedication and hard work on the part of the police, the overall impression was described by Canter as one of 'great confusion'. This was hardly surprising given the lack of theoretical underpinning but the detectives were intent on a change of plan. 'At the senior levels of the police force, at least, there was an attempt to move beyond a craft, based solely on experience and knowledge of the law, to something more professional, using scientific procedures, methods and theories as central to their investigations rather than as an optional extra' (page 34).

They began looking in greater detail at the assailant's behaviour during each rape.

- What exactly was said to the victim before the assault?
- Were the victims' clothes pulled off, torn off or cut off?
- What sort of threats were made?
- What sort of sexual activity took place?
- How did the assailant deal with the victim after the assault?

All these details were fed into a computer (an innovation, since all previous documentation had been done by hand) in order to indicate the degree of similarity and difference between the crimes. Two lines of investigation were then taken; looking at each individual attack and looking at the changes that had occurred over time.

With respect to the behaviour shown at the scene of each rape, Canter used two principles from social psychology in his investigation. First, the concept that the type of 'relationship' (if any) that the assailant tried to form with the victim might reflect his relationships with others. In this case a relationship had been made; the rapist talked to his victims, asking them questions about their personal life and even showed some consideration to them. Secondly, the degree of domination he exercised over the victims would also provide clues. He had only used enough control to rape and was therefore probably not a very powerful or secure individual.

The investigation into the way in which the assaults had changed over time indicated that the assailant had learned directly from his own experience of the crimes, and that this had made him more subtle and sophisticated. There was an indication that he was familiar with police procedures; on one occasion he combed the pubic hair of his victim in order to remove his own hairs. This implied that he had at least been questioned by the police, if not charged.

On 28 July 1986, Canter produced the following preliminary profile (Canter, 1994, pages 50–2).

- Residence: has lived in the area circumscribed by the first three cases since 1983.

- Marital status: probably lives with wife/girlfriend, quite possibly without children.

- Age etc: mid to late twenties; light hair, about 5 ft 9 in.

- Occupation: probably semi-skilled job, involving weekend work or casual labour from June 1984 onwards. Job does not bring him into a lot of contact with public, in all probability.

- Character: keeps to himself but has one or two very close men friends. Probably very little contact with women, especially in work situation. Has knowledge of the railway system along which attacks happened.

- Sexual activity: the variety and mixture of his sexual actions suggest considerable sexual experience.

- Criminal record: was probably under arrest at some time between 24 October 1982 and January 1984. His arrest may not have been a sex-related crime at all but an aggressive attack, possibly under the influence of alcohol (or drugs?).

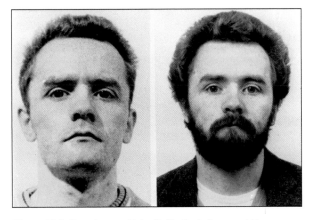

Figure 12.2 Two photos of John Duffy, the 'railway rapist'

What factors led to this particular profile? It was the result of an enormous amount of information; let us consider just one aspect – that he was in a sexual relationship, married or cohabiting. More of the men who are convicted of rape are unmarried than are married, so

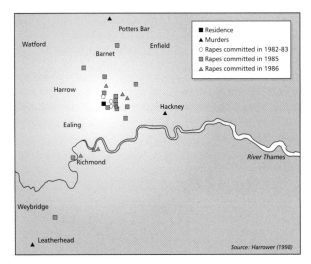

Figure 12.3 The 'map' of Duffy's offences, which enabled David Canter to compile an offender profile

why was a different conclusion drawn in this case? The rapist was sexually experienced as shown by the variety of sexual practices used in the rapes. He approached the women beforehand, often asking for directions or using a similar subterfuge. He was at ease with approaching strange women without fear of rebuff, interested enough to ask them questions about their own relationships and felt comfortable about being in control of them. All of this could be used to hypothesise that he was, or had been, in a sexual relationship. This relationship was likely to have been abusive; by the time the rapes were happening, this relationship may have broken up completely (this was later found to be the case). This single example serves to illustrate how every aspect of the profile is the result of painstaking analysis of the minute details of the crimes, not the result of 'flashes of inspiration' that provide the sudden 'turnabout' in the investigation so beloved of fiction.

In November 1986 John Duffy was arrested and later convicted; he was sentenced to life imprisonment. Duffy was initially on a list of 2000 suspects but not a prominent one, being placed 1505th. His arrest was the result of the fact that he so closely fitted the profile that the police had mounted a large-scale surveillance operation to watch him; his activities convinced police that he was the rapist and murderer responsible for this series of crimes.

How close was the profile? Duffy lived in Kilburn (which fitted the area mentioned in the profile); he was 29 years old; he was separated from his wife with whom, in the later stages of the relationship, he had had an abusive relationship; he was a travelling carpenter for British Rail; he had a prior criminal record (for stealing; he had also been accused of raping his wife at knife point). The analysis had been extraordinarily accurate.

It is worth noting two further points from this case study. First, Canter was able to use not only the successes in this profile but also the inaccuracies in order to improve profiling methods. Secondly, some very important clues were gained about the accuracy of eye-witness testimony (discussed earlier in this chapter), one of which is that rape victims are not always accurate in their physical description of the assailant but they are very good indeed at accurately recalling the actions that took place.

media watch

Murder on his mind

Britain's prisons abound with killers who thought they could outwit Paul Britton. From seemingly inconsequential details of a murder scene, Britton can construct a character sketch that gives an insight into the mind of the killer. He pioneered offender profiling in this country and has been called in to more than 100 cases.

Television's Cracker was inspired by his work (though Robbie Coltrane's rambling, fumbling, gambling addict is a world away from Britton). His subjects have included Fred and Rosemary West, James Bulger's killers and Colin Ireland, who murdered five gay men in London in 1993.

Behind the public profile, however, there has been a long career as a clinical forensic psychologist, working with patients who pose a danger to society. His book about offender profiling, The Jigsaw Man, was a bestseller. Now retired from the NHS, he has written a new book, Picking Up the Pieces, based on his clinical casebook. It is a chilling read.

"If you are looking at a murder you have to understand fully the destruction of another human being. The idea of anyone getting a buzz out of it leaves me very uneasy.

"You have to get to know the victim in order to find out what you need to know about the killer. It's more personal than 'she was a woman, 5ft 6in, fair hair'. You have to get to know how she responded to her killer.

"And when you get to know someone that well, the pain they endured touches you. In each case you leave a bit of yourself behind. It erodes you."

The Sunday Times, 12 November 2000

1 What kind of 'inconsequential details' from a crime scene might help to give clues to the character of the offender?

2 Why do you have to understand the victim in order to understand the perpetrator?

Evaluating offender profiling

Earlier, we briefly considered some criticisms of specific profiling methods; now we will look in more detail at evaluating profiling.

Limitations

The main limitation of profiling is that it may only be appropriate for specific types of crimes, mainly those stemming from psychopathology, such as serial murders upon which the US approach is based. Holmes and Holmes (1996) list other types of crimes appropriate to psychological profiling:

- sadistic torture in sexual assaults;
- evisceration (tearing out of the gut/bowels);
- postmortem slashing and cutting;
- motiveless fire setting;
- lust and mutilation murder;

- rape;
- satanic and ritualistic crime;
- paedophilia.

Limited though this list may be, such crimes, although comparatively rare, are so horrific that the need to apprehend the offender is of paramount importance. This leads, however, to another problem, namely that when attempting to assess whether profiling works, there are so few real-life cases that it can be difficult to effectively analyse its contribution.

Does profiling work?

Some researchers believe that profiling is ineffective, unnecessary and unhelpful. Campbell (1976) maintains that profiles offer no more information than could be obtained from the local bartender; that they are so vague and ambiguous as to be no more than common sense and the only reason the police take any notice of them is that they are impressed by the qualifications of academics. His comment that 'psychologists confronted with real-life murder mystery can't do any better than a college student could do with the same materials put in front of him' (page 119) is now over 25 years old but is still being quoted, for example, by Oleson (1996). Despite this, there has been a steady increase in the demand for offender profiling advice (Copson, 1996). Let us take a look at some of the attempts to assess its usefulness, first by looking at satisfaction surveys and then at one piece of direct research on its effectiveness.

Satisfaction surveys

Douglas (1981) (whose study is often attributed to Pinizzotto (1984) who reported on it) conducted an internal review for the FBI on the costs and benefits of profiling. His findings reflect those of many other such studies – that profiling does not often lead to the direct identification of the suspect but that the peripheral benefits are considerable and far outweigh the costs. In the 192 cases considered in this review, profiling identified the suspect in only 15 cases but in 77 per cent it helped to focus the investigation. In general, the procedures used in profiling improved thoroughness, investigators estimated that it saved many days' work and all users agreed that the service should continue.

Britton (1992) conducted a review evaluating British initiatives in offender profiling. Questionnaires were sent to CID chiefs and focused on establishing how far profiling advice had led to the arrest of suspects. Judged on these criteria, the responses were negative; there was little evidence that profiles were either accurate or had contributed to any arrests. Nevertheless, most respondents expressed the view that their experience of profiling led them to believe that it had potential, which, as long as it was done

with caution, was worth developing.

Jackson et al (1993) conducted a survey to assess the satisfaction of officers of the criminal justice system in The Netherlands for whom profiles had been compiled. Since there were only 20 respondents, interviews rather than questionnaires were used. Overall, there was a high level of satisfaction but, as in previous studies, the profilers appeared to be better at offering advice on how the investigation should be conducted than on generating profiles. The researchers commented that this is an important type of success but is extremely difficult to measure.

In Britain, Copson (1996) produced a report for the Home Office on the effectiveness of profiling.

Direct research into the effectiveness of profilers

Pinizzotto and Finkel (1990) compared five groups on their ability to write profiles of a homicide and a sex offence; both cases that had been closed. The groups were expert profilers, detectives with profiling experience, detectives without profiling experience, clinical psychologists and undergraduates. Profilers were significantly more accurate than non-profilers on the sex offence but not as accurate as detectives without profiling experience on the homicide case. This suggests that 'old fashioned experience may be far more important in profiling a case than training in psychological profiling' (Oleson, 1996, page 13).

In conclusion, there is no magic to profiling. Building up a picture of an offender requires painstaking systematic evidence gathering in order to work out how he thinks and behaves. The television character Cracker may be able to depend on seemingly brilliant insightful hunches but the real world does not operate in such a manner. There are enormous problems with trying to assess the usefulness of offender profiling, especially when the profiling methods of investigators are so idiosyncratic. What is essential is a detailed analysis of the factors that are and are not useful in profiling in order to provide a uniform, effective theoretical structure to advise on how it should be conducted. As Canter (1989) comments:

> 'It is ... essential that psychologists involved in this work seize the initiative by developing and testing explanatory frameworks for the advice they give. If they do not they will soon rejoin the ranks of the astrologers and numerologists, whose contributions are found to be of value on some occasions, but whose lack of scientific discipline precludes the evolution of cumulative principles that will improve the effectiveness of their contribution.' (page 16)

research
now

is offender profiling really necessary?

Copson G. (1995) Coals to Newcastle? Part 1: a study of offender profiling. Police Research Group. Special Interest Series: Paper No 7. London: Home Office Police Department.

aim: there is no systematic approach to offender profiling in Britain, rather there are many individual approaches which have resulted in arguments about the nature of the process and how far it is or can be developed as a science. Although many profiles have been used by British police, no independent scientific assessment has been conducted to evaluate its usefulness.

This paper is part of a wider programme of research into offender profiling by the Home Office Police Research Group (PRG). The objectives of this PRG research programme are twofold:

● to establish whether offender profiling can significantly improve the proficiency of the experienced detective

● to devise appropriate ways of delivering any benefits of offender profiling to the police service.

procedure: a survey using a questionnaire. A questionnaire was considered the most appropriate method for two main reasons. There were too many respondents to use interviews and it was considered that the impersonal questionnaire would minimise the risk of bias being introduced that might influence police officers' responses. Great care was taken not to invite opinions (since these are contaminated by prejudice, misconception, pride and other such factors). What was sought was the professional judgements on the service provided by the profilers.

Questionnaires were sent to police officers who had used profilers.

findings: the response rate was 81 per cent. There were 184 returned questionnaires, just over 60 per cent of which concerned murder investigations; the majority of these murder investigations (at least 60 per cent) did not involve any secondary sexual motive. The study's main interest, as indicated by the title 'Coals to Newcastle', was whether or not profilers provided any information that was not already available. This proved a difficult question to answer since there are so many complex variables, but over 50 per cent of respondents felt that the profilers had provided something extra and over 80 per cent reported that the advice given by the profiler had been useful – on the face of it a very positive statistic. However, only 14 per cent of respondents reported that it had assisted in solving the case. In less than 3 per cent of cases had it led to the identification of the offender. How, then, had it been useful? The main way was that it furthered the understanding of the case and/or of the offender or it provided expert reassurance from the profiler that the judgements of the investigating team were sound. The benefits of offender profiling were seen mainly not so much in identifying the offender but in having an intelligent second opinion that may provide new ways of approaching the case, thereby enabling the officers involved to look at it from a new angle. It seems that profiling does assist in solving crimes but its effect is indirect rather than direct.

conclusion: one important finding from this particular survey was that profilers are all very different in their approach and that satisfaction or otherwise depended very much on the individual profiler. At present in Britain at least there is little consistency of approach, therefore overall assessment of usefulness is extremely difficult if not impossible.

where to now?

▶ **Canter D. (1994) *Criminal Shadows*. London: Harper.** This is the personal account of the profiling of the 'Railway Rapist' and the scientific principles underlying profiling. It's a very intriguing read.

▶ **Holmes R.M. & Holmes S.T. (1996) *Profiling violent crimes: an investigative tool* (2nd edn). California: Sage Publications.** This is a very accessible, interesting, up-to-date book on all aspects of profiling, including that of fictional characters. The authors use many fascinating case studies to illustrate virtually every point made. An excellent, effortless read.

what do you know?

1 Outline three goals of offender profiling.

2 Describe what is meant by the expressions 'bottom up' and 'top down' when applied to offender profiling. Compare and contrast these two approaches.

3 Discuss research that investigates the usefulness and limitations of offender profiling.

Jury decision making

The jury system is based on the principle that a group of representative people should reach an objective decision about whether or not the law has been broken. As early as the eleventh century in Britain, the neighbours of a person accused of wrongdoing were asked to consider the evidence and come to a verdict. This method of justice has traditionally been held in such high regard that it is used in many democratic countries. The jury lies at the core of

our judicial system, so factors affecting the decisions they make and the processes by which these decisions are reached are of paramount importance in operating a fair system of justice. These include the electing of a foreperson, the effects of minority influence and social pressure or conformity, and the characteristics of the defendant, such as their attractiveness or ethnic group.

Conducting research on trial procedures and court decisions

The study of real jury deliberation is prohibited in the UK and USA, so it is necessary to use less direct methods to study them and this inevitably involves questions of ecological validity. Two main alternatives to studying actual juries have been employed: mock (or simulated) juries and shadow juries.

Mock juries

Mock juries are made up of a group of participants who are asked to consider a case and make judgements about it. The case is often presented as a written, summarised scenario rather than in any other form (such as a film or video clip). An example of the type of trial material presented in such a study is given on pages 126–7. The type of judgements made include degree of responsibility (sometimes of the victims as well as the defendant), guilt or innocence of the accused and the type of sentence that might be deemed appropriate. The problems and limitations with such an approach include the following:

● Often the participants are students and are therefore not representative of the general population;

● The scenarios that give an account of the case are usually brief and even if they represent the presentation of a real-life case, they do not involve any of the complexities of such a trial. Reading a brief summarised report of a criminal case is worlds apart from spending a considerable amount of time listening to evidence from both sides, seeing and hearing the witnesses and defendant, and assessing the summing up of the court prosecutor, the defence lawyer and the judge;

● Any judgements made have no consequences for a real person, whereas in a real-life situation, these can obviously be very serious indeed. This is perhaps the most crucial difference of all between real and artificial jury situations.

On the positive side, the use of mock juries does allow psychologists to investigate effects that are of great significance in ensuring a fair trial but cannot be researched in real court cases. The systematic manipulation of variables, while others are kept constant, means that it is possible to study the effect of such factors as the defendant's appearance, age or ethnic group, the amount of damage done and how the order of presentation of evidence affects the final decision reached by jurors.

Shadow juries

The shadow jury method involves selecting a group of people (usually 12) who are eligible for jury service and asking them to sit in the public gallery to hear all the evidence, then retire to somewhere quiet to consider their verdict, while all deliberations are recorded. This method avoids some of the most significant problems of mock juries although not the question of consequences. Unlike the mock jury method, it does not allow the researcher to explore the effect of systematic manipulation of variables but does have considerably greater ecological validity. This method is far less frequently used than simulations, probably because of practical problems such as obtaining volunteers prepared to participate in a study lasting several days.

Abbreviated Version of Stimulus Trial, *Commonwealth of Massachusetts v. Johnson*

Indictment

The defendant Frank Johnson is charged with killing Alan Caldwell with deliberate premeditation and malice aforethought.

The Defendant's Plea

The defendant, Frank Johnson, pleads NOT GUILTY.

Officer Richard Harris

On May 21st at about 11:00 P.M. I was on my usual foot patrol when I heard shouts from the direction of Gleason's Bar and Grill and hurried in that direction. From across the street I saw Caldwell (the victim) hit the defendant Johnson in the face. Johnson staggered back against the wall, then came forward and raised a knife above his head with his right hand. I yelled, "Frank, don't do it." But he plunged the knife downward into Caldwell's chest. Caldwell had fallen to the ground by the time I reached the scene. I apprehended Johnson, phoned for a police cruiser and an ambulance.

Cross-examination. I had a clear view of the fight from across the street approximately 75 feet away. I did not see anything in Caldwell's hand although I could not see Caldwell's right hand which was down by the side away from me. Johnson did not resist arrest, but he did say, "Caldwell pulled a razor on me so I stuck him." (This last statement was declared inadmissible by the trial judge.) The knife Harris retrieved from the ground near Caldwell is introduced as evidence. It measures eleven inches from end to end.

State Pathologist, Dr. Robert Katz

I found the following items on the body of Alan Caldwell: a ring, a watch, and small change in the right front pocket, and a straight razor in the left rear pocket. Caldwell was killed by a stab wound to the heart between the third and fourth ribs. I was unable to determine the angle at which the knife entered Caldwell's chest. His blood alcohol level was .032. This is enough alcohol that Caldwell may have been drunk. Caldwell had numerous surgical scars on his body. There were other scars of undetermined origin. The straight razor is introduced as evidence.

Patrick Gleason

I am the owner of Gleason's Bar and Grill. That night I had occasion to run to the window because there were some shouts outside. Actually, I expected it because I had watched Caldwell and Johnson leave the bar together a few minutes before. Through the window I saw Johnson raise his hand up and stab Caldwell. I didn't see anything in Caldwell's hand. Caldwell and Johnson didn't come to the bar together. First, Johnson and his friend Dennis Clemens arrived at about 9:00 P.M. and later Caldwell arrived. Then later, Caldwell and Johnson were talking at the bar and then they walked outside together. On the way out Caldwell put his watch in his pocket. Earlier in the day Johnson and Caldwell had both been in the bar. At that time they were arguing. Caldwell pulled out a razor and threatened to kill Johnson. A couple of patrons said something to Johnson and he left. That was earlier in the afternoon – before this fight in the evening.

Cross-examination. There was a neon light in the window which partially obstructed my view and I could only see Johnson and Caldwell at an angle. Frank Johnson has a reputation for peacefulness and has never caused trouble in the bar. (The judge does not allow Gleason to testify about Alan Caldwell's reputation.)

Dennis Clemens

I stopped at Frank Johnson's home on the evening of May 21st and asked Johnson to join me for a drink at Gleason's, which is where we usually go. Before we went in the bar, we looked around. We didn't see anything. At about 9:30 P.M. Caldwell entered, and after a while motioned Johnson to come and talk. In a few minutes, Johnson and Caldwell left the bar. I could not hear what they said, but went near the front door which was open. I heard a few shouts, saw Caldwell punch Johnson to the

---

ground, and begin to attack him with a razor. Johnson tried to hold Caldwell off but Caldwell attacked, there was a scuffle, Caldwell staggered back, and after about twenty seconds fell to the ground. I didn't go outside to stop the fight because it happened so quickly.

Cross-examination. Johnson and I did not go to Gleason's looking for Caldwell, and Johnson was reluctant to go into Gleason's until we had assured ourselves that Caldwell was not there. I saw the razor clearly in Caldwell's right hand. I didn't see the knife in Johnson's hand because of the angle of the two men.

Janet Stewart

I am a waitress at Gleason's Grill, and on the night of the fight I noticed both Caldwell and Johnson in the grill before the fight. There was shouting outside. When I ran outside I saw Caldwell on the ground. I also noticed Caldwell's car, which I recognized, was parked illegally in front of the grill and would have obstructed a view of the fight from across the street.

Frank Johnson

I was in Gleason's Grill on the afternoon of May 21st. A woman asked me to give her a ride somewhere the next day. Alan Caldwell immediately came over screaming at me and threatening me; he pulled a razor and threatened to kill me. I was quite upset and frightened and I went home and spent the day with my wife and six children until 9:00 P.M. when Dennis Clemens came by and suggested we go out for a drink. When we got to Gleason's Grill, I was afraid to go in but was finally convinced when we could find no evidence that Caldwell was in the grill. Later Caldwell entered and sat at the bar. Twenty minutes later Caldwell motioned me over in a friendly way and suggested we go outside. Caldwell was calm and friendly and I thought he wanted to talk. Once outside though, Caldwell became angry, threatened to kill me, and then hit me in the face with his right fist. The blow knocked me back against the wall and stunned me but I noticed that Caldwell had pulled his razor again. I unthinkingly reached for my fishing knife, pulled it out and held it in front of me to keep Caldwell away. But Caldwell rushed in with his razor and lunged on the fishing knife. The next thing I remember is Officer Harris arriving at the scene. I almost always carry my fishing knife because I am an avid fisherman and my wife does not like the knife to be lying around where the smaller children may pick it up. I couldn't get away from the fight because I was knocked down and cornered against the wall. I reached for the knife instinctively and tried to protect myself. I didn't mean to kill Caldwell.

Cross-examination. I don't think I had my knife with me in the afternoon but I don't really know because I carry it with me a lot.

Judge's Instructions

Now I want to define the elements of the charges against the defendant. These definitions are essential to determining which verdict you should return. The Commonwealth has charged the defendant with murder in the first degree. You actually have four verdict alternatives: murder in the first degree, murder in the second degree, manslaughter, and not guilty by reason of self defense. Murder in the first degree is a killing committed with deliberately premeditated malice aforethought. Both first and second degree murder require malice aforethought. This includes feelings of hatred or ill will, but is more than that. It means any intentional infliction of an injury where there is a likelihood of causing death. Malice may be inferred from the intentional use of a deadly weapon without just provocation or legal excuse. If you find a killing with malice, then you must return a verdict of at least murder in the second degree. To return a verdict of first degree murder, you must find that the killing was performed with deliberately premeditated malice aforethought. Deliberate premeditation is a sequence of thought processes. You must be convinced that a plan to murder was formed. It is the sequence of thought, not the time taken that determines premeditation; it may take place over weeks, days, hours, or only seconds. First the deliberation and premeditation, then the resolution to kill, then the killing in pursuance of the resolution.

The third verdict alternative is manslaughter. Manslaughter is a killing without malice, a killing resulting from a sudden passion or heat of blood produced by a reasonable provocation or sudden combat. Reasonable provocation requires more than just words or insults or a general dislike or general feeling of anger. Your final verdict alternative is self defense. If you find that the killing was in self defense then the defendant is not guilty of a crime and should be found "not guilty". The right to self defense arises from a threat to one's life but does not come into existence at all until the defendant has exhausted all reasonable means to escape from the confrontation and once the threat is over, the right evaporates. The method one uses to defend oneself can only be reasonable, but this judgment is made with some consideration for the frailties of human impulses in a stress situation. If the defendant does not have a reasonable fear of great bodily harm or has not exhausted all reasonable means of escape or has used more than reasonable force to protect himself, then self defense does not apply and the defendant is guilty of at least manslaughter. Since the defendant has raised the issue of self defense, the burden is on the Commonwealth to prove it was not a situation of self defense. Finally, remember it is your duty to find the defendant guilty of the more serious charge of which he is in fact guilty beyond a reasonable doubt. If the Commonwealth has failed to prove the elements of the charged offenses, it is your duty to find the defendant not guilty.

Influences on jury decision making

Characteristics of jurors

Jurors will inevitably bring to the courtroom their own preconceptions and theories. People are not raised in a vacuum and the fact that their own personal experiences and other characteristics will impinge on decision making should not necessarily be a cause for concern. However, if jurors have very closed-minded attitudes, in particular if they show open racial prejudice, then this obviously compromises any chance of defendants having a fair trial. Lloyd-Bostock (1988) quotes a case from 1950s America in which a black youth was charged with aiding and abetting the interstate transportation of a stolen car. When jurors were interviewed after the trial, it turned out that several had been racially biased. Two in particular had made comments to the effect that the defendant should be found guilty because 'niggers are just no good' and 'niggers ought to be taught to behave'. To add insult to injury, they were not deterred from making such remarks by the presence of a black female juror. Although this occurred in the 1950s, there is evidence that we cannot afford to be complacent about this type of racism occurring at the present time, especially in cases where a black man is accused of sex crimes against a white woman (Lloyd-Bostock, 1988).

Size of the jury

People often assume that a jury comprises 12 individuals and although this is true in Britain, it is no longer the case in the US. Indeed one lawyer, Melvin Tatsumi, attempted to have a jury of just one person because he believed this to be preferable to relying on 'mob mentality'. This request was accepted at first but overturned on appeal. In the now famous constitutional case of *Williams v Florida* (1970), Williams challenged his conviction on the grounds that there were only six people on the jury. The Supreme Court refused to overturn the verdict, on the basis that a six-person jury could operate as effectively as a 12-person one, and such juries are now permitted in American courts except when the death penalty is a possible sentence. However, most of the evidence presented in favour of smaller juries was scant in the extreme and based on opinions and anecdotes (Zeisel, 1971). The small amount of social psychological research used was completely misinterpreted (Saks, 1974).

Despite the ruling by the Supreme Court, psychological studies show that there are significant differences between the way small and large juries operate, and that larger juries tend to be fairer. There are several reasons for this. For a start, larger juries obviously having a greater chance of being representative of the general population. Saks (1977) summarises the other advantages as follows.

1 Larger juries spend more time in deliberation.

2 They spend a greater proportion of their time in discussion (as opposed to vote taking and other activities).

3 Larger juries show more accurate recall of the testimony.

4 The pressure to conform despite being unconvinced is not as extreme in large groups as in small ones. When there is only one person who disagrees with the rest, that person is more likely to feel very uncomfortable about not going along with the majority view. But if they are a member of a larger jury they stand more of a chance of finding an ally than if they were serving on a small jury.

5 Larger juries tend to produce more consistent verdicts.

On the whole then, smaller juries may save money but it very doubtful whether they are as effective as larger ones.

Characteristics of the defendant

Physical attractiveness

Heroes are handsome and villains are ugly, or so we learn from films and books. It would appear that this stereotype is not confined to the media but operates in real life, for research indicates that people do believe that villains have a certain type of facial appearance, one that may be described as 'tough' or 'hard'. One of the most distinguishing features of such a stereotype is that criminals are unattractive. Conversely, attractive people are rarely considered capable of behaving criminally. Dion, Berschied and Hatfield (1972) coined the expression 'What is beautiful is good' to describe findings that demonstrate that attractive people have a considerable advantage in life. The stereotype they enjoy is to be judged as more intelligent, confident, happy, assertive, serious and truthful than people with average looks.

So do we assume that ugly people are more likely to commit crimes than beautiful ones? In mock jury situations, or in real life, does someone's facial appearance affect the sentence they are given or even whether or not they are judged guilty? Iniquitous though it may be, the answer to both of these questions appears to be 'yes'.

Saladin et al (1988) showed participants eight photos of men and asked them to judge how capable they considered them to be of committing each of two crimes: murder and armed robbery. Overall, the attractive men were considered less likely to have committed either crime than the unattractive ones. This and other studies indicate that, compared to unattractive individuals, attractive people are not only seen as less likely to commit a crime, they are also viewed more sympathetically by jurors and judges and are treated more leniently when deemed guilty. This *attractiveness effect* is strongest with serious but non-fatal crimes such as burglary, and when females are being judged (Quigley et al, 1995). An exception to this rule occurs if people are considered to be using their attractiveness for illegal material gain, such as in performing confidence tricks or in fraud.

In a meta-analysis of 80 studies using mock juries, Mazzella and Feingold (1994) found it was an advantage for the defendant to be physically attractive. This reliable experimental effect does not appear to be restricted to the psychology laboratory but also occurs in real courtroom. Downs and Lyons (1991) analysed the fines and bail payments of 1500 defendants accused of minor crimes and asked police officers, who were not told the purpose of their assessments, to rate them on attractiveness. The results showed that, even when the seriousness of the crime was controlled for, attractiveness was negatively correlated with the amount of bail or the fine imposed by the judge. Attractiveness, however, appeared to be irrelevant when imposing fines or setting bail payments for more serious crimes (McKelvie & Coley, 1993).

Stewart (1980) sent observers into courtrooms to rate defendants on various traits, including physical attractiveness. The results were similar to those found in simulated jury studies: when seriousness of the crime and ethnic group were controlled for, there was a significant negative correlation between attractiveness and length of sentence. In other words, attractive people received shorter sentences than unattractive people accused of a similar crime. In this study only one rating of attractiveness was made. Stewart later extended his research by asking the observers sitting in the courtroom to rate defendants not only on physical attractiveness but also on cleanliness, neatness and quality of dress. Using a seven-point scale, defendants were rated as attractive–unattractive, dirty–clean, sloppy–neat and well dressed–poorly dressed. Over a two-year period, 60 defendants were observed and it was found that those who were perceived as attractive, clean, neat and well dressed were treated with greater leniency than were those rated lower on these four dimensions. However, although attractiveness affected sentencing, it did not affect whether or not the defendant was convicted or acquitted.

Recent evidence suggests that the effect may be more complex as indicated in the study described below.

research now

gender and ethnic group – sources of bias for jurors

Abwender D.A. & Hough K. (2001) Interactive effects of characteristics of defendant and mock juror on US participants' judgement and sentencing recommendations. *Journal of Social Psychology* 141: 603–15

aim: to investigate two possible interactions, between defendant attractiveness and juror gender and between defendant and juror ethnicity.

procedure: 207 black, hispanic and white participants formed mock juries and were presented with a scenario of a fatal road accident in which the defendant's ethnic group or physical attractiveness was varied.

findings: an interaction was demonstrated between gender and attractiveness. While female jurors treated an unattractive defendant more harshly than an attractive one, male jurors showed the opposite pattern. An interaction was also demonstrated between juror and defendant ethnic group. The black participants showed an in-group bias, being more lenient when the defendant was presented as a black rather than white person, whereas hispanic participants showed the opposite leniency. White participants did not exhibit an ethnicity-based leniency.

conclusion: gender, attractiveness and ethnicity all appear to affect jury decision making but they do so in complex ways. Jurors of different genders and ethnic groups do not necessarily show consistent patterns of same-gender or same-ethnic group biases, and males and females respond differently to the characteristic of attractiveness in a defendant.

Ethnicity

Duncan (1976) investigated the role of ethnicity in judgements of blame. He varied the ethnic group of the perpetrator and victim in a videotape of a potentially violent situation. Participants observed the scene (believing it to be occurring in another room) and judged a particular act (an ambiguous shove). This was judged as more violent when performed by a black than a white individual. Do such differences arise in the real world? Stewart (1980) looked at the sentencing received in 67 criminal court cases in which the defendant did not received a 'flat sentence'. A systematic pattern emerged relating ethnicity and punishment; white defendants received consistently more lenient sentences than non-white defendants. Many studies have been conducted since then to investigate factors affecting the influence of ethnicity in court settings.

Pfeifer and Ogloff (1991) found that, in a mock jury situation without specific instructions to the jurors, white participants were significantly more likely to judge a black than a white defendant to be guilty. Skolnick and Shaw (1997) investigated the *black racism* hypothesis using a mock jury situation. Participants read a transcript of a fictitious murder trial in which the defendant's ethnic group was varied (black or white). Black jurors, unlike white jurors, displayed biased judgements; they were more likely to vote not guilty and were more lenient in their sentencing when the defendant was a black person. In their meta-analysis, Mazzella and Feingold (1994) found no overall effect of ethnicity on mock jury decisions, although punishment was affected by ethnic group. However, Johnson et al (2002) manipulated ethnic group (black or white) of the defendant by altering a massage read by participants about a criminal case. The participants, who were all white, made more situational attributions about the white defendant and suggested more lenient punishments. In a study using both black and white participants, Wuensch et al (2002) used a mock jury to investigate the effect of ethnic group on the judgements in a sexual harassment case. They experimentally manipulated the ethnicity of the litigant (black or white) and found that mock jurors favoured their own ethnic group. Some recent studies have, however, demonstrated more complex effects (see Abwender & Hough, 2001, page 129).

This is extracted from an article by Clare Dyer on the *Guardian* website, 25 June 2002.

Jurors behaving badly

The right of a jury to keep its deliberations secret is sacrosanct. But what happens when it threatens to cause a miscarriage of justice?

Imagine you are an Asian man on trial for arson, facing the prospect of years in jail if you're found guilty. Your fate is in the hands of 12 men and women chosen at random from the electoral roll. But what if some of those jurors are racist? Suppose they make disparaging remarks in the jury room about your appearance, your accent, your poor English and your business integrity. Comments such as 'They're all the same. I've worked with them in Birmingham. I know what they're like.' Or 'The only reason he's got a clean record is because he's never been caught,' and 'He would have been better off staying in India.'

That's what happened during Sajid Qureshi's trial at Mold crown court in October 2000, according to one of the jurors who convicted him by an 11–1 majority and saw him sent down for four years. In a letter to the court six days after his conviction, she claimed that some of her fellow jurors seemed to have already decided their verdict from the start, that one juror fell asleep during the evidence, that another was deaf and that some tried to bully others. Enough, you might think, to raise serious doubts about whether Qureshi had a fair trial.

But not enough for the court of appeal [which] refused him permission even to launch an appeal. The stumbling block was the Contempt of Court Act 1981, which bans anyone – and that includes judges –

from inquiring into the secrets of the jury room. If trial by jury was to be preserved, allegations could be investigated only while the trial was still going on.

British society is riddled with racism, Sir David Calvert-Smith, director of public prosecutions, contends. The police, the crown prosecution service and the prison service have all admitted institutional racism.

Yet, while inquiry after inquiry investigates possible racism elsewhere in the system and makes strenuous efforts to weed it out, no one can inquire into the prejudices of juries.

John Spencer, professor of law at Cambridge University, argues, 'If juries are composed of 12 people chosen from the electoral roll at random, it is inevitable that they will sometimes be dominated by people who are racists, or are irresponsible and silly. Our legal system is gravely deficient if it fails to guard against this obvious danger.'

The ban's potential for wrongful convictions did not escape the appeal court judge Sir Robin Auld when he drew up his blueprint last year for radical reform of the criminal justice system. His recommendations will form the major part of a criminal justice bill. The ban, Sir Robin argued, was 'indefensible and capable of causing serious injustice'. He recommended that the curtain should be lifted far enough to allow trial judges or the appeal court to look into allegations of bias or improper behaviour by jurors which could have led to an unfair trial.

The lord chief justice, Lord Woolf [said] he would be reluctant to allow judges to investigate jury deliberations.

Professor Spencer, one of 12 consultants appointed to the Auld review, takes issue with that stance. He describes the ban as 'quite unacceptable', adding: 'I think … this involves a real risk of genuine miscarriages of justice. And even if it would involve cost and trouble, and even though there would be false allegations for every genuine allegation, nevertheless if people are risking long terms of imprisonment for things they didn't do in consequence of it, it shouldn't be permitted.'

Spencer argues that the court of appeal's decision in Qureshi's case is 'to put it mildly, questionable'. He says the ruling is 'almost certainly incompatible with article 6 of the European convention on human rights, which guarantees defendants a "fair hearing" before a tribunal that is "independent and impartial" '. More fundamentally, he adds, 'the refusal of the legal system to investigate a serious allegation of jury bias or misconduct is objectionable because it amounts to a refusal to intervene where there is a serious risk that the defendant was convicted, not because the jury thought him guilty, but because it did not like him'. Spencer argues that the danger of false complaints can't justify ignoring them all, since we happen to know that some allegations are true. In one recent case it emerged that some jurors had used a ouija board to try to contact the murder victim to find out who had killed him.

The court was able to look into the allegation, verify its truth and quash the conviction only because the jurors had done it in the hotel where they staying overnight and not in the jury room.

Spencer calls for urgent action to prevent future miscarriages of justice and puts forward three options: lift the ban and let the court investigate; have the judge sit with the jury during their deliberations; or tape-record jury deliberations. Spencer's preferred option is tape-recording; he suggests that the tape could be sealed and locked away, to be opened if plausible allegations of jury misconduct surface later. 'Taping the discussions would make the jury take care in all cases and it would mean there was some valid record.

'The police fought the taping of interviews but they gave in, and the result is that we have confidence in police interviewing suspects in a way we never did before. I think we would end up with greater confidence in jury trial because we would know, if it derailed badly, there would be some means of checking.'

Discuss the evidence suggesting that members of a jury such as those described above will not make fair judgements.

A recent Home Office report, *Race and the Criminal Justice System* (published in November 2002) confirms that there are still many inequalities. The report identifies the following issues for people from ethnic minorities:

- They commonly have worse experiences in the criminal justice system.

- They are over-represented as clients within the system but under-represented as employees of criminal justice services and agencies.

- In 2001/2002, black and Asian people were respectively eight and three times more likely to be stopped and searched than white people.

- In 2001/2002, black people were four times more likely to be arrested than white people.

In response to the report, the Home Office intends to devise a programme of action and support to address these issues in order to meet the requirements of the Race Relations Act.

Other factors

Although attractiveness and ethnic group are two of the most important factors that have been shown to influence judges and juries, other features do have an effect. Berry and McArthur (1985) found, in a mock trial study, that defendants with 'baby' faces were more likely than those with mature ones to be found guilty of negligence in not warning customers of the possible dangers of the products they were selling. Those with mature features were more likely to be considered guilty of deliberately deceiving their customers by telling lies about their products.

Dixon, Mahoney and Cocks (2002) investigated the effect of regional accent on the attribution of guilt. One hundred and nineteen participants listened to a recorded exchange between a suspect and a policeman. The suspect's accent was varied; it was either a standard British accent or a Birmingham accent. In the latter condition, the suspect was rated as significantly more guilty.

However, not all studies have found a relationship between defendant features and jury decisions. Bull and McAlpine (1998) suggest this may reflect a publication bias; studies finding no effect of appearance on judgements may have been rejected for publication. Nevertheless, studies strongly suggest that people do assume that there is a relationship between facial appearance and criminality, and they are agreed on which particular face fits a particular crime. This, together with the evidence that, at least in some instances, real-life court decisions are affected by facial appearance, should be a matter of considerable concern.

where to now?

The following is a good source of further information on factors affecting jury decision-making:

 Wrightsman L., Niezel M. & Fortune W. (1994) *Psychology and the legal system* **(3rd edition). California: Brooks/Cole.** Chapters 13 and 14 consider the dynamics of jury decision making with many examples from case studies of actual trials. It is very detailed but fascinating. The other chapters are equally absorbing and relevant to the study of criminal psychology.

Processes involved in jury decision making

Attribution biases in jurors

As we saw earlier (see page 107), attribution biases can affect people's beliefs about why someone behaved the way they did. Like witnesses, members of a jury may be biased in their judgements of guilt or innocence and the degree to which an individual is considered responsible for his or her actions. For example, in Duncan (1976)'s study (see page 130) situational attributions were assigned when the perpetrator was white but dispositional ones when they were black. This accounted for the greater leniency towards white defendants. One particular example of an attribution bias that can affect jurors is explained below.

The just world hypothesis

Lerner (1980) suggested that people have a need to believe in a world that is just and fair, a world in which people get what they deserve. In this way we can protect ourselves from the unpalatable truth that we could fall victim to the cruel twists of fate.

However, this belief is often strongly challenged by the fact that we regularly hear about events that involve the suffering of innocent victims and the unjust treatment of people. Rather than surrender our belief in a just world, we find ways of interpreting the causes of people's behaviour in such a way that it restores our faith in a just world. There are several ways in which this can be done.

- We can blame victims for their own misfortune. For example, we can accuse a victim of burglary of being careless and not securing their property adequately.

- We can vilify the character of victims, so they are perceived as deserving of their fate. For example, we may believe that battered wives provoke their abusive husbands or even have a personality type that is attracted to such behaviour.

- We can help the victims or compensate them in some way.

The tendency to disparage victims is another example of the fundamental attribution error because too much emphasis is put on the person and not enough on the situation. Although believing in a just world is common, there are marked individual differences in the strength of this belief. A strong believer in a just world is relatively unsympathetic to victims of misfortune and is also unlikely to take account of mitigating circumstances that may lead someone to commit a crime. Such individuals are more likely to be biased in their judgements as jurors.

One of the most disturbing aspects of the just world hypothesis is the attitude that is sometimes expressed towards rape victims. 'She must have led him on', 'She was asking for it walking home that late at night', 'What does she expect dressed like that?' are the kinds of comments often heard in media reports of rape. Bell et al (1994), using a simulated jury situation, asked male and female college students to consider four different incidents of rape, two of which concerned rape by a stranger and two of which involved date rape. Both males and females placed considerably more responsibility for what happened when the victim knew her assailant than when he was a stranger, and males ascribed more blame to the victim in both conditions than did females.

We don't have to denigrate the victim if there is an alternative means of restoring our belief in a just world. The study reported below demonstrates that when it is possible to compensate the victim, we do not ascribe more blame to one victim than another, but the amount of compensation offered differs according to circumstances. In this study people awarded greater compensation to an older woman than a younger one, indicating that we try to restore our belief in a just world by offering compensation to the victim in proportion to what we believe they deserve.

research
now

how do beliefs in a just world impact on attributions of responsibility and awards of monetary damages?

Foley L.A. & Pigott M.A. (2000) Belief in a just world and jury decisions in a civil rape trial. *Journal of Applied Social Psychology* 30(5): 935–51

aim: when an unjust event occurs, there are several ways in which our belief in a just world can be restored. For example, when a person is raped, people often ascribe responsibility to them for what happened, otherwise the event is too unfair to fit comfortably with their view of the world. An alternative way of restoring faith in a just world, if the opportunity arises, is to award the victim some compensation. The more innocent the person is judged to be, the greater the amount of the compensation that will be awarded. If the opportunity exists to offer compensation, then there is no need to ascribe responsibility to someone who is raped.

The general aim of this study is to investigate the impact of people's belief in a just world on attributions of responsibility and awards of monetary damages in a civil rape case.

This was done by testing two hypotheses:

Hypothesis 1. Younger plaintiffs and older plaintiffs will be held equally responsible for rape.

Hypothesis 2. Older women will be awarded more monetary damages than will younger women.

(Additional hypotheses were tested that are not reported here.)

procedure:

Design: this is an experiment, using an independent groups design. The independent variable was the age of the rape victim (young or old); the dependent variables were the percentage of responsibility attributed to the plaintiff and the amount of monetary damages awarded to them.

Participants: the participants were in two groups:

a) 47 students of Psychology (undergraduates); 37 females, 10 males, with a mean age of 20.3 years.

b) 59 jury-eligible residents of the same state; 21 males, 38 females, with a mean age of 48.5 years.

Scenario: the participants were given an account of the situation in which the rape occurred. A female nurse, who worked variable shifts, was raped in her apartment by an employee of the apartment owner. Before the rape occurred, the plaintiff complained several times to the apartment owner that someone was entering her apartment. She asked to have the locks changed, but he refused. He said that no one was ever allowed into an apartment without his being present. The rapist, the pool maintenance man, used the master key that hung in the owner's office to enter the apartment. The plaintiff was suing the owner for damages.

Materials: two different photographs of the rape victim, who was a white woman. The photographs had been generated by a computer so that the features were the same but one victim was young (described as 27 years old) whilst the other was considerably older (described as in her mid-60s).

findings: hypothesis 1 was found to be accepted: there was no significant difference in the amount of responsibility attributed to women based on their age. Usually, an older, more respectable victim would be considered to be less responsible than a younger one, but in this case the prediction was that the mock jurors would not need to perceive the older victim as less responsible as they could award her more money. This was indeed the case, since the second hypothesis was also accepted: participants awarded significantly higher monetary damages to the older woman than they did to the younger one, despite the two plaintiffs being perceived as equally responsible for the incident.

conclusion: the awarding of these different amounts of damages appears to support the Just World Hypothesis. Nevertheless, it would be advisable to consider some alternative explanations. It is possible that participants believed the older woman to be more psychologically damaged and/or to have sustained more severe physical injuries from the incident and therefore would need to take more time off work. However, it could also be argued that the younger woman has a greater life expectancy and would therefore be expected to suffer for a longer period of time than the older woman. Future research is needed to determine the rationale behind the decision to award more compensation to the older victim but it does appear to offer support for the Just World Hypothesis in that the older woman was offered more compensation.

One way of restoring our belief in a just world is to offer compensation and the amount of damages will be related to how responsible we feel a person is for their fate. In this case, the older woman was probably considered to be more 'innocent' than the younger one, even though this judgement was not a conscious one. Therefore she was considered worthy of higher compensation in order to restore the world to being a fair place.

Pollard (1992) has reviewed many studies looking at judgements about victims and attackers in depicted rapes. He reports that, generally, females make more pro-victim judgements than males do, as do those people with non-traditional sex-role attitudes. The victim's dress and past history also have a consistent effect in that the more scantily or provocatively dressed and the more sex partners the victim has had, the less sympathy they receive. Pollard points out that not all results found in experiments are directly relevant to a trial situation: for example, data on sentencing has no direct application since juries don't recommend sentences. Nevertheless, such studies do shed light on some of the attitudes with which jurors enter the court. In this chapter we are mainly concerned with influences on jurors but it is important to acknowledge the importance of these findings to other legal aspects. As Pollard comments:

> Attitudes of individuals to some extent determine the legal processes and have direct bearing on related issues such as whether a victim will report the rape. Given the prevalence of rape and the infrequency of reporting (especially in the case of those rapes that are likely to produce jury trials about consent), jury behaviour is not the only interest. Identification of the social attitudes endemic to the population in which rape flourishes is perhaps a more important goal … work on the attribution of responsibility paradigm has contributed to this goal (page 322).

The following is a good source of further information on the processes involved in jury decision-making:

▶ **Hastie R. (ed.)** *Inside the juror: the psychology of juror decision making.* **Cambridge: Cambridge University Press.** The Story Model is one paper in this very interesting book which covers many of the influences on how juries reach their verdicts.

The interpersonal influences on jury decision making

Once the evidence has been heard, the jury is ushered into a room and given brief instructions by the judge about how to proceed. The judge informs them of relevant legal concepts, tells them about verdict options (whether a majority verdict or unanimous one is required and what that majority must be), instructs the jury members to disregard extralegal factors (such as inadmissible evidence) and advises them on how to conduct their deliberation. We will now consider some of the psychological processes that underlie the reaching of a final verdict.

Electing a foreperson

Before any deliberation takes place, the jury selects a foreperson or leader who is responsible for calling for votes, liaising between the judge and jury and announcing the verdict to the court. The foreperson is not necessarily a leader in the sense of controlling proceedings or being more influential than others, but more often than not it is the foreperson who takes on that role.

Several factors influence who becomes the foreperson. Strodtbeck and Hook (1961) conducted a series of impressively realistic simulated jury studies in order to examine in detail the procedures involved. With the co-operation of the court, Strodtbeck and colleagues chose people from a remaining jury pool, used *voir dire* to eliminate the biased ones, played them a recording of the trial and then asked them to retire and reach a verdict. This research, and evidence both from real-life and other mock jury studies, showed that certain people are more likely than others to be chosen as the leader.

In the main, people who have previously served on a jury, those of high socio-economic status and those who spoke first were most likely to be selected. Men rather than women are also preferred as a leader. Kerr et al (1982) found that in 179 real-life trials in which half the jurors were women, in only 10 per cent of cases was a woman selected as the leader. Factors other than the individuals involved can also be influential. Strodtbeck et al found that people who sit at the 'head' of a rectangular table are more likely than those sitting at the side to be chosen. This may not, of course, be independent of individual factors, since a confident middle-class man who has served on a jury before may seat himself in such a position. In summary, then, as Ainsworth and Pease (1987) comment '… the person most likely to be chosen as foreman is an upper-class male who sits at the end of the table and opens the discussion. These findings are important as the person elected foreman may have more influence in the group than any other member' (page 71).

Group polarisation and conformity

The opinions of the majority are hugely influential in the final decisions made within a group and juries are no exception to this rule. Hastie et al (1983) found that if the first decision favoured acquittal, then in 86 per cent of cases a not guilty verdict was returned. If at the outset the majority favoured a guilty verdict, then in 90 per cent of cases, that was the final outcome.

The study of group processes reveals that when a majority of group members favour one side, discussion usually results in the group moving to an even stronger position, a phenomenon known as *group polarisation*.

classic
research

grouped jurors judge greater guilt

Myers D.G. & Kaplan M.F. (1976) Group-induced polarization in simulated juries. *Personality and Social Psychology Bulletin* 2(1): 63–6

aim: to test the effect of group-polarisation on jury decision making.

procedure: 60 students, in a simulated jury setting, were asked to respond to eight hypothetical traffic cases. In these cases the implication of guilt towards the person to blame was varied (either high guilt or low guilt). In small groups, the participants discussed only four of the cases (two high guilt and two low guilt) and then had to respond again to all eight cases.

findings: after discussing low guilt cases, participants were more likely to be more extreme in their judgements of innocence and more lenient in their recommended punishments. Conversely, after discussing high guilt cases, participants tended to shift towards making more harsh judgements of guilt and punishment. These shifts occurred only on cases that had been discussed. For the four cases that were not discussed, participants gave similar answers to those in the first phase of the study.

conclusion: the simulated jury discussions caused polarisation of judgements, supporting the idea that exposure to a group situation induces a polarisation in group, and consequently individual, judgements.

Social psychologists explain group polarisation in terms of the need to make sense of the social world. Interviews with jurors and studies of mock juries show that the majority has a powerful influence over the minority. The extent of this influence is surprisingly strong, as shown by Asch (1955), whose studies are described on page 137. If people are prepared to deny the clear evidence of their own eyes on a simple task, as 75 per cent of the participants in this study did at least once, consider how much more powerful the influence of the majority may be when considering whether they are right or wrong in a far more ambiguous situation. The experience of being in a small minority, especially a minority of one, can create considerable anxiety, which is reduced by conforming to the majority decision.

Studies of conformity such as those by Asch give us valuable insight into the conditions under which a majority may influence a small minority. But jurors do not simply sit round a table and express a single decision, they are involved in a deliberation process during which each member gives his or her own opinion and seeks to influence others. How does the majority have its influence and why this influence is so strong?

The strength of majority influence

Smith and Mackie (1995) suggest that there are several factors that operate in favour of the majority position:

- **When the majority is offering a certain opinion the arguments are more numerous and varied.** The minority of the jurors who disagree with the majority are likely to be presented with a set of persuasive arguments that they had not previously considered and this is likely to move them towards the majority view (Hinsz & Davis, 1984).

- **Information and opinions shared by several members of a group tend to be discussed for longer than views held by one person.** Stasser and Stewart (1992) devised a situation in which the majority of members of a group shared certain information but other information was only given to a single individual. Even though the group was specifically instructed to discuss all the information, they focused almost entirely on that which was shared, to the virtual exclusion of the non-shared information.

- **Majority arguments are usually more compelling than minority ones.** When several people make the same arguments, it has more impact than one offered by a single individual. People generally believe that if several individuals have come to the same conclusion, it is probably correct. Therefore the arguments advanced by the majority of jurors tend to be very persuasive and move the group further towards the extreme of their original opinion.

- **Majority views tend to be expressed more convincingly than minority views.** With the benefit of knowing that most people are on their side, members of a majority use a forthright and argumentative style that is compelling (Kerr et al, 1987). This may account for members of a majority being viewed as more confident, logical and intelligent than those of a minority (McLachlan, 1986), resulting in the likelihood that they will convert them. Once again, the end result is group polarisation.

classic
research

what is the effect of a majority influence on a minority?

Asch S.E. (1955) Opinions and social pressure. *Scientific American* **193(5): 31–5**

---

aim: to investigate the effect of a majority influence on a minority of one, using a simple perception task.

procedure: this is a laboratory study using a total of 123 participants from three different institutions.

On each series of trials a group of 7–9 young male students were seated at a table to take part in a perception task. Only one of them was a true participant and he was seated in the penultimate or last seat; the remainder were confederates.

The experimenter told them that they would be comparing the lengths of lines and then showed two large white cards. On one there was a single vertical line, called the standard. On the other there were three vertical lines of varying length, one the same length as the standard, the other two substantially different in length from it. The students were asked to choose the one that was the same length as the standard. The students gave their answers in turn, starting at number one and proceeding around the table.

Before the study started, the confederates were requested to give the same incorrect answer on certain crucial trials. On the first two trials they gave the correct answer, and on some of the remaining ones, so as to reduce the possibility of the naive participant suspecting the collusion. There were 18 trials in each series; on 12 of these the majority responded incorrectly. In only a few cases did the participant actually show suspicion: when this happened the experiment was stopped and the results were not counted.

Variations on the basic study:
(a) The number of people seated around the table was varied from two (one confederate plus the true participant) to 16 (15 confederates).

(b) A single dissenter (placed in a position before the participant) stated the correct answer. The participant was no longer on his own in his judgement.

(c) A single dissenter answered differently from the other confederates but incorrectly (he chose the other incorrect card).

findings:
The basic study: an incorrect answer (one that agreed with the majority) was given in 36.8 per cent of the trials.

There were considerable individual differences in the amount of conformity. About 25 per cent of participants never agreed with the incorrect judgements of the majority. In contrast, some individuals went with the majority nearly all the time. Those who were independent did not, as a rule, succumb to the majority even over a large number of trials.

Interviews at the end of the study established different reasons for independence and yielding.

Reasons for independence: some firmly believed in their own judgements; they were responsive to the majority but were able to recover from doubt and re-establish their equilibrium.

Others believed that the majority was correct but nevertheless felt obliged to 'call the play as they saw it'.

Reasons for yielding: some believed that they were wrong and the majority was correct.

Others said they did not want 'to spoil your results'. These participants believed that the majority were sheep going along with the first respondent or that the majority were victims of an optical illusion, but these suspicions were not sufficient to make them give an answer they believed to be correct.

Some believed themselves to be deficient and defective and felt they must hide this from the others.

Interestingly, all the yielding participants underestimated the frequency with which they conformed.

The size of the majority: when the true participant was only one of two, he invariably remained independent and did not conform. Conformity rose to 13.6 per cent of trials when there were two confederates and to 31.8 per cent when there were three. After that, the conformity rate remained steady regardless of the size of the majority.

The effect of breaking unanimity: the presence of a supporting dissenter had a striking effect. It reduced the amount of yielding to less than a quarter of what it had been. The fellow dissenter was warmly regarded and felt to inspire confidence. Even when the other dissenter chose a different incorrect response, yielding was reduced, although not as much as with an agreeing dissenter.

Conclusion: the fact that conformity is so strong that people will deny the evidence of their own eyes is a matter of concern. This raises questions about education methods and the values that guide our conduct. Nevertheless, the capacity to be independent should not be underestimated; those who participated agreed without exception that independence was preferable to conformity. Their actions, however, did not match their beliefs.

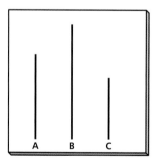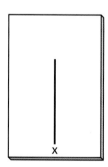

Example of cards used by Asch (1955)

The majority view is more likely than the minority one to be accepted because this view is expressed more often, is discussed more and in greater depth, seems more compelling and is presented more persuasively than the opinions of the minority. This quantitative and qualitative advantage leads to group polarisation.

Minority influence

In the classic and brilliant film, *Twelve Angry Men*, a lone juror, played by Henry Fonda, persuades a sceptical jury to change their original view and acquit a young man of a murder charge. For anyone interested in psychology the film makes compulsive viewing. You see the questioning of what appeared originally to be very convincing witness testimony, you experience the raw prejudice of certain jury members and gain insight (as they do) into the causes of their bigoted views.

Real life is seldom as dramatic as the cinematic world and, as we have already seen, minorities in situations such as a jury room rarely win the day. Nevertheless, they do occasionally convert the majority and the way in which this is done has been studied in detail by Moscovici (1976, 1980, 1985). He maintains that the success of minorities is dependent on the behavioural style of the individuals involved. If the minority is consistent and flexible, and their arguments are relevant, then they may eventually win over the opinions of the majority. The first of these factors, the consistency with which the group defends and advocates its position, is the most crucial. This consistency must be maintained between the minority group and over time. If the minority members agree among themselves and continue to do so, they may persuade the majority to question its own assumptions and seriously consider those of the minority. To be successful, those people in the minority must not appear to be rigid and dogmatic but flexible in their approach and willing to discuss the reasons why they disagree with the majority.

Figure 12.4 A scene from the film *Twelve Angry Men*

Just as we looked at why majorities are influential, it is appropriate to consider why some minorities are successful in converting others to their point of view. Nemeth (1977) suggests that when majorities are faced with a consistent minority sticking to their guns, they are puzzled and try to work out why they are so convinced they are right and so determined to express publicly these unpopular views. The majority is therefore prepared to scrutinise these minority views and, on occasions, be convinced by them. Even when minorities fail to sway people initially, they may start a questioning process that discon-

certs the majority and may eventually lead to change.

The character played by Henry Fonda behaved with such consistency and confidence that he swayed the jury. However, in real jury rooms establishing a minority consensus and maintaining it with consistency and confidence are so difficult that minorities rarely win over majorities.

A unanimous or a majority verdict?

One of the reasons why a minority is rarely influential may be the fact that not all jury decisions have to be unanimous. In Britain a jury does not have to be in total agreement; a majority of 10 to 2 is sufficient to secure a conviction. In the US the rules vary from state to state, with respect to both the size and unanimity of juries. Nowadays few states allow a less-than-unanimous verdict in criminal trials, although many do so for civil cases.

There are important implications for the interaction of group size and majority verdicts. As mentioned earlier in the chapter, in the ruling *Florida v Williams* (1972) the US Supreme Court ruled that a 5 to 1 majority was the equivalent of a 10 to 2, citing Asch's work in support of this contention. Even a cursory reflection on Asch's research shows this to be a gross misinterpretation; the presence of one ally (a fellow dissenter) reduced conformity drastically, so a minority of two, even when opposed to 10 people, is much stronger than a minority of one and less likely to be persuaded.

The effect of using a majority versus a unanimous verdict system was investigated in mock trials by Nemeth (1977). He asked student jurors to make decisions about the guilt or innocence of a person charged with murder and organised the juries so that they included some members initially in favour of acquittal and some who were initially predisposed towards conviction. Some juries were required to reach a unanimous verdict while others were allowed to reach a verdict based only on a two-thirds majority. Some significant differences emerged between the two groups. Compared to the majority-verdict groups, those who had to reach a unanimous decision debated for longer, were more likely to take account of minority views and were more confident in their final decision. More significantly, they were also more likely to change from their original judgement. Hastie et al (1983) conducted a similar study using 69 mock juries and requiring either a 12 to 0, a 10 to 2 or an 8 to 4 verdict. Compared to the juries requiring a unanimous verdict, those requiring a majority one spent less time discussing and more time voting and they did not continue any deliberation after the required majority had been reached. As in the previous study, these jurors were less confident and less satisfied with the decisions they had made. Perhaps even more disturbing is the observation by

Hastie et al that when a unanimous verdict was not required the jurors who were in the majority used coercive, forceful and bullying tactics to try to persuade those who disagreed with them.

The general opinion of social psychologists is that a majority verdict reduces the effectiveness of juries. There may, however, be some occasions on which it is useful. If, for example, a single bigoted juror insists on sticking to an opinion despite it not being based on any evidence ('I don't care what anyone says, you can tell by looking at that lad that he did it'), then at least they can be ignored. Nevertheless, the overall verdict is that expressed by Brehm and Kassim (1996), when they state that 'it is clear that this procedure weakens jurors who are in the voting minority, breeds close-mindedness, inhibits discussion and leaves many jurors uncertain about decisions' (page 487).

Conclusions

In conclusion, research into the workings of juries and

where to now?

The following social psychology textbooks contain a section on jury decision making and are good sources of further information on the interpersonal influences involved:

▶ **Brehm S.S. & Kassim S.M. (1996)** *Social psychology*, **3rd edn. Boston and Toronto: Houghton Mifflin Company.** See Chapter 12.

▶ **Forsythe D. (1987)** *Social psychology.* **California: Brooks/Cole.** See Chapter 10. Although this book is a little dated now, it is brilliantly written and still has many relevant points to make.

▶ **Brigham J.C. (1991)** *Social psychology*, **2nd edn. London: HarperCollins.** See Chapter 13.

▶ **Hewstone M., Strobe W., Stephenson G. (eds) (1996)** *Introduction to social psychology*, **2nd edn. Oxford: Blackwell.** See Chapter 18.

their effectiveness is difficult to conduct as the observation of real juries during their deliberations is not permitted. Social scientists must therefore rely on the use of mock juries or shadow juries. These methods can never provide a completely valid picture of how juries come to their final verdict but they can and do provide valuable insights into the decision making process. From such research, psychologists have shown how factors including interpersonal influences within the jury such as leader selection, conformity and characteristics of the defendant can affect jury decision making.

what do you know?

1   Describe and evaluate research into the influences on decision making processes in juries.

2   (a) Describe **two** factors that influence jury decision making, such as minority influence and the election of a foreperson.
    (b) Evaluate studies investigating the effects of the factors you have described in part (a).

3   With respect to juries, discuss the possible effects of conformity on jury decision making.

13 Social and media influences on criminal behaviour

what's ahead?

On 20 April 1999, Eric Harris and Dylan Kiebold raided the school they attended in Littleton, Colorado, murdered 12 students and a teacher and wounded 23 others before shooting themselves dead. Although the causes of such behaviour are obviously complex and multiple, it was noted that the boys spent a great deal of time playing the video hate game 'Doom' and that for a school project they had produced a video in which, dressed in trenchcoats and carrying guns, they killed school athletes. Is it possible, the general public, sociologists, media researchers and psychologists ask, that a continuous diet of violent films, television programmes and games is a major cause of aggression and therefore a significant contributor to crime?

This view is far too simplistic for some theorists who claim that the media is being used as a scapegoat by parents, teachers and society to deflect the blame away from them. A judge in the US recently threw out a case against 25 media companies after a 14-year-old schoolboy shot dead three girls at a prayer group in 1997. The victims' parents claimed that the 'one hit, one kill' pattern used by the young killer mimicked that of video games. The judge, however, commented that 'Tragedies such as this simply defy rational explanation, and courts should not pretend otherwise.'

In this chapter we take a critical look at research into the effects of the media on antisocial aggressive behaviour, including some recent work on the effects of violent video games. We consider the conditions under which children may be most susceptible to social and media influences, including the effects of families and of self-fulfilling prophecies.

Figure 13.1 A woman is reunited with her daughter following the shootings at Columbine High School, Littleton, Colorado, in April 1999

Are media influences a problem?

There is no doubt that children are exposed to a great deal of media violence. Eron (1995) estimated that by the end of primary school a child is likely to have seen 8000 murders and more than 100,000 other acts of violence on television and video. Such has been the concern regarding the possible relationship between media violence and violence within society, including the possibility of 'copycat' crimes, that this has been the focus of several public commissions and reports designed to influence social policy (Wood et al, 1991).

The debate about the extent of media influence is not a new one: many years ago Bandura, a major proponent of social learning theory, expressed the view that viewing of violence could encourage imitative aggression in children. His research, which you will have learnt about at AS (see *Angles on Psychology*), paved the way for many studies investigating the possible link between media violence and violence within society. Such research, however, is beset with methodological problems and various techniques

141

have been used in an attempt to obtain some answers. Before looking at the research itself, we will describe and evaluate each of these methods.

interactive angles

Think back to your AS course. When you studied the learning approach you will have considered how, according to social learning theory, behaviour can be acquired through exposure to models. Look at a range of media sources (such as children's comics, advertisements, magazines, films, television programmes, books, videos and computer games) and identify:

- models demonstrating aggressive or criminal activities;

- how effective these models might be (for example, are they famous or powerful or targeted to appeal to a particular audience such as children);

- whether there is any evidence that their behaviours are being imitated;

- if these actions are being rewarded (either indirectly – if the model is a hero for example – or directly, such as by the player of a game 'winning' through the use of computerised violence).

Methods used to investigate media influences

There are four main methods by which the link between media violence and aggression has been investigated (see also Chapter 29, on methods). These methods are laboratory experiments, field experiments, natural experiments and correlational studies.

Laboratory experiments

These are investigations carried out in a laboratory or similarly controlled environment and usually compare two matched groups on their level of aggression when one has been exposed to some form of media violence (such as a film clip or video game) and the other has been exposed to something similar, and equally engaging, but with no violent content. The participants are then given the opportunity to aggress (or so they believe), by, for example, pressing a button marked 'hurt' to deliver a painful stimulus to another

person (the pain is never delivered) and the level of aggression between the two groups is compared.

Sometimes, in addition to this, a repeated measures design is used in which levels of aggression are rated before and after viewing violent material.

This method has the important advantage that, being experimental, it can establish cause and effect. However, such studies have been criticised for their lack of ecological validity; there is a world of difference between pressing a button marked 'hurt' and being deliberately cruel to others following exposure to media violence in a natural setting. Doubts have understandably been expressed about whether laboratory findings will generalise to real life. Another problem with this method is that it only measures short-term effects.

Ethical concerns have also been voiced. Does the experimental provision of opportunities for violence encourage such behaviour? An example of such a study is that of Bandura (1965), see page 144.

Field experiments

These are experiments carried out in more natural settings, such as the home of the participant or a boarding school. They have greater ecological validity than laboratory studies but, like the latter, they look only at short-term effects. It is difficult to control extraneous situational variables, such as how much other violence the children witness or whom they associate with, so there can be less confidence in judging cause and effect. Examples of this type of research include that of Leyens et al (1975) (see page 146) and Parke et al (1977) (see page 146), in which an institutional setting was used.

Using this technique, Troseth (2003) demonstrated that children as young as two years of age could use information they had seen on a video. Over a period of two weeks, the participants could watch themselves 'live' on the family television. When subsequently tested on their ability to find a toy that they had seen on a live video being hidden in another room, they could utilise this information effectively, enabling them to complete a task that children of this age would normally find very difficult. Most of the children also transferred this ability to using another symbolic medium, that of still pictures, to complete the searching task. These findings suggest that even very young children can acquire information from visual media and apply this knowledge to their own behaviour.

Natural experiments

These are studies carried out in a real-life setting in which the independent variable (the degree of exposure to violent media) exists already so cannot be

research now

spoiling for a fight?

Yukawa S., Endo K. & Yoshida F. (2001) The effects of media violence on aggression: focus on the role of anger evoked by provocation. *Japanese Journal of Psychology* **72(1): 1–9**

aim: to investigate how prior provocation and exposure to media violence affect cognition, emotion and aggressive behaviour.

procedure: half of a group of 60 male undergraduate participants were provoked by a confederate (posing as another participant) to induce anger. All participants then viewed one of three videos differing in their content: highly violent, violent with a high entertainment level or non-violent. The participants' pulse and eyeblink rates were measured during viewing and, following this, each participant described the thoughts and affective reactions they experienced in relation to the video. Finally, each participant's aggression towards a confederate was measured.

findings: the anger elicited through provocation by the confederate and a high level of violence in the video combined to produce negative thoughts and emotions and this, in turn, facilitated aggressive behaviour towards the confederate.

conclusions: media representations of violence can cause negative thoughts and feelings. Under some situations, such as when provoked, this is likely to result in the expression of aggressive behaviour.

---

controlled. These studies have a reasonably high level of ecological validity but it is impossible to clearly establish cause and effect since other factors and changes will also be influential. Opportunities for such investigations are rare but recently one has become available; that of the island of St Helena (Charlton et al, 2000) (see page 147).

Correlational studies

These studies look for a positive correlation between the level of aggression expressed by individuals (by using personality tests, self-ratings or crime statistics) and the amount of media violence experienced. Some studies follow individuals from childhood through to adulthood, so they have the advantage of looking at very long-term relationships; others measure short-term effects. Their main limitation is that of all correlational studies: they cannot establish cause and effect. A positive correlation may arise because experiencing media violence causes aggression, but this is not the only possible explanation. It may be that aggressive children (and adults) seek out violent films and games or that children brought up in a violent household and subculture are exposed to media violence, but it is the general upbringing, rather than the media influences, which causes the high levels of aggression. Examples of such studies include Eron et al (1972) (see page 146),

Eron and Huesmann (1986) (see page 146) and Phillips (1983, 1986) (see page 146).

Studies investigating the effects of media violence

Laboratory experiments

Bandura, the founder of social learning theory, conducted early laboratory experiments into the effects of viewing violence that you will recall from AS. He used laboratory studies to demonstrate that children imitate aggressive models. His famous Bobo doll studies in which young children watched an adult either beat up the large inflatable doll or simply play non-aggressively with other toys, showed that young children imitate aggressive acts and learn from the models new ways of aggressing (Bandura et al, 1961). The study on page 144 demonstrated this, and also showed that if a person is seen to be punished for acting aggressively then children are unlikely to imitate them. This is important because much media violence is seen to be rewarded, either directly or indirectly. The 'good guys' often use violence to get their own way and are hailed as heroes (or very occasionally heroines) for so doing.

classic
research

how do children respond to TV violence?

Bandura A. (1965) Influence of models' reinforcement contingencies on the acquisition of imitative responses. *Journal of Personality and Social Psychology* **1(6): 589–95**

aims:

1 To observe children's responses to seeing a television presentation of an aggressive model who is seen either to be punished, rewarded or to have no consequences for the behaviour.

2 To see how many of the novel aggressive responses the child will imitate when induced by rewards to do so.

procedure: this is an experimental study with a carefully controlled independent variable, that is, whether the model is punished, rewarded or no consequences occur.

The participants were 33 boys and 33 girls aged between 3 years 6 months and almost 6 years. The children were assigned randomly to one of three treatment conditions of 11 boys and 11 girls.

The children viewed the televised film on their own. The film lasted five minutes and involved a character called Rocky being abusive to an adult-sized plastic Bobo doll. The content of the film is described in the paper as follows:

'First, the model laid the Bobo doll on its side, sat on it, and punched it on the nose whilst remarking, "Pow, right in the nose, boom, boom." The model then raised the doll and pommeled it on the head with a mallet. Each response was accompanied by the verbalisation, "Sockeroo … stay down." Following the mallet aggression, the model kicked the doll about the room, and these responses were interspersed with the comment, "Fly away." Finally, the model threw rubber balls at the Bobo doll, each strike punctuated with "Bang". This sequence of physically and verbally aggressive behaviour was repeated twice.'

The ending of the film differed according to the conditions; there were three of these:

(a) Model-rewarded condition: the model was given drinks, called a 'strong champion' and congratulated on the aggressive performance.

(b) Model-punished condition: the model was given a good telling off, called a bully, spanked with a rolled-up newspaper and threatened with a more serious spanking if it happened again.

(c) Non-consequences condition: no extra ending was added to the basic film.

After viewing the film, each child spent 10 minutes in the test room, which was equipped with a Bobo doll, balls, a mallet, dart guns, farm animals and a dolls house. Two observers, who did not know which condition the child had been assigned to, recorded their behaviour and noted the number of imitated behaviours they performed.

After a short break, the children were offered a sticker and juice for each physical or verbal response they reproduced. They were asked to show what Rocky did and what he said in the film.

findings: children in the no-consequences and the model-rewarded condition imitated significantly more aggressive behaviours than the model-punished group. There was no difference between the no-consequences and the model-rewarded groups.

In the second part of the study, when children were offered rewards to recall the behaviour of the model, there was no difference between the groups. They could all repeat a considerable number of the aggressive actions. The use of positive incentives had completely wiped out any previous performance differences.

conclusion: although the administration of punishment reduces whether or not children imitate aggressive behaviours, it does not influence the degree to which they learn them.

research
now

look, listen and learn?

Vidal-Vazquez M.A. & Clemente-Diaz M. (2000) The attraction of media violence. *PSICO* 31(2): 49–80

aim: to investigate adolescents' views of media violence and assess the cognitive and emotional effects of watching violence in the media.

procedure: the participants were 203 males and females, aged 13 years. They were shown 15-minute excerpts from three videos, depicting: action without violence, socially acceptable violence and unjustifiable violence. The participants' views about media violence were tested before and after watching the videos.

findings: one key result emerged – that viewing violence caused a more positive assessment of, and greater attraction, to violence, even in participants who had expressed a negative view prior to watching the videos.

conclusions: viewing media violence affects both children's judgements of the acceptability of violence and its appeal, and could therefore affect their perceptions of acceptable social behaviour in the real world.

Correlational studies

Longitudinal studies

Eron and his colleagues conducted a longitudinal correlational study of a large number of children over more than 20 years. Although the findings may be somewhat dated they are worth considering because the length of the study permits conclusions about long-term effects of television violence. At the beginning of the study, in 1960, Eron et al measured the TV violence level of the programmes the children watched and the aggressiveness of 875 seven and eight year olds and found a positive correlation between the two. Ten years later, with 475 of the original sample remaining, they measured the same two variables and found a negligible correlation (Eron et al, 1972). However, a comparison during the teenage years of violence viewed and aggressiveness found an even stronger positive correlation in the boys, though not in girls. Furthermore, the more television violence the boys had watched at the age of eight, the more likely they were to have been convicted of violent crimes at the age of 30 (Eron & Huesmann, 1986). The methodological problems inherent in such longitudinal studies applied in this case; only 55 per cent of the original sample were available, so they may not have been representative. It is also quite possible that those participants who were predisposed to be aggressive sought out violent television programmes to watch or that a common factor, such as harsh parental punishment, produced children (and, later, adults) who were both aggressive and enjoyed watching others suffer. Nevertheless, while recognising the limitations of the correlational method, the researchers concluded that watching TV violence can cause aggression in later life.

Correlational studies

Huesmann proposes that the cumulative effect of media violence does not only reveal itself in crime statistics but is implicated in general antisocial behaviour such as inconsiderate driving and the use of harsh corporal punishment on children. The pervasive influence of violent television, argues Huesmann, is to make all forms of aggression more acceptable.

Eron (1995) maintains that television violence teaches children attitudes that condone violence and offer examples of specific aggressive behaviours, such as giving someone a good thump, as a way of solving problems. Television violence differs in important ways from that shown in films, fairy stories or at the theatre because these are perceived as fantasy. Not only is a great deal of television violence quite realistic but a child sees a great deal of it – in many homes the television is on most of the time.

Somewhat different correlational research was conducted by Phillips (1983, 1986) who investigated whether there was an association between violent crime and the newspaper and television coverage of 18 heavyweight boxing matches. He found that homicide death rates rose after each of these boxing matches, peaking at about three days afterwards. Phillips even found that murders of white males increased after the defeat of a white boxer and homicides of African-Americans increased following the defeat of an African-American fighter.

Not all correlational studies show a relationship between viewing violence and aggressive behaviour. Over a three-year period, Milavsky et al (1982) found only a small association between viewing violent television and levels of aggression. They concluded that the influence of violent television was extremely weak compared to the family and social environment, a point to which we will return.

Hagell and Newbury (1994) compared the television and video viewing habits of 78 young offenders with those of a school control group and found that the delinquents reported watching no more violent television and having fewer television sets or video recorders. They were also less able to name favourite television programmes and had more difficulty naming a television character they emulated. They were typically to be found on the streets getting into trouble rather than indoors watching television. Significantly, though, they tended to come from chaotic, deprived, unhappy homes.

Field studies

A classic field study on media violence was conducted by Leyens et al (1975) in a correctional home for boys. The amount of aggression shown by the boys was measured both before and after a week of watching either violent films (such as *Bonnie and Clyde* and *The Dirty Dozen*) or non-violent ones. Those boys who watched the violent films showed considerably more aggression in the week after watching them than in the week before, whereas those who had seen the non-violent films showed no increase at all.

Parke et al (1977) conducted a similar study, also on juvenile offenders, in three different institutions. These boys were split into two groups matched on the amount of aggression shown in the course of one week. On each of the next five days they were shown either non-violent or violent films, all judged to be equally exciting. Trained observers coded the amount of violence the boys showed during the days of the study and found that the boys watching the violent films were more aggressive than those who had watched neutral films. In addition to this, the boys who had seen the violent films were more likely to give what they believed to be an electric shock to opponents in a game when provoked by them.

Both of these studies used a sample of delinquent boys, so their findings cannot be generalised to most youngsters. They do, however, demonstrate that media violence may increase the antisocial tendencies of youths who are already very aggressive.

research
now

the imitation of school violence after the Columbine High School massacre

Kostinsky S., Bixler E.O. & Kettl P.A. (2001) Threats of school violence in Pennsylvania after media coverage of the Columbine High School massacre: examining the role of limitation. *Archives of Pediatric and Adolescent Medicine* **155(9): 994–1001**

aim: to investigate whether the cluster of bomb threats and other school violence that occurred after the Columbine High School massacre in Colorado, USA, were due to imitation. The massacre had received much media attention, for example, it was reported that the boys, former students at the school, had made a film threatening to kill students and had used their own website to publicise their hatred of the school and desire to kill staff and students.

procedure: the researchers examined a database of threats of school violence reported to the Pennsylvania Emergency Maintenance Agency in the 50 days after the massacre. The daily frequency of threats of violence and their geographical location were recorded.

findings: 354 threats were logged during the 50 days following the massacre (compared to the one or two threats typically logged per year). The frequency of the threats peaked just over a week after the incident and more than one-third occurred on days 8, 9 and 10.

conclusions: the successive threats of school violence appeared following media coverage of the Columbine massacre, suggesting that they were imitative threats. The researchers suggest that the risk of imitation should be considered in the way such incidents are reported.

A natural experiment: the St Helena study

Recently an opportunity arose to investigate the effects of the introduction of television to a small community. The island of St Helena became the site for a natural experiment when satellite television became available there in March 1995. Video cameras were installed in two school playgrounds and, before and after television was introduced, children aged between three and eight were filmed through lunch and playtimes. Analysis of the videos before the introduction of television showed that the great majority of the children were well adjusted and hard working; in fact the three and four year olds were considered to be among the best behaved in the world.

So did this change after the introduction of television? Not at all. Even though the violent content of the programmes was slightly higher than in the UK (46 per cent as opposed to 41 per cent) and there was no watershed, the amount of hitting, kicking, pushing and pinching was just the same after the introduction of television as it was before. Teachers also rated the children as just as hardworking and co-operative as they had ever been (Charlton et al, 2000).

Conclusions to be drawn

So what we can conclude from all of these findings? Obviously the issue is a complex one and much as the popular press may like to draw simplistic conclusions and suggest even more facile solutions, psychologists and media researchers have a responsibility to weigh up the argument in a rather more considered fashion.

One major problem that besets any attempt to assess the effects of media violence is outlined by Livingstone (2001):

> Almost irrespective of the academic legitimacy of claims for media effects, such claims tend to be addressed within a context in which the mass media are constructed as a scapegoat for, or deflection from, broader cultural and political anxieties (concerning say, childhood, sexuality, crime, unemployment or the underclass). The urgency of this moral and political agenda complicates, or even undermines, careful assessment of the academic research literature. (page 29)

Certainly much of the research indicates that exposure to excessive violence can affect some viewers some of the time. Huesmann and Malamuth (1986) comment that the great majority of field and laboratory studies indict media violence as a factor in the development of aggressive behaviour. Nevertheless, it is only one factor and even the researcher most convinced of the detrimental effects of media violence would not argue that exposure to it alone would be sufficient to make a person behave aggressively. Cumberbatch (1997) argues that right from the time of 'Penny Dreadfuls' the media has been used as a scapegoat. He considers that the link between media violence and criminal acts is greatly exaggerated and founded more on moral panic fuelled by newspaper hysteria than on factual evidence. He lists some of the criminal acts, including the Hungerford massacre, that were supposedly the result of copycat crimes and argues that none was supported by convincing evidence.

TV wrestling in the dock over death of girl, 6

The death of six-year-old Tiffany Eunick has shocked America. The little girl's alleged killer is a boy of 13 who is said to have pounded her skull until it was flat, and to have beaten her so badly that her liver was split.

Her attacker's line of defence has caused further alarm. Lionel Tate, one of the youngest defendants to face a murder charge, claims that his actions were inspired by professional wrestling on television.

Tate's assertion puts the flamboyant and aggressive image of wrestlers such as Hulk Hogan and The Rock next to him in the dock of the Florida court where his trial began last week. Central to his defence is his lawyer's claim that the killing was the result of the boy copying moves he had seen in bouts televised by the Worldwide Wrestling Federation (WWF).

According to his lawyer, Jim Lewis, the teenager – who weighs almost 10st but has the mental age of an eight-year-old – was incapable of distinguishing between the mock brutality and phoney personas of the WWF and the real harm he was capable of inflicting. The defence calls Tiffany's death a 'horrible accident'.

Although at least four other children have died in incidents linked to copycat violence from wrestling shows, the Florida case is the first to put the blame squarely on the effects of television. It comes at a time of growing concern about the impact of screen violence on children and teenagers.

A report released last week by David Satcher, the United States Surgeon General and the country's most senior public health official, stated: 'A substantial body of research now indicates that exposure to media violence increases children's physically and verbally aggressive behaviour in the short term.'

The allegations are being vigorously countered by the WWF, which is shown in Britain on Sky TV. The federation is suing Mr Lewis for defamation after remarks he made on television chat shows. The WWF, which insists that children can distinguish between screen fiction and reality, has also successfully blocked attempts by the boy's defence team to force star wrestlers including The Rock – otherwise known as Dwayne Johnson – to give evidence during the trial.

The issue of media violence is particularly sensitive in America after a series of violent rampages by children and teenagers, including the 1999 Columbine High School massacre in Denver, in which 12 pupils and a teacher were shot by two pupils who later killed themselves.

An unsuccessful attempt to sue the video-game industry for $33 million (£22 million) was made by the parents of three children killed by another armed pupil in Paducah, Kentucky, in 1997. The killer, Michael Carneal, 13, claimed to have been influenced by violent videos, films and internet sites.

Last week's report by the Surgeon General was originally commissioned by President Clinton in the wake of Columbine. It found that violence in children was usually the result of a combination of factors, of which poverty and abuse were the most significant.

While it concluded that children became more aggressive after watching some television programmes and videos, the report noted that this behaviour did not usually translate into violence against others, except among children who were already disturbed.

A separate study by Stanford University in California, published this month, compared the actions of two primary school classes, one of which had been discouraged from watching television for almost two weeks. The research team found that the group that cut down its viewing by more than a third was almost 50 per cent less likely to engage in aggressive playground behaviour than other pupils.

Sunday Telegraph, 21 January 2001

1 Why might it be unwise to generalise from this particular case to the effects that watching wrestling might have on children in general?

2 What arguments may be advanced in the defence of the media, that it is being being used as a scapegoat and the fundamental causes of violence cannot be laid at its door?

where to now?

The following are good sources of further information on studies into the effects of media violence:

▶ **Newson E. (1994) Video violence and the protection of children.** *Psychology Review* **1(2): 2–6** This article discusses a very controversial paper by the author published after the judge's comments at the trial of Jamie Bulger's murderers that 'I suspect that exposure to violent video films may, in part, be an explanation'. Since there was little evidence that the boys had ever watched the film *Child's Play 3*, the debate became very contentious. It is answered in the following article.

▶ **Cumberbatch G. (1997) Media violence: sense and common sense.** *Psychology Review* **3(4): 2–7** In this article Cumberbatch reconsiders the link between media violence and behaviour, looking very critically at the research.

▶ **www.chelt.ac.uk/ess/st-helena/faq.htm** This website gives the background to the St Helena study and links to other websites that provide a list of relevant research references.

▶ **Gunter B. & McAleer J. (1997)** *Children and television.* **London: Routledge.** This provides an accessible summary of research investigating the effects of television on a range of children's behaviours.

It is common sense to note that ordinary people do not murder and maim simply because they watch a gruesome film. Most of us just chat about it to our friends. We will now explore how factors interact to enhance or inhibit the effects of media violence.

The effects of violent video games

Despite the fact that playing video games has been a popular entertainment for children and adolescents for a number of years, until recently it attracted little research. Video games differ in important ways from television. The player or players are actively engaged in the action and can change the course of events. and, unlike television, which is watched by all ages, video games are largely designed for the young.

In the 1980s few video games had a violent content but through the 1990s many games were introduced featuring destruction and killing and now violent games tend to dominate the market. Dietz (1998) sampled 33 popular games and found that nearly 80 per cent of them were violent in nature and, rather worryingly, over one-fifth of these portrayed violence towards women. It is unsurprising that concern has been expressed that they may encourage aggression, indeed their adverse effect could be greater than that of television because of the active involvement of the players. Of particular concern is the argument that some video games encourage racism and sexism by providing children with a world populated by the worst of such stereotypes (Provenzo, 1991).

Do video games increase aggression?

The argument as to the effects of playing violent video games on aggression is, like that of television, con-

Figure 13.2 Trigger or release

tentious, with some researchers arguing that it increases aggression while others (eg Griffiths, 2000) argue that the case is by no means proven. Emes (1997) has expressed the Freudian view that video game playing is cathartic and as such may be a useful means of coping with pent-up and aggressive energies.

A series of correlational studies looked at the relationship between measures of aggression (including self-reports, teacher ratings and peer reports) and video game playing habits. A positive correlation was found in three out of four of these studies (Dominick, 1984; Fling et al, 1992; Lin & Lepper, 1987). However, it is important to remember that aggressive youngsters may seek out violent games to play. This, coupled with the fact that there was no record made of whether the games played were violent or non-violent, means that we cannot conclude from these studies that playing the games was the cause of the aggression ratings.

Wiegman and van Schie (1998) argue that intense engagement with a violent game can increase aggressiveness. They reviewed 12 studies, all of which showed that playing violent video games is liable to increase aggression in the players. However, Griffiths (2000) points out

research now

do violent video games cause aggressive thoughts and behaviour?

Anderson C.A. & Dill K.E. (2000) Video games and aggressive thoughts, feelings, and behaviour in the laboratory and in life. *Journal of Personality and Social Psychology* **78(4): 772–790**

aims: the general aim was to investigate video game violence effects and broaden the understanding of media violence in general. Specifically, the aim was to begin laying down empirical evidence to test the GAAM formulation (discussed next in 'what's new?').

procedure: there were two studies which used different methods, a correlation and an experiment, chosen because these were considered to have strengths that complement each other and surmount each other's weaknesses.

Study 1: the correlation
The variables to be correlated were long-term exposure to video game violence and a set of other variables, the most important being aggressive behaviour and delinquency, both aggressive and non-aggressive.

There was a total of 227 participants, 78 males and 149 females, all psychology students.

Participants completed self-report questionnaires to measure:

● aggressive behaviour;

● delinquency;

● irritability and trait aggressiveness;

● the amount of time spent playing video games in general;

● the amount of time spent playing violent video games.

Study 2: the experiment
A pilot study was conducted to select two video games, one violent, one non-violent. The games selected were Wolfenstein 3D and Myst; this pair were chosen because they produced no difference in physiological measures, difficulty, enjoyment, frustration and action speed (however, Wolfenstein was rated more exciting than Myst). It was important to control for physiological arousal to avoid this becoming an extraneous variable.

Wolfenstein has a blatant violent content, realism and human characters. The human hero can choose from an array of weaponry; the goal is to kill Nazi guards and thereby advance through the levels to the ultimate goal of killing Hitler. Myst is an interactive adventure game designed to be non-violent. It is a fast-paced, thinking game in which players attempt to align geometric figures as they fall down a computer screen.

There was a total of 210 participants, 104 females and 106 males, all psychology undergraduates.

Participants were matched on high or low irritability, then divided by gender and each group was then given either violent or non-violent video games to play. The procedure was that each participant played the game three times, twice in the first session and once in a second session approximately a week later. In the first session, they completed an affective measure (how they felt), a world view measure and a cognitive measure (what they were thinking).

After playing the game for the third time, participants played a game in which they had the opportunity to give an opponent a blast of noise (no noise was actually administered). All games were arranged so that all participants won and lost the same number of contests. This noise level was used as a measure of aggression.

findings:
Study 1: There was a positive correlation between the amount of time spent playing violent video games and both aggressive personality and delinquent behaviour, both aggressive and non-aggressive.

Study 2: The participants who played a violent video game behaved more aggressively towards an opponent than did those who played a non-violent video game.

conclusion: in the short term playing a violent video game increases aggression, presumably by encouraging aggressive thoughts. The researchers suggest that longer term exposure might alter the person's basic personality structure, making them more likely to have aggressive thoughts and feelings and to behave aggressively. Because of the active nature of these games, this effect is probably stronger than that of watching violent television and films. Consumers and parents of consumers should be aware of these potential risks.

that there are at least 11 others that have not yielded the same results.

Several experimental studies have used a design in which children play either a non-violent or violent video game and are then assessed on aggressiveness. Many of these studies demonstrate that levels of aggression are significantly higher after playing the violent games than after playing the non-violent ones. However, there is a very important confounding variable not controlled in these studies. The games played were not matched on difficulty, enjoyment or excitement. As pointed out by Anderson and Dill (2000) and Bushman (1995), violent materials tend to be more exciting than non-violent materials, so the effects could have been the result of higher excitement levels induced by the violent games. Thus the crucial difference between these studies and that of Anderson and Dill is that the games used in the recent research have been matched on these key variables.

interactive angles

Imagine you are on the board of governors at your local primary school. You are concerned about the level of aggression children are displaying in the playground. You feel that this may be due to their exposure to violent media at home. Prepare a document for parents, which, backed up by evidence, presents them with an understanding of the role media influences can play in the observational learning of aggressive behaviour. If you can, try to set up a classroom debate in which the board of governors are confronted by angry parents who contest this view.

GAAM: General Affective Aggressive Model (Anderson & Dill, 2000)

This new model is designed to describe a multi-stage process by which aggressive personality and certain situational variables lead to aggressive behaviour. It integrates existing theories, such as Bandura's Social Learning Theory, and the data derived from the researchers' own studies (described previously in 'research now'). It explains the processes that are involved in both the short-term effects and the long-term effects of video game violence.

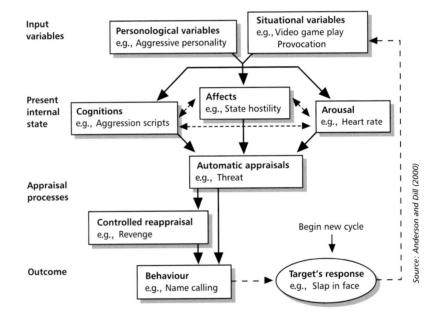

Figure 13.3 Single episode General Affective Aggression Model: short-term effects of video game violence

Source: Anderson and Dill (2000)

Short-term effects

As figure 13.3 illustrates, when people with an aggressive personality play a violent video game (especially one in which they experience frustration), this arouses feelings of anger within them, accompanied by biological arousal (such as increased heart rate) and aggressive thoughts, possibly involving revenge. The particular content of the game can influence the aggressive thoughts and behaviours that are shown. For example, being insulted may cause a person to think how to return the insult in a harmful way. More importantly as far as video game playing is concerned, playing a violent game increases the *accessibility* of aggressive thoughts.

Whether an aggressive response is made depends on the person's usual mode of responding. Well-learned behaviours (called, in this model, scripts) come to mind relatively easily and quickly and are expressed fairly automatically. People who score high on aggressive personality have a relatively well-developed and easily accessible array of aggression scripts that are easily activated by relatively minor provocation. What is more, aggressive people have cognitions (thoughts) that encourage violent reactions, such as thinking that there is more violence than there really is, and that the best way to solve problems is to use aggression.

In sum, playing a violent video game primes aggressive thoughts, including aggression scripts. The short-term effects of both an aggressive personality and playing a violent video game have the short-term effect of increasing aggressive responses.

Study 2 in Research Now was designed to test the short-term effects of violent video game playing and, by showing that participants who played a violent video game behaved more aggressively than those who played a non-violent game, it supported the GAAM model.

Long-term effects

The long-term effects of playing violent video games are illustrated in figure 13.4. This demonstrates that each time people play violent video games, it reinforces the following:

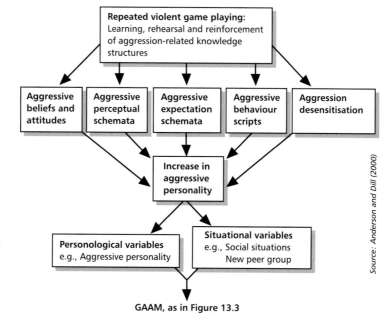

Figure 13.4 Multiple episode General Affective Aggression Model (GAAM): long-term effects of video game playing

Source: Anderson and Dill (2000)

- watchfulness for enemies;

- aggressive action against others;

- expectations that others will behave aggressively;

- positive attitudes towards the use of violence;

- beliefs that violent solutions are effective and appropriate.

In addition to this, repeated exposure to scenes of violence desensitises people to its consequences. Taken together over a long period of time these effects change the individual's personality. Habitual video game players can become more aggressive in outlook and behaviour than they were before the repeated exposure. As the person becomes more aggressive, their whole social environment changes. Their interactions with teachers, parents and non-aggressive peers worsen and they seek out more delinquent peers with whom to associate.

Study 1 in 'research now' was designed to test this part of the model and by demonstrating a positive correlation between a person's level of exposure to violent video games and their aggressive behaviour, it was supportive.

for and against

the media encouraging antisocial behaviour

+ correlational longitudinal studies show a consistent positive relationship between the amount of violent television watched and levels of aggression

+ laboratory and field experimental studies also show that watching violent television and films or playing violent video games can cause certain people to behave in an aggressive and antisocial manner

− correlations do not show that viewing media violence *causes* aggressive behaviour. People who are aggressive may seek out violent programmes to watch, or a third factor, such as a violent family, may be responsible for the connection

− the media are being used as a convenient scapegoat so that more deep-rooted problems in society can be absolved of blame

− psychodynamic theorists argue that viewing aggression may be *cathartic* and therefore reduce violent behaviour, not increase it

where to now?

The following are good sources of further information on the effects of violent video games:

▶ **Griffiths M. (1998) Violent video games: are they harmful?** *Psychology Review* 4(4).

▶ **Griffiths M. (1997) Video games and aggression.** *The Psychologist* 10(9).

▶ These two articles cover essentially the same material but the 1997 one is the original and much more detailed. For the purposes of A-level, the *Psychology Review* article is quite sufficient. Griffiths looks critically at empirical research into violent video games.

Criminal behaviour and the self-fulfilling prophecy

Self-fulfilling prophecy

For reasons that we have just explored, those discussed in chapter 12, and others, some individuals may be more likely to be assumed to be the perpetrators of crime. This expectation of others may act causally; once an individual has, or feels they have, the label of a criminal, they may alter their behaviour to fit with that expectation. This is an example of a *self-fulfilling prophecy*. Smith and Mackie (2000) define the self-fulfilling prophecy as 'The process by which one person's expectations about another become reality by eliciting behaviours that confirm the expectations' (page 94).

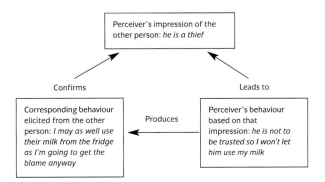

Figure 13.5 The self-fulfilling prophecy: we behave in the way people expect. How does a housemate's beliefs affect our behaviour?

Based on Smith & Mackie (2000), page 94

So, we would predict that when a person expects us to behave in a criminal or aggressive way, this would cause us to act in ways that confirm their expectations. This was the finding of Jahoda (1954) who studied delinquency rates among the Ashanti in Western Africa. The Ashanti people traditionally choose *kradin*, or 'soul names' for their male children according to the day of the week on which they were born. As they also believe that a boy's (but not a girl's) day of birth affects temperament; this has the potential to be self-fulfilling. Monday's boys (with *Kwadwo* as part of their name) are thought to be placid, whereas Wednesday's boys (with *Kwaku* in their name) are believed to be violent and aggressive. Jahoda's findings, that over a five-year period almost 22 per cent of violent offences recorded in court were committed by boys with 'Wednesday' names but 'Monday's boys' accounted for only 6.9 per cent, supported the idea that the boys 'lived up to their names'. Jahoda concluded that, rather than confirming the Ashanti superstition about day of birth dictating an individual's character, these results showed that it was the cultural expectation that selectively enhanced aspects of their development. Because the boys were aware both of the prophecy (the nature of children born on different days) and their own birth-day (indicated by their name) they were treated differently and grew up with particular beliefs about themselves, thus ensuring that their traits fulfilled expectations.

interactive angles

Do you know what day you were born on? British children may learn the rhyme:

> Monday's child is fair of face;
> Tuesday's child is full of grace.
> Wednesday's child is full of woe;
> Thursday's child has far to go.
> Friday's child is loving and giving;
> Saturday's child works hard for his living,
> But the child that is born on the Sabbath day
> is bonny and blithe and good and gay.

Unlike those in Western Africa, children growing up in Britain are unlikely to fulfil the prophecy of this verse. Suggest two reasons why not.

In another investigation supporting self-fulfilling prophecies, Levy and Hartocollis (1976) looked at the incidence of violence in two psychiatric units. One unit was staffed by a typical, mixed, female and male staff, the other had an all-female staff. When compared over a year, the unit staffed only by women had no incidents of violence at all, in contrast to the mixed staff unit, which had 13 violent incidents. Levy and Hartocollis concluded that '... the expectation of violence among psychiatric patients and the consequent use of male nursing aides to control violence may represent a self-fulfilling prophecy' (page 429).

Conclusions

Serious antisocial aggression is determined by multiple factors. Obviously the relationship between media violence and aggression is a complex one and the answer to the question 'Does media violence cause increased aggression and crime?' is 'it depends ...'. It depends on a great many things. It depends on the individuals who are watching the programme, the family life they have, the society in which they live. It depends on who they watch it with and on the exact content. It depends on how much other media violence they are exposed to and on the expectations of others. Concerns over the amount of violence seen by children have justification. The American Psychological Association Commission on Violence and Youth reported in 1993 that 'There is absolutely no doubt that higher levels of viewing violence on television are correlated with increased acceptance of aggressive attitudes and increased aggressive behaviour.' However, we still cannot dismiss the idea that a violent society, or norms within subcultures, are responsible both for the enjoyment of violent films and games and for increased antisocial behaviour. Perhaps, as the researchers from the St Helena project comment (Charlton et al, 2000), we need to look more closely at the way in which society is structured and the support systems it provides before we lay the entire blame for antisocial and criminal behaviour at the feet of the media.

what do you know ?

1 Evaluate **four** ways in which the influence of the media on aggressive behaviour has been investigated.

2 Describe and evaluate **one** study that shows how children may imitate what they see in films.

3 'Blaming the media for criminal and antisocial behaviour is simply a way of shifting the blame from the family and society'. With reference to psychological research, discuss this point of view.

4 What factors may mediate the effects of media violence?

5 Discuss how the self-fulfilling prophecy may account for some instances of criminal behaviour.

14 Preventing crime and treating criminals

what's ahead?

The criminal justice system can use punishments to deter individuals from re-offending and, while many offenders are imprisoned or fined, some will experience treatment programmes that aim to improve their behaviour and reduce the chances of them reoffending. Behaviour modification, social skills training and anger management are the programmes we will describe and evaluate in this chapter. Outside the prison service, there are many people and agencies working to reduce or prevent crime. The crime rate in New York in the 1980s was escalating at such a rate that the extreme policy of 'zero tolerance' was adopted. We will explore whether this policy of clamping down on petty crime is successful.

Therapies used for treatment of offenders

Behaviour modification

The principles of learning have not only been used in the laboratory but have also been applied in many real-life settings, such as classrooms, mental hospitals and prisons. The use of operant conditioning in such real-world settings is called *behaviour modification*.

Many behaviour modification programmes rely on a technique called the *token economy*, in which desirable behaviour, such as co-operation and compliance, is reinforced by the use of tokens. These tokens have no intrinsic value but can be exchanged for primary reinforcers. When used in prisons, most of the programmes also involve the use of negative reinforcement (the removal of something unpleasant) and punishment (the implementation of something unpleasant) in order to reduce undesirable behaviour such as non-compliance and aggression. Tokens may be exchanged for privileges, such as watching television or going into the exercise yard, while a typical punishment would be isolation.

Token economy programmes tend to have a direct, short-term effect on specific behaviours. For example, Hobbs and Holt (1976) recorded the effects of introducing a token economy to young delinquents across three small institutional units while the fourth unit acted as a control. Tokens were given for behaviours such as obeying rules, doing chores properly, co-operative social interactions and appropriate behaviour when queuing for meals. Extra positive reinforcers such as soft drinks, sweets, leisure activities, cigarettes and passes home were also used. The programme showed a significant increase in the targeted behaviours compared to the group not involved in the programme. Other studies show that token reinforcement also works with adult prisoners (Ayllon & Millan, 1979). However, Ross and Mackay (1976) reported a deterioration in behaviour when such a programme was used with delinquent girls, but such results are unusual.

Although these programmes are popular, especially in the US, not many of them have been evaluated in terms of the conduct of the offenders after release. Moyes et al (1985) reported limited success with hospitalised behaviourally disordered males and females with a criminal history. After a year they had had fewer contacts with the police than a control group of similar patients, but after two years there was no difference. One long-term follow-up failed to find any benefit at all from the token economy programme (Rice et al, 1990).

Perhaps the most important concern with behaviour modification is its potential for violation of civil rights. Many programmes rely heavily on negative reinforcement (such as the removal of privileges until the offender complies) rather than positive ones, with little or no emphasis on new skills. There are ethical objections to prisoners having to 'earn' basic rights, such as recreation time, food or drink, by behaving compliantly, particularly as these are some of the most effective reinforcers.

Opinion on the use of behaviour modification is sharply divided. Some researchers argue that offenders need to feel responsible for their treatment, not have it imposed on them. Others maintain that such programmes make the whole prison environment more bearable and humane for all concerned; after all, the behaviours that are targeted for reduction are those that hurt others and make life unpleasant in the institution.

for and against

the use of token economies with offenders

+ it is successful in changing specific behaviours under controlled conditions

+ it requires little training and can be done by paraprofessionals

+ it is economical

+ it quickly controls unmanageable behaviour

+ it can be easily evaluated and researched

− it requires a high degree of commitment from everyone who is evenly remotely involved in the programme

− although relatively simple to operate in controlled conditions, it is extremely difficult in an actual prison. There are many other sources of reinforcement and punishment, such as approval of other prisoners or threats by them

− its effects have not convincingly been shown to generalise from institutions to life in the real world, nor to have long-term effects

− having to 'earn' basic needs may be seen as an infringement of human rights

Social skills training

Social skills are those skills, such as making eye contact, standing a certain distance from someone and turn-taking during conversation, which make social interactions run smoothly. We learn them as children and take them for granted as adults. If we do not have these skills or if we use them clumsily, we make others and ourselves feel extremely uncomfortable, as anyone who has tried to have a conversation with an individual who makes no eye contact or stands too close is well aware. Many offenders are believed to be lacking in these skills and social skills training is a technique aimed at improving competence in social interactions. The programmes assume that being deficient in these skills is associated with offending and that acquiring such skills will reduce rates of reoffending. Neither of these assumptions has gone unchallenged.

Social skills training (SST) is one of a number of cognitive-behavioural programmes, which are all based on the principle that attitudes and thoughts (cognitions) affect behaviour. There is a variety of SST programmes, all of which have certain common elements. Clients are first taught the skills by a combination of modelling, instruc-tion, role play and rehearsal. They then attempt to re-enact these skills themselves in various arranged situations and receive feedback on their performance, the emphasis being on the use of social reinforcement such as praise. They are also given homework assignments, which aim to help them practise and consolidate the skills they have learned in various situations, including real-life ones for those who are not incarcerated.

Some programmes start by teaching certain non-verbal skills, known as *micro-skills*, such as eye contact, gesture and posture, and then move on to all-round skills such as how to maintain a good conversation, how to interact with members of the opposite sex or how to negotiate (eg Hollin et al, 1986). The type of situation that might be practised is how to enter a room full of strangers, how to return faulty goods to a shop, how to politely decline getting involved in a drinking binge when you've already had enough, and how to say what you want to say without being embarrassed and 'tongue-tied'.

Results of SST

Feedback from social skills training programmes is mixed. Goldstein (1986) reviewed 30 studies of SST used with aggressive or delinquent teenagers and found that various skills such as the use of appropriate eye contact and how to negotiate with a probation officer had been learned. However, Goldstein et al (1989) found that only 15–20 per cent of trainees could use the skills they had learned during training in a more real-life situation. These researchers did, however, manage to increase this to 50 per cent by providing additional teaching.

Some other programmes report improved self-esteem and a feeling of greater control over life (a shift to a more internal locus of control) (Spence & Marziller, 1981). However, in this programme, individuals in a control group who received no training but spent an equal amount of time discussing their problems showed an equivalent improvement in self-esteem, so perhaps attention alone is the key to improvement. With respect to locus of control, Hollin et al (1986) found no change in individuals to whom they gave SST.

Rates of recidivism (reoffending) are a longer term measure of effectiveness of SST. When the conviction records of individuals in the Spence and Marziller programme were examined six months later, the SST group appeared to have benefited, but when asked about offending this group reported having committed more offences. There is evidence that both the appearance of a suspect and their general demeanour (bearing and expression), including the amount of respect shown, can affect whether an adolescent is detained by the police for questioning (Piliavin & Briar, 1964). In this case, it may be that the lads trained in SST were better at talking to the police and therefore less likely to be arrested.

There have been very few studies that have investigated the effects of SST on recidivism. Hollin (1990) has made two important points in this respect. First, there simply is no research to show whether or not lack of social skills is associated with offending and, secondly, in some SST programmes, there has been no evidence that the participants who received it were actually lacking in the skills in the first place.

It seems reasonable to conclude that short-term changes in social behaviour can be achieved with SST, but it has yet to be shown that they are either long-lasting or that they can be generalised to real-life situations. As Blackburn (1993) suggests, it may be a useful programme for offenders who have very serious social difficulties, but 'the available evidence does not warrant the routine use of SST in correctional settings' (page 357). Hollin (1990) also comments that SST alone is unlikely to be a cure for crime but it can be a powerful means of personal change.

Anger management

Anger management programmes are based on the idea that anger is a primary cause of violent criminal acts and once offenders can learn to control this anger, bad behaviour in prisons will decrease, as will rates of recidivism. Anger management is a cognitive-behavioural approach (see also pages 28–34), which originated in North America in the mid-1970s. Its aim was to teach individuals how to apply self-control in order to reduce interpersonal anger (Towl, 1993, 1995), with the long-term goal of reducing disruptive behaviour (Law, 1997). Holbrook (1997) used anger management successfully with a group of prison inmates. The male inmates selected for the programme had a history of reactive aggression so were considered to be the most likely to benefit. Following the intervention, they showed a reduction in scores on a measure of vengeance, that is, the tendency to take revenge.

There is a variety of such programmes that are run in many prisons as well as in other settings. One anger management programme used in Britain is outlined below.

Results of anger management programmes

With the increasing use of anger control programmes in prisons, it is crucial to determine their effectiveness. Studies of effectiveness are few, and the results range from very limited to substantial. On the negative side, Law (1997) reported that only one individual who completed

what's
new?

the National Anger Management Package

Keen (2000) provides an example of the preparation and delivery of an anger management course within a young offender institution, conducted with young male offenders aged between 17 and 21 years. The programme, first devised in 1992 and updated in 1995, was developed by the Prison Service in England and Wales and is known as the National Anger Management Package (Prison Service, 1995).

The aims of the course are as follows:

- to increase course members' awareness of the process by which they become angry
- to raise course members' awareness of the need to monitor their behaviour
- to educate course members in the benefits of controlling their anger
- to improve techniques of anger management
- to allow course members to practise anger management during role plays

The course involves eight two-hour sessions, the first seven over a 2–3 week period, with the last session a month afterwards. The details of the course are as follows (for more details see Towl & Crighton, 1996).

Keen's experiences of using the course are generally positive, though there are various predictable problems with young incarcerated males, such as failure to bring the anger diary to sessions, grins and sniggers at the mention of 'bodily arousal' and a certain degree of egocentrism which can make relationships and progress in the group a little difficult at times. Overall, though, the feedback from the individuals completing the course indicates that they have increased their awareness of their anger management difficulties and have increased their capacity to exercise self-control.

an eight-session course showed any improvement. In contrast, Hunter (1993) reported considerable improvements in certain specific areas, such as a reduction in impulsiveness, depression and interpersonal problems. The effectiveness of programmes in producing these short-term benefits is shown in 'research now'.

research
now

do anger management courses work?

Ireland J. (2000) Do anger management courses work? *Forensic Updates* 63: 12–16

aim: to assess the effectiveness of a brief group-based anger-management programme with a sample of male young offenders.

procedure: a quasi-experimental design was used in which there were two comparisons made:

- pre- and post-programme scores for a 'treatment' (experimental) group
- two scores taken at the same interval for the 'awaiting treatment' (control) group.

The design: this is a quasi-experimental design because the two groups are not equivalent. In real-world research it is not possible to randomly assign individuals to each group. It would have been possible to carry out research using the experimental group only, comparing pre- and post-programme scores but the control group gives the design extra experimental rigour.

The participants: the experimental group consisted of 50 prisoners who had completed the anger management course. The control group consisted of 37 prisoners who had been assessed as suitable for the course but had not yet completed it. The two groups did not differ significantly in terms of age, offence and level of angry behaviours reported prior to completing the course.

The programme: the anger management used in this study was an adapted version of the national package which was developed in the UK by Clark (1988). It includes 12 one-hour sessions run over a three-day period.

Measures used to assess prisoners on suitability for the course: there were two measures:

1   A cognitive-behavioural interview. This consisted of various questions concerned with how often they lost their temper, what provoked this temper loss and what happened when it occurred.

2   Wing Behavioural Checklist (WBC) – a checklist completed by prison officers concerning 29 different angry behaviours with scores of 0, 1 or 2 for how often any particular prisoner had shown them in the previous week.

3   A third measure, the Anger Management Assessment questionnaire (AMA), which was a self-report questionnaire completed by the prisoners, consisted of 53 items which could indicate an anger problem.

All prisoners in the study had been deemed suitable for the course on the basis of these measures.

Pre- and post-test measures: Pre-test scores were obtained for both groups of participants two weeks before the start of the course and eight weeks later (after course completion for the experimental group and while the control group remained on the waiting list).

findings:

Wing-based measures: there was a significant reduction in wing-based angry behaviours in the experimental group but no difference in the control group.

AMA: the experimental group scored significantly lower on self-reported angry behaviours after completion of the course. There was no difference for the control group.

Overall, 92 per cent of the prisoners in the experimental group showed improvement on at least one measure; 48 per cent showed improvement on both the AMA and WBC; 8 per cent showed a deterioration on both measures after completing the course.

conclusion: short-term measures indicate that this programme was a success and significantly reduced the disruptive behaviour of these offenders in the prison. Future research could usefully be directed at assessing the characteristics of the 8 per cent who showed no improvement. There is also a need for future research aimed at long-term evaluation of such interventions.

Evaluation of anger management programmes

The effectiveness of anger management programmes to reduce recidivism in violent offenders is called into question by several researchers. Although it may seem common sense to propose that anger is a serious problem among those convicted of violent crimes such as assault, researchers disagree about whether there is a link between anger and violent crime. For example, while Zamble and Quinsey (1997) argue in favour of such a relationship and propose that uncontrolled anger is a risk factor in predicting violence and recidivism, others dispute it (eg Muirhead, 1997).

Prominent among those who do not believe that anger is a primary cause of violent criminal acts are Loza and Loza-Fanous (1999). They argue that many of the research findings linking anger with violence and rape were based on laboratory studies using students (eg Zillman, 1993) or offenders' own explanations of their violent acts (Zamble & Quinsey, 1997). In fact they maintain that:

> Unfortunately, most of the opinions supporting a link between anger and violent behaviour, rape, or recidivism are based on speculations with very little empirical support such as results of valid and reliable psychometrics (page 492)

They studied 271 Canadian male offenders, comparing a group of violent offenders with non-violent ones and a group of rapists with non-rapists. Violent offenders were those who had committed crimes such as murder, assault and robbery with violence. The non-violent offenders had a history of moderate or minor offences such as fraud or property offences. Using several psychometric measures of anger, they found no difference between violent offenders and non-violent offenders and between rapists and non-rapists on anger measures. Loza and Loza-Fanous argue that not only are anger treatment programmes ineffective with violent offenders, they have the potential to be harmful by encouraging the offender to attribute his violent actions to anger for which he cannot be blamed, rather than taking full responsibility for his actions.

Anger management programmes have, as we have seen, proved to be useful in controlling aggressive antisocial behaviour in prisons, but there needs to more research into the relationship between anger and crime before an assessment of its use and effectiveness in reducing rates of recidivism among violent criminals can be made.

for and against

anger management as an effective treatment for criminal behaviour

+ some research shows that these programmes are an effective means of reducing antisocial behaviour in prisons

+ the programmes may provide criminals with greater insight into the causes of their behaviour and offer alternative ways of responding to provocation

– some researchers argue that there is no link between anger and violent crime, which is often done in a cold, calculated manner

– there is a lack of research into whether or not these programmes have any long-term benefits in preventing recidivism

where to now?

The following is a useful source of further information regarding anger management courses:

▶ **Loza W. & Loza-Fanous A. (1999) The fallacy of reducing rape and violent recidivism by treating anger. *International Journal of Offender Therapy and Comparative Criminology* 43(4): 492–502.** This gives an interesting evaluation of anger management courses which is complementary to the 'research now' article, allowing you to appreciate two very different angles on the use of such courses.

Zero tolerance

One method by which crime has been tackled is the use of a policy known as zero tolerance. *Zero tolerance* policing has its roots in an approach nicknamed 'broken windows', developed by Kelling and Wilson in 1982. They argued that if one broken window was not repaired in a building, then others would be broken and the building vandalised, followed by other buildings, then the street and the neighbourhood. The area would soon go into rapid decay and act as a breeding ground for serious crime such as drug dealing and prostitution. This would lead to a downward spiral in which respectable law-abiding citizens would leave the area and crime rates would escalate. An unrepaired window is a sign that no one cares and therefore more damage will occur.

The original idea behind 'broken windows' was that there should be more police 'on the beat', who negotiated acceptable public behaviour and worked with the neighbourhood to maintain a decent standard of behaviour. However, since it was first proposed, zero tolerance policing has become a much more punitive policy, based on cracking down on minor offences such as offensive language, loitering and begging, in the belief that this will help reduce more serious crimes as well.

The term 'zero tolerance' was consequently applied to other areas of public policy, some of which were concerned not so much with policing as with changing attitudes. One such policy was a campaign against domestic violence, sexual assault and child abuse in various countries including Britain.

We will take a look at two programmes based on zero tolerance: the first one is a campaign in New York to reduce the very high crime rates by a severe clampdown on all crime; the second is a community-based project designed to prevent violence against women.

Zero tolerance of street crime in New York

The argument in favour

By the late 1980s and early 1990s, New York had the unenviable reputation of being one of the most crime-ridden cities in the world. William Bratton, who eventually became Police Commissioner of the City of New York, describes his experience in arriving in New York in 1990:

> I remember driving from LaGuardia Airport down the highway into Manhattan. Graffiti, burned out cars and trash seemed to be everywhere. It looked like something out of a futuristic movie. Then as you entered Manhattan, you met the unofficial greeter for the City of New York, the Squeegee pest.

Welcome to New York City. This guy had a dirty rag or squeegee and would wash your window with some dirty liquid and ask for or demand money. Proceeding down Fifth Avenue, the mile of designer stores and famous buildings, unlicensed street peddlers and beggars everywhere. Then down into the subway where every day over 200,000 fare evaders jumped over or under turnstiles while shakedown artists vandalised turnstiles and demanded that paying passengers hand over their tokens to them. Beggars were on every train. Every platform seemed to have a cardboard city where the homeless had taken up residence. This was a city that had stopped caring about itself ... The City had lost control. (pages 33–4)

Once Bratton had taken up his position in 1994, the problems were tackled on many fronts. Seven thousand extra police officers had been employed since 1990 and a programme of clear-cut goals and priorities was begun. In addition to serious crime, particular attention was to be paid to actions that interfered with quality of life (such as public drinking), graffiti and other minor street crime. Crime hotspots were to be identified to which patrol officers, detectives and narcotics officers were assigned. Twice-weekly meetings were held at which the Department's top executives were called to account for the previous month's crime statistics and asked about plans for the following month.

In three years the city's crime rate dropped by 37 per cent and the homicide rate by over 50 per cent. In answer to critics who suggested that crime rates were somehow massaged, Bratton responded by pointing particularly to

Figure 14.1 Problems in New York City

the figures for homicide, which is a crime that cannot easily be covered up or over-reported. He believes that this approach, involving decentralisation and coordination, is a successful way of policing, as borne out not only by the crime statistics but also by the fact that New Yorkers now feel safer and the city is slowly revitalising itself. Long-term problems still exist but the foundations for dealing with them have been firmly laid.

The argument against: short-term fix, long-term liability?

Pollard (1998), Chief Constable of Thames Valley Police, urges caution in the use of the policy of zero tolerance. He argues that the crime reduction in New York is not necessarily a direct result of this policy, since crime has fallen elsewhere in America, including cities such as San Diego in which the approach is very different. The success in New York, he maintains, may be due in no small part to an extra 7000 police officers (a huge increase), greater accountability and an enormous pressure to reduce crime such that the rates would have fallen regardless of the particular policy adopted.

Pollard describes zero tolerance as being aggressive, uncompromising law enforcement based on ruthlessness in cracking down on low-level crime and disorderliness, including acts that are not, strictly speaking, criminal, such as drinking but not being drunk, and vagrancy that involves lying on the edge of a pavement but not blocking pedestrian access. More worryingly, it may involve the harassment of the mentally disturbed who are doing nothing other than causing discomfort in others by their strange behaviour. It is interesting to note that while Pollard describes zero tolerance as based on heavyhanded aggressive tactics, Dennis (1998) describes it as 'humane, good-natured control'.

While not disagreeing at all with the philosophy behind the 'broken windows' approach, Pollard argues that this theory was based on a solution to crime that includes a wide variety of tactics, with the police working in close cooperation with other social agencies, rather than a quick, uncompromising response to petty crime and disorder. Without this the policy creates an atmosphere of distrust between the police and public, which destroys any opportunity for future effective policing. 'Going in heavy' provides a short-term fix at the expense of a long-term solution and can become positively counterproductive. As Pollard says, once this policy has been operational for some time:

It may then be too late. Firstly, the police will have lost touch with the community. Confidence will have drained away. Tensions will have risen. It will then need only a spark to ignite serious disorder, as happened in Los Angeles following the Rodney King case. We know about these in England too. They happened in our own inner cities in the 1980s, and we have learned hard lessons of our own. (pages 55–6)

Pollard points out that decay and disorderliness in a neighbourhood have many causes and these need to be tackled in a planned way, not just by papering over the cracks. This can only be done if the police work in close cooperation with many other agencies, such as with the refuse collection service so that the area is tidy, with the education and youth departments, with social services and with the probation department. In this way it is not just the physical environment that is attended to but other problems as well such as the lack of amenities for the young, design of buildings that encourage crime (see chapter 25) and the failure of public services. Such a policy tackles the root causes of crime and disorder rather than offering a superficial solution.

It is very difficult to make objective judgements on the success of any policy because each era and area is different. Comparisons between America and Britain are especially difficult not least because of the gun culture in the US, which does not exist in Britain. With respect to New York, this is a unique city – Pollard himself acknowledges that Bratton was faced with a crisis that required drastic action and that he should be congratulated on his success. He does, however, urge great caution in assuming that a policy of zero tolerance would necessarily be the best policy elsewhere.

The use of zero tolerance policies in other domains has also proved problematic. Skiba and Peterson (2000) found that despite the increased use of zero tolerance procedures in schools, there was little evidence that this had improved school safety or student behaviour. They suggest that this is because a zero tolerance policy alone cannot teach students to solve inter- or intra-personal problems without resorting to disruptive behaviours. Similarly, Lennings (2000) reviewed studies investigating the therapeutic use of zero tolerance regimes with intravenous drug users. Success was measured in several ways including changes in drug use, drug-related crime and morbidity, but concluded that there was little significant evidence for the effectiveness of the policy.

research
now

zero tolerance and crash rates in US teenagers

**Ulmer R.G., Preusser D.F., Williams A.F., Ferguson S.A. & Farmer C.M. (2000) Effect of Florida's gradu-
ated licensing program on the crash rate of teenage drivers.** *Accident Analysis and Prevention* **32(4):
527–32**

aim: to assess the effectiveness of a zero tolerance approach to drink-driving and various other traffic restrictions
on young adolescents in Florida.

procedure: the state of Florida introduced new laws regulating young drivers including:

- for the first three months holders of learner's licences were not allowed to drive between 1900–0600h;
  thereafter they could drive until 2200h;
- all drivers under 18 years had strict limits on the number of traffic violations they could accumulate;
- all drivers under 21 years were subject to a zero tolerance law for drinking and driving.

findings: in Florida there was a 9 per cent reduction in fatal injuries and non-fatal injuries during 1997, the first
year of the zero tolerance approach. There was an age related pattern to the results. Fifteen year olds showed the
greatest reduction followed by 16 year olds and then 17 year olds. There were no reductions among teenagers in
Alabama, a neighbouring state that did not implement a zero tolerance policy, nor in 18 year olds in Florida.

conclusion: the strategy appeared to be effective in reducing crashes, especially in younger drivers. However, the
effect was not particularly great and did not extend to all age groups for whom the zero tolerance approach
applied.

Zero tolerance applied to violence against women

The first UK project based on zero tolerance was
launched by Edinburgh City Council in November 1992
and run by the Zero Tolerance Charitable Trust (ZTCT).
This ongoing campaign aims to highlight the prevalence
and nature of male violence towards women and to challenge some of the attitudes that made it appear
acceptable.

The need to change attitudes was revealed in research
undertaken by the Trust. They interviewed over 2000
young people aged between 14 and 21 years in Glasgow,
Fife and Manchester. The results were quite shocking.
Half of the boys and a third of the girls thought there
were some circumstances in which it was acceptable to
hit a woman or force her to have sex. Over a third of boys

(36 per cent) thought they might use violence in future
relationships and both boys and girls thought that forced
sex was more acceptable than hitting. Over half of the
young people interviewed knew someone who had been
hit by a male partner and exactly half knew someone who
had been sexually abused (Burton et al, 1998). Group discussions revealed that although hitting women was
considered 'unmanly' and 'cowardly', it was seen as OK
to hit your wife if she nagged; one young man commented
that, 'Some women just need a slap to the jaw and put
into the bedroom to calm down'. It is interesting to note
that the young people who took part in these focus group
discussions welcomed the opportunity to express their
opinions and discuss issues in depth, rather than simply
being told that certain types of behaviour are wrong.

The Trust tackles the problem of male violence to women
on many fronts. It lobbies the Government, commissions

research and develops educational intervention and training programmes. It has initiated a three-year advertising campaign to raise awareness and change attitudes, including a series of television advertisements, which began in December 2000. It also provides quality practical support for abused women and children.

One such programme targeted at school children and started in January 2001 is known as Respect. It involves the development of primary and secondary curriculum materials, support materials for teachers and youth workers and a publicity campaign involving school posters and bus side advertising. The idea is to prevent violence before it happens. It encourages boys and girls to develop healthy relationships based on equality and mutual respect, and emphasises that violence against women is unacceptable in any context and should not be tolerated.

At present it is too early to evaluate the effect of Respect, but it appears to be a very necessary and positive step on the road both to educating youngsters and to encouraging a healthier, more positive and happy attitude not only to women but also to relationships in general.

where to now?

The following are good sources of further information on zero tolerance:

▶ **Dennis N. (ed) (1998) *Zero tolerance. Policing a free society* (2nd edn), IEA Health and Welfare Unit. Lancing: Hartington Fine Arts Ltd.** A series of papers written by various members of the criminal justice system and academic departments on both sides of the Atlantic, though mainly in Britain. It contains classic papers by Dennis and Bratton and a useful editorial discussing the principal issues surrounding zero tolerance.

▶ **www.cabinet-office.gov.uk/womens-unit/fear** A Home Office site that looks at zero tolerance projects concerned with violence towards women across the country.

▶ **www.zerotolerance.org.uk/splash.htm** The website address of the Zero Tolerance Charitable Trust and provides details of their various projects.

The Zero Tolerance Charitable Trust is at 25 Rutland Street, Edinburgh, EH1 2AE and will provide full reports of its work.

Conclusions

Neither the treatment of offenders nor the prevention of crime is easy to achieve. Programmes designed to treat offenders in prisons, such as behaviour modification, social skills training and anger management are difficult to assess in terms of effectiveness and have met with variable success. This is hardly surprising given the wide range of prison management systems, types of programme and personnel responsible for the implementation of them, and the enormous variety of offenders and offences.

There have been many attempts to tackle crime by changing the type of environment that is believed to harbour it. The policy of zero tolerance adopted in New York was considered by many to be a successful and a necessary, if somewhat drastic, answer to a crisis. It may not, however, necessarily generalise to other environments and cultures.

what do you know?

1 (a) Describe and evaluate **two** techniques used to control aggression.

(b) Explain the psychological principles behind these techniques.

2 (a) What is meant by 'zero tolerance'?

(b) Describe and evaluate evidence that suggests zero tolerance is

(i) effective in controlling crime;

(ii) ineffective in controlling crime.

3 'Within the school there is a zero tolerance drug policy and an emphasis on information, with peer groups used. Vulnerable students are targeted and introduced to such sports as canoeing as well as other activities.' Source: *Teachers*, January 2003

Use evidence to evaluate the effectiveness of zero tolerance policies such as the one described above.

Individual differences in sporting behaviour

what's ahead?

The purpose of this chapter is to discuss the concept of individual differences in human behaviour, and the ways in which these can be explained, measured and related to sporting behaviour. Two approaches to individual differences have been particularly influential in sports psychology. *Trait theories* suggest that we can think of individual differences as a set of stable personality characteristics (traits), each of which is formed by an interaction of genetic and environmental influences. There has been a large body of research into the extent to which particular personality traits are associated with participation in sport, choice of sport and sporting success. The role of social development in sporting behaviour has also been investigated. *Social learning theory* is discussed in detail, and the influence of social factors, including family, gender and culture, are considered. Finally, we discuss whether sport has a positive or negative influence on children's social development.

Trait theories of personality

The term *personality* refers to those aspects of human nature that vary from one person to another – in other words what each of us is like as an individual. It is difficult to be more precise than this in a definition because each theoretical approach sees personality as something slightly different (Engler, 1999). When we talk about someone as a particularly lively or anxious person we are looking at them in terms of their personality characteristics or traits and thus adopting a *trait* approach.

Traits are stable and measurable personality characteristics. Trait theorists are interested in how many traits we need to explain human personality, the measurement of these traits, and the relative importance of genes and environment in the development of each personality trait. As compared to other models of personality, trait theorists place considerable emphasis on the role of genes as well as environment in our individual differences. Genes can affect our personalities by influencing the physical characteristics of the nervous system so that we all have slightly different nervous systems, which thus respond differently to our environment. We might, for example, have a nervous system that requires a lot of stimulation before we can experience excitement. This might predispose us to seek out the social stimulation of a team sport or the physiological arousal of a high-risk sport. Trait theorists measure personality by means of *self-rating inventories*, personality tests in which the respondent receives a set of questions or statements and chooses a response, for example, ticking yes/no to a question or choosing one of several statements that best

describes them. Each trait theory of personality has its own self-rating inventory to measure the traits identified by the theory.

Eysenck's theory

Hans Eysenck (1952) suggested that personality can be understood by just two 'supertraits'. The first of these is *extroversion*, which describes the extent to which someone is lively, sociable and impulsive (an extrovert), or alternatively quiet and solitary (an introvert). The second trait is *neuroticism*, which describes the extent to which someone is emotionally stable and unflappable (a stable person), or emotionally unstable, moody and flappable (a neurotic). By looking at someone's extroversion and neuroticism we can classify them as one of four personality types or *temperaments*. These are shown in figure 15.1.

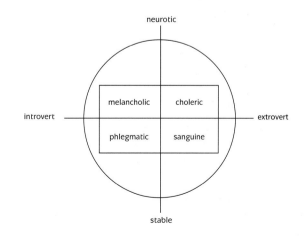

Figure 15.1 Eysenck's four personality types

Melancholic individuals are highly introverted and neurotic. This combination makes them unsociable, pessimistic and anxious. Cholerics are extrovert and neurotic, leading them to be touchy, restless and changeable. Phlegmatic individuals are introvert and emotionally stable, and are thus careful, thoughtful and calm, whereas those classified as sanguine are stable and extroverted. They are the most carefree, lively and easy-going people.

The biological basis of personality

Eysenck (1967) suggested that both extroversion and neuroticism can be explained in terms of individual differences in the nervous system. According to Eysenck we all feel comfortable with around the same level of physiological arousal, however, the amount of stimulation needed to achieve this level differs according to how strongly our nervous system responds to the environment. Introverts are characterised by an easily excitable *reticular activating system (RAS)*, an area of the brain responsible for control of its level of arousal in order to allow sleeping and wakefulness; hence to achieve their comfortable level of arousal they seek out situations where there is relatively little stimulation. Extroverts, on the other hand, are characterised by a less excitable RAS, hence they require more stimulation to achieve a comfortable level of arousal. This leads extroverts to be more lively and sociable in their behaviour. Neuroticism can be explained in terms of how strongly the nervous system (in particularly an area of the brain called the *limbic system*) responds to stress. People high in neuroticism are those who respond particularly strongly to stress because of their highly reactive limbic system.

Measuring personality

Eysenck developed a self-rating inventory, the EPI (Eysenck Personality Inventory), in order to measure extroversion and neuroticism. According to their responses to the items on the EPI, people are given two scores between 0 and 24, their E-score representing their extroversion and their N-score representing their neuroticism. The first four items from the EPI are shown in table 15.1. Questions 1 and 3 make up part of the E-scale and 2

and 4 are from the N-scale. Answering 'yes' to 1 and 3 would give you points on your E-score, and answers in the affirmative to 2 and 4 would gain points on the N-score.

In his later work, Eysenck (1975) added an additional 'supertrait', which he called *psychoticism*. Those studying clinical or abnormal psychology should be aware that this term is not synonymous with the clinical term 'psychotic', but contains elements of clinical psychosis and psychopathy. Someone high in psychoticism is distinguished by their tough-mindedness and detachment from reality. To be tough-minded means to be cold, antisocial, lacking in empathy and impulsive. According to Eysenck, those high in psychoticism also find it hard to distinguish fact from fantasy and lose contact with reality. Recent versions of Eysenck's self-rating inventory, now called the EPQ (Eysenck Personality Questionnaire), incorporate a third subscale to measure psychoticism.

Cattell's theory

Like Eysenck, Raymond Cattell was interested in identifying the underlying aspects of personality that can explain individual differences in behaviour. However, he disagreed that personality can be reduced to two or three 'supertraits,' instead proposing 16 fundamental aspects of personality.

Surface and source traits

Cattell (1965) made the important distinction between surface traits and source traits. *Surface traits* are observable aspects of people's behaviour, for example, honesty. Cattell noted that these surface traits tend to cluster in the same people; thus people high in honesty are usually also highly disciplined and thoughtful. He suggested that because these surface traits tend to be present in the same individuals, they may be result of a single underlying *source trait*. In this example the source trait was identified

Table 15.1 Items from the EPI

	Yes	No
1. Do you often long for excitement?	[ ]	[ ]
2. Do you often need understanding friends to cheer you up?	[ ]	[ ]
3. Are you usually carefree?	[ ]	[ ]
4. Do you find it very hard to take no for an answer?	[ ]	[ ]

Table 15.2 Cattell's 16 source traits

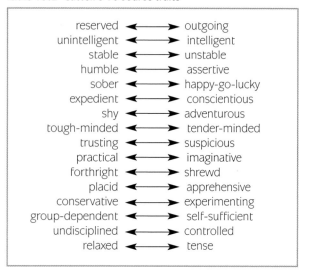

reserved	⟷	outgoing
unintelligent	⟷	intelligent
stable	⟷	unstable
humble	⟷	assertive
sober	⟷	happy-go-lucky
expedient	⟷	conscientious
shy	⟷	adventurous
tough-minded	⟷	tender-minded
trusting	⟷	suspicious
practical	⟷	imaginative
forthright	⟷	shrewd
placid	⟷	apprehensive
conservative	⟷	experimenting
group-dependent	⟷	self-sufficient
undisciplined	⟷	controlled
relaxed	⟷	tense

as *ego strength*, the spectrum between being controlled and undisciplined. Cattell proposed 16 of these source traits. These are shown in table 15.2.

Measuring personality

Cattell (1965) produced a self-rating inventory to assess people on each of the 16 source traits. This personality test is known as the 16PF (standing for 16 personality factors). The original 16PF asked 160 questions, 10 of which assess each source trait. There have been a number of versions of the 16PF. Table 15.3 shows 4 of the 10 questions used to assess ego strength in an early version. Answers 1a, 2b, 3a and 4a indicate good ego strength.

Table 15.3 Items from the ego strength subscale of the 16PF

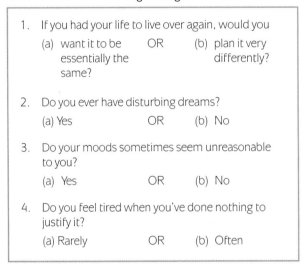

1. If you had your life to live over again, would you
   (a) want it to be essentially the same? OR (b) plan it very differently?

2. Do you ever have disturbing dreams?
   (a) Yes OR (b) No

3. Do your moods sometimes seem unreasonable to you?
   (a) Yes OR (b) No

4. Do you feel tired when you've done nothing to justify it?
   (a) Rarely OR (b) Often

Costa and McCrae's 5-factor model of personality

Perhaps the most popular trait theory in contemporary personality psychology is the 5-factor model, developed by Costa and McCrae (1985). These five factors include extroversion and neuroticism (similar to Eysenck's 'supertraits'). In addition, *openness* describes the tendency to appreciate experience and tolerate the unfamiliar. Highly open people are curious, creative and imaginative. Those low in openness are conventional and narrow in their interests. *Agreeableness* describes the extent to which one is, at one extreme highly compassionate and trusting, or at the other extreme cynical, antagonistic and ruthless. The final trait is *conscientiousness*, a similar idea to Cattell's trait of ego strength. Conscientiousness describes the extent of our organisation, persistence and motivated. Highly conscientious individuals are disciplined, punctual and ambitious. At the opposite end of the spectrum are individuals who are aimless, unreliable and hedonistic (pleasure-seeking).

The fundamental lexical hypothesis

One of the principles of the 5-factor theory is that the most important aspects of personality will be those that occur frequently in our use of language, and in a wide variety of languages. Twenty years before the 5-factor theory was formally developed, Norman (1963) analysed the descriptions people made of one another and concluded that they could be divided into five aspects of personality, very similar to those of the 5-factor theory. More recent reviews (eg John, 1990) have supported the idea that people in a diverse range of cultures describe people principally according to these five characteristics.

Measuring personality

Costa and McCrae (1985) developed a self-rating inventory known as the NEO-PI, which stands for the neuroticism, extroversion and openness personality inventory (the first version just measured these three traits and the name stuck, despite the addition of agreeableness and conscientiousness). The NEO-PI has a different format from the EPI and the 16PF. There are a total of 181 statements to which respondents indicate their agreement on a 5-point scale, ranging from strongly agree to strongly disagree. Table 15.4 shows four of the 40 items of the E-scale of the NEO-PI.

For these four statements a high E-score is indicated by agreement with the statement. Some items, however, are reversed. Thus agreement to the statement 'You never smile when you talk to friends' would be scored negatively and reduce your E-score.

Table 15.4 Items from the E-scale of the NEO-PI

	SA	A	?	D	SD
1. You enjoy talking to strangers.	[ ]	[ ]	[ ]	[ ]	[ ]
2. You like talking to family members.	[ ]	[ ]	[ ]	[ ]	[ ]
3. You tell other people that you like them.	[ ]	[ ]	[ ]	[ ]	[ ]
4. You are a very friendly person.	[ ]	[ ]	[ ]	[ ]	[ ]

Research into personality traits and sporting behaviour

There have been many attempts to try and link personality traits to sporting behaviour. Broadly, we can classify research into two categories; linking personality to participation in and choice of sport, and linking personality to success in sport. A classic study by Schurr et al (1977) investigated both of these relationships.

The Schurr et al study remains of interest to sports psychologists because of the large sample size and the use of the 16PF, which yields interesting results because of the large number of personality variables it measures. However, there are problems with this and similar studies. The sample, consisting of young adult American middle-class males, was highly unrepresentative of sporting participants on a global level. Moreover, the factors that make someone participate and succeed in sport in the social setting of a university may be quite different from those operating under other circumstances. The definition of an athlete as someone participating in sport at university level has also been criticised for being too specific, giving us little information on the characteristics of those who take part in sports at both the more casual recreational level and the elite level.

classic
research

what is an athlete?

Schurr K.T., Ashley M.A. & Joy K.L. (1977) A multivariate analysis of male athlete personality characteristics; sport type and success. *Multivariate Experimental Clinical Psychology* 3: 53–68

aim: the aim of the study was to investigate the relationship between personality traits, as measured by the 16PF, and sporting behaviour. Three aspects of sporting behaviour were looked at; sporting participation, choice of sport and sporting success.

procedure: participants were 1596 male American university students. They were classified as athletes or non-athletes. An 'athlete' was defined as someone who participated in sport at the university at inter-university level. Their involvement, type of sport and level of success (defined by awards) were noted, and they were administered the 16PF. Relationships between each of Cattell's 16 personality variables and the three sporting variables were calculated (hence the study is said to be *multivariate*).

findings: athletes emerged as significantly different from non-athletes in three ways. They were less anxious, more self-sufficient and more objective. There were also differences between athletes opting for team and individual sports. Team players were more anxious, dependent and extrovert but less imaginative than individual athletes. No relationship emerged between any of the 16 personality factors and sporting success.

conclusion: personality is an important determinant of both participation in and choice of sport. However, it is unrelated to success in sport as defined by receiving sporting awards.

Research into personality and participation in sport

Eysenck et al (1982) suggested that people high in psychoticism and extroversion are more likely to take up a sport than others. This is because sport can provide both the social and physical stimulation craved by extroverts, and because those high in psychoticism are suited to the competitiveness and assertiveness/aggression involved in sport. Some, though by no means all research has supported Eysenck's position. Francis et al (1998) compared Irish female students who participated in university hockey clubs with a control group of female students with no formal involvement in sport. The hockey players scored significantly higher in extroversion and psychoticism as measured by the EPQ. Although these results support Eysenck's view we need to remember that university hockey players cannot be taken as representative of athletes as a whole. Hockey is a team sport in which players typically build a close-knit team identity, and the high levels of extroversion found in hockey players may reflect team players rather than athletes *per se*.

Figure 15.2 Hockey players are often highly extrovert

In a study of leisure activities, mood and personality in 275 adults, Hills and Argyle (1998) found that those who participated generally in competitive sport or exercise in general were higher in extroversion and psychoticism than others. This study has the advantage of including a wider range of participants than was typical of earlier studies, and further support's Eysenck's ideas. So far, however, no consistent picture has emerged of the relationship between extroversion and psychoticism and sporting participation (Kremer & Scully, 1994).

A small body of research has also examined the relationship between neuroticism and participation in sport. Egloff and Gruhn (1996) compared 80 endurance athletes (distance runners and triathletes) with 73 non-athletes on extroversion and neuroticism. The athletes emerged as more extroverted and less neurotic than the control group. As well as providing information on neuroticism, this study is useful in identifying extroversion as a characteristic of individual as well as team sports. In a recent Slovakian study by Sevcikova et al (2000) 213 children aged 10–14 were assessed on their daily activity, exercise and nutrition, and administered the junior EPI. Children high in neuroticism were significantly lower in physical activity and less likely to participate in sport. They also came out worse in nutritional habits. Interestingly, the authors suggest a different causal relationship between personality and sport from Eysenck's – namely that participation in exercise and other health-enhancing behaviours such as good nutrition actually reduces neuroticism. This is important in terms of using sport to enhance children's psychological development (discussed further on page 175).

(discussed further on page 175).

interactive angles

How would you describe your own personality in terms of traits like extroversion and neuroticism? What sports do you like? Does the relationship between your personality and choice of sport mirror the findings of sport psychology?

Research into personality and sporting success

Tutko and Ogilvie (1966) proposed that athletic performance could be explained in terms of personality traits. They suggested 11 traits associated with performance; aggression, 'coachability', conscientiousness, determination, drive, emotional control, guilt-proneness, leadership, mental toughness, self-confidence and trust. These were measured by a self-rating inventory called the *athletic motivation inventory* (AMI). It is generally agreed nowadays that the AMI had some serious flaws, both in the traits it identified (there is for example little evidence for leadership or coachability as stable traits) and in the items used to measure them. It is thus of little use in predicting performance.

Contemporary research using more widely accepted personality tests has provided some support for the idea that personality can impact on performance. Garland and Barry (1990) categorised 272 American university football players into different levels of skill and tested them with the 16PF. They found that four traits were significantly associated with skill; tough-mindedness, extroversion, group-dependence and emotional stability. Between them these traits accounted for 29 per cent of the variance in skill level. However, not all studies have found significant results. In a study by Feher et al (1998) 67 rock-climbers were assessed on their skill level and given a battery of personality tests including the EPI. No personality characteristics were associated with rock-climbing skill.

Clearly these two studies found very different results, but there are a number of possible factors that may have led to this. One obvious difference lies in the sports studied.

Rock-climbing, although it involves co-operation, is not a team sport in the same way as American football, so we would expect extroversion and group-dependence to be less important. Rock-climbing is also less competitive than American football; hence we might expect tough-mindedness to be less of an issue. However, the two studies also used different personality tests and involved different populations, so we cannot assume that the nature of the sport was the principal reason for the different findings of the two studies. This is a good illustration of the difficulty in reaching hard and fast conclusions about personality and sport; two equally sound approaches to researching the issue can produce completely contradictory conclusions.

Although the 5-factor model of personality is currently the most widely accepted theory in personality psychology, it has made very little impact on the field of sports psychology. This may now change, however, as a recent study by Piedmont et al (1999) shows some interesting relationships between the five factors and sporting performance.

for and against

using personality traits to predict sporting behaviour

+ there is some evidence linking personality traits to participation in and choice of sport

− early attempts to predict performance using the AMI failed

+ some newer research using modern personality tests has found relationships between personality and performance

− results of contemporary studies remain highly inconsistent, varying according to the sport, the criteria for assessing performance and the choice of personality measure

research now

can the 5-factor model predict athletic performance?

Piedmont R.L., Hill D.C. & Blanco S. (1999) Predicting athletic performance using the five-factor model of personality. *Personality & Individual Differences* **27: 769–777**

aim: although the most widely accepted trait approach to personality is now Costa and McCrae's 5-factor model, there has been almost no research linking the approach to sporting participation or performance. The aim of this study is to test whether the five personality factors are associated with either estimates or objective measures of sporting success.

procedure: 79 women footballers were assessed for the five personality factors of extroversion, neuroticism, openness, agreeableness and conscientiousness, using a *semantic differential scale*, where each question involved the respondent choosing which of two opposite adjectives best described them. Statistical information on each player's performance was collected and their coaches were asked to rate their performance.

findings: significant relationships were found between coaches' ratings of players' performance and extroversion and neuroticism scores, good performance being associated with high E-scores and low N-scores. Between them E and N accounted for 23 per cent of the variance in coaches' ratings. However, there was no relationship between extroversion or neuroticism and objective measures of performance in the form of game statistics. Conscientiousness was associated with statistics, however, accounting for 8 per cent of the variance.

conclusion: the fact that extroversion and neuroticism were associated with coaches' assessments of performance but not with more objective performance data suggests that coaches' assessments may be highly inaccurate, and the validity of previous studies using such assessments to measure performance may be deeply flawed. Conscientiousness may in fact be the most important personality variable in athletic performance.

where to now?

The following are good sources of further information about personality traits and sport.

▶ **Pervin L. (1993) *Personality*. New York: Wiley.** Gives a good account of the major trait theories, including those discussed here.

▶ **Kremer J. & Scully D. (1994) *Psychology in sport*. Hove, Taylor & Francis.** A highly critical look at research into personality and sport.

what's new?

reversal theory, telic dominance and sport

Reversal theory was developed by Michael Apter (eg Apter, 1993). It is a general theory of human motivation and explains personality in terms of individual differences in motivational style. According to Apter, we all have some times when we seek out situations that lead to low physiological arousal (this is called being in a *telic* state), and other times when we seek out situations that produce high arousal (this is the *paratelic* state). Some individuals spend more time in a telic state and are said to be telic dominant. Others are more often in a paratelic state and are known as paratelic dominant individuals. Telic dominance can be assessed using a self-rating inventory called the telic dominance scale (TDS). The TDS contains 42 items and assesses people on three subscales, serious-mindedness, planning orientation (tendency to plan ahead) and arousal avoidance. Items from the serious-mindedness subscale are shown in table 15.5.

Table 15.5 Items from the telic dominance scale (Murgatroyd, 1978)

Here are some alternative choices. If you had an open choice, which of the following alternatives would you usually prefer?

1. Compiling a short dictionary for financial reward.
   Writing a short story for fun.
   Not sure.

2. Going to an evening class to improve your qualifications.
   Going to an evening class for fun.
   Not sure.

3. Leisure activities that are just exciting.
   Leisure activities that have a purpose.
   Not sure.

4. Improving a sporting skill by playing a game.
   Improving a sporting skill by systematic practice.
   Not sure.

Kerr (1997) has suggested that telic dominance affects choice of sport, sporting achievement and the response of the individual to the pressure of competition. Because arousal is associated with high risk, we would expect highly paratelic dominant people to prefer high-risk sports, whereas telic dominant individuals might prefer more low-risk activities. This hypothesis was tested in a study by Chirivella and Martinez (1994), in which participants in a high-risk sport (parasailing) were compared for telic dominance with those opting for a medium-risk sport (karate) and a low-risk sport (tennis). As expected there were significant differences between the three groups, parasailors being the most paratelic dominant and tennis players the most telic dominant.

A number of studies have investigated the relationship between telic dominance and sporting achievement. Snell (1991) compared professional and amateur triathletes using the TDS. No differences were found in serious-mindedness or planning orientation, but professionals scored significantly lower on arousal avoidance, suggesting that an important factor in success is being able to cope with the additional pressure (hence arousal) of professional level sport.

where to now?

The following is a good source of further information about reversal theory and sport.

> **Kerr J.H. (1997)** *Motivation and emotion in sport*. **Hove: Taylor & Francis.** Contains a much more detailed account, both of reversal theory itself and its application to sport.

Social development and sporting behaviour

Whereas trait theories of personality are concerned with identifying stable and largely in-born aspects of personality, social developmental psychologists are more concerned with the influences of the social environment on the individual differences in our behaviour. While these two approaches to explaining individual differences sound contradictory, it is important to remember that both approaches are valid; although we do have stable personality traits, we also learn patterns of behaviour, some of which are quite specific to particular situations. It is thus important to look at social development as well as traits if we are to understand individual differences in sporting behaviour. One theory of social development, Bandura's social learning theory, has been particularly influential in sports psychology.

Social learning theory

Observational or *social learning* occurs when one individual, known as the *learner*, acquires a new behaviour by imitating another individual, known as the *model*. Social learning theory (Bandura, 1977) is an approach to personality development that places particular emphasis on the way children's individual behavioural patterns develop as a result of their imitation of models. Bandura proposed four requirements that must be met for observational learning to occur. These are: *attention* to the model; *retention* of the observed behaviour; *reproduction* of the observed action; and *motivation* to generate the learned behaviour in return for a reward. Attention is clearly vital, as without it the behaviour cannot be perceived. However, it is also necessary to be able to recall the sequence of actions observed. You also have to be able to reproduce the behaviour. Finally, you need to be motivated to demonstrate the newly acquired skill. This motivation comes from the perception of the rewards available for reproducing the behaviour. We can either receive a reward after imitating the behaviour or witness the model being rewarded (this is called *vicarious reinforcement*).

One important variable in determining whether or not behaviour is imitated is the nature of the individual model. Duck (1990) suggests that the extent to which the model resembles the observer may determine their effectiveness as a model, thus same-sex models are more effective than opposite-sex models. Other important attributes of effective models include power, social status and likeability. All social animals, including humans, are more likely to imitate the behaviour of individuals with high social status in their community. This means that parents, teachers, high status peers and public figures such as sporting stars are all potent models. The fact that professional athletes enjoy high social status and are thus role models for young people makes it essential that they conduct themselves in a 'sporting' manner. The ways in which sport can impact on children's development is discussed in detail on page 174.

Unlike trait theorists, who see personality as largely in-built and stable across a range of situations, social learning theorists see personality as a set of learned patterns of behaviour, some of which may be quite specific to a situation (Mischell, 1973). An advantage of adopting a social learning approach is that it can explain why some people behave quite differently in sport as opposed to other parts of their lives. For example, you may have come across people who are mild-mannered and peaceful in most situations, but who are highly aggressive on the sports field – you might in fact say that they become a 'different person' (a term that trait theorists would find hard to explain). This situation specific behaviour might be the result of imitating an aggressive role model, who might be a parent, teacher or high profile athlete and receiving either direct or vicarious reinforcement for doing so.

for and against

social learning theory

- **+** social learning provides an explanation of how we learn from our family and other role models

- **+** social learning also explains the importance of high-profile athletes as role models

- **−** some aspects of individual differences are perhaps better explained by trait theories

- **−** it can be hard to look retrospectively at the influence of role models on an existing characteristic

The influence of the family

Both common sense and psychological research suggests that our family influences us all in our social development. Social learning theory suggests that family members provide both role models (especially same-sex high-status family members) and sources of reinforcement. This can affect sporting behaviour in a number of ways. Children imitate sporting techniques witnessed when spectating. Spectating with family members is also important because children can receive vicarious reinforcement when family members are heard to praise athletes. Indeed, the very attention given to athletes when a family spectates together is a vicarious reinforcer. Because sport is widely considered a socially valuable activity, it is also likely that children who imitate athletes will be directly reinforced by praise from family members.

The idea that families are a source of social influence on sporting behaviour is supported by a recent study by Jambor (1999). In this study 165 parents of 5–10-year-old children who did or did not participate in football were questioned on their beliefs and attitudes about sport. The parents of football players differed significantly from those of non-players, having more positive beliefs about sport, for example, in terms of health benefits and being more likely to take part in sport themselves. It seems that modelling of sporting behaviour is thus one factor in children's participation, but that parental attitudes and beliefs also have an effect, independent of modelling. It may be that family influences also moderate the effect of other variables such as gender. In a survey of 145 women (average age 21 years) Miller and Levy (1996) found that although women showed concern about being sufficiently 'feminine' if they participated in sport, this effect was sharply reduced if their mother was a sporting participant.

interactive angles

As a group, record for each person the sport in which you take part most frequently and the favourite sport of your same-sex parent. Using a chi2 test calculate the association between parental and offspring choice of sport. Does it seem that parental preference influenced your own sporting behaviour?

The influence of gender

The term *gender* refers to the psychological as opposed to the biological aspects of being male and female. Biological *sex* differences have an obvious influence on sporting performance, but what is subtler and perhaps more interesting is the way in which issues of gender affect sporting behaviour. Our perceptions of what is appropriate masculine and feminine behaviour can have profound effects on our actions, and this is clearly important in sport. Typically, boys and girls are socialised into different patterns of behaviour. For example, girls are much more likely to be nagged at in childhood not to get dirty (Kremer & Scully, 1994). They also tend to have role models who maintain stereotypically feminine behaviour that does not normally involve wallowing in mud! Clearly this is likely to lessen the chances of girls' involvement with any sports such as rugby and hockey that necessarily involve getting muddy. Girls are also likely to receive positive reinforcement for displaying the 'feminine' characteristics of passivity, submissiveness, dependency, low aggression and low need for achievement (Cox, 1998). Clearly these qualities are not helpful in sport.

So, to what extent does gender affect sporting attitudes and behaviour? In the Miller and Levy study (above) women did display some anxiety about the femininity of sports participation, although this was mediated by other factors such as maternal sporting participation. Concerns about femininity and sport may begin in early adolescence. When Hagger et al (1997) surveyed 9–11-year-old English children on their attitudes to sport they found that both boys and girls were overwhelmingly positive in their perceptions of sport, and no gender differences emerged. However, in a study by Guillet et al (2000) (see below), the extent to which the individual identifies themselves as stereotypically masculine or feminine, proved to be a powerful influence on adolescent girls' decision to maintain or quit sport.

Further research suggests that in adults there can be considerable difficulty in combining an athletic identity (ie seeing oneself as an athlete) and a strong feminine identity. Lantz and Schroeder (1999) assessed athletic identity using a self-rating inventory called the *Athletic Identity Measurement Scale* and the Bem Sex-Role inventory in 173 male and 236 female athletes. Athletic identity was positively correlated with masculinity and negatively correlated with femininity. Essentially this means that athletic identity involves adopting characteristics that we strongly associate with masculinity and rejecting those we associate with femininity.

Interestingly, although most research has supported this association between athleticism and the traditional masculine identity, an alternative type of male athlete has recently been studied, who does not conform to the traditional masculine role. Beal (1996) investigated 41 US Colorado skateboarders, using a combination of techniques including participant observation and interviews. Results confirmed that skateboarders have a subculture quite distinct from that of more conventional sport. The values of authority, conformity and competition, which characterise the traditional athlete, were rejected in favour of an emphasis on self-control, self-expression and open participation. Nonetheless it was clear that skateboarders considered their sport to be masculine.

research
now

girlies don't play handball!

Guillet E., Sarrazin P. & Fontayne P. (2000) 'If it contradicts my gender role I'll stop': Introducing survival analysis to study the effects of gender typing on the time of withdrawal from sport practice: a 3-year study. *European Review of Applied Psychology* **50: 417–21**

aim: gender role typing is the extent to which we identify ourselves as masculine, androgynous (having a balance of masculine and feminine characteristics) or feminine. The aim of this study was to assess whether gender role type would predict the tendency of adolescent girls to drop out of handball, a 'masculine' sport.

procedure: 336 French schoolgirls aged 13–15 were assessed for gender type using a self-rating inventory called the *Bem Sex-Role Inventory*. All participants took part in handball at the start of the study, but could opt to drop it. They were followed up for just under three years to see whether their sex role was predictive of their decision to maintain or cease their participation in handball.

findings: 173 days after the initial assessment 87 per cent of girls classed as androgynous were still playing handball as opposed to 62 per cent of those classified as feminine. After 498 days the figures were 80 per cent and 60 per cent respectively. After 823 days 76 per cent of androgynous and 56 per cent of feminine girls were still playing handball.

conclusions: sex role predicted dropout from handball, a masculine sport. This suggests that as long as many women have a traditional 'feminine' identity and some sports are thought of as 'masculine' there will be problems maintaining women's participation in those sports.

The influence of culture

The term *culture* refers to the sets of beliefs, practices, values and customs that characterise a group of people. These groups can be regional, ethnic or self-defined. Cultural differences between ethnic groups have been those most extensively studied in psychology. Psychologists are interested in the similarities between cultural groups (these similarities are collectively known as *etic*) and differences between them (collectively known as *emic*). If, as we have seen, our families influence us in our development of sport-related behaviour, then culture operates at a wider level, influencing what values, beliefs and customs we learn from the family.

One way in which cultural beliefs affect our sporting development relates to where we attribute success and failure. Morgan et al (1996) studied black, native American and white field and track athletes' perceptions about the influences on sporting success. Whereas the white athletes tended to see success as something unchangeable (the 'you've either got it or you haven't' attitude), the black and native American athletes placed much more emphasis on effort, and saw success as something to be earned. This has a clear implication for the

effort we might expect each cultural group to go to in preparing for competition.

There are also cultural differences in aggressive attitudes and behaviour in sport. Ferraro (1999) compared cultural attitudes to authority and aggression in American and Asian athletes. The Asian respondents emerged as less aggressive and angry than Americans, and more disciplined and work-oriented. The benefits of Asian cultural attitudes in the sporting arena are clear.

Sport as an influence on social development

A commonly held assumption concerning sport is that participation, particularly by children, is in some significant way 'character-building'. Courage, discipline, dedication and perseverance are widely believed to increase as a direct result of playing sports (Drewe, 1998). Actually there are strong arguments for the potential positive and negative influences of sport. On one hand, sport does provide positive role models and offers opportunities for young people to experience both co-operation and

Figure 15.3 Skateboarders have a distinct culture with a different idea of masculinity from most sports

and there is a surprisingly small body of research demonstrating the benefits to social development of sporting participation.

Hastie and Sharpe (1999) looked at the development of 20 Australian adolescents classified as 'at risk' (of crime, social problems, educational failure etc), who participated in 20 sessions of 'Kangaroo ball' in which the coaching particularly emphasised fair play. Compliance with teachers, quality of interpersonal interaction and leadership were assessed before and after the programme, and were found to be significantly improved. Although the findings of this study are encouraging, we should remember that it may not be representative of the general effects of sporting participation. Coaching was especially designed to foster prosocial development, and may thus be rather different from the PE teaching and coaching most young people receive. Furthermore, the participants were not representative of young people as a whole.

The case against sport as a positive influence on social development

While both witnessing and participation in sport undoubtedly has the *potential* to help prosocial development, and it can be seen to be beneficial under certain circumstances, this is not necessarily to say that sport is a positive influ-

competition. On the other hand, there is considerable question as to whether in reality athletes succeed in providing positive role models, and there is a worrying body of literature suggesting that athletes are more prejudiced and sexually aggressive than other people. We can look at both sides of the debate.

The case for sport as a positive influence on social development

There is no doubt that sport provides an opportunity for adults to model and reinforce the 'sporting' attitudes of fairness, effort and self-discipline. Numerous successful adults attribute their success, at least in part, to having participated in sport. Certainly spectators witness dedication, courage, discipline and perseverance on almost every sporting occasion. Moreover, socially disadvantaged groups such as minority ethnic groups, who sometimes lack high profile role models, can benefit from seeing members of their community publicly succeeding in sport (Krane, 1998). Indeed, the stereotypes held of minority ethnic groups by others may be changed for the good in response to sporting success. This 'commonsense' analysis should not satisfy psychologists, however,

Figure 15.4 One reason for the success of black athletes is the cultural belief that sporting success is earned by hard work

ence on the development of most young people. Although numerous successful adults speak fondly about their sporting youth, there is a question of cause and effect to consider before we take this too seriously. Physically energetic, competitive and determined people are likely to succeed in sport and their careers, thus although they may *attribute* their success to sport, it may be that both sporting and career success owe more to their personality traits and other learning experiences. As Krane (1998) points out, most psychological research has focused on athletes, and we know almost nothing about the futures of those who have negative childhood experiences of sport.

As regards the effects of spectatorship and modelling, there are many cases in which athletes model antisocial as well as prosocial behaviour. Waxmonsky and Beresin (2001) are particularly critical of the values modelled in professional wrestling. Wrestling in the entertainment guise depicted on television (as opposed to the pure sport form) includes frequent verbal intimidation and cheating, directly opposed to the traditional values of sport and those which might benefit children's social development. Vicarious reinforcement through witnessing professional wrestlers win matches using cheating and intimidation may be a negative influence on children's social behaviour.

Some research suggests that sport may be associated with distinctly antisocial behaviour, including violence and intimidation, and with antisocial attitudes such as sexism and homophobia. Harry (1995) assessed attitudes towards women, gay men and lesbians in 304 American university students, and tested whether these attitudes are associated with their *sports ideology*. A 'sports ideology' was defined as the life attitudes stereotypically associated with athletes; conservatism, authoritarianism, elitism and competitiveness. It was found that in men, though not women, students high in sports ideology were more sexist and homophobic than others. Interestingly, when Craig (2000) compared students' responses to scenarios in which male athletes and non-athletes battered women, responses were more positive towards the athletes, suggesting that in some way violence to women by athletes was expected and even socially accepted.

It may be, however, that although there is an association between athletic participation and unhealthy attitudes to women, this may not be a simple causal relationship. Caron et al (1997) assessed athletic participation, competitiveness, hostility to women and attitudes to rape in 104 male students aged 18–24. There was no overall difference in sexual aggression between participants and non-participants in sport, however, highly competitive people were both more supportive of rape and more likely to participate in sport. This suggests that it is competitiveness rather than sporting participation per se that is linked to sexual aggression.

To play or not to play?

We have seen that sport has the potential to be of benefit to children's social development, but also that modelling of negative social behaviour can be a negative influence and that a 'sports ideology' can be associated with prejudice and support of rape. One important factor affecting the extent to which sport is a positive influence appears to be the values put across during teaching and coaching. In one study of the coach's role, Shields (1999) assessed the frequency of verbal intimidation, physical intimidation and actual violence in basketball and football, and looked for associations between each of these and the setting, pressure and coaching style. Coaching was the only factor associated with any of the three antisocial behaviours, suggesting that the nature of coaching and teaching have great power over the social behaviour of athletes. Although there is no suggestion based on the research looked at here that we should cease to encourage children to participate in sport, teachers and coaches need to pay attention to the risks of over-competitiveness and the existence of a 'sports ideology'.

where to now?

The following is a good source of further information on social development and sport.

 Gervis M. (1991) Children in sport. In Bull S. (ed) *Sport psychology: a self help guide.* **Marlborough: Crowood.** A practical guide to working with children in sport.

Conclusions

Trait theories see individual differences in terms of personality traits, characteristics that are stable across time and a range of situations. There is some evidence for links between traits and sporting participation, but there is also some question over cause and effect relationships – sport may affect personality as well as being affected by it. There is also some evidence for a link between sporting success and personality traits. However, recent research has shown that we need to be careful about what criteria we use for success, and that personality accounts for only a relatively small proportion of the variance in sporting success.

Social factors, including the influence of family, gender and culture, have also been firmly linked to individual differences in sporting behaviour. Some psychologists have found Bandura's social learning theory to be a helpful basis for understanding social influences. One of the most interesting questions concerning individual differences is the extent to which sport can have positive and negative effects on social development. While it appears that sport can be a positive influence, there is also research highlighting the risks of developing competitive attitudes and a 'sports ideology'.

what do you know?

1 What are personality traits? To what extent can they be linked to sporting participation and success?

2 Contrast trait and social learning perspectives on individual differences in sporting behaviour.

3 How might sport act as an influence on children's social development?

16 Motivation and sport

what's

The aim of this chapter is to better understand people's motives for participating in sport, and to examine ways in which this understanding can be applied to improving athletes' motivation to train and compete. We begin by examining the distinction between intrinsic and extrinsic motivation, and question the common assumption that increasing the tangible rewards available to athletes improves their motivation. We also look at achievement motivation, and discuss the factors that might make an athlete more or less motivated to achieve, including achievement orientations. The remainder of the chapter is devoted to two cognitive approaches to understanding and improving motivation. Self-efficacy refers to our belief in our ability to perform a task; and attribution refers to our beliefs about the causes of events, including success and failure. Sport psychologists work to manipulate both the self-efficacy and attributions of athletes in order to improve their motivation.

The importance of motivation

When athletes are highly motivated 'they work hard in training and give 100% effort when competing' (Duda & Pensgaard, 2002, page 49). They also tend to respond better to difficulties, which can include a losing streak, injury or loss of confidence. It is important for all those who employ, coach or teach athletes to understand the ways in which their own behaviour can affect the motivation of the athlete. We should also consider the importance of motivational factors in the decision by non-exercisers to take up sport.

Intrinsic and extrinsic motivation

An important distinction to make if we are to understand the range of motives underlying sporting participation and achievement is between intrinsic and extrinsic motivation. *Intrinsic motives* are those that come from within the individual. We might, for example, relish the physical sensations experienced in sport, and derive personal satisfaction from improving our performance. Competition provides us with excitement, and training with friends can be a happy social experience. What these factors have in common is the pleasure associated with sport.

Extrinsic motives are the external rewards that we can gain from taking part and succeeding in sport. These include the obvious rewards such as trophies and lucrative prizes and contracts, but also less obvious yet nonetheless potent rewards such as social status and attractiveness. A recent study by Martin et al (2000) suggests that people who participate in sport are considered more attractive

than non-exercisers. A group of 627 men and women aged 18–30 were given descriptions of a young man or woman and asked to rate them on a number of variables. In one condition the target individual was described as a regular exerciser and in the other condition they were described as a non-exerciser. Both men and women rated the individual as more attractive (regardless of the sex of the target) if they participated in exercise. One factor in the decision to participate and to succeed in sport may thus be the enhancement of one's personal image.

Intrinsic motivation

Research has strongly supported the importance of intrinsic motivation, both in the decision to participate in sport and in achieving a good performance. Studies to assess people's reasons for taking part in sport have tended to find that people report intrinsic rather than extrinsic motives. Ashford et al (1993) interviewed 336 English adults (chosen on the basis of their use of a community sports centre) in order to ascertain why they participated in sports. Four intrinsic motivators emerged from their responses; physical well-being, psychological well-being, improvement of performance and *assertive achievement* (defined as achieving personal and competitive goals).

Because intrinsic factors are so important in sporting participation, a key aim of research has been to improve our understanding of what influences intrinsic motivation. Amorose and Horn (2001) assessed 72 American college athletes aged 17–19 on their intrinsic motivation at the beginning and end of their first year of inter-college level participation. They were questioned about the time put in on training, their coaching and whether they had sports scholarships. Neither scholarship status nor time had any impact on the extent to which the participants maintained their initial levels of intrinsic motivation. However, the behaviour of coaches had a profound impact. Those whose coaches spent more time in instruction and less time in *autocratic* behaviour (ie throwing their weight about) tended to display significant increases in their intrinsic motivation during the year.

interactive angles

As a group, record your own motives for participating in sport. What factors emerge as most important overall? To what extent are they intrinsic motives?

The additive principle

Clearly most individuals are strongly influenced by intrinsic factors in their motivation to take part in sport and to try to achieve good performances. Common sense suggests that if we throw some extrinsic motivation into the equation as well, then we will increase the athlete's total motivation. This is known as the *additive principle*, shown in the equation below.

Intrinsic motivation + Extrinsic motivation = Maximum motivation

There are numerous extrinsic rewards available to top-class athletes. As well as the high salaries paid to some professionals, there may be prize money and sponsorship money. Athletes also have high social status and are likely to be considered a good sexual 'catch'. Until the 1970s it was standard wisdom to provide athletes with extrinsic rewards in order to make use of the additive principle. However, organisational psychologist Edward Deci (1972) challenged this practice with a series of experiments, which suggested that in fact the introduction of extrinsic rewards undermines rather than enhances intrinsic motivation.

There are limitations of studies like this. They take place in laboratory conditions and make use of artificial tasks that bear little resemblance to real life sports scenarios (ie they lack *ecological validity*). However, there are a huge number

classic research

when rewards go wrong

Deci E.L. (1972) The effects of contingent and noncontingent rewards and controls on intrinsic motivation. *Organisational Behaviour & Human Decision Processes* 8: 217–29

aim: in both organisational and sports psychology, it had long been assumed that motivation could be increased by adding an additional extrinsic reward in the form of money and/or escaping a punishment. This study set out to directly test the assumption. Although this study was a simulation of what happens in the workplace rather than in sport, it was hugely influential in sports psychology.

procedure: the study took the form of a laboratory experiment involving 72 participants. They were given standard workplace tasks under several conditions. In a control condition they received no payment, punishment or feedback on performance. In experimental conditions they were offered either a flat payment, performance-related payment, punishment should they fail to perform well or verbal feedback on their performance. In each condition intrinsic motivation was assessed.

findings: offering payment not tied into performance had no effect on intrinsic motivation. However, performance-related pay, punishment and negative feedback all reduced it. Positive feedback enhanced intrinsic motivation.

conclusion: introducing extrinsic motivators in the form of rewards and/or punishment leads to decreased intrinsic motivation. Positive verbal feedback is different because it enhances the pleasure taken in performing skills and hence enhances intrinsic motivation.

of well-documented cases where talented athletes have turned professional, accessed greater extrinsic rewards and promptly lost their enjoyment of their sport (ie their intrinsic motivation) and so ceased to perform well (Cox, 1998). Factors that might lead to this decline in intrinsic motivation include greater competitive stress, heavier training schedules and reduced personal choice. In some cases turning professional and making a good living may also mean adapting to a different and less intrinsically enjoyable sport altogether. For example, a British kick boxer wishing to turn professional and remain in Britain would have to take up professional boxing.

Further evidence against the additive principle comes from comparisons of intrinsic motivation between athletes who compete purely for pleasure and those at higher competitive levels. Fortier et al (1995) compared the intrinsic motivation of Canadian university team-level athletes with that of students who participated in university sports clubs for recreation and found it to be significantly higher in the latter group. Another way of investigating the additive principle involves following up athletes whose extrinsic rewards have just increased. Sturman and Thibodeau (2001) tracked the performance of 33 American baseball professionals for two seasons before and two seasons after they signed lucrative new contracts. There was a sharp decline in performance as measured by batting average, number of home runs etc immediately following the new contract, and lasting for around one season. This suggests that the players' intrinsic motivation was undermined by their increase in salary. Of course, not every player in every sport has their intrinsic motivation undermined by money; it may be that those who do not lose motivation in response to money are those for whom money has little meaning. Consider the following extract from an interview with golfer Jose Maria Olazabal.

media watch

The following extracts are taken from an interview with Jose Maria Olazabal, featured in the *Sunday Times*, 5 May 2002, page 20.

In response to a question about money: 'That's not a factor,' he said. 'I want to play and to win because it's a tournament I've always enjoyed being part of. When I draw up my training schedule it's one of the first ones I circle on the list.'

In other regards, Olazabal's itinerary is a famously curious business. While most players head for the most lucrative events, the 36-year-old picks tournaments that offer agreeable surroundings and a level of competition that inspires him. He has been known to reject offers of huge appearance fees and has remained loyal to Sergio Gomez, who has managed his entire professional career.

'Sometimes you have to give something to get something, so it balances out. Money has nothing to do with it. It's about trying to find out how good I can be.'

1 What evidence can you pick out from the above interview to suggest that Olazabal's motivation is intrinsic rather than extrinsic?

2 Suggest why his motivation remains good after considerable success and extrinsic reward.

Figure 16.1 Jose Maria Olazabal has ignored the extrinsic rewards of his success and focused on improving his game

for and against

the additive principle

+ common sense suggests that motivation is greatest if sport provides both enjoyment and tangible rewards

+ extrinsic rewards may improve performance in some competitors depending on their motivational style

− most studies have found that in fact extrinsic rewards undermine intrinsic motivation

− there are also numerous cases of athletes who have lost motivation when they have gained access to extrinsic motivators

Improving intrinsic motivation by coaching

If simply adding extrinsic motivators appears to undermine rather than improve intrinsic motivation, what can we do to improve athletic motivation? The answer seems to be to work to make participation in sport more pleasurable. As we have seen from the work of Amorose and Horn (2001, page 177), sport can cease to be pleasurable when coaches adopt an autocratic stance towards athletes. Duda and Pensgaard (2002) suggest a number of ways in which coaches can work to improve intrinsic motivation; coaches need to focus on instruction and emphasise the importance of the link between improved technique and success. They need to give personal feedback, acknowledge that athletes can make mistakes and treat all participants as important. This is in direct contrast to the approach of bullying, humiliation and exclusive encouragement for the already-successful elite employed by the stereotypical sadistic PE

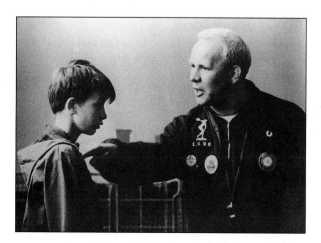

Figure 16.2 Autocratic behaviour by teachers and coaches can demotivate young athletes

teacher portrayed on television in *The Grimleys* and at the cinema in *Kes*.

where to now?

The following are good sources of further information about intrinsic and extrinsic motivation.

▶ **Gill D. (2000)** *Psychological dynamics of sport.* **Champaign: Human Kinetics.** Gives detailed coverage of this issue, in particular explanations for the failure of the additive principle.

▶ **Duda J. & Pensgaard A.M. (2002) Enhancing the quantity and quality of motivation: the promotion of task involvement in a junior football team. In Cockerill I. (ed)** *Solutions in sport psychology.* **London: Thomson Learning.** A useful practical account of how to improve intrinsic motivation.

Achievement motivation

Competitive sport by definition involves measuring our performance relative to that of other athletes. Even individual exercise and training involves measuring oneself against previous personal performances. What both these situations have in common is that they involve *athletic achievement*. One of the important differences between individual athletes is the extent to which they are motivated to achieve highly. In some cases this appears to be the greatest single factor in an athlete's success, driving them to train and compete hard enough to overmatch stronger opponents. There have been a number of theories that aim to explain why individual athletes differ so much in their achievement motivation. We will look here at two approaches, first, the traditional *McClelland-Atkinson model* and then the more recent *achievement orientations* approach.

The McClelland-Atkinson model

According to McClelland and Atkinson (eg McClelland et al, 1961), we can understand achievement motivation in terms of two factors, namely, motivation to succeed and fear of failure. The motivation to succeed is understood in this theory to come from intrinsic motivation, ie the pleasure derived from participating in sport (as discussed on page 178). Fear of failure is determined by our individual levels of competitive anxiety. Whenever we enter a sporting situation we experience an *approach-avoidance conflict*, ie we want to approach the situation in order to enjoy taking part. At the same time we also want to avoid it to escape the anxiety that taking part would produce. If the intrinsic motivation to take part in a sporting activity is greater than the anxiety we feel over the competitive situation then we will be motivated to achieve highly in the event. This can be expressed as an equation:

Achievement motivation = Intrinsic motivation – Competitive anxiety

Individuals who are high in intrinsic motivation and low in anxiety are likely to be motivated to succeed at high levels. Those who are low in intrinsic motivation and high in anxiety are likely to experience considerable difficulty in competitive sport. Those who have moderate intrinsic motivation but high anxiety levels might enjoy sport but find it very difficult to compete at a high level where competitive anxiety is likely to be greater.

In later developments to the McClelland-Atkinson model, the role of extrinsic motivation was taken into account as well as intrinsic motivation and anxiety. Thus, if intrinsic motivation is low and anxiety high, it may still be possible to produce high levels of achievement motivation by introducing extrinsic motivation. In other words, if we don't particularly enjoy a sport and competition makes us anxious, we may still be motivated to succeed if success will give us a sufficiently attractive reward such as a trophy or prize money.

The principles that intrinsic motivation is important for success and that excessive anxiety can put us off competing are not controversial. Furthermore, the model is helpful in understanding why athletes respond differently to different levels of competition. However, there are serious limitations in the McClelland-Atkinson model. The principal problem is that it cannot be used to predict successful performance. Research has found that those high in achievement motivation as calculated from intrinsic motivation and anxiety do not consistently do better in competition than those low in achievement motivation. A further problem is that the model does not take account of gender differences in achievement motivation. It seems that women may still fear to enter into competition even when intrinsic motivation is high and anxiety low.

for and against

the McClelland-Atkinson model

+ it appears to be true that high levels of intrinsic motivation predict good performance and that, at least under certain circumstances, high anxiety predicts poor performance

– the McClelland-Atkinson formula does not reliably predict good performance

– the model does not appear to apply as well to women as to men

Achievement orientations

Nicholls (1984) distinguished between two types of achievement motivation, which appear at different stages of development. These achievement orientations are a product of how the athlete explains their perceived ability. *Task orientation* appears between two and six years of age. Task-oriented children judge their competence on the basis of how well they performed the task at the last attempt. High levels of effort are judged to be evidence for high levels of competence. A change takes place in the way a child comes to view their athletic competence at around six years. The *ego-oriented* child judges their competence based on their performance relative to that of others. In adulthood we can use information about our past performances and the performances of others to judge our competence. Athletes can be classified as task oriented or ego oriented according to their tendency to rely on one source of information rather than the other. Contemporary research supports the existence of both task and ego orientations, but suggests that individuals may exhibit signs of both; ie they are not mutually exclusive and can exist in the same person. Table 16.1 compares the characteristics of task and ego-oriented athletes.

Table 16.1 Comparison of task and ego-oriented athletes

	Task oriented	Ego oriented
Criterion for judging success	Past personal performances	Comparison with others
Judged cause of success	Practice and skill development	Chance and natural ability
Response to difficulty/failure	Persistence	Cheating

Achievement orientations are one of the most researched topics in sports psychology, and some important applications have come out of research. Zahariadis and Biddle (2000) have used the approach to better understand people's motives for participation in sports. A group of 412 11–16 year olds were assessed for their achievement orientation and questioned about their reasons for taking part in sport. A clear relationship emerged between reasons and orientations. Task-oriented young people cited team spirit and skill development as their main reasons for taking part in sport, whereas those classified as ego oriented were more concerned with extrinsic rewards such as their social status. This understanding is important, as it helps us realise that not all young people are influenced by the same sporting motivators. We might also wish to identify ego-oriented youngsters in order to encourage them to adopt a more task-oriented approach.

Environments as well as individual athletes can be classified as task or ego oriented (Cox, 1998). A task-oriented environment is one in which there is a focus on the mastery of skills. An ego-oriented environment places its emphasis on comparisons between the abilities of individual athletes. The latter can be extremely harmful to the motivation of low ability participants, who simply experience the humiliation of comparison with more skilled athletes in response to their efforts. It is widely agreed that a task-oriented environment is preferable to an ego-oriented environment (European Federation of Sport Psychology, 1996).

Figure 16.3 The Wing Chun Federation provides an excellent example of a task-oriented environment. Reproduced by permission of Alan Gibson and Wing Chun Federation

One way in which sports psychologists can enhance athletic motivation is to help athletes develop a healthy blend of task and ego orientations. In a recent study of golfers, Steinberg et al (2001) compared the progress of 72 novice golfers who were assigned to one of four training conditions. In one condition training focused purely on competition, in the second it was based purely on task-mastery, in the third there was a balance between mastery and competition and in the fourth condition there was no systematic orientation towards tasks or competition. After six weeks only the group with combined training orientations had significantly improved their performance.

for and against

achievement orientations

+ research has supported the distinction between task and ego-oriented athletes, although some individuals may be high in both types of motivation

+ the approach has important applications in coaching and teaching, in particular in creating a task-oriented environment

+ by understanding the role of both types of achievement orientation psychologists can improve the motivation of individual athletes

where to now?

The following is a good source of further information about achievement orientation.

▶ **Cox R.H. (1998)** *Sport psychology: concepts and applications*. **Boston: McGraw-Hill.** Gives a detailed account of the theories of achievement motivation discussed here, and in addition a number of alternative approaches.

Cognitive approaches to improving motivation

There are a number of ways in which psychologists can work with athletes to improve their motivation. Based on the research looked at so far, for example, we can see that we could work to increase intrinsic motivation and minimise the impact of extrinsic motives, reduce competitive anxiety and increase achievement motivation, particularly the task-oriented variety. Another approach to improving motivation involves changing people's *cognitions*, ie the way they think about sport and in particular about themselves in relation to sport. Two ways of doing this are to work on self-efficacy and attributions.

Self-efficacy

Bandura (1982) introduced the now-important concept of self-efficacy to sports psychology. Self-efficacy is related to self-esteem, but the two concepts are quite distinct. Whereas self-esteem is the emotional experience of how we feel about ourselves, *self-efficacy* refers to our beliefs about our abilities. As well as being a cognitive rather than emotional phenomenon, self-efficacy differs further from self-esteem in being *situation-specific*. Whereas our self-esteem is fairly constant and generalises across quite different situations, we can have different self-efficacy in different situations. Self-efficacy can be affected by a number of factors. These factors were the subject of an investigation by Chase (1998).

research
now

what gives children their beliefs in their sporting abilities?

Chase M. (1998) Sources of self-efficacy in physical education and sport. *Journal of Teaching in Physical Education:* 18: 76–89

aim: it is well established that self-efficacy is an important factor in athletic performance. It is also believed that experience, for example, of winning and losing, affects self-efficacy. The aim of this study is to investigate in more detail the sources of self-efficacy in children, and to see whether these sources change according the age of the child.

procedure: 24 children aged 8–14 years were individually given semi-structured interviews. These interviews focused on children's beliefs in their sporting abilities and where these beliefs came from. The content of children's responses was analysed in three age groups; 8–9, 10–12 and 13–14 years.

findings: there were common factors that appeared to influence the self-efficacy of children, irrespective of their ages. All respondents cited praise and encouragement as important. There were also age-related differences, however, with older children focusing more on victories and comparison with the performance of peers as sources of self-efficacy. Peers and coaches became more important sources of information with increasing age.

conclusion: children used a number of sources of information to establish their self-efficacy, including social comparison, results of competition and verbal feedback. Older children are more influenced by competition results and social comparison, however, verbal feedback remains important irrespective of age.

Our beliefs concerning our abilities are an important influence on performance.

By manipulating an athlete's self-efficacy, ie their beliefs about what they are capable of achieving under particular circumstances, sports psychologists can boost performance considerably. In a classic demonstration of the impact of self-efficacy Wells et al (1993) randomly divided student participants into three groups and gave them weight-lifting tasks. In one condition the participants were given accurate feedback about how much they were lifting. In another condition they were misled into believing they were lifting heavier weights, and in the final condition they were misled into thinking they were lifting lighter weights. The three groups were then compared on how much they could lift, and the group who believed that they had lifted heavier weights than they really had were actually able to lift the most. This demonstrates both the power of self-efficacy and the ease with which a good coach can improve it, not necessarily by lying to athletes but by emphasising the positive aspects of their performance. Clearly self-efficacy has some limitations, and no amount of self-belief is going to allow a 1.5-m (5-ft) tall man to compete at top-level basketball, or a slower than average runner to make the Olympic squad. However, where athletes are reasonably well matched it is often self-efficacy that can determine the outcome of a contest.

for and against

the importance of self-efficacy

+ there is strong evidence that high levels of self-efficacy are associated with improved performance

+ we have a good understanding of how to influence athletes' self-efficacy; hence we can directly manipulate performance by means of self-efficacy

— self-efficacy probably only determines the outcome of a contest if the athletes are fairly well matched

Attribution

We all have an innate desire to try to understand why people (including ourselves) behave as we do. In particular we have a strong tendency to *attribute* behaviour to either the nature of the individual (an internal attribution) or the situation in which the behaviour occurred (an external attribution). In sports psychology, attribution of success and failure is particularly important. If we attribute our successes to our individual nature and our failures to the situation, we are likely to maintain a healthy self-esteem. Actually there is a tendency to do

this, even in the face of a certain amount of evidence to the contrary. This phenomenon is known as *self-serving bias*. Women are less prone to self-serving bias than are men, as are people who suffer from depression, and are thus more likely to attribute success to external factors and failure to internal factors. Some typical reasons given to explain success and failure are shown in table 16.2.

Biddle and Hill (1992) carried out an experiment in which success and failure were manipulated in order to see what sort of attributions were made and what effect these attributions had on athletes. Fifty-eight students were asked to fence for the first time. The judges manipulated the results of each bout so that some participants consistently won and others consistently lost. Their attributions and self-esteem were then measured. Those who made internal attributions for success and external attributions for failure had significantly higher self-esteem. The effect was particularly powerful in the 'losers', among whom those who made internal attributions for their failure developed particularly low self-esteem.

Weiner's theory of attribution

Weiner (1972) proposed that we can attribute our successes and failures to one of four factors; ability, effort, luck or the difficulty of the task. Which of these four attributions we make depends on two factors, *stability* and *locus of control*. Stability refers to the individual's belief in the changeability of an outcome. A person's locus of control is their tendency to believe in their own control over their lives. Stability and locus of control interact to produce the attribution of ability, effort, luck or task difficulty, as shown in table 16.3.

Table 16.2 Examples of internal and external attributions for success and failure

good self-esteem →		poor self-esteem →	
Internal attributions for personal successes	**External attributions for personal failures**	**Internal attributions for personal failures**	**External attributions for personal success**
I am really talented	The ref was biased	I'm as bad as Julia at tennis	I got a lucky shot in
I played a blinder	The pitch was too soft	I must be past it	By the laws of chance we had to win eventually
I always do best under pressure	No one can get a look in when she's in this form	I always crumble under pressure	We only won because half their first team was injured

Table 16.3 Weiner's model of attribution

	Internal locus of control	**External locus of control**
Stable	Ability	Task difficulty
Unstable	Effort	Luck

If we win a match and attribute the win to our ability, we are saying that the victory is due to a stable characteristic (ie we would win again) and that we were able to influence the outcome (internal locus of control). If we attribute it to effort we are saying that we influenced the result (internal locus of control), but that the result is unstable, ie it might change if we repeated the contest. If we believe that our victories are due to

our behaviour, but that we need to train hard if we are to continue to win, then we are likely to be highly motivated. If we perceive our victories as due to an easy task (such as a weak opponent) or simply to luck (external locus of control), then that will provide poor motivation to work hard for future contests. With regard to our losses, if we attribute them to ability then we are viewing loss as unchangeable and hence there is little

what's new?

counterfactual thinking

Sometimes our attributions about sporting successes and failures are quite unrealistic. This type of thinking is called *counterfactual thinking* (or CFT), because it runs counter to the facts of the incident in question (Roese, 1997). Sometimes our tendency to make attributions leads us to think negatively about events that are over, and over which we no longer have any control. This can lead athletes who have underachieved in competition to 'torture' themselves, dwelling on their failure and agonising over how things might have turned out differently. This is called *upward counterfactual thinking*. Alternatively we might be unrealistically positive, thinking about how much worse things might have been. This is called *downward counterfactual thinking*.

CFT is most likely when an outcome is negative, unexpected and upsetting, and when the result constitutes a near miss. Woolfson (2002) cites the example of England's World Cup quarterfinal in 1998, when David Beckham was sent off after petulantly kicking out at an Italian player after an aggressive tackle. Although the score was level at the time of the incident and England were by no means certain to win had Beckham remained on the pitch, England's loss was almost universally attributed to his actions. Interestingly, had England been clearly losing at the time, there would probably have been little attention given to Beckham's action – this illustrates the importance of the near miss in activating CFTs. In a study of winners at the 1992 Olympics, Medvec et al (1995) analysed the faces of bronze and silver medal winners for signs of happiness (without access to information about the results), and found that bronze medal winners were happier than winners of silver medals. This suggests that the silver medal winners were dwelling on how closely they had missed out on the gold medal – an upward CFT – again illustrating the importance of the near-miss phenomenon.

Both upward and downward counterfactual thinking have the potential for both positive and negative consequences. Upward CFT can clearly be a depressing experience if it just leads us to relive unhappy and humiliating experiences, wishing we had done something differently. However, it can also point us in the direction of where we need to improve. Thus a tennis player who takes a thrashing from an inferior opponent might feel humiliated and dwell on this, but if it leads her to work on her serve it may improve her performance in the long run.

Downward CFT has a defensive function, and may make us feel better after something has gone wrong; for example, a footballer who breaks a leg after being tackled might be comforted by the thought that if the tackle had been a little higher they might have had serious knee damage and had their career ended all together. However, downward CFT can lead an athlete to become complacent. Thus the martial artist who scrapes through a brown belt grading and then dwells on this achievement, ignoring the nearness of failure and the harder task of gaining a black belt is likely to lose the necessary motivation to continue training hard (this is known as the 'brown belt blues'). Martial arts instructors often introduce new challenges and work students particularly hard after a grading in order to avoid this.

motivation to work hard in future contests. If, however, we attribute loss to insufficient effort, then we are likely to try harder next time.

Weiner's model has a clear application in working with athletes to maintain good motivation in the face of victories and losses. This technique is called *attribution training* or *attributional therapy*. Studies have supported the principle that we can improve an athlete's motivation and importance by attribution training. Orbach et al (1999) investigated the effectiveness of attribution training with 35 novice tennis players. They received false feedback over 4 training sessions, in order to lead them to attribute successes to internal factors. The players changed their attributions in response to the feedback, as was hoped, and these changes led to improved self-esteem and performance.

There are, however, limitations to Weiner's understanding of attribution. A number of studies have attempted to classify attributions into Weiner's four categories of ability, effort, task difficulty and luck, but not all have agreed as to how comprehensive these categories are. Some studies have found that as few as 45 per cent of athlete's responses to winning and losing fit neatly into these categories.

Conclusions

Motivation is an important factor in sporting participation and performance. An important distinction is between intrinsic and extrinsic motivation. The former is generally more important to athletes than the latter, and attempts to increase motivation by giving athletes large material rewards have usually undermined rather than improved

performance. There are wide individual differences in the achievement motivation of athletes. The traditional McClelland-Atkinson model, which explains achievement motivation in terms of an approach-avoidance conflict between intrinsic motivation and competitive anxiety, has fallen out of favour with psychologists. Modern sports psychology places considerable emphasis, however, on the distinction between task and ego achievement orientations, and understanding this distinction can be applied in a number of ways in order to improve achievement motivation. Sports psychologists also work to enhance athletic motivation by changing athletes' cognitions regarding their ability (self-efficacy) and their understanding of their successes and failures (attribution). Studies have supported the effectiveness of both these cognitive interventions.

where to now?

The following are good sources of further information about cognitive techniques for improving motivation.

▶ **Woolfson S. (2002) Reflections on past events: the role of social cognition in sport. In Cockerill I. (ed) *Solutions in sport psychology*. London: ITP.** Provides a more detailed account of CFT.

▶ **Cox R.H. (1998) *Sport psychology: concept and application*. Boston: McGraw-Hill.** A good, detailed account of both attribution and self-efficacy.

for and against

the importance of attribution

╋ it is well documented that we place great emphasis on making attributions about our sporting successes and failures

━ theories of attribution, such as Weiner's, have limited validity because they do not explain all athletes' attributions of success and failure

╋ attribution training can improve self-esteem and performance

╋ understanding counterfactual thinking has further enhanced the range of techniques available to improve motivation

what do you know?

1 Distinguish between intrinsic and extrinsic motivation and discuss their importance in athletic motivation.

2 (a) Describe **one** theory of achievement motivation.

(b) Evaluate the theory you described in (a).

3 (a) Describe **one** study of self-efficacy in sports psychology.

(b) Assess the extent to which self-efficacy impacts on performance.

17 Social and physiological influences on performance

what's ahead?

We have already looked at the importance of individual differences and motivation in sporting performance. In this chapter we consider two further sources of influence, the social and the physiological. The former includes social facilitation, the influence of the presence of other people. We look at the positive effects audiences and competitors can have, and also consider the negative social influence of social loafing, in which team members take it easy, and let others do the work. We also look at team cohesion – the closeness of a team' and its possible effects on performance. In the second half of the chapter we consider the effects of both physiological arousal and anxiety on performance. Of particular current interest in sport psychology are theories of the anxiety-performance relationship, in particular catastrophe theory and zones of optimal functioning.

Social facilitation

The term 'social facilitation' refers to the effects the presence of others can have on the performance of a task. These effects can be positive or negative. *Co-action effects* are the effects of performing alongside other people as opposed to alone. This can be in the form of competition or co-training. The importance of co-action was demonstrated by Triplett (1898) in one of the first studies in sports psychology. Children were asked to wind fishing reels as fast as they could. In one condition

they were alone and in another they performed the task in a group. The children were significantly faster when performing the task together than when alone. Co-action effects are important in training for individual sports such as running.

Audience effects

We don't have to perform alongside others for social facilitation to take place; just being watched has a similar effect. The effects of an audience were demonstrated in a classic study by Michaels et al (1982).

classic research

how to spoil a game of pool!

Michaels J.W., Blommel J.M., Brocato R.M., Linkous R.A. & Rowe J.S. (1982) Social facilitation and inhibition in a natural setting. *Replications in Social Psychology* **2: 21–4**

aim: the aim of the study was to test the effects of an audience on the performance of pool players in the natural surroundings of a bar. More specifically, the researchers wanted to know about the different effects an audience has on performers of differing levels of expertise.

procedure: the design of the study was a field experiment, conducted in a university bar. First, researchers watched students playing pool and classified them according to ability (as measured by the percentage of successful pots). They then approached tables where players were classified as below average or above average in skill. A group of four researchers stood by the target table and watched the game, noting the subsequent performance of the players.

findings: the presence of the four researchers appeared to have a significant effect on the performance of the players at the target tables. The effects were different, however, for the above average and below average players. The above average players increased their percentage of successful pots, whereas the below average group declined in performance.

conclusion: an audience has a significant effect on performers of a range of ability. However, they have different effects on high and low ability competitors, improving the performance of the former and reducing performance of the latter.

Figure 17.1 Expert pool players perform better with an audience but novices tend to play worse

Not all recent studies have shown the same effects as the Michaels et al (1982) study. When Geisler and Leith (1997) tested the effect of an audience on the number of penalty shots scored out of 10 by 40 Canadian ex-university soccer players, no difference emerged in the number of goals scored in private or in front of an audience. One important difference between these two studies is the social situation, and it may be that the pool players in the Michaels study (who were unused to spectators) were more intimidated by the close attention of four physically very close observers than the experienced football players were at performing in front of their audience.

Ability and the specifics of the social situation may not be the only factors affecting whether audiences have positive or negative effects on performance. Another factor appears to be the personality of the participants. Graydon and Murphy (1995) administered 50 male students the EPI (see page 166 for details), and identified 10 extroverts and 10 introverts. These 20 participants were given the task of serving a table tennis ball into a grid. In one condition they did this alone and in another condition they did it in front of an audience. The extroverts performed better in front of an audience, whereas the introverts did better alone.

Home advantage and disadvantage effects

An important practical application of research into audience effects is in understanding the implications of playing in home and away matches. The home advantage effect (HAE) operates when performance is enhanced by the presence of a large supportive home audience. The importance of the HAE phenomenon was demonstrated by Nevill and Cann (1998), who looked at the size of home crowds and scores in home-wins in English and Scottish football matches between 1985 and 1996. When home crowds were large, the home team score was typically higher than when the home crowd was smaller.

Although the existence of the HAE is well documented, the opposite phenomenon of the home disadvantage effect (HDE) also exists, and can cause problems for home teams playing under conditions of high pressure. Wright et al (1995) demonstrated the existence of the HDE in an analysis of American ice hockey scores in home and away games. In high-pressure matches, for example when a championship was at stake, home teams performed less well than those playing away. One likely explanation for the HDE (Baumeister and Steinhilber, 1984) is that players feel more closely evaluated by their supporters, and that this is a particular problem where there are a large number of supportive spectators.

Explaining social facilitation effects

There are a number of ways in which social facilitation in sporting situations can be explained. Zajonc (1965) explained the phenomenon in terms of drive theory (discussed in more detail on page 194). According to drive theory, performance improves with increased physiological arousal, provided the task is simple and/or the performer has a high level of expertise. However, when the task is complex or the performer is inexpert, then increased arousal harms the performance. Zajonc suggested that the presence of other people leads to increased arousal. This means that the presence of others will improve expert performance and harm inexpert performance.

Zajonc's explanation is well supported by research. In the Michaels study for example, expert pool players potted more balls when watched, whereas poor players made fewer pots. The results of the Geisler and Leith study are also consistent with drive theory; the situation created by

The following extract is taken from an article by Martin Smith, published in *Daily Telegraph*, 29 March 2002, page S3.

> Sheffield Wednesday's record at Hillsborough [their home ground] this season has been abysmal, to say the least. They have won five games there, and, desperate times requiring desperate measures, the independent supporters association are asking fans to turn up for tonight's match against Coventry in yellow away shirts. Paul Register, the WISA chairman said: 'We've been scratching our heads about why we play so well away and so poorly at home.'

1 Using your knowledge of the home disadvantage effect, suggest a reason why Sheffield Wednesday might have played so badly at home in the 2001–2002 season.

2 How would you have advised the club to tackle the problem?

Figure 17.2 Sheffield Wednesday suffered from the home disadvantage effect in the 2001–2002 season

the researchers would be unlikely to impact particularly on the arousal levels of football players accustomed to playing in front of an audience, hence we would not expect to see much effect on their performance.

Although Zajonc appears to be correct as regards the effect of the presence of others on performance, he failed to explain *why* arousal should increase in response to the presence of others. Unless we understand this, we cannot begin to understand home advantage and disadvantage effects. However, Cottrell (1968) proposed a credible explanation for the link between presence of others and arousal in the form of *evaluation apprehension*. This is the anxiety we feel in response to being judged by others. If we are highly competent in the task we are performing, then we are likely to enjoy being judged on our performance, hence our arousal may increase somewhat, but we are unlikely to be overwhelmed by anxiety. If, however, we are not competent, then when we realise we are being evaluated we are likely to become too anxious to perform well.

The major advantage of Cottrell's approach over that of Zajonc is that it provides an explanation for home advantage and disadvantage effects. Home advantage effects are strongest in low-pressure situations where the audience is likely to be relatively uncritical. However, in critical matches the home crowd is likely to be extremely picky about the performance of the home player or players, hence they are likely to suffer from evaluation apprehension.

Social loafing

Audience and co-action effects occur because the presence of others increases arousal and effort. However, when performers are acting in concert rather than alone the opposite effect can occur, as each individual makes less effort. The French engineer Ringelmann first noted this phenomenon of *social loafing* in the 1880s. He measured how hard one man pulled on a rope then how hard each man pulled as their number increased. By the time there were eight men pulling, Ringelmann calculated that each was only putting in half the effort of the single man.

Social loafing is a potential problem in any team sport, but is perhaps most evident when each member of the team has the same role as the others and when each performs at the same time. Thus, there is little opportunity for social loafing in a sprint relay because we can easily evaluate the performance of each member of the team as they run separately. Neither, in rugby, can a scrum half or hooker indulge in social loafing because their role in the team is highly specific and so open to evaluation. However, it is difficult to see how hard any particular forward is pushing during a scrum, and it is similarly hard to measure the contribution of any one rower in a coxless four. These athletes may thus be vulnerable to social loafing. As a coach or teacher, we can reduce social loafing in these situations by giving individual feedback to team members and, where possible, giving each member of the team a particular responsibility or goal prior to a contest.

Figure 17.3 It is very difficult to see how much effort is made by each player in a scrum

Clearly, one factor in the likelihood of social loafing taking place is how easily identifiable the effort made by individuals is. Another factor appears to be the athlete's *goal orientation* (see page 182 for a discussion). Swain (1996) performed a study of social loafing, in which 96 Year-10 boys (average age 15 years 6 months) were assessed for goal orientation and given the task of running a 30-m sprint under three conditions. In the first condition they ran individually; in the second they ran in teams but each boy's time was recorded; and in the third they ran in teams but only the team time was recorded (thus their own performance was not identifiable). Ego-oriented participants ran significantly slower in the third condition, but there was no difference in the performance of task-oriented athletes across the three conditions. This has a clear practical application for coaching and managing teams. Ego-oriented athletes are likely to indulge in social loafing if they think they are not being watched, therefore it is important that their performance *is* observed in training and fed back to them. We might also attempt to increase an athlete's task orientation or even deselect them if they have a strong tendency to loaf.

interactive angles

The coach of your local children's football team is worried about social loafing in some of the team members. What advice would you give them about how to reduce social loafing?

The following is a good source of further information about social facilitation in sport.

 Gill D. (2000) *Psychological dynamics of sport*. **Champaign: Human Kinetics.** Contains a useful chapter on social facilitation.

Team cohesion

The term 'cohesion' literally means to stick together. In the context of sport, we think of a team as highly cohesive if it 'sticks together', ie it is a close-knit united group. Widmeyer et al (1985) identified two aspects of team cohesion, namely *group integration* and *individual attractions to the team*. Each team member has a view of the team as a unit (group integration) and of every individual within it (individual attractions). They may also have different perceptions of the team and its members as regards task-achievement (ie sporting performance) and social life.

It is thus possible to think of your teammates quite differently as individuals and as a team, and as people and co-competitors. We might, for example, see them as collectively nice but ineffective, individually nice but collectively obnoxious, socially unpleasant both individually and collectively but effective co-competitors etc. Carron et al (1985) devised a psychometric test called the Group Environment Questionnaire (GEQ), which can be used to measure team cohesiveness. The GEQ considers group integration and individual attractions, and both the task achievement and social life of a team.

So what determines the cohesiveness of a team? In a recent study, Holt and Sparkes (2001) studied an English university football team over the course of eight months of a season. Data was gathered by observation and interviews. Based on these, the researchers concluded that four factors affected team cohesion; a clear role for each member of the team, willingness of make personal sacrifices for the good of the team, quality of communication between team members and shared goals for the team as a whole.

Team cohesiveness and performance

There is a large body of research to suggest that team cohesiveness is associated with performance, ie the more close-knit the team the more successful they tend to be. Gould et al (1999) interviewed athletes and coaches for the American Olympic teams in eight sports, assessing a number of factors including team cohesion, commitment, confi-

dence, experience, social support and practical problems such as travel arrangements to the Games. Performance in the Games was classified in terms of how it related to expectations, ie did they do better or worse than their past performances would predict? It emerged that teams with low cohesiveness were more likely to underperform, but that cohesiveness was just one of several important factors affecting performance. Experience, commitment and social support were also associated with success at the Games.

It seems then that teams higher in cohesion tend to be more successful. However, this does not necessarily mean that the cohesion caused the performance. A problem with the Gould et al study is that it was *retrospective*, looking at cohesiveness after the performance. It may be that the teams who performed well became closer as a result, and that teams that underperformed drifted apart in their disappointment. A number of studies have tried to determine the extent to which cohesion affects performance and performance affects cohesion. Slater and Sewell (1994) assessed team cohesion in three male and three female university hockey teams at the beginning, middle and end of the season. They also assessed team performance by means of scores at the same three points in the season. They used a procedure called *cross-lagged correlation* to analyse the cohesiveness-performance relationship. This means that the relationship between early cohesiveness and later performance and between early performance and later cohesiveness were calculated. Actually, early cohesiveness predicted later performance *and* early performance predicted later cohesiveness, but the stronger relationship was between early cohesiveness and later performance, suggesting that team cohesion is an important factor in determining performance, and that performance is a less important factor in cohesiveness.

Not all studies have supported this relationship, however. In an experimental study, Grieve et al (2000) randomly assigned male basketball players to three-person basketball teams, and tried to manipulate teams so as to create either high or low levels of team cohesiveness. Each team was then assessed for cohesiveness, given a series of games and then assessed once again for cohesiveness. In this study there was no relationship between cohesiveness before the games and performance, however, successful performance was associated with high levels of cohesiveness at the end of the games. These findings suggest that cohesiveness does not influence performance but that performance *does* influence cohesiveness.

The studies of Grieve et al and Slater and Sewell lead us to quite different conclusions regarding the cohesiveness-performance relationship. So why have these studies found such different results? One answer may lie in the type of sport being studied, and a further related answer may be team size. Slater and Sewell looked at hockey teams, which are fairly large at 11 a side, and which are noted for their tendency to be highly cohesive. The Grieve et al study on the other hand looked at teams of three, which may be simply too small for cohesiveness to affect performance, and used basketball, which may be less affected by cohesiveness than hockey. It is useful to look at cohesiveness in different sports because it shows that we should not assume that the cohesiveness-performance relationship is the same in different sports. One recent study compared the influence of competitive success on team cohesiveness in two quite different sports, rugby and swimming.

research now

the effects of winning and losing on different types of team

Kozub S.A. & Button C. (2000) The influence of competitive outcome on perceptions of cohesion in rugby and swimming teams. *International Journal of Sport Psychology* 31: 82–95

aim: it had previously been established that performance both affects team cohesiveness and is affected by it. However, little was known about the differential effects in different sports. The aim of this study was to compare the effects of competitive outcome on team cohesion in two different sports, rugby and swimming.

procedure: 60 male rugby players and 60 male swimmers completed the General Environment Questionnaire (GEQ) immediately before and after each of a series of competitions. Changes in the group integration and individual attractions in relation to both task achievement and social life following wins and losses could thus be seen.

findings: no changes were noted in swimmers or rugby players in relation to the social life of the team. However, the team's task-related group integration and individual attractions did alter according to the outcome of each match, and the effects were different in the two sports. In both sports the task-related individual attractions increased during each competition, regardless of the outcome. In swimmers the task-related group integration scores also rose, regardless of the outcome. However, for the rugby players task-related group integration rose slightly following a win but fell sharply following a loss.

conclusions: some aspects of team cohesiveness appear to be affected by the outcome of competition. The effects are different in different types of sport. This suggests that previous research has underestimated the complexity of the performance-cohesiveness relationship.

for and against

cohesiveness as a factor in performance

+ studies such as that of Gould et al have found an association between cohesiveness and performance
+ cross-lagged correlations such as that of Slater and Sewell have found that early cohesiveness is associated with later performance
− some studies, eg Grieve et al, have found no links between early cohesiveness and later performance
− there is much that we do not yet understand about the cohesiveness-performance relationship, for example differences between sports

where to now?

The following is a good source of further information about team cohesiveness:

▶ **Scully D. (2002) 'The team just hasn't gelled'. In Cockerill I. (ed)** *Solutions in sport psychology*. **London: Thomson Learning.** Presents a useful and quite critical account of research in this area.

Arousal, anxiety and performance

At the top level of sporting competition there is little difference in skill, fitness or motivation. Perhaps the most important factor separating winners from losers at this level is the ability of the participants to cope with arousal and anxiety (Jones, 1991). Let us first distinguish between the terms 'arousal' and 'anxiety'. *Arousal* is our general level of physical and psychological activation. We are low in arousal when we are tired, bored or sleeping, and we are high in arousal when we are excited, anxious or angry. High and low levels of arousal can thus both be positive or negative experiences. *Anxiety*, however, is a negative emotional state in which we experience high arousal accompanied by worrying. Psychologists have made important distinctions between state and trait anxiety, and between cognitive and somatic anxiety.

Distinctions between types of anxiety

State and trait anxiety

You should recall the term 'trait' from chapter 15. A trait is a stable personality characteristic that remains fairly constant across a range of situations. An athlete high in *trait anxiety* is thus consistently anxious. *State anxiety*, on the other hand, refers to the anxiety experienced before and during competition. The concept of state anxiety is probably of more use in sports psychology, as it is the anxiety we experience while participating in sports that directly impacts on our performance and is open to reduction by psychological techniques. Martens et al (1990) have developed a self-rating inventory called the Competitive State Anxiety Inventory-2 (CSAI-2) to assess state anxiety. Items from the CSAI-2 are shown in table 17.1.

Cognitive and somatic anxiety

The term 'somatic' comes from the Greek *soma*, meaning body. Somatic anxiety is thus bodily anxiety, the physical sensation of anxiety. This involves increased heart and breathing rates, along with 'butterflies in the stomach', the feeling of blood being diverted away from the digestive system. Cognitive anxiety, by contrast, refers to anxiety in the mind. This takes the form of anxious thoughts, for example of doubts about one's own ability, and of mental images, such as of scenes of losing.

The relationship between arousal and performance

We can look at the impact of both arousal and anxiety on sporting performance. There are two traditional approaches used to explain the relationship between arousal and performance, drive theory and the inverted-U hypothesis. Note that in one sense both these theories are outdated as contemporary sports psychologists usually find it more helpful to consider the relationship between performance and anxiety as well as arousal. Drive theory and the inverted-U hypothesis do however still have some practical applications.

Drive theory

Hull (1943) proposed *drive theory* as a general explanation of human performance and motivation. According to drive theory, there are three major factors influencing performance; the complexity of the motor task, physiological arousal and learned tendencies to respond to a task in a certain way. The higher the level of physiological arousal, the more likely we are to adopt our dominant response to a situation, ie the learned tendency to respond in a particular way. If the task is a simple one and our dominant response is the correct one, then higher arousal will be associated with better performance. This can be expressed as an equation:

$$\text{Performance} = \text{Arousal} \times \text{Habit}$$

Drive theory can also be shown graphically – see figure 17.4.

Table 17.1 Items from the CSAI-2

		Not at all	Somewhat	Moderately so	Very much so
1	I am concerned about this competition	1	2	3	4
2	I feel nervous	1	2	3	4
3	I feel ill-at-ease	1	2	3	4
4	I have self-doubts	1	2	3	4

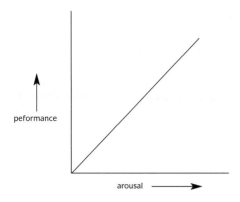

Figure 17.4 The relationship between performance and arousal for an expert performer performing a simple motor skill

If, however, the task is a complex one involving fine motor skills, or if the athlete has acquired bad habits and the dominant response for the situation is wrong, high levels of arousal will inhibit performance. Because arousal level is greater in competition than in practice, and increases according to the importance of the competition, drive theory predicts that the best performances of high-level athletes will take place in high-level competition. Drive theory also predicts, however, that, because novices are more likely to have bad habits, they would be more likely to make mistakes under pressure. An important application of this principle is that if novices are to acquire better skills, they need to practise under conditions of low arousal, ie with minimal spectators and minimal competition.

Drive theory has been useful in explaining why top-level athletes achieve their personal bests in competition and why novices tend to crack under the pressure of high-level competition. Empirical evidence for drive theory comes from studies of social facilitation (reviewed on page 187) in which social conditions that we would expect to lead to high arousal have positive effects on expert performances and negative effects on novice performances. However, drive theory fails to explain instances where even expert athletes become too aroused and make errors. It also fails to take account of the type of arousal experienced or psychological factors that may accompany arousal such as cognitive anxiety.

for and against

drive theory

+ drive theory can explain why experts do best under pressure, whereas novices do worse

+ this understanding can be used by coaches to help athletes reach the optimum level of arousal

– it cannot easily explain why experts make errors in simple tasks under pressure

– it cannot explain the influence of cognitive anxiety on performance

Inverted-U hypothesis

The inverted-U hypothesis originated from Yerkes and Dodson (1908). The principle is that for every motor task we can carry out there is an optimum level of physiological arousal. Performance is best at this level and drops off when arousal rises above or falls below it. This relationship is shown in figure 17.5.

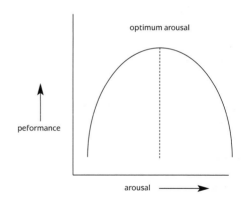

Figure 17.5 The inverted-U hypothesis

The optimum level of arousal for a task depends on the complexity of the motor skills used to perform that task. For a complex task involving fine motor skill, such as placing a dart in the bull's-eye, low levels of arousal are preferable. For gross tasks such as weightlifting, the optimum arousal level is much higher.

Support for the inverted-U hypothesis comes from studies of athletes' perceptions of what factors affect performance. Thelwell and Maynard (2000) asked 198 county level English cricketers (100 batsmen and 98 bowlers) what they

Figure 17.6 As weightlifting requires power rather than fine motor skills, performance is best with a high level of arousal

considered to be the most important variables affecting their performance. Optimum level of arousal emerged in the top four factors affecting both batsmen and bowlers (the others were self-confidence, a pre-match routine and following a performance plan).

Understanding optimum levels of arousal has an important application in mental preparation for competition. Before a snooker or darts match players aim to achieve relatively low levels of arousal. This is the reason why darts players drink alcohol during competition and why beta blockers (drugs that control heart rate and blood pressure) are considered an unfair advantage in snooker. On the other hand a sport involving gross motor skills and the application of power requires a process of 'psyching up' to raise arousal levels. Some athletes have rituals to help them do this, a classic example being the Maori Haka display used by the New Zealand 'All-Blacks' prior to rugby matches.

An advantage of the inverted-U hypothesis over drive theory is that it can explain why even world-class athletes make serious errors under conditions of high arousal – fine motor skills become unsupportable at high levels of pressure and arousal even in experts. However, most psychologists now believe that we cannot explain the complex relationship between level of performance, the nature of the required skills and the situation by reference to arousal alone. Instead, most modern approaches focus on the performance-anxiety relationship, and it is to this that we now turn.

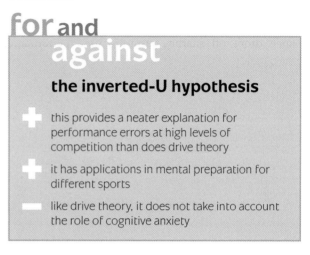

for and against

the inverted-U hypothesis

+ this provides a neater explanation for performance errors at high levels of competition than does drive theory

+ it has applications in mental preparation for different sports

− like drive theory, it does not take into account the role of cognitive anxiety

The anxiety-performance relationship

The emphasis in modern sports psychology is more on anxiety than arousal as a predictor of performance. Two theories have emerged as particularly influential in understanding the role of anxiety; these are Fazey and Hardy's *catastrophe model* and Hanin's *zones of optimal functioning*.

The catastrophe model

A problem with the inverted-U hypothesis is that it predicts that a small increase in arousal above the optimum will have only a small impact on performance. Fazey and Hardy (1988) pointed out that under some conditions a very small increase in arousal beyond the optimum level can lead to a *performance catastrophe*, ie a massive fall-off in performance. According to Fazey and Hardy the main factor affecting when performance catastrophes occur is cognitive anxiety. Catastrophes occur when levels of cognitive anxiety are high and not at other times. Figure 17.7 shows the relationship between arousal and performance under conditions of low and high cognitive anxiety.

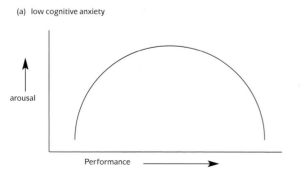

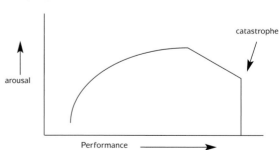

Figure 17.7 The relationship between arousal and performance under conditions of low and high cognitive anxiety

According to Fazey and Hardy, then, the inverted-U hypothesis is not worthless, but it only explains what happens under conditions of low cognitive anxiety. However, when cognitive anxiety is high then there comes a point just above the optimum level of arousal where performance drops off sharply, resulting in a performance catastrophe.

The catastrophe model is hard to test directly, partly because cognitive anxiety is hard to assess during performance. However, there is evidence to suggest that athletes' best and worst performances occur when their cognitive anxiety is particularly high, and that under high cognitive anxiety performance drops off sharply when the optimum arousal level is exceeded. In a study by Hardy et al (1994), eight expert crown green bowlers bowled three balls at a jack on two consecutive days. On one day, prior to bowling they were given neutral instructions designed to create low cognitive anxiety and on the other day they were given a different set of 'threatening' instructions designed to create a state of high cognitive anxiety. The CSAI-2 confirmed that cognitive anxiety was in fact higher in this condition. To increase physiological arousal the participants were given shuttle-runs to perform and their heart rates were individually monitored. The relationship between arousal as measured by heart rate and performance could thus be measured in conjunction with low and high cognitive anxiety. Results supported the catastrophe model. In the low cognitive anxiety condition the performance-arousal relationship showed a weak inverted-U. Under the high cognitive anxiety condition, however, performance was better, but dropped off sharply when arousal became too high. The results are shown in figure 17.8.

It is important to note that although high levels of cognitive anxiety are associated with performance catastrophes they are also associated with the best performances. An important application of the catastrophe model and the research surrounding it is to show that cognitive anxiety can be a help as well as a hindrance to athletes (Hardy, 1996). Although studies like that of Hardy et al (1994) do support the catastrophe model, they are few in number and can be criticised on the basis that the cognitive anxiety induced in artificial conditions is quite different to that experienced by athletes in competition (ie they lack ecological validity). The difficulty in testing the catastrophe model more conclusively has proved frustrating to psychologists. Moreover, the idea that high levels of cognitive anxiety can enhance performance remains controversial (Gill, 1992).

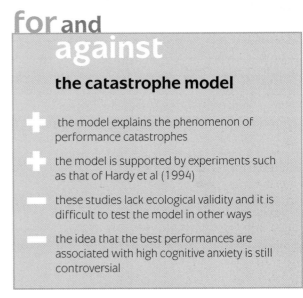

for and against

the catastrophe model

+ the model explains the phenomenon of performance catastrophes

+ the model is supported by experiments such as that of Hardy et al (1994)

– these studies lack ecological validity and it is difficult to test the model in other ways

– the idea that the best performances are associated with high cognitive anxiety is still controversial

Zones of optimal functioning

Yuri Hanin identified a further limitation of traditional theories of the relationship between anxiety and performance. Both drive theory and the inverted-U hypothesis fail to take account of individual differences in athletes' responses to anxiety. Hanin (1986) measured the precompetitive anxiety scores of 46 elite female rowers and noted that there was a wide range of scores (mean score 44, range 26–67). This wide variety of anxiety levels in highly successful athletes suggested that different athletes thrive

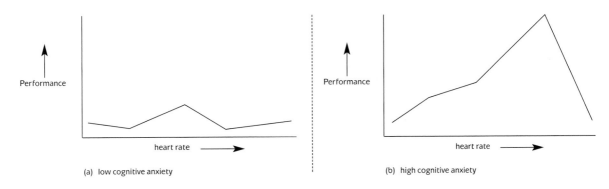

Figure 17.8 The relationship between arousal and bowls performance under conditions of low and high cognitive anxiety (adapted from Hardy et al, 1994)

on different levels of anxiety. Hanin suggested that each athlete has their own preferred level of anxiety – the individual zone of optimal functioning or IZOF – and that their performance would suffer if their anxiety went below or above this preferred level. In general, athletes competing in team sports have a lower IZOF than competitors in individual events (Randle and Weinberg, 1997).

There is some empirical support for the idea that athletes do best when at the level of anxiety they prefer. In a study of field and track athletes Inlay et al (1995) investigated anxiety during seven competitions and found that 63 per cent of the athletes judged to be in their 'zone' performed well, while 31 per cent performed badly. This provides some support for the IZOF construct. More recently Russell and Cox (2000) assessed IZOF in 55 college basketball and American football players by measuring their positive and negative emotions during performance. Performances were also assessed. As in the Inlay et al study, athletes judged to be 'in the zone' because they reported positive rather than negative emotions did perform better but only moderately so.

It thus appears that there is such a thing as an individual zone of functioning, and that achieving it during competition leads to moderate improvements in performance. It is clearly useful to recognise that not all athletes require precisely the same level of precompetitive anxiety. This is not to say, however, that the idea is uncontroversial. By definition an athlete's IZOF is difficult to measure and even more difficult to explain. It remains unclear for example to what extent the 'zone' is a cognitive state and to what extent it is a state of physiological arousal. Perhaps the greatest virtue of the IZOF construct is its *meaningfulness* to athletes and coaches, who have found it extremely helpful to think of mental preparation as putting the athlete in the zone.

where to now?

The following are good sources of further information about the influence of arousal and anxiety on performance.

▶ **Landers D.M. & Boutcher S.H. (1993) Arousal-performance relationships. In Williams J.M. (1993)** *Applied sport psychology.* **Mountain View: Mayfield.** Takes a practical view of applying the theories described here in real-life situations.

▶ **Kremer J. & Scully D. (1994)** *Psychology in sport.* **Hove: Taylor & Francis.** A critical discussion of traditional and modern theories of performance.

Conclusions

There are a number of social and physiological factors affecting sporting performance. The presence of audiences and competitors tends to enhance performance. However, under conditions where the effort made by a particular individual is hard to identify, and in particular where athletes are ego-oriented, team members may be

for and against

IZOFs

➕ studies have confirmed that individual athletes have different preferred levels of anxiety

➕ there is moderate support for the idea that athletes perform better when 'in the zone'

➕ athletes and coaches have found the idea of the 'zone' helpful in preparation for competition

➖ IZOF is difficult to measure and explain

what do you know?

1 (a) What are social facilitation effects?

(b) Discuss alternative theories of social facilitation.

2 Describe and evaluate research into social loafing.

3 (a) Describe one study of the relationship between team cohesiveness and performance.

(b) Discuss the relationship between team cohesiveness and performance.

4 Compare and contrast two theories of the relationship between performance and arousal and/or anxiety.

vulnerable to social loafing, reducing their personal effort and letting other team members take the strain. Team cohesiveness appears to be another important social factor affecting team performance. In general, highly cohesive teams perform better, although it is unclear to what extent the cohesiveness actually leads to the performance, and to what extent the relationship extends to a wide variety of sports.

Physiological arousal and anxiety are also associated with performance, although there are a number of competing theories, which explain these relationships. The traditional approaches of the arousal-performance relationship – drive theory and the inverted-U hypothesis – have practical applications and some empirical support, but in recent years psychologists have turned to more complex theories that focus on the relationship between performance and anxiety as opposed to arousal. These include the catastrophe model and individual zones of optimal functioning. Each of these theories has practical applications but a limited body of empirical support.

18 Attachment

what's ahead?

In this chapter we will be looking at the importance of our earliest relationships; how they come about and how they can affect us in later life. Having briefly examined the process of attachment formation, we can go on to look at the work of John Bowlby, from whom many of our current ideas about attachment come. We shall also look in depth at the work of Mary Ainsworth, who extended Bowlby's theory with the idea that children can be classified as having different attachment types according to their behaviour towards their primary carer. We examine research, looking at the later consequences of attachment type, both with regard to intellectual and social development, and consider what factors influence attachment type. We then look at attachments across the world and consider the different meanings attachment might have in different cultures. In what's new? we will look at a recent development – the discovery of atypical or *disorganised* attachments associated with neglect and abuse. Finally, we shall look at the social constructionist view of attachment and the social implications of emphasising the mother as the major influence on children's development.

What is attachment?

An attachment is a two-way emotional bond in which people depend on each other for their sense of security. Attachment is characterised by proximity seeking (wanting to remain close to each other), distress at being separated and pleasure at being reunited. Although we form attachments throughout our lives, psychologists are particularly interested in the attachment that forms between babies and their primary carers. Note the term *primary carer*. Psychologists normally only use the word 'mother' if they are referring to the biological mother, and 'mother' is generally used in this book when we are looking at studies that have looked in particular at biological mothers.

Bowlby's attachment theory

John Bowlby's (1951, 1958, 1969) theory of attachment remains the dominant explanation in psychology today. There are several strands to the theory, and we shall restrict ourselves here to looking at four areas in particular:

- maternal deprivation hypothesis
- the evolutionary basis of attachment
- social releasers and instinctive parenting responses
- internal working models.

Figure 18.1 John Bowlby

Maternal deprivation hypothesis

The most fundamental of Bowlby's ideas was that the development of an attachment in early life is an essential aspect of a child's development. Before going on to develop attachment theory-proper, Bowlby (1951) proposed the *maternal deprivation hypothesis*. This stated that a child requires the continuous presence of a primary carer throughout a sensitive period lasting at least the first 18 months to 2 years. Bowlby (1951) identified two particularly serious consequences of the failure to form an attachment or serious disruption to the attachment during this sensitive period (for example prolonged separation from the primary carer).

- **Affectionless psychopathy:** This is the inability to experience guilt or deep feelings for others. Naturally this interferes enormously with one's relationships in later life. It is also associated with criminality, as affectionless psychopaths find it difficult to appreciate the feelings of their victims and so lack remorse.

- **Developmental retardation:** Bowlby proposed that there is a critical period for intellectual development and that if children are deprived of a maternal relationship for too long they would suffer retardation, i.e. very low intelligence.

Bowlby provided evidence for the link between affectionless and psychopathic behaviour and early experience in a classic study conducted at the child guidance clinic where he worked.

Taken at face value, the *Forty four thieves* study provides powerful evidence for a link between early disruption to attachments and later emotional impairment. However, when we look more closely at the study we can see some important design flaws, which detract somewhat from its credibility (Flanagan, 1999). Firstly, information about

classic
research

can disruption to attachment cause affectionless psychopathy?

Bowlby J. (1946) *Forty four juvenile thieves*. London: Balliere, Tindall & Cox

aim: Bowlby believed that prolonged separation from the primary carer during the first two or three years of life could cause permanent emotional damage. One way in which this damage manifests itself is affectionless psychopathy. Bowlby aimed in this study to see whether teenage criminals who displayed affectionless psychopathy were more likely to have had an early separation than those who had not.

procedure: 44 of the teenagers referred to the Child Guidance Clinic where Bowlby worked were selected on the basis that they were involved in criminal activity, and that they were living with their biological parents. Bowlby interviewed them in order to assess whether they exhibited signs of affectionless psychopathy. This was identified by lack of affection to others, lack of guilt or shame at their actions and lack of empathy for their victims. Bowlby also interviewed the families of the adolescents in order to establish whether the children had had prolonged early separations from their primary carers in their first two years. Bowlby then matched up those young people who had been classified as affectionless psychopaths with those who had had prolonged maternal deprivation in the first two years. A control group of non-delinquent young people was established in order to see how commonly maternal deprivation occurred in the non-delinquent population.

findings: the results were striking. Of the 14 children identified as affectionless psychopaths, 12 had experienced prolonged separation from their mothers in the first 2 years. By contrast, only 5 of the 30 delinquent children not classified as affectionless psychopaths had experienced similar separations. Of the 44 people in the non-delinquent control group, only 2 had experienced prolonged separations.

conclusions: the young criminals who had a prolonged separation in their first 2 years were several times more likely to exhibit affectionless psychopathy than those who had no such separation. This provides strong support for Bowlby's maternal deprivation hypothesis.

the early separation was collected *retrospectively* during interviews. This relies on the participants' accuracy of recall, not to mention their honesty, hence it does not carry the same weight as information obtained from an objective source such as medical records. Secondly, Bowlby himself carried out both the interviews and the psychiatric assessments. As he knew what he was expecting to find, he may have been biased in his assessments. It is now standard procedure in this type of study for researchers to assess participants without knowing any details that might predispose them towards bias. This is called a *double blind* procedure.

media watch

Spain in shock as girls admit murder 'to become famous'

Two teenage girls hacked to death a schoolfriend because they wanted to become famous and enjoy extreme experiences, they confessed to a judge near the southern port of Cadiz. The case has stunned Spain and prompted psychologists to warn that lack of family affection is producing a generation of young psychopaths.

Clara Garcia Casado, 16, was found dead early on Saturday on scrubland in the town of San Fernando, bearing more than 18 knife wounds and with her head almost severed.

Psychologists warned that cold-blooded violence by alienated youngsters was increasingly common. One said abusive family relationships could produce personality defects in adolescents. Such character flaws flourished in a climate that was seen to encourage violence and risk-taking.

Source: *The Independent*, 31 May 2000

1 The psychologists quoted in the article appear to have been influenced by Bowlby's ideas. How might have Bowlby explained this case?

2 Reading ahead, how have ideas changed since Bowlby's maternal deprivation hypothesis, and what factors might we now implicate in the behaviour of these two murderers?

Contemporary psychologists generally believe that, while early relations with the primary carer are very important, Bowlby overstated his case in his early work. They believe that children are more resilient to early experiences – for example temporary separation from their primary carer – than he gave them credit for. In fairness to him, Bowlby did later acknowledge this (Bowlby, 1957). Maternal deprivation hypothesis opened up a debate about the possible effects of day care on children that continues today. We shall look at this in detail in chapter 3.

One way in which our ideas have changed since Bowlby's time is that most psychologists would make a distinction between deprivation and privation. *Privation* occurs when no attachment is formed, whereas *deprivation* takes place when a child is separated from an attachment figure after an attachment has been formed (Rutter, 1981). Bowlby did not distinguish between deprivation and privation, and nowadays psychologists tend to associate the very serious effects of affectionless psychopathy and retardation with *privation* rather than deprivation.

Bowlby's ideas developed considerably following research in the 1950s and 1960s. What follows is sometimes called *attachment theory-proper* and is considered as a separate theory from maternal deprivation hypothesis.

The evolutionary basis of attachment

Bowlby had an interest in *ethology*, the study of animal behaviour, as well as in child development. He noted that other species apart from humans formed attachments, and suggested (Bowlby, 1957) that there may be evolutionary advantages to the formation of secure attachments. Think back a million or so years ago to more dangerous times. Wolves and other predators posed a serious threat to humans and for obvious reasons children were among the most vulnerable individuals. Children who maintained close proximity to their carers and who returned often to them for comfort were less vulnerable to predation. Attachment, which led to children maintaining proximity, was thus *adaptive*, i.e. it increased the chances of survival.

Evolutionary psychology has developed considerably since Bowlby's time, but his ideas remain sound. An influential contemporary view on evolution and attachment comes from Jay Belsky and colleagues (eg Belsky, 1999). Belsky proposes that parents instinctively respond to the nature of their own environment with different parenting styles that lead to different types of attachments and hence to different patterns of adult relationships in their offspring. These patterns of attachment are adaptive in equipping individuals for particular environments. High levels of environmental stress, associated with a dangerous environment, lead to relatively harsh and inattentive parenting styles and hence to an adult attachment style (insecure), suited to coping with a high-mortality environment. It is adaptive **not** to form close relationships when the environment is sufficiently dangerous to make it likely that attachment figures will die early and violent deaths. The social and emotional difficulties faced by insecurely attached individuals in the current low mortality environment of Europe and America can be seen an evolutionary leftover from a time when insecure attachment was adaptive.

All evolutionary explanations in psychology present us with something of a problem, and Bowlby's idea of an evolved tendency to form attachments is no exception. While we can make logical links between attachment in different species and speculate about what might have been adaptive for humans a million years ago, there is no *direct* evidence for the evolution of any human behaviour. That said, evolution is generally accepted as an influence on infant behaviour and this aspect of Bowlby's theory is not generally considered controversial.

Social releasers and parenting responses

Bowlby noted that infants are born with a set of instinctive behaviours, including smiling, sucking, gesturing and crying. He proposed that these have evolved in order to maximise the chances of being well looked after and hence surviving. He famously said:

Babies' smiles are powerful things, leaving mothers spellbound and enslaved. Who can doubt that the baby who most readily rewards his mother with a smile is the one who is best loved and best cared for? Bowlby (1957, page 237)

Bowlby called these behaviours *social releasers*. Their function is to elicit instinctive parenting responses from adults. The interplay between social releasers and parenting responses is the process that builds the attachment between infant and carer. Failure on the part of the carer to provide the appropriate parenting response to the child's social releasers leads to psychological damage. This is a crucial aspect of Bowlby's theory as it means that the most important factor in a child's development is the effort and skill of their primary carer. We shall revisit this idea when we examine the social constructionist critique of attachment theory – that it allows mothers to be blamed for anything that goes wrong in a child's development.

Subsequent researchers have observed the interplay between social releasers and parenting responses proposed by Bowlby. Brazleton *et al* (1979) systematically observed mothers and babies during their interactions, and noted that both mothers and babies imitated each others' movements and took turns to initiate a new movement. They

Figure 18.2 This baby and adult are clearly interacting successfully

called this *interactional synchrony*. The researchers also tried asking the mothers to ignore the babies' signals. It was found that the babies quickly became concerned and some curled up and became motionless. Brazleton's findings support Bowlby's ideas about social releasers and the importance of responding to them.

It is important to emphasise that when Bowlby talked of 'parenting' or 'mothering' he did not mean that the carers need to be the biological parents or that the primary carer need be the biological mother. He did, however, believe that it was necessary for there to be a primary carer or carers who would spend a considerable amount of time with the infant during their first two to three years. Bowlby believed that the first two to three years of a child's life are crucial to its social development. These years are thus a *sensitive period*, and if a successful attachment is not formed during this time it will be more difficult to form one later on.

Internal working models

One of the most important aspects of Bowlby's theory was his idea of internal working models (Bowlby, 1969). Bowlby proposed that the developing child formed a mental representation of their first attachment relationship and that this would have profound effects on their later relationships and on their own success as a parent. He called this mental representation an internal working model. If the child internalises a working model of attachment as kind and reliable, they will tend to bring these qualities to their future relationships. If, however, they are neglected or abused, there is a chance that they will reproduce these patterns. Bowlby believed that patterns of behaviour were transmitted down through families through the formation of internal working models.

It is something of a myth that only those who have had model upbringings can be successful parents themselves, and that those who have been abused as children will necessarily go on to become abusers themselves. However, it does seem to be true that, as Bowlby suggested, people's mental representations of their early experiences of being parented affect their own formation of attachments with their children. This was demonstrated in a study by Fonagy et al (1993). They assessed pregnant women's internal working models using a standard interview called the adult attachment interview (AAI). They then measured how securely attached their babies were at 12 and 18 months. It emerged that those mothers who reported insecure attachments with their own parents tended to be those whose babies displayed insecure attachment towards them. This strong association between mothers' reports of their own maternal attachment and their attachment with their own babies is powerful evidence for the importance of internal working models.

Bowlby's ideas

+ Bowlby appears to be correct in stating that the formation of the child's first attachment(s) is important to its future development

− it does seem, however, that Bowlby underestimated children's ability to survive delayed attachment and periods of separation from the primary carer (see chapter 19)

+ there is strong evidence for Bowlby's idea of social releasers, for example from the Brazleton study

+ there is also strong evidence for the importance of internal working models in affecting people's attachment with their own children

− although Bowlby's view of attachment as having evolved because it is adaptive is highly credible, it is very difficult to test, so we have to take it 'on faith'

where to now?

The following are good sources of further information about the work of John Bowlby:

▶ **Bowlby J. (1988)** *A secure base*. **London: Routledge.** Based on a series of introductory lectures by Bowlby on the field of attachment. Less technical than most of Bowlby's writing, so a good starting point for people wishing to read some Bowlby.

▶ **Holmes J. (1993)** *John Bowlby and attachment theory*. **London: Routledge.** A detailed account of the life and works of Bowlby.

▶ **Jarvis M. (2003)** *Psychodynamic psychology: classic theory and contemporary research*. **London: Thomson learning.** Contains a more advanced account of Bowlby's work, along with an account of contemporary research.

Van Ijzendoorn (1995) performed a meta-analysis of 18 similar studies conducted in a range of countries, and this association between parental and infant attachment was supported.

Mary Ainsworth's theory: classifying and explaining attachment types

A number of researchers, sometimes called the *NeoBowlbyites* because of their emphasis on the importance of attachment, have researched extensively the factors associated with the development of attachments and the long-term effects of the first attachment. In a naturalistic observation study, based in family homes, Ainsworth (1967) observed children's behaviour with caregivers and strangers, and proposed that different attachment types could be seen, based on the independence shown by playing infants, the anxiety they displayed when left alone or with a stranger and their response to being reunited with the primary carer. Based closely on this observational study, Ainsworth and Wittig (1969) developed a laboratory procedure to classify attachment types. This is called the *Strange Situation*, and it is still the most popular procedure for classifying attachments.

Classifying attachment types – the Strange Situation

This is a laboratory procedure designed to determine how securely attached a child is to the primary carer. The rationale is that infants display different behaviour towards the primary caregiver and towards strangers according to the security of attachment. The *Strange Situation* has eight episodes, lasting three minutes each. These are shown in table 18.1 and the diagram on page 206.

Table 18.1 The Strange Situation

1. The caregiver and the child are placed in an observation room.
2. The child is left free to explore.
3. A stranger enters and speaks to mother, then attempts to play with child.
4. The carer leaves the child and stranger alone.
5. The carer re-enters and the stranger leaves.
6. The carer leaves the child alone.
7. The stranger re-enters and tries to play with the child.
8. The stranger leaves and the carer re-enters.

Based on the Strange Situation, Ainsworth et al (1978) proposed three types of attachment:

● *Type A* – **avoidant**; these children play independently and do not show distress when the mother leaves nor make contact when she returns. Between 20 and 25 per cent of British children aged 12 to 18 months are classified as type A (van Ijzendoorn and Kroonenberg, 1988).

● *Type B* – **securely attached**; these children play independently and do not show much distress in episodes 3 and 4. They greet the carer positively when she returns. They are likely to be distressed in episode 6 when left alone. They require and accept comfort from the carer in episode 8. Between 60 and 75 per cent British children aged 12 to 18 months are classified as type B.

● *Type C* – **resistant (or ambivalent)**; these children explore less in episode 2 than others. They are very distressed on being left with a stranger but, although they rush to the carer on her return, they do not readily accept comforting. Around 3 per cent of British and 15 per cent of American infants are classified as type C.

So how useful is the Strange Situation as a test of attachment? A large number of studies have confirmed that children classified as type B according to the Strange Situation go on to do better in tests of both intellectual and social development than those classified as types A or C (see above). The Strange Situation thus has good *predictive validity*, ie it can predict how a child will turn out. On the other hand, there is some question as to precisely what the Strange Situation actually measures. How distressed a child becomes in the anxiety-provoking stages 4, 6 and 7 could depend as much on their temperament as their attachment (see above for a discussion of temperament). Temperament does not, however, predict the child's responses to the primary carer's return in stages 5 and 8 (Sroufe, 1985), so it does appear that the test measures something more than temperament.

The origins of attachment type – sensitive responsiveness

Like Bowlby, Ainsworth believed that the major determinant of the quality of a child–parent attachment was the quality of care provided by the primary carer. She saw the crucial ingredient of successful parenting as *sensitive responsiveness*, ie how successfully the parent picks up and responds to the child's signals. Tracy and Ainsworth (1981) tested whether there was an association between which mothers displayed low levels of sensitive responsiveness and which babies developed insecure attachments. They observed mothers interacting with their babies in their own homes and rated them on a scale

1. The caregiver and the child are placed in an observation room.

2. The child is left free to explore.

3. A stranger enters and speaks to mother, then attempts to play with child.

4. The carer leaves the child and stranger alone.

5. The carer re-enters and the stranger leaves.

6. The carer leaves the child alone.

7. The stranger re-enters and tries to play with the child.

8. The stranger leaves and the carer re-enters.

Figure 18.3 The eight stages of the Strange Situation

of sensitivity. The babies were meanwhile given an attachment classification based on the Strange Situation. It was found that the mothers of insecurely attached children (types A and C) tended to be less responsive to the child and to cuddle them less than did mothers of the type B children, supporting the idea that responsiveness is important in the development of secure attachments.

In a recent meta-analysis of 41 studies, Atkinson et al (2000) concluded that sensitive responsiveness was associated with attachment security, but that as the time gap between assessment of sensitivity and assessment of infant attachment type increased, this association became weaker. This suggests that although sensitivity is important in developing the initial attachment type, other influences come to bear later and these may modify the influence of sensitive responsiveness.

Interestingly, it seems that a primary carer's sensitivity is related to her own attachment to her primary carer. In a recent study Levaenan and Silven (2000) assessed the attachment of 49 Finnish mothers to their own mothers by interview and then recorded them interacting with their infants. A strong relationship emerged between the sensitivity of the mothers and their own reported attachment to their mothers, suggesting that quality of maternal attachment is a major factor in determining mothers' sensitivity. This is not to suggest that a mother's sensitivity is fixed or that a mother with a poor relationship with her own parents cannot be an effective primary carer. Recent studies have tested the idea that primary carers can be trained to be more sensitive. For example, Juffer et al (1997) trained 30 pairs of adoptive parents in sensitive responsiveness. They found that they showed higher levels of sensitive responsiveness than untrained controls, and that a higher percentage of children of the trained parents were classified as securely attached.

A weakness of Ainsworth's approach to explaining the formation of different attachment types seems to be that she did not take account of individual differences in the temperament of children and the contribution this can make to attachment type. Children with type B attachments come from the complete spectrum of temperament types (Sroufe, 1985), but it seems that type A attachments are associated with both controlling and rejecting parenting (Vondra et al, 1995), and with a temperament characterised by low sociability and low emotional reactivity (Fox et al, 1991). Similarly, type C attachments are associated with both under-stimulating and unresponsive parenting (Vondra et al, 1995) *and* an irritable temperament (Goldsmith & Alansky, 1987). It thus seems that sensitive responsiveness is one important influence on attachment type but it is not the whole story. This is important because a by-product of research into sensitive responsiveness has been the *blaming* of parents of insecurely attached infants for not being sensitive enough. This is most unhelpful for parents already struggling with a difficult baby.

Training in sensitive responsiveness like that performed by Juffer et al can be particularly useful in supporting parents of children with difficult temperaments. Van den Boom (1994) offered training to 50 mothers of babies aged 6 months assessed as having an irritable temperament. At 12 months they were compared to a control group of 50 irritable babies whose parents had not had the training. It was found that, unlike the control group, the number of securely attached babies in the training condition had increased significantly.

Later consequences of attachment type

Attachment researchers have gathered considerable evidence linking attachment type to both social-emotional and intellectual development. Hazan and Shaver (1987) investigated the relationship between adults' romantic love behaviour and their infant attachment type. They printed a 'love quiz' in a newspaper, which included items related to their parental attachment and to their dating behaviour. It was found that those people classified as securely attached according to their descriptions of their relationship with their parents tended to be those who reported that they believed in long-term relationships, trusted their partners and were not threatened by intimacy. The insecurely attached adults appeared to have much greater difficulty in their relationships. This study tells us not only that the patterns of the first relationship are reflected in adult relationships, but that a secure attachment gives us a head-start when it comes to falling in love.

Of course the Hazan and Shaver study has its limitations. It relied upon respondents to a newspaper quiz, by definition not a representative sample of the population because most of us do not reply to newspaper quizzes. None the less, the principle that a secure attachment to a primary carer is helpful when forming adult relationships is well supported by more rigorous research. We can look in detail at one such study.

There is also a body of research linking attachment type with cognitive development. Frankel and Bates (1990) gave two-year-old children a series of tasks involving practical problems including joining two sticks together to extract a toy from a tube and weighing down one end of a see-saw in order to reach a biscuit on the other end. In all such tasks securely attached children did better than those without a secure attachment.

Meins (1997) performed a series of studies comparing securely and insecurely attached children on a variety of cognitive tasks. In one study mothers of 30 securely attached and 18 insecurely attached infants aged 12 to 13 months were trained to record the children's use of

research
now

do women with insecure attachments have relationship difficulties as adults?

McCarthy G. (1999) Attachment style and adult love relationships and friendships: a study of a group of women at risk of experiencing relationship difficulties. *British Journal of Medical Psychology* 72: 305–21

aim: results of previous studies had suggested a link between attachment type and the type of adult friendships and romantic relations experienced. The aim of this study was to see whether women known to have had poor attachments in their childhood were experiencing difficulties in their adult relationships.

procedure: 40 women aged between 25 and 44 years (mean age 36) were identified as being likely to have insecure attachments on the basis that, as children, they had been identified in previous studies as having insecure attachments to their primary carers. They were asked to take part in the study by means of a letter, then interviewed in their own homes. A standard interview called the Adult Personality Functioning Assessment (APFA) was used to find out as much as possible about their friendships and romantic relationships during the previous five years. The participants also completed a questionnaire (from Hazan and Shaver) designed to indicate their attachment type, a test of depression called the Beck Depression Inventory (BDI) and a test of self-esteem.

findings: as expected there was a much higher rate of insecure attachment in this sample than in the population as a whole. Only 43 per cent were classified as securely attached, as opposed to about 65 per cent in the whole population. The women with the secure (type B) attachments were significantly more likely to have successful romantic relationships and friendships. They also tended to have better self-esteem. Participants with avoidant (type A) attachments had the greatest difficulty in romantic relationships, while those with ambivalent (type C) attachments had the poorest friendships. There was no relationship between attachment classification and mood as measured by the BDI. Twenty per cent of the women had abnormal attachments characterised by both avoidant and ambivalent behaviour. Overall these women experienced the greatest relationship difficulties.

conclusion: attachment type predicts relationship difficulties in adult women. Type A attachment is particularly associated with problems in romantic relationships, while type C is particularly associated with problems in friendships. Atypical attachments, ie those not falling within types A, B or C appear to cause the most problems of all.

language. At 19 months the records were analysed. Children were classified as 'faster' in language acquisition if they have a vocabulary of 25 words or more at 19 months and 'slower' if their vocabulary is less than 25 words. Seventy-seven per cent of the securely attached group as opposed to only 12 per cent of the insecurely attached group were classified as 'faster' in their development of language.

Culture and attachment

Studies of attachment across different cultures, using the Strange Situation, have revealed wide variations in the proportions of securely attached infants. Van Ijzendoorn and Kroonenberg (1988) combined results of a large number of studies in a variety of countries and produced percentages of infants classifiable as avoidant, securely attached and resistant in these different cultures. Some of these are shown in table 18.2.

Table 18.2 percentages of attachment types in different cultures. From Van Ijzendoorn and Kroonenberg (1988)

	Avoidant	**Secure**	**Resistant**
Britain	22	75	3
West Germany	35	57	8
USA	21	65	14
China	25	50	25
Japan	5	68	27

As you can see, it appears at first that there are some differences in the proportions of different attachment types in these cultures, but we cannot accept such a conclusion uncritically. Takahashi (1990) has suggested that the Strange Situation is simply not appropriate for testing different cultures because of differences in maternal behaviour. Thus the Japanese children had no opportunity to show avoidant behaviour in the final stage of the Strange Situation as mothers inevitably went straight to them and picked them up.

An alternative explanation for differences in rates of attachment types across nationalities comes from Grossman and Grossman (1990). They suggest that attachment has different meanings in different cultures. Thus, what we call 'avoidant' in Britain and America might be called 'independent' in Germany. As independence is valued more highly in German than British or American culture, we would expect a higher proportion of type A attachment in Germany. As you can see in table 18.2 this is in fact the case.

The cross-cultural study of attachment poses an important challenge to the ideas of Bowlby and Ainsworth, who saw attachment as universal. If attachment has different meanings in different cultures, then it may be that the usefulness of attachment theory and research is *culture-bound*, ie it is applicable in Anglo-American culture but not world-wide.

where to now?

The following are good sources of further information on the ideas of Mary Ainsworth:

▶ **Gross R. (1997) Attachment theory, extensions and applications.** *Psychology Review* **4(1): 10–13.** An excellent account of aspects of adult behaviour, including romantic relationships, work and religiosity that are associated with different attachment types.

▶ **Jarvis M. (2003)** *Psychodynamic psychology: classic theory and contemporary research.* **London: Thomson Learning.** An advanced account of Ainsworth's ideas, in particular sensitive responsiveness.

▶ **Schaffer H.R. (1996)** *Social development.* **Oxford: Blackwell.** Includes an excellent chapter on the causes and effects of attachment types.

for and against

Ainsworth's attachment types

+ the Strange Situation appears to reliably distinguish between securely and insecurely attached infants

– temperament as well as attachment affects infant behaviour in the anxiety-provoking parts of the Strange Situation. We therefore need to be cautious about labelling a child insecurely attached based on how much anxiety they show on separation from the primary carer and the presence of a stranger

+ many studies have found, in line with Ainsworth's theory, that the style of maternal behaviour (that we could call sensitive responsiveness) towards infants is associated with particular attachment types

– contrary to Ainsworth's theory, in which attachment type can be accounted for entirely by sensitivity, it seems that infant temperament is also associated with attachment type

+ attachment type does predict later social and intellectual development

– attachment type is just one of several influences on development, and Ainsworth, like Bowlby, may have underestimated the impact of other factors

– although the majority of infants fall into types A, B and C, a small but significant proportion have atypical attachments, that are not accounted for by Ainsworth's classification

– Ainsworth's classification appears to be culture-bound. It is unclear whether this is due to the different meanings of attachment to different cultures or the difficulties in measuring attachment in different cultures

what's
new?

atypical attachments

We can think of Ainsworth's types A, B and C as normal variations in attachment style, and 85–90 per cent of children fall into one of these categories (Main & Solomon, 1986). However, there are a minority of children who have atypical attachments that fall outside these classifications. In the Gerard McCarthy study for example (page 208), women who showed the characteristics of both type A and type C attachments emerged as having the most serious difficulties in their adult relationships. Mary Main and Judith Solomon (1986) have called this category of mixed avoidant and resistant behaviour type D attachment (combined avoidant and resistant behaviour is also sometimes known as type AC). Type D children placed in the Strange Situation may alternate between avoidant and resistant behaviour, or they may combine them, maintaining proximity but avoiding contact and resisting when cuddled. They may also freeze or move very slowly. Typically they appear afraid of the primary carer and may prefer the company of the stranger.

Type D or *disorganised/disoriented attachment* is associated with a number of situations that interfere with the development of a more typical attachment. For example, Radke-Yarrow et al (1995) found that 23 per cent of infants of depressed mothers and 42 per cent of infants of mothers suffering manic depression (in which periods of depression alternate with periods of euphoria or irritability) had type D attachments. It appears that depression, especially manic depression, can interfere with the capacity of primary carers to respond sensitively and consistently to babies.

Carlson et al (1989) compared the attachments of 22 children identified as needing help from Social Services because they had suffered abuse or neglect with those of a control group of 21 children. The two groups were matched for poverty and other social factors. Eighty-one per cent of the maltreated group had type D attachments as opposed to 19 per cent of the control group. This shows clearly that maltreatment by a carer can have a dramatic effect on attachment, and is presumably linked to the high incidence of psychiatric problems in adults who suffered emotional, physical or sexual abuse in childhood.

The studies of Carlson et al (1989) and Radke-Yarrow et al (1995) tell us that type D attachment is associated with certain situations, but it is only very recently that researchers have begun to link specific patterns of behaviour on the part of the primary carer with the development of type D attachment. Lyons-Ruth et al (1999) assessed the attachment types of 65 infants aged 18 months. Their mothers were videotaped interacting with them at home. Maternal behaviours that were associated with type D attachments included frightened or frightening behaviour and the consistent failure to respond to clear infant signals. The researchers also looked at the possible role of infant behaviours, but the type D infants appeared to have no less skill in communicating their wishes to the carers than those characterised as types A, B or C; they were simply not responded to. This study therefore supports the idea that type D attachment is a product of behaviour on the part of the primary carer.

There is a substantial body of research showing that type D attachment leads to serious disadvantages for children. Whereas having a type A or C attachment influences development consistently but only to a moderate degree, type D attachments can have disastrous consequences. In the McCarthy study the women classifiable as type D had the most serious relationship difficulties, both with regard to friendships and romantic involvement. In the Meins study of language acquisition (above), type D children were found to have the smallest vocabulary of the four attachment types.

where to now?

The following is a good source of further information regarding disorganised attachment:

 Vondra J.I. & Barnett D. (1999) Atypical attachment in infancy and early childhood among children at developmental risk. *Monographs of the Society for Research in Child Development*. Oxford: Blackwell.

The social constructionist challenge to attachment theory

We have already looked at the idea that attachment has different meanings in different cultures. The social constructionist perspective is concerned with how the meaning we attribute to attachment in Anglo-American culture may have arisen as a result of social and historical factors. Erica Burman (1994) has identified how a number of such factors might have influenced the development and popularity of attachment theory. For example, much of Bowlby's early work on maternal deprivation took place immediately after the Second World War, a time when soldiers were returning home and seeking to take back the jobs that had been done predominantly (for the first time) by women during the war. This meant that men were set to benefit at the expense of women from a theory that emphasised the importance of women's mothering role. The government also benefited from the social construction of women as mothers rather than workers as it gave them a way to tackle post-war unemployment. It may thus be that the tremendous popularity of attachment theory in the 1950s was due to the fact that it served the needs of the male-dominated society.

Burman (1994) goes on to suggest that the attachment perspective is fundamentally misogynist (anti-women), because it lays the blame for anything that goes wrong in an individual's development firmly at the door of their mother. Women who are not 'model mothers' (this can include those who work or study, who have an active social life or are single parents) tend to be judged to be in some way immoral. This helps secure men's dominant position in society by placing restrictions on the 'acceptable' activities of women. The concept of sensitive responsiveness has caused particular problems, because it suggests that the only 'good' mothers are those who focus exclusively on the needs of their baby. Measures of sensitive responsiveness may also be discriminatory in that they tend to find higher scores in middle-class than working-class primary carers, so helping to reinforce the idea that middle-class norms are somehow the 'correct' ones to which all women should aspire.

The social constructionist approach is helpful in reminding us that there are social inequalities – between men and women and between working and middle classes – and that these can be an important influence on the development of psychological thinking. However, before we become too outraged and throw out the baby with the bath water it is worth considering the social benefits that have come from attachment theory and research. Day care and hospital care have been revolutionised by the principle that children should be allowed as much contact as possible with their primary carer and be provided with a substitute attachment figure when appropriate. This is why nurseries and other childcare settings now often employ a *key-worker* for each child, who builds a relationship with them and takes prime responsibility for their welfare. Prior to Bowlby's time it was customary to *forbid* childcare workers to become attached to children in their care, and this made hospital and nursery care unnecessarily traumatic for children.

A further benefit to women of the attachment approach has been in putting a value on mothers and motherhood. This was certainly Bowlby's aim (Holmes, 1993), as opposed to the oppression of women. Remember that prior to Bowlby's time, women were discriminated against in employment *and* undervalued as mothers, so Bowlby certainly did not make life harder for women in general. A particularly controversial aspect of Bowlby's work was his view that parenting ideally requires two parents (Bowlby, 1988), and that it is extremely unwise for a woman without a partner to deliberately have a child. From a social constructionist perspective, this fosters the view that single parents are immoral and irresponsible, and has legitimised discrimination against single parents. On the other hand, we can also use attachment research to argue that, given the importance of parenting and the isolation and lack of support faced by many single parents, it is especially important that single parents are given every support possible. It is thus perhaps unwise to associate attachment theory with a particular political ideology.

interactive angles

Psychologists place considerable value on not promoting theories that can have negative social consequences, for example restricting the freedom of mothers. However, they are also committed to scientific research and discovering the truth. Attachment is a particularly tricky area because research strongly supports attachment theory and it has important practical applications, however it is felt by many to impose unreasonable pressure on mothers.

1 Make a list of the pros and cons of attachment theory.
2 On balance, where do you stand?

where to now?

The following is a good source of further information about social construction and attachment:

▶ **Burman E. (1994)** *Deconstructing developmental psychology*. **London: Routledge.**
A fascinating book, looking at a number of aspects of child development and exploring their historical and political influences and implications.

Conclusions

Attachment theory, derived from the work of Bowlby and Ainsworth, is a highly influential perspective on child development. Its fundamental principles that the formation of an attachment with a primary carer in infancy is (at least partly) the product of sensitive and responsive parenting, and that a secure attachment greatly advan-

tages the child in its later development, are upheld by contemporary research. However, traditional attachment theory has neglected the importance of infant temperament, which may be as important as sensitive responsiveness in the development of attachment types and the child's personality. Attachment theory is also firmly bound up in Anglo-American culture and has proved difficult to apply to a range of cultures.

Attachment theory has proved invaluable in understanding the relationship between early experience and later development. It has led to vast improvements in childcare facilities in nurseries and hospitals, and helped professionals understand and intervene in families at risk of passing on patterns of abuse and neglect through generations. On the other hand, as the social constructionists have emphasised, attachment theory has been used to discriminate against women and aid attempts to put them 'back in the home' by constructing a view of the 'good mother' as being focused exclusively on childcare.

what do you know?

1 Define social releasers.

2 Outline **one** study into maternal deprivation.

3 What is sensitive responsiveness? What other factor appears to be important in determining attachment type?

4 Outline **one** study into the long-term effects of attachment type on future development.

5 Why might attachment be a culture-bound concept?

6 Outline **two** ways in which social constructionists believe that attachment theory has disadvantaged women.

19 Early experiences: deprivation and privation

what's ahead?

In this chapter we will be looking at various experiences that children can have, both typical and atypical, and discussing children's responses to and the possible long-term consequences of these events. There will be a degree of overlap with the subject matter of chapter 2, because of course one thing that may be affected by childhood experiences is attachment. We will begin by distinguishing between different types of childhood experience, then go on to look at the possible effects of short-term separation from primary carer with a particular focus on day-care, and long-term separation resulting from parental separation or the death of a parent. We shall then look at privation, which occurs when children are orphaned before they have the chance to form an attachment, and in cases of severe neglect and abuse. Adoption often follows privation and we can examine studies into the development of children who have suffered privation, then been adopted. Finally, in 'what's new?' we can look at the concept of the *developmental life path* and examine the importance of early experiences for later development.

Classifying different types of early experience

In chapter 2 we looked at Bowlby's ideas about attachment, including his *maternal deprivation hypothesis* – the idea that failure to form a secure attachment or experiences that disrupt this attachment lead to serious long-term consequences for the child, both in their intellectual and social development. As previously discussed (page 200), Bowlby has been criticised in his early work for not distinguishing between short and long-term separations from carers, and between *deprivation*, ie separation after the formation of an attachment and *privation*, the failure to form an attachment (Rutter, 1981). In contemporary research, we tend to classify deprivation experiences into three categories:

● **Short-term separation** – as occurs when working primary carers make use of day-care provision or the infant or carer has a short stay in hospital.

● **Long-term separation** – as occurs when families split up and one parent gets custody of the child, or when one or both parents die.

● **Privation** – as occurs when a child is orphaned very young and receives institutional care, or when a child is severely neglected or abused by carers so that an atypical attachment is formed.

In this chapter we will be examining research under these three headings.

Short-term separation

Hospitalisation

Before Bowlby's work became influential the conventional wisdom surrounding children in hospital was that, provided their physical care was good, they would experience few difficulties. It was thus standard practice for parents to be allowed very little access to their children when they were in hospital. Robertson and Bowlby (1952) created quite a stir when they filmed a two-year-old girl called Laura when she went into hospital for eight days for a minor operation. Laura deteriorated throughout the eight days and by the end of her stay she was severely withdrawn and no longer showed trust or affection towards her visiting mother. Robertson and Bowlby filmed several more children in hospital and, based on their observations, proposed three stages children go through when experiencing this type of separation.

1 **Protest**: children at first were often panic-stricken and upset. They cried frequently and tried to stop their parents leaving.

2 **Despair**: after a time, children cried less frequently, but became apathetic and uninterested.

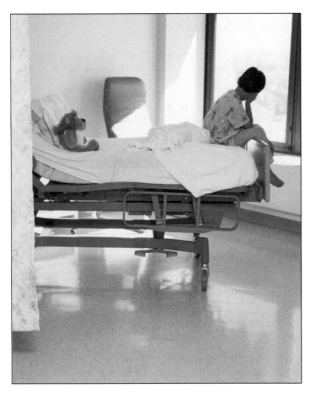

Figure 19.1 The trauma of surgery can be made worse by being separated from parents

3 **Detachment**: children eventually began to take an interest in their surroundings. However, if they reached this stage, children frequently rejected their primary carer.

Subsequent research has revealed that not all children go through the stages described by Robertson and Bowlby. There are in fact wide individual differences in children's reactions. Kirkby and Whelan (1996) reviewed research into the effects of hospitalisation on children. They concluded that, although it **can** have negative consequences, there are many variables that impact on the effects. These include the age of the child and the quality of their parental attachments, the seriousness of the condition and the severity of the medical intervention. However, Robertson and Bowlby made a huge contribution to our understanding of the effects of hospitalisation, and as a consequence of their work hospitals now go to great lengths to reduce the trauma of hospitalisation for children, for example encouraging parents to be around as much as possible.

Day-care

Day-care is a routine part of the lives of a huge and steadily growing number of children. Nowadays, economic circumstances mean that it is has become the norm for both parents in two-parent British and American families to work. Given what we have said about the importance of attachment and Bowlby's suggestion that disruption to attachment can result from prolonged separation from the primary carer, the question is begged; does day-care harm children?

Different researchers have found wildly differing results as regards the effects of day-care on children. Andersson (1996) followed up 128 Swedish children who had been in day-care in early childhood, and assessed them on their intellectual and social-emotional development at 13 years. Their development was compared with that of a control group who had had full-time maternal care in their early childhood. It emerged that the children who had spent time in day-care scored higher in both measures of academic achievement and social skills. This study indicates that day-care can have very positive effects.

On the other hand some research has shown that day-care is associated with insecure attachment, behavioural difficulties and intellectual deficits. Baydar and Brooks-Gunn (1991) surveyed over 1000 families and found that if mothers started work in their first year the children were more likely to be reported to have behavioural difficulties or poor intellectual development. In a *meta-analysis* (combining the results of several past studies weighting the results of each study according to the sample size) of 101 studies of day-care published between 1957 and 1995, involving a total of 32,271 children, Russell (1999) found that, overall, research has shown negative rather than positive effects for day-care. However, the majority of research included in Russell's analysis involved middle and upper-middle class families in which the mother returned to work from choice rather than necessity. While evidence regarding the effects of day-care is mixed, there is no doubt whatsoever about the effects that *poverty* can have on children's development (Cross et al, 1998). If working and using day-care facilities frees a family from poverty it is likely ultimately be beneficial for the child.

Yet other studies have found mixed results in the relationship between day care and development. Belsky and Fearon (2002) assessed children's attachment prior to entering day care, and followed them up through their experiences of maternal or day care. They found that negative effects of day care were associated with type A (avoidant) attachment only. This suggests that securely attached infants and those with type C attachments can use day care with little or no risk, provided they are not very young or the hours away from the primary carer are not excessive. Harr (1999) measured emotional adjustment and academic attainment in 628 children and found very few differences between children of mothers who did not work and those who worked full time. However, once children reached school age, those children whose mothers worked part-time were better adjusted than those of full-time employed mothers. Interestingly, children's emotional adjustment and academic progress were positively associated with mothers' satisfaction with their parent/worker status. This supports the common-sense view, often neglected by psychologists, that it is *happy* mothers rather than working or non-working mothers who are the most successful parents. This study has important implications in terms of informing mothers' decisions as to whether to work – it *is* legitimate for mothers to consider their own wishes.

Why are research findings so inconsistent?

As is often the case in psychology, it seems that the issue is more complex than it first appeared, and just asking whether day-care *per se* is a good or a bad thing is simply the wrong question. The results of different studies conflict because there are several factors that can influence whether day-care has positive, negative or no effects. We have already established that whether the mother wishes to return to work is one important factor. The age at which day-care commences may be another. Most of the

research that has found negative effects of day-care has looked at children whose primary carer returned to full-time work in the child's first year. There is almost no evidence that day-care in older children can have any harmful effects.

The number of hours in day care per week may also be a factor. Belsky (2002) examined aggression and defiance in pre-school children (as measured by teacher ratings) in relation to time spent in day care in the first, second, third and fourth sixth-month periods of children's lives. The more time children spent in day care, in particular during the first year, the higher the levels of aggression and defiance. Belsky concludes that it is long hours in early infancy spent in day care that can have negative effects.

Another important factor in determining the effects of day-care is the type and quality of day-care provided. It is estimated that unregistered childminders outnumber those registered and inspected by Social Services by two or three to one. Yet research has found that many unregistered childminders provide poor care. Nursery care can run into different problems. While nurseries typically

What the Gurus say

'We know that daycare doesn't do children any harm, especially if it is of good quality'

Tony Munton, London University's Institute for Education

'When a child's mother dies, that is a terrible tragedy. But we impose that tragedy on every child when we leave them to go to work'

Kathy Gyngell, Full Time Mothers Association

'It is best for babies to have something close to full-time mother care for six months at least'

Penelope Leach, childcare author and expert

'The entire debate has been hijacked by a feminist clique. You can always go back to work, but the damage done in the early years can never be rectified'

Patricia Morgan, Institute of Economic Affairs

The Observer, 10 October 1999

1 From your reading of the research reviewed in this chapter, to what extent would you agree with each of the four statements?

2 What might have influenced each of these 'gurus'? Think about psychological theory and possible political factors

have a stimulating environment and well-trained staff, they also tend to have a lower staff:child ratio and a higher turnover of staff, thus limiting the ability of children to form attachments.

A highly controversial recent line of research has suggested that the association found in some research between insecure attachment and use of day care may actually be an artefact, not of the effects of day care itself, but of the parents that choose to use it. It is well established that parents with insecure attachments are more likely to have insecurely attached infants. If it were demonstrated that insecure parents are more likely to use day care, then it might be that this can account for the association between day care and insecure attachment. This idea was tested in a recent study by Koren-Karie (2001).

for and against

day-care

+ some research has found beneficial effects for good quality day-care

− a larger body of research has revealed negative effects of day-care

+ most of this research showing negative outcomes for day-care has involved very young children and much has involved poor quality day-care

+ research has revealed that poverty resulting from not working, and frustration resulting from not working when mothers wish to, have negative consequences for children. Using day-care can help avoid these situations

research now

insecure parents are more likely to use day care

Koren-Karie, N. (2001) Mothers' attachment representations and choice of infant care: centre care vs home. *Infant & Child Development* 10: 117–27.

aim: a number of studies have suggested that children in day care are more likely to have insecure attachments than those who have full-time maternal care. It has been widely assumed that the day care is a cause of the attachment insecurity. However, it may be that some other factor, for example the attachment security of the primary carer, influences both the use of day care and the child's insecure attachment. The aim of this study is to investigate whether mothers with insecure attachments are more likely to use day care.

procedure: 76 mothers (mean age 27 years, 7 months) took part in the study. Thirty-eight had chosen to return to work and use nursery care. The two groups were matched for age and socio economic status. The attachment status of all the mothers was assessed during a standard one-hour interview called the adult attachment interview (AAI).

findings: overall, most mothers were classified as type B (securely attached). However, a much larger percentage of the insecurely attached parents opted for nursery care than did the securely attached mothers, the vast majority of whom opted for exclusive care of their baby.

conclusions: insecurely attached mothers are more likely to use nursery care than securely attached parents. It may be this maternal characteristic, not day care itself that leads to the higher percentage of insecurely attached infants amongst those who use day care.

where to now?

The following are good sources of further information on the effects of day-care:

▶ **Cowie H. (1995) Child care and attachment. In Barnes P. (ed) *Personal, social and emotional development of children.* Oxford: Blackwell.** Very clearly written with a good selection of research.

▶ **Flanagan C. (1999) *Early socialisation.* London: Routledge.** Contains a very clear but detailed and up-to-date account of day-care research.

Long-term separation

This type of separation is associated with parental separation and death of a parent. Although these events are less frequent than short-term separation, a large number of children do experience them. It appears that these events are traumatic for children and can have lasting effects.

Parental separation

Some readers will have parents who are divorced. It is important as we look at the possible consequences of divorce to realise that there are a number of factors that determine the effects divorce has on children. The differences reported between children of divorced and intact couples are typically quite small and do not apply to all children.

Richards et al (1995) has identified a number of typical effects of parental separation on children. You should note that these differences are very small, although they occur in many cases:

- Lower levels of academic attainment.
- Higher rate of behavioural problems.
- Earlier average ages for beginning sexual relationships, leaving home, cohabiting and marrying.
- More distant relationships with family as an adult.
- Lower socio-economic status and psychological well-being as an adult.

An important question you might ask is whether children are more affected by parental conflict or *discord* within an intact family or by parental separation/divorce/remarriage, collectively called *family reordering*. This is important to families in discord who have to make a decision whether to reorder or remain intact, based partly on their beliefs about the effects on the children. The results of studies seeking to find out whether reordering or discord is worse for a child are mixed. A classic study by Cockett and Tripp (1994) aimed to compare directly the effects of discord with those of divorce.

A problem with using this type of study to compare the effects of reordering and discord is that it is impossible to truly match the groups. It is possible that the reordered group's greater incidence of problems was due to some form of greater conflict or lesser reason for staying together that triggered the family split rather than the split itself. Logically, there *must* be something different in the reordered and intact groups because something led one group of families to remain intact while the others separated.

Other studies have suggested that parental discord can cause more problems for children than family reordering. Fergusson et al (1992) used a different approach to try to tease out what factors in family problems affect children most. They examined a group of 1265 children who had been studied each year, up to the age of 13. The rates of parental separation, reconciliation, arguments, violence and sexual problems were recorded each year. At 13 years the rate of criminal offending was noted and the rates of offending were looked at in relation to each of the above variables. Significant associations with offending were found for all the variables measured, apart from parents' sexual problems. The most significant factor was parental discord, measured by the number of arguments. Another study by Jekielek (1998) supports the idea that family discord is more damaging than reordering. Responses from 1640 children aged 6 to 14 in the *National Longitudinal Surveys of Youth* were analysed, and indications of anxiety and depression were compared in intact without discord families, intact with discord families and reordered families. Children in both reordered and discordant families showed significantly more signs of anxiety and depression than those in intact families with discord; however children who remained in families suffering high levels of discord displayed the highest levels of anxiety and depression of all.

An important question you might wish to ask, particularly if your own parents are separated and you are beginning to wonder what the effects might have been on you, is why some children are so much more affected than others by family reordering. We have already seen from the Cockett and Tripp study that most parents neither prepare children adequately prior to separation nor make adequate arrangements for children to keep in regular touch with the absent parent. There is also evidence to suggest that the temperament of the child affects chil-

classic
research

how do divorce and separation really affect children?

Cockett M. & Tripp J (1994) Children living in reordered families. *Social Policy Research Findings* 45, Joseph Rowntree Foundation.

aim: a number of studies have shown that children whose parents have separated are at increased risk from social and educational problems. Cockett and Tripp set out to investigate the effects of family reordering and discord on children, and what factors children reported as particularly difficult during reordering. This was the first major study that involved interviewing children themselves about their responses to family reordering.

procedure: 152 children and their parents were assessed and divided into three groups. One group consisted of reordered families, those who had separated and who may have joined other families. The second group were those who were still in intact families suffering serious discord. The third group consisted of those in intact families suffering no serious discord. The three groups were matched for age, sex, socio-economic status and maternal education. Children in each group were assessed by interviews and questionnaires on their self-image, their social life, their school success, their behaviour and their health. They were also questioned in depth about their experiences of family reordering, for example how their parents had prepared them for separation and what provision was made for keeping in touch with the absent parent.

findings: on all measures of emotional adjustment and academic success the children of reordered families came out worse than the intact groups. Those from intact families experiencing discord followed next, while children from intact families without discord had fewest problems. Children who had three or more successive reorderings generally came off worst on all measures. Only a small minority of children had been prepared for the parental split, and fewer than half had regular contact with the absent parent. Children who had several reorderings tended to have less support from extended families.

conclusion: the obvious conclusion from these results is that parental separation and divorce are more harmful to children than parental discord, and this study is often reported as showing that family reordering *per se* is harmful to children. However, it is perhaps more interesting to look at how badly most parents appeared to manage their separation as regards the child's welfare. It is likely that the poor outcomes for children in reordered families could be minimised by preparation before the event and by proper contact after the event.

dren's responses. Some children have a particularly *resilient* temperament, and are significantly less affected by reordering than more sensitive children (Nair, 1999).

Are the effects of parental death different?

As you might expect, it seems that separation from a parent by death has different psychological effects on children from separation by family reordering. Certainly the circumstances are different. In the case of parental divorce children may blame themselves for the parent leaving. The stress resulting from integrating into a new family as the remaining parent remarries is likely to come sooner. On the other hand it is likely that the absent parent will not be entirely gone from the child's life. Bifulco et al (1991) studied 249 women whose mothers had been lost before they were 17 years old, either through family reordering or death. The whole group suffered more from depression and anxiety disorders than the norm for the population. However, the highest rate of depression occurred in those whose mother had died in the first six years of their life. The same effect did not occur for women whose mother had *left* during the first six years. This implies that parental death at a young age has more serious effects than parental divorce.

The following are good sources of further information about the effects of family re-ordering and discord.

▶ **Cockett M. & Tripp J. (1994) Children living in reordered families. Social Policy Research Findings 45, Joseph Rowntree Foundation.** A fascinating and fairly non-technical paper intended for a general as well as psychological audience. Very influential, but contains a number of findings not often discussed, therefore well worth reading in full.

▶ **Das Gupta P. (1995) Growing up in families. In Barnes P. (ed) Personal, social and emotional development of children. Oxford: Blackwell.** An excellent account of the issues discussed here.

Privation

Privation occurs when children never have the opportunity to form an attachment to a primary carer, or when any attachment they do form is distorted due their treatment by carers. This means that prived children do not experience the close relationship most of us enjoy in childhood, and it seems that this lack of an early close relationship can have serious effects on children.

While we are confident that privation *can* produce serious social-emotional and intellectual problems for children, what remains open to debate however is the extent to which these effects *inevitably* result from privation, and the extent to which they can be *reversed*. As you can imagine, there would be serious ethical problems with any kind of controlled experimental study on privation in humans, as this would mean deliberately inflicting privation on infants knowing that it would harm them! We do, however, have two sources of evidence that help us understand the effects of privation:

● case-studies of severely abused children;
● studies of children in institutional care from an early age.

Case-studies of severely abused children

There have been a tragically large number of cases of children who have suffered privation because of the treatment they received at the hands of those responsible for them. If we examine two cases with very different outcomes we may be able to tease out some of the factors that affect how serious and permanent the effects of privation are.

1 Koluchova (1972, 1991) described the case of two identical twin boys (generally known in Britain as the 'Czech twins'). The twins were born in 1960, lost their mother shortly after birth and were cared for in an institution for a year before being fostered by an aunt for a further six months. Their father then remarried and the twins were reared by a cruel stepmother who kept them locked in a dark, cold closet the whole time and regularly beat them severely. When rescued at the age of seven, the boys were severely retarded and had no speech. They were terrified of adults. After two years of intensive institutional care including physiotherapy, speech therapy and psychotherapy, a pair of exceptionally caring and attentive sisters fostered the boys. By the age of 14 they showed no social-emotional or intellectual deficits. By 20 they both showed above average intelligence, and were working and experiencing successful romantic relationships. They both did National Service in their 20s, and later married and had children. Both are reported (Clarke & Clarke, 1998) to have successful relationships and careers.

2 Curtiss (1977) has described the case of Genie. Genie was discovered and rescued at the age of 13 years. She had been kept tied to a potty by day and tied into a sleeping bag at night by her father who believed that she was brain-damaged. Genie was regularly beaten, especially when she tried to communicate verbally, and she received virtually no intellectual stimulation or affection. She had developed little language and she was indifferent to adults. When rescued Genie was fostered for a time by a teacher, then by one of the psychologists studying her. She showed consistent progress and developed limited language and attachments to her carers. However, when funding for the research was withdrawn she was returned to Social Services and cared for by a succession of foster-parents. In one foster-home she was severely beaten for vomiting, and this traumatised her greatly, causing her to lose the language skills and emotional stability she had developed. She was briefly reunited at this point with the psychologists, to whom she expressed considerable anger. Genie was eventually settled with an adult foster-carer, who understandably did not wish her to have anything to do with psychologists again. We thus have no recent information on her condition.

We can see that at the time of their rescue, both the Czech twins and Genie displayed considerable emotional disturbance and intellectual deficits. However they went on to have very different outcomes. By comparing the cases of Genie and the Czech twins we can see three major differences that may have contributed to the difference in outcome:

- Whereas Genie was largely alone throughout her childhood (although her mother claimed to have a relationship with her), the Czech twins were able to form a close attachment to each other. Thus technically they had not suffered *privation* at all, rather very severe *deprivation*.

- The Czech twins were rescued at a much earlier age than Genie. It seems likely that the younger we can intervene in cases of privation the better the chances of success.

- Following their rescue the Czech twins received excellent care from their foster-carers. By contrast, Genie was abused again and this triggered a worsening in her condition.

We should be very cautious in assuming that these differences in circumstances account for the difference in outcome in the two cases. Because the cases were recorded *retrospectively* we cannot be sure about what other factors affected the children prior to their discovery. Furthermore, Genie's father may have been correct in his belief that she had suffered brain damage as well as being appallingly treated. We can see, however, that early intervention and good after-care are helpful when dealing with privation.

Studies of institutionalised children

The study of institutional care is very much tied up with the study of adoption. Adoption gives psychologists the chance to study the extent to which any effects of early institutional care can be reversed later. Perhaps the most influential study of institutional care and adoption was begun by Tizard and Rees (1974) and followed up by Tizard and Hodges (1978), and Hodges and Tizard (1989). We can look at this series of studies in some detail.

classic
research

should children taken into care remain there, be restored to their family or be adopted?

Hodges J. & Tizard B. (1989a) IQ and behavioural adjustment of ex-institutional adolescents. *Journal of Child Psychology and Psychiatry* 30: *53–76*

Hodges J. & Tizard B. (1989b) Social and family relationships of ex-institutional adolescents. *Journal of Child Psychology and Psychiatry* 30: *77–98*

aim: the aim of this series of studies was to compare the development of children who had been taken into institutional care at a very young age under the three possible conditions that could follow, i.e. remaining in an institution, being adopted or being restored to their biological family.

procedure: a total of 65 children took part in the study. All had been in institutional care since prior to 4 months of age: 24 had been adopted; 15 had been restored to their biological families; and 26 were still in institutional care. All were about 4½ years old at the time of the initial study. All the children in a home setting (ie not in an institution) had been there at least 6 months when assessments were made. The design was a naturalistic experiment in which development in each of the three conditions of institutional care, restoration and adoption could be compared. Assessment of development was carried out by interviewing carers and teachers, by observation and by IQ tests. Both intellectual and social development were assessed. Assessments were carried out again at 8 years of age (Tizard & Hodges, 1978). By this time 25 children were adopted, and a further 3 were in long-term foster homes. Thirteen were now restored to their original families. The participants were assessed once more at 16 (Hodges & Tizard, 1989).

findings: at 4½ years, the adopted group had the lowest number of reported behavioural problems. Both adopted and restored children were more visibly affectionate and attention-seeking than is typical of children who have always lived with their family. The restored group differed from the adopted group in displaying more 'clingy' behaviour. Of those still in institutions, the majority showed clingy behaviour and most were said by staff to 'not care deeply about anyone'. At the age of 8, the differences between the groups had increased. The adopted group were now generally reported as having strong attachments to their carers, although they were generally slightly more physically affectionate than is typical of children who have always lived with their biological parents. Only half of the mothers in the restored group felt that their child was attached to them, and these children displayed less than the usual levels of physical affection. At school, all three groups were reported by teachers to be unpopular with peers, restless and aggressive in comparison with other children. At 16, the adoptees had family relationships indistinguishable from those of children who had always lived with biological parents, although they still had some problems getting on with their peers. On all measures of intellectual development and academic attainment the adopted group did far better than the restored or institutional groups.

conclusion: spending time in institutions as an infant had some lasting effects, irrespective of whether infants were restored to their families, adopted or remained in institutions. This suggests the effects of privation are only partially reversible. However, the outcomes were considerably better following adoption than either of the alternatives. We need to be clear, though, about what this series of studies does and does not show. There was no attempt to match adoptive carers with the biological parents in the restoration group. The adoptive parents were older, wealthier, better educated and more likely to have stable family lives and previous experience of child rearing than the mothers in the restored group. They were also more motivated than the biological parents, most of whom reported mixed feelings about taking back their children. This is **not** therefore an experiment showing that restoring children to biological parents is harmful. It **does** show that, following a poor start in life, children are more likely to make up lost ground if they have experienced and committed carers.

Following the fall of President Ceaucescu in Romania in 1990, much public attention in Europe and America was focused on the plight of the many children left in crowded and understaffed Romanian orphanages. A large number of these orphans were adopted, including in Britain, and the progress of 111 such orphans was followed up by Michael Rutter and colleagues.

Rutter et al (1998) aimed to see the extent to which good care could make up for very poor early institutional experiences. A secondary aim was to compare the Romanian adoptees with a group of British adoptees in order to see whether some of the effects often observed in privation are due to maternal deprivation itself, or to the physical hardships associated with privation. Adoptees were followed up to the age of 4 years and measured with developmental tests of physical and intellectual development. On arrival in Britain the Romanian children were developmentally delayed. About half showed signs of mental retardation and they tended to be severely underweight (half were in the bottom 3 per cent of children their age). The British children did not show these delays, showing that factors other than maternal deprivation had contributed to the delays in the development of the Romanian children. At 4 years, the Romanian children had caught up with the British group on both physical and intellectual development. There was a rela-

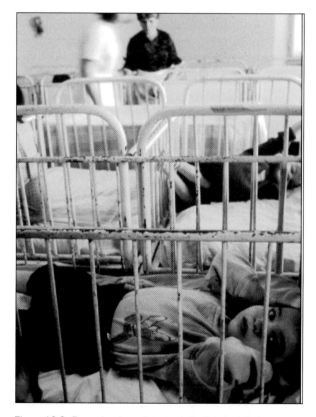

Figure 19.2 Romanians in orphanages following the fall of Ceaucescu lived in very poor conditions

tionship between age at adoption and development at the age of 4. The older the child on adoption, the less ground they had made up.

Given the results of studies like Rutter's and of case-studies such as the Czech twins, we can be reasonably optimistic about the prospects for children who have suffered early privation and who then receive good care. However, high-quality care is absolutely essential, and the earlier it begins, the better the child's chances of healthy development.

interactive angles

Summarise the arguments for the reversibility of privation. You should be able to include at least one case study and one empirical study on each side of the argument.

what's new?

the life path approach to understanding early experiences

Clarke and Clarke (1992, 1998) have reviewed the evidence for the impact of early experiences on later child development and challenged the popular view that particular experiences *will* lead to particular later effects. They reviewed many of the studies we have looked at in this chapter and noted that in no case do *all* participants in a particular condition go on to develop in the same way. In the series of Tizard studies for example, not all the adopted children developed better socially or intellectually than all the restored or all the institutionalised children, although there were fairly large differences in the average development achieved by the three groups. Similarly, in the studies of attachment we looked at in chapter 18, not all securely attached children did better than all insecurely attached children, even though overall a secure attachment did seem to give them an advantage.

What this means is that particular experiences have a *probabilistic* effect on development, ie they affect the *likelihood* of certain outcomes, not the certainty. However serious an early experience, there is always a next stage of development for the child to enter with new opportunities and pitfalls. Thus children with secure attachments are more likely to do well at school because they are more likely to have good relationships with peers and teachers. However, if they do not develop these relationships (and some will not due to other factors) then their attachment no longer places them in such good stead. The converse is that a child who has suffered early hardship, but who has particularly good care from an adoptive family and/or particularly dedicated and skilled teachers, can overcome completely a poor start. Thus early experience puts us on a particular life path, but later experience, both good and bad, can alter this developmental path. Clarke and Clarke cite the case of the Czech twins as an example of children whose life paths involved multiple experiences, initially negative in the form of their mother's death, their early institutionalisation and their abusive step-parenting. However, they also had a number of positive experiences in the form of their attachment to each other and their excellent care when adopted.

The Clarkes' approach is not to suggest that early experience is not important – it clearly is. However, all children carry on developing along a 'life path' regardless of particular experiences, and no individual experience, however extreme, can determine future development; it can only be one of several influences on it. The life path approach is not only helpful in understanding why early experiences do not have identical experiences on all children, it is also highly optimistic, and gives professionals and adoptive families a way of looking beyond experiences that have disadvantaged children.

The following are good sources of further information on privation:

▶ **Flanagan C. (1999) Early privation and developmental catch-up.** *Psychology Review* **6(1): 24–5.** A simple but very up-to-date review of research following the adopted Romanian orphans.

▶ **Skuse D.H. (1993) Extreme deprivation in early childhood. In Messer D. & Dockerell J. (1999) (eds)** *Developmental psychology, a reader.* **London: Arnold.** An excellent account of case studies of privation and the implications of findings.

▶ **Clarke A.D.B. & Clarke A.M. (1998) Early experience and the life path.** *The Psychologist* **11: 433–6.** A fascinating look at how early experience can affect but does not necessarily determine later development.

▶ **Hodges J. (1996) The natural history of non attachment. In Bernstein B. & Brannen J. (eds)** *Children, research and policy.* **London: Taylor & Francis.**

Conclusions

When talking about the long-term effects of early experience, most psychologists have found it helpful to look at short-term separation, long-term separation and privation separately. Short-term separation takes place most commonly when working mothers make use of day-care. Results concerning the effects of day-care are mixed, with the larger body of evidence showing negative effects. However, most of the research showing negative consequences for children of working mothers has involved very young children and poor day-care. There is also research showing that maternal poverty and frustration can have serious consequences for children, so there remains a strong argument for mothers to work and make use of day-care. The most common cause of long-term separation is family reordering. Findings are clear that children from families with discord or reordering are disadvantaged, but it remains unclear whether discord in intact families or parental separation have the more serious effects. The effects of the death of a parent may be more serious than those of family reordering.

Privation is perhaps the most serious early experience a child can have. By looking at the cases of Genie and the Czech twins we can tease out some of the factors that influence the severity of privation and the prospects for recovery. Studies of prived and later adopted children have yielded mixed results, but we can say that the outlook for prived children is reasonably optimistic provided adoption is early and by committed parents. Clarke and Clarke (1998) have suggested that we can best conceive of the effects of privation and other early experiences as probabilistic influences on the life path of the child. This means that they increase the probability of certain outcomes but do not determine them.

what do you know?

1 Outline one study into the effects of hospital treatment on children.

2 Based on psychological research, outline one argument for and one argument against day-care.

3 What are discord and reordering in families, and how might each affect a child's development?

4 What have adoption studies taught us about the reversibility of privation?

5 What is a life path, and how has the idea affected our understanding of the effects of early experience?

20 Friendship and play

what's ahead?

In this chapter we will be looking beyond children's initial relationships with their families to *peer relationships*, ie their relationships with other children. We shall look at the typical development of friendships in childhood and adolescence, and what factors might affect individual differences in children's abilities to form friendships and their popularity with other children. It is then interesting to consider children's friendships in cultural context and look at friendships in different cultures. Tied up with peer relationships is play. We can identify several categories of play and examine factors that may affect individual differences in play. In *What's new?* we will look at the study of rough and tumble play. We shall then look at two important theoretical perspectives on play, the cognitive-developmental approach, which emphasises the importance of play in intellectual development, and the psychodynamic approach, which emphasises the emotional significance of play. Based on a psychodynamic understanding of play we shall finish by introducing the therapeutic value of play and the use of play in child psychotherapy.

The development of friendships in children

In early childhood, children's most important relationships are those with their primary carer and other family members. Relationships with peers are initially far less significant than those with family members. However, the importance of peer relationships increases throughout childhood and by mid-adolescence most young people tend to use friends as their primary sources of social and emotional support. So what benefits does friendship have for children? Erwin (1998) has suggested a number of gains that children derive from being in stable friendships. Childhood friendships serve as a training ground for future relationships in which social skills, such as getting one's own way and resolving conflict, can be developed. They also give children experience of intimacy with peers and sensitivity for other people's needs. The experience of friendship can compensate to some extent for earlier poor relationships in giving children valuable experience of intimacy. Friendship also allows children to make *social comparisons* with peers, ie they can compare their own behaviour with that of others and modify it where it appears to differ from the norm. A stimulating environment is associated with good intellectual development. Clearly social interaction with peers is one source of such stimulation, so friendship can aid intellectual development. Friendship also provides social and emotional support, particularly important during conflict with family.

Changes in friendships with age

From about six months of age, children can be seen to show interest in their peers. Vandell et al (1980) observed that if two infants are given the opportunity to interact they will typically look at each other, touch, imitate each other's movements, smile and vocalise at each other. However these interactions are not normally sustained longer than a few seconds. In the second year of life, peers become a real focus of attention, and although toddlers generally maintain proximity to their primary carer they will spend considerable time looking at other toddlers if they are present in the room (Lewis et al, 1975). Interestingly, toddlers are more likely to try to interact with another toddler if that toddler is interacting with an adult. In a study by Tremblay-Leveau and Nadel (1996) French infants of 11 and 23 months were placed in pairs in a room with a familiar adult. Some spontaneous interaction took place between the toddlers but this increased dramatically when the adult played with one of them. Toddlers were five times as likely to initiate contact with the other toddler at 11 months and eight times as likely to do so at 23 months when the other was interacting with the adult.

Hinde et al (1985) have defined friends as children who choose to play together more than 33 per cent of the time. According to this criterion Hinde et al observed that 20 per cent of 18 month olds and over 50 per cent of 4 year olds had stable friendships. Newcomb and Bagwell (1995) compared interaction between friend and non-friend peers and described four main differences. Firstly

Figure 20.1 These two children are displaying the signs of friendship

friends played together more frequently. Secondly the type of play was different, being more likely to involve fantasy and extended periods of speech. Thirdly, although friends were involved in just as much conflict as non-friends they were much better at *resolving* conflicts. Finally, friends were much better at helping each other with difficult tasks. At primary school, behaviour between friends and non-friends becomes increasingly different, and friendships increase steadily in complexity and intimacy. Children's beliefs about friendship also change during their school years. O'Brien and Bierman (1988) asked American children and adolescents aged 9, 13 and 16 to describe friendship groups. The younger participants defined friendship groups as those who did things together. By adolescence the criterion for belonging to a friendship group had shifted to sharing values and appearance.

The formation of friendships

We have already looked at how children's friendships change with age. This is sometimes referred to as the *vertical* development of friendship. However friendship also develops *horizontally*, ie individual friendships change over time. Levinger and Levinger (1986) have developed a five-stage model to describe the typical course of children's friendships.

1 **Acquaintance** – Relationships begin with casual contact. At this stage it is important that two children come into close contact regularly; thus most friendships form between children who live near one another or go to the same school. Children do not necessarily establish contact with all the peers with whom they come into regular contact, but usually choose to interact with those who are attractive and socially skilled.

2 **Build-up** – After establishing casual contact, children go through a process of getting to know each other. This does not follow a set pattern, but may happen quite gradually – for example when two neighbouring children meet up regularly over a period of weeks – or in one go – for example when two families go on holiday together. Common attitudes and interests are established at this stage, as is trust.

3 **Continuation and consolidation** – Friendship is now established, but if it is to be maintained certain conditions must be met. Children expect each other to disclose intimate information and secrets, and may break off friendships if this is not forthcoming. Children also need to demonstrate trust and the ability to share in order to keep relationships going.

4 **Deterioration** – Most friendships decline over time. As in the build-up stage, there is no set pattern to deterioration. Some children simply grow apart due to differing interests. If friends at the same primary school go to different secondary schools they are likely simply not to bother maintaining the friendship. Permanent falling-out following conflict is more common in adolescents than younger children. In very young children, some friendships simply fail because the children do not have the social skills to maintain them.

5 **Ending** – When relationships have deteriorated they typically end altogether. There may be a formal ending where former friends announce that they are no longer so, or they may simply start to avoid contact with one another.

The Levinger and Levinger model is useful in reminding us that relationships are not static but are constantly changing and developing. There are, however, some fairly obvious limitations. Different stages are particularly important for children of different ages; thus the consolidation stage is more significant in older children and adolescents. Of course, not all friendships begun in childhood and adolescence deteriorate or break down. Some are maintained throughout life and others may enter a moratorium, for example when a child moves house or school, only to be picked up later. They may alternatively simply end at this point without a deterioration stage.

Individual differences in children's popularity

You will know from your own experience that some children have more friends than others, and that some children tend to be liked by the majority of peers while others are ignored or even actively disliked. Coie and Dodge (1983) identified five categories of *sociometric status* or popularity type. Children were asked to categorise their peers as 'liked most' or 'liked least' and every child was categorised according to their tendency to be identified as liked most or least.

- **Popular children** were identified as those who tended to be categorised by peers often as 'liked most' and seldom as 'liked least'.

- **Average children** were identified as moderately and equally likely to be categorised by peers as 'liked most' or 'liked least'. Children tended not to have strong opinions for or against them.

- **Controversial children** were identified as being frequently categorised as both 'liked most' and 'liked least'. They were therefore very popular with some peers and very unpopular with others.

- **Neglected children** were identified as those rarely categorised as 'liked most' or 'liked least'. They appeared to be little noticed by their peers.

- **Rejected children** were identified as those frequently categorised as 'liked least' and rarely as 'liked most'. They were thus the most unpopular group.

Factors affecting sociometric status

Physical attractiveness

A number of factors can impact on children's popularity. Physical attractiveness appears to be one factor. Coie et al (1983) rated children for attractiveness, then asked members of peer groups to rate each other as 'most liked' and 'most disliked'. A strong relationship emerged, with the most attractive children being those most likely to be categorised as 'most liked' and the least attractive children as those most likely to be categorised as 'least liked'. Cash (1995) reports that facial disfigurement seriously handicaps children socially, as it interferes with non-verbal communication and so makes the affected child more difficult to interact with. Langlois et al (1995) examined parental attitudes towards physically unattractive children from infancy and discovered that premature and disfigured babies tended to receive less attention and lower expectations from adults. There may thus be a *self-fulfilling prophecy* at work here, in which physically unattractive children are not less popular with peers merely because they are unattractive to **them**, but because their development has already been adversely affected by adult attitudes.

Social skills

While there is no doubt among child psychologists that some children are more socially skilled than others or that highly skilled children are more likely to have successful relationships with their peers, exactly what the essential social skills are has proved much more difficult to pin down. Coie and Dodge (1988) had American boys of 6 to 9 years old rate each other as 'most liked and 'most disliked',

then observed classroom behaviour and questioned teachers about the strengths and weaknesses of each child. It emerged that three social factors were associated with high popularity; sporting prowess, skilful use of humour and *pro-social* (generous) behaviour. Asher et al (1990) looked at rejected children and concluded that they were more aggressive and critical than the other sociometric types, and that they were more likely to be hyperactive. Rejected children often play alone, sometimes in games typical of younger children (Rubin et al, 1983).

It is, however, difficult to untangle cause and effect from these findings. Children may make themselves unpopular by being critical, aggressive and immature, **or** it may be that they become critical and aggressive, and regress to immature behaviour **in response** to rejection by their peers. Ladd and Golter (1988) set out to test whether social incompetence led to unpopularity or whether unpopularity resulted in behaviour normally classified as socially incompetent. Researchers followed children aged 3 to 4 for a year, assessing popularity and social behaviour three times. It was found that early argumentative behaviour predicted later unpopularity. It seems then that rejected children are less socially skilled than others, and that their lack of social skill leads to their being rejected.

Attachment

In chapter 18 we looked at theory and research in the area of attachment, and concluded that the security of a child's attachment to its primary carer was an important factor in

Figure 20.2 Some children lack the social skills to become popular

its later development. Securely attached children (type Bs) tend to have better peer relationships than insecurely attached children. Remember that type A attachment is characterised by *avoidant*, ie distant, unemotional behav-

iour and type C by *resistant*, ie bad-tempered behaviour. If these patterns of relating to others persist through childhood and characterise other relationships apart from that with the primary carer, you can imagine that they would

research
now

is bullying behaviour related to attachment?

Myron-Wilson P. & Smith P.K. (1998) Attachment relationships and influences on bullying.
Proceedings of the British Psychological Society 6(2): 89–90

aim: previous research using American child participants had established that type A (avoidantly attached) children are at increased risk of being bullied at school. This study aimed to test this idea and also to test whether there was an association between attachment type and participation in bullying behaviour, either as a bully or victim.

procedure: 196 children aged between 7 and 11 years from a South East London primary school took part in the study. All children were assessed for attachment type and quality of relationship with parents using a test called the *Separation Anxiety Test*, which looks at how distressed a child becomes on being separated from their attachment figures and a *Parenting Styles Questionnaire*, which assesses children's perceptions of their relationship with their parents. Involvement with bullying, both as a perpetrator and victim were examined by a test called the *Participant Roles Scale*, in which each child identifies their peers as either a bully, a victim of bullying or uninvolved in bullying. Children were then divided into types A, B and C attachment, and the number of bullies and victims identified by peers in each category were counted.

findings: securely attached (type B) children were assessed by their peers as very unlikely to be involved in bullying, either as a perpetrator or victim. Type A (avoidantly attached) children were the most likely to be identified by peers as victims of bullying, while type C (ambivalently or resistantly attached) children were the most likely to be rated by peers as bullies.

conclusion: attachment classification is associated with bullying behaviour. Securely attached children are less likely than insecurely attached children to be involved with bullying, either as bully or victim. Taking bullying as a negative social behaviour and the avoidance of bullying as a positive social behaviour, we can say that insecure attachment predicts some of the most negative types of interaction between peers.

cause problems for children. Research has found that type A children tend to have the lowest social status among peers (LaFreniere & Sroufe, 1985) and are most likely to be bullied (Troy & Sroufe, 1987). A recent study by Myron-Wilson and Smith (1998) confirmed this and further suggested that type C children are the most likely to be bullies.

Attachment type is not merely associated with popularity and positive patterns of social interaction with peers, but also with the formation of friendships. Kerns (1994) studied interactions between pairs of 4-year-old friends with secure and insecure attachments. It emerged that pairs of securely attached friends had

more successful and positive interactions than pairs where one had an insecure attachment. The implication of this is that securely attached children will find it more rewarding to interact with each other, while insecurely attached children, who would benefit most from interacting with securely attached peers, are likely to find themselves isolated (Erwin, 1998). There is some evidence that the relationship between attachment, popularity and friendship is different in adolescents than in younger children. Kerns and Stevens (1996) found that securely attached adolescents had more frequent and successful interactions with peers than insecurely attached individuals, but they were no more likely to have close friendships.

Benefits for children of popularity and friendship

Earlier in this chapter we identified some of the possible benefits of having friends. We can now explore this idea further, and look at the separate question of whether popularity is also of benefit in children's development.

Erwin (1998) has suggested that friendships convey benefits to children, both in terms of their social and intellectual development. We can consider evidence for both of these benefits. In terms of social benefits, having friends is, unsurprisingly, associated with lower levels of loneliness (Jones et al, 1982). In adolescence, when peer relationships become increasingly important and friends replace family as major sources of social support, loneliness for friendless individuals becomes an increasing problem, and loneliness is one of the most frequently reported problems in adolescence (Shultz & Moore, 1989). Friendship is also associated with fantasy play (see page 230 for a discussion), which is in turn associated with the development of social competence. Connolly and Doyle (1984) looked at the time spent and the complexity of pretend play in children and found that both were greater in pairs of children who exhibited signs of friendship. This suggests that friendship advantages children in their social development because it increases the type of play that aids social development.

There is also evidence that friends aid cognitive development. Below we look at Vygotsky's theory of cognitive development and studies showing that children learn quicker if they are in co-operative pairs and groups. In a study by Pellegrini and Melhuish (1998), 28 pairs of children were observed in tasks of *literate language*. Literate language can be defined as children's talk about their own mental processes. It was found that pairs of friends were more likely to use literate language than pairs of non-friends. It was also found that the use of literate language predicted good performance in school-based tests. This has an important implication: children who have friends are advantaged in school work, and one thing that may improve the performance of children who are not doing well at school work is friendship.

Having secure friendships thus appears to give children an advantage in social and cognitive development. A separate but related line of research has looked at whether popularity in childhood predicts the course of later social development. Parker and Asher (1987) reviewed studies that looked at whether sociometric status, aggression or shyness predicted early school leaving, criminality or adult mental health problems. It was found that aggression and peer rejection were associated with early school leaving and involvement with crime. Shyness did not predict later school dropout or criminality. None of the measures of popularity showed any consistent relationship to mental health problems.

Children's friendships and culture

Friendships in childhood vary in ways that reflect the culture in which the children are growing up. Whiting (1986) compared social contact in children of 20 communities in various parts of the world and found massive variations in the time children spent with parents, siblings, extended family and friends. At one extreme, the Kung Bushmen of the Kalahari Desert in Botswana live in nomadic extended family groups; thus children tend to have very little contact with peers outside the family. At the other extreme (Tobin et al, 1989) children in the Kibbutzim of Israel live from a very early age with other children and not with their parents at all.

Different cultures have different values, and these will impact on children's friendships. Anglo-American culture is highly *individualistic*, ie a strong value is placed on the independence and freedom of the individual. In individualist cultures we place much emphasis on friendships as sources of individual enjoyment and of individual social and intellectual development. We thus encourage children to have friends, both in educational and social situations, for their own benefit. However, in more *collectivist* cultures there is much less emphasis on the importance of the individual and so friendship tends to be seen as less important, and commitment to family and other members of the community are seen as more important (Harrison et al, 1995).

Children's opportunities to make friends and particularly to choose some peers over others as friends are constrained by the practices of their culture, which in turn are influenced by geographical and economic factors. In the education system of Britain and America, most children come into contact with a very large number of peers but are required to spend a great deal of time in the company of children of the same sex and exactly the same age. This cultural norm encourages children to choose their friends among their own age and sex (Montmayor & Van Komen, 1985). Within those limits they can use criteria like physical attractiveness, social competence and sociometric status to make their friendship choices. These bases on which Anglo-American children choose their friends are not universal however. In other societies, for example those which are nomadic or live in small settlements, children are much less likely to be routinely segregated from a young age by age and sex, nor are they likely to have regular contact with such a large number of children in total. This means that children who live in small communities are more likely to have cross-sex friendships and to associate with children of a variety of ages (Whiting & Edwards, 1988).

It is important to remember that most of the research concerned with children's friendships you have encountered in this chapter has been conducted in Britain and America. From looking at this research you might have concluded certain 'facts' about the patterns and effects of friendship and popularity. You should be wary, however, of trying to apply the results of studies conducted in Britain and America to all children.

where to now?

The following are good sources of further information about children's friendships.

▶ Erwin P. (1998) *Friendship in Childhood and Adolescence*. London: Routledge A simple and user-friendly overview of research into all aspects of children's friendships.

▶ Smith P. (1998) Social development. In Eysenck M. (ed) *Psychology, an integrated approach*. Harlow: Longman Includes some good information on sociometrics and the use of social skills training to improve children's popularity.

Play

For the remainder of this chapter we will be looking at children's play. Children spend a great deal of time engaged in play and psychologists have suggested that play is important in intellectual, social and emotional development. The importance of play was recognised in the early 20th century. Educational experts began to champion the role of play in education. Susan Isaacs (1929) described play as 'the child's work' and A.S. Neill, founder of the famous Summerhill School in England, where lessons are voluntary, described childhood as 'playhood'. Play certainly has benefits for children's development, although psychologists are still debating just *how* important it is and in precisely what ways it aids children's development.

Categories and types of play

An early but still very influential system for classifying types of play comes from Mildred Parten (1932). Below, we look at her research in detail.

Parten's classification of play is still important in contemporary psychology, and it is accepted as one valid way of

classic research

how do children play?

Parten M. (1932) Social participation among pre-school children. *Journal of Abnormal and Social Psychology* 27: 243–69

aim: the aim of the study was to examine the different ways in which children played when adults were not guiding them. More specifically, Parten aimed to classify play activity in terms of the different types of interaction that took place between children. A secondary aim was to look at how the nature of social interaction during play changed with children's age.

procedure: sessions of free play, ie play in which adults did not intervene or direct, were observed in an American nursery school. The participants were children aged between 2 and 5 years. Parten classified the children as either occupied or unoccupied. The play activities of the occupied children were carefully noted and later classified according to the social interactions involved.

findings: children's activities were classified into four types:

● *Solitary play* – children play alone with their own toys and make no effort to get close to other children. Children engaged in solitary play are not influenced in their play by the activities of nearby children.

● *Parallel activity* – the child is still playing independently and does not directly interact with surrounding children, but may be in closer proximity to peers, and is influenced by them in choice of toys. Play is thus around but not with peers.

● *Associative play* – children play the same game together. The common game is a major topic of conversation, and toys are swapped and borrowed. There is, however, no organisation to the game; thus there is no competition or co-operation.

● *Co-operative play* – children play games that have rules and involve a division of labour. There may be competition, for example in sporting activities, or there may be co-operation to achieve a goal, for example in building a model. There may be role-play in which adult activities are imitated. Typically one or more of the children direct the activity of the others.

The different categories of play were found to be associated with different ages. The younger children spent most of their time in solitary and parallel play, whereas the older children spent more time in associative and co-operative play.

Conclusion: play can be categorised in terms of the interaction between children into four categories. The time spent in each of these categories varies according to the age of the child. Older children tend to have more complex social interactions than do younger children.

classifying children's play. However, the approach only tells us about how children interact while playing. It does not tell us much about what they are *doing* (Faulkner, 1995). We can now look at some of the different activities that fall under the heading of play.

Pretend play

Pretending or *fantasy* is an important part of children's play, and pretence of one sort or another dominates most play activities. Think back for a moment to your own childhood. You probably enjoyed a number of different pretend activities. During solitary play you may have pretended to be in an adult role, for example by doing housework or you may have pretended that your toy soldiers were actually fighting. In co-operative play you may have adopted a role, such as a doctor in a game of 'doctors and nurses'.

The beginnings of pretending in play can be seen as early as 12 to 15 months (Smith et al, 1998). Early pretend play tends to involve real objects or objects that closely resemble the objects they are symbolising. Fein (1975) found that 93 per cent of 2 year olds would imitate an adult making a toy horse drink from a plastic cup. However, only 33 per cent imitated the pretence of the horse drinking when a shell was used instead of a plastic cup. Most studies of this type were conducted in laboratory settings, using artificially created conditions and a limited choice of toys. It was not until recently that psychologists began studying the development of pretend play in natural surroundings. Haight and Miller (1993) conducted a longitudinal study into the development of pretence in play, conducted in children's homes.

Dramatic role-play

Dramatic role-play is the term given to play in which children act out adult roles **together**. This is a particular type of pretend play. By 3 to 5 years children act out quite complex roles, including policeman, fireman and princess, and

these regularly form part of children's co-operative play. First (1994) observed the emergence of early dramatic role-play in younger children. Five families with 2-year-old children took part in the study. Parents were taught to record signs of role-play and they were regularly interviewed to keep up to date with developments in their children's play. The first game involving role-play emerged in the three girls at 2 years 4 months. First called this the 'leaving game'. The leaving game involves one partner pretending to leave and the other pretending to cry. One of the participants was recorded to say:

> *'I'm going. You alone. You cry.' (Jane, 2 years 5 months)*

This is typical of the leaving game. Interestingly in this excerpt Jane is taking on the role of leaver. In fact children typically swap roles in the leaving game. In the First study, boys developed dramatic role-play rather later than the girls did – 2 years 7 months and 2 years 10 months respectively. However, with such a small sample we cannot say whether this is representative of all boys.

Factors affecting the content of pretend play

An interesting question concerns what determines the content of pretend play. We can look here briefly at three areas; culture, gender and family factors. Some games such as the leaving game may be universal. Another likely universal is that dramatic role-play involves imitating adult roles, but these roles vary according to the culture of the child. Curry and Arnaud (1984) videofilmed and analysed the play of children in five American cultures: Appalachians from West Virginia; Mexican Americans from Texas; black Americans from Texas; Native Americans from Montana; and a mixed group of City children from Pennsylvania. Several universals emerged across the groups. Dramatic role-play in all cases involved domestic play involving food preparation, family roles such as parent–child and sibling interaction, the use of toys to symbolise objects from the children's experience,

classic
research

how and when do children pretend?

Haight W.L. & Miller P.J. (1993) *Pretending at home: early development in a socio-cultural context.* **Albany: SUNY Press**

aim: earlier research had shown that children in laboratory situations given particular objects to play with tend to use them for pretend activities. However, relatively few studies had looked at the pretend activities children choose to spend time doing, given a full choice of toys in their home environment. The aim of this study was to observe the development of pretend play in children in their home environment from 1 to 4 years.

procedure: the participants were four girls and five boys. They were aged 12 months at the beginning of the study. The study was longitudinal, ie the same participants were tracked over a period of time. The participants were followed up from 12 months until 48 months, assessing pretend play every 4 to 6 months (seven times in total). Each child was videofilmed playing at home for 3 to 4 hours at a time. The frequency and type of pretend play and whether pretence was alone or in conjunction with another person was noted in each session.

findings: as expected the sophistication of pretend play increased with age. A more surprising finding that had not been picked up in previous observations of children playing alone in a psychology laboratory was that even in young children most pretend play was with another person rather than alone. Overall, 75 per cent of incidents of pretend play were social rather than solitary. In the younger children the primary carer was the most likely partner in pretend play. By 4 years pretend play was equally likely to be with the primary carer or with a peer. Episodes of pretend play with another person tended to be longer than episodes of solitary pretence.

conclusion: most pretend play is social rather than individual. Social pretend play is more complex than individual pretend play. The partner for social pretend play is initially the primary carer, but peers become more important in older children.

medical personnel and patient interaction and finally aggression, including to and from monsters. There were, however, differences in the play of the five groups, reflecting their different cultures. For example, while all the cultures played some games involving medical personnel, the settings varied from a city hospital to a rural surgery.

We can see then that culture is one influence on the specifics of play content, although perhaps not the general themes. There are also differences in the play of boys and girls. Boys spend more time in rough-and-tumble play than girls, and their dramatic role-play reflects adult male roles, whereas girls spend more time in role-playing household tasks (Stone, 1981). Tarullo (1994) asked 7-year-old boys and girls to compose a story and tell it using a selection of toys. This is a task of pretend play. Boys' narratives tended to contain more violence, and to describe events in the third person – he did, she did etc. Girls' narratives also contained conflict but it was less likely to be of a physical nature and they tended to use

the first person, ie they identified themselves as one of the characters. Girls were more likely to describe how characters in the stories **felt**.

Family factors can also influence the content of children's pretend play. Dunn (1988) reported that children with older siblings who instruct them in play become involved in co-operative pretend play at a younger age than first or only children. Remember that in the First (1994) study (which involved children without siblings) the leaving game did not appear until after 2 years. Dunn reports that among children with siblings 15 per cent were engaged in pretend play at 18 months and 80 per cent by 2 years. The content of play also reflects particular events in the child's home. Dunn et al (1999) compared the pretend play of 40 'hard to manage' children with a control group and found significantly more violent fantasy in the 'hard to manage' group, who were more likely than the control group to have experienced poor parental relationships and an unstable home environment.

Theories of play

We have already said that some types of play, such as rough-and-tumble play, are not easily explained by major theoretical perspectives. However, bearing that limitation in mind it is still worth looking at two perspectives, each of which probably explains well some of the characteristics and benefits of play. The *cognitive-developmental* perspective sees play as important in facilitating intellectual development, while the emphasis of the *psychodynamic* perspective is on emotional expression in play. You should

rough-and-tumble play

Rough-and-tumble play or play fighting occupies up to 10 per cent of children's time spent in play (Smith, 1998). Until recently however it has attracted relatively little attention from psychologists. Play fighting does not fit neatly into categorisations of play such as that used by Parten, nor is it easily explained by the major theoretical perspectives on play (we shall move on to discuss these shortly). So what exactly is rough-and-tumble play? It involves grappling and wrestling, chasing and kicking. To adults, this type of behaviour is hard to distinguish from real fighting, and children are often mistakenly disciplined when they play fight. The frequency of rough-and-tumble fighting peaks in middle childhood and is greater in boys than girls (Pellegrini & Smith, 1998).

In spite of its violent appearance, however, play fighting appears to only occasionally lead to real violence, and injuries are rare (Schafer & Smith, 1996). There are unwritten but strict rules governing rough-and-tumble play. Participants laugh frequently in order to signal their friendly intentions and blows either do not land at all or they are 'pulled'. Stronger children frequently take turns to let weaker children win (this is called reversal). Play fights turn into real fights either when one child accidentally hurts another or deliberately breaks the 'rules' and takes advantage of a momentary advantage to hurt the other participant. Pellegrini (1994) investigated individual differences in children's behaviour in rough-and-tumble play and found that rejected children (see above for a discussion) were the most likely to break rules. This appears to show a lack of social skills and may contribute to their rejected status.

Figure 20.3 Rough-and-tumble play looks violent but relatively rarely leads to real fights

Rough-and-tumble play is apparent in a wide range of human cultures, as well as in many animal species. We may take it then that this type of play has not just resulted from imitation of violent role models, but serves some purpose. The benefits of play fighting include strength and endurance training, learning how to really fight and the establishment of hierarchy of dominant and submissive children. Pellegrini and Smith (1998) reviewed the evidence and concluded that the most important function is probably the latter, and that there is little evidence that rough-and-tumble is important in developing fighting ability. Bjorklund and Brown (1998) have suggested that a further function is to provide a break from the demands of intellectual activity.

where to now?

The following are good sources of further information regarding different types of play:

▶ **Faulkner D. (1995) Play, self and the social world. In Barnes P. (ed) *Personal, social and emotional development of children.* Oxford: Blackwell.** A good account of research into a variety of categories of play behaviour.

▶ **Smith P. (1998) Social development. In Eysenck M. (ed) *Psychology, an integrated approach.* Harlow: Longman.** Particularly useful account of rough-and-tumble play.

bear in mind that play is probably important in both these domains and that the two approaches are complementary rather than in competition. It is also worth remembering that there may other functions of play, such as the development of social skills, that are not accounted for by the major theories of play.

The cognitive-developmental perspective on play

The cognitive-developmental perspective on child development is examined more fully in chapters 18 and 19, and in Jarvis et al (2000) *Angles on psychology.* Briefly though, this approach is concerned with children's intellectual development. The best-known figure in cognitive-developmental psychology is Jean Piaget, and we can begin by looking at his views on play.

Piaget's theory of play

Piaget saw the nature of children's play as developing in line with their general intellectual or cognitive development. He emphasised that children play because they

enjoy it rather than in a conscious attempt to promote their intellectual development, but that none the less different forms of play could be linked to the development of cognitive abilities at particular ages. He identified three types of play particularly associated with different ages:

● **Mastery play** (1–2 years) – this is associated with Piaget's sensorimotor stage of development, in which the child is beginning to learn about itself and its environment. Mastery play involves imitating, repeating and mastering the actions of other people. The purpose of play at this stage is thus to improve the child's mastery of its own body and behaviour.

● **Play stage** (3–6 years) – this is associated with Piaget's preoperational stage, in which children are developing symbolic thought, ie the ability to use symbols such as language to think with, as well as physical actions. At this stage children begin to use objects symbolically, for example toys come to represent other people and objects. Piaget saw this kind of symbolic play as essential for the child to fully develop symbolic thinking.

● **Game stage** (7+) – this is associated with Piaget's concrete and formal operational stages. By the start of the concrete operational stage children have developed intellectually to the point at which they can begin to see things from the perspective of other people. This ability means that they can begin to play successfully together, and co-operative play becomes possible.

Piaget's fundamental ideas that the sophistication of play increases with age, and that symbolic play is associated with intellectual development, have largely stood the test of time. Nowak-Fabrykowski (1995) has suggested that playing with letters in the preoperational stage facilitates the development of reading, and that the symbolic use of objects (such as a cardboard box to represent a castle) enhances children's developing creativity. Symbolic play may also be important in helping the child construct their mental representation of the world.

Piaget's idea that co-operative play does not become possible until the child achieves concrete operational thinking

interactive angles

Read the following examples of play. Which example belongs in which of Piaget's classifications?

1 Having watched a film involving submarines on television, a child takes the cardboard centres of kitchen and toilet rolls and plays with them, pretending they are submarines.

2 A child repeatedly climbs on to a sofa and jumps from it on to the floor (until told off by its exasperated parents).

3 Two children play 'doctors and nurses'. They examine each other using toy stethoscopes.

does neatly explain why co-operative play is much more common in older children than younger. However, Piaget's ages are probably slightly 'out'. Remember that in Parten's (1932) observation, the majority of children spent most time in co-operative play by the age of 5, well before they reach Piaget's concrete operational stage. Another finding that is rather tricky for Piaget's theory to explain comes from Dunn and Munn (1985), who observed that much younger children (80 per cent of 2 year olds) who received instruction from their older siblings were capable of genuinely co-operative play. This finding is much more easily explained by the approach of another cognitive-developmental psychologist, L.S. Vygotsky.

Vygotsky's theory of play

Vygotsky agreed with Piaget on many points including stages of development. However, he placed a great deal of emphasis on the *zone of proximal development* (ZPD), the gap between what a child can achieve on its own and what it can learn under instruction from an 'expert'. This is rather different from Piaget, who saw children's capabilities as being limited by their developmental stage. Presumably in the Dunn and Munn study, young children who had instruction from older siblings were at the upper end of their ZPD, and so were more advanced than the children observed by Piaget, even though they were at the same stage of development.

Vygotsky saw learning as happening between people rather than taking place in isolation, and that an important part of cognitive development is the taking on board (internalising) of a set of 'tools'. In children's early development the term 'tools' can be taken quite literally. Hayes (1998) gives the example of a child learning that it can make more noise by banging a drum with a spoon than with its hand – the

spoon is thus a tool. However, tools also include language, rules and social conventions, which are specific to the culture in which the child grows up. To Vygotsky (1967) play was important because it creates a zone in which children can interact with more expert peers and so internalise these mental tools. Vygotsky (1970) emphasised in particular the importance of rules in play. He suggested that all play has rules, because when a child pretends to be someone else or pretends a toy is something else, then they and their toys have to obey the rules governing those objects or people. Every time the child chooses to restrict its play according to rules, it reinforces its understanding of the rules that govern the world. When an expert peer, such as an older sibling, instructs the child in the rules of a game the child takes on board more rules of its culture.

The influence of Vygotsky's ideas has grown in recent years, and they are widely supported by research. Dunn and Munn's study demonstrates that children who receive expert instruction during their play can advance beyond their stage of cognitive development. This in turn indicates that play is a medium in which children learn from others – the central point of Vygotsky's theory. Vygotsky's ideas are also supported by cross-cultural studies, such as that of Curry and Arnaud (1984), which show that children practise culture-specific roles in their dramatic role-play.

Figure 20.4 This type of game may help children understand what people are thinking

One assumption of Vygotsky's approach (like that of Piaget) that has been challenged, however, is the idea that cognitive development is a generalised phenomenon, and that play assists cognitive development as a whole. Recent research has linked play with specific rather than general aspects of cognitive development, in particular with the development of *theory of mind*.

Play and theory of mind

Despite its slightly confusing name, theory of mind is not a psychological theory. Instead, it refers to the child's individual 'theory' or understanding of other people's minds. The acquisition of a theory of mind is an important part of cognitive development, because it allows the child to understand and so successfully interact with other people. Think back to the Haight and Miller study on page 231. They found that 75 per cent of children's pretend play was with another person. To share a pretend idea requires – and perhaps helps develop – the child's theory of mind. Fonagy et al (1997) have suggested that sharing a pretence during play is a key element in developing an understanding of what others are thinking.

for and against

cognitive-developmental theories

+ Piaget's theory explains why games become more complex as children get older, and why co-operative play becomes more common than solitary play

− Piaget's theory does not explain why children with older siblings have more co-operative play than others

+ other theories, such as that of Vygotsky, do address the weaknesses of Piaget's explanation

− cognitive-developmental theories alone do not explain the emotional significance of play

The psychodynamic approach to play

In contrast to the cognitive-developmental approach to play, psychodynamic explanations have centred on its emotional significance. From a psychodynamic perspective, play represents conflicts or anxieties that the child is working through. We have already looked at First's (1994) study of the 'leaving game'. In the leaving game children and their primary carers act out a sequence of leaving one another, the left partner pretending to cry. What might be the emotional significance of such a game? Two year olds are firmly attached to their primary carer (although of course they may have other attachments as well), and a feature of attachment is distress at being separated from the attachment figure. Two year olds have virtually all experienced some separation from their primary carer and been distressed by the experience. A psychodynamic explanation of the leaving game might thus be that it represents the child's expression of its distress when left.

Freud's theory of play

The psychodynamic study of play began with an observational study by Freud (1922) of an 18-month-old boy. The boy would throw all his toys as far away as possible while saying 'o-o-o-oh', which according to his mother meant 'go away'. He then threw a wooden reel over the side of the cot by the string, saying again 'o-o-o-oh', then pulled it back into view by the string, expressing great pleasure at its return. This pattern of behaviour was repeated frequently. Freud interpreted this game as representing the departure and return of the child's mother. A year later, at the age of 30 months, the child would say 'go to war' while throwing the reel away. The reel represented the parents, initially the mother and later the father, who could be made in pretend to leave and return *under the control of the child*. Based on this case, Freud proposed that children have a *power instinct*, ie a wish to be in control of events, and that play provides this sense of feeling in control. Freud introduced the idea of a *compulsion to repeat* traumatic experiences, in dreams and in play, and so gain mastery over negative events.

Studies of the emotional significance of play

Looking at the classic studies of Freud (1922) and First (1994), we can begin to appreciate both the necessity and the difficulties in adopting a psychodynamic approach to play. It seems extremely likely that, given the emotional nature of children, play does serve some emotional as well as intellectual function. So Freud's explanation seems credible, but it is also highly *speculative*, ie the logical link between Freud's observations and his theory are not obvious, and there are numerous other possible explanations for the child's play with the reel of string. Freud himself conceded that looking at 'a single case of this kind yields no sure conclusion' (1922:14). So is there more scientific evidence to support the idea that play can be a way of mastering negative feelings? Experimental studies are limited by ethical considerations – clearly we can't deliberately traumatise children just to see what will happen to their play. However, there have been some ingenious studies in order to get around this problem. Barnett (1984) used a naturally occurring situation of high anxiety – children's first day at nursery school – to test the effects of play on anxiety. Children were individually assessed for their level of anxiety by measuring their galvanic skin response (how sweaty they became). They were then assigned to two groups, one of which listened to stories while the other group had free play. It was found that the anxiety levels of the high-anxiety children declined much more in free play than in listening to stories, and that the high-anxiety children in free play had spent significantly more time in pretend play than low-anxiety children. This study clearly demonstrates that pretend play serves a role in the reduction of anxiety.

In a more recent study by Watson (1994), 18 children aged between 4 and 6 years were told the story of Hansel and Gretel individually in their day-care centres. Recorded sound effects were used to add to the anxiety-inducing effect of the story. Children were rated as low, medium or high anxiety according to their posture, expression and speech. They were then left alone in the room and invited to play with their choice of toys. The toys had been selected so that children had a choice between sets of toys related and unrelated to the Hansel and Gretel story. A strong correlation (0.81) emerged between the anxiety of the child as assessed while listening to the story, and the correspondence between play and the story.

Warren et al (2000) investigated whether the anxieties expressed in the play of 35 children aged 5 corresponded with anxiety-related behaviour. Play was observed and recorded in themes of negative expectations of self, others and experiences. Parents and teachers completed an assessment of the children's behaviour at same the time and again a year later. The themes expressed in play were strongly predictive of children's anxiety at home and school. This study indicates that the systematic analysis of children's play can be a good indicator of likely anxiety-related problems later.

These studies clearly show us that play is of emotional significance to children, as well as being a medium of intellectual development. This is supportive of Freud's approach, fitting in well with both a compulsion to repeat negative experiences and an attempt to gain mastery over negative events. Of course there may be reasons other than those suggested by Freud to explain why play has emotional significance.

A further way of investigating the emotional significance of play comes from studies of play therapy, in which children who have suffered trauma can use play in the presence of a therapist in order to work through the trauma and gain mastery over the event. It is to this area that we now turn.

where to now?

The following is a good source of further information regarding theories of play:

  Slade A. & Wolf D.P. (eds) (1994) *Children at play: clinical and developmental approaches to meaning and representation.* **Oxford: Oxford University Press.** Reports a selection of studies primarily relevant to understanding the relationship between play and emotional development.

The therapeutic value of play

We have already looked at the way in which children express and master difficult feelings. Play is thus therapeutic in itself. It follows, then, that play can be a useful tool in psychological therapies, predominantly though not exclusively with children. Play can be used in several approaches to psychotherapy, but in this chapter we will concentrate on the psychodynamic approach to child psychotherapy. Central to the psychodynamic treatment of children is the Freudian idea that children play in order to master their negative emotions, such as anxiety or anger. Play can also serve to communicate feelings. Children may lack the ability of older people to talk about the things that are on their minds, but they can express themselves through play, and a therapist can pick up much information about a child's state of mind from the child's play.

A fascinating and touching example of this type of communication comes from Hobson (1985). Hobson was having trouble getting Stephen, a 15-year-old boy, to talk until he began a game called the squiggle. Hobson drew a squiggle and asked Stephen to add to it. Stephen drew a small boat, turning the squiggle into a large wave. Hobson drew a pier and Stephen added a waving figure to the boat. Knowing that Stephen had been traumatised by a separation from his mother Hobson drew a waving woman on the pier. Stephen drew rain across the whole picture, indicating sadness.

Hobson's case example illustrates the usefulness of a play technique in communicating with a reluctant young person. However, you can also see that it is an intensely *subjective* process, ie it relies on the individual interpretations of a therapist. This subjectivity raises the hackles of many psychologists who are committed to a more scientific approach.

In adult psychodynamic therapies, patients are encouraged to *free associate*, ie to say whatever comes into their minds in the belief that this will lead them to bring up things that are bothering them. In child psychotherapy 'free play' can take the place of free association, as children with a problem who are left to play without direction will tend to express and explore that problem in their play.

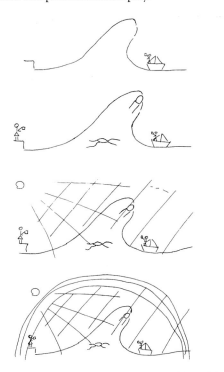

Figure 20.5 Four scenes from the squiggle game. From Hobson (1985)

The nature of a child's play can initially be a source of information with which the therapist can assess the child's psychological state. Parsons (1999) described the case of Mary, an 8-year-old girl who played with toy animals in her first therapy session. She began to put up toy fences around the animals. The therapist commented on the fact that the animals were fenced in, whereupon Mary enacted a furious fight between lions and tigers. The therapist judged that Mary was an angry child, but had been hiding her aggressive feelings. The fences symbolised the way in which she had been keeping her anger trapped inside herself and the battle symbolised the hidden feelings.

In another case, Melzak (1999) described the case of Pascal, a refugee whose father had just died a political prisoner in Zaire. Pascal repeatedly played out fantasies with dolls, puppets or plasticine figures, all of which ended in death and destruction. Each 'death' was accompanied by a 'shrug of inevitability'. The therapist's interventions involved reminding Pascal that not all stories had to end in death and that real men (like his father) are not superheroes and can be killed. After a year of therapy in which the violent games continued, Pascal accepted what the therapist said and his violent games ceased. Only at that point did he begin to mourn the death of his father. Perhaps the most famous case in child psychotherapy comes from Axline (1947), who described the case of Dibs.

classic
research

the case of Dibs

Axline V.M. (1947) *Dibs in search of self*. London: Penguin

background: at the age of 5 years Dibs was referred to Axline, a clinical psychologist specialising in play therapy, for very disturbed behaviour. At school Dibs would play alone and bite and scratch other children when they tried to interact with him. He would violently resist any attempt to take him home from school. Dibs's father was a successful scientist and his mother was a surgeon, who had given up her job when Dibs was born. Both parents believed that Dibs was suffering from brain damage or retardation. Adults who worked with him at school, however, suspected that his problems were emotional in origin.

the therapy: in the first session Dibs painted. At this point he revealed for the first time that he could read by reading out the labels of different paints. He was very reluctant to leave the session. The following week Dibs played with a doll's house and closed all the shutters and doors, then drew a lock on the front door. He commented 'A lock that locks tight with a key, and high hard walls. And a door. A locked door' (page 42). Axline noted that Dibs was concerned with locked doors. Dibs then played with finger paint, but commented 'Oh come away Dibs. It is a very silly kind of paint. Come away!' (page 44). In another session shortly after this Dibs commented that he was glad to come to therapy but sad to leave the therapy room. When Axline asked him if he took any of the gladness with him he responded by burying three toy soldiers in sand and saying 'This makes them unhappy. They cannot see. They cannot hear' (page 67). He dug them up but said of one 'this is papa' and punched it to the ground repeatedly.

By now you might have picked up some of what Dibs was feeling. Being locked up seemed to be an issue, and Dibs was clearly very angry with his father. Dibs's father picked him up that day, and was obviously embarrassed by Dibs, saying 'can't you stop that senseless jabber?' when Dibs tried to speak to him. The next day Dibs's mother came to see Axline and told her how, when they got home after the therapy Dibs's father had commented that Dibs was 'babbling like an idiot', whereupon Dibs had attacked him and been locked in his room. Dibs's mother then confessed that Dibs's birth had been accidental and that it had ruined her career and angered her husband. They had both resented Dibs, and found it difficult to relate to him. A week later Dibs took down the locked front door to the doll's house. He sang 'I hate the walls and the doors that lock and the people that shove you in. I hate the tears and the angry words and I'll kill them all with my hatchet and hammer their bones and spit on them' (page 85). Here Dibs appears to be expressing his anger; whether towards just his father or to both parents is unclear. In taking down the front door of the doll's house it seems that he may have been, in Freud's terms, mastering his feelings about being locked up. Note also the clarity of expression from a 5 year old who had been considered brain-damaged or retarded only a few weeks before.

During the period of Dibs's therapy his behaviour at school gradually improved. He would speak to his teachers and he even began to show some interest in other children. However he still had a lot of anger towards his father. In one session Dibs asked to play in Axline's office rather than the play room. He dictated into her tape recorder; 'Once upon a time there was a boy who lived in a big house with his mother and father and sister. And one day the father came home to his study and the boy went in without knocking. "You are mean man" the boy cried "I hate you. I hate you. Do you hear me I hate you." And the father began to cry. "Please" he said, "I'm sorry for everything I did. Please don't hate me!" (page 159). Dibs had feared his father, but it seems that he was now overcoming that fear, using fantasy play. Outside the therapy Dibs's relationship with his father improved. A week after therapy finished Dibs's IQ was tested and he scored 168, in the top 1 per cent of the population. By then he had no emotional difficulties.

Research into play and therapy

We have already looked at the case of Dibs, who showed remarkable improvements in his emotional state following play therapy. However case-studies alone are not enough of a basis on which to judge the effectiveness of play therapy, because we cannot know for certain that Dibs's improvement was a direct result of the therapy, or that he would not have got better over time without intervention. There is, however, a body of more systematic research into the therapeutic value of play that has painted a broadly positive picture. Fonagy and Target (1994) examined the records of approximately 800 children treated psychoanalytically at the Anna Freud centre in London for anxiety and depression. Most treatments lasted between one and two years. Over 80 per cent of the children were completely free of symptoms at the end of the therapy. Of course child psychotherapy consists of more than play, and studies like this do not really demonstrate that play per se is therapeutic. However, other studies have looked more specifically at the effects of play therapy. LeBlanc (1999) performed a *meta-analysis* on a large number of studies of different techniques used in therapy with children. Meta-analysis involves combining the results of several past studies weighting the results of each study according to the sample size. He concluded that the use of play was associated with a moderate but consistent improvement in the effectiveness of therapy with children.

Other studies have looked at the impact of therapy based exclusively or almost exclusively on play as opposed to psychotherapy involving play as one of several techniques. Sloan (1999) examined whether play therapy could be used to reduce aggressive behaviour in children. Twenty-two children from New York State referred for aggressive behaviour were allocated to one of two conditions. In one condition, play therapy involving aggressive games was used. In the other condition more usual non-aggressive play therapy was used. After 10 sessions the children in both groups experienced a significant decline in aggressive behaviour. This suggests that play therapy is effective for reducing aggression, irrespective of whether it involves aggressive activities.

for and against

psychodynamic explanations

+ there is ample evidence for the emotional significance of play. Play can be used to predict children's later anxieties

+ play can be used therapeutically with great effect

− psychodynamic theory alone does not satisfactorily explain the significance of play to cognitive development

ment. Play includes a number of different activities. Different types of play are associated with different ages. There are also some sex differences, with boys spending more time in rough- and-tumble play. There are two particularly important theoretical perspectives on play. The cognitive-developmental approach, particularly associated with the theories of Piaget and Vygotsky, sees play as important in facilitating children's intellectual development. The psychodynamic approach, particularly associated with the work of Freud, places more emphasis on the emotional significance of play. Building upon the work of Freud, therapists successfully use play to help children express and master emotions.

what do you know ?

1 What are horizontal and vertical changes in children's friendships? Give examples of each.

2 What is sociometric status? Outline **one** way in which sociometric status can be classified.

3 Outline **one** study into the benefits of either popularity or friendship in childhood.

4 Outline **one** way of classifying children's play.

5 What factors affect the content of children's pretend play?

6 Describe **one** theory of play.

7 How can play be used in a therapeutic setting?

where to now ?

The following are good sources of information on the therapeutic value of play:

▶ **Axline V. M. (1947) *Dibs in search of self.* London: Penguin.** An absolutely fascinating and touching case study. Don't read it in public if you want to look hard though – it will make you cry!

▶ **Sylva K. (1994) The therapeutic value of play. *Psychology Review* 1.** A clear and simple overview of the therapeutic use of play.

▶ **Lanyado M. & Horne A. (1999) *The handbook of child and adolescentpsychotherapy.* London: Routledge.** Contains a number of case studies and a particularly useful chapter on research findings on the effectiveness of psychodynamic interventions with children, including the use of play.

Conclusions

Both friendship and play appear to be important aspects of children's development. Children's popularity is affected by a number of factors including physical attractiveness and social skills. Attachment type is associated with popularity and with bullying behaviour. Both popularity and the successful formation of friendships are associated with benefits in social and cognitive develop-

21 Substance abuse

what's ahead?

This chapter aims to explore the psychological issues surrounding the abuse of drugs. We begin by explaining some central concepts such as dependence, tolerance, withdrawal and relapse. We then look at the ways that drugs act on the nervous system, discussing the action of a range of drugs on neurotransmitters and synapses. The physiological and psychological effects of drugs are described, including the long-term consequences of use and the effects of abstinence. Finally, key factors affecting drug abuse, including psychological, social and cognitive determinants such as drug availability, culture and expectation are discussed.

Concepts in understanding drug abuse

Dependence and withdrawal are used in ICD-10 (see chapter 1) as indicators of mental and behavioural disorders due to psychoactive substance abuse (other characteristics include psychotic disorders and amnesia). The named drugs of abuse in ICD-10 are: alcohol, cannabis, sedatives, hypnotics, cocaine, stimulants (including caffeine), hallucinogens, tobacco and volatile substances (solvents). Some of these drugs will be discussed later in the chapter. First we will explain some of the terms that are used to describe the psychological and physiological effects of drugs.

● *Physical dependence* refers to a compulsion to keep taking drugs and has largely replaced the term addiction. It results from the regular and heavy use of drugs such as alcohol, heroin, cocaine or tranquillisers. For a dependent user, sudden absence of the drug results in withdrawal.

● *Withdrawal* or the *abstinence syndrome* is the experience of physically painful and unpleasant symptoms suffered by a physically dependent user as the effects of the drug wears off. These may include vomiting, shaking, headaches and convulsions, although they vary from drug to drug. Physically dependent users need to continue to take the drug just to avoid feeling ill.

● *Psychological dependence* is more common than physical dependence and can occur with any drug. The user believes that they need to keep taking the drug in order to function. They may feel unable to

cope in the absence of the drug. It is possible to become psychologically dependent upon many things: work, other people or gambling for instance. These behaviours become compulsive; the individual assumes that they cannot exist without them. Psychological dependency may also contribute to the experience of physical dependence.

● *Tolerance* is the development of a need for greater amounts of a drug, with repeated use, in order to achieve the same effect. It occurs as the body adapts, probably because taking the drug causes the nervous system to increase the number of receptor sites for that class of molecule. Tolerance occurs with many drugs, such as alcohol, heroin and amphetamine. Within some drug categories, such as the opiates (heroin, morphine etc) and tryptamines (LSD, mescaline and psilocybin), prolonged use of one drug in the group results in the development of tolerance to the others. This is called *cross tolerance*.

● *Relapse* refers to the return to drug-use of a previously recovered user.

The physiology of drug action

The immediate action of a drug is caused by its interaction with a receptor (normally intended for a neurotransmitter), which affects the function of neurones within the central nervous system. For many psychoactive drugs, the classes of receptors involved are known, providing us with an insight into the short-term action of these drugs.

Drugs may be classified in a number of different ways, each having uses in different settings. For our purposes, two classifications are useful. Firstly, drugs may be distinguished by their effects on behaviour. So, for example, drugs may be:

- *sedatives* (induce sleep), eg alcohol;
- *stimulants* (induce wakefulness and activity), eg amphetamine;
- *hallucinogens* (cause perceptual distortions), eg LSD;
- *analgesics* (including *narcotics*, control pain), eg heroin.

Alternatively, drugs may be classified according to their physiological action. Thus drugs may be categorised into those that:

- facilitate or mimic an existing neurotransmitter – *agonist*;
- inhibit or block the effect of an existing neurotransmitter – *antagonist*.

How can drugs mimic or block neural transmission? As you may recall from your study of physiological psychology at AS, nerve cells (or *neurones*) pass messages from one cell to the next by a chemical process across the gap between cells (the *synaptic cleft*). This process, called *synaptic transmission*, is caused by the release of molecules from the presynaptic membrane, which diffuse across the synaptic cleft and attach to specific receptors on the postsynaptic membrane (the edge of the next cell). The molecules are called *neurotransmitters* and are released in response to an action potential (an electrical signal) moving along the length of the neurone (its axon) to the very end (the axon terminals). Here, the cell surface forms many minute synaptic knobs, massively increasing the surface area for communication with adjoining neurones. When the neurotransmitter molecules attach to the postsynaptic receptor sites of an excitatory synapse in large enough amounts, a new action potential is generated (see figure 21.1 below).

Many 'neurotransmitters' are, more accurately, neuromodulators. Most (if not all) of the messages sent into and around the brain use the neurotransmitters glutamate and GABA (gamma-aminobutyric acid). Glutamate has an excitatory effect (increasing the probability of action potentials) and GABA an inhibitory one (reducing the probability of action potentials). The effects we attribute to different compounds, such as the involvement of serotonin with sleep or endorphins with pain relief, are, in fact, neuromodulatory effects. The molecules involved are *neuromodulators* because they facilitate or suppress the effects of neurotransmitters such as glutamate and GABA.

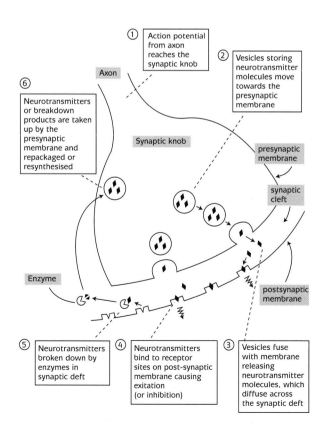

Figure 21.1 (a) Normal functioning of the synapse

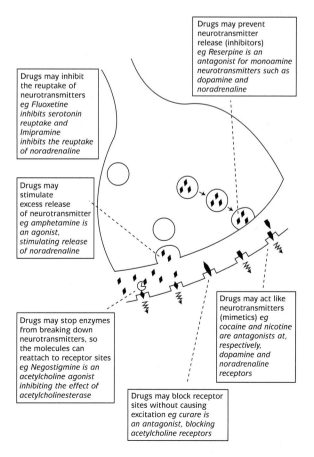

Figure 21.1 (b) Action of drugs at the synapse

Finally, some neurotransmitters attach to more than one types of receptor site. These are then given different names (such as the nicotinic and muscarinic acetylcholine receptors, see page 246–7). Below table 21.1 summarises the neurotransmitters and neuromodulaters we will refer to in this chapter.

Drugs can act in a number of ways (see table 21.2). Agonists generally resemble the chemical structure of the neurotransmitter they mimic. As a consequence, they can fit into the postsynaptic receptor site, and have the same effect as the neurotransmitter itself, causing excitation of the next neurone. Sometimes this effect is enhanced as the drug molecules, unlike the neurotransmitter they are mimicking, get 'stuck' in the receptor site, thus causing repeated excitation. Alternatively, the drug molecules may not be broken down effectively by enzymes in the synaptic cleft, so they can diffuse back to the receptor sites, causing further excitation.

Antagonists have the opposite effect, preventing or inhibiting the effect of neurotransmission. Commonly this occurs because the drug molecules simply block the receptor sites. If the drug is similar in chemical structure to the neurotransmitter it may attach to the receptor site with greater affinity, that is, more firmly, so preventing the neurotrans-

mitters from attaching to the receptor site and reducing postsynaptic excitation (see figure 21.1 on page 241).

Some drugs can have other effects, either at the synapse or on other neuronal processes. An agonistic effect may be produced by a drug that prevents the breakdown of a neurotransmitter in the synaptic cleft or its reuptake into the presynaptic membrane. This interference will accentuate the effect of the neurotransmitter, increasing excitation. An antagonistic effect may be produced by blocking the production or release of neurotransmitters from the presynaptic neurone. In addition, some drugs bind to different receptor sites on the postsynaptic membrane from those used by the neurotransmitter they are affecting.

Cocaine

Cocaine affects receptor sites for monoamine neurotransmitters (noradrenaline and dopamine and, to a lesser extent, serotonin). It increases activity in these neurones by blocking the reuptake of molecules of neurotransmitter from the synaptic cleft, so that they re-stimulate the postsynaptic membrane. Cocaine thus acts as a potent agonist, affecting neurones both centrally and peripherally (hence its use as a local anaesthetic in the latter case). The enhanced activation of postsynaptic receptors

Table 21.1 Examples of neurotransmitters, their chemical structure and some of their functions

Name of molecule	Molecular group	Role	Effects
Glutamate	Amino acid	Neurotransmitter	CNS excitation
GABA (gamma-aminobutyric acid	Amino acid	Neurotransmitter	CNS inhibition
ACh (acetylcholine)	Choline	Neuromodulater	Excitation at neuromuscular junctions, parasympathetic part of the ANS, some areas of the CNS, eg the pons (an area of the brain stem) where it is involved in sleep
Dopamine	Monoamine	Neuromodulater	CNS inhibition and excitation; involved in movement, attention and reinforcement, eg learning and the addictive nature of drug abuse
Noradrenaline	Monoamine	Neuromodulater	Sympathetic part of the ANS, some areas of the CNS
Serotonin	Monoamine	Neuromodulater	Found in the CNS, involved in sleep and dreaming, arousal and eating
Endorphins	Opioid	Neuromodulaters and neurotransmitters	Found in the CNS, involved in analgesia, defensive behaviours (hiding, fleeing) and reinforcement

Table 21.2 Non-synaptic effects of drugs on neurotransmitters

Example of drug	Action of drug on neurotransmitters	Use and psychological effects of drug
α-methyl-dopa	Disrupts the synthesis of noradrenaline by replacing a key molecule during production resulting in the synthesis of non-functional molecule (a *false transmitter*)	Previously used in treatment of hypertension (high blood pressure)
Tricyclic antidepressants (eg Imipramine)	Prolonged use causes down-regulation of genes controlling the manufacture of noradrenaline receptors, that is, there is an effect on the nuclei of adrenergic neurones that causes fewer receptor sites to be maintained on the pre-synaptic membrane	Antidepressant
Monoamine oxidase inhibitors (eg iproniazid)	Cause down-regulation of genes involved in serotonin receptor production (as described above for tricyclics and noradrenaline receptors)	Antidepressant
Reserpine	Prevents the movement of noradrenaline into storage granules in the synaptic knobs, so it is broken down in the cytoplasm Less noradrenaline is therefore available for release into the synapse	Previously used in treatment of hypertension (high blood pressure) and as a traditional treatment for mental illness
Alcohol	Prevents neurotransmitter release in response to action potentials in the axon by inhibiting the opening of voltage-sensitive calcium ion channels that are responsible for the intracellular changes that cause the movement of vesicles towards the pre-synaptic membrane (in neurones using any neurotransmitter system)	CNS depressant, causing inhibition of social restraint, impaired co-ordination, aggression and coma

in the presence of cocaine in the CNS is the cause of its psychological effects, which include a sense of euphoria, insomnia and appetite suppression.

The presence of excess dopamine prevents further release by having a negative-feedback effect on the presynaptic membrane (North, 1992). As a consequence, some hours after cocaine use, when it has been removed from the synaptic cleft, the user suffers a 'crash' – contrary sensations to those experienced under the influence of the drug. The effect is an unpleasant, depressed state.

Heroin

Natural opiate drugs, such as codeine and morphine, are derived from the opium poppy, hence this group of drugs are called *opiates*. Heroin (dihydromorphine), a synthetic opiate, affects several neurotransmitter systems. Pert and Snyder (1973) identified the receptors to which opiate drugs attach. These receptors exist to receive input from endogenous (internal) opioids called *endorphins* (*endogenous morphines*). The key roles of endorphins are to reduce the experience of pain and to provide reinforcement.

By stimulating endorphin receptors, heroin inhibits the release of GABA. Because GABA serves to inhibit dopamine release, the effect of heroin is to facilitate the release of dopamine. The effects of heroin include analgesia, euphoria and withdrawal from reality. Under medical supervision as a painkiller, dihydromorphine is rarely dependence forming but is readily so when used in an uncontrolled way. One reason for this is that heroin, like endorphins, acts on the brain's reward system.

Cannabis

The active chemical found in the cannabis plant, *Cannabis sativa*, is delta-9-tetrahydrocannabinol (a cannabinoid). Medically, cannabis produces effects such as analgesia, sedation, appetite stimulation (used with cancer patients) and reduction of pressure in the eye (for glaucoma patients). However, it also has effects such as interfering with perception (including time) and affects learning and memory.

media watch

Court clears MS patient who used cannabis openly

A disabled man who admitted using cannabis to ease the pain of Multiple Sclerosis was cleared of charges for growing the drug ... [used for] reducing his constant pain ... [He] now uses morphine – a drug that leaves him feeling sick ... 'I know quite a few other MS sufferers who use cannabis. It really works and has no side effects,' he said. ... [He] is hoping to take part in Government-sponsored trials in which disabled people would be legally allowed to take tablets made from a cannabis derivative.

From Independent, 1 March 2000

To what extent can you explain and justify the opinions expressed in this article?

Cannabis use appears to be habit forming rather than causing dependence as users do not experience intense symptoms of withdrawal. One reason for this is because cannabinoids dissolve into body fat where they are stored and slowly released (Julien, 1998). As a consequence, users may test positive for the drug long after they last used it. The discovery of molecules with a cannabinoid structure in chocolate has led to the suggestion that these compounds may be responsible for the craving associated with chocolate consumption. However, when Di Marzo et al (1998) extracted the compounds from various foods including cocoa and investigated whether they would be digested if administered orally, insufficient reached the bloodstream to have measurable effects on the central nervous system.

Cannabinoid receptors were discovered relatively recently compared to those for other drugs, by Devane et al (1988). These receptors are found in various brain regions including the hippocampus and cerebellum. Their absence from areas such as the medulla that control vital functions (breathing, heartbeat etc) accounts for the fact that even large doses of the drug are not lethal. As with the isolation of endogenous opioids (the endorphins) following the discovery of opiate receptors,

research now

mice with the munchies

Fride et al (2000) reported in *New Scientist*, 8 July 2000

aim: to investigate the effect of cannabinoids, the active ingredient in cannabis, on feeding. The property of cannabis to stimulate eating is utilised help cancer and AIDS patients by increasing appetite. Cannabinoids have been detected in human milk and may play a role in the early development of newborns.

procedure: newborn mice were injected with a cannabinoid antagonist, a drug that blocks the natural effect of cannabis-like substances in the body. The mice were then injected with the active component in cannabis, in a dose sufficient to swamp the receptors and counter the effect of the antagonist.

findings: none of the mice treated with the antagonist fed from their mothers. Some died within a week and, if they survived, they developed slowly. Following treatment with the cannabis derivative the mice fed and grew normally.

conclusions: the cannabis antagonist acted to inhibit the feeding response and cannabis counteracted this effect, suggesting that endogenous cannabinoids trigger the ingestion of food.

the search for cannabinoids (endogenous substances that would attach to the receptors) has been successful. The cannabinoid anandamide is manufactured by neurones and probably serves as a neurotransmitter (Di Marzo et al, 1994). One of the functions of anadamide is to inhibit a type of serotonin receptor (Fan, 1995) that is involved in mediating nausea. This accounts for the efficacy of cannabis in combating nausea such as experienced by cancer patients receiving chemotherapy.

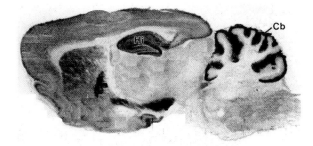

Figure 21.2 The autoradiogram of a rat brain shows the areas that have receptors for cannabinoids. These include the cerebellum (Cb) and hippocampus (Hi). The hippocampus plays a role in the consolidation of memories, which may account for memory losses associated with cannabis use

Alcohol

Unlike the other drugs that we have considered, alcohol acts on the brain in more diverse ways. Although it facilitates GABA activity and decreases serotonin activity (Fils-Aime et al, 1996), it also has direct effects

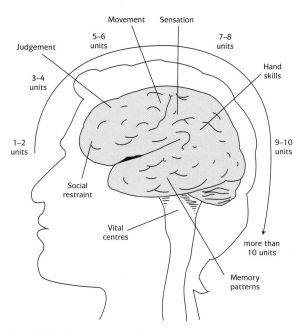

Figure 21.3 The progressive effects of alcohol intoxication

on neuronal membranes and a range of other effects. Cornwell and Cornwell (1993) suggested that the specific pattern of behavioural effects of alcohol intoxication is due to progressive inhibition of cortical areas from the front to the back of the brain, culminating in brain stem inhibition (see figure 21.3 above).

Table 21.3 below summarises the cellular and psychological effects of a range of drugs acting on different neurotransmitters systems.

Table 21.3

Chemical drug name (or active ingredient)	Source	Neurotransmitter or synaptic process affected	Mode of action	Immediate psychological effects
lipid receptors				
cannabis (delta9-tetrahydro-cannabinol, THC)	plant derived, from *Cannabis sativa*	cannabinoid receptors	stimulates cannabinoid receptors that have an inhibitory effect on neurotransmitter release	CNS activation in areas including the brain stem, cerebellum, cortex and hippocampus. Causes analgesia, sedation, appetite stimulant, reduces pressure in the eye. Interferes with perception (including time), affects memory
alcohol				
alcohol	fermented by yeast from sugar	various: GABA, glutamate and serotonin receptors	inhibits GABA and glutamate receptors	CNS depressant, causing inhibition of social restraint, impaired co-ordination, aggression and coma

Chemical drug name (or active ingredient)	Source	Neurotransmitter or synaptic process affected	Mode of action	Immediate psychological effects
drugs affecting cholinergic neurones				
nicotine	plant derived, from *Nicotiniana tabacum*	nicotinic ACh receptors	stimulates ACh receptors (agonist)	CNS stimulant
curare	plant derived from a woody vine	nicotinic ACh receptors	block ACh receptors (antagonist)	paralysis of lung muscles, hence asphyxiation unless breathing is artificially assisted (as it is when curare is occasionally used during surgery)
atropine	plant derived from *Belladonna*	muscarinic ACh receptors	block ACh receptors (antagonist)	dilates the pupils, affects memory
negostigmine	synthetic	inhibits the effect of the enzyme (AChE) responsible for breaking down ACh	facilitates the effect of ACh (agonist)	relieves the symptoms of myasthenia gravis a muscle-weakening disease
drugs affecting monoamine neurones				
Imipramine (tricyclic antidepressant)	synthetic	noradrenaline	inhibits reuptake of NA (agonist)	elevates mood in depression
L-DOPA	synthetic precursor to dopamine	taken up by neurones and converted to dopamine	facilitates the effect of endogenous dopamine (agonist)	relieves symptoms such as limb rigidity in patients with Parkinson's disease
reserpine	derived from the root of the plant *Rauwolfa*	prevents storage of monoamines in synaptic vesicles	inhibits release of monoamines (antagonist)	traditionally used to calm victims of snake bites and for treatment of mental illness. Also reduces high blood pressure
amphetamine	synthetic	dopamine (also stimulates release of NA and dopamine from synaptic knobs)	stimulates relaease of dopamine and inhibits its reuptake (agonist)	stimulant causing apparent energy
cocaine	plant derived from coca leaves	dopamine and NA	blocks reuptake (agonist)	euphoria, talkativeness. Also occasional use as a local anaesthetic
chlorpromazine	synthetic	dopamine	blocks receptors (antagonist)	reduces overactivity of dopamine neurones characteristic of schizophrenia

Chemical drug name (or active ingredient)	Source	Neurotransmitter or synaptic process affected	Mode of action	Immediate psychological effects
3,4-methylene-dioxymeth-amphetamine (MDMA) (Ecstasy)	synthetic	serotonin (5-HT receptors)	stimulates receptors by preventing the retention of serotonin within the presynaptic membrane	emotional closeness, apparent increase in sensory awareness, rush of energy
Prozac (fluoxetine)	synthetic	serotonin (5-HT receptors)	inhibits serotonin reuptake (agonist)	elevates mood in depression
fenfluramine	synthetic	serotonin (5-HT receptors)	inhibits serotonin reuptake and facilitates release (agonist)	appetite suppressant
lysergic acid diethylamide (LSD, acid)	synthetic, originally derived from fungus (ergot, *Claviceps purpurea*)	serotonin	inhibits serotonin release in some brain areas (eg raphe nuclei), facilitates in others (eg forebrain), ie both antagonistic and agonistic functions	hallucinations and visual distortions
amino acid receptors				
phencyclidine (PCP)	synthetic	additional binding site on glutamate receptors	inhibits the effect of glutamate (works indirectly), also affects opioid type σ receptors	cognitive disruption, altered body image, euphoria, dreamlike state
ketamine	synthetic	additional binding site on glutamate receptors	inhibits the effect of glutamate (works indirectly)	general anaesthetic, causes detached sensations, a rush of energy and hallucinations
benzodiazepines (eg diazepam – Valium and chlordiazepoxide – Librium)	synthetic	additional binding site on GABA receptors	promotes GABA activity (works indirectly)	tranquillisers, reduce anxiety, promote sleep and muscle relaxation
barbiturates (eg phenobarbital)	synthetic	additional binding site on GABA receptors	promotes GABA activity (works indirectly)	reduce anxiety, promote sleep
peptide receptors				
dihydromorphine (heroin)	synthetic	opiate receptors	facilitates endorphin activity (agonist)	analgesic
nalaxone	synthetic	opiate receptors	inhibits endorphin activity (antagonist)	reverses opiate intoxication (counters overdose)

The effects of drug use

Cocaine

Cocaine produces intense feelings of self-confidence and energy. It shows tolerance and leads to severe psychological dependence. Withdrawal symptoms may include 'cocaine bugs', a sensation of creatures crawling under the skin. This hallucination is probably caused by sensory neurones firing spontaneously. It may be so strong that attempts are made to cut them out. If the effects are this grotesque, why is cocaine abused?

Cocaine is very highly addictive; taking it generates a desire for more. Every species of animal tested will self-administer cocaine for its powerful reinforcing effects. Even when self-administration of cocaine is punished, a person will still want more of the drug (Johanson and Fischman, 1989). This craving becomes part of the withdrawal syndrome that includes depression, anxiety, loss of co-ordination, tremors and sleepiness. In chronic use at high doses, interpersonal conflicts arise and toxic paranoid psychosis may develop. The user becomes hyperreactive, paranoid and impulsive. Their altered perceptions of reality may lead to aggressive or homicidal responses to imagined persecution (Mendelson and Mello, 1996). Neuropsychological disorders have been identified in 73 per cent of cocaine abusers seeking treatment (Rounsaville et al, 1991).

The consequences of cocaine addiction for physical and mental health are severe. This is in part because cocaine abuse is often associated with abuse of other drugs, including alcohol and heroin. However, the reinforcing effect of cocaine across species suggests that abusers do not have an inherent pathological condition that inclines them towards cocaine abuse (Julien, 1998). Cocaine demonstrates a strong tolerance effect, so dependent users may take very large doses, as much as 150 mg (effects are apparent at 8 mg). The problems of cocaine abuse are magnified by the effects on the family and financial concerns. These threats contribute to the user's fears, so exaggerating the symptoms of withdrawal.

Opiates

Drugs from the opiate group are often referred to as *'hard'* drugs, although this term may be applied to any drug capable of producing physical dependence. Heroin causes a brief sensation of euphoria and a relatively lasting feeling of well being – initially. Tolerance develops rapidly and equivalent doses merely maintain the user in a bearable condition. The immediate symptoms of withdrawal include pain, nausea, diarrhoea, sweating, extreme anxiety and depression. During prolonged abstinence, dependent users suffer continued depression and

anxiety, decreased self-esteem, abnormal responses to stress and an increased incidence of other psychiatric disorders (Brooner et al, 1997).

Jaffe (1993) proposes several behavioural explanations for opioid use:

- seeking euphoria (positive reinforcement);
- avoidance of withdrawal (negative reinforcement);
- self-medication of opioids to relieve dysphoric or painful affective states from which dependence develops;
- initial experimentation in search of euphoria by individuals with pre-existing psychopathology leads to dependence;
- individuals with deficient endorphin systems seek to correct the imbalance by using drugs;
- repeated use of opioids permanently alters the function of the endorphin system so that normal functioning is no longer possible without additional opioids;
- withdrawal and drug effects become linked through environmental cues and moods. Either source can then initiate the recall of the distress of withdrawal, so it is avoided.

Cannabis

Pope et al (1998) reported little effect of daily cannabis use on memory. They did find that frequent users were somewhat poorer on a test where they had to mimic simple card matching rules demonstrated by the experimenter, adapting whenever the rule changed. Whilst slight, such an impairment could be significant in a rapidly changing environment such as on the road. The findings were from well-controlled samples but even these results raise issues of validity. Why, for instance, did they find smaller performance decrements in female participants than in males? Fletcher et al (1996) compared chronic users and non-users over a 20-year period. The users demonstrated greater impairment of memory and attention, but the differences were subtle and the chronic users' abilities were still within the normal range. They concluded that 'no evidence exists for the severity of health risks associated with the use of other drugs'. These results conflict with other studies, which demonstrate impaired ability to attend to tasks and filter out irrelevant information (Lundqvist, 1995; Solowij, 1995).

Chronic cannabis use is associated with 'dropping out'. Musty and Kaback (1995) found that as many as 50 per cent of adolescents admitted to a substance abuse treatment programme were found to have depressive symptoms. It is not clear, however, whether this is a consequence or cause. Are depressed teenagers more likely

Spiders on drugs can't spin straight

Stoned spiders produce way-out webs, scientists have discovered. On marijuana they spin only so much, then decide it doesn't matter any more. On Benzedrine, a well-known upper, the results are, to say the least, hallucinatory.

Give the little arachnids a spot of caffeine and they can do no more than throw a few threads together at random.

The insect spins with terrific speed but without any clear thought given to planning.

The result is a tangled web indeed – a spaghetti-like mess which leaves great holes through which its intended victims can fly.

One recruit, fed a dose of chloral hydrate, a well-known soporific, dozed off before it had got started.

The information was gathered by scientists from NASA, America's space programme.

… The researchers, from NASA's Marshall Space Flight Centre in Alabama, think spiders could replace other animals in testing the toxicity of chemicals.

By analysing the state of the webs after the spiders have been fed certain substances, they believe they can better predict the toxicity of new medicines.

… NASA spokesman Jerry Berg denies the research is frivolous.

For one thing, spiders are cheaper to use than higher-order animals like rabbits and less likely to engender complaints from the animal welfare lobby.

'It follows a long tradition of using lower life-forms like insects and even bacteria in research', he says.

S. Dalton/NHPA

From *Daily Express*, 28 April 1995

Marijuana   Benzedrine   Caffeine   Chloral hydrate

Research the effects of marijuana (cannabis), Benzedrine (a benzodiazepine or drug – like Diazepam – used to reduce anxiety), caffeine and chloral hydrate (a now rarely used hypnotic – it induces sleep). Using this information, the comments in the text and your knowledge of animal experimentation from Unit 6 Issues, Perspectives and Debates, develop reasoned arguments for and against the use of animal models to explore the effects of drugs on humans.

to use cannabis? Estimation of the problem arising from cannabis dependence is hindered by the way statistics are gathered. For instance, the number of people receiving treatment for cannabis use in the US is inflated by those arrested or who test positive in random checks at work. They may opt for rehabilitation as an alternative to prosecution or being fired.

Alcohol

In the long term, alcohol abuse leads to the development of tolerance, although this is largely a metabolic adaptation that reduces apparent intoxication without affecting the reinforcing qualities. Alcoholics therefore appear to get less drunk, but still enjoy it. Physical dependence develops from chronic drinking, and withdrawal symptoms include hallucinations, confusion, disorientation, vomiting, sleep disorders and psychomotor agitation. This syndrome is referred to as delirium tremens (DTs). Long-term alcohol abuse may lead to Korsakoff's syndrome, an irreversible dementia caused by alcohol damage to neurones as well as much non-psychological damage.

Alcohol dependency, previously referred to as alcoholism, is a chronic, progressive and potentially fatal disease. It is characterised by impaired control over drinking, preoccupation with alcohol, continued use despite adverse consequences, and distortions in thinking, most noticeably denial. Genetic, psychosocial and environmental factors influence its development, and Cornwell and Cornwell (1993) estimate that 500,000 Britons suffer serious alcohol dependency. Why do so many people abuse alcohol? Research suggests that one reason for alcohol abuse may be as a means to self-medicate for underlying psychological problems such as depression (eg MacAndrew, 1989).

Factors affecting drug abuse

There may be many reasons for starting, or continuing, to abuse drugs (Plant, 1987 – see below). Some of these are discussed in detail in the remainder of the chapter.

interactive angles

Why do people use drugs?
Hedonism – drugs can be fun to use.

Availability – people use drugs because they are there.

Cultural/subcultural factors – different groups in society may develop differing beliefs and practices with regard to different drugs.

Biological predisposition – the idea that it is something in a person's biological or genetic make-up.

Personality peculiarities – such as being extrovert, introvert or neurotic.

Intelligence – drug users are either more or less intelligent than average.

Mental health – users often have (pre-existing) psychiatric problems.

Sex – males are more likely to use drugs than females.

Age – eg young people may use drugs to deal with uncertainties.

Self-medication – people with problems may use drugs in an effort to make themselves feel better or more stable.

Basic human need – altered states of consciousness are attractive to humans and can be achieved through drug use or through meditation, music, sport or religion.

Curiosity – people are interested in what drug effects are like.

Self-destruction – people with suicidal tendencies may be attracted to heavy drug use

To attempt to resolve personal problems.

Family disturbance – people from 'broken' or 'disturbed' homes may be at risk.

Unemployment or educational problems.

Socio-economic class and deprivation.

Peer pressure.

Anti-authority views.

Delinquency – users may have criminal records before they begin to abuse drugs.

Occupation – doctors have high rates of alcoholism; students have a high incidence of illegal drug use.

Historical reasons – the types of drugs abused depend on the 'fashion'.

Alienation – people who feel they have little to invest or future in society may be inclined to abuse drugs.

Deviance amplification – by making something illegal it may become more attractive.

from Plant (1987)

Using resources such as your library or the Internet, investigate any two of these issues.

Addiction

The word 'addiction', for many people, conjures up images of sick-looking heroin users injecting themselves. Since many drug users do not fit this pattern confusion arises over the meaning of the term so it is best avoided. When used, it refers to the condition of a person whose whole life is ruled by the need to buy and take drugs to the extent that they may be unable to function normally in society. Such individuals are generally heavy users of drugs such as heroin or cocaine. Therefore, it is preferable to refer to 'dependent users' rather than 'addicts'.

Learning theory

You will probably already be aware of three learning theories; classical conditioning, operant conditioning and social learning theory. Each of these has been used to explain some aspects of drug use. To recap briefly, *classical conditioning* is the formation of an association between a known or *unconditioned stimulus* (the UCS) and a new, *neutral stimulus* (the NS) such that the NS (which becomes the *conditioned stimulus* or CS) acquires the properties of the UCS to initiate a response (the CR). So, the same behaviour that began as the unconditioned response (UCR) now appears as the conditioned response (CR). *Operant conditioning* is the acquisition of a new response to a stimulus through the processes of reward (reinforcement) or punishment. *Social learning* occurs when an individual becomes capable of a new behaviour because they have observed and imitated that behaviour in another individual, the model.

Classical conditioning

Classical conditioning can explain some aspects of the effects associated with drug use. For example:

Prior to conditioning:

going out for a drink → *relaxation*
UCS → UCR

This relationship exists perhaps because people enjoy socialising, company or playing pool.

During the association phase:

going out for a drink + alcohol → *relaxation*
UCS + CS → UCR

Repetition of this pairing results in conditioning, such that:

alcohol → *relaxation*
CS → CR

The conditioned stimulus of alcohol has thus acquired the association of relaxation.

Unconditioned stimuli may be external, such as being with particular people or at the pub, or internal, such as feeling depressed, anxious or happy. This may be problematic as external stimuli can be avoided (for example not going out with friends who smoke if you are trying to give up) but internal cues cannot. The phenomenon of *discrimination* in classical conditioning (in which CRs are acquired to only one of a similar range of possible stimuli) could account for people being able to resist smoking at work but being unable to do so when out with friends. *Generalisation* occurs when a CR is triggered by stimuli similar to the CS. As a result, withdrawal symptoms (for example, anxiety) may act

as triggers to resume a drug taking habit that was dependent on internal cues. Such habits are therefore hard to break.

Classical conditioning can also account for some instances of overdose. In addition to the development of tolerance, CSs associated with a drug-taking habit can trigger a classically conditioned physiological response that prepares the body for the arrival of the drug. Using a medical example, the blood sugar level of diabetics falls in response to the expectation of an insulin injection; this is a compensatory reaction brought about by classical conditioning. Intravenous drug users (IVDUs) may develop a classically conditioned expectation of the arrival of a drug dose in response to the stimuli associated with drug preparation (needles and syringes for example). Unlike medically supervised diabetics using insulin, a heroin user cannot guarantee the strength of the dose they are administering. The *compensatory reaction hypothesis* suggests that, if the preparation is unusually strong and the body has acquired a compensation reaction in response to doses of lower strength, the physiological effect of the drug will be far greater than the user's body is prepared for. The consequence is effectively an overdose and the situation may be fatal.

Operant conditioning

Positive reinforcement increases the frequency of a behaviour. Drug use may be reinforcing if it is associated with social acceptance (for instance when peer pressure to smoke exists). Leventhal and Cleary (1980) reported that teenagers may start smoking if they have friends who smoke, suggesting that the social norm within a group is important in the initial determination of drug use. Morgan and Grube (1991) investigated the effect of peer group pressure on drug use. They suggested that peer group closeness would be a critical factor in determining drug use since social influence is affected by the closeness of relationships. They investigated the effects of peer group (best friend, other good friends and other people of their age) on drug experimentation and maintenance of substance use. They found that 'closeness' was a good predictor of drug use, several good friends being an important factor in the initiation of drug taking. The 'best friend' was uniquely influential in maintenance of drug use. These findings have important implications for drug education; familiar, rather than anonymous, peers may also be more effective at delivering preventative messages.

Peer pressure has been demonstrated to affect health behaviours positively. Mosbach and Leventhal (1988) identified four different peer groups within a junior high school. They found that students belonging to the 'dirtballs' (boys who were poor, had personal or school-related problems, and tended to smoke and use other drugs) and 'hotshots' (mainly popular and academically successful girls) made up only 15 per cent of the sample but 56 per

Figure 21.4 Drinking habits may be acquired through observation of models

for and against

learning theory as an explanation of drug use

+ classical conditioning can account for the acquisition of some drug habits

+ some rehabilitation programmes are also based on the classical conditioning paradigm, using aversion therapy

+ the processes of generalisation and distinction can account for the differences individuals may show in their drug use in different settings and for some aspects of dependency

+ operant conditioning can explain the maintenance of drug habits

+ methods of drug use may be acquired through observation, for example the drinking wine from a stemmed glass but beer from a mug (Sussman and Ames, 2001)

− evidence from family studies may be explained by genetic rather than learned factors

The avoidance of withdrawal symptoms would act as a *negative reinforcer*, perpetuating the drug taking habit because cessation results in unpleasant effects. The effects of withdrawal have been discussed earlier in the chapter (on pages 240, 248, 250). Many drugs act on the dopamine reward system (as discussed on page 243). This can account for their addictive properties and the tendency of users to ignore other aspects of life. For a dependent heroin or cocaine user the euphoric effect and avoidance of withdrawal are sufficiently reinforcing that they can override basic needs and standards.

Social learning theory

Young people may acquire drug-use habits from observing significant others such as their parents. Smoking is more common in children who have a parent who smokes (USDHHS, 1989). Evidence suggests that problem drinking also runs in families (Sher et al, 1997) although it is difficult to determine the extent to which this is a result of the children's environment or genetic. Twin and adoption studies (eg Cloninger et al, 1981; Bohman et al, 1981) suggest that both components are important.

Psychological factors affecting drug use

The feeling that users of drugs such as opiates and cocaine describe as a 'rush' or 'high' is called *euphoria*. It is experienced as an intense pleasure but is short lived and, although users may continue to take increasing amounts of the drug in search of the effect, it becomes harder to achieve due to the effects of tolerance. In drugs that cause physical dependence, it is progressively replaced instead by feelings of normality when on the drug and withdrawal without it. Thus, euphoria may account for the initial desire to continue to take a drug, but physical dependence maintains this need.

The concept of *salience* refers to the importance of the drug-taking behaviour within the individual's life. When salience is high, the focus of the user's activities centres around their drug habit as seen in dependent users of alcohol, heroin and cocaine. When they are not taking the drug they are thinking about it. So, once dependent, users experiencing salience may be unable to draw their attention away from their drug habit, making attempts at abstinence difficult and exacerbating the effects of withdrawal.

Personality characteristics

An individual's personality may also affect their drug use. Most individuals with substance abuse problems have psychiatric disorders in addition to their drug dependence (Horner and Scheibe, 1997). Self-medication has been identified as a reason why many users begin taking drugs, for instance in the use of nicotine and alcohol. Julien

cent of the smokers. The 'jocks' (mainly boys who were keen on sport) and the rest of the student population were much less likely to smoke. Within these groups, peer pressure acted against smoking.

(1998) suggests the following possible reasons for self-administration of drugs to treat psychological distress:

- nicotine acts as an antidepressant;
- alcohol reduces anxiety, sensitivity and inhibitions so increasing socialisation, helping the individual to cope;
- cocaine and amphetamine elevate mood and temporarily avert feelings of worthlessness;
- opioids reduce physical and psychological pain, enabling the individual to deal with otherwise intolerable situations;
- cannabis has a calming, sedative effect combined with a feeling of well being, which could be used to relieve the effects of anxiety, depression or social isolation.

interactive angles

Return to the reasons for opioid use listed on page 248. Use learning theory and differences in personality characteristics to account for at least four of the explanations offered.

Whilst cocaine shows patterns of abuse across social groups, this may be explained by accessibility. It is not likely that personality factors play a significant role in cocaine use, as it is powerfully reinforcing for absolutely everyone and everything. The effects of cocaine differ from those of alcohol in that, although animals will self-administer cocaine once they are dependent, dependency only develops following enforced exposure. Any differences that exist between people must therefore arise at the stage of trying cocaine rather than in the risk of becoming dependent.

Children with ADHD often gain relief, surprisingly, from the use of stimulants and many are treated with methylphenidate (Ritalin). Recent evidence suggests that such children may be a high-risk group for later cocaine abuse. Schenk (1998) studied the effect of priming rats with amphetamine (a stimulant similar to methylphenidate). They were more likely to self-administer cocaine than control rats. She believes that children who take methylphenidate are three times more likely to abuse cocaine in adulthood. Lambert (1998) suggests that, as adults, they are also more likely to smoke.

Some individuals may be more tempted by the appeal of drugs and use seems to be dependent upon the image the drug portrays. For example, MDMA was originally sold by dealers as *Empathy*. When this failed to appeal to young people, it became known as *Ecstasy* (Yeoman, 1995). McCann and Ricaurte (1993) compared the personalities of 30 Ecstasy users with 28 volunteers who had not taken the drug. The participants who had taken Ecstasy were less hostile and showed greater restraint and control. These are aspects of behaviour thought to be mediated by serotonin, the neurotransmitter upon which Ecstasy works. The findings may reflect differences in initial personality of the users compared to non-users or, alternatively, could reflect changes that occur after use. The users had, on average, each taken the drug 95 times over about five years. It is possible that Ecstasy use could affect behaviour or personality as prolonged use has been shown to result in damage to serotonin neurones in the brain and to impair long-term memory (Reneman et al, 2001).

Another characteristic associated with drug taking is *sensation seeking*, which is a trait encompassing the desire to find and participate in novel, complex and intense sensations and experiences (Zuckerman, 1994). Sensation seeking individuals are characterised by a willingness to take financial, physical, social and legal risks in search of such opportunities. Sensation seeking has been linked to smoking (Zuckerman et al, 1990), alcohol use (Stacy et al, 1993) and the use of other drugs such as cannabis (Ames et al, 2002). Furthermore, high sensation seekers seem to be at greater risk from drug excesses such as alcoholism (Zuckerman, 1987; Sayette & Hufford, 1997).

for and against

personality differences as an explanation for drug abuse

+ some personalities may be more susceptible to drug taking in an attempt to self-medicate

+ personality differences have been identified between Ecstasy users and non-users

− such differences may be consequent upon drug taking rather than causal

+ personality factors and subsequent drug use (such as in ADHD) may be additive in their effects

+ high sensation seekers are more likely to try drugs and are at greater risk of subsequent dependence

research
now

arousal and anxiety in Ecstasy users

Wareing M., Fisk J.E. & Murphy P.N. (2000) Working memory deficits in current and previous users of MDMA ('Ecstasy'). *British Journal of Psychology* 91: 181–8

aims: to investigate the effects of long-term Ecstasy use on memory, arousal and anxiety.

procedure: current, past and non-Ecstasy users were tested on cognitive functioning and were given a self-report questionnaire on arousal and anxiety.

findings: both users and ex-users showed some cognitive impairment compared to the non-users, making more information processing errors. There were significant differences in anxiety; users (both current and previous) were more anxious than non-users. The arousal scores of previous users were higher than the non-users' controls, whereas those of current users were lower.

conclusion: following weekend Ecstasy use, users may experience a decline in arousal during the middle of the week. This may arise from the destruction of some serotonin pathways in the brain and abnormal growth in other areas in response to exposure to Ecstasy.

Social factors affecting drug use
Drug availability

Availability of drugs can be separated into three aspects:

- *ease of distribution* refers to the existence of a mechanism for transporting drugs to different locations. This may depend on physical location (such as being near a port) or a 'business structure' that allows drugs to be moved with little resistance;

- *access* is a measure of individuals' knowledge about how to obtain drugs from sources after distribution;

- *acquisition* refers to the ability of an individual to get drugs for themselves, for example, through trust, money or prostitution (see figure 21.5 below).

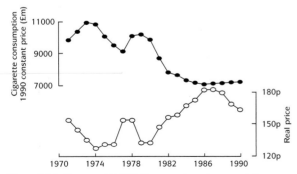

Figure 21.5 Townsend (1993) illustrates how the cost of cigarettes affects smoking. Drug use is directly related to the acquisition aspect of availability in this instance; when smoking is expensive, people smoke less

- Some regional areas may provide greater drug availability than others. For example, Sussman and Ames (2001) suggest that drug use in the US is greater in areas that are in close proximity to New York City and Los Angeles as these are major centres for drug distribution.

Peer groups may provide a route for both access and acquisition. According to Robinson et al (1997), the step from trying cigarettes to being a regular smoker is influenced by whether members of the friendship group smoke, approval from the peer group and being offered cigarettes by friends. The workplace may also be a route for drug access and acquisition. Frone (2003) reports workplace substance availability as a risk factor in on-the-job alcohol and marijuana use.

Cultural factors affecting drug use

Sources of information about cultural norms include the Internet, television and films. Indeed, the images and language used may be responsible for promoting drug use. Cinema idols or rock stars can be powerful role models and repeated exposure of them pictured smoking cigarettes or taking heroin may influence the cultural norm. Wills et al (1996) found that advertisements linking smoking to social popularity and sensation-seeking cues may be influential in the onset of smoking.

Differences in normative structure can also account for differences between cultural groups with respect to drug use. Many French children grow up drinking wine with meals and buying wine in shops so the norm is for 'wine as a food' rather than an alcoholic drink. In contrast, in the US, where the purchase of alcohol is illegal under the age of 21, children do not drink at all. The difference between attitudes to cannabis between The Netherlands (where recreational use is legal) and countries such as the US (where it is not) represents a similar variation in cultural norms. The importance of social norms within the peer group is a further example of the effects of normative structure and was discussed on page 251–2.

Cultural differences also exist in the use of medicines. French people and, to a lesser extent Italians, use more prescribed tranquillisers and antidepressants than Britons or Germans. The French Research Centre for the Study and Documentation of Health Economics (CREDES, 1994) compared the prescribing habits of doctors in the four nations. They measured consumption of tranquillisers, including sleeping tablets and drugs for treating anxiety, in Defined Daily Doses (DDD), the amount that would be required by a 75-kg person. French doctors prescribed about four times as many DDDs per thousand people as their counterparts in Britain or Germany and two-and-a-half times as many as in Italy. Yet the WHO (1995) found no greater incidence of mental illness in French people. Instead, French doctors appear to be more likely to prescribe drugs and less likely to advise other treatments, such as counselling. This suggests that a cultural norm of antidepressant use affects the rate at which such medicines are prescribed.

There may also be cultural differences in the reaction to some drugs, for example, alcohol intoxication. Alcohol dependency is a biological concomitant of excess drinking, which arises in all societies where alcohol is consumed; drunkenness, however, is not. The behaviours associated with the influence of excess alcohol consumption are at least partly culturally determined. While drunken Westerners become depressed, angry or aggressive, this loss of control is not automatic but learned (MacAndrew & Edgerton, 1970). For example, Tahitians are peaceful and civil under the influence of alcohol. In contrast, communities such as the Native Americans who have been exposed to examples of violence in response to alcohol consumption, will learn these behaviours and begin to display them. This suggests that problems arising from drug abuse may be, in part, a consequence of social constructs.

Cognitive factors affecting drug use

Expectation

Expectancy theory (Rotter, 1954) proposes that an individual's anticipation of particular consequences of drug use leads to their experience of those effects. For example, cultural expectations about the effects of alcohol lead to different effects in different cultures (see page 254). This suggests that users develop a cognitive construct for the outcomes of drug use. Fromme et al (1997) suggest that early observations or experience of alcohol use tend to have positive rather than negative outcomes. The resulting positive outcome expectancy can then contribute to the initiation and continuation of the behaviour (Sussman et al, 1996).

The expectancy effect can account for the efficacy of *placebos* – inert substances that offer relief from symptoms. They are given in experimental situations in place of active drugs to control for the bias that may be created by the experience of being treated. In medical settings, placebos have been found to offer some relief in acne, allergies, asthma, cancer, diabetes, dementia, insomnia, multiple sclerosis and obesity (Haas et al, 1959). Even sham operations (where the patients believe they have been operated on but no surgery has been completed) have been found to be as effective as real bypass operations at relieving the pain of angina (Diamond et al, 1960).

Conclusions

Drugs can enhance or inhibit neuronal functioning either because they are structurally similar to neurotransmitter molecules or, less commonly, by acting on enzymes or the presynaptic membrane. Many drugs act

---

for and against

cultural factors as an explanation of drug abuse

+ patterns of drug consumption and anticipated effects may be culturally determined through opportunity or expectation

— the globalisation effect of the Internet may obscure some cultural differences

— Rushton (1997) suggests that research on drug use by young people fails to consider participants' own knowledge and insights. She discusses the subcultures of drug users who may have different 'careers' in drug use. It may therefore be difficult to identify clear cultural effects

classic
research

I can't feel the pain

Levine J.D., Gordon N.C. & Fields H.L. (1979) The role of endorphins in placebo analgesia. In Bonica J.J., Liebeskind J.C. & Albe-Fessard D., *Advances in Pain Research and Therapy* **(vol 3). New York: Raven Press**

aims: to investigate the placebo effect.

procedure: participants were given a baseline measure of sensitivity to pain. They then received a placebo injection and were told it was a painkiller. After further pain sensitivity testing the participants were given a second injection. They were again told it was a painkiller but it was in fact nalaxone, an opiate antagonist (that blocks the body's defence against pain).

findings: the initial injection reduced sensitivity to pain but the second restored the participants' pain sensitivity.

conclusion: although the initial injection produced a placebo effect, this was abolished by the second injection. This suggested that the placebo effect is mediated by the body's natural endorphins (opiate-like molecules secreted in the brain in response to pain).

on more than one neurotransmitter system but often the effects of a drug clearly relate to the role played by the neurotransmitter that they mimic. Cocaine is a monoamine agonist that produces euphoria and strong physical dependency. Heroin is a synthetic opiate that mimics the effects of natural endorphins, producing analgesia and, initially, euphoria but tolerance leads to the disappearance of this effect. Both of these physically addictive drugs cause unpleasant withdrawal symptoms so users find abstinence difficult. Cannabis acts on cannabinoid receptors and produces effects such as distorted perception and appetite stimulation. It may result in memory loss and persists in the body in fatty tissue long after use has ceased. Alcohol has a range of actions on the CNS and consequently produces many different behavioural effects. Withdrawal symptoms include hallucinations, vomiting and sleep disorders, and chronic alcohol consumption leads to tolerance and physical dependence.

Learning theories, including classical and operant conditioning and imitation, all offer explanations for the acquisition and maintenance of drug-taking behaviour. Differences in personality may also account for some variation in risk between individuals. Heroin and alcohol dependency may arise in individuals with psychological disorders as an attempt to self-medicate and high sensation seekers are more likely to try drugs and to become dependent on them. Drug availability also affects risk. If drugs are easier to obtain, because of geographical area, cost or contact for example, individuals are more likely to try them. Cultural differences can account for differences in use of illegal, legal and prescription drugs and for variation in the behavioural responses experienced during intoxication. These latter differences may be the consequence of expectancy effects, as users develop a cognitive construct for the effects of drug use.

where to now?

▶ **Carlson N.R. (1998)** *Physiology of behavior.* **London: Allyn & Bacon.** This text is very biological, providing a good overview of drug action.

▶ **Sussman S. & Ames S.L. (2001)** *The social psychology of drug abuse.* **Buckingham: Open University Press.** This text provides an in-depth coverage of social, cultural and personality factors affecting drug use.

▶ **Vines G. (1994) I'm relaxed, you're drunk.** *New Scientist*, **10 December 1994: 35–8.** A readily accessible article discussing the ways in which culture can alter the effects of alcohol.

▶ **Cornwell A. & Cornwell V. (1993)** *Drugs, alcohol and mental health.* **Cambridge: University of Cambridge Press.** The small handbook provides a wealth of information about the biology and psychological and social consequences of drug abuse.

▶ **http://www.hda-online.org.uk/downloads/ pdfs/smokingmedia.pdf** This website describes the history of anti-smoking campaigns in Britain.

what do you know?

1 (a) Define tolerance, withdrawal and relapse as used in the context of drug abuse.

   (b) Distinguish between psychological and physical dependence.

2 Using **two** named examples, describe the mechanisms of drug action and explain how this accounts for the short-term effects of these drugs.

3 Use learning theory to describe **two** ways in which drug abuse may be explained.

4 Personality, social, cultural and cognitive factors are known to affect drug use. Discuss how any **two** of these factors can account why people may abuse drugs.

22 Stress

what's **ahead**

We begin the chapter by considering the concept of stress, internal and external stressors, and how they can interact. We then describe the biological processes involved in the stress response looking at the involvement of the nervous system, hormones and the immune system, including a review of psychoneuroimmunology. In addition, we explore examples of biological, social and psychological factors that affect our experience of stress. Finally, we look at the ways in which we can cope with stress.

The concept of stress

Stress is a reaction, both physical and psychological, to circumstances that are perceived to be negative and threatening to the individual. The elements of the situation that provoke such a response are called *stressors*. Some kinds of stimuli, under particular circumstances, may become stressful. Stressors could affect us in one of two ways:

- *physiologically* by affecting body functioning such as altering pulse rate, blood pressure and the immune system or by changing hormone levels;
- *psychologically* through sensitivity changes in cognitive functioning and emotions such as fear or anger.

Some of these responses are, of course, adaptive; they help us to respond to potential dangers. However, they evolved to protect us when our environment was somewhat different from that in which we now live. For example, the need to be able to run fast is far more use when trying to chase a woolly mammoth, or escape from a sabre-toothed tiger, than when trying to cope with too much homework or rush hour traffic!

Factors involved in the explanation of stress

Stressors can be categorised as either *internal* (individual) or *external* (environmental). These two classes of stressor can also operate in combination.

Internal factors and stress

Some stressors are internal; that is they originate within us. The sensation of anxiety can arise without any obvious stimulus from the outside yet it can make us stressed. Although such feelings may be irrational and without an apparent cause they can nevertheless be very stressful. A range of thoughts and feelings may be stressful, such as worrying about things that might never happen or feeling that you

have let someone down even when you haven't. Pain is also an internal source of stress; a nagging headache or chronic back pain could act as a stressor. Similarly, being ill or unable to sleep are internal experiences that can induce stress. Lying in bed fretting about being tired the next morning because you can't fall asleep is stressful even though there may be no external trigger for your sleeplessness.

External factors and stress

When we consider the external factors affecting stress, the focus is on sources of stress in the physical and social environment. Life Events Theory (Holmes & Rahe, 1967) identifies key occurrences that are stressful such as bereavement, divorce, redundancy, retirement, or moving schools (see Roberts & Russell (2002) *Angles on Environmental Psychology* for details of this theory). In approaches that focus on external factors, stress is seen as something that happens *to* you rather than something that happens *within* you. You suffer stress when levels of stressors, such as the pressures of work, become too high. Thus we find physical situations such as crowding or noise, and social situations such as missing the person you love, or being forced to engage with people whom you dislike, stressful. Pollution, fear of crime and weather conditions such as extreme heat or cold can all act as external stressors. It is important to note that some of these stimuli may not always be deemed to be stressful; a cool dip when you are hot and bothered or the loud noise of a concert are experienced positively, whereas cold or noise may be stressors in other situations. Such differences may arise because of context or as a consequence of the way the stimuli are interpreted, thus neither internal nor external explanations alone are sufficient.

Interactional factors and stress

This approach suggests that stress arises from an interaction between the environment and the individual's response to it. Importantly, this approach emphasises the psychological factors that allow some of us to cope with more stress in our environment than others. Lazarus's appraisal model (see

Roberts & Russell (2002) *Angles on Environmental Psychology*) incorporates such an interaction. It suggests that the way an individual perceives and responds to a stimulus, that is, how they cope, determines their experience of stress. When the individual judges their resources to be inadequate in comparison to their perception of the challenge they feel stressed. This helps to explain why the relationship between a potential stressor and the stress an individual suffers is not a simple one. People may differ in the way they appraise, and therefore tackle, the demands of a situation as well as in their personal resources.

This approach provides a more complete account of stress. Stress begins with the appearance of a stressor in the environment (or within us) and we assess whether this is indeed a problem. If we judge that it is, then there is an emotional and physiological response. A behavioural response follows as a way of dealing with the emotional and physiological aspects of the situation. Thus the individual experiences stress if they appraise the situation to be difficult (or impossible) to cope with.

The physiological response to stress

The physiological response to stress is mediated by two bodily systems. The *autonomic nervous system* (ANS) is composed of two approximately antagonistic (oppositely acting) subsystems, the sympathetic and parasympathetic branches. The ANS acts rapidly to stimulate physiological changes such as breathing and heart rate as well as affecting the second element, the endocrine system. Hormones (chemical messengers) provide a slower communication route through the body. They are released into the bloodstream by glands in response to signals from nerves or from other glands. Together these glands and their hormones comprise the *endocrine system*.

Autonomic nervous system

When we are faced with an emergency, the sympathetic branch of the autonomic nervous system responds quickly, preparing us for 'fight or flight'. The sympathetic nervous system (SNS) also sends impulses to the endocrine system, which responds by releasing hormones that enhance the preparation for action. This mechanism, which links the SNS to the *adrenal medulla* (the inner part of the adrenal glands), is called the sympathetic adrenal medullary system (SAM). Although the sympathetic response is very fast, allowing us to respond quickly to an emergency, its effects are short lived.

Endocrine system

The effects of the endocrine system are slower but longer lasting. The hormone adrenaline is released from the adrenal

medulla in response to stressors, as are related neurotransmitters (catecholamines) including dopamine and noradrenaline. This elevated level of catecholamines during stress may be responsible for some of the effects of stress on health such as hardening of the arteries. The *adrenal cortex* (the outer region of the adrenal glands) also releases certain hormones, corticosteroids, under conditions of stress. These processes are discussed further on page 261.

General adaptation syndrome

Selye (1947) described the body's response to stress and began to explore the links between the nervous system, the endocrine system and illness. He induced stress in rats by using stressors including heat and fatigue. The rats showed the same physiological responses regardless of the nature of the stressor; they had enlarged adrenal glands, shrunken lymph glands and stomach ulcers. Selye proposed that the body responded to any stressor by mobilising itself for action, a response he called the *general adaptation syndrome* (GAS). This response has evolved to help the individual to deal with emergency situations such as fleeing physical danger. Selye identified three phases to the body's response to stress through which we pass if a stressor persists over time:

- *alarm reaction* – the body's mechanisms to deal with danger are activated;

- *resistance stage* – the person struggles to cope with the stress, and the body attempts to return to its previous physiological state;

- *exhaustion stage* – if the stress persists and the body cannot return to its previous state, physical resources will become depleted, eventually leading to collapse.

We now know a great deal more about the precise mechanisms controlling the response to stress that Selye observed.

Sympathetic adrenal medullary system

In the initial response to stress, we perceive a potentially threatening stimulus and the sympathetic branch of our autonomic nervous system prepares the body quickly for action. The sympathetic response also causes the release of hormones, adrenaline and noradrenaline (also called epinephrine and norepinephrine respectively), from the adrenal medulla. The combined effect of the sympathetic adrenal medullary system (SAM) ensures that we are physically prepared to respond to the environmental threat, for instance by fighting or fleeing. The SAM therefore controls responses to acute (short-term) stressors. The effects of the sympathetic response and hormones are shown in figure 22.1.

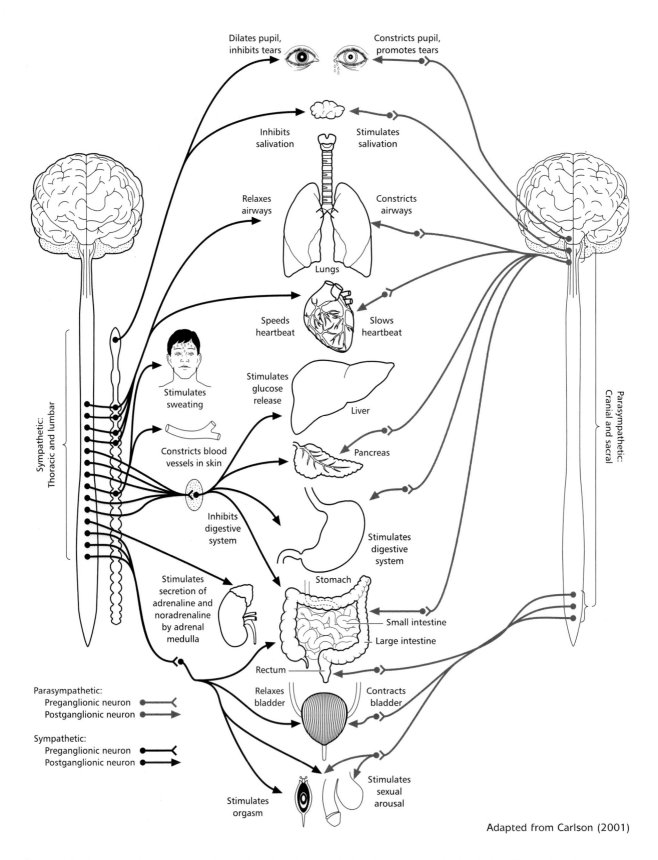

Dilates pupil, inhibits tears

Constricts pupil, promotes tears

Inhibits salivation

Stimulates salivation

Relaxes airways

Constricts airways

Lungs

Speeds heartbeat

Slows heartbeat

Stimulates sweating

Stimulates glucose release

Liver

Constricts blood vessels in skin

Pancreas

Inhibits digestive system

Stimulates digestive system

Stomach

Stimulates secretion of adrenaline and noradrenaline by adrenal medulla

Small intestine

Large intestine

Rectum

Relaxes bladder

Contracts bladder

Stimulates orgasm

Stimulates sexual arousal

Sympathetic: Thoracic and lumbar

Parasympathetic: Cranial and sacral

Parasympathetic:
Preganglionic neuron
Postganglionic neuron

Sympathetic:
Preganglionic neuron
Postganglionic neuron

Adapted from Carlson (2001)

Figure 22.1 The autonomic nervous system has two branches, the sympathetic and the parasympathetic, which work approximately antagonistically (in opposition to each other). Sympathetic responses, such as to a stressful situation, tend to occur in unison as the sympathetic chain of ganglia lying alongside the spinal cord activates all the sympathetic functions simultaneously. In contrast, the parasympathetic system, that is active when we are relaxed, can activate target organs individually

interactive angles

Complete the table below that lists some of the functions of the two parts of the autonomic nervous system.

Sympathetic effects	Parasympathetic effects
Increased heart rate	
Increased blood pressure	
Dry mouth	Maintenance of saliva production
Dilated pupils	
Dilated blood vessels in muscles	
Contracted blood vessels around system	Blood supply to digestive system is increased to remove products of digestion
Increased sweating	
Increased breathing rate	

The sensation of 'butterflies in the stomach' is caused by the contraction of blood vessels around the gut. This ensures that the blood supply can be directed to the muscles, supplying them with more oxygen and carbohydrates for metabolism if physical action becomes necessary. You have probably experienced this response when frightened, for example before going into a psychology exam! If the stressor is removed, parasympathetic activity in the ANS returns levels of adrenaline and noradrenaline to normal.

The hypothalamic pituitary-adrenocortical axis

If the stressor is not removed the body responds differently, reducing levels of adrenaline and noradrenaline and increasing levels of three other hormones:

- *cortisol* breaks down fatty tissue, releasing soluble fats and stimulates the release of glucose from the liver. This means that the muscles can obtain more energy from the blood;

- *aldosterone* increases blood pressure, maintaining the body ready for action;

- *thyroxine* increases the body's metabolic rate. This means that the stressed person can extract energy from food more quickly. Thyroxine also increases the rate at which food travels through the gut, allowing energy to be quickly obtained from the food currently in the gut.

The release of corticosteroids such as cortisol from the adrenal cortex (the outer part of the adrenal glands) is controlled by another hormone, adrenocorticotrophic hormone (ACTH) from the pituitary gland. ACTH is in turn secreted in response to the release of corticotropin-releasing factor (CRF). CRF is a peptide (a small protein) released by the parvoventricular nucleus, a region of the hypothalamus. Soendergaard and Theorell (2003) reported raised cortisol levels in refugees, particularly when they were experiencing distress in significant others (such as close friends or relatives) and excessive demands on everyday life.

Injection of CRF into the brain produces responses similar to those associated with aversive situations supporting the belief that some aspects of the stress response are caused by CRF. For example, Swerdlow et al (1986) found that CRF increased the startle response shown by rats to a loud noise. This link between the hypothalamus, the pituitary gland and the adrenal cortex is referred to as the hypothalamic pituitary-adrenocortical axis (HPA) and can trigger the release of corticosteroids to minor but unpredictable changes. If these are not threatening, the response diminishes as cortisol feeds back to the hypothalamus and pituitary gland to limit further releases of CRF and ACTH. If, however, the situation is sustained – in the case of a chronic stressor – the action of the HPA is maintained by the forebrain.

If the stressor remains for long enough, and is severe enough, we may become exhausted. Examples of such severe and prolonged stressors include torture, being hunted or working in a high-demand profession such as teaching. Exhaustion occurs when the body's supplies of energy are used up. This may result in collapse and sometimes death. Furthermore, these systems are adapted to protect us from environmental stressors present in our evolutionary history – such as being chased by a sabre-toothed tiger – but we are now exposed to rather different problems – sitting in a traffic jam is stressful but the alarm reaction is unlikely to be helpful here. One consequence of this may be that our biological endowment of coping strategies fail to deal effectively with our fast pace of life causing chronic SAM activation rather than leading to HPA activity. The effects, such as prolonged elevation of pulse rate and blood pressure, would put strain on the cardiovascular system with, perhaps, the consequence of increased levels of cardiovascular disorders. Where coping is less effective, for example, because control is limited – another characteristic of modern living – HPA activity will be triggered. Where such stressors are chronic, immunosupression may result as corticosteroids such as cortisol affect immune functioning.

The two systems, the SAM and HPA, have been represented here as independent although, in reality, they are not. The neurotransmitters noradrenaline and serotonin, natural endorphins, and the hormone cortisol, all act as intermediaries between the two systems.

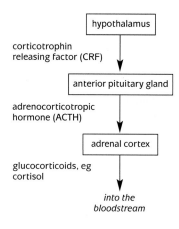

Figure 22.2a **Hypothlamic pituitary adrenal axis (HPA)** *(in response to a chronic stressor)*

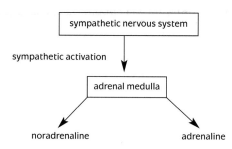

Figure 22.2b **Sympathetic adrenal system** *(in response to an acute stressor)*

for and against

physiological explanations of stress

— much of the evidence supporting physiological explanations is based on animal research. There are problems in applying this to humans since we can only equate physiological and not psychological effects – we cannot know whether animals 'feel' stressed in the same way as humans even when their physiological responses are equivalent

＋ deciphering hormonal and neural changes can help us to understand the link between stress and illness. Such knowledge can direct both further research and health education and treatment strategies

— this approach to stress does not take account of either the effects of different types of stressor in the environment or individual differences in people's responses to those stressors

＋ physiological explanations can account for both short-term increases in the immune response under acute stress and long-term immunosuppression in response to chronic stress

＋ physiological explanations may be able to account for increased susceptibility to cancer for individuals under stress

Stress and the immune system

The *immune system* is a collection of structures and mechanisms that our bodies use to fight off disease. The *lymphatic system* consists of branching vessels that drain tissue fluid containing micro-organisms away from the cells of the body back into the blood. Various kinds of white blood cells called *lymphocytes* are responsible for different aspects of the immune response (see table 22.1). Changes in levels of these cells and their products (immunoglobulins) can be measured and related to levels of stress (Pitts & Phillips, 1998).

Table 22.1

Cell type	Immunological role
B lymphocyte	Multiply in response to specific infections and produce *antibodies* (proteins called immunoglobulins) that bind to antigens on the cell surface of invading micro-organisms thereby labelling them for destruction
T lymphocyte	Recognise, engulf and destroy body cells that have been infected, for example, by a virus. They therefore tend to multiply during illness
Natural killer cell	Selectively target and destroy suspect cells including cancerous cells

Cooper et al (1988) stated that the top 20 fatal illnesses in Britain are all caused or made worse by stress. The high levels of cortisol resulting from prolonged stress are associated with allergic responses. This means that allergic conditions such as eczema and asthma are made worse for some people by prolonged stress. Rheumatoid arthritis, an autoimmune disorder causing painful inflammation of the joints, is worsened by stress (Zautra, 1998). Here, the effects of stress are indirect, resulting from physiological changes that occur in response to stress. In other situations, stress appears to affect health more directly by impairing our ability to fight disease. Bereavement (Schleifer et al, 1983), marital disruption (Keicolt-Glaser & Glaser, 1986) and the examination period for students (Keicolt-Glaser et al, 1994) all cause reduced immune functioning.

An alternative strategy for observing the effects of stress upon immune functioning is to test susceptibility to infection. Cohen et al (1993) used a nasal drip to administer either a cold virus or saline solution. The participants were then quarantined and asked to complete measures of their stress levels. Outcome was assessed by observing both infection (multiplication of the cold virus) and clinical disease (symptoms of a cold). Participants whose stress ratings were high were significantly more likely to become infected and to develop symptoms. In a subsequent study, Cohen et al (1998) found that the risk of infection increased progressively with the duration of exposure to a stressor. A parallel effect can be demonstrated for the rate of wound healing. Students are 40 per cent slower to recover from a standardised mechanical injury during exam time, when they are most stressed, than during vacations (Marucha et al, 1998).

Recent research suggests that whilst long-term stress appears to induce immunosuppression, resulting in an increased risk of infection and disease, short-term stress may trigger an enhancement of the immune response. In psychologically challenging situations, such as public speaking, confrontational role play and difficult computer games, increases in natural killer cells and other lymphocytes has been observed (Evans, 1998). The explanation for these differences seems to lie in the two physiological systems controlling the stress response. The SAM (see page 259) seems to be temporarily activated in short-term acute stress; an effective evolutionary response enabling organisms to mobilise resources to fight possible infection caused, for example, by injury. Such elevated responses would, however, be damaging in themselves if prolonged. In contrast, one of the functions of the HPA axis (see page 261), activated when stressors are chronic, is to regulate the immune system inducing immunosuppression.

There is also considerable evidence for a link between stress and cancer although none indicates that stress causes cancer. Animal studies, such as that of Seligman and Visintainer (1985), have found that rates of cancer in laboratory animals increase when they are stressed. Similar results have been obtained in studies of humans. Eysenck (1988) followed up nearly 400 individuals and found that death rates from cancer were higher for those who reported greater levels of stress at the start of the study. Normally the immune system finds and kills cancer cells before they can establish themselves as a tumour. Clearly, if our immune systems are functioning less efficiently, then cancerous cells are less likely to be eliminated. This is arises because, as Herbert and Cohen (1993) reported, natural killer cell activity is consistently impaired by stress. Strategies such as smoking, which some people use in an attempt to reduce stress, actually make things worse by introducing carcinogens (chemicals that can cause cancer) into the body.

what's new?

Psychoneuroimmunology

Psychoneuroimmunology (PNI) is a field that is investigating the effect of the mind on the function of the immune system. Although not new (the term was first introduced in 1964) it has recently attracted considerable attention. At a basic level, it is trying to find out why our attitude or state of mind affects our susceptibility to, or recovery from, illness. As we have seen in this chapter, when we are stressed the functioning of our immune system (our immunocompetence) is reduced. In addition, the way we think can improve our immune response. Pettingale et al (1985) found that women with breast cancer who denied or fought their illness survived, on average, five years longer post diagnosis. However, Salmon (2000) observes that such personality factors may be linked to better survival for entirely different reasons – a person with 'fighting spirit' may eat more, helping themselves, or may attract better care from staff because they are perkier. Iljas (2001) used PNI to examine the effects of two techniques for complementary medicine (qi gung and scalp acupuncture) on the fatigue, pain and depression suffered by patients with multiple sclerosis. She found some significant effects for each treatment; scalp acupuncture relieved fatigue and qi gung elevated mood.

Keller et al (1994) suggested that the key aim for psychoneuroimmunological research was to understand the relationship between:

- psychological distress;
- immune system functioning; and
- the development of disease.

In reality, few studies investigate all three of these variables simultaneously. Ben-Eliyahu et al (1991) injected rats with tumour material, tested their immune function (natural killer cell level) and observed the course of the disease (the occurrence of metastases) under two experimental conditions (stress within one hour or 24 hours of the injection). They found that individuals receiving the stressor and injection together had more metastatic growth (ie the cancer spread more rapidly). Research such as Marucha et al (1998, described on page 263) has succeeded in demonstrating a similar three-way relationship in humans. Immunological abnormalities have been linked to disorders such as schizophrenia, depression and Alzheimer's disease (Schwarz et al, 2001). The differences in such immune-related pathophysiology may lead to new, specific treatment strategies.

De Groot et al (2002) investigated the effects of social stress on the immune response of rats after inoculation with pseudorabies virus. Stressed individuals (that had encountered an aggressive conspecific nine times between inoculation and testing) were rated for the extent of wounding following these encounters. Wounded animals showed more severely impaired immune responses than non-injured animals. Their production of protective antibodies had been suppressed and they produced fewer virus-specific interleukins. This suggests that it is the combination of physical damage and psychological stress that compromises immune functioning.

Working with human participants, Gruzelier et al (2001) used hypnosis to examine immune functioning, mood and health of students during the examination period. Hypnotised participants were given suggestions of increased alertness, concentration and happiness. In addition they engaged in guided imagery relating to either immunity or relaxation. Blood levels of various lymphocytes, natural killer cells and blood cortisol were measured and the participants reported their illnesses. Participants who engaged in the immune-related imagery suffered fewer viral illnesses (such as colds or influenza). All participants receiving hypnosis experienced less decline in one lymphocyte type compared to a control group, but those who received the immune-related imagery were more successful in buffering the stress induced decline of a range of lymphocytes.

where to now?

▶ **Kalat J.W. (1998)** *Biological Psychology.* **London: Brooks/Cole.** Covers both the autonomic nervous system and the physiology of the stress response in detail.

▶ **Pinel J.P.J. (1997)** *Biopsychology.* **London: Allyn & Bacon.** Discusses the biology of the effects of stress on the functioning of the immune system in an accessible way.

▶ **Sapolsky R.M. (1994)** *Why zebras don't get ulcers.* **New York: Freeman.** A highly readable account of stress, stress-related illnesses and coping. It has great examples and doesn't have too many references.

▶ **Cassidy T. (1999)** *Stress, cognition and health.* **London: Routledge.** This has a short but interesting section that looks at our changing understanding of the physiology of stress from Selye to psychoneuroimmunology.

Teachers are taking more than five days off sick a year on average as problem pupils and staff shortages wreck government attempts to curb absenteeism... The number of teachers taking early retirement on health grounds has also shot up by 10 per cent... Education Ministers are expected to unveil official figures ... showing teachers took up to 2.7 million days off sick last year, equivalent to about 5.5 days for the average teacher... Although the Department of Education and Skills is expected to blame thuggish behaviour among pupils for part of the rise, with teachers laid low by stress and in some cases physical injury, teaching unions said the Government was to blame...

'Pressure on teachers in recent years has got worse and worse, ...' said [the] general secretary of the National Union of Teachers. 'If you are overworked and overstressed, then your ability to recover from an illness is always hampered...' [T]he number of teacher retirements on the grounds of ill health rose from 2,350 in 1999–2000 to 2,610 in 2000–2001.

From *Observer*, 26 May 2002

Explain how the view that 'If you are overworked and overstressed then your ability to recover from illness is always hampered' can be justified by empirical evidence.

Factors affecting the experience of stress

In addition to categorising stressors as internal or external, it is possible to identify particular factors that exacerbate the stress response. Biological factors, that is, physiological responses within the individual, may arise as a consequence of internal stressors such as pain or external ones such as the disruption of bodily rhythms. Social factors include those situations in which the source of stress is directly related to the presence of others, for instance in crowds or arguments. Finally, psychological factors are characteristics within us, such as our personality, that affect the way in which we respond to a potentially stressful situation.

Biological factors affecting stress

Disruption of bodily rhythms

Commuting by air, often spending only short periods of time at the destination, for example, to attend meetings at international venues, can lead to stressful symptoms such as poor sleep, tiredness and gastrointestinal symptoms. This phenomenon, known as *jet lag*, is the fatigue experienced by air travellers as a consequence of crossing

time zones such that their circadian rhythm is desynchronised from the local zeitgebers (for a full discussion of jet lag, see *Angles on Psychology*). Since it is often difficult to sleep on long-haul flights, passengers will suffer the stressful effects of both sleep loss and desynchronisation. Physiologically, the effects of jet lag arise because the body clock continues to work on the rhythm established at home. The traveller's needs, in terms of food, sleep and concentration, are therefore dictated by their internal schedules rather than being tuned to local time. Staying in a new location will allow the traveller to adapt, as zeitgebers such as daylight entrain the suprachiasmatic nucleus to a new circadian rhythm. However, in the short term, the traveller must cope with the discrepancy between the body's needs and immediate demands such as attending meetings. They will feel tired during the daytime but unable to fall asleep at night because their internal clock is out-of-tune.

Waterhouse et al (2000) investigated the effects of an eastbound flight crossing ten time zones on passengers. The participants experienced sleep disturbances and felt more irritable (until day 4) and felt fatigued until day 5. They were still suffering significant signs of jet lag by the sixth (and final study day) after arrival at their destination. Similar effects are experienced by airline crew but, because they are exposed to desynchronisation more often, the stressful effects may accumulate. Cho et al (2000) investigated the effects of repeated jet lag on airline staff. The average salivary cortisol levels of cabin crew were used as an indicator of circadian disruption and were compared to levels for the ground crew. The cabin crew, who experienced repeated jet lag, showed elevated cortisol levels on an average working day.

Pilots run greater cancer risk

Airline pilots on international routes have rates of skin cancer up to 10 times higher than expected, according to research published today.

Those who regularly flew through five time zones had an even greater risk, 25 times higher than the general population, the researchers say in *Occupational and Environmental Medicine*.

Dr Vilhjálmur Rafnsson, of the University of Reykjavik, Iceland, said exposure to cosmic radiation, disruption to body rhythms and a lifestyle which includes more sunbathing than average could be to blame.

From *Daily Telegraph*, 17 February 2000

Using your understanding of physiological psychology, justify Dr Rafusson's opinion that disruption to body rhythms could be to blame for increased cancer risk in pilots.

Shift work also disrupts the body's biological clock. Each time a shift is changed workers must readjust to a new schedule. For those on a nightshift this is even more difficult as the zeitgeber of daylight cannot help to synchronise their internal clock with the demands of their working hours. In addition to the biological disruption, other problems may arise as facilities and the family follow a daytime routine while the night-worker attempts to operate on a different pattern. Fenwick and Tausig (2000) found evidence for both family stress and health problems associated with working non-standard shifts.

Shift work is a characteristic of the health care profession. Taffinder et al (1998) investigated the effect of sleep deprivation on surgeons' dexterity during a simulated operation. They found that surgeons suffering overnight sleep deprivation made 20 per cent more errors, were 14 per cent slower than those who had had a full night's sleep and were more stressed.

Social factors affecting stress

One social situation that we commonly find stressful is a crowded place such as a shop or concert. Many studies have investigated the stressful effects of crowding experimentally, on both humans and animals.

Crowcroft and Rowe (1958) studied the effect of restriction of space on colonies of house mice (see also page 344–5). They found that, in crowded conditions, the mice populations increased and then levelled off. This was because the female mice had lost the ability to reproduce. However, these results may not have been the consequence of stress. There was little fighting among the animals and the females' reproductive capacity returned if the colonies were allowed space in which to disperse. Similar results were obtained by Calhoun (1962) using rats. Under crowded conditions, dominant animals defended space and remained in better health than submissive ones. See Chapter 27 for a detailed discussion of crowding and stress in humans which shows that high density living, such as is experienced in cramped student accommodation, results in physical signs of stress, ill health and reduced social contact and social support.

Psychological factors affecting stress

Personality type

The type A personality

Two doctors, Meyer Friedman and Ray Rosenman, began their research into the role of the type A personality, with a casual observation of the state of their waiting room furniture. The pattern of wear on the upholstery of some of the chairs was unusual; rather than the typical pattern of wear on the seat, the front edge and arms had worn out first. They later observed that the chairs were those used by coronary patients – they had a tendency to sit on the edge of their seat, leaping up frequently to enquire how much longer they would be kept waiting for their appointments. The possibility of a connection between the heart conditions and tense, frenetic behaviour of these individuals led to the proposal of 'hurry sickness' later renamed *type A behaviour* (Friedman & Rosenman, 1974).

Using a structured interview, questionnaire or self-report method it is possible to classify people into personality types on the basis of patterns of behaviour. Type A individuals tend to be highly competitive, aggressive, impatient and hostile, with a strong urge for success. Their behaviour tends to be goal directed and performed at speed. In contrast, people with type B behaviour are relatively laid back, lacking the urgency and drive typical of type A individuals. Some individuals do not fall clearly into either category and are termed type X.

Forgays et al (2001) investigated the relationship between the stress of parenting and type A behaviour in mothers. They examined the stress levels and behaviour patterns of 174 mothers in Italy, including both women working outside the home and at-home mothers. They found those with higher type A behaviour patterns experienced more stress; higher maternal stress in employed mothers and more stressful interactions with the child in those at home.

The risk of stress-related illnesses, such as coronary heart disease (CHD), is greater for type A individuals than for type B (Rosenman et al, 1975; Haynes et al, 1980). This could be a direct physiological consequence of some underlying difference, for example in the endocrine responses of different individuals or an indirect effect arising from the behavioural difference. Type A behaviour of itself may not necessarily cause stress; an individual with this personality type may tend to expose themselves to more stressful situations, such as a high pressure job, or may experience situations such as queuing as more annoying. Even if the cause is psychological, the effect must still be mediated by a biological process. One significant difference in this respect is hostility. The tendency for people displaying type A behaviours to be aggressive may lead them experience more conflicts with others, for example, when driving. Several studies (eg Perry & Baldwin, 2000) have found that type A behaviours are associated with aggression on the road.

A likely candidate for a physiological link to CHD is the neurohormonal system, specifically the effects of hormone levels on atherosclerosis (hardening of the arteries due to fatty deposits lining the inside walls of the vessels). Type A individuals show elevated heart rate, blood pres-

sure, skin conductance and catecholamine response. These are all changes associated with the stress response. This resembles the chronic activation of the sympathetic adrenal medullary system described on page 259.

Not all studies demonstrate a clear relationship between stress and type A behaviour. Freeman et al (2000) suggested that the political violence in Northern Ireland would increase the stress experienced by members of the population and it would be expected that individuals demonstrating type A behaviours would be more severely affected. However, when Freeman et al compared the stress levels in groups of dental students from Belfast in 1992 and during the 1994–6 ceasefire they found no effect related to type A behaviour. The students' personalities did not seem to affect their experiences of stress although other factors, such as gender and social support, were important.

Hardiness

Kobasa (1979) studied the stress levels, personalities and health of business executives. She found that, of those who were highly stressed, the individuals who did or did not become ill differed in terms of a personality factor she called *hardiness*. There are three key characteristics of a hardy personality, these are:

● *commitment* – a sense of purpose and involvement in events and activities;

● *control* – a belief that one can influence events in one's own life;

● *challenge* – a perception of change as positive and representing an opportunity for growth rather than a threat.

The hardy executives were less ill, perhaps because their approach to life allowed them to meet problems as potentially beneficial and therefore less stressful. As a result they may take more direct action in the face of stress, such as problem-focused coping strategies, enabling them to tackle rather than avoid issues.

Kobasa's original study only looked at males although subsequent investigations have demonstrated similar effects in women. Rhodewalt and Zone (1989) assessed the illness and depression ratings of women with high and low hardiness scores. They found that hardy women suffered lower rates of illness and depression following undesirable life changes than non-hardy women. The women also appeared to differ in their interpretation of life changes. High and low hardiness scorers did not experience significantly different numbers of stressful events, but, of those reported, more events were classified as undesirable by the non-hardy group. This suggests that it is the way in which hardy individuals appraise potentially stressful events that buffers them against the negative effects of stress.

for and against

a link between stress, health and type A personality

+ the link between type A behaviour and stress is supported by empirical evidence

– not all research evidence demonstrates a link between stress and type A behaviour

+ the link between type A and health, such as CHD, has been supported by several studies including prospective ones

+ the link between type A and CHD reflects an independent risk, that is, it is unrelated to other factors, for example, if type A individuals were more likely to smoke (another risk factor for CHD)

– different measures of type A personality do not necessarily correlate with one another and generate different relationships to CHD

– one study has reported a link between increased risk of CHD and type B personality

– the results of studies may not generalise well, for instance, because they have used participants of only one gender

Bartone (2000) examined the results of studies investigating the role of hardiness in offering resilience to stress. Based on observations of members of the armed forces during the Gulf War in 1991, the findings suggested that hardiness provides a significant buffer against the stress experienced during the conflict. However, not all evidence suggests that hardiness is an effective moderator of stress. As part of a wider study, Wellbrock (2000) investigated the relationship between stress and the personality variable of hardiness in police officers under stress. In her initial analysis she found that hardiness was related to the symptoms of trauma that were experienced but, after accounting for the stress experienced by officers, hardiness did not predict the degree of trauma related symptoms.

Locus of control

There is good evidence that having control over one's situation is a contributory factor in illness and health as we have seen in the response of the HPA (page 261) and the effect of lack of control in crowded environments (page 345). Langer and Rodin (1976) showed that the simple manipulation of personal control in elderly clients in a retirement home affected their health and longevity. Langer and Rodin manipulated control by giving the clients a talk, a plant for their room and the opportunity to see a film. In the experimental group the talk stressed personal responsibility, the individuals were asked where they would like the plant put and which night they would like to see the film. The other groups' talk did not focus on responsibility and they were told – rather than asked – where the plant would be placed and when they would see the film. The residents who experienced greater control were happier and healthier, and more active, alert and sociable. When the researchers returned after 18 months they also found that the group with induced

for and against

hardiness as a personality factor affecting the experience of stress

+ there is good evidence that people with hardy personalities become less ill when under stress than individuals with lower hardiness scores

+ recent evidence suggests that a hardy personality may reduce the likelihood of 'burnout' when under pressure (Sciacchitano et al, 2001)

+ the notion of hardiness has encouraged researchers to look closely at those individuals who exhibit successful responses to stressors rather than just those who do not

– it is unlikely that a single personality factor dictates the extent of the effect of stress on an individual. There may be other effects or hardiness may in fact be composed of many elements rather than just three

– hardiness may be nothing more than positive affect. The effects of better coping might simply be explained by more positive appraisal and interpretation of events in the individual's life

– hardiness may have an indirect rather than direct effect on illness. Hardy individuals may be more likely to engage in successful health-related behaviours, thus experiencing less risk of illness

responsibility also lived longer; their death rate was 15 per cent compared with 30 per cent for the comparison group. These findings suggest that control, or the perception of control, may be an important factor in determining our health.

The way individuals appraise their role in controlling their own lives also appears to be important. Rotter (1966) identified a personality variable he called the *locus of control*. People who attribute control to factors they cannot govern, such as chance or the behaviour of other people, are described as having an *external* locus of control. Those who believe that they are responsible for actions that affect themselves have an *internal* locus of control. This internal-external dimension may also relate to health behaviour. Strickland (1978) suggested that individuals with an internal locus of control may engage in more preventive measures such as avoiding accidents and being informed about their own health.

The precise role of locus of control in the context of health has been investigated using the Health Locus of Control (HLC) scale, developed by Wallston et al (1978). This measure, which looks specifically at an individual's beliefs about the factors that determine their health outcomes, assesses three dimensions, these are:

- **internal health locus of control** – this aims to determine the extent to which the individual feels able to be responsible for their own health and uses responses to such items as 'The main thing that affects my health is what I myself do';

- **powerful others' control over health** – this aims to measure the individual's belief in the role that other, significant, people (such as doctors, nurses, family and friends) play in their health and uses items such as 'Whenever I don't feel well, I should consult a trained professional';

- **chance health locus of control** – this aims to assess the role that the individual assigns to pure 'luck' (or otherwise) and uses items such as 'No matter what I do, if I am going to get sick, I will get sick'.

Norman et al (1998) investigated the link between HLC and health-related behaviour. They surveyed 11,000 people using the three factors listed above and the individuals' health behaviours including smoking, alcohol use, exercise and diet. The participants were compared on each

research
now

healthy choices

Steptoe A. & Wardle J. (2001) Locus of control and health behaviour revisited: A multivariate analysis of young adults from 18 countries. *British Journal of Psychology* 92: 659–72

aim: to investigate the relationship between health locus of control (HLC), health values and health related behaviours in a diverse sample.

procedure: a group of 4358 female and 2757 male university students aged 18–30 years, from 18 European countries, were tested on three measures: HLC, health values and 10 health-related behaviours (physical exercise, not smoking, limited alcohol consumption, regular breakfast, daily tooth-brushing, seat belt use and consumption of fruit, fat, fibre and salt).

findings: there was a significant difference in the behaviours exhibited by individuals with the highest compared to the lowest internal HLC scores. Those with the lowest scores were 40 per cent more likely to engage in five of the health-compromising behaviours (exercise, daily tooth-brushing, eating fibre and avoiding salt and fat). Similarly, those with the highest chance HLC scores were 20 per cent less likely to select the healthy option for more than half of the behaviours (not smoking, limited alcohol consumption, regular breakfast, daily fruit, eating fibre and avoiding fat).

conclusion: low internal HLC and high chance HLC are associated with poor health choices. A low internal score suggests that the individual does not believe that they can affect their own health for the better, so they do not try. A high chance score indicates that the individual believes that factors outside their control influence their health and that their own behaviour is therefore irrelevant.

of the three factors and not only did the 'internals' (who scored highly on all three measures) engage in more health-protective behaviours, but also those individuals who gained low scores on all three measures. These two groups were more health conscious than individuals with mixtures of high and low scores on the three measures.

Support for the HLC was also obtained by O'Carroll et al (2001) in relation to the response of individuals who had suffered a myocardial infarction (heart attack). Many patients fail to seek help when they are having a heart attack and O'Carroll et al found that a high HLC was the best predictor of delay in seeking medical attention. Because these individuals believe that chance is a major factor determining their health (rather than, say, their own actions), they do not seek help soon enough and their delay, in these circumstances, could be fatal. O'Carroll et al suggest that attempts to modify the beliefs of people at risk could reduce their response time and therefore increase survival rates.

Conversely, people can engage in health-compromising behaviours such as drug-taking, unprotected sex or over-eating. Individuals with a high score on the chance dimension of HLC, whose beliefs suggest that whatever they do will have little effect on their health, would be expected to be less aware of, or ignore, risks to health.

where to now?

▶ **Walker J. (2001)** *Control and the psychology of health*. **Buckingham: Open University Press.** This book contains a wealth of information about the role of control and perceived control in health including a thorough coverage of the development and use of the Health Locus of Control scale.

▶ **Cassidy T. (1999)** *Stress, cognition and health*. **London: Routledge.** This text provides sections on a range of social factors affecting stress and explores factors such as Type A and hardiness as well as other personality types.

▶ **Rajaratnam S.M.W. & Arendt J. (2001)** *Health in a 24-h society. The Lancet*, **358: 999–1005.** This provides an excellent review of the effects of shift work on many aspects of health.

Hodgson (2001) used a student population to investigate perceived risk, risk-taking behaviour and HLC. The results showed a link between these variables, suggesting that – for adolescents at least – those who believe that their health status is determined by chance factors are more likely to engage in risky activities.

Coping with stress

Folkman et al (1986) define coping as 'the person's cognitive and behavioural efforts to manage (reduce, minimize, master, or tolerate) the internal and external demands of the person-environment transaction that is appraised as taxing or exceeding the resources of the person'. Coping thus represents the ways in which we attempt to deal with aspects of the world that we find are beyond our normal means to fight.

One way that people attempt to cope with stress is through the unconscious use of *defence mechanisms*. These are an important aspect of Freudian theory and were discussed in detail in *Angles on Psychology*. To protect ourselves from painful, frightening or guilty feelings that might cause us stress, we unconsciously deny ourselves access to these thoughts or change the way that we interpret them. These mechanisms include:

● *displacement* – the redirecting of emotions;

● *regression* – the use of childlike strategies to comfort ourselves;

● *repression* – the blocking of a memory so that it cannot be recalled.

If a stressful situation, such as an argument at work, makes us angry we may use displacement and express our anger on other people, such as our family. Alternatively, we may become stroppy and difficult – acting the child – and use regression to avoid having to deal with the real issues. It is not uncommon in severe cases of stress, such as child abuse, for the victim to have no recollection of the stressful events themselves; this would be described as repression.

Stress management strategies

Sources of stress can be tackled from an external or internal perspective, that is, coping strategies can be either *problem-focused*; aiming to reduce the causes of stress or *emotion-focused*; aiming to manage the negative effects on the individual. In any situation, a combination of these strategies may be employed.

Problem-focused strategies

Problem-focused strategies include discussing the situation with a professional, relying on one's own past experiences to tackle the issue and dealing with the situation one step at time.

Emotion-focused strategies

Emotion-focused strategies include keeping busy to take one's mind off the problem, preparing oneself for the worst, praying for strength and guidance, ignoring the situation in the belief that the problem will go away and bottling feelings up. Other strategies are listed in table 22.2 below.

How effective are the strategies?

It seems obvious that problem-focused strategies are better because they deal with the cause. However, it may be beyond the scope of the individual to effect change, so emotion-focused solutions may be essential to enable the individual to feel less stressed about the situation. For example, individuals may be powerless to alter the direction of wind blowing air pollutants from foreign countries or to reverse the effects of an industrial accident. There may also be cultural factors affecting methods of coping. Frydenberg et al (2003) compared the way young people from different cultures dealt with their concerns. They found that, although all adolescents seemed to cope by working hard – perhaps to 'take their mind off the prob-

lem' – there were some differences. Palestinian and Colombian students focused more on social support and action, spiritual support and worrying, than Australian and German students, who rated physical recreation more highly among their coping strategies. These differences suggest that it may be important to ensure that coping strategies reflect community values.

Of the emotion-focused strategies, evidence suggests that long-term avoidance may be ineffective (Nolen-Hoeksema & Larson, 1999). In fact, avoidance strategies may even be damaging. Epping-Jordan et al (1994) found that in patients using avoidance strategies, the progression of cancer was faster.

Resources to help with stress management

Different individuals, circumstances or situations may lead to the availability of differing resources to assist with coping. Wealth may offer the means to overcome many stressors (through avoidance or protection) but it may not provide a solution to inescapable sources of stress. Here, intra-personal resources may be of greater significance. Wealth has been demonstrated to be linked to reduced stress, but this does not apply to everyone (tending only to be important at the lower end of the socioeconomic scale; Dohrenwend, 1973). Neither is wealth a buffer against all sources of stress; it is not particularly important following bereavement for example (Stroebe and Stroebe, 1987).

Table 22.2 Stress management strategies

Source of stress	Emotion-focused strategy	Problem-focused strategy
Noisy children playing outside	Trying to remember that children need to play and it's good for them to be outside (being objective)	Talking to a friend on the telephone (discussing the situation)
Noise from a nearby lawn-mower	Accepting that the grass will look nicer afterwards (seeing positive side of situation)	Closing the windows (taking a positive action)
Cigarette smoke from a nearby table in a non-smoking area of a restaurant	Snapping at the waiter (taking anger out on others)	Contemplating asking the waiter to request that they stop or moving yourself (considering alternative solutions)
Fumes from a local factory	Eating or smoking more (trying to reduce tension)	Trying to find out what the emissions are and why they are released (investigating the issue)

Some examples of strategies that may be employed in response to environmental stressors (NB These are not intended to represent the best ways to cope!)

Table 22.3 Resources for coping with stressors

Type of resource	Examples	Ways they may be employed
Material	Wealth	Having more money might enable people to live in rural areas with lower air pollution or fewer noisy neighbours
Educational	Published research (including posters, leaflets and media information) schools, Internet	Knowing how to protect an employee from hearing damage in a noisy environment or harassment at work
Physical	Strength, health	Individuals without asthma may be more tolerant of some air pollutants
Intra-personal	Skills, abilities and personality characteristics such as determination and self-esteem	One individual might be better able to work effectively in a crowded office than another
Social	Family, friends, pets, neighbours, community organisations	Being able to talk to a dog about the journey home may alleviate some of the annoyance about traffic jams

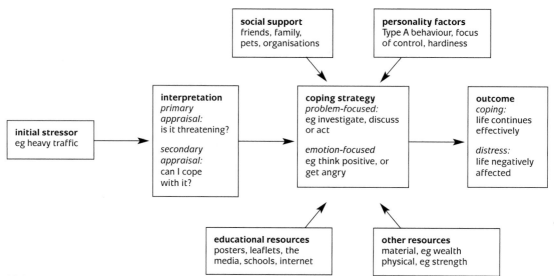

Figure 22.3 Appraisal, available resources and coping strategy can all influence the outcome of exposure to a stressor

Social resources

People gain help, reassurance and other forms of assistance from their interactions with others (including their pets), which helps them to deal with stress; this is called *social support.* As we saw on page 269, one way that people help to combat the stress of living in a time of political violence is to rely on the support of others. How can an individual's social contacts provide support during stressful experiences? The kinds of support offered by social networks has been categorised in a number of different ways (eg Cohen and Wills, 1985; Stroebe and Stroebe, 1987). These are summarised by Stroebe (2000):

- *emotional support* – providing empathy, care, love and trust;

- *instrumental support* – consisting of direct help such as caring for children or offering transport;

- *informational support* – providing routes to knowledge and understanding that will help the individual to cope with their problems;

- *appraisal support* – providing information that will specifically help the individual's self-evaluation, such as being able to compare oneself to another individual.

When social support is measured, two different approaches can be taken. Measures of *perceived support* consider the respondent's description of individuals they could rely upon for assistance, such as who they could discuss an intimate problem with or ask for advice. Alternatively, we can measure *received support*, that is the actual frequency with which an individual has received specific supportive behaviours from others. These two measures appear to be linked, but the relationship is not strong (eg Dunkel-Schetter and Bennett, 1990). This may be the consequence of the ways in which different individuals use others to assist them – they may talk to one person often or many people occasionally, for example. Surprisingly, perceived support may be a better predictor of health status than actual support.

Studying actual support is relatively simple; the Inventory of Socially Supportive Behaviors (Barrera et al, 1981), for example, asks respondents about specific supportive behaviours in the domains of emotional, tangible, cognitive-informational and direct guidance support. An average is generated for each respondent based on the total number of occurrences of such assistance in the previous four weeks. Perceived support can also be assessed using questionnaires, such as the Interpersonal Support Evaluation List (ISEL) (Cohen et al, 1985). The ISEL measures four sources of social support: tangible, appraisal, self-esteem and belonging. There is good evidence to show that social support is an important variable in health status.

interactive angles

Consider the following potential social resources that could relieve stress for someone enduring a personal crisis such as a relationship breakdown. How would you categorise them using the Stroebe (2000) model?

Money, companionship, encouragement, leaflets about the problem, doing their washing, finding case studies of other people with similar difficulties, giving them web addresses for Internet support groups, offering compliments that boost their self-esteem, taking them to local groups dealing with their issues.

Interpretation of the results of studies such as Berkman and Syme (see page 274) is problematic as there are issues of both validity and reliability with self-report measures of health status. In a subsequent study, House et al (1982) used more objective measures of health including blood pressure, cholesterol level, respiratory functions (breathing) and electrocardiograms (heart function). They, too, found that after a 10–12-year fol-low-up period, the mortality risk was approximately double for people with a low level of social support.

One explanation of how social support affects health is the *buffering hypothesis*. This proposes that social support protects the individual from the negative effects of stress either by enabling socially supported individuals to appraise stressful situations differently or by enhancing their ability to cope with the stressor. For example, an effective social network may enable a stressed individual to appraise redundancy in a less damaging way because they recognise that they have people who can offer them advice or financial assistance. Alternatively, the individual may deal with the redundancy better precisely because they have those sources of advice and assistance.

If the buffering hypothesis is correct, we would only expect to see the effects of social support when stress levels are high. This is rather like the consequence of inoculation against a disease; if you have an influenza injection you appear identical to someone who has not, until you are exposed to the flu virus – under these conditions, your vaccination protects you against the disease. Likewise, the effects of buffering only become apparent when the stressed individual's own resources are insufficient. DeLongis et al (1988) investigated the stress levels, self-esteem and health of 75 married couples. Those individuals in unsupportive relationships (that is, low social support) with low self-esteem became more ill in stressful situations than did the individuals in supportive relationships with high self-esteem.

As an alternative to the buffering hypothesis, the *main effect hypothesis*, suggests that an absence of social support is, in itself, stressful and is the cause (rather than consequence) of ill health. Social encounters are often positive and rewarding experiences and community membership can provide us with a sense of belonging and raise our self-esteem. This would imply that social support would be important to health, regardless of stress levels, hence the main effect hypothesis would predict that people with stronger social networks should be healthier regardless of the stressors they encounter. The difference between the predicted effects of the main effect and buffering hypotheses is illustrated in figure 22.4 overleaf.

The main effect hypothesis is also supported by empirical evidence. Lin et al (1979) investigated the relationship between social support and psychiatric symptoms. They used information about participants' interactions with friends and neighbours and their community involvement as measures of social support. They found that those individuals with higher levels of social contact had lower levels of psychiatric symptoms irrespective of their stress levels. This supports the main

classic
research

more mates – live longer!

Berkman L.F. & Syme S.L. (1979) Social networks, host resistance, and mortality: a nine-year follow-up of Almeda County residents. *American Journal of Epidemiology,* **109: 186–204**

aim: to investigate the relationship between social support and health.

procedure: a group of 6928 men and women aged between 30 and 69 were asked to complete self-reports on physical health, cigarette smoking, alcohol consumption, obesity and physical activity. In addition, they were assessed for social support, looking at four social relationships (marriage, contacts with extended family and friends, association with the church and membership of other organisations). This information provided a Social Network Index (SNI) that weighted intimate relationships more heavily. Baseline health status was controlled to ensure that individuals who may have been ill at the time of the survey, so were unable to maintain their social contacts, did not skew the results.

findings: those individuals with a low SNI had roughly twice the mortality risk of high scoring individuals over the nine-year follow-up period.

conclusion: social support seems to predict health status with higher social support relating to better health.

effect hypothesis. However, as this was a correlational study, it is possible that individuals with psychiatric symptoms found it more difficult to establish or maintain social contacts; causality between the two variables cannot be determined.

It would appear that when social support is measured as the absolute number of different social contacts that could be relied upon, results appear to be consistent with

the main effect hypothesis. However, if social support is assessed functionally, in terms of the roles that social contacts can play in offering support, the buffering hypothesis is supported (Bishop, 1994).

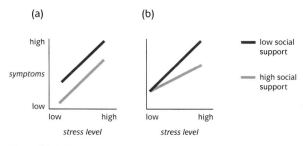

(a)   (b)

low social support

high social support

Figure 22.4 These graphs illustrate the effects of stress on symptoms of ill health as predicted by (a) the main effect hypothesis and (b) the buffering hypothesis. Graph (a) shows that social support would protect against ill health irrespective of stress levels, whereas graph (b) indicates that social support would buffer against the effects of stress, protecting against ill health only when stress levels are high. The angle of the 'high social support' line in graph (b) would depend on the power of the buffering effect. If social support offered complete protection against the negative effects of stress on health the line would be horizontal. A steeper line would suggest that the effect of buffering was only partial

Figure 22.5 Research on the aftermath of disasters such as Three Mile Island discusses the coping strategies, such as social support, employed by people from the locality in their attempts to deal with the stress that arises from actual or suspected exposure to pollution. Those residents around the Three Mile Island site who had lower levels of social support showed higher levels of stress (Fleming et al, 1982). In addition, Collins et al (1983) found that residents who focused on managing their feeling in response to the disaster (an emotion-focused strategy) were less stressed than those who attempted to take direct action (a problem-focused strategy)

for and against

social support explanation of stress

+ empirical evidence suggests that individuals with better social support networks are healthier and live longer

– self-reporting of measures of health and of social support affect the reliability and validity of evidence for the effects of social support on health

+ social support may affect mental as well as physical health

– evidence suggesting a link between health and social support is correlational so the dependence of the effect of social support cannot be determined

Educational resources

In Chapter 23 we discuss health education in detail and look at different theories that explain how our health behaviours are controlled. One way that we can mediate the effects of stress on our health is to be informed as knowledge underlies our health beliefs and attitudes, and is therefore important (although not exclusively so) in the development and change of our health behaviours. One of the roles of educational resources is therefore to provide us with knowledge and understanding about our behaviour under stress, and to suggest strategies that we may employ to minimise and cope with stressors and reduce the associated health risks.

interactive angles

If you have already studied the concepts in chapter 23, you might like to use them to consider how you would plan a strategy for helping to reduce stress before reading on.

The Mental Health Foundation, the Health Education Board for Scotland and the Royal College of Psychiatrists, among many others, provide educational information about stress. Broadly, this information covers:

- explaining what stress is;
- the effects or symptoms of stress;
- why being stressed is a problem;
- the causes of stress;
- potential ways to deal with stress.

Educating people to the risks of stress enables them to make informed decisions about taking action against the effects of the stressors on their health. In order to do this they must be aware both of the causes of stress that they are experiencing and the possible courses of action they can take to reduce the stressors or minimise their effects. Thus information about sources of stress and positive courses of action are very important, especially to the deployment of problem-focused strategies (see page 272). In addition, such information would provide the basis for judgements of perceived vulnerability to stress and seriousness of its effects, perceived barriers to taking action against stress and benefits of doing so. These components form the basis of health belief model (see page 291).

Explaining about stress

One factor that affects our ability to cope with stress is our understanding of our condition or situation. Educational information that outlines what stress is can help people to feel that they can overcome their condition as it indicates that they can gain control over the symptoms they may be experiencing. According to both the theory of planned behaviour (pages 294–5) and self-empowerment approaches (see page 306) an individual's perceived behavioural control or self-efficacy is important in following through health behaviours. The importance of control is also important in understanding why some individuals become more stressed than others, for instance in locus of control theory (see page 268 of this chapter).

Symptoms of stress

Informing people about the effects or symptoms of stress has two benefits. Those people who are aware that they are suffering from stress may be reassured that the symptoms they are experiencing are 'normal' – that is, characteristic of stress – and shared (unfortunately) by many other people. In addition, individuals who are suffering from stress but are unaware of their condition would benefit from information to identify the problem. They may have feared that their symptoms were due to some other condition about which they may have worried unduly. In both cases such knowledge may encourage the individual to take action to protect themselves from stressors in order to avoid such symptoms. According to the health belief model, knowledge about symptoms an individual was already suffering with would indicate to them the extent of their vulnerability, hence may encourage them to take steps to protect themselves.

What is stress?

Stress can be defined as the way you feel when you're under abnormal pressure. For example, if you are speaking in public for the first time, if you are rushing to catch the last train home, or if you are made redundant.

All sorts of situations can cause stress. The most common, however, involve work, money matters and relationships with partners, children or other family members. Stress may be caused either by major upheavals and life events such as divorce, unemployment, moving house and bereavement, or by a series of minor irritations such as feeling undervalued at work or dealing with difficult children. Sometimes there are no obvious causes.

Stressful events that are outside the range of normal human experience, for example, being abused or tortured, may lead to post-traumatic stress disorder (PTSD). …

Some stress can be positive and research has suggested that a moderate level of stress makes us perform better. It also makes us more alert and can help us in challenging situations such as job interviews or public speaking. Stressful situations can also be exhilarating and some people actually thrive on the excitement that comes with dangerous sports or other 'high-risk' activities.

But stress is only healthy as a short-lived response. Excessive or prolonged stress can lead to illness and physical and emotional exhaustion. Taken to extremes, stress can be a killer.

From Mental Health Foundation website

Which psychological theories explain the descriptions of stress given in the extract above?

Symptoms of stress

Stress can damage physical health, social relationships and the way we function at work and at home. It is important to remember that the following symptoms may have nothing to do with stress but they are often danger signals which should not be ignored:

- physical signs like headaches, insomnia, indigestion, high blood pressure
- behaviour aspects such as poor work performance, accidents, poor relationships at home and work, dependence on tobacco, drugs and alcohol
- emotional factors such as irritability, lack of concentration, anxiety, depression.

Mental and physical ill health are a personal loss to your employees and a cost to your company whether they mean sick pay for those who stay home or poor performance from those who come to work. A quick response can prevent the situation deteriorating further and may well lead to considerable improvements for both you and your employees.

From Health Education Board for Scotland website

1 Many different symptoms of stress are described above; how can they be accounted for?

2 How might a stressed person recognise their vulnerability to stress after reading this information?

Why stress matters

Modern society is competitive and success is valued highly compared to, say, community driven ideals. As a consequence, we may accept that stress is an inevitable part of people's lives so may be reluctant to act in response to rising stressors. This inertia can result in chronic stress responses that, as we have seen earlier in the chapter (pages 262–6), can be very harmful. Educating people to the risks of stress enables them to make informed decisions about taking action against the effects of the stressors on their health. The health belief model suggests that people need both to perceive themselves as vulnerable and to see changing their behaviour as advantageous to improving their health. Furthermore, the theory of reasoned action (page 294) suggests that where subjective norms are counter to good health behaviours, people are less likely to change. Educational strategies aiming to tackle stress therefore need to challenge the role played by society in passively accepting stress as a consequence of modern life.

Why stress matters

Mental ill-health or distress is a major cause of sickness absence from work, reduced productivity and staff turnover. Stress is the root cause of a lot [of] mental ill-health, especially anxiety and depression.

- Work-related stress is estimated to be the biggest occupational health problem in the UK, after musculoskeletal disorders such as back problems.
- Nearly 3 in every 10 employees will have a mental health problem in any one year – the great majority of which will be anxiety and depressive disorders.
- Mental health problems account for the loss of over 91 million working days each year.
- Half of all days lost through mental ill-health are due to anxiety and stress conditions.

Stress is a necessary part of everyday life. Indeed, some degree of stress or pressure is considered healthy. Underemployment can lead to boredom, apathy and a loss of energy and motivation. But conversely, excessive stress lead[s] to fatigue, impaired judgment and decision making, exhaustion and the onset of serious health problems – both mental and physical.

Physically, stress is implicated in the development of coronary heart disease, certain types of cancer, and a host of other ailments including stomach ulcers, skin rashes, migraine, asthma, and increased susceptibility to infections.

The psychological effects of stress can be just as damaging. Increased anxiety, irritability, disturbed sleep, poor concentration and aggressive behaviour can increase the risk of accidents and disrupt relationships both at work and at home. Individuals under stress are often inclined to smoke more, drink more alcohol, and consume excessive amounts of caffeine, thus increasing irritability, sleep impairment, etc., in a vicious circle. Exposure to prolonged stress will increase the risk of serious mental health problems, including depression and disabling anxiety conditions, as well as alcohol misuse.

From Mental Health in the Workplace booklet, Mental Health
Foundation website

1 Later in the booklet it is made clear that, with adequate support, people suffering from stress recover when the stressors are reduced. At least 20 problems caused or exacerbated by stress are listed above. What advantages might a stressed individual perceive in changing their behaviour?

2 In what ways does this information fail to challenge the subjective norm that we should expect modern life to be stressful?

Causes of stress

In order for people to improve their health behaviours they need to be aware of the causes of stress that they are experiencing. This will enable them to take steps to avoid or reduce these stressors to prevent them-selves from becoming chronically stressed. Again, the health belief model would suggest that such advice should, in order to be most effective, indicate the benefits to the individual in changing their health behaviours.

What can give rise to stress at work?

- lack of control over work
- under-utilisation of skills
- too high a workload, no or few challenges
- low task variety
- high uncertainty, eg due to poorly defined roles and responsibilities, lack of clear priorities and targets, job insecurity
- low pay
- poor working conditions, eg noise, overcrowding, excessive heat, inadequate breaks
- low interpersonal support, eg via inadequate or insensitive management, hostility from colleagues
- undervalued social position

From *Mental Health in the Workplace*, a booklet from the Mental Health Foundation. Accessed online at http://www.mentalhealth.org.uk

Take any three of these points and, using psychological theories and studies, explain how they may cause stress.

Potential ways to deal with stress

When people have sufficient understanding of their own stress and its causes they need to know how to take appropriate action. The final role of education about stress is to inform people about the possible courses of action they can take to reduce the stressors or minimise their effects. In order for individuals to benefit from such resources once they know that they are available, they must feel able to access them. Education about dealing with stress must break down the barriers that exist to seeking help in these circumstances. This is important as, according to the health belief model, people will fail to change their health behaviours if the barriers they perceive are greater than the perceived benefits.

interactive angles

Find some different sources of information on dealing with stress; you might try your doctors' surgery, a local counselling service and the Internet. Critically consider the advice given in the documents. Can you decide what strategies are being recommended? Justify the advice offered on the basis of the empirical evidence available to support each strategy.

where to **now?**

▶ **Brannon L. & Feist J. (2000)** *Health psychology: an introduction to behavior and health,* **London: Wadsworth, Thomson Learning.** This has a detailed coverage of stress and coping.

▶ **http://www.mentalhealth.org.uk** This website provides a range of information about dealing with stress.

Coping with stress

There are several things that you can do to help yourself cope. For things that happen every day, it can be useful to think of your stress as a puzzle to be solved:

- Work out the situations that stress you, and how you behave.

- Work out how you could behave differently in these situations, so that you feel more in control of them.

- Imagine how other people might behave if you acted differently.

- Rehearse some of these different ways of behaving. It might be a bit embarassing, but try doing it out loud with a friend.

- Be prepared to fail the first time you try it out in real life – but be prepared to try again!

- List all the things you can think that would make things easier or less stressful – write them down on a piece of paper…

Ask yourself: *'Is there another way of dealing with the problem which will work better for me than the one I usually use?'*

Thinking like this can be useful even when you are faced with less common situations, like being bullied, being offered drugs, involved in the start of a fight with a friend, or being threatened on the street. For these really tricky situations, it's even more important to rehearse what you're going to say and how you're going to behave.

If you can't cope, get help

Sometimes stress gets on top of you. Especially when the situation causing the stress goes on and on, and the problems just seem to keep building up. You can feel quite trapped, as if there is no way out and no solution to your problems. If you feel like this, it is important to get help.

People you might want to talk to could be

- parents, a family member or family friend

- a close friend

- a school nurse, teacher or school counsellor

- a social worker or youth counsellor

- a priest, someone from your church or temple

- the Samaritans (telephone 0345 90 90 90).

Your family doctor or practice nurse may also be able to help. They may suggest that you sees someone from your local child and adolescent mental health service – a team of professionals specially trained to work with young people. They include child and adolescent psychiatrists …, psychologists, social workers, psychotherapists and specialist nurses. They will respect your wishes about confidentiality and about the type of help you would like.

From Royal College of Psychiatrists website

The information above is taken from a booklet designed to enable children and adolescents to cope with stress. Identify some of the barriers it attempts to help them overcome and some of the benefits it identifies.

Conclusions

Stress is caused by a range of factors, both internal, such as our own thoughts or pain, and external, such as pressures of work or crowds. Biological factors such as the disruption of body rhythms and personality type may increase our susceptibility to the effects of stress. These factors can interact, compounding the effects on our ability to cope. The bodily stress response is mediated by both neural and hormonal processes. The sympathetic adrenal medullary system responds quickly to immediate threats while the hypothalamic pituitary-adrenocortical axis maintains a prolonged response to chronic stressors.

The effects of stress on the immune system are indirect. Although short-term stress may enhance our immune response, in the long term stress induces immunosuppression. As a consequence, chronic stress increases the risk of succumbing to infections and cancer. Psychoneuroimmunology investigates the link between stress, immunity and disease. Recent discoveries have shown that state of mind (both positive and negative) can affect the progression of disease and other research has investigated the effectiveness of alternative therapies and the link between immunity and mental health disorders.

what do you know ?

1 Describe and distinguish between the physiological responses to short-term and long-term stressors.

2 Evidence suggests that stress and immunity are linked. Discuss some of this evidence and evaluate the research methods used in such investigations.

3 Describe and evaluate **one** problem-focused and **one** emotion-focused stress management strategy.

4 Biological, social and psychological factors can affect our experience of stress. Discuss, using evidence, the effects of any **two** of these kinds of factors.

23 Health promotion

what's  ahead ?

In this chapter we will explore ways in which people can be encouraged and educated to avoid or limit health problems such as stress and drug abuse. We will look at primary prevention methods including the importance of hygiene and adequate nutrition and the part social skills can play in reducing health problems. Two models of health behaviour, the health belief model and the theory of reasoned action, are discussed in detail. We explore how they enable us to understand health behaviour and the implications they have for health education. Finally, we consider health education programmes and how they can be used to raise awareness and change attitudes towards health issues.

Health promotion, health behaviour and health habits

People tend to engage in behaviours that impair their health, and fail to commit to activities that could protect or improve their health. *Health promotion* aims to enable people to gain control of, and therefore enhance, their own health. This may be achieved through lifestyle changes, such as taking exercise, eating a different diet or reducing alcohol consumption and through preventative practices such as breast and testicular self-examination and dental check-ups. Those activities that people do to maintain or improve their health are called *health behaviours*. People who engage in poor health behaviours not only compromise their health in the short term but may also develop poor *health habits*, that is, they may acquire firmly established health related behaviours that are detrimental. We begin to develop health habits at 11 or 12 years old and they may become so automatic that we perform them without awareness. Can you actually remember cleaning your teeth this morning?

Good health habits are important. Belloc and Breslow (1972) asked almost 7000 Californians about seven health habits: sleeping seven to eight hours per night, not smoking, eating breakfast every day, having no more than two alcoholic drinks per day, getting regular exercise, not eating between meals and not being more than 10 per cent overweight. The participants were also asked about illnesses they had suffered and how disabled they had been, for example, how many days they had taken off work in the last year. Those who engaged in more good

health habits had fewer illnesses and were less 'disabled'. When the participants were followed up almost 10 years later, those who engaged in the seven health habits were found to have a lower mortality rate (Breslow & Enstrom, 1980).

Table 23.1 Primary prevention measures

positive health behaviours:
eating a balanced diet
eating less fat, salt and cholesterol
eating more fruit and vegetables
regular dental check-ups
self-examination (breast/testicular)
taking exercise
keeping vaccinations current
practising safe sex
regular cervical smear test
wearing a seat belt

avoidance of health-compromising behaviours:
stopping smoking
stopping drug misuse
reducing alcohol consumption
avoiding stress

Primary prevention

Primary prevention aims to prevent disease in currently healthy individuals by developing good health habits and discouraging poor ones. Two strategies logically follow from this approach to health. Firstly, behaviour change can be used to encourage people to substitute good health behaviours for poor ones, as in programmes to help people to lose weight by altering their eating habits and exercise patterns. Secondly, programmes may aim to discourage people from ever developing poor health habits, for example, educational campaigns to dissuade teenagers from starting smoking or trying drugs. It is preferable to stop people from acquiring bad health habits but this may be difficult for a number of reasons:

- the range of behaviours known to be threatening to health is limited, for example, tobacco, opiates and cocaine have each, historically, been believed to be beneficial to health;

- early intervention may be hindered – school-based programmes will be too late to protect young people against poor health habits acquired in the home. Children of smokers are more likely to smoke than those of non-smokers;

- cognitive limitations of children younger than school-age may prevent full comprehension of the need for health behaviours;

- developing successful strategies to prevent the acquisition of poor health habits depends on understanding this process but our knowledge of the development of such processes is poor;

- during the time when people acquire health-compromising behaviours they fail to recognise or accept the long-term threat, therefore lack any incentive to avoid the behaviour.

Hygiene

Historically, greater advances in health have been made through improved understanding of hygiene, that is avoiding infection through cleanliness, than have been gained through modern medicine.

Helman (1994) suggests several aspects of culture that affect hygiene (either positively or negatively) and therefore affect health. Different cultural practices may:

- encourage or neglect personal hygiene;

- determine whether, or how often, hair is washed and cut;

- affect choice of clothing – how often it is washed and how tightly it fits (tailored clothing may provide an environment that encourages fleas or lice);

- dictate the frequency of bathing and whether it is communal or private.

Other hygiene factors that contribute to health include food storage, preparation and cooking; water sources (for drinking and bathing); disposal of human waste; and the location and care of pets and domestic animals (Helman, 1994). These issues may be at least in part culturally determined. For example, the burial of human bodies near to the source of drinking water supplies can cause contamination. Cultural practices may favour or reject cremation, an alternative that would reduce the risk.

A classic study into hygiene behaviours was conducted by Janis and Feshbach (1953) and is described below.

classic
research

dental horrors don't help!

Janis I.L. & Feshbach S. (1953) Effects of fear-arousing communications. *Journal of Abnormal and Social Psychology* **48: 78–92**

aims: to test whether fear is an effective motive to induce a change in health behaviour.

procedure: three 15-minute films were made of illustrated lectures presenting information about the dangers of poor oral hygiene. The recordings differed in the degree to which they were intended to elicit fear:

- strong – focused on pain (eg from tooth decay) and other risks such as blindness and cancer, and used photographs of decayed mouths;

- minimal – used diagrams and X-rays, avoided serious consequences other than decayed teeth and cavities;

- moderate – created an intermediate level of fear.

Each film was shown to a group of students and a fourth group saw no film. Those students who saw the films were asked how they felt immediately afterwards and completed questionnaires about their dental hygiene one week before and one week after viewing the film.

findings: the strong fear appeal film created the greatest immediate concern and participants expressed greater motivation to look after their teeth. It also aroused the most interest but was rated negatively as it was unpleasant. After one week, however, the high fear arousal group could remember less information and the minimal fear group demonstrated the greatest change in behaviour, with 36 per cent (compared to 8 per cent of the strong fear appeal group) reporting improved oral hygiene habits.

conclusion: although fear appeals generate strong emotional responses, these do not necessarily translate into changes in health behaviours such as dental hygiene. The fear elicited by such strong communications does not motivate health behaviour but results in individuals ignoring the problem or minimising the importance of the threat as a result of their fear.

Further studies have contributed to our understanding of the cognitive and behavioural constraints upon hygiene. Pinfold (1999) used a range of media to convey messages about hand and dish-washing to combat diarrhoeal infections in a population in the Khon Kaen province of Thailand. The use of posters, stickers, leaflets, comic books, songs, T-shirts, badges and a slide show combined to produce an increase in both health behaviours as indicated by presence of traces of faeces on the fingertips. Schools were more active in the programme than were villages and school children demonstrated a significant increase in knowledge about hygiene. Although knowledge was related to recall of the messages contained in the media, this increased knowledge did not necessarily result in improved hygiene-related behaviours.

what's new?

reducing the risk of infection through needle sharing

Needle sharing by intravenous drug users (IVDUs) is a significant risk factor in the transmission of disease because blood remaining in a needle or syringe can be injected directly into another user. Failure to engage in hygienic alternatives (sterilising needles or cleaning them in bleach) results in a high infection rate. It has been estimated that, in Edinburgh, 60 per cent of drug users who inject are HIV-positive (Plummer, 1988). In addition to AIDS, other diseases, such as hepatitis B and C, can also be transmitted via this route. Whilst it is possible that needle sharing correlates with other high-risk behaviours, evidence suggests that use of shared IVDU equipment is the major source of infection. Page et al (1990) found that 104 of the 230 IVDUs they studied were HIV-positive. They not only shared needles but used the same container of water to clean their syringes and prepared injections from shared drug sources, increasing the risk of spreading disease.

In a study conducted by Newmeyer et al (1989) many IVDU participants shared needles and, although they cleaned their equipment, this was in general just rinsing in water. Needle sharing often arises because needles are in short supply, for example, when it is illegal to possess them outside a medical context. Newmeyer et al's findings suggested that, of possible strategies for reducing infection (including ceasing drug use, injection of drugs or sharing of equipment), only the option of disinfecting shared equipment was acceptable to most

IVDUs. Newmeyer et al concluded that, since changing sexual practices of IVDUs (another high risk factor) would be harder than changing needle-use, the latter was a better focus for interventions to improve health-related behaviours. However, Longshore et al (2001) have confirmed that the HIV antibody is detectable not only in needles but in other injection supplies. Furthermore, they have found that attendance at needle exchange programmes (NEP) is associated with not only a lower incidence of needle sharing but also greater likelihood of cleansing the skin before injection and less sharing of cookers used to prepare drugs for injection. They conclude that NEPs are an underexploited opportunity to promote risk reduction beyond the avoidance of needle sharing.

A San Francisco primary prevention campaign to encourage IVDUs to sterilise their equipment. The 8-ft high 'bleachman' distributing packets of bleach was backed up by an advertising campaign

Junkieboden is a federation of Dutch self-help groups, which was involved in the establishment of the first syringe exchange for IDVUs in The Netherlands. Since the needle exchange network was formed, many more individuals have joined treatment schemes even though the number of IVDUs in Amsterdam has remained constant. The rate of HIV infection has decreased over the same time period (Marks et al 2000). Blakey and Frankland (1995) worked with a target group of prostitutes in Cardiff. The women were provided with information about safer drug use and (in addition to employing safer sex strategies) they reported needle exchange use and reduced needle sharing.

Several studies investigating the use of NEPs suggest that they make a significant contribution to the reduction of the spread of disease among IVDUs (Vertefeuille et al, 2000; Longshore et al, 2001; Gibson, 2001). Miller et al (2001) interviewed attenders at a syringe exchange programme (SEP) in Oslo, Norway between 1992 and 1997, and found that syringe sharing declined significantly over time. HIV prevalence remained low and neither SEP attendance nor the number of syringes exchanged increased. This suggests that the SEP was contributing to the control of disease without increasing drug use. Similarly, Yoast et al (2001) reported on exchange, free distribution and legal pharmacy sales of needles and syringes, and found these neither increased existing drug use nor led to the initiation of drug use.

Nutrition

Health behaviours relating to nutrition most obviously include weight control but also relate to healthy eating in terms of the provision of sufficient and appropriate nutrients. According to Seidell and Rissenen (1998) 14 per cent of the population of England are clinically over-weight to an extent that their obesity will adversely affect their long-term health. The additional demands placed on health services resulting from poor nutrition accounts for the interest governments show in promoting healthy eating habits. Chronically obese people are at greater risk from heart conditions and diabetes than non-overweight people.

Our Healthier Nation

The governmental consultation paper 'Our Healthier Nation' states that:

'A good diet is an important way of protecting health. The amount of fruit and vegetables people eat is an important influence on health. Unhealthy diets, which tend to include too much sugar, salt and fatty foods are linked to cancer, heart disease and stroke as well as tooth decay. Research suggests that a third of all cancers are the result of a poor diet.'

What health behaviours and health habits do people acquire that perpetuate healthy or unhealthy diets?

In many parts of the world food is in short supply; malnutrition and starvation are appallingly common. In stark contrast, the difficulty for inhabitants of developed countries with regard to nutrition is, most significantly, weight control, although eating disorders and poor diet are also problematic (eating disorders are discussed in chapter 11). We have evolved to attend to the nutritional needs of active hunter-gatherers, thus we are highly motivated to consume high calorie, and therefore fattening, foods. As a result we prefer the taste of fatty and sugary foods, even though we probably do not need them in terms of energy output. The task for psychology is therefore not simply to understand the desire to over-eat but to identify effective ways to control eating.

Psychological explanations of health behaviours relating to food

We believe that we have biologically determined desires for food, as illustrated by the 'food cravings' of premenstrual and pregnant women. Conversely, some aspects of our eating habits are acquired; we might learn that we don't like sprouts, so avoid them, or refuse to eat raspberry ice cream because we were once sick after eating some and – rightly or wrongly – formed an association between the two. Finally, we may have beliefs about eating that are dictated by our culture. 'Spinach is good for the blood' and 'Carrots help you to see in the dark' are two such guiding principles (each with a measure of genuine biological foundation). To what extent are these factors of biology, learning and culture, determinants of our health behaviour in relation to nutrition?

Biological explanations

An evolutionary explanation, as proposed at the beginning of this section, can account for the tendency of people to over-eat. Not everyone, however, does so. Differences between people may be accounted for by variation in metabolic rate, with obese people tending to have lower rates, utilising energy from food more efficiently so that surplus intake is ultimately converted to fat. Evidence from twin studies suggests that there may indeed be inherited components to both basal metabolic rate and the storage of excess energy as fatty rather than lean tissue (Bouchard et al, 1990). These explanations, however, can only account for the way in which excess food is utilised, not the amount that is consumed. This must be controlled by other factors.

Homeostatic theories suggest that our bodies have biological systems that monitor and adjust some aspect of our physiology, such as blood glucose (glucostatic theory), blood fat (lipostatic theory) or weight (set point theory). Each suggests that biological processes, such as hunger, metabolic rate and the laying down of fat, are controlled to maintain the particular variable around an optimum.

In set point theory (Brownwell & Wadden, 1992) the hypothalamus (a region of the brain) determines a bodyweight at which an individual will maintain a consistent weight independently of moderate changes in food intake. Each individual's weight is 'set' at a particular point. Thus, according to set point theory, when an individual eats a little more than they need to for weight maintenance, their metabolic rate rises, the energy consumed is used up more quickly and they feel less like eating. Conversely, if they eat too little, the body responds with increased efficiency, lowering the rate at which energy is used, and increasing the motivation to eat. As a result, small increases or decreases in food consumption make little difference to long-term weight. This accounts for the failure of crash diets – in the absence of sufficient food, the body may simply conserve energy by lowering the metabolic rate so food is 'burned' more slowly.

Experimental evidence supporting set point theory comes from investigations of extreme eating. Keys et al (1950) observed the effects of systematic starvation on healthy young men. Thirty-six Second World War conscientious objectors chose to participate in the study instead of signing up for active service. After three months of normal eating and monitoring, the aim was to subsequently reduce the participants' body weights to 75 per cent by giving them only half the amount of food they had chosen to eat previously. During the six-month reduced intake phase, their diet provided sufficient nutrients to avoid actual starvation. After rapid initial weight loss, rations had to be reduced further to achieve continued loss, although this did result in most of the participants reaching the 25 per cent loss target. Following this phase, re-feeding to return to the previous weight produced a much faster change in weight suggesting that deviations away from the set point are opposed by bodily processes – the men were hungry and lethargic during starvation but ate up to five meals a day during the re-feeding phase.

In a study into the effects of overeating conducted by Sims and Horton (1968), prisoners volunteered to consume excess food in order to gain approximately 2 stone. Their physical activity was restricted and they had access to ample, tasty food. As in the starvation study, initial weight change was rapid but as weight gain slowed the men had to eat around double their normal intake of 3500 calories per day. Some men failed to reach their target, one despite eating 10,000 calories a day! When the men's diets were reduced, they all lost weight although some found returning to their previous weight difficult. Again these results suggest an internal regulatory system exists to maintain the set point. In both studies the body responded by altering both metabolism and behaviour; when starved the participants were continuously hungry and inactive whereas those in the overeating study found food repulsive. However, in both studies there was a ten-

dency for some individuals to settle above their previous standard weight, suggesting that the internal optimum may be affected by other factors.

Biological determinants of weight, such as metabolic rate and levels of fat cells, may have some genetic contribution. In a study comparing the weight of adopted children to that of their natural and adoptive parents, there was a relationship between the former but not the latter (Stunkard et al, 1986). Similarly, identical twins of obese natural parents tend to be obese even when reared apart (Stunkard, 1988). Together, these findings imply that inherited factors do play a part in determining weight. They do not, of course, suggest that the environment is unimportant. Indeed, even family trends may be explained by environmental rather than genetic factors. Mason (1970) found that 44 per cent of the dogs owned by obese people were also obese, compared to only 25 per cent of dogs with normal weight owners.

However, the key factors that affect weight loss or gain are eating and exercise. These behaviours are not inherited. Other factors must therefore be considered in the explanation of healthy eating habits.

Behaviourist explanations

Learning theories (as you may recall from your AS work) explain different ways in which animals, including people, may acquire behaviours. Classical conditioning suggests that we learn associations between a 'new' situation (the neutral stimulus, NS) and an 'old' one (the unconditioned stimulus, UCS) to which the individual already exhibits a behaviour (the unconditioned response, UCR). Repeated pairings of the NS and UCS result in the generation of a behaviour resembling the UCR in response to the NS. Once this association has been established, the NS is called the conditioned stimulus (CS), and the resulting response, the conditioned response (CR). The acquisition of behaviours such as comfort eating may be explained using classical conditioning. Chocolate (UCS) tastes nice so makes us feel good (UCR). In a situation where we are unhappy (NS) we can experience an elevation in mood (UCR) by eating chocolate (ie pairing the NS and UCS), thus we learn to cheer ourselves up with food (CR).

In operant conditioning, behaviours that are followed by pleasant consequences (reinforcers) are performed more often, those with unpleasant consequence (punishers) less often. Unhealthy food-related behaviours are often rewarding – chips and chocolate taste nice – thus they are reinforcing and performed more often. Whilst such behaviours do have unpleasant consequences on health (negatively affecting teeth, weight and the heart), their effects are delayed so are ineffective punishment.

Social learning theory suggests that people can acquire behaviours by observing and copying the actions of others.

Thus we may like sweets because we see other children enjoying them but dislike vegetables if our siblings protest about eating them. Parents will be powerful models for the amount and type of food a child learns to enjoy.

Cultural explanations

Culture can account for some differences in food related behaviour including constraints, such as imposed by Ramadan or Lent, and expectations, such as the consumption of rich foods for celebrations. In addition, cultural preferences may guide choices, for example, traditional foods may continue to predominate in the diet long after international trade has made other foodstuffs readily available.

interactive angles

Use the Internet or other resources to investigate food preferences of a range of cultures. Find out the extent to which these have precedents in religion or have arisen because of locally available resources, such as particular plants or animals or the constraints of a hot climate. Some examples might be eating fish on Fridays, use of different cooking fats such as lard or olive oil, cooking curries or excluding pork from the diet.

Food availability is clearly a factor in healthy eating and although the presence of excess food will not necessarily result in weight gain, where the abundance includes a variety our food selection may be unhealthy. As we have observed, fatty and sugary foods taste nicer and may thus be chosen in preference especially where cultural factors instruct our choices. Eating dessert when we are already full depends both on the taste and the social incentive. Variety itself also plays a direct role. Sclafani and Springer (1976) investigated the effect of a wide and variable diet on rats. The experimental animals had free access to supermarket foods including cheese, salami, bananas, chocolate chip cookies, marshmallows and chocolate and increased in weight by 269 per cent! Since supermarket shopping and access to good storage facilities such as freezers enables people to maintain a huge diversity of foods in their homes, healthy eating behaviours may be compromised by the powerful effect of novelty on satiation.

Society provides powerful role models, for example, within the family and on television. Wadden and Brownell (1984) found that an average each American child watches 10,000 commercials for food every year. Approximately half of these were for cereals, a third advertised sweets or biscuits and just 5 per cent were for products that did not contain sugar and none at all were

for vegetables. The study also found that 75 per cent of mothers selected foods chosen by their children, suggesting that advertising directly influences children's diets.

Since, until very recently, food has been in short supply, fatness, rather than thinness, has been culturally endorsed as a sign of health and prosperity. Today, however, developed countries value lower body weights. To examine the changing perception of attractive body shape in women, Garner et al (1980) studied the body weights of Miss America contestants and Playboy centrefolds from 1959 to 1978. In both groups body weight declined relative to average weight for the general population. In a similar study conducted by Wiseman et al (1992) for Miss America from 1979 to 1988, the contestants became significantly thinner. These results seem to reflect a cultural preference for thinness. This change in society's ideal conflicts with the trend in average body weight, which is on the increase, hence the dissatisfaction of many people with their size. One study reports that two-thirds of women and more than half of the men questioned were trying to lose, or avoid putting on, weight (Serdula, 1993).

Table 23.2 Implications of explanations of food-related behaviours for health promotion

---

biological

- people are powerfully motivated by the taste of food, especially sweet and fat-rich flavours
- weight control programmes need to be tailored to individuals to combat the effect of different set points

behaviourist

- there is a need to counter-condition or unlearn associations that have been built up between unhealthy food and positive emotions or comfort
- healthy food must be perceived to be as rewarding as unhealthy food
- reinforcements are less effective if they are not immediate
- role models must exhibit positive behaviours toward healthy but not unhealthy foods

cultural

- children's food choices are affected by advertising and this is not necessarily countered by adults' shopping behaviour
- cultural differences in eating habits may mean that different health issues arise within different cultural groups

interactive angles

Use biological, psychological or cultural explanations to account for the following food-related differences in behaviour:

- a child who is bullied in the lunch queue eats the vegetarian option in order to avoid his classmates although he eats meat at home. Later in life he doesn't like eating meat in restaurants;

- two people of the same height and gender who eat identical diets and take the same exercise are not the same weight;

- advertisements for chocolate often use images suggesting sex appeal;

- a family that encourages 'finishing everything on your plate' regardless of whether you are hungry finds that the children grow into adults who are indiscriminate eaters;

- parents who tend to overeat have children who also to overeat.

Social skills

The aim of social skills training as a primary prevention measure is to enable people to identify their personal and social needs, and to develop the skills required to meet those needs. For instance, many smokers report that they smoke in order to reduce social anxiety so finding alternative means to relax could be beneficial. Since the largest group of new smokers is young people, it would be effective to equip youngsters with the social skills to enable them to avoid taking up smoking at all. One way to achieve this is to teach relaxation techniques as part of a self-management strategy allowing individuals to find alternatives to smoking for coping with difficult social situations. Self-management strategies used with smokers encourage the participant to self-observe and monitor when smoking occurs, the circumstances under which it occurs, and their own reactions. Self-reward techniques can then be used to separate smoking behaviour from the environmental cues with which it is associated.

In addition to dealing with the emotional consequences of the social environment, training must equip individuals with the social skills to respond appropriately to interactions. Bachman et al (1988) investigated the success of a programme used in schools to enable young people to say

'no' to drugs. Students were encouraged to talk to each other about drugs, to state their disapproval of drug taking and to say that they did not take drugs. The aim was to create a new social norm that was anti drug taking and to give the participants experience of refusing drugs. The programme claimed to have succeeded in changing attitudes to drugs and reducing cannabis use.

Klesges et al (1986) investigated the effects of a workplace-based six-week training programme to help smokers to stop, which was organised as a competition between different work sites. The programme used cognitive behavioural therapy to teach workers skills to assist their progress. A control group did not receive the intervention. At the end of the programme, 31 per cent of the intervention group but only 22 per cent of the control group had given up smoking. However, in a follow up 18 months later, more of the intervention group who participated in the competition had resumed their smoking habit but overall – including worksite members who did not participate in the competition – there was still a greater reduction of smoking at the sites exposed to the intervention.

interactive angles

Abraham and Sheeran (1993) recommended the use of skills training to encourage safer sex. They suggested teaching skills that young people could use in the following contexts:

- buying condoms;

- negotiating condom use with a partner;

- use of condoms;

Furthermore, several teaching strategies were proposed, including:

- tuition;

- role-play;

- feedback;

- modelling;

- practice.

Using the ideas of contexts and teaching strategies suggested by Abraham and Sheeran (1993), devise ways to teach people about either healthy nutrition or an aspect of hygiene.

Injuries to cyclists are common but could be reduced in severity by the wearing of appropriate helmets. Could a change in children's social skills help to achieve this? Sacks et al (1991) estimate that fatal head injuries to cyclists could be cut by almost 90 per cent if all cyclists wore helmets, but sadly few do. Kann et al (1998) found that only 12 per cent of high school students regularly wear helmets when riding their bicycles. Stevenson and Lennie (1992) suggest that the 'nerd factor' associated with wearing helmets is a barrier for young people. The theory of reasoned action would suggest that the social norm needs to be changed; children need to believe that their peers view helmet wearing as fashionable to increase the likelihood of them following advice to wear them. Farley et al (1996) used a range of strategies to increase cycle helmet wearing by 5 to 12 year olds that included activities intended to change attitudes and beliefs about wearing helmets. The effectiveness was judged by measuring helmet use by children in cities exposed to the intervention compared to areas that were not. Although over a four-year period helmet use increased regardless of the intervention, the likelihood of children wearing cycle helmets increased more in those cities where the intervention was used, with the percentage of children wearing helmets rising from 1.3 to 33 per cent.

Explaining health behaviour

Health belief model

The health belief model (HBM) is a cognitive model that attempts to explain health behaviours by considering the variables that affect our decision making in relation to health-protective and health-compromising behaviours. It is thus an information processing model of the reasoning behind our beliefs and the way that they control our readiness to engage in health behaviours. The HBM was originally proposed by Hockbaum (1958) and has been adapted several times (eg Rosenstock, 1966; and Strecher et al, 1997).

classic
research

screen savers

Hochbaum G.M. (1958) *Public participation in medical screening programmes: a sociopsychological study* (Public Health Service Publication 572). US government Washington DC: Printing Office

aims: to investigate the factors affecting people's participation in a health screening programme.

procedure: 1200 adult residents of cities participating in a new tuberculosis screening programme were asked about their beliefs about tuberculosis in relation to themselves and whether or not they had attended screening clinics.

findings: two factors were found to predict the likelihood of people participating in the scheme; whether the individual:

● felt personally at risk from catching tuberculosis;

● believed that early identification and treatment of the disease would be effective.

Eight per cent of those people holding both of these beliefs went for screening but only 20 per cent of those who held neither.

conclusion: health behaviours are closely related to specific health beliefs. Therefore, a key to effecting change in people's health behaviour is to understand how decisions affecting health are made and thus how the beliefs and consequent behaviour can be altered.

The HBM is composed of five core beliefs that are affected by a range of external variables. The findings of Hochbaum's study provided the basis for these components and the way in which they interact to affect health behaviour on the basis of external cues. The components are:

1 *perceived vulnerability* – the individual's assessment of the risk that they will be affected by the condition (susceptibility);

2 *perceived seriousness* – the individual's assessment of how bad the effect will be if they are affected (severity).

Together, perceived vulnerability and seriousness determine the individual's perception of the threat posed by the disease. So, for example, a person who is asthmatic may recognise that this is a lethal condition (high perceived seriousness), but believe that because they don't get breathless during exercise they do not need to be concerned (low vulnerability). Where some threat exists, the individual must determine the extent to which engaging in a particular health behaviour will protect them. This is a balance between barriers and benefits:

3 *perceived barriers* – aspects of the situation that disincline the individual from taking action. These may be financial (cost of prescriptions), situational (living in a rural area a long way from a hospital) or social (not wanting to inconvenience other people by being off work). Time, effort and the perception of obstacles would also act as barriers to effective health behaviour;

4 *perceived benefits* – possible gains for the individual such as alleviating pain or anxiety, improving health or reducing health risks.

Together, the perceived barriers and benefits present the individual with a cost-benefit analysis. For example, Abraham et al (1992) studied Scottish teenagers, who were well aware of the seriousness of the risk of HIV infection, their vulnerability to it and the benefits gained by using condoms. However, condom use by the participants was prevented because the perceived barrier of costs, including loss of pleasure, awkwardness of use and anticipated conflict with their partner exceeded the perceived benefits to avoiding infection.

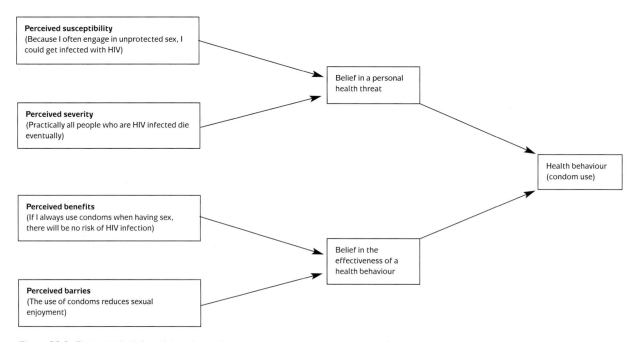

Figure 23.2 The health belief model can be applied to aspects of sexual health (source: Stroebe de wit, 1996)

The fifth core belief of the HBM is:

5 *cues to action* – for us to exhibit a health behaviour, even when our cost-benefit analysis judges it to be necessary, we need a *cue to action*, that is an immediate trigger to initiate the appropriate behaviour. This may be internal or external. For example, we may believe

that we should stop smoking because it is a serious threat to our health, recognise our vulnerability and know that stopping would be advantageous. However, we may only do so when we develop severe chest pains (internal cue) or a relative dies of lung cancer (external cue).

media watch

When 25-stone Karina Buiskool got stuck in a turnstile while getting on to a fairground ride, she knew she just had to lose weight.

'I finally forced my way in but it seemed like I was there hours with everybody staring at me' said the 36 year old. Her embarrassment led to such a determination to diet that she has shed 13 stone – a typical weight for a grown man – in just 30 months.

Padraic Flanagan, *Daily Express*, 20 November 2002, page 17

This excerpt describes the way in which one woman, who had been seriously over-weight to an extent that would have been a serious risk to her health, ultimately lost weight. How would the Health Belief Model explain the significance of the event described above?

The five core beliefs of the HBM should predict the likelihood that a particular health behaviour will arise in a given situation. Consider an example of a stressed individual with a high cholesterol level who believes that changing their eating habits to reduce their fat intake is going to reduce their risk of dying of a heart attack. That individual is more likely to persevere with the diet despite disliking the diet than a person who holds the belief that the fuss about cholesterol levels is all hype (low perceived seriousness) or that no one in their family has heart problems so they are not at risk (low vulnerability).

Evidence suggesting that knowledge is important in bringing about appropriate health behaviours suggests that the provision of health information is worthwhile. Rimer et al (1991) found that women who had more knowledge about breast cancer were more likely to have regular mammograms and O'Brien and Lee (1990) demonstrated that manipulating knowledge about pap tests (for cervical cancer) by showing women an informational video resulted in both increased knowledge and healthier behaviour.

interactive angles

Taking the example of someone who is obese and at risk from heart disease, identify the following as examples of perceived benefits, barriers, vulnerability, seriousness or cues to action and decide which person would be likely to embark on health-protective behaviours:

Fred

'My chances of having a heart attack are low'

'I don't want to turn into a jogging-junkie'

'Exercising cuts down the risk of a heart attack but even sporty people still have them'

'People who have heart attacks generally recover and go back to work'

Jake

'Heart attacks kill people'

'I feel ready to start exercising more'

'My neighbour had a heart attack and was younger than me'

'I guess that being stressed increases my chances of having a heart attack'

'Getting fit will make me more attractive too'

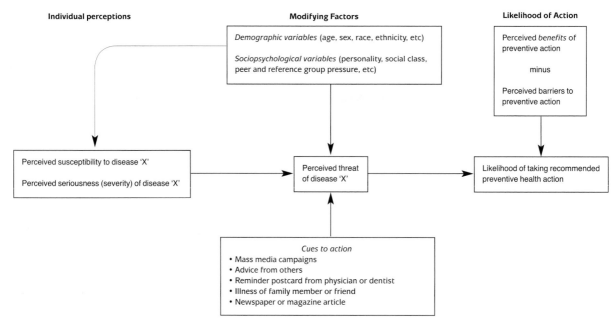

Figure 23.3 The health belief model (source: Becker & Maiman, 1975)

Using the health belief model

The health belief model can be used to interpret behaviour in a number of contexts, for example to understand why some people make use of disease prevention schemes and screening tests but others do not. Haefner and Kirscht (1970) found that people were more likely to use disease prevention measures and attend health screening services including physical examinations and x-rays if they were exposed to interventions that stressed vulnerability and effectiveness of the particular health behaviour in combating the risk. Thus, the HBM can not only help us to understand health behaviours but to effect change to improve people's health.

Applying the health belief model to some of the studies described above we can see how health campaigns may be made more effective. In the case of Abraham et al's (1992) study of condom use the HBM would suggest that AIDS campaigns should have focused not on vulnerability and seriousness but on overcoming barriers to condom use in order to be effective.

Making use of disease prevention

Schemes for disease prevention include immunisations, self-examination (of the breasts or testicles) and effective tooth-brushing and flossing. The reason for encouraging people to engage in preventative measures is clear; it reduces health risks and early detection makes treatment easier. The likelihood of people participating in these health-promoting behaviours can be predicted using the health belief model. Furthermore, an understanding of the factors affecting people's participation or non-participation can direct health promotion campaigns.

interactive angles

Parental reasons for non-immunisation:

- risk/benefit ratio – perception that the risks of contracting the disease outweigh the benefits of being immunised;

- individual risk – belief that the societal statistics that public health planners use do not apply to their child. Further, the parents believe that they can protect the child from exposure;

- ambiguity aversion – aversity to options with ambiguous outcomes such that parents will prefer a straightforward Yes/No assessment of the likelihood of their child contracting a disease. When there is a disagreement about potential risk they will err on the side of caution;

- omission bias – preference for acts of omission over acts of commission;

- 'free riding' – assumption that since most of their children's peers have been vaccinated they are protected.

From Meszaros et al, 1996, page 698

Identify how the issues raised above would affect a parent's decision making about whether to have their child immunised according to the health belief model.

Immunisation protects against disease by administering a vaccine to individuals before the infectious agent has been encountered. Vaccination is effective against diseases such as whooping cough (pertussis), measles, mumps and rubella (MMR) and many more. In an interview study of mothers in north-west England, New and Senior (1991) found that less than 75 per cent had had their children fully immunised. One reason for not having their child vaccinated against whooping cough was the risk to the child from the pertussis vaccine, that is, the perceived barriers were too great. Research from both the UK (Reddy, 1989) and the US (Lewis et al, 1988) has found that parents give the reason 'the child was sick at the time of the appointment' for non-attendance for vaccinations. However, at least in the case of the English study, when the parents were telephoned, the child in fact only had a cold. This suggests that the benefits of vaccination were not perceived to be sufficiently high to overcome other concerns. Lewis et al, also suggesting the illnesses were minor, consider that adverse media reports and other causes of parental concerns may have deterred parents from completing their child's vaccination series. Again this suggests that the perceived benefits of vaccination do not outweigh the perceived barriers.

interactive angles

Use newspapers from the library or the Internet to find reports on the public response to MMR vaccination and its potential link to autism. Consider how the health belief model would explain the effect of such publicity on parental choices with regard to immunisation.

Murray and McMillan (1993) investigated the effectiveness of the HBM as a predictor of whether women would employ breast self-examination as a preventative measure against breast cancer. A sample of 391 women completed questionnaires about their health behaviours including the frequency of breast self-examination. The participants also rated items reflecting their health beliefs, such as: 'my chances of getting cancer are great' (susceptibility); 'I am afraid to even think about cancer' (seriousness); 'if cancer is detected early it can be successfully treated' (benefits); and 'I just don't like doctors or hospitals' (barriers). In addition they provided information relating to their knowledge about cancer, their confidence in performing self-examination and whether any family member had ever had cancer.

The findings showed that breast self-examination was related to many variables including knowledge and perceived benefits. Demographic variables such as age and social class also affected participation; young, professional women were more likely to use breast self-examination. The best predictor of appropriate action in this context was *self-efficacy* – an individual's confidence in their own ability to perform a behaviour. Women who were more confident about carrying out breast self-examination were more likely to do so. This evidence suggests that health promotion should aim to improve women's confidence in their ability to perform self-examination and to provide opportunities to practise the skills.

Making use of screening tests

Screening tests include cervical smear tests for women, ultrasound scanning and amniocentesis that investigate unborn babies, and x-rays (such as mammograms to detect breast cancer). As with disease prevention measures, screening enables health professionals to detect diseases early and treat them more effectively. Participation in these health behaviours can be predicted, and appropriate directions for health promotion ascertained, using the health belief model.

As part of the study described above, Murray and McMillan (1993) investigated the power of the HBM to predict attendance at cervical cancer screening tests (the cervical smear or pap test). The women were asked about the number of tests they had had and why they had been tested (asked to be, doctor suggested it, routine post-natal check up etc). When compared to measures of health beliefs, it was found that cervical smear testing (like breast self-examination) was related to knowledge and perceived benefits in addition to other variables. The best predictor in this case was 'barriers' that is, the women were more likely to have smear tests if they perceived little threat from the health service, the examination itself or the result. In terms of health promotion this suggests that attendance at cervical smear testing could be improved by education that aimed to reduce anxiety experienced by women about the consequences of the investigation. In addition, the benefits of cancer screening are also perceived to be low. Several studies have found that a common reason for non-attendance at cancer screening is that women believe that cervical smear tests are not necessary (eg Harlan et al, 1991), or only important when symptoms were present (eg Slenker & Grant, 1989). This suggests that perceived vulnerability is also low.

McCaul et al (1996) conducted a meta-analysis (that is, combined the results of many studies) to investigate factors affecting utilisation of mammography (x-ray screening for breast cancer). There was a strong relationship between family history and attendance, suggesting that perceived vulnerability (as well as actual risk) played an important part in motivating women to attend. Bernstein Hyman et al (1994) found that women who did not attend a scheduled mammogram appointment perceived fewer benefits than those who did. In the absence of a relationship between attendance and perceived vulnerability, they suggested that other factors, such as knowledge, are more important in determining health behaviour with regard to mammography. This implies that more information about the risks of breast cancer and the importance of mammography would improve attendance rates for screening.

for and against

the health belief model

+ a strong body of evidence supports the ability of the HBM to predict health actions in contexts preventing AIDS (Aspinwall et al, 1991), conducting self-examination of the breasts (Champion, 1990) and dental care (Ronis, 1992)

+ the HBM can explain failure to engage in health behaviours even when vulnerability is recognised because people underestimate their own levels of health risk compared to others (Weinstein, 1987) and may lack cues to action or perceive insurmountable barriers

+ participation in screening programmes can be predicted by the HBM

+ the HBM has provided direction for health education, such as focusing on ways to limit barriers to health behaviours

— variables such as perceived susceptibility may not be measured in the same way in all evaluations of the model

— the HBM considers each health belief in isolation rather than the way the factors interact to affect health behaviour

— some health behaviours, including habits such as dental hygiene or smoking, do not fit the model suggesting that the HBM is an incomplete explanation

— some factors affecting health behaviours, such as dieting or exercise, may be motivated by non-health-related reasons such as a desire to look good

— other factors, such as self-efficacy (Schwarzer, 1992), may be important in determining health behaviour

+ the HBM can be adapted to include new beliefs, for example, Becker and Rosenstock (1987) proposed the addition of perceived control and Strecher and Rosenstock (1997) recommended the inclusion of self-efficacy

— conflicting evidence suggests that healthy behaviour may be related to low susceptibility (Langlie, 1977) and low seriousness (Janz & Becker, 1984) beliefs

— HBM is a cognitive model, aiming to explain the reasoning behind people's health behaviours. As such, it cannot take account of non-cognitive factors like emotions: failure to go for a vaccination even when the appropriate beliefs are held may be accounted for by a phobia of needles but this emotional component would not fit neatly into the HBM

— Smeldslund (2000) observes that some of the underpinning assumptions of HBM are true by definition and therefore lack explanatory value. If our health behaviour is affected by our perceived susceptibility, which is in turn affected by our knowledge, then we must have knowledge in order to feel susceptible at all: we cannot be aware that we are at risk if we do not know that the risk exists! Therefore, knowledge is not a factor that affects perceived susceptibility but is a necessary prerequisite

The theories of reasoned action and planned behaviour

Ajzen and Fishbein (1980) proposed the theory of reasoned action, which predicts the performance of a behaviour on the basis of behavioural intention, that is, it assumes that action is the product of the intention to perform a behaviour. This theory has been updated (Ajzen, 1985, 1991) to include other factors such as the importance of an individual's confidence that they can succeed in changing their behaviour. This new version of the model is called the theory of planned behaviour (TPB).

The theory of planned behaviour

Ajzen's (1985) *theory of planned behaviour* proposes that actions, such as health behaviours, are determined by a combination of *behavioural intention* (deciding to achieve a goal) and *perceived behavioural control* (believing that you can or cannot perform a behaviour). So, if we consider the example of someone who wants to give up smoking, the two factors can be distinguished: firstly, wanting to be a non-smoker (behavioural intention), perhaps to avoid feeling excluded by non-smoking friends; and secondly, believing that you can achieve the goal (perceived behavioural control), for example feeling that you have the strength to overcome the unpleasant effects of nicotine withdrawal. The importance of both factors is illustrated by the findings of Schifter and Ajzen (1985) in their study of weight loss in female students. Individuals who expressed both the intention to lose weight and perceived that they would be able to limit their calorie intake over the six weeks of the study lost more weight. This shows that intention only predicts healthy behaviour when perceived behavioural control is high.

Behavioural intention itself may be determined by attitude (which is affected in turn by knowledge) and by subjective norms arising from our beliefs and inclination to comply with these values. *Attitudes* are the product of an individual's beliefs in the outcomes of the health behaviour in question and that individual's evaluation of these outcomes. *Subjective norms* are the individual's beliefs about the value other people (individuals or groups) place on that individual's health behaviour and the extent to which there is a motivation to follow these expectations. There are two components to subjective norms; normative beliefs about how others expect us to behave and motivation to comply. Considering the smoker again, they may believe that smoking is damaging to the lungs and heart and may value health and fitness, resulting in an attitude that will make them more likely to give up. In this respect TPB resembles the health belief model as it considers the role of beliefs in affecting behaviour. The smoker may also consider subjective norms such as how their family feels about smoking (normative beliefs) and may be compelled to follow the family's example or advice (motivation to comply). The relationship between behavioural intention and action has been supported empirically. Research has successfully applied TPB to a range of health behaviours, including smoking (Norman & Tedeschi, 1989), weight loss (Schifter & Ajzen, 1985) and breast cancer detection (Montano & Taplin, 1991). Eagly and Chaiken (1993) report successful application of the model to other health behaviours such as blood donation, contraception, consumption of junk food, dental hygiene, having an abortion and smoking cannabis.

Michie et al (1992) found that behavioural intention was a good predictor of the likelihood of pregnant women attending health information classes. Those women who, prior to delivery, expressed an intention to attend classes were more likely to do so once their baby was born. However, factors such as the attitude of the baby's father also contributed to attendance.

Van den Putte (1991) reported that attitudes and subjective norms were good predictors of behavioural intention and that intentions were moderate predictors of actual behavioural outcome.

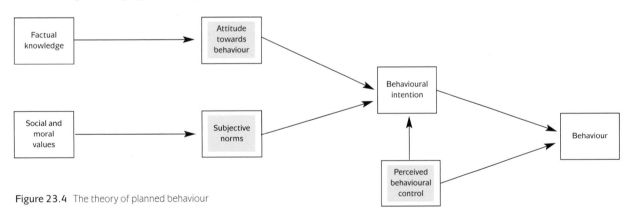

Figure 23.4 The theory of planned behaviour

Perceived behavioural control is the product of internal factors, such as knowledge, abilities and intrinsic motivation ('will power') and external factors, such as opportunity (eg the effect of the weather on participation in sport) and dependence on others (eg needing a lift to the gym). In support of TPB, Armitage and Conner (1998) found that perceived behavioural control, in addition to attitudes and subjective norms, reliably predicted behaviour.

Brubaker and Wickersham (1990) investigated the use of testicular self-examination (TSE) by young men following instruction in the procedure. The participants were also given a questionnaire to establish their attitudes towards TSE, their beliefs about subjective norms, the effectiveness of TSE as a means to detect testicular cancer (ie outcome), their own effectiveness at TSE (self-efficacy) and their intention to perform TSE in the future. When followed up later, the results showed that both attitude towards TSE and beliefs about subjective norms (such as the extent to which they felt other people wanted them to practise TSE) significantly predicted intention to perform TSE.

research
now

when you think dieting's easy, it is

Povey R., Conner M., Sparks P., James R. & Shepherd R. (2000) Application of the theory of planned behaviour to two dietary behaviours: role of perceived control and efficacy. *British Journal of Health Psychology* 5: 121–39

aims: to test the theory of planned behaviour (TPB) in the context of dieting to find out whether perceived control and self-efficacy are good predictors of behaviour.

procedure: questionnaires were used to measure variables relevant to the TPB including initial intentions to eat either five portions of fruit and vegetables a day (for 144 participants) or a low-fat diet (for 143 participants) and subsequent behaviour (whether the dietary principle was followed) a month later. The individual components of perceived behavioural control (perceived control and self-efficacy) and their determinant beliefs were also tested.

findings: the TPB variables were found to be good predictors of intention to eat fruit and vegetables or reduce fat intake, with self-efficacy being a more consistent predictor than perceived control. These factors also predicted eating behaviour, although the correlation was weaker. The determinant beliefs of attitude and subjective norms were also important. Attitude related strongly to intention to eat a low fat diet (although less so for eating fruit and vegetables). Subjective norms predicted intention only for eating fruit and vegetables.

conclusion: self-efficacy was in general a better predictor of intention than perceived control, which suggests that a person's perception of their ease or difficulty of engaging in a behaviour is an additional and important factor affecting that person's intention to perform that behaviour. Thus both self-efficacy and perceived behavioural control may be important determinants of intention and behaviour. The findings suggest that TPB should include self-efficacy as a separate variable and that health promotion strategies that aim to change dietary habits should target people's attitudes and self-efficacy.

Having the intention to perform a behaviour does not necessarily lead to the behaviour arising. We may have decided that we need to diet after Christmas but we may not actually do so. We are more likely to fulfil an intention if it is specific; 'I will not buy chocolate' is more likely to be successful than 'I will eat less'. Latency also affects the link between intention and behaviour. We are more likely to follow an intention through if we perform the behaviour immediately after deciding to do so. Hence, 'I will swim daily, starting today' is more likely to work than saying 'I will start swimming at the end of the holiday'. Thus the theory of planned behaviour can account for both individual influences in health behaviour (such as attitude or intention) and local influences (such as the availability of information), as well as the effects of physical factors and socio-cultural constraints.

Being able to predict health behaviour is clearly useful in planning health promotion campaigns, although the effectiveness of any chosen strategy depends on the factors most salient in the decision-making process. For example, in the choice between bottle and breast feeding, women seem to be affected more by attitudes than by subjective norms (Manstead et al, 1983). Conversely, a woman's decision to have an abortion seems to be more strongly affected by perceived social pressure, that is, subjective norms, than by her attitudes (Smetana & Alder, 1980). Findings such as these have important implications for health promotion. Health behaviours that are most strongly affected by the individual's attitudes are more likely to change if the individual is exposed to persuasive information than if the behaviour is under the control of subjective norms. In contrast, behaviours that are primarily the product of subjective norms will be affected by attempts to change beliefs about expectations.

Rutter (2000) used the TPB to predict attendance of women at mammography sessions (to assist early detection of breast cancer). A group of 1215 participants who had not been screened before completed questionnaires to indicate attitudes, subjective norms, perceived behavioural control over attendance and intention to attend breast screening. Those women with a strong intention to attend were the most likely to do so, both at their first and follow-up screening (three years later). In line with TBP, their intention was predicted by attitude, subjective norms and perceived behavioural control. The findings suggest that screening rates might be improved in those women who do not attend, by focusing on subjective norms – why other people might wish them to attend.

The difference between behaviours primarily driven by behavioural intention compared to perceived behavioural control also warrants a different approach to health promotion. Where behavioural intention is not the best predictor of behaviour, this raises the question, why not? The issue here is to ascertain the reasons why behaviour and intention are not related. Stroebe (2000) suggests that such situations are rare, and that where behaviour is largely the product of perceived behavioural control there is, in fact, very little variation in intention between individuals, thus perceived behavioural control becomes a much more potent cause of action. More commonly, behaviour is governed predominantly by behavioural intention so, as well as the factors of attitude and subjective norms that we considered on page 295, the contribution of perceived behavioural control also has to be considered. The case of failed AIDS campaigns provides an appropriate example. In 1990 de Wit et al reported a questionnaire study of secondary school children, assessing their health-related knowledge about AIDS and the following variables in relation to condoms:

- attitudes towards their use;
- perceived norms of use;
- perceived behavioural control over use;
- intention to use them.

The test was administered before, and two weeks after, the students saw a health education programme on AIDS. Although this intervention increased knowledge about AIDS, it did not affect health behaviour; condom use by the students did not increase. This was because condom use was governed not by knowledge or perceived susceptibility but by attitude to condom use, and perceived norms and effectiveness. These findings have clear implications for improving health education. More emphasis should be given to changing attitudes to condom use, subjective norms and individuals' perception of their own effectiveness.

for and against

the theory of planned behaviour

+ the theory can effectively predict health behaviour on the basis of behavioural intention

− not all evidence supports a strong correlation between intention and behaviour (Six, 1996)

+ the theory takes into account variables other than intention (eg perceived behavioural control)

+ the theory takes individual variables into account because people vary in terms of both intention and perceived control.

− the model may not be a good predictor of health behaviour for low income, relatively uneducated samples (Bishop, 1994)

− the model does not account for how these non-volitional factors affect behaviour

+ includes the role of constraints on behaviour that are outside the individual's control

where to now?

▶ **Bennett P. & Murphy S. (1997) *Psychology and health promotion*. Buckingham: Open University Press.** This text covers both the health belief model and the theory of planned behaviour as well as some newer approaches to explaining health behaviours.

▶ **Ogden J. (2000) *Health psychology, a textbook*. Buckingham: Open University Press.** This discusses nutrition and has a thorough coverage of both theories of health behaviour discussed in this chapter.

Health education programmes

Health education programmes attempt to change people's health behaviours from health-compromising to health-enhancing ones. This may be attempted through different routes according to the model being followed. For example, *fear arousing appeals* should, according to the health belief model, increase perceived vulnerability but this approach has little success. Warner (1977) found only small, transient reductions in smoking (of 4 to 5 per cent) following scares in the US in the 1950s and 1960s. It could also be argued that a 'shock-horror' approach to discouraging drug use is as counterproductive because it emphasises the seductive qualities of any drug.

Kelley (1979) reported on the effectiveness of a *mass media campaign* to increase the percentage of car drivers wearing seat belts (which stood at 6.3 per cent for city driving in 1968). Using cable television to segregate experimental groups, Kelley ensured that some households saw professionally made seat belt advertisements frequently over a nine-month period (estimated at two or three times a week), while others did not. Using car licence plates to identify drivers from the two experimental areas, observers counted the number of drivers wearing seat belts after the experimental period. The shocking conclusions were that the campaign had had no effect on seat belt use; drivers from the experimental group did not alter their behaviour at all during the test period. Kelley concluded that mass media campaigns are an ineffective way to attempt to alter health behaviour.

Informational appeals aim to promote good health by providing people with the knowledge to make better health behaviour choices. However, information presented in campaigns may be interpreted differently by individuals than by those with a wider perspective. In population terms, nearly 10,000 in every 1,000,000 male smokers

Figure 23.5 A new source of health information are internet chat rooms

aged 35 will die before reaching 45, because of their habit. From the perspective of the individual however, this is only a 1 per cent chance – the odds are on survival. It is difficult to persuade individuals that they are at risk, therefore campaigns need to identify and focus on other routes to changing behaviour. Nevertheless, access to information may still be a barrier. One relatively new source of health information is the Internet. Condon (2001) describes the successful use of Internet chat rooms by the director of San Francisco's Stop AIDS project, Marcel Miranda. The Internet, Miranda suggests, offers a way of getting information about HIV and safe sex to groups who would otherwise remain uninformed.

Experts divided on whether shock tactics will deter young people

The parents of a 21-year-old university dropout who died of a heroin overdose last night justified their decision to release graphic photographs of her blackened corpse as part of an educational video.

Pauline Holcroft, the mother of Rachel Whitear, a one-time psychology and sociology student, who was pictured still clutching the syringe used for her fatal fix, said: 'We realised when we agreed to release them they would be distasteful to some people but we felt they were a very important part of the film.'

... [T]he 22-minute film ... charts the effect her descent into addiction had on her middle-class family. ...

Mrs Holcroft added: 'I think we are focusing too much on one small part. The exposure of these photographs is an important part of the film, but it's only one part and others are equally important.' Poems written by Ms Whitear as she fought unsuccessfully to overcome her addiction were more emotive.

'The feedback we have got from parents is excellent. Practically 100% of children said it would make them think they couldn't do this to their families,' Mrs Holcroft said.

As the graphic images were displayed on news stands yesterday, opinion was divided on whether such shock tactics would work, with some drugs specialists warning that such images would have little effect on drugs deaths, which have almost doubled from 864 in 1993 to 1,662 in 2000. ...

Lynn Clare, project manager of the support group Parents Against Drug Abuse, said: ... 'It probably won't have any more of an effect on children because they don't equate themselves with this and they tend to think they are fairly indestructible. When the Leah Betts picture was shown, it caused a lot of interest but it didn't stop people taking ecstasy.'

Herefordshire local education authority – which has produced the video which charts Ms Whitear's descent to a lonely death in a flat in Exmouth, Devon – says that students who had seen it had been affected because it 'challenges the stereotypical image of a drug user'. ...

Statistics from the national crime survey suggest that the number of ecstasy users rose from 9 per cent of 16–29-year-olds in 1996, the year after Leah Bett[s]'s death, to 12% in 2000, the last available figure, while heroin use doubled to 2%.

From *Guardian*, 2 March 2002

Justify the opinion of some experts that the video described above would be unsuccessful in its aims to reduce drug-taking by young people.

Alternative strategies include raising awareness and changing attitudes. In presenting information to people in order to promote change, Taylor (1995) suggests that it should:

- be colourful, vivid, virtually statistics-free and use case histories;
- come from an expert source;
- discuss both sides of the issue;
- have the strongest arguments at the beginning and end of the message;
- be short and clear;
- have explicit rather than implicit conclusions;
- not be too extreme.

Figure 23.7 An example of a postcard, targeted at teenagers, printed (in bright purple and orange!) by the fpa (Family Planning Association). Designed by Feel Agency for Contraceptive Awareness Week 2002.

There are XIII (13) methods of contraception, your doctors surgery, family planning clinic or pharmacy, or the fpa (0845 310 1334, *www.fpa.org.uk*) can provide you with information.

To what extent does it follow the principles advocated by Taylor (1995)?

Attempts to change attitudes to health behaviours, as is envisaged by the theory of planned behaviour, can employ the same persuasive techniques described on page 364.

QUIT SMOKING

If not
for yourself
then for
your children
and
grandchildren!

Source: www.gasp.org.uk

Do you think that this advertising campaign fulfils the criteria suggested by Taylor (1995)?

Raising awareness

As we have seen in relation to many areas, such as hygiene (page 282), nutrition (page 285) and road safety (page 289), the first step in encouraging improved health behaviour is to increase awareness of healthy and unhealthy options.

interactive angles

Major campaigns have been launched to raise awareness of specific risks, such as AIDS and meningitis. Find out about these using resources in your library or on the Internet. What kinds of messages are used to inform people? Do they impart knowledge? If so, does it relate to seriousness, vulnerability or other aspects of the disease? Does the information attempt to alter beliefs or attitudes? Do they try to influence subjective norms or people's perceptions or their own behavioural control?

The two models of health behaviour we have considered, the health belief model (pages 291–4) and the theory of reasoned action/planned behaviour (pages 296–9) both suggest that awareness is important in promoting health behaviours. The HBM suggests that awareness is essential to making assessments of vulnerability and seriousness that combine to enable the individual to make a judgement of the threat posed by a disease. In addition, knowledge about the benefits of a particular health behaviour and ways to overcome barriers enable the individual to sway their cost-benefit analysis in favour of engaging in healthier behaviours. Awareness is also important from the perspective of the TPB. Here, knowledge is a prerequisite in the formation of attitudes towards health behaviours. Inadequate awareness or misinformation would lead to poor health behaviour choices, therefore it is the role of health promotion to ensure that people are aware of sufficient and appropriate resources so that they can make informed choices.

Changing attitudes

It is clear that awareness or understanding of issues alone is insufficient to guarantee an improvement in health behaviours. People must be encouraged to change their beliefs and attitudes before behaviour changes can occur. However, as the discussion of the Yale model of persuasive communication (page 362–6) shows, changing attitudes is difficult and, like improving knowledge, does not guarantee a change in behaviour. Kirscht et al (1978) found that threat messages about weight control in obese children (that should have induced a change in maternal attitude) did indeed affect behaviour (the children lost weight). This shows that attitudes can affect behaviour. However, Leventhal and Cleary (1980) failed to change health behaviour; even when smoker's attitudes were manipulated by stimulating feelings of vulnerability they did not stop smoking.

interactive angles

Return to the following descriptions of studies reported earlier in this chapter:

- Bernstein Hyman et al (1994)
- Hochbaum (1958)
- Haefner and Kirscht (1970)
- Murray and McMillan (1993)
- O'Brien and Lee (1990)
- Rimer et al (1991)

For each study, identify the nature of the information that the participants needed in order to improve their awareness of health risks and justify your explanation using either the HBM or TPB.

media watch

Scenes of a student's death could backfire

Shock campaigns against drug use are not new. Neither are concerns about their efficacy. A report to the Teachers Advisory Council on Alcohol and Drug Education in 1986 criticised such tactics and pointed out they had failed in other areas.

The 1950s educational film *Reefer Madness* was intended to shock American younsters into avoiding cannabis. Instead, it helped to create the image of cannabis as cool and desirable and became a cult classic.

In the mid-1980s, the Government responded to a surge in heroin use with a television and poster campaign featuring a wasted youth with the caption: 'Heroin screws you up.' Dozens of posters went missing as the boy in them became a teenage pin-up. Within months 'heroin chic' appeared on the catwalks.

Three years ago a video called *The Trap* featuring real addicts and a staged overdose was shown to 11-year-olds at 50 primary schools in the Rhondda Valley, South Wales. The area still has a massive heroin problem.

More recently the Leah Betts poster campaign – featuring her photograph under the headline 'Sorted. Just one ecstasy tablet killed Leah Betts' – was quickly hijacked by the pro-ecstasy lobby, who released a rival poster: 'Distorted: You are just as likely to die from eating a bay leaf as from an ecstasy tablet.' …

The video of Rachel's addiction and death … 'makes teachers and parents feel better, but the actual value is highly questionable,' said Hunt. 'Videos like this allow schools to tick the "drugs education" box and feel that they have done what they need to do. Actually talking to schoolchildren about heroin – a drug they are very unlikely to be exposed to – as opposed to tobacco or alcohol – which they almost certainly will be – doesn't make sense.'

From *Observer*, 3 March 2002

The extract above refers to the video described on page 298–9. To what extent do you think that this video, and the previous drugs education resources described, would be successful at changing attitudes to drug use?

interactive angles

The following studies, reported earlier in this chapter, suggested that poor health behaviour choices were the result of the attitudes of the individuals. For each example, identify the attitude in question and suggest how it would need to change to encourage healthier behaviours:

- Abraham et al (1992)

- Brubaker and Wickersham (1990)

- de Wit et al (1990)

AIDS education programmes

Acquired immune deficiency syndrome (AIDS) is a condition diagnosed by the presence of specific secondary diseases, caused by infection with the human immunodeficiency virus (HIV), which destroys helper T cells, part of the body's defence system (see page 262). Infection with HIV makes the body vulnerable to the secondary diseases that characterise AIDS, such as pneumonia and the rare skin cancer Karposi's sarcoma, in addition to causing a complex of symptoms including fever and fatigue.

There may be a long period of incubation of HIV, commonly five to eight years, without the appearance of any symptoms associated with the infection. During this time, and subsequently, the infected individual presents a health risk to others if (and only if) they engage in behaviours that can transmit the virus. These include activities in which infected bodily fluids (blood or semen) can pass between individuals. Vaginal, anal and oral sex all carry such risks as does the sharing of needles and syringes for injection of drugs (see page 283–4). Physical contact, kissing, sharing crockery and contact with tears and saliva do not represent a threat to health. Although the virus can be traced in all bodily secretions, you would have to drink several buckets of saliva in order for it to represent any risk! Since infectious individuals may be unaware of their status and cannot be identified in the first few years of infection, all people exposed to routes of infection are at risk and should engage in health-protective behaviours.

Treatments for AIDS are being developed but prevention continues to be the best strategy for promoting health in this context. However, most evidence suggests that the health promotion programmes attempted so far have been largely unsuccessful. Worldwide the number of infected individuals is still increasing and, although infection in the UK appears to have reached a plateau, more people are still becoming infected. One group for whom the risk of infection is still increasing is intravenous drug users (IVDUs), because blood contact via non-sterile equipment is a route to infection. They are therefore a key target for health education programmes. The development of such programmes has much to learn from the failure of early campaigns. We will look at these now.

When awareness of AIDS first emerged in the early 1980s the highest risk groups were considered to be homosexual males and intravenous drug users. Unprotected sexual intercourse carries a high risk of transmission (especially for the recipient), so early campaigns used fear-arousing appeals to attempt to encourage safer practices, emphasising non-penetrative sex and cutting down the number of sexual partners. The campaigns relied on posters, leaflet drops to households and information provided via television, radio and print media. Despite the high profile of these campaigns, young people still reported a sense of invulnerability to HIV. The campaigns did result in some increase in knowledge about HIV and AIDS, but this was not always accurate as lay beliefs and stereotypes affected they way in which people interpreted new information. So, although considerable information was available, few people altered their behaviour. Woodcock et al (1992) reported that participants offered justifications for high-risk behaviours such as believing that the risk of AIDS had been blown out of proportion or that their partners were not promiscuous. Temoshok et al (1987) compared the beliefs of gay, bisexual and heterosexual men about HIV. The gay and bisexual men had higher levels of knowledge about HIV than heterosexual men and some studies have found a change in the behaviour of gay and bisexual men to reduce risk (eg Curran et al, 1985), although many continued with unsafe sex (Kelly et al, 1990). In contrast, no change was identified by Simkins and Ebenhage (1984) in the heterosexual population.

More recent campaigns have concentrated on safer sex and the use of condoms as a barrier against HIV infection. Importantly, they have also attempted to change the behaviour of heterosexuals, who are currently the fastest growing risk group. The World Health Organisation estimates that more than 90 per cent of new HIV infections are the result of heterosexual transmission. The General Household Survey, comparing British households between 1983 and 1991, indicated a small increase in the use of condoms, especially by younger people. One reason for the reluctance of heterosexuals to change their

Figure 23.8a Early AIDS awareness campaigns used fear – arousing appeals and provided information

Figure 23.8 b Recent campaigns have focused on changing behaviour and beliefs about risk

Our Healthier Nation

The governmental consultation paper 'Our Healthier Nation' states, under the heading 'publicity campaigns' that:

'The Government will continue to use publicity campaigns on issues such as occupational health, road safety, drink-driving, anti-drugs initiatives, safe sex, and smoking.'

Design a publicity campaign on one of the topics listed above using the ideas in this chapter. Write an accompanying document to the government justifying your choice of strategies.

behaviour is the mistaken belief that AIDS is limited to minority groups (homosexuals or intravenous drug users). This myth of invulnerability results in people denying that they are at risk so failing to alter their health behaviours appropriately. Another consequence of the myth is that it perpetuates a climate of blame directed at those groups and a stigmatisation of people with AIDS (Pitts & Phillips, 1998).

Skills training, as discussed earlier in the chapter (pages 288–9), is an alternative health promotion approach. Kelly et al (1989) employed a behavioural intervention with a group of gay men. This included risk reduction information, sexual assertiveness training and the promotion of social support groups to discourage high-risk behaviours. Compared to controls on a waiting list, those who were randomly assigned to participate reported greatly reduced unsafe sexual behaviours and this change had been maintained by the follow-up eight months later.

Self-empowerment models of health promotion offer an alternative strategy to that proposed by social cognition theories (such as HBM and TPB). The aim of the *self-empowerment approach* is to give the individual the information and skills to make healthy choices through the ability to control their physical, social and internal environments (Marks et al, 2000). In addition to skills training (discussed above and on pages 288–9), other techniques employed include assertiveness training, group work, problem solving and educational drama. This technique has been used with young people in a range of HIV-preventative interventions. The techniques used by Abraham and Sheeran (1994) included:

- rehearsing the interactions involved in situations such as buying condoms;
- rehearsing the possible interactions in sexual negotiations;
- questioning sexual scripts where negotiation is prevented;
- peer education programmes;
- programmes aimed to identify and overcome personal obstacles to HIV prevention.

Such initiatives, Abraham and Sheeran argue, offer the opportunity to develop skills and promote self-efficacy, which is a good predictor of behavioural intention and behaviour (Bandura, 1992). This technique probably offers a more powerful approach than simply providing information to raise awareness or attempting to manipulate attitudes.

Smoking education programmes

Anti-smoking campaigns

Anti-smoking campaigns tend to change attitudes but not behaviour. They encourage people to want to give up, but do not increase success. They do, however, have some benefits. They provide information; most smokers now know it is bad for them and have instilled an anti-smoking attitude in the general population that can help smokers who are trying to quit. When many smokers, affected by the same advertising campaign, decide to quit together they create for themselves a supportive social network, which is central

interactive angles

Find out about World AIDS Day or AIDS Awareness Week health campaigns using the Internet or local health promotion resources. Looking at the way the materials used have been designed, can you justify their approaches using the health belief model or the theory of planned behaviour? See if you can develop and implement a programme for raising AIDS awareness at your school or college. Prepare a briefing document explaining the strategies you would like to employ.

to their success. Advertising campaigns are also important in stopping non-smoking adults from taking up the habit (Warner and Murt, 1982).

Prevention programmes

While advertising campaigns may be effective in stopping the potential adult smoker, these individuals have already managed to resist smoking during adolescence. Why do increasing numbers of young people still take up smoking despite their early exposure to dissuasive material?

Effectiveness of prevention programmes may depend on their timing. The concept of a window of vulnerability suggests that there is an age at which children or young adults are likely to begin to abuse drugs. For nicotine dependence, this occurs when children are first exposed to their peers smoking. School anti-smoking campaigns should therefore target this age group.

Workplace smoking

Prevention can also be exercised through banning smoking. This is typical of many workplaces and educational buildings. Parry et al (2000) investigated the effectiveness of a smoking ban implemented in a Scottish university. The potential benefits of such a ban would be to:

- reduce opportunities for smokers to smoke so they may cut down;
- protect non-smokers from the effects of passive smoking;
- reduce smoking-related litter.

Bans may either restrict areas available for smoking, for instance by providing a designated area, or prohibit smoking within the buildings. The latter was chosen in this case.

The result, however, was that smokers congregated at entrances (where littering increased) and, as a result, the profile of smoking within the university was raised rather than lowered. In addition, perceived discrimination against smokers resulted in increased sympathy for them. So, while the objective of improving air quality inside the buildings had been achieved, any reduction in smoking by staff needed to be approached in a different way.

Social inoculation

Evans et al (1988) proposed social influence intervention as a preventative measure to reduce uptake of smoking by school children. This suggests that smoking is acquired, at least in part, by modelling the behaviour of others. When children see other individuals apparently enjoying what they know to be high-risk behaviours, their fears are reduced and the potential positive consequences enhanced. To counter this, children should be exposed to high-status, non-smoking models (Evans, 1976). This would be more effective in a context of behavioural inoculation. This, like vaccination, exposes the individual to a weakened dose of the offending agent in order for them to develop resistance against it. In this context children could be allowed to develop their own (strong) counter-arguments against a (weak) message in favour of drug use.

Taking smoking as an example, three stages follow from Evans's social influence intervention programme:

- information about the negative effects of smoking should be presented in a way that appeals to adolescents. This needs to focus on the immediate disadvantages, which are tangible to teenagers, such as smelling of smoke, being unpleasant to kiss, having yellow fingers or the cost (ie raise perception of barriers);

- positive images of non-smokers must convey independence and self-reliance. These raise adolescents' expectations of themselves as independent thinkers, while depicting smokers as vulnerable to advertising (ie raise perception of benefits);

- the peer group should facilitate non-smoking rather than smoking. This can be achieved using older, respected, non-smoking students to convey information about how to resist the temptation to smoke when invited (ie alter subjective norms).

In assessing the effectiveness of such programmes, Elder et al (1993) found that the participants had learned how to refuse cigarettes, but this did not relate to cigarette use, that is, the adolescents had learned how to say no but continued to smoke. Flay et al (1992) suggest that intervention programmes are only effective in stopping experimental smokers, who would cease of their own accord anyway. They do not tackle the problem of those destined to become adult smokers. An alternative is to teach life skills (see pages 288–9), enhancing the self-esteem of adolescents in order to bolster their ability to resist peer pressure to smoke. This technique appears to be as effective as intervention programmes (Botvin et al, 1980).

An application of Flay's inoculation model employed in the US is peer resistance training. This aims to help children to resist pressure to use drugs by teaching refusal skills and reinforcing group norms against drug abuse.

Benefits from such schemes include improved self-esteem and communication and delayed onset of alcohol, cigarette and cannabis use. However, these initial gains tend not to persist for longer than a year (McAlister et al, 1980). In Britain, peer education is used to encourage youngsters to take responsibility to achieve and sustain a drug-free lifestyle. Messages from peers are arguably more effective with young people than more traditional health education from adults (Quirk et al, 1993).

where to now?

- Tones K. & Tilford S. (2001) *Health promotion: effectiveness, efficiency and equity.* Cheltenham: Nelson Thornes. This text provides a wealth of information about health promotion and its application to a variety of settings.

- Rachel's Story. A 22-minute video about the life and death from a heroin overdose of Rachel Whitear. This shock-tactic video is an example of the failure of fear-arousing health promotion material.

- www.ash.org.uk is the Action on Smoking and Health website. It provides information on all kinds of support for people trying to give up smoking.

- www.quit.org.uk also provide practical advice for giving up.

- http://smoking.netdoctor.co.uk provides a free 90-day email advice programme on stopping smoking.

- www.avert.org/newsukhist.htm is a collection of HIV and AIDS related news reports from the UK.

- www.avert.org/historyi.htm provides a pictorial history of AIDS from 1986–99, covering health education campaigns.

for and against

health promotion

+ mass media appeals have the potential to reach large numbers of people

+ promotion can be based on strategies developed from health behaviour models, improving their effectiveness

− despite their coverage, television campaigns to reduce alcohol and drug abuse have been unsuccessful (Morrison et al, 1976)

− campaigns may fail because people are unwilling to believe that they are vulnerable to health risks

− even when people accept the existence of health risks this may not be sufficient to motivate a change in behaviour

− the factual approach to drug education has been criticised as simplistic. It ignores personality and social factors such as drug availability, and promotion in the case of cigarettes (Nutbeam et al, 1993)

+ research with specific target populations can identify a focus for campaigns (such as reducing barriers or changing subjective norms) rather than just providing information about dangers

− by making people aware of their responsibility for their own health, health education may be engendering a culture of blame (Stroebe, 2000). Information fuels arguments such as 'I've looked after myself and am healthy, you are ill therefore it must be your own fault'. This is characteristic of the effects of AIDS campaigns

− even when campaigns are successful at transmitting the intended message, they may fail because people find it hard to act on their intentions

− evaluation of drug-related health promotion schemes is often confounded by contamination between groups through peer influence, advertising and the media (Nutbeam et al, 1990)

Conclusions

Primary prevention strategies aim to encourage positive health behaviours by providing information that warns of risks to health without inducing fear. Such strategies can be used to improve health behaviours relating to hygiene and nutrition. In the case of healthy eating, biological explanations suggest that genetic factors affect our health, such as the predisposition to obesity. Metabolic rate, fat cells and weight all appear to have inherited components. Eating habits may also be acquired, by classical or operant conditioning and through social learning. Foods may become associated with emotional states and may act as a reinforcer (or punisher). We may imitate the amount or type of food that role models consume. Cultural factors may determine aspects of health behaviours, such as the types of food we eat and when we eat them.

The health belief model attempts to explain health behaviours by considering the way in which we process information relating to health issues. It suggests that, in relation to any health behaviour, we have five central beliefs about our vulnerability, the seriousness of the condition, potential barriers to and benefits of taking evasive action and cues that trigger the behaviour. When these variables favour action over inaction, positive health behaviour should occur. This explanation can successfully account for preventative behaviours such as immunisations and self-examination, and for attendance or non-attendance at screening tests.

The theory of planned behaviour suggests that health behaviours are determined by the intention to act and the extent of perceived behavioural control. When an individual both intends to engage in a health behaviour and feels that they have the power to do so, they will take action. Intention is determined by factors such as knowledge, attitudes and subjective norms, while perceived behavioural control may be affected by self-efficacy as well as intrinsic motivation and external factors. The theory can help to direct health campaigns by identifying why people fail to engage in health behaviours, for example, to promote breast feeding or condom use.

Health education programmes can therefore be based on the findings of research, not only on the success of previous campaigns, but also on the predictions of the health belief model and the theory of planned action. In addition to, and perhaps more importantly than, providing information to raise awareness, health promotion programmes need to change attitudes to health and health behaviours.

what do you know ?

1 The following factors could affect an individual who is thinking about giving up smoking: the existence of many non-smoking restaurants; the belief that smoky clothes is unpleasant; a desire to combat the effects of smoking on the individual's own asthma; the knowledge that they can stop themselves from starting again once they have said they've given up.

(a) Describe the theory of planned behaviour.

(b) Explain how each of the factors listed would relate to the theory of planned behaviour.

2 Rise in sexual diseases blamed on young people's complacency:

> Sexually transmitted diseases are spreading at a faster rate than they were before the hard-hitting Aids campaign of the 1990s because young people have become complacent… The report, *Sexually Transmitted Infections* (STIs), found the rise in infections was worst among people aged 18 to 24, and it urged television soaps and dramas to include stories where characters catch STIs. Far greater investment in health services was also needed to allow GPs to screen for [sexually transmitted diseases]… The Department of Health said a safe sex information programme would be announced later this year.
>
> From *Independent*, 27 February 2002

(a) Using the health belief model, explain how the following excepts from the article above can be justified:

(i) the complacency of young people;

(ii) the importance of television soaps and dramas;

(iii) the role of GP screening services.

(b) What advice would you give, based on the health belief model, to assist in the development of a new safe sex information programme?

3 (a Define primary prevention.

(b) Discuss how primary prevention strategies can be implemented in relation to **either** hygiene **or** nutrition.

4 Health behaviours can be approached from a range of psychological perspectives including biological, behaviourist and cultural explanations.

(a) Describe **two** of these perspectives in relation to health behaviour.

(b) Evaluate these two perspectives.

(c) Compare and contrast the two perspectives that you have discussed.

5 (a) Using one example of a health campaign, such as AIDS or smoking education programmes, describe the techniques that have been employed.

(b) Discuss how the chosen campaign has tried to raise awareness and change attitudes relating to health.

24 Personal space and territoriality

what's

In this chapter we will examine the role that personal space and territory play in human behaviour. For example, what happens when somebody invades that space? Why do humans need territory? We will also examine individual differences in the need for personal space including gender differences and cultural differences.

Personal space

What is personal space?

Think about how it feels to have someone stand very close to you, or what it is like to be on a crowded bus or train. It probably makes you feel a little stressed and irritable, and that is because someone is invading your *personal space*. Katz (1937) was the first person to discuss the term 'personal space'. Bell et al (1996, page 275) define it as a '... portable, invisible boundary surrounding us, into which others may not trespass. It regulates how closely we interact with others, moves with us, and expands and contracts according to the situation in which we find ourselves.' Thus our personal space is like a bubble. It changes shape and size depending on the social context.

interactive angles

Describe how you would feel on a crowded bus, when you are with your best friend or when you are meeting someone for the first time. How does your personal space differ in each situation? Does the 'bubble' around you change for each situation?

Hall (1963) distinguished between zones of personal space (called *spatial zones* by Hall) based around interpersonal relationships that we may have.

Theories of personal space

There are numerous theories as to why we require personal space. Bell et al (1996) describe four main theories:

Table 24.1 Spatial zones

Distance	Usual activities and relationships	Input to the senses
Intimate (0.0–1.5 feet [0.0–0.45 m])	Contact is intimate (for example, comforting another or having sex). Physical sports such as judo and wrestling allow invasion of the intimate zone	Touch is the basic mode for communication. We are intensely aware of other sensory information. Such as smell and heat emitted from another person
Personal (1.5–4.0 feet [0.45–1.2 m])	Friends are allowed to get within this zone, especially those who are close to us. Your usual everyday interactions will trespass into this zone too	Speech is the key source of sensory input from others (more so than touch). However, research has shown vision to be a key source of sensory input too (see Gale et al, 1975, page 8)
Social (4–12 feet [0.45–3.66 m])	People we do not really know personally, but whom we meet quite regularly, are allowed in this zone. Business-like contacts are also allowed to enter this zone	Sensory input from other people is now rathe minimal. Vision is less crisp, speech is still easily processed but touch is now impossible
Public (more than 12 feet [3.66 m] away)	This is for formal contact; for instance, for someone giving a public speech	Very little sensory input, usually only from speech. Non-verbal communication takes over as a main source of information

- **Arousal theory**. When people invade our personal space we usually become aroused, that is, we develop a heightened awareness. As a result, we try to make sense of this arousal and this dictates how much space we feel that we require. For example, when we meet someone for the first time (such as on a date), we may either feel good or nervous. Either of these situations could arouse us. In the first situation (feeling good), we may require less personal space than in the second situation (feeling nervous), as we have understood why we are aroused and acted upon that reason.

- **Behavioural constraint theory**. According to this theory, we require personal space because, without it, we feel that our behavioural freedom is being taken away. We experience this when people get too close.

- **Overload theory**. We maintain an optimum personal space for each situation in order to avoid being bombarded with too much information. This over-stimulation needs to be avoided otherwise we cannot cope with the situation because we are too busy processing stimuli such as facial details, smells and touch.

- **Stress theory**. This theory suggests that we keep personal spaces so that we do not get stressed about close proximity. Basically, it subsumes the above theories into a more general explanation. Chapter 27 looks at the stressful effects of crowding.

interactive angles

Draw the shape below several times on separate sheets of paper. Imagine that you are standing at the intersection of the lines, facing in the direction of '4'. How close would you allow someone to stand to you before you felt that they were invading your space? Mark across each line in order from one to eight, then join up the marks. Repeat this for several different scenarios – a friend, a stranger, your teacher, someone you fancy. You could also try comparing males and females or the effects of different contexts: at a party, at work etc. Look at the different shapes that are produced.

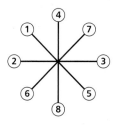

What problems can you see with the technique?

The technique described in above is called the *comfortable interpersonal distance scale* (CIDS) (Duke & Nowicki, 1972). It is one way to measure the personal space that people require in different circumstances. The technique allows participants to identify when the interpersonal distance become 'too close' in a range of imaginary situations. It is a good technique because it is ethically sound; it does not place people in unpleasant situations. However, people could lie when completing the CIDS, not imagine the scenario very well or be inaccurate at judging the distance at which they would become uncomfortable. Also, because it is an artificial set-up, the findings may not generalise to everyday behaviour.

Individual and cultural differences in personal space

Individual variables seem to affect our levels of tolerance to having our personal space invaded these include prior knowledge of the situation, perceived danger, gender and culture. In addition, Sanders (1978) discovered that personal space is affected by the menstrual cycle. Females ranging from 17 to 27 years of age completed a menstrual cycle questionnaire and it was discovered that they tended to maintain a larger personal space during the menstrual period compared to the approximate middle of the cycle.

Prior knowledge and personal space

Prior knowledge about a situation affects the amount of personal space that we wish to have. Feroleto and Gounard (1975) examined how close individuals would sit to an interviewer in relation on their expectations about the situation. Twenty participants took part in the study; 10 college students and 10 older adults from a residential home. In both groups of participants, half were told to expect an unpleasant interaction and half were told to expect a pleasant interaction. Those who were told to expect an unpleasant situation sat significantly further away compared to those expecting a pleasant situation. The older adults seated themselves further away in both conditions (unpleasant and pleasant). This would appear to indicate that older adults require larger personal spaces, as they may feel more threatened in an interpersonal situation.

Perceived danger and personal space

Skorjanc (1991) examined the personal space of participants in relation to the perceived violence level of a criminal. Participants in the study were primed (given information beforehand) to believe that a person they were about to meet in a room was a violent offender, a non-violent offender or someone who had never committed a criminal offence. The measurement of personal space was taken as the number of seats away from the 'criminal' that each individual participant chose to sit. The results showed that, on average, the participants sat much closer to the person they had been told was a non-offender compared to the two 'criminals'. There was little difference in the mean number of seats between the participant and either the violent or the non-violent offender. Therefore, attitudes about individuals can affect our personal space preferences in social situations.

Gender and personal space

Gender has long been assumed to be one area in which differences are marked with respect to personal space. Early research showed that females have a smaller personal space, especially in same-sex interactions (Andersen & Leibowitz, 1978; Larsen & LeRoux, 1984). Maier and Ernest (1978) asked adults to rate levels of touch in a series of hypothetical situations. Consistent findings emerged: both males and females believed that people, irrespective of gender, would prefer to be touched by a female. Also, both genders reported that females place more emphasis on touch compared to males. However, observational studies have reported there is no difference in the number of times a man and woman touch (Henley, 1973; Willis et al, 1978; Greenbaum & Rosenfeld, 1980; Major, 1981). On the other hand, Bell et al (1996) noted that females interact at a closer distance compared to males when with people that they like or find attractive.

So, in some studies females are found to be more positive about same-gender touch than males. However, an examination of potential cultural differences in same-gender touch has suggested that there are consistent differences between the genders. Willis and Rawdon (1994) examined female and male students from Chile, Spain, Malaysia and the United States. They all completed the same-sex touch scale (developed by Larsen and LeRoux, 1984), that measures the importance we place on touch in interactions with the same sex: the higher the score, the more importance was placed on touch in same-sex interactions. The average scores for each gender in each nationality are shown in the table below, out of a maximum score of 100:

Nationality	Female	Male
United States	70.6	58.3
Malaysia	54.3	46.1
Chile	64.6	56.8
Spain	69.8	61.9

As can be seen, irrespective of culture, females had more positive scores towards same-sex touch compared to males. With respect to culture, the Malaysian students had the most negative scores. The Spanish males were

the most tolerant of all males of same-sex touch. Of all groups, females from the US had the most positive scores. Of course, the research has its limitations, in that the measure was via a questionnaire rather than actual observation of interactions. However, it does identify cultural and gender differences in personal space.

Figure 24.1 There are cultural differences in personal space distances

Little (1968) examined cultural differences over 19 different social situations in a sample of Americans, Swedes, Greeks, Italians and Scots. The participants had to place dolls at distances that reflected where they would stand in real social situations. The situations that they had to assess included: two good friends talking about a pleasant topic; a shop owner discussing the weather with his assistant; two people talking about the best place to shop; and two strangers talking about an unpleasant topic. Below is a graph of the average

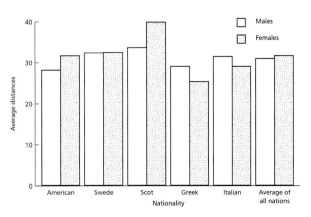

Figure 24.2 Average distances over 19 social situations (source: Little, 1968)

distances (in twelfths of an inch [1 inch = 2.54 cm]) over the 19 different social situations.

As can be seen, on average, the Greeks placed the dolls at shorter distances, while the Scots placed them at greater distances, compared to the other nationalities.

Consequences of invading personal space

The effects of invasion of personal space have been investigated in a variety of ways. One study involved directly invading the personal space of men in a public lavatory to see if this affected arousal levels.

classic
research

a lav-oratory experiment!

Middlemist R.D., Knowles E.S. and Matter C.F. (1976) Personal space invasion in the lavatory: suggestive evidence for arousal. *Journal of Personality and Social Psychology* **33(5): 541–6**

aim: to investigate the proposal that invasion of personal space produces arousal.

procedure: the setting was a men's public lavatory. According to the researchers, this was an ideal set-up as 'norms for privacy' were already in place (the spaces between the urinals), so the effect that distance had on arousal could be easily measured. The men's public lavatory contained three urinals. Sixty participants were randomly assigned to one of three conditions: (1) the experimenter stood immediately next to the participant; (2) the experimenter stood at the other end of the three urinals to the participant; or (3) the experimenter was absent. Two key measures were taken. The first was a measure of how quickly the participant began to urinate. The second measure was how much time he took to urinate.

findings: the closer the experimenter stood, the longer it took for the participant to begin urination. Also, the closer the experimenter stood, the less time it took the participant to 'complete' urination.

conclusion: the evidence suggests that invasion of personal space in men produces physiological changes associated with arousal. (The sympathetic autonomic nervous system arousal relaxes the bladder therefore inhibiting micturation. This is caused by the social stimulus of company affecting the autonomic nervous system via the central nervous system.) The more the personal space was invaded, the more aroused the men became. However, the ethics of the research must be questioned!

Another study that examined arousal levels, linked to the invasion of personal space, was conducted by Gale et al (1975). They measured both *direct invasion* (closeness of a person) and *indirect invasion* (looking at the participant). For the 18 participants, an electroencephalogram (EEG) reading was used as a measure of arousal. The conditions involved a male experimenter either looking directly at the participant, or looking away, at distances of 2, 4, 8, 16 or 32 feet (0.6, 1.2, 2.4, 4.8 or 9.7 m) from the participant. The results showed that the greatest level of EEG arousal was when the experimenter was looking at the participant from a distance of 2 feet (0.6 m) away. The EEG arousal measures diminished the further away the experimenter was from the participant. However, for each distance, the EEG readings showed more arousal when the experimenter was looking at the participant compared to when the experimenter was looking away.

Gender differences in the responses to invasion have been found, for example, in a classic study by Fisher and Byrne (1975).

classic
research

girls just wanna have space!

Fisher J.D. & Byrne D. (1975) Too close for comfort: sex differences in response to invasions of personal space. *Journal of Personality and Social Psychology* **32(1): 15–21**

---

aim: there were two main aims of this study: (1) to examine gender differences in the invasion of personal space; and (2) to examine how gender affects the ways in which we indicate to others the boundaries of our personal space.

procedure: for the first aim, Fisher and Byrne's confederates (people who knew what the experiment was about) invaded the personal space of 62 males and 63 females in a university library in a number of ways. They either sat next to the participants, sat one seat away from the participants or sat opposite the participants, for five minutes. After the invasion had taken place, Fisher and Byrne asked each participant to complete a questionnaire about the experience. Questions were asked about how the participants felt during the invasion of their personal space (for example, how happy they felt, how attracted they were to the confederate, their perceived level of crowding and so on).

For the second aim, a different researcher was used, who was not told about the aim of the research (this is called the 'single-blind' technique). The researcher had to observe 33 males and 33 females and record where they placed their personal belongings on a library table.

findings: from the first study, distinct gender differences emerged. Males disliked being invaded by someone approaching from opposite them, but did not mind someone invading the space next to them. For females, the opposite pattern emerged: people could invade the space opposite to them, but they disliked invasion when someone sat next to them. The following tables of means highlight this trend across all measures taken on the questionnaire:

Table 24.2 Happiness and attractiveness rating

		Sitting next to	**Sitting opposite**
Happiness rating – the higher the score, the more happy the participant was	Male	29.15	23.57
	Female	23.46	26.79
Attractiveness rating – the higher the score the more attracted the participant was to an opposite-sex confederate	Male	10.99	9.14
	Female	9.87	10.14
Perceived level of crowding – the higher the score, the more the participant felt crowded	Male	11.48	17.04
	Female	16.60	14.76

The results of the second study backed up those reported in the first study. Males were more likely to place their personal belongings in front of them, while females were more likely to place personal belongings next to them – both males and females were setting up barriers to defend their least favourite direction from which they could be invaded.

The chart below shows the number of 'barrier placements' observed on the table at which the participants were seated:

	Barrier next to person	Barrier opposite person
Male	9	15
Female	17	6

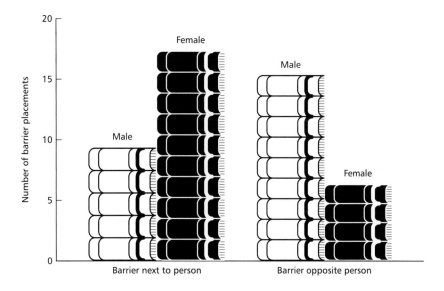

Figure 24.3 Number of barrier placements

conclusion: from this study, it is clear that males do not like to have the space in front of them invaded. Females do not like to have the space next to them invaded. Both genders defend this invasion by setting up barriers to stop people getting too close.

According to Sinha and Sinha (1991), lack of personal space (through continual invasion) may well affect our ability to complete tasks. They manipulated social density by changing the number of people in a room (the higher the social density, the more chance there is that your personal space will be invaded) and asked the participants to perform difficult or easy tasks. They also measured the personal space of all participants using a *stop-distance technique*: that is, a person approaches and the participant says 'Stop' when he or she begins to feel uncomfortable. The social density and the size of the individual's preferred personal space had effects on performance of difficult tasks, but not simple ones. Those participants who preferred a large personal space perceived a high social density to be more crowded than to those who had a small personal space. This could be because the participants who had large personal spaces were more likely to perceive that their personal space was being invaded. Those with a small personal space, however, would not perceive invasion so readily therefore would report less crowding. These perceptions only differed in difficult tasks. During a simple task all participants, irrespective of the size of their personal space, perceived little crowding.

Kaya and Erkíp (1999) were interested in the levels of personal space that are comfortable when we withdraw money from an automatic teller machine (ATM, or cash-point). They observed people waiting to withdraw money under low-density and high-density conditions. A total of 100 observations were conducted under both density conditions. They also interviewed a selection of participants. Personal space was predictably invaded more often under high-density conditions, but also if the participant perceived the space to be narrow around the ATM (these perceptions were measured using a questionnaire that asked them about the space in the ATM hall). There was, however, no difference in the amount of personal space that the participants felt was necessary under the differing density conditions. People wanted privacy when withdrawing money. Gender did not play a main role in the need for personal space in this situation, although participants of opposite genders kept greater distances between themselves and other ATM users. One gender difference reported was that females' approach to males was more distant compared to males' approach to females (for example, in the low-density condition, 76 per cent of females kept more than 46 cm away from males, while for males approaching females this figure was only 46 per cent).

Brodsky et al (1999) investigated invasions of personal space in real-life courtroom trials. They found that attorneys were more likely to invade the personal space of witnesses during cross-examinations (questioning a person who you are not defending) than during direct examinations (questioning a person who you are defending). This technique might be assumed to be intended to make the witnesses 'crack under pressure', but Brodsky et al noted that this technique was ineffective.

Territory

What is territory?

Bell et al (1996, page 304) define territoriality as follows: '… (it) can be viewed as a set of behaviours and cognitions a person or group exhibits, based on perceived ownership of physical space'. This may be permanent, as in owning a house, or temporary, as in controlling your office space but not directly 'owning' it.

Altman (1975) noted that we have three different types of territory (see table 24.3 below).

Table 24.3 Three types of territory

Type of territory	Occupation of territory/ perception of ownership	The extent to which we 'personalise' the territory
Primary territory (for example, own home, office space, bedroom)	*High* degree of occupation and perception of ownership. We believe that we permanently own the territory, and others believe this too	The territory is personalised in great detail, so that the owner has complete control, and others recognise this almost immediately after entering the territory. Uninvited intrusion can have serious consequences
Secondary territory (for example, a classroom)	*Medium* degree of occupation and perception of ownership. We believe that we are one of only a limited number of users of the territory	Personalisation occurs to some extent, but only when the occupancy of the territory is legitimate. For example, within about one month of a new class starting, each person will have his or her own seat, in which he or she will usually stay for the rest of the year. That person legitimately 'owns' that seat during every lesson
Public territory (for example, an area on a beach, or a seat on a bus)	*Low* degree of occupation and perception of ownership. We believe that we are one of countless people who use this piece of territory	Personalisation tends to be temporary, as we may not revisit the territory for some time. We tend not to defend this territory in the way we would if it were primary or secondary territory

The functions of territory: social organisation and maintenance of privacy

So, on the basis of what we have seen about the importance of territory, what could be the functions of territory for humans?

Territory as a social organiser

Taylor (1978) suggests that one of the functions of territory is to allow us to organise ourselves sensibly (see table 24.4 below).

Table 24.4 Importance and functions of territory

Type of social situation	The function of the territory in terms of organisation
A public place (for example, on a beach or in a library)	It organises a person's space. It allows you to try to dictate the amount of personal space that you would like within that territory
Primary territory (for example, your bedroom or your desk at work)	It again organises a person's space. It allows you to tell others that you need some solitude. It allows for intimate behaviour to occur. It also allows an outlet for self-expression and personal identity
Small groups, usually face-to-face (for example, with close friends)	It organises the function of the group. It can aid communication between the group members, with both verbal and non-verbal cues being picked up more easily. Also, 'home court' advantage can play a role (see Schwartz and Barsky, 1977). That is, you feel more confident with things when they are part of your group's territory and not another person's. For example, in sport, most teams will perform better when playing 'at home'
Communities and the neighbourhood	It organises larger areas of territory as an 'in-group' area or the 'in place to be'. It gives a sense of belonging to a larger group of people. You sense that you can trust the people who commonly use the territory

Is there a similar sense of territory in the workplace? We spend a great deal of our time there, so is territory important for job satisfaction? Meijanders et al (2000) examined whether having your own 'personal' desk or having to share a desk space had an effect on job satisfaction.

what's new?

hotdesking

Meijanders et al (2000) showed that primary territory does have an effect on personal identity, as proposed by Taylor (1978). They examined the regulation of privacy in an office that was non-territorial (that is, where workers use any available desk that happens to be free at a particular time – this is called **hotdesking**) compared to a traditional 'one person per desk' office. The main results showed that employees in both types of office were satisfied with the set-ups. However, the way in which this satisfaction was maintained differed between the two groups of employees. Compared to the employees in the traditional office, those in the non-territorial office placed less emphasis on their personal identities at work. There was no difference between the group identity levels for both sets of employees. This can be explained by Taylor's (1978) model, noted above, as the employees in the non-territorial office were 'deprived' of a definite territory and therefore the opportunity to assert their personal identities. This had a detrimental effect on satisfaction. The consequences that this might have with regard to future job satisfaction, or whether it predicted the length of time that someone might spend in their job, were not reported.

Another avenue of research has looked into whether personalising your office space (for example, with photographs and personal items) has an effect on job satisfaction. Wells (2000) examined the role of personalisation on satisfaction in 20 companies in California.

research
now

a messy office is a happy office!

Wells M.M. (2000) Office clutter or meaningful personal displays: the role of office personalisation in employee and organizational well-being. *Journal of Environmental Psychology* **20: 239–55**

aim: to examine the role of territory in the workplace, especially whether personalisation of office space has an effect on employee well-being and organisational well-being (for example, how much a person likes to work in a particular environment, the morale of workers, and so on).

procedure: Wells surveyed 338 office workers from 20 companies in Orange County, California, on the amount of personalisation allowed at work and how they personalised their own office spaces.

findings: for employee well-being, three aspects played a role:

- As the number of personal items displayed on or around a desk increased, so did satisfaction with the work environment.

- There was an association between how much the employee would like to personalise and how much was allowed.

- The more employees were allowed to personalise, the more they were satisfied with the work environment.

Also, satisfaction with the work environment was strongly related to job satisfaction. Those who were happy with their physical work environment were more likely to be satisfied with their job. For organisational well-being, the companies that allowed more personalisation of work space reported a more positive work environment, a more positive social climate among employees, greater levels of worker morale and reduced staff turnover. Finally, females tended to personalise more with items related to personal relationships (especially family, friends and pets), and had more trinkets and more plants compared to males. The only aspect of personalisation where males exhibited higher levels than females was with regard to sport.

conclusion: this research shows the importance of primary territory – as defined by Altman (1975) and then Taylor (1978) – in the formation of a personal identity, and the subsequent satisfaction of being able to show it to other people.

Territory as a means of maintaining privacy

A sense of territorial ownership appears to be important for many individuals and families. Peluso (2000) examined low-income groups in Brazil, with the idea that a sense of territory to protect the 'self' from the adversities of outside life would be evident, as there appear to be 'grand' ideas about the potential benefit, intimacy and privacy of owning a home. Indeed, this is what Peluso discovered when she interviewed low-income families. Some of the poorest inhabitants of Brasilia considered their houses to be comfortable and adequate for a private life, an important function of territory. However, many of the interviewees did indicate a desire for improvement by stating that they would like, among other things, a bigger and better home. This shows that people want territory to allow them to feel protected.

The homeless population of Rio de Janeiro also shows levels of territorial behaviour that are linked to home ownership (dos Santos & Duarte, 2000). Observations of homeless people revealed many symbolic forms of behaviour that were indicative of territorial occupation. For example, the use of barriers or urban equipment allowed the homeless to 'map out' bedrooms, bathrooms and

Figure 24.4 Having a personalised desk can improve job satisfaction

kitchens. Therefore, a sense of territory appears to be important in a variety of circumstances.

Conclusions

Personal space appears to be needed for a variety of reasons, and it changes depending on the circumstances in which we find ourselves. Research has revealed gender differences and cultural differences in personal space. Psychologists have also examined our reactions to invasion of the personal space around us. Again, gender differences have been reported. Invasion of personal space also appears to cause us stress and to affect our ability to complete tasks. In the courtroom, it is used of by lawyers – but to no real effect – when cross-examining witnesses, in an attempt to intimidate them.

Territory also plays a key role in our behaviour, allowing us to organise the space around us and feel a sense of personal and social identity. Cirumstances that reduce territory at work – for example, 'hotdesking' – make employees place less emphasis on personal identities at work. Allowing personalisation of territory has a positive effect on worker morale.

what do you know?

1 (a) Define personal space.

   (b) Discuss **one** individual and **one** cultural difference in personal space.

2 Distinguish between the concepts of territory and personal space and discuss the consequences of invasion of personal space.

3 'Humans are territorial animals. We use our territories as social organisers and as a means to maintain our privacy.' Discuss the importance of territory and assess **two** functions, such as those mentioned in the quote above, that territories may fulfil for people.

25 The effect of architecture on behaviour

what's ahead?

In this chapter, we will examine the role that architecture plays in our behaviour. The effects of architecture on communication and residential satisfaction will be explored. The work of Oscar Newman on defensible space and its effect on crime and vandalism will be examined with respect to defensible space including the Pruitt-Igoe housing project and the Van Dyke Estate. Finally, we will consider good and bad practice in architectural design.

The effect of architecture on communication

The architecture, design or layout of a room can have a considerable effect on our communication. For example, there are two main types of chair layout that can affect the amount of interaction we have in a room. The first is the sociofugal design. This kind of design is used to keep people apart. It usually features fixed seats that face away from each other such as in airport departure lounges or hospital waiting rooms. The second type is the sociopetal design, which promotes interaction between people, usually with movable seats that are placed facing towards each other. This design can be seen in hotel function rooms and primary school classrooms.

interactive angles

Have a look around your college and make a list of sociofugal and sociopetal designs. What design is used in your library, or your refectory? Do the designs go along with the intended purpose of the room?

Recent research has examined the design of study areas and whether it affects communication, and hence the ability to concentrate and work.

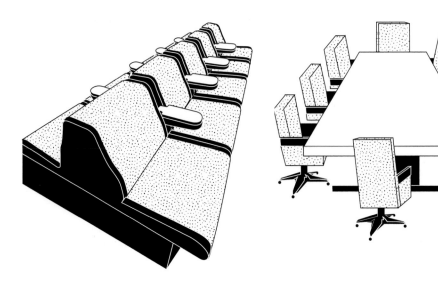

Figure 25.1 Sociofugal and sociopetal designs

research
now

the blues may not make you sad!

Stone N.J. (2001) Designing effective study environments. *Journal of Environmental Psychology,* **21: 179–90**

aim: to examine how a person's ability to study is affected by setting (open plan or private), colour of room (blue, white or red) and type of task (reading or mathematics).

procedure: a total of 144 students took part. Each student was randomly assigned to one of 12 conditions from the combinations of setting, colour and type of material as noted above. The open plan and private settings were as shown opposite:

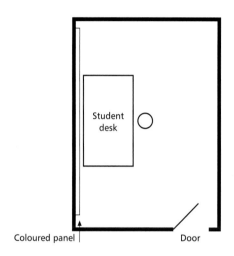

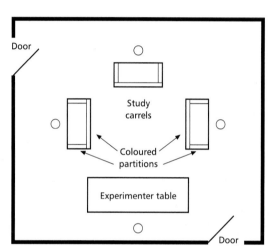

Source: Stone (2001)

In each condition, the participants were either given a mathematics test or a reading comprehension test. After completing the tasks, the participants had to complete questionnaires that measured mood, satisfaction and motivation.

findings: Stone found that there were some differences between the conditions. For example:

● On average, the participants experienced the most positive mood in a blue open-plan room, and experienced the least positive mood in a red open-plan room.

● For the private room, the colour red brought about the most positive mood.

● Participants were the most satisfied with their performance in the white private room and the blue open-plan room.

● There was little difference in the amount of privacy the participants felt they had between the open-plan room and the private room.

● Participants performed significantly worse in the reading task, irrespective of the setting, if the surroundings were red. They performed better in white surroundings.

conclusion: there were some differences between the two settings (open plan and private) on the measures taken. For example, room colour had effects on satisfaction with performance in the tasks and on mood.

The effect of architecture on residential satisfaction

Lawton et al (1975) examined whether there was any relationship between type of residential building (size, sponsorship of building and height of building) and well-being in older adults. They discovered that residents of non-profit-making privately sponsored housing had higher friendship scores and were more involved in activities compared to other types of dwellings. Those in small communities also had high friendship scores alongside higher residential satisfaction and activity levels. However, the cause might have been that friendly people had chosen to live in such places.

The main factor that affected residential satisfaction was the size of the community in terms of number of units. The smaller the number of units, the more satisfied the people were. Height of building had a negative effect on residential satisfaction. That is, those who lived in taller buildings were less satisfied with where they lived.

Studying residential satisfaction in Vietnam, Hanazato (2000) noted the differences between dwellers in two types of housing: pencil-housing (large, privately owned dwellings) and apartments (small, government-run dwellings). The former type of housing is popular, but poor ventilation and lack of building regulations mean that there is a wide range of conditions and, subsequently, of satisfaction levels with the dwelling. In the latter type of housing, satisfaction is increased only with increased space and extensions are often undertaken. Hanazato concluded that there needs to be more control over the housing situation in Hanoi, Vietnam, for there to be overall improvements to dwellings. So, both the condition of the building (for example, ventilation) and the amount of space affects satisfaction with a residence.

The work of Oscar Newman

Newman (1972) introduced the concept of defensible space to psychology, following after the work of Jane Jacobs. The term refers to an area of physical space that can be perceived as clearly belonging to someone. Any visitors to this space would quickly realise that it is someone else's territory. The idea of defensible space was generated because Newman had noted that many 'new' high-rise residential developments of his time had failed, as evidenced by their rapid decay and high crime rates. Newman proposed that this was because people had no control over the secondary territory (see Altman, 1975; see also page 314) within or around the buildings; for example, lobbies, staircases, lifts, parking areas and communal gardens. Residents were not able to feel any ownership of territory surrounding their living quarters. They therefore had a reduced capacity for surveillance over these areas and they could not distinguish between people who lived in the same building as themselves and those who did not. This lack of ownership led to a reduced sense of 'community'.

According to Taylor et al (1984), defensible spaces could reduce crime for a number of reasons:

● Spaces that look 'defended' could well lead potential burglars to believe that the residents will actively respond to them trespassing on this secondary territory.

● Defensible spaces may well increase a 'sense of community', leading to a more cohesive residential group. As a result, people may feel 'safer' and therefore use the defended space more, which will lead to more contact with neighbours. This, in turn, could make people more inclined to intervene if a non-resident enters the defensible space.

● Defensible space may increase people's territorial functioning. As areas become characterised as 'defensible', people will act accordingly and come to the defence of those areas when necessary.

Newman (1972) then argued that if defensible spaces were deliberately designed into new multi-dwelling buildings, residents would feel more ownership over certain areas, and that this would increase informal surveillance and promote some form of cohesion within the community. That is, people would be more likely to 'look out for one another and their properties'. As a result, crime should decrease and a sense of community would be introduced. Newman recommended that certain features in the design of buildings could easily increase the amount of defensible space. These included using boundary markers that would show others where the territory was located. For example, pathways, fences and hedgerows would tell others that the territory was defended. Another approach would be to strategically arrange the windows on a building so that semi-public areas could be watched over by many of the residents. This could help to encourage positive social interaction between members of the community, so that the amount of surveillance increased.

On page 322, we will look at examples that have been shown to be good and bad with respect to Newman's ideas of defensible space.

Newman and Franck (1982) tested the relationship of physical design to crime as outlined in defensible space theory by examining housing developments in America. A total of 2655 residents were surveyed about defensible space. Newman and Franck found some support for the idea that the size of the building affects personal crime and fear of crime; the smaller the building, the lower the fear and reality of criminal activity. This was the case when participants felt control over the spaces around their apartments and used the spaces outside their apart-ment as territorial markers. However, the effect of build-ing size on fears of personal crime was not as strong as Newman had originally hypothesised in his defensible space theory.

Ham-Rowbottom et al (1999) examined defensible space theory by assessing police officer's judgements of the vul-nerability of residences to burglary. Although Newman's original ideas focused on multi-occupancy dwellings, his work has been applied to other types of dwellings (for example, houses).

research now

will your house get burgled?

Ham-Rowbottom K.A., Gifford R. and Shaw K.T. (1999) Defensible space theory and the police: assess-ing the vulnerability of residences to burglary. *Journal of Environmental Psychology* 19: 117–29

aim: to examine how the theory of defensible space applies to police officer's assessments of the vulnerability of different houses to burglary.

procedure: 41 police officers were shown a series of 50 photographs of detached houses. Each house had been scored on 55 physical cues that were believed to be good indicators of defensible space. The police officers had to rate each house's vulnerability to burglary on a seven-point scale, from 'highly likely' to 'not likely'.

findings: a total of 10 physical cues were correlated with less vulnerability to burglary (in order of importance based on correlation coefficients):

- at least three-quarters of the house is visible from the road

- at least three-quarters of the yard is visible from the road

- a glass panel is not located next to the front door

- a garage is present

- the front door is solid, with no glass

- the backyard is separated from the front yard by an actual barrier

- more windows are visible from the road

- the front door is visible from the road

- the distance from the road is less than 20 feet (6 m)

- a neighbour's house is visible in the photograph.

conclusion: it would appear that – as judged by police officers – the more physical barriers there are and the greater the road surveillability is (for example, from windows at the front of the house), the less likely a house is to be burgled. This finding is in line with defensible space theory. According to the police, the more physical barriers there are around a house, the less likely it is that it will become a victim of burglaries and other crimes.

Figure 25.2 Which house do you feel would be more likely to be burgled?

However, defensible space does not always deter burglars. MacDonald and Gifford (1989) surveyed 43 males who had been convicted of breaking and entering. The participants were shown 50 photographs of single-family dwellings and had to rate each one on a seven-point scale of vulnerability to burglary. The houses for which surveillance was easy were rated as less vulnerable to burglary. However, territorial displays (for example, fences) actually increased the attractiveness of the house to burglary. It was argued that these features, designed to deter trespassing as Newman stated, indicated that the house contents might be of value, as the occupants had chosen to defend their space in such an overt way. Also, barriers can help rather than hinder burglars, as they make it easier to climb into the property and can give them somewhere to hide.

Brower et al (1983) identified a problem with defensible space theory: it fails to take account of social factors. They surveyed 40 residents, some of whom perceived that they lived in a high-problem neighbourhood and others who perceived that they lived in a low-problem neighbourhood. The participants were shown pictures of a variety of residential backyards. All participants interpreted pictures with real barriers and plants as having a deterrent towards burglars, because the occupant had strong territorial attitudes. However, for those in a high-problem neighbourhood, the territorial displays were seen as being a less effective deterrent. Therefore, the social context overrode the idea that defensible space would deter people from entering. That is, if the neighbourhood is believed to have a high crime level, defensible space appears to be less important.

It appears that the work of Newman (1972) still has an impact on the design of urban areas. For example, Yildirim and Kulodlu (2000) observed that in Turkey the planning process for urban open areas has to take environmental factors into consideration. If certain factors, such as defensible space, are ignored, this will ultimately lead to the failure of the plans for the building, causing financial and aesthetic damage to the entire project.

Good and bad practice in architectural design

After Newman had proposed the idea of defensible space, researchers examined housing developments and crime rates to see whether his ideas could be translated into the real world.

The Van-Dyke estate

One such examination of defensible space theory looked into two adjacent housing estates in New York City. The two estates were called Van Dyke and Brownsville. The Van Dyke estate consisted of a series of 14-storey buildings, separated by small areas that had little or no defensible space. In contrast, the Brownsville estate consisted of six X-shaped buildings only three storeys high. As a result, the entrances were less frequently used and were easy to watch over; non-residents could be more easily spotted compared to the Van Dyke estate. Within the Brownsville buildings, children played in the hallways and stairwells, and it was common for residents to leave their doors open, again making it easier to protect the immediate space. Due to the greater levels of defensible space in the Brownsville estate, there were stronger bonds between the residents, there was less crime and maintenance costs were reduced.

The Pruitt–Igoe project

Another example that demonstrates poor design with regard to defensible space is the Pruitt–Igoe project in St Louis, USA (Newman, 1972). The estate was built in 1954, with the ethos of 'no wasted space'. The project was constructed to relocate 12,000 people into 43 buildings, each 11 storeys high. The entire complex had 2762 apartments, was expensive to build and had:

- narrow hallways that led to the apartments;
- no semi-private areas in which people could meet (so no areas to oversee);
- wall tiles designed so that graffiti could be easily removed;

interactive angles

Have a look at the website which has photographs of buildings designed with defensible space in mind:
http://www.eslarp.uiuc.edu/la/LA338-S00/part1/a/cpted.html

Identify the characteristics that would make the defence of territory easy and decide how each feature contributes. Suggest alternative designs that may have preceded these that would have been less readily defensible.

Figure 25.3 Entrance to Van Dyke houses – no defensible space, high crime rates and a 'run-down' appearance

interactive angles

Can you think of any other reasons why the Pruitt–Igoe project was a failure? Use your knowledge from this chapter so far to see if other reasons besides defensible space could explain the problems that arose.

The Pruitt–Igoe research, which had suggested that defensible space was necessary for the reduction of crime, was backed up by a study conducted by Sommer (1987). He compared the crime rates in high-rise university halls of residence compared to those in cluster halls, which have more defensible space. The latter were seen to have much lower rates of crime and vandalism.

Figure 25.4 Central grounds of Van Dyke houses

- indestructible light fittings;
- radiators and lifts that were vandal-resistant.

It is curious that the project managers appeared to be 'expecting trouble' by introducing the features above. But they were correct. After a few years, the entire project was in disarray. Within the buildings there was broken glass and rubbish, the 'indestructible' features had been destroyed, many windows were boarded up or smashed, the lifts had been repeatedly used as toilets and the top floors were no longer lived in. Crime and vandalism were common place; the car park was littered with semi-destroyed cars and the children's playground covered in broken glass. By 1970, only 16 of the 43 buildings were still lived in. In 1972, the entire project was demolished. Many people believed that the lack of defensible space had caused the downfall of the Pruitt–Igoe dream.

Figure 25.5 Brownsville houses from the street – a considerable amount of defensible space and low crime rates

Shon and Kim (2000) have noted that Korean policy has reverted back to a supply of housing that is sustainable (presumably with defensible space so that degradation is lessened and sustainability is increased) compared to a mass production of housing, which – as we have seen from the Pruitt–Igoe example – may not be the best type of housing to design.

Brunson (2000) has examined the Department of Housing and Urban Development (HUD) in America, as they have recently invested millions of dollars in the regeneration of urban areas using defensible space theory. Brunson notes that some regenerations have worked, lowering crime levels and bringing about a more cohesive community. However, not all have been so successful. Therefore, Brunson investigated whether defensible space was linked to residents' experiences of safety and a sense of community in public housing. A total of 91 residents were surveyed. All were living in an area with a moderate amount of defensible space. Those who defended their near-home space reported that the neighbourhood felt safer and that there was a more cohesive community, compared to residents who did not defend their near-home space. Also, those who spent time outside more often reported that the neighbourhood was a safe place. Those who participated in 'greening' activities believed that the community was more cohesive. This evidence supports Newman's (1972) idea that defensible space makes the community more cohesive and safer to live in.

Blossom (2000) notes that interior designers are over-looked in community design work. They often help to produce healthier interior environments, which must increase aspects such as residential satisfaction. Blossom states that there has been too much emphasis on building systems (as in the Prutt–Igoe case, for instance), where the focus has been on the actual exterior nature of the building. Interior features may well have an effect on people's perceptions of urban areas.

interactive angles

List the advantages and disadvantages of segregating older adults in terms of the type of housing in which they live.

for and against

defensible space theory

+ it appears that when residential areas are constructed with defensible space, crime rates decrease (for example, the Brownsville estate)

+ there are examples in which residential areas have suffered higher levels of crime and vandalism when no defensible space has been present (for example, Pruitt–Igoe and Van Dyke)

– social factors may have been overlooked in the original theory. If the area has a notorious reputation for crime, then defensible space may not help to reduce it

– burglars tend to see more defensible space as an indicator that properties have something to hide

where to now?

▶ **Dwyer D. (2001) Angles on criminal psychology. Cheltenham: Nelson Thornes.** Has a good section discussing Oscar Newman's approach in relation to criminal behaviour.

▶ **http://www.defensiblespace.com** This is Oscar Newman's own website, with links to other sites including one from which Newman's publication *Creating defensible space* can be downloaded.

▶ **http://www.nhi.org/index.html** This is the website of the US National Housing Institute. The NHI journal, *Shelterforce,* is available online and has an relevant articles about defensible space including one by Oscar Newman.

Conclusions

Architecture appears to have a considerable effect on our behaviour and on the way in which we communicate with each other. Sociofugal designs keep us apart, while sociopetal designs bring us together. The number of buildings around us could have an effect on how satisfied we are with the place in which we live. Oscar Newman introduced the idea of defensible space, a semi-public area that is clearly 'owned' or looked after by someone. He had the idea that these areas should reduce crime rates in residential areas. There is some support for his ideas and modern residential buildings are constructed with areas of defensible space. Previous residential areas that failed to make use of defensible space saw an increase in crime rates, and some were even demolished.

**what
do you
know ?**

1. (a) Describe what Oscar Newman meant by defensible space.

   (b) Use evidence to assess how useful the concept of defensible space has been in efforts to reduce vandalism and crime.

2. Discuss the effect of architecture on residential satisfaction.

3. Describe examples of good and bad practice in architectural design with respect to defensible space and justify why you have classified them as successes or failures.

26 Environmental stress

what's ahead?

In chapter 22 we looked at the concept of stress and the physiological effects of stress on the body. In this chapter we will explore a range of sources of environmental stress, including noise, pollution and travelling to work. We will then consider research evaluating the importance of these stressors and the effects that these stressors can have on our behaviour. Finally, we will look at the ways in which we can cope with sources of stress.

Sources of environmental stress

Many aspects of our environment act as stressors. Being kept awake at night by street lights, feeling jet lagged or getting lost in a crowd, can all contribute to making our lives stressful. In this section we consider noise, pollution and travel as sources of stress.

Noise

The intensity of *sound* (volume) is measured in decibels (dB). Individuals vary in their threshold of hearing; that is, the quietest sound that they can detect.

In the context of environmental psychology, *noise* refers to sounds that are unpleasant. A sound must be 'unwanted' in order to be categorised as noise; the sound of your favourite track played loudly on your own stereo is pleas-

dB	Example		
140	Painfully loud		*Painfully loud*
130	Machine gun fire at close range		
120	Maximum vocal effort		
110	Music at a concert		
100	Chainsaw		
90	Lawn mower		*Hearing damage after 8 hours*
80	Underground train		
70	Fast traffic		
60	Busy office		
50	Conversation		*Quiet*
40	Residential area at night		
30	Clock ticking		*Very quiet*
20	Leaves rustling		
10	Normal breathing		
0			*Hearing threshold*

Table 26.1 The decibel scale

Figure 26.1 Why is your own phone a perfectly acceptable sound, but the calls of others an irritating noise?

ing, but the noise of same music heard through the wall from your neighbour when you're trying to sleep is annoying. Clearly, volume is not the only factor that affects the distinction between wanted and unwanted sounds.

Glass and Singer (1972) identified three key variables that could affect the extent to which we experience sounds as unpleasant; that is, dimensions along which a sound becomes a noise:

- volume;
- predictability;
- perceived control.

research now

noisy student halls

Ng C.F. (2000) Effects of building construction noise on residents: a quasi experiment. *Journal of Environmental Psychology* 20: 375–85

aim: to investigate the psychological and behavioural effects of noise on students living in a hall of residence adjacent to a construction site.

procedure: ninety-four students accommodated in an all-female hall of residence completed a questionnaire about the effects that they experienced relating to the construction of a building nearby. The students were housed in three wings of the hall, providing a comparison between those nearest to, furthest from and in an intermediate position in relation to the noise, the closest being within 5 m of the site. In addition, some students kept an activity log, sound level measurements were taken, observations were made of window opening and closing, and student turnover and achievement were recorded.

findings: students living in the wing nearest to the construction site were exposed to louder noise and showed significant behavioural differences compared to those in the central or furthest wing. Students living in the noisiest wing were distracted significantly more often, were more likely to be awakened by the noise and had more difficulty with studying and relaxing. The noise interfered with television viewing, conversations and telephone calls. These students coped by speaking more loudly, keeping their windows closed and leaving their rooms. However, there were no differences between residents in different wings with respect to their attitude towards the construction, nor with respect to their academic success.

conclusion: noise has significant psychological and behavioural effects on a young, student population, although even the students exposed to the greatest noise did not demonstrate long-term effects of stress. There appear to be few effective strategies to reduce loudness, but students do take action – such as closing windows – which may help to counter the effects by increasing perceived control.

Volume

Higher-intensity sounds are clearly more disruptive. Above 90 dB, sounds become disturbing, interfering with conversation, for example. In addition, louder noises demand more attention, and increase arousal and stress to a greater extent. However, loudness is not the same as volume. *Volume* is the measurable increase in magnitude of vibration in the air; it is an objective measure of sound intensity (sounds increase in volume as the amplitude of the waves increases). *Loudness* is a subjective measure of the perceived intensity of the sound. This may be affected by several factors:

● *context* – sounds appear louder against a quiet background (when the music in a bar stops, you find that you are shouting);

● *habituation* – we become insensitive to repeated, monotonous sounds (if you live near a railway, you may cease to notice loud but continuous noise from trains);

● *pitch* – we attend readily to high-frequency sounds (the screech of an over-excited young child is difficult to ignore).

Stevens (1956) demonstrated that, across most of the audible range, increasing the volume tenfold produces an approximate doubling of loudness. This relationship is illustrated in figure 26.2. The relationship between intensity and loudness breaks down for very quiet sounds, below 20 dB, where loudness appears to change more rapidly (that is, changes in loudness more closely match changes in volume).

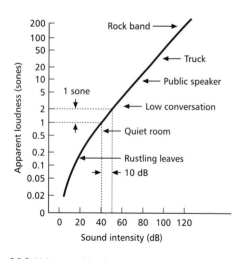

Figure 26.2 Volume and loudness – across most of the audible range, a doubling of loudness (measured in 'sones') requires a tenfold increase in intensity of a sound (measured in decibels)

Belojevic et al (2001) tested participants' ability on a mental arithmetic task under noisy conditions (with recorded traffic noise at 88 dB(A)) and in quiet conditions (42 dB(A)). Extroversion and introversion were also measured using the Eysenck personality questionnaire. The introverts (but not the extroverts) suffered impaired concentration and greater fatigue in the noisy compared to the quiet condition, although accuracy was not affected.

Repeated or continuous sounds appear less loud over time; this is *habituation*. As we habituate to the stimulus of the sound, its apparent loudness decreases; this is called *auditory adaptation*. Exposure to intense sounds can induce auditory fatigue, which causes a persistent reduction in apparent loudness.

Postman and Egan (1949) exposed listeners to an intense (115 dB) noise for 20 minutes. Recordings of their subsequent sensitivity showed that there was an immediate, significant hearing loss, which did not reverse for several days (see figure 26.3).

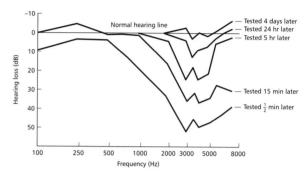

Figure 26.3 Even brief exposure to loud sounds can have a detrimental effect on hearing. Postman and Egan (1949) found a measurable loss in hearing even 24 hours after exposure to a short burst of loud noise

Predictability

In addition to acoustic factors (for example, volume and pitch), non-acoustic variables such as predictability alter the effect of noise on mood (Green & Fidell, 1991).

Figure 26.4 Consider how annoying the occasional cough or sniff is in an exam room. It breaks your concentration far more than the continuous hum of the heater

A loud 'clonk' that comes at regular intervals is less disturbing than one that occurs irregularly. For example, the predictable ticking of a clock is less annoying than the erratic scuttling of a pet hamster. This is because we are more likely to be able to ignore an intrusive stimulus that we can anticipate than one we cannot. As a consequence, we can adapt to predictable but not to unpredictable noise. Corah and Boffa (1970) exposed participants to a loud noise either with or without prior warning. Those participants who were told about the noise (that is, those for whom it was predictable) experienced less subjective stress. According to Corah and Boffa, this predictability enabled the participants to feel that they had control over the stimulus. Noises that are unpredictable demand more attention and increase arousal and stress.

Perceived control

Being able to control a noise reduces the likelihood of it becoming a problem. A noise that can be stopped, muffled or avoided is less disturbing. If you have control over the noise, such as when you are using a lawnmower, it is less irritating for you – because you can stop the noise whenever you like – than for your neighbour, who has no control over its cessation. Similarly, if the neighbours can block the sound out by closing windows, the noise becomes less annoying to them. Even if they choose not to take any action, they benefit from the sense of having the potential to regain control over the noise. The knowledge that one can avoid a noise, by choosing to go out shopping while the neighbours are mowing, has a similar effect; again one can opt not to and still benefit. However, if you exercise your perceived control and it proves to be ineffectual (you close the windows but can still hear the lawnmower, or you go out in the morning only to find that your neighbours have delayed mowing until the afternoon), the stress of your failure to control the situation will be greater. Ultimately, this can result in *learned helplessness*, the failure to exert control even when it becomes possible. This occurs because prior learning has taught us that attempts to control the situation are not effective. Evans (2000) reports that children and adults exposed to noise, crowding, traffic congestion or pollution develop responses, such as poor decision making, that resemble learned helplessness.

Individual differences

Unsurprisingly, loud, unpredictable, uncontrollable noises are the most psychologically distressing. In addition to these factors, Borsky (1969) found that necessity, concern, perceived health risk and satisfaction also affected a person's value judgement about whether a noise was annoying. Two further factors – fear and sensitivity to noise – have been shown to be important.

- *Necessity – whether the cause of the noise is seen to be a worthwhile activity.* A lawnmower at least cuts the grass, while loud music may be seen to have no useful function (and is therefore perceived as more annoying).

- *Concern – whether the person responsible is believed to care about those who are disturbed by the noise.* Neighbours who choose to do DIY at night appear to have little concern for the disturbance that they are causing, and the noise is therefore more annoying than, say, their baby crying.

- *Perceived health risk – whether those exposed to the noise fear that they may be damaged by their enforced exposure.* Office workers who believe that noise from a nearby construction site could damage their hearing will find the noise more annoying than those who do not.

- *Satisfaction – whether the individual is content with his or her environment in general.* A neighbour who is in other respects satisfied with the locality will be less disturbed by the noise from a lawnmower than one who is already engaged in a dispute with other residents.

Whether or not an individual associates a noise with a fearful stimulus may affect his or her aversion to that noise. An individual who associates a particular noise with fear will experience greater distress than someone who does not. Thus the buzzing of a wasp against a window will be more problematic for someone who is afraid of insects than for other people.

Some people find noise more aversive than others do; they have higher *noise sensitivity*. This may be due to some personality trait or due to a differing sensitivity to sound, so they may be more intolerant of noise because it is more intrusive for them. It is possible that these two factors are related; people who are more reactive to sound may additionally be more bothered by it (Taylor, 1984). However, this alone does not appear to be sufficient to explain individual differences in annoyance caused by noise (see Staples et al, 1999, page 56).

Sensitivity versus disturbance

Zimmer and Ellermeier (1999) compared measures of noise sensitivity, including behavioural and emotional responses to environmental noises at work, during recreation and while sleeping. They also tested objective disruption during a cognitive task and compared this to the participants' subjective noise sensitivity ratings. Only a weak correlation was found, which suggests that the self-reported effects of noise sensitivity are greater than the actual disruption. The effects of noise sensitivity on annoyance must therefore be mediated by emotional reactions to noise.

research
now

are planes a perk or a pest?

Staples S.L., Cornelius R.R. and Gibbs M.S. (1999) Disturbance from a developing airport: perceived risk or general annoyance? *Environment and Behavior* **31: 692–710**

aim: to investigate whether people differ in their levels of annoyance according to the long-term benefits they perceive from the disturbance caused by aircraft noise.

method: 901 residents living in close proximity to airports were assessed using the Environmental Noise Risk Scale (ENRS) to measure the costs and benefits that they associated with having an airport close by. They were also tested on a noise sensitivity scale, rating themselves on statements such as 'I find it difficult to study in a noisy setting' and 'I cannot sleep when even a minor noise is present'.

results: participants showed a stronger relationship between the ENRS score and the extent to which they were disturbed by the noise than between sensitivity and disturbance. If they were able to perceive economic and community benefits, such as employment opportunities and convenience, rather than focusing on the adverse environmental effects of the airport, they were less likely to be disturbed by the airport noise.

conclusion: cost–benefit analysis may be more useful than sensitivity testing in analysing the likely impact of noise on an individual. Where perceived benefits exceed perceived costs, people are likely to be less affected by noise disturbance regardless of their sensitivity level.

Sources of environmental noise

Whilst many sounds can become 'noise', for instance, if they are loud, some sources of noise, including occupational and transportation noise, present an ongoing problem for many of us.

Occupational noise refers to the unpleasant sounds to which people are exposed in the workplace. There are two reasons why workplace noise is so disruptive. First, in the workplace people need to concentrate, but as noise demands attention and increases arousal the task will be more difficult. Secondly, workplace noise, particularly in offices, tends to be *wide-band noise*; that is, it is composed of a range of frequencies. This makes it particularly difficult to mask using white noise (unpatterned sound, containing a wide range of frequencies, like 'static'). In other settings, the problem may be volume; for example, construction workers may be regularly exposed to volumes of 100 dB, aircraft mechanics to 88–120 dB and coal miners to 95–105 dB (Raloff, 1982). Inside a large barn full of pigs, a farmer may be exposed to 110 dB, or even more at feeding time (Health and Safety Executive, 1995).

Transportation noise refers to the unpleasant sounds generated by motor vehicles, trains, aeroplanes and other means of transport. One of the reasons why transportation noise is a problem is because it is so loud. Bronzaft

Figure 26.5 Noise in the workplace can be distracting and difficult to mask as well as loud

et al (1998) found that approximately 70 per cent of residents living beneath an airport flight path reported being troubled by noise from aircraft.

research now

planes in the parks

Mace B.L., Bell P.A. & Loomis R.J. (1999) Aesthetic, affective and cognitive effects of noise on natural landscape assessment. *Society and Natural Resources* 12: 225–42

aim: many beauty spots, such as the Grand Canyon in the USA and the English Lake District, attract air traffic as well as visitors on the ground. People who may have walked many miles in pursuit of 'restoration' and 'escape' in the natural environment are perturbed to find their isolation violated by helicopters and aeroplanes. The aim of this study was to measure the extent to which enjoyment of the natural environment was affected by noise.

procedure: in a laboratory simulation, helicopter noise at 40 dB or 80 dB was played while participants viewed slides of national park scenes. Participants recorded their feelings and rated the slides for scenic beauty.

findings: participants' feelings of annoyance, solitude, tranquillity, freedom and naturalness were all negatively impacted by the noise, in both the quiet and loud conditions. Furthermore, ratings for scenic beauty (even for some of the most breathtaking views) were reduced by the noise.

conclusion: noise both presents a source of annoyance and directly reduces the pleasure experienced from the surrounding environment. Aircraft noise in areas of outstanding natural beauty is an issue that is in need of further attention.

Figure 26.6 Noise can reverse the stress-reducing effects of the natural landscape

The noise from Concorde (a supersonic jet – one that can fly faster than the speed of sound) on the runway may be as much as 100–120 dB. This is 10–20 dB louder than a subsonic jet. Bell et al (2001) report that a single flight by a loud aircraft is as disturbing as 10 flights by a plane that is 10 dB quieter. In addition to being very loud, transportation noise is intermittent and therefore more disturbing – and may continue into the night, when it is more apparent in contrast to the quiet of nightfall.

The research by Staples et al (1999) accounts for the findings of Fidell and Silvati (1991) that little reduction in the annoyance caused by noise is achieved by adding sound insulation to homes near an airport. Similarly, Nivision and Endresen (1993) studied residents living on a busy street, measuring their health, sleep anxiety levels and attitude towards the noise. Although noise levels were unrelated to either their health or sleep, a strong relationship emerged between the participants' subjective view of the noise to which they were exposed and the number of their health complaints.

Pollution

Like noise, pollution is an everyday concept. We think of oil tanker spills and billowing smoke from factories. These, and many less visible sources of pollution, result in the contamination of the environment with harmful or poisonous substances. How does this action become a source of stress?

Pollution is not just a recent phenomenon: the seepage of human and animal waste into waterways, for example, has plagued communities for centuries. What has changed, however, is the nature and the scale of the pollution for which we are responsible. For example, radioactive waste is invisible but deadly, and chemical plants and tankers

have vast capacities, so that accidents can cause extensive damage and the effects may be long-lasting, such as in the case of nuclear contamination. Furthermore, because of the nature of modern pollutants and the power of their sources (governments and multinational companies), people who are affected may feel that the situation is out of their control. This helplessness enhances their fear.

Air pollution

We can see or smell some pollutants, but there are others that we cannot detect. Carbon monoxide, for example, is an odourless and colourless gas, but it can be fatal. What makes us concerned about pollution? The level of pollution, perceived or absolute, is not the only factor that affects the stress levels associated with a pollutant. The

Table 26.2 Atmospheric pollutants and their sources or causes

Atmospheric pollutant	Sources or causes
Particulates	Cigarette smoke Incinerators Vehicle exhausts
Sulphur dioxide (SO2) Carbon monoxide (CO) Particulates	Smoke from fires burning fossil fuels
Carbon monoxide Nitrogen dioxide (NO2) Hydrocarbons	Vehicle exhausts
CFCs (chlorofluorocarbons)	Aerosols and old refrigerators
Nitrogen dioxide	Industry

research
now

muddy waters and heavy metal

Eiser J.M., Podpadec T.J., Reicher S.D. & Stevenage S.V. (1998) Muddy waters and heavy metal: time and attitudes guide judgements of pollution. *Journal of Environmental Psychology* **18: 199–208**

aim: to study the changing attitudes of residents living close to the source of river pollution over time following contamination of the River Fal, and to investigate factors affecting differences in perception of risk.

method: residents around Falmouth, Cornwall, were sent questionnaires following an environmental incident in which toxic heavy metals such as cadmium and zinc were washed out of a disused mine and into the River Fal. The questionnaires were sent out soon after the event and after 8 months had elapsed. These asked about the perceived seriousness of the spillage (such as the potential effects on employment – for example, fishing or tourism – and at home, as in the contamination of non-mains water) and whether this was believed to be a chance accident or a predictable event for which someone should have been responsible.

findings: the participants' estimates of the seriousness of the contamination (in terms of visible effects, and toxicity of shellfish and drinking water) were higher immediately after the incident than after 8 months, and women were more concerned than men. Those participants asked immediately after the event believed that the toxic effects would be longer lasting than those questioned later. With regard to responsibility, the respondents at 6 weeks were more likely to assign blame than those asked later, and women were more likely to attribute responsibility than were men.

conclusion: one factor affecting the perceived risk was gender. In general, women were more concerned than men about the potential damage caused by pollution and with assigning responsibility. Both genders became less pessimistic about the effects of the spillage with time. This change may not be related to any real reduction in risk, but to habituation.

nature of the pollutant matters too. Smells emerging from oil refineries or breweries are perceived to be more annoying than emissions from a chocolate factory (Winneke & Kastka, 1987).

Rankin (1969) found that members of a community who were concerned about air pollution did not complain because they believed that their protests would be ineffective. Such feelings of apathy increase the stress associated with the pollutant. As with noise pollution, even a perception of control over the situation reduces stress. Rotton et al (1979) reported that perceived control over air quality when exposed to a malodorous substance was more important than the level of pollution in determining the level of tolerance of the situation. Feeling less helpless serves to reduce frustration and therefore lowers the stress experienced as a result of the environmental insult.

As with noise, those people who are most anxious are more aware of the threat posed by a pollutant (Navarro et al, 1987). Their fears, unabated by reassurances of safety or reinforced by apathy, can therefore create more stress. Familiarity may also increase the stress associated with a pollutant, although it may also make people less concerned (Medalia, 1964).

Travel

Travel, over short or long distances, can be a source of stress. Road rage could happen on a short trip to the shops, an employee who takes the same route to work every day may experience fatigue and a long-haul passenger may suffer the effects of jet lag.

Rathbone and Huckabee (1999) conducted a review of the literature, legislation and preventive measures in use across the USA. They distinguish between road rage and

road rage

A study of 526 drivers, conducted by the Automobile Association (AA) Road Safety unit in 1995, found that 90 per cent had experienced 'road rage' incidents during the preceding 12 months. Ward and Waterman (2000) define road rage as the expression of aggressive behaviour towards other road users, in response to an angry (emotive) appraisal of the traffic context. Motorists reported being both the recipient and cause of road rage – both of which are stressful. It is interesting that there is a discrepancy between the numbers of each form of behaviour conducted and experienced. This may be explained by subjective perceptions of threat by the recipient. For example, tailgating is frequently experienced but apparently less often performed, perhaps because we perceive the threat of encroachment while failing to recognise our intrusive behaviour towards others. This view is supported by the environmental approach – taken, for instance, by Joint (2000) – which suggests that the car is an extension of our personal space, and is thus defended against invasion by another vehicle cutting in.

Driving behaviour	Percentage of drivers experiencing this behaviour from other motorists	Percentage of drivers admitting to engaging in this behaviour towards other motorists
Aggressive tailgating (driving very close behind)	62	6
Flashing lights	59	45
Aggressive or rude gestures	48	22
Deliberate obstruction	21	5
Verbal abuse	16	12
Physical assault	1	<1
Any other form of road rage	12	40

Road rage experienced and conducted by motorists
http://www.reportroadrage.co.uk/aastat.htm

aggressive driving. The former is uncontrolled and criminal, while the latter – although potentially dangerous and often constituting a driving offence – is not a criminal offence. They suggest that road rage is most frequent on Friday afternoons at peak travel times, during fair weather, in congested, urban areas. They observe that, although relatively infrequent, the apparent randomness of the victims and perpetrators of road rage frightens the public. This fear is exacerbated by a lack of information about the precursors that lead to road rage incidents and of ways in which to defuse potentially dangerous situations.

Further evidence that aspects of the environment, rather than internal factors such as personality, are responsible for aggressive driving comes from a study conducted by Ellison-Potter et al (2001), using a driving simulator. The

research
now

the anger of road rage

Parkinson B. (2001) Anger on and off the road. *British Journal of Psychology* 92: 507–26

aim: to investigate whether the anger expressed in 'road rage' is different from that experienced in other contexts.

procedure: a group of 64 undergraduates described two recent experiences in which they had become angry (one while driving, the other not). They were compared on various measures and the participants indicated how angry they felt in a range of different situations on the road by choosing from a series of statements to describe their driving.

findings: anger was experienced more frequently while driving than in non-driving situations. The target for this aggression was a stranger when driving but this was not the case for the non-driving incidents.

conclusion: these differences may arise as the costs attached to being aggressive may be less if you are not face-to-face and communication is more difficult, probably due to the physical distance between road users.

results showed that when students believed that they could not be identified, because they had been told that they were in a convertible with the roof up, they drove more aggressively, had more accidents and killed more virtual pedestrians! The belief that they were visible had the opposite effect, resulting in safer driving (for the effects of anonymity on behaviour, see page 350–3). Aggressive bumper stickers and road signs also made drivers more aggressive but driver anger, a measure of personality, did not appear to be related to aggressive driving. This suggests that making drivers identifiable (for example, printing work telephone numbers on vans) and reminding people to drive courteously (such as signs on Scottish roads, which say 'Frustration causes accidents, please allow passing') could help to reduce driver aggression.

Commuting

'Home-working' is increasingly becoming possible as communications networks offer greater flexibility, enabling employees to do their jobs away from the formal workplace. In contrast, as long-distance travel becomes faster, easier and more familiar, so more people are travelling very long distances to their work. People may spend several hours a day commuting, and in addition to the time penalty, they may experience problems on the roads (diversions, hold-ups and, increasingly, gridlock) and on the railways (cancellations, delays and derailments). Such delays inevitably lead to stress, as time is wasted and deadlines are missed. Increasing stress in commuters,

both on the road (Gaulin et al, 1989) and on public transport (Costa et al, 1988), has been demonstrated.

The amount of difficulty experienced on any journey can be measured objectively as impedance. This has two elements: *physical impedance* – that is, the actual obstruction to travel encountered (which can be operationalised as the time taken to complete a journey divided by the distance travelled) – and *subjective impedance* – that is, the individual's perception of the problems encountered on the journey. Cassidy (1992) showed that physical impedance rather than distance travelled was the better indicator of perceived stress and health consequences of commuting. An unimpeded long-distance trip is less stressful than a short but interrupted journey. Therefore, a driver can cover many miles if the traffic is free flowing, but a short, queue-ridden trip is more stressful. When covering long distances, a traveller may take the opportunity to work or relax (such as reading on a long flight or train journey) or to learn a new language (using tapes in a car stereo). These options are more readily available to the user of public transport (as their attention is not required for driving), but these commuters report higher levels of perceived stress. This may be the result of the higher perceived control available to drivers in terms of personal space as well as progress (Cassidy, 1997).

For the commuter who spends many hours on the road, there is an additional risk – that of fatigue. Trying to concentrate on a demanding task such as driving when we are in a trough of our circadian cycle is both stressful and

media watch

Road rage and space-defending space wagons

Commenting on the causes of 'Road-Rage', Matthew Joint, MSc, BSc, MCIT, Head of Behavioural Analysis

Human beings are territorial. As individuals we have personal space, or territory, which evolved essentially as a defensive mechanism – anyone who invades this territory is potentially an aggressor. The car is an extension of this territory. If a vehicle threatens this territory by cutting in, for example, the driver will probably carry out a defensive manoeuvre. This may be backed up by an attempt to re-establish territory, flashing headlights or a blast of the horn are perhaps most commonly used for this purpose. However, this may not always succeed in communicating the full depth of our feelings. As it is usually difficult to talk or even shout to the offending driver, other non-verbal communication (offensive gesticulations) may be employed. Confrontations of this nature are not uncommon and are usually defused as the vehicles move away from each other.

In some circumstances, the defending driver may wish to go one step further and assert his dominance. Many drivers admit to having chased after a driver to 'teach him a lesson', often pressing him by moving to within inches of his rear bumper. This is comparable to the manner in which a defending animal will chase an attacker out of its territory. However, the result of such behaviour in drivers is, of course, potentially fatal.

Some of the worst cases of 'Road-Rage' have occurred where the opportunity for the vehicles to separate and go their own ways does not present itself. Gesticulations and aggressive manoeuvres have been exchanged in a rapidly degenerating discourse. Worked up into a rage, one or both drivers have then got out of their vehicles and physically attacked their adversary and/or his vehicle.

Drivers can adopt simple strategies that help keep frustration, anger and rage in check.

Never assume that an apparently aggressive act was intended as such. We all make mistakes. So don't bite back. If we take an example from studies of animal behaviour in the wild, the dominant animal in a group will rarely get involved in petty fights and disagreements. Although confident in his ability to defeat any opponent, there is always the risk of injury.

Source: http://www.reportroadrage.co.uk

Using the concepts and research discussed in chapter 24, analyse the evidence for the ideas presented in this article.

dangerous (for a discussion of circadian rhythms, see Jarvis et al, 2000). In particular, drivers on very familiar journeys who are tired or out of phase with their biological clocks are at risk of losing concentration. Driving without awareness, a condition in which drivers become mesmerised and fail to attend to road conditions, is a particular risk.

Commuting by air, often for short periods of time to attend meetings at international venues, can lead to poor sleep, tiredness and gastro-intestinal symptoms. This phenomenon, known as jet lag, is the fatigue experienced by air travellers as a consequence of crossing time zones, such that their circadian rhythm is desychronised from the local zeitgebers (for a full discussion of jet lag, see Jarvis et al, 2000). Since international travel results in sleep loss, commuters experiencing jet lag will suffer both the effects of sleep loss and desynchronisation of the body clock and the local zeitgeber.

A further source of stress for air travellers relates to the relative confinement of airline seating. This has several consequences. First, invasion of personal space is inevitable, because neighbouring passengers are well within the intimate zone (see chapter 24) and while territory is demarcated by the arm rests and seats themselves, the breaching of these boundaries is inevitable.

A second factor that causes stress on aircraft is the prolonged immobility. This has health implications that are now becoming apparent in direct relation to air travel. Staying still, particularly where legroom and hence movement is restricted, increases the risk of deep vein thrombosis (DVT). Such potential problems serve to exacerbate the stress associated with long-haul travelling. Furthermore, the dry atmosphere on aeroplanes and the tendency to consume (free) alcohol causes thickening of the blood, increasing susceptibility to DVT.

The following are good sources of information about environmental stress:

▶ **http://www.hse.gov.uk** – the Health and Safety Executive website is a useful source, with many pages devoted to noise at work.

▶ **http://www.le.ac.uk/psychology/acn5** – Adrian North's website describes many of the studies that he has conducted into the effects of noise.

▶ **http://www.reportroadrage.co.uk/experts.htm** and **http://www.reportroadrage.co.uk/aastat.htm** – these websites provide details of reports on road rage.

▶ **http://www.drivers.com** and **http://my.webmd.com** – both have interesting articles about road rage incidents and ways to reduce risk.

The consequences of stress

Effects of stressors on performance

Cohen et al (1973) investigated the effects of urban noise on the development of children's reading ability. They compared children living on different floors of a high-rise block over a busy New York City highway. Children lower in the block were exposed to greater noise levels and (despite similarities in social class and exposure to air pollution) were poorer readers than children living on higher floors. Cohen et al suggest that this may be related to the impaired hearing of the chil-

dren on the lower floors (see page 69). Similar results were obtained by Bronzaft and McCarthy (1975), in their comparison of the reading ability of children at the same school who worked in classrooms adjacent to or away from elevated railway tracks. The reading skills of the children exposed to the noise from the railway were inferior to those of the children on the quiet side. Noise can interfere with the perception of speech sounds; for instance, masking the difference between /p/ and /b/. This could delay the development of verbal skills and reading. Alternatively, the children on the noisy side of the building may have suffered from the 11 per cent loss in teaching time experienced in the classrooms adjacent to the railway.

Evans et al (1995) compared children living adjacent to Munich International Airport with children from less noisy urban areas (see also page 71). Both memory and reading performance were better in children from the quieter neighbourhoods. These differences may be the direct effects of noise or a consequence of other behavioural differences observed; the children from the airport district were more readily frustrated and annoyed and had poorer motivation.

Performance at work is also affected by noise, not just in obviously noisy settings such as construction sites and airports, but in offices and industrial plants too. Banbury and Berry (1998) suggest that the background noise generated by voices is particularly troublesome. Because we tend to 'tune in' to conversations, they are more likely to interfere with our own concentration and communication. Acton (1970) found that we can, however, learn to adapt to working in a noisy environment. Workers from an industrial setting, accustomed to higher noise levels, were more effective at communicating against a background of loud noise than were university employees, whose workplaces are typically quieter.

Although there is little evidence that noise affects workplace productivity directly, it could impact upon effectiveness through employee communication, morale or fatigue. If so, reducing workplace noise could boost productivity indirectly. This might be achieved by the use of sound-absorbing materials on the floors, ceiling and walls, using sound insulation around noisy pieces of equipment and replacing older machinery with newer, quieter models. An alternative technique is to mask noise; for instance, with a constant hum or piped music (see page 59).

Experimentally, air pollution with an unpleasant smell has been shown to affect performance on a complex task (proofreading) but not a simple one (arithmetic). In reality, we may be most likely to suffer the effects of air pollution; for instance, from traffic fumes, when we are engaged in the relatively complex task of driving. How

classic
research

it's a shocking noise

Geen R.G. and O'Neal E.C. (1969) Activation of cue-elicited aggression by general arousal. *Journal of Personality and Social Psychology* 11: 289–92

---

aim: to investigate whether exposure to loud noise increases the incidence of aggressive behaviour and whether this adds to the arousing effect of viewing aggressive media.

method: participants were shown a film that was either violent (a prize-fight) or non-violent (a sports film). They were then placed in a situation in which they believed that they were administering electric shocks to another individual (who was, in fact, a confederate of the experimenter and received no shocks). During this phase of the experiment, the participants were exposed to either noisy or quiet conditions.

results: exposure to either the violent film or the noisy conditions increased the number of shocks given by the participant. The effect was greatest with the violent film and noise in combination.

conclusion: noise increases aggressive behaviour, as measured by the likelihood of administering shocks, and exacerbates the effects of viewing aggression, suggesting that noise may promote aggression by increasing arousal.

---

are driving skills affected by the levels of a major pollutant, carbon monoxide? Beard and Wertheim (1967) found that time judgement was impaired by exposure to carbon monoxide, while Breisacher (1971) reports a reduction in manual dexterity and attention with raised carbon monoxide levels. Similarly, Lewis et al (1970) found that participants exposed to air taken at approximately exhaust-pipe height from a busy road did not perform as well as those breathing 'clean' air on information processing tasks. Clearly, the heavier the traffic is and the more dangerous the driving conditions are, the worse our performance may become.

Effects of stressors on social behaviour

As noise can affect attention, arousal and stress, it is likely to have an effect upon social interactions. It seems to have the effect of making people unpleasant; they are more aggressive and less helpful.

Sauser et al (1978) found that participants exposed to a loud noise during a management simulation were likely to assign lower salaries to fictitious job applicants. Loud noise seems to reduce the probability of altruistic behaviour. Page (1977) conducted a field experiment in which a pedestrian (a confederate) dropped a package near a construction site. Under different noise conditions created by the use of a pneumatic drill, the incidence of passers-by stopping to help was recorded. Fewer passers-by helped in noisy conditions, especially when the noise was very loud.

Matthews and Canon (1975) investigated the interaction between the effect of noise on helping behaviour and another factor known to influence the likelihood of altruism, apparent need. The experimenters contrived a situation in which a pedestrian dropped some books on a city street. Two variables were manipulated in the staged incidents; whether the pedestrian's arm was in a cast and noise generated by a nearby lawnmower. Although the noise reduced altruism in both conditions, the effect was most marked in the reduction of offers of help when the pedestrian's arm was in a cast.

Results such as these may have arisen because people simply do not attend to so many social cues when they are confronted with the sensory overload of a loud noise. For instance, in Matthews and Canon's 'noisy' condition people simply may not have noticed the cast. Alternatively, the noise may affect mood, making people less inclined to help when in a noisy environment.

From the results of a study conducted by Yinon and Bizman (1980), mood seems to be a less important factor than attention. The mood of participants was manipulated by giving them positive or negative feedback on a task that they had performed. During the task, they were exposed to either loud or quiet noise. Finally, the participants were

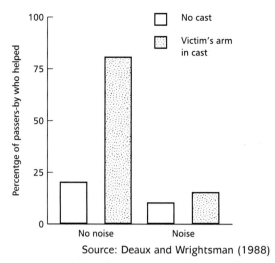

Source: Deaux and Wrightsman (1988)

Figure 26.7 Passers-by are less likely to help when conditions are noisy

asked for help (by a confederate of the experimenter). If noise affected altruism by having a detrimental effect on mood, it would be expected that the combination of loud noise and a negative report on performance would reduce the likelihood of helping. However, Yinon and Bizman found that in the loud noise condition there was no difference between helping by participants who had received positive or negative feedback. As there was a difference in the low-noise condition, these results suggest that the effect of the loud noise overrides that of feedback, either distracting the participants from the negative feedback or justifying it. It seems that interference from a stressor such as noise is more important than mood in determining social behaviour.

Air pollution can also affect social behaviour. For example, Chapko and Solomon (1976) reported a reduction in visitor numbers to attractions, such as New York City zoo and an aquarium, when air pollution rose to unhealthy levels. Asmus and Bell (1999) exposed participants to foul smells, mimicking the effects of malodorous pollution. They found that this made the participants feel unpleasant, reduced their willingness to help and increased the likelihood of anger and flight behaviour. These findings support those obtained in the field by Rotton and Frey (1985), who used archive data to demonstrate that high levels of ozone were associated with increased complaints about household disturbances. The effect of such pollution may be either to increase aggressive behaviour (hence actually elevating levels of disturbance) or it may increase sensitivity to disturbance (thus elevating the incidence of complaints). Air pollution may increase the risk of aggression as well as reducing the likelihood of helping behaviour (Jones & Bogat, 1978; Cunningham, 1979). Furthermore, the stressful effects of major life events seem to be exacerbated by air pollution (Evans et al, 1987).

One particularly frequent source of air pollution that causes stress to others is cigarette smoke. In a study of office productivity, Harris et al (1980) found that 35 per cent of office workers smoked, but the smoking of nearby co-workers distressed 26 per cent of the non-smoking majority. In a shopping centre, people on public benches left more quickly if a smoker, rather than a non-smoker, joined them (Bleda & Bleda, 1978). Jones and Bogat (1978) found that volunteers would administer higher levels of aversive noise to another person if they were exposed to cigarette smoke. It is not yet clear whether these responses are a direct physiological response to chemicals in the smoke itself or are simply due to the annoyance that it causes.

Strategies for coping with environmental stressors

Folkman et al (1986) define coping as 'the person's cognitive and behavioural efforts to manage (reduce, minimize, master, or tolerate) the internal and external demands of the person-environment transaction that is appraised as taxing or exceeding the resources of the person'. Coping thus represents the ways in which we attempt to deal with aspects of the world that we find are beyond our normal means to fight.

Like any source of stress, environmental stressors can be tackled from an internal or external perspective; that is, coping strategies can be either emotion-focused, aiming to manage the negative effects on the individual, or problem-focused, aiming to reduce the causes of stress. In any situation, a combination of these strategies may be employed. Emotion-focused strategies may include keeping busy to take one's mind off the problem, preparing oneself for the worst, praying for strength and guidance, ignoring the situation in the belief that the problem will go away and bottling up one's feelings. Problem-focused strategies may include discussing the situation with a professional, relying on one's own past experiences to tackle the issue and dealing with the situation one step at time. Other strategies are listed in table 26.4.

How effective are the strategies?

It seems obvious that problem-focused strategies are better, because they deal with the environmental cause. However, it may be beyond the scope of the individual to effect change, so emotion-focused solutions may be essential to enable the individual to feel less stressed about the situation. For example, individuals may be powerless to alter the direction of wind blowing air pollutants from foreign countries or to reverse the effects of an industrial accident.

Of the emotion-focused strategies, evidence suggests that long-term avoidance may be ineffective (Nolen-

Table 26.3 Sources of stress

Source of stress	Emotion-focused strategy	Problem-focused strategy
Noisy children playing outside	Trying to remember that children need to play and it's good for them to be outside (being objective)	Talking to a friend on the telephone (discussing the situation)
Noise from a nearby lawnmower	Accepting that the grass will look nicer afterwards (seeing the positive side of the situation)	Closing the windows (taking a positive action)
Cigarette smoke from a nearby table in a non-smoking area of a restaurant	Snapping at the waiter (taking anger out on others)	Contemplating asking the waiter to request that the smoker stops, or moving yourself (considering alternative solutions)
Fumes from a local factory	Eating or smoking more (trying to reduce tension)	Trying to find out what the emissions are and why they are released (investigating the issue)

Hoeksema & Larson, 1999). In fact, avoidance strategies may even be damaging. Epping-Jordan et al (1994) found that in patients using avoidance strategies, the progression of cancer was faster.

Different individuals, circumstances or situations may lead to the availability of differing resources with which to cope. Whilst having wealth may offer the means to avoid many environmental stressors (through avoidance or protection), it may not provide a solution to inescapable sources of stress. Here, intrapersonal resources may be of greater significance. Wealth has been demonstrated to be linked to reduced stress, but this does not apply to everyone (tending only to be important at the lower end of the socio-economic scale: Dohrenwend, 1973). Neither is wealth a buffer against all sources of stress; for example, it is not particularly important following bereavement (Stroebe & Stroebe, 1987).

Gaining control

Earlier in the chapter (page 329) we considered the importance of the sensation of control over a situation to an individual's perception of stress. In many situations, having, or believing that you have, control over a situation helps to alleviate some of the effects of an environmental stressor.

Table 26.4 Resources for coping with environmental stressors

Type of resource	Examples	Ways in which they may be employed
Material	Wealth	Having more money might enable people to live in rural areas with lower air pollution
Educational	Published research, schools, Internet	Knowing how to protect an employee from hearing damage in a noisy work environment
Physical	Strength, health	Individuals without asthma may be more tolerant of some air pollutants
Social	Family, friends, pets	Being able to talk to a dog about the journey to work may alleviate some of the annoyance about traffic jams
Intrapersonal	Skills, abilities and personality characteristics, such as determination	One individual might be better able to live effectively in crowded conditions than another

Social support

People gain help, reassurance and other forms of assistance from their interactions with others (including their pets), which helps them to deal with stress; this is called social support.

Coping with stressors at work

The work environment is a common source of stress in the lives that we lead today. Most of the ideas that we have looked at so far have considered how the individual can cope with stressors. This attitude in the workplace puts the responsibility for stress management on the employees, whereas in fact some of the sources of stress could (and for greater efficacy should) be managed by the employer. Increasingly, companies are placing job-stress issues on the agenda. What can be done to reduce stress at work? In chapter 25 we looked at issues of architectural design including the layout of offices, one factor that can help to relieve stressful aspects of working life.

where to now?

The following are good sources of information about coping with stress:

▶ **Brannon L. & Feist J. (2000) Health psychology: an introduction to behavior and health. London: Wadsworth, Thomson Learning.** This offers detailed coverage of stress and coping.

▶ **http://www.stressfree.com** This website focuses on the problems of work-related stress. It considers the measurement of stress as well as strategies for coping.

▶ **http://www.workhealth.org/ prevent/prred. html** This is a more academic site that considers employer-based changes to reduce workplace stress.

Conclusions

Stressors present in the environment, such as noise, pollution and problems with road rage and air travel, are all clearly major sources of stress in modern life. Factors such as predictability and perceived control affect the extent to which we experience these factors as stressful. Such sources of stress can have a negative impact on our performance, such as making people less effective and impairing learning; and alter social behaviour, making people more aggressive and less helpful. We can attempt to overcome the effects of stressors through problem-focused and emotion-focused strategies, the former being more effective but not always possible.

what do you know?

1   (a) Describe **one** study into the effects of a named source of environmental stress.

(b) Evaluate the study you have described in part (a).

(c) Discuss the effects that the environmental stressor you named in part (a) can have on behaviour.

2   (a) Describe **two** strategies for coping with environmental stressors.

(b) Assess the effectiveness of the strategies you described in part (a).

3   'Modern life is stressful. Too much noise, too much pollution, and the hassle of getting to work can all affect us.' Using your knowledge of environmental psychology, discuss how stressors such as those mentioned in the quote affect human behaviour.

27 Crowding and high-density living

what's

We begin this chapter with a consideration of the nature of crowding in both humans and animals. We then describe and assess the effects of high density living on human including our health, social behaviour and performance. Finally, we discuss theories of crowding, including deindividuation, contagion and emergent norm theory.

What is crowding?

There are two ways in which we use the word crowd. When we refer to a crowd, we mean a large, cohesive gathering of individuals. When we use the term to *crowd*, or *crowding*, we mean the act of coming together to form a tightly spaced group. The *density* of the population is the number of individuals per unit area. In a laboratory this can be artificially manipulated by varying either the number of individuals (*social density*) or the available space (*spatial density*). Laboratory studies are often (but not always) conducted with animals. In some instances, it is possible to observe the effects that different densities have in naturalistic settings. Studies of crowding using people are generally naturalistic, thus avoiding ethical and practical issues. Crowding for humans also refers to the way we feel when exposed to either too many people or insufficient space; in other words, the subjective experience of crowding.

Studies of crowding in animals

Animals have been used to study the effects of increasing both social density and spatial density by varying the number of individuals or available space. While on the surface they seem to have the same effect (more individuals per unit area), there are differences. An increase in social density results in an increase in the number of individuals with which any particular individual must interact, and thus there is a potential for social problems. An increase in spatial density generates the key problem of too little space.

Some of these effects on fecundity described by Crowcroft and Rowe (1958) may have been a consequence of lack of exercise rather than crowding per se. Indeed, Schneider (1946) reversed the loss of fecundity in caged house mice by introducing exercise wheels.

Calhoun (1962) observed the behaviour of a group of rats as it grew to overpopulation and found that dominance relationships also affected response to crowding. The dominant animals defended space and remained in better health than the submissive animals. The latter became confined to a small area of the available space, were more aggressive and were abnormal in their reproductive behaviour and success (96 per cent of offspring died before weaning). Whilst this study clearly demonstrates the negative effects of crowding on social behaviour and reproduction, it can be criticised in several ways. The experiment designed by Calhoun was neither high in ecological validity (rats in the wild would not be confined, they would disperse) nor a simple manipulation of density (as territoriality was also a variable). However, similar patterns of response have been demonstrated in other species, such as frogs (Dyson & Passmore, 1992), pigtail monkeys (Anderson et al, 1977), pigs (Pearce & Patterson, 1993) and hens (Channing et al, 2001; see page 344). It may be possible that the reduction in reproductive success in crowded conditions occurs independently of the effects of aggression. Within a colony of naked mole rats, sexual suppression mediated by pheromones (airborne chemical signals) released by the queen accounts for the infertility of most of the males and females (Sherman et al, 1992).

As a consequence of his findings, Calhoun (1971) proposed a mechanism by which crowding could have its effect upon animals. He suggested that each species has an *optimal group* size at which the individuals within it can tolerate the balance between beneficial and non-beneficial contacts with others. Beyond this size, the costs of social contacts (for example, competition and aggression) outweigh the benefits (for example, food sharing and ease of mate location).

An alternative explanation for the effects of crowding was offered by Christian (1955) in his social stress theory. This suggests that high-density existence leads to social conse-

classic
research

cramped conditions and non-mating mice

Crowcroft P. & Rowe F.P. (1958) The growth of confined colonies of the wild house-mouse (*Mus musculus* L.): the effect of dispersal on female fecundity. *Proceedings of the Zoological Society of London* 131: 357–65

aim: to investigate the effect of the restriction of space on colonies of house mice, with particular respect to *fecundity* (reproductive capability).

procedure: seven colonies were established, each consisting of one adult male and two adult females. Each colony was housed in a pen with high metal walls and eight nest boxes measuring 6 feet (1.8 m) square. Some of these animals had access to much larger pens (more than 100 square feet [9.3 m²]) after 32 or 40 weeks.

findings: in crowded conditions the mice populations increased and then levelled off. The failure to reproduce once a certain population density was reached appeared to be the result of non-fecund (infertile) females. This did not appear to be a direct effect of stress, as aggression was not observed between the females and none sustained injury. In crowded situations the female mice were found to have low fecundity because they could not be penetrated by the males and had inactive ovaries. In addition, they had thread-like uteri and excessive fat deposits. Those animals that remained in crowded conditions did not return to a fecund condition, whereas colonies that dispersed into larger pens showed an increase in birth rate, indicating a return to fecund status.

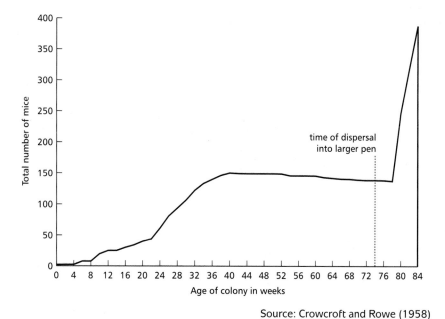

Source: Crowcroft and Rowe (1958)

Figure 27.1 Effect of space availability on population growth

conclusion: these results suggest that, for mice at least, populations have a self-regulatory mechanism for limiting reproduction when the population density is high. This appears to act on the reproductive capacity of the females through a reversible change in their physiology and anatomy.

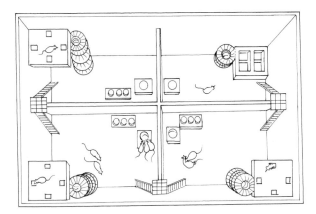

Figure 27.2 Calhoun (1962) observed the change in behaviour of a colony of rats as the pen became overpopulated. In response to crowding, animals in the *behavioural sink* area (the bottom two areas) became aggressive, had higher mortality rates in the females and their reproductive success was reduced

quences that are stressful, such as fighting and competition for food or territory. This would result in a stress-like response mediated by the adrenal glands (see chapter 22). Increased levels of adrenalin could then be directly responsible for the behavioural and physiological changes that have been identified. Recent experimental evidence from Haller et al (1999) suggests that crowding-induced social instability is more stressful for female rats than for males, resulting in weight gain and hormonal changes associated with stress. Male rats experienced greater stress-related changes in response to increased aggression.

This supports the social stress theory, as it demonstrates that crowding may trigger physiological changes associated with stress.

research
now

happy hen housing

Channing C.E., Hughes B.O. & Walker A.W. (2001) Spatial distribution and behaviour of laying hens housed in an alternative system. *Applied Animal Behaviour Science* 72: 335–45

aim: to compare the behaviour of hens in differing social densities.

procedure: perchery-housed laying hens were kept in colonies of eight different sizes from 323 to 912 individuals per pen from age 12 weeks. They were observed from 26 to 61 weeks of age, at 8-week intervals.

findings: in the smallest and largest colony sizes, more standing and fewer feeding behaviours were observed. The distribution of individuals was uneven throughout each pen and this variation was greatest in the larger colony sizes, with individual counts of up to 41 hens per m³.

conclusion: high social density within a pen leads to uneven distribution of hens and greater crowding in some areas. This may have adverse implications for the welfare of perchery-housed hens. There appears to be an optimum colony size at which birds distribute themselves more evenly and move and feed more freely.

A response to stress may account for the behaviour of wild colonies of Norway lemmings (*Lemmus lemmus*) when the population increases. Contrary to popular belief, this small, hamster-like rodent of the Arctic tundra does not make the ultimate sacrifice in the face of population explosion and head for the nearest cliff to hurl itself off. Rather, colonies reach a size at which they migrate to disperse to new feeding and breeding grounds. These migrations may consist of several thousand individuals, predominantly young males. En route to new territories, the lemmings may encounter mountains, rivers and the open sea. While lemmings are good swimmers, and will generally only enter water when there is land in sight, they may swim into open water when many individuals accumulate at the water's edge. As a consequence, many drown (McFarland, 1999).

for and against

studies on crowding in animals

+ crowding research has provided evidence for the physiological effects of crowding, including stress and reduced fertility

+ crowding research has provided evidence for the behavioural consequences, such as increased aggression and changes in dominance and sexual behaviour

— studies of crowding cause stress to animals, and so raise ethical issues

— studies that manipulate spatial density are confounded by consequent effects on space per individual and absolute space available

— studies that manipulate social density are confounded by consequent effects on space per individual and group size

+ the effects of social and spatial density manipulations may be the indirect result of changes in behaviour, such as territoriality, rather than the direct consequences of crowding

+ the findings of animal research may help to improve the conditions under which animals are housed; for instance, in zoos and farms

Studies of crowding in humans

To what extent are the findings from animal studies replicated in the literature on humans? This is difficult to answer, as although laboratory experiments into crowding are conducted, long-term investigations into the effects on humans tend to be naturalistic observations, which means that the results are not directly comparable. The study described below attempted to test Calhoun's 'optimal group size' idea, investigating the pay-off between frustrating and beneficial interactions with others.

Social density

As with animals, studies of social density in humans suggest that crowding results in negative consequences. For example, Saegert (1975) reported increased anxiety during a task performance under crowded compared to uncrowded conditions.

As well as worsening difficult situations, crowding also seems to affect the pleasure that we derive from positive situations. Stewart and Cole (2001) reported that backpackers visiting the Grand Canyon National Park had poorer-quality experiences if they encountered more groups of other people. Crowding in the natural environment seemed detrimentally to affect their enjoyment. Similar effects have been demonstrated in the work environment. Rishi et al (2000) assessed the work satisfaction of employees at a bank in Bhopal, India. They found that work satisfaction was negatively correlated with crowding; the more crowded the employees felt, the less satisfied they were. The following study illustrates the way in which social density affects our perceptions of crowding.

Spatial density

With regard to human responses to increasing spatial density, there seems to be a gender difference; males experience more negative mood states in high compared to low spatial density environments, the reverse being the case for females (Freedman et al, 1972). In chapter 24 we discussed gender differences in personal space, which could explain this finding. Alternatively, it may be the result of differences in response to socialisation. Women tend to be more friendly, seeking opportunities to associate with others, whereas men tend to be competitive in their social encounters, and thus may view others close by as a threat (Deaux & LaFrance, 1998). However, some studies report no differences between the genders in their preferences for isolation (see, for example, Demirbas & Demirkan, 2000).

Recent evidence suggests that the sensation of crowding is affected not only by our perception of density but by our expectations — if we correctly anticipate crowds, this helps us to tolerate them.

classic
research

people, privacy and perceived crowding

Baum A. & Valins S. (1977) *Architecture and social behavior: psychological studies of social density.* **Hilldale, NJ: Erlbaum**

aim: to investigate the balance between the benefits of increased opportunities to interact as density increases and the costs of such enforced encounters.

procedure: the perceptions and behaviour of occupants of two different types of university halls of residence were compared. The accommodation was either corridor-style or suite-style, each offering the same amount of space per individual, the same number of individuals per floor and the same facilities (bathroom and lounge). They differed only in the number of other individuals sharing those facilities (either 4 to 6 in suites and 34 on corridors) and hence the number of different interpersonal encounters (in other words, the social density varied).

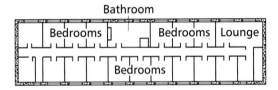
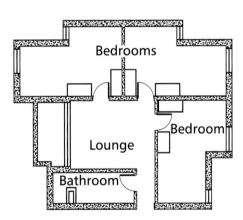

Figure 27.3 People, privacy and perceived crowding (based on: Baum and Valins (1977))

findings: residents in corridor-style accommodation perceived their floors to be more crowded. They felt that they had to engage in inconvenient and unwanted social interactions, and wanted to avoid other people. Their feelings of helplessness were reflected in their social skills. They were less likely to initiate a conversation with a stranger or to reach a consensus after a discussion and were less socially assertive and competitive.

conclusion: exposure to a large number of other people, especially when the group lacks social structure, has negative consequences. Behaviour becomes less sociable because of enforced, uncontrollable personal contacts. Individuals living in high-density accommodation learn that they have little control over their social environment. This leads to feelings of helplessness and a tendency be less assertive and to avoid social interactions.

Effects on health

Animal studies have shown that high-density living may affect health because there is a greater risk of the spreading of disease (Hoogland, 1979) and the same effect may arise in human populations (Paulus, 1988). Studies of death rates in prisons suggest that inmates in higher-den-sity settings are at greater risk, even when factors such as violent deaths have been controlled for (see figure 27.4).

Evans (1979) reports that varying spatial density – for instance, by putting 10 people in an 8 foot by 12 foot (2.4 m by 3.6 m) room – increased blood pressure and other physiological indicators of stress. Students living in high-

research
now

the benefits of being on top

Kaya N. & Erkíp E. (2001) Satisfaction in a dormitory building: the effects of floor height on the perception of room size and crowding. *Environment and Behavior* 33: 35–53

aim: to investigate the effects of room location (floor height) on students' perception of the size of their room and how crowded they felt.

procedure: residents occupying two dormitory blocks (one for men and one for women) at Bilkent University, Ankara, were studied. The identical five-storey buildings contained identical rooms and had equal densities. The occupants were surveyed with regard to their perception of their room size, privacy and satisfaction.

findings: residents on the highest floor perceived their rooms to be larger and felt less crowded than residents on the lowest floor. Participants who perceived their rooms as being larger expressed greater feelings of privacy and were more satisfied with their dormitory rooms.

conclusion: the perception of density, as well as the actual density, affects the sensation of crowding and hence satisfaction with accommodation.

density accommodation make more frequent visits to the infirmary (Baron et al, 1976) and Fuller et al (1993) report a higher level of physical illness in crowded condi-

tions. Fleming et al (1987) compared the effect of a challenging task on blood pressure and heart rate of people living in crowded or uncrowded neighbourhoods. Those

research
now

crowded shops and crabby shoppers

Machleit K., Eroglu S. & Mantel S.P. (2000) Perceived retail crowding and shopping satisfaction: what modifies the relationship? *Journal of Consumer Psychology* 9: 29–42

aim: to examine the relationship between retail store crowding and shopping satisfaction.

procedure: a total of 1006 participants were used in two field and one laboratory experiment to investigate the importance of high density on emotions and satisfaction.

findings: shopping satisfaction was shown to be reduced by the emotions associated with crowding. However, this effect was moderated by expectations of crowding and personal tolerance for crowding. These relationships were found in both laboratory and field settings.

conclusion: people who expect shops to be crowded and who are relatively tolerant of crowds are more likely to find shopping satisfying under high-density conditions than those who have less realistic expectations or are less tolerant.

for and
against

studies on crowding in humans

➕ laboratory experiments are well controlled and are comparable to animal studies

➖ laboratory experiments of crowding lack ecological validity

➖ laboratory studies of crowding in humans can only study the short-term effects

➕ research has shown that crowding affects social behaviour, causing people to become less sociable, avoid one another and take less interest in their neighbours

➕ expectations of crowding as well as actual density affects our experience of crowding

Pandey (1999) asked participants living in high-density or low-density areas of Gorakhpur City, India, about their health status. A positive relationship between crowding and illness was found; that is, people living in more crowded areas exhibited poorer physical and mental health. These people also reported a strong sensation of crowding (in other words, there was a positive correlation between objective crowding and feelings of crowding) and reduced perceived control. However, Chan (1999) tested 414 urban residents from the hyperdense metropolis of Hong Kong and found that residents in spatially constrained dwellings did not necessarily feel crowded. Where architectural designs met expectations – that is, the participants were satisfied with their physical surroundings – this helped to alleviate feelings of crowdedness.

Not only may high-density living conditions pose greater health risks, but it also seems to impair our ability to care for our own health. Menezes et al (2000) studied a range of factors that could have been related to discharged psychiatric patients failing to comply with outpatient treatment. The only variable associated with poor compliance was residential crowding. Patients living in very crowded homes were twice as likely to miss outpatient appointments as those living in less-crowded homes.

Effects on social behaviour

Baum and Valins (1977) showed that increasing the apparent social density by increasing the number of people encountered affects social behaviour. Under crowded conditions, people became less sociable, less assertive, avoided one another and took less interest in their neighbours. At higher social densities, for instance, with three people sharing a room rather than two, room-mates' perceptions of each other become less positive (Baron et al, 1976). Crowding appears to reduce our liking for individuals, as well as for social interaction in general. Furthermore, the effects of crowding on social interaction seem to reduce our ability to seek out others when we need them. Lepore et al (1991) found that individuals who had high levels of social support lost this buffering effect after eight months in crowded conditions; they no longer sought the assistance of other people as a resource in times of psychological distress. Crowding results in withdrawal: it seems to erode the social support networks that are most important in stressful situations.

Crowding also impacts on prosocial behaviour; that is, the extent to which people will help others. Bickman et al (1973) compared helping behaviour across three conditions: high-density, medium-density and low-density dormitories. The experimenters 'accidentally' dropped envelopes that had been stamped and addressed into each dormitory and observed the helping behaviour – that is, the number of envelopes that were picked up and put into

participants experiencing chronic crowding demonstrated greater cardiovascular reactivity (higher heart rates and blood pressure) than those from uncrowded environments. The effect of crowding seems to be an enduring one, affecting performance even away from the stressful environment itself.

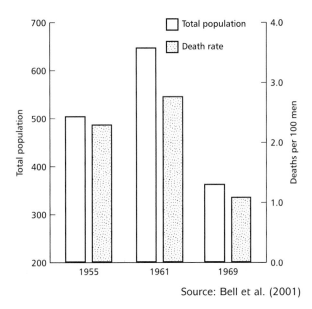

Source: Bell et al. (2001)

Figure 27.4 A higher population size in a prison setting is associated with a higher mortality rate (Paulus et al, 1978)

the postbox. The graph illustrates the rate of prosocial behaviour in each condition. Crowded conditions seemed to reduce the likelihood of helping fellow residents.

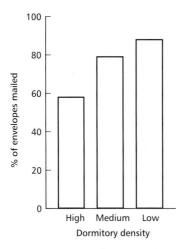

Source: Bickman et al (1973)

Figure 27.5 Residents in crowded dormitories are less likely to pick up and post apparently lost items of mail for other residents

If crowding reduces prosocial behaviour, does it also increase antisocial behaviour? The evidence here seems to be contradictory, with effects dependent on age, gender and access to resources (Bell et al, 2001). Since much research on the effects of crowding on aggression is conducted in laboratories, its validity in the real world is questionable. However, research conducted in settings such as prisons (see figure 27.6) avoids this criticism – although, arguably, the prison population may not be representative in terms of aggressiveness.

Patterns similar to those of Cox et al (1984) have been found with both elderly residents in long-term care and young people in crisis centres. Morgan and Stewart (1998) found that increased social and spatial density were associated with more disruptive behaviour in elderly residents with dementia, while Teare et al (1995) found that the probability of problem behaviour arising in young people at a shelter increased as it became more crowded. In hospital settings with psychiatric patients, Ng et al (2001) and Nijman and Rector (1999) have found that occupancy levels affect the behaviour of patients, with crowded conditions leading to increased verbal and physical aggression.

Effects on performance

If crowding detrimentally affects our physiology and social behaviour, it seems likely that it will also have negative effects on task performance. If so, this would have implications for the ideal density experienced in learning and working environments. Although early studies suggested that there was no decrement in performance with increased density (see, for example, Freedman et al, 1971), subsequent studies, using more complex tasks, have demonstrated some effects (see, for example, Aiello et al, 1975). Since crowded conditions raise arousal level, the Yerkes–Dodson law would predict that we would perform better on simple tasks in relatively crowded conditions, but relatively poorly on more difficult tasks under similar circumstances (see figure 27.6).

Karlin et al (1979) found that students living in crowded accommodation (with three people in a room designed for two) suffered a decline in their grades. More recently, Bruins and Barber (2000) conducted a field experiment on 80 members of the public recruited outside a super-

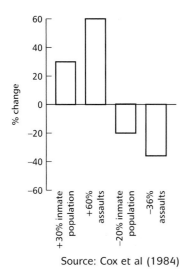

Source: Cox et al (1984)

Figure 27.6 Cox et al (1984) found a strong relationship between density in prisons and inmate aggression

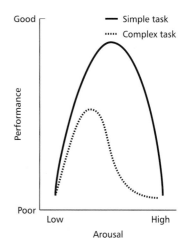

Figure 27.7 The Yerkes–Dodson law predicts a relationship between arousal level and performance on tasks of differing difficulties. According to this law, when we are highly aroused (such as in crowded situations), we perform best on simple tasks

market during crowded or uncrowded periods. The participants were required to complete a 'shopping list' of physical and mental tasks. Under crowded conditions the performance of the participants, particularly on the mental tasks, was impaired.

Crowd behaviour

So far, we have only considered the effects of crowding, particularly those pertaining to high-density living; that is, the consequences of chronic exposure to crowded conditions. Psychologists are also interested in the processes that lead to the formation of short-term crowds, such as are seen at demonstrations or public events. Such crowding falls under the term 'collective behaviour', which can be defined as spontaneous in origin, structureless and dependent upon stimulation from within (Milgram & Toch, 1969). Several theories have been proposed to account for the behaviour of people in crowds, three of which are discussed below.

Contagion

Le Bon (1879) suggested that the behaviour of an individual within a crowd is irrational and uncritical; an individual within a crowd loses the measure of the norms that usually govern his or her behaviour and so becomes 'primitive': hence mob violence results. Contagion theory thus suggests that riotous behaviour spreads through a crowd like a contagious disease. Le Bon proposed four situational determinants of crowd behaviour:

- *suggestibility* – individuals become more inclined to respond to the ideas of others, especially when proposed in an authoritative manner and in the absence of a clear leader;
- *social contagion* – individuals within a crowd arouse and respond to one another, thereby amplifying the intensity of their interactions;
- *impersonality* – individuals lose their appreciation of others as people and so cease to treat them as such;
- *anonymity* – within a crowd each individual loses his or her sense of individuality and hence the responsibility for his or her own behaviour.

Of these, social contagion and anonymity have continued to receive the attention of psychologists as key issues in crowd behaviour. When an individual is anonymous, as in a crowd, he or she may lose his or her sense of being an individual. Festinger et al (1952) called this process deindividuation. Group members cease to pay attention to individuals as individuals, thus losing their self-consciousness and with it the belief that they are accountable for their own actions – moral responsibility shifts from the individual to the group. This loss of the internal constraints that normally inhibit socially unacceptable behaviour could therefore explain the criminal activity of crowds – such as the looting and violence seen during riots. The concept of deindividuation is discussed further below.

Social contagion has been observed in animals: behaviour patterns demonstrated by some animals appear in others that can see or hear them. For example, one barking dog is liable to set off all the others in the neighbourhood. Such social transmission of behaviour can also be seen in people – when one person yawns, those around that person find it irresistible not to follow suit. Although this resembles social learning, it is much simpler. Unlike social learning, contagion does not require that a new behaviour is learned; nor does it demand that the models for the behaviour are in any way responsible for tutoring those acquiring the behaviour. Contagion simply occurs when a pre-existing behaviour is triggered in one individual by observing that behaviour in another. Thus, for individuals in a crowd, the nature and intensity of their interactions is likely to escalate; once aroused, individuals seek an outlet for their intense emotions. Horton and Hunt (1976) report an incident in which the victim of a lynch mob was protected by the mayor, resulting in the redirection of the attack on to the mayor. Once incited to attack through social contagion, the group sought an alternative target for their aggression.

Members of a crowd may also share aspects of behaviour, emotions and motivation because of the nature of the crowd; for example, people at a concert all enjoy the same music. Durkheim (1898) suggested that *controlled emotional contagion* (the spread of feeling in a peaceful situation) can be useful in allowing the expression of otherwise pent-up feelings. This tendency of like-minded people to congregate forms the basis of *convergence theory* – the suggestion that crowds are composed of similar individuals because they 'converge' or come together. Benewick and Holton (1987) found that members of a congregation of 80,000 at Wembley Stadium in 1982, attending a mass said by Pope Paul, reported strong feelings of unity with other members of the crowd.

Deindividuation

Diener (1979) suggests that, once within a crowd, an individual loses his or her sense of separateness, because self-awareness is blocked and the person is unable to monitor his or her own behaviour. We frequently perform certain forms of behaviour without self-awareness, but we are accustomed to returning to a higher level of conscious control when the situation or outcome is unexpected, or when we feel that we are being judged.

media watch

How can the ideas of Durkheim (1898) help us to understand the behaviour of the crowd paying tribute after Princess Diana's death?

According to Diener (1979), self-regulation is also lost when we become part of a crowd, and this results in deindividuation. Without the appropriate self-regulatory restraints, we become less concerned about others' opinions of our behaviour, less rational and more impulsive. These are exactly the kinds of behaviour that we see in crowds.

How does being part of a crowd result in this change in behaviour? Prentice-Dunn and Rogers (1982) suggest there are two routes via which socially inappropriate behaviour in crowds could increase. These derive from two kinds of self-awareness, private and public. *Private self-awareness* refers to the self-regulation described by

interactive angles

Think about situations in which you lack conscious awareness of yourself as an individual. Generate a list of circumstances or activities where you 'do it without thinking'. These might include actions that you perform often that have become automatic, such as doing up buttons, and instances of social behaviour where you 'know the protocol', such as replying to 'Hello, how are you?' or requesting a bus to stop.

To what extent is this crowd demonstrating the impulsivity and lack of rationality predicted by Diener (1979)?

Diener: it is our conscious attention to our own beliefs, feelings and behaviour. *Public self-awareness* is the extent to which we care about how other people regard our behaviour.

Being part of a crowd can reduce private self-awareness because our attention shifts from ourselves to others: the noise, arousal and participation in events cause us to focus 'outwardly' on the situation around us. This, in turn, results in a lowering of attention to ourselves, so we are less aware of our internal beliefs and standards, and thus an internal state of deindividuation arises. We experience a loss of individual identity and become more likely to perform kinds of behaviour that we would otherwise regard as unacceptable.

Public self-awareness is also affected by the presence of a crowd, since we become relatively anonymous as the number of other people increases. Other factors such as wearing masks or identical clothing also increase our sense of anonymity. In addition, larger groups result in *diffusion of responsibility*; we feel less accountable when

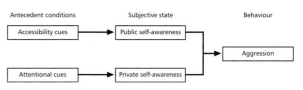

Source: Prentice-Dunn and Rogers (1982)

Figure 27.8 A model of the independent effects of different types of self-awareness impacting on behaviour in a crowd (Prentice-Dunn & Rogers, 1982)

there are other people around – the responsibility is shared (that is, diffused) when the numbers in a crowd rise, so no particular individual feels responsible. Since people feel that they can neither be identified nor held responsible for events, this will compound their disregard for social norms and laws.

The importance of anonymity is supported by evidence such as that of Zimbardo (1970), who demonstrated experimentally that identically dressed participants whose faces were covered (who were therefore unidentifiable members of a group) delivered stronger electric shocks than participants who were dressed normally and wore name tags. This suggested that deindividuation was related to an increase in antisocial behaviour (however, see also Johnson & Downing, 1979, page 100). Mullen (1986) studied lynchings reported in newspapers between 1899 and 1946. He found a strong relationship between mob size and the atrocity of the crime; the larger the group was, the more aggressive and destructive were their actions. This suggests that

members of larger groups did indeed lose their self-awareness to the group, felt less identifiable and less responsible, and were therefore more antisocial in their behaviour.

Finally, Prentice-Dunn and Rogers (1982) suggest that when the effects of the loss of private and public self-awareness are combined with behavioural cues, such as weapons and aggressive models, aggression and other socially inappropriate forms of behaviour arise.

classic
research

nurses get nicer

Johnson R.D. & Downing L.L. (1979) Deindividuation and valence of cues: effects on prosocial and antisocial behaviour. *Journal of Personality and Social Psychology* 37: 1532–8

---

aim: to investigate the effects of deindividuation on the incidence of antisocial behaviour.

procedure: participants were either dressed in robes with hoods (having negative connotations, such as association with the racist Ku Klux Klan group or with executioners) or in nurses' uniforms (having positive associations with helping and caring). In addition, the participants were either identifiable – they had name tags on their costumes – or anonymous. Photographs were taken of each individual and each was told that these were on view to other participants, thus achieving individuation and deindividuation conditions. The participants were required to decide the level of shock to be administered to another person if the participant failed to perform a task correctly.

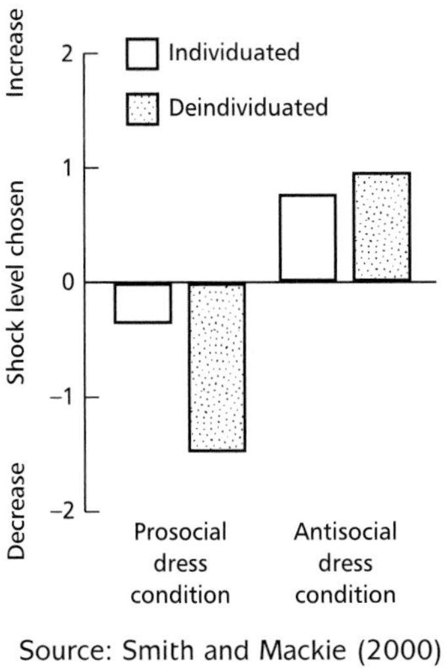

Source: Smith and Mackie (2000)

Figure 27.9 Effect of pro and antisocial on shock selection

findings: clothing with aggressive associations increased the likelihood of participants using higher shock levels, and this effect was increased when the participants were deindividuated. Prosocial clothing resulted in lower shock levels, and this effect was also exaggerated when the participants were deindividuated; that is, the nurse-like participants gave even lower shocks when they felt anonymous.

conclusion: the effects of increasing deindividuation increases people's tendency to follow salient social norms, in this instance to behave in keeping with their 'uniform'. Antisocial behaviour was thus only increased in those participants who wore aggressive-style clothing. This suggests that deindividuation does not result in a freeing from internal standards, but in people altering their behaviour in accordance with the social norms of the group with which they are identified at the time.

for and against

deindividuation

➕ it can explain people's actions when 'deindividuated', or when they believe they cannot be identified

➕ it explains the apparently irrational and impulsive nature of behaviour seen by members of crowds

➖ it cannot explain why some crowds become violent and others do not: it takes no account of the intent of the crowd

Emergent norms

From the research that we have looked at so far, it is clear that some groups become antisocial while others become prosocial. We have not yet considered a theory that can explain how these differences in outcome arise. Contagion theory (page 350) can explain how a crowd might become riotous if some angry individuals exacerbate feelings of aggression and desire for revenge in those around them. Also, deindividuation theory would predict that the behaviour of individuals will contravene societal norms as they become unconstrained. Emergent norm theory enables us to explain how members of a group might in fact be conforming to a new, emerging set of standards for behaviour. Turner and Killian (1972) suggest that two key factors need to be present for crowd behaviour to change:

● the crowd must develop a new – that is, *emergent* – norm for behaviour (such as aggression);

● individuals in the crowd should be identifiable, thus increasing social pressure on them to conform to the new norms.

This contradicts the predictions of deindividuation theory in that it relies on individuals being identifiable. In a test of the two explanations, Mann et al (1982) produced evidence to suggest that both emergent norm formation and deindividuation may occur. The former was supported, as participants behaved more aggressively when told that the group norm was aggressive. The latter was also supported, as identifiable participants were less aggressive than anonymous participants.

research now

is litter the norm?

Cialdini R.B., Reno R.R. & Kallgren C.A. (1990) A focus theory of normative conduct: recycling the concept of norms to reduce littering in public places. *Journal of Personality and Social Psychology* 58: 1015–26

aim: to find out whether evidence of people behaving contrary to a social norm caused others to adopt this new standard of behaviour.

procedure: five separate studies were conducted, two of which are described here. In study A, participants were observed as they crossed a car park that was either clean (anti-littering norm) or littered (pro-littering norm). Half of the participants saw a confederate dropping a leaflet that said 'THIS IS AUTOMOTIVE SAFETY WEEK. PLEASE DRIVE CAREFULLY' and all, on returning to their car, found an identical leaflet under their windscreen wiper. The participants were observed to see whether this leaflet was dropped into the environment around the vehicle.

In study B, conditions were created by introducing different amounts of litter along a path on different occasions (between none and 16 items of rubbish). Passers-by were given leaflets and observed as they turned a corner and walked along the previously littered path, to see whether and how quickly they dropped their leaflet.

findings: Study A: participants more often dropped litter in a littered environment than in a clean one, and this effect was greater when attention to the norm was reinforced by seeing the confederate littering. However, they were less likely to drop litter in the clean environment when the confederate did so; again, their attention was being drawn to the norm (of anti-littering in this case).

study B: the participants were more likely to drop their leaflet if the path was already littered; and the more litter there was, the more likely they were to do so. Virtually all participants who had not littered by the end of the path placed their leaflets in a rubbish bin that was visible only when they reached the end of the path.

conclusion: the litter appeared to draw the participants' attention to the prevailing norm: where that was disregard for the environment, this induced littering behaviour. The participants' perceived an emerging norm (which may have differed from their internal standards) and behaved accordingly.

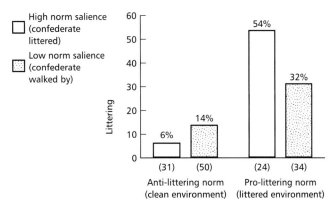

Source: Cialdini et al (1990)

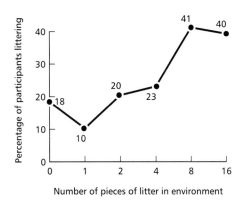

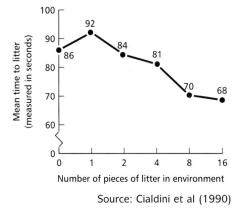

Source: Cialdini et al (1990)

The findings of Mann et al can be explained by Postmes and Spears's (1998) proposal that the process of deindividuation results in individuals being more likely to respond to emerging group norms, which are reliant on the situation or context. This arises because deindividuation has three characteristics:

- a decreased focus on personal identity (but not a loss of self-awareness);
- an increased responsiveness to situational group and context norms;
- it is neutral with respect to general social norms.

This can therefore explain why crowds behave differently: deindividuation may or may not occur, and when it does, the behaviour of the crowd will be affected by the locally arising emergent norms. Furthermore, it can explain the selectivity of behaviour exhibited by members of a crowd.

Reicher and Potter (1985) studied scientific and lay accounts of the riot that arose in the deprived area of St Paul's, Bristol, in 1980. They concluded that the police raided a café in the belief that illegal drinking was taking place. When they tried to leave, bricks were thrown and they requested back-up. A 3000-strong rioting crowd amassed but, contrary to the predictions of contagion theory or deindividuation, the rioters were not an irrational, irresponsible mob. Instead, they were highly selective in their destruction, for example:

- damage to property was restricted to police buildings, banks and other symbols of the establishment, rather than local shops or houses;

- damage to other property (such as cars) was restricted to those believed to be unmarked police vehicles;

- the effects of the riot were confined to the St Paul's district and did not spread to other parts of the city;

- the rioters denied that they had lost their sense of identity – rather, they felt a strong sense of pride in their community.

These findings suggest that the attention of members of the crowd shifted from themselves as individuals to a focus on other members of the group. Since the emerging group norm was one of specific aggression towards the establishment, this provided a cue for the behaviour of others. This theory is based on the ideas of social identity theory (see Jarvis et al, 2000). Reicher's (1984) view sees the rioters as an 'in group' who adopted a shared social identity (based on their location and behaviour) and could justify their behaviour because the initial police presence was judged to have been illegitimate.

Reicher's explanation would support the findings of Marsh et al (1978) after an extensive study of football supporters. They concluded that much of the fans' behaviour followed established social rules, which imposed restrictions on their aggressive behaviour, and that uncontrolled violence was more likely to arise when police intervention interfered with the fans' own self-regulation. Similarly, Waddington et al (1987) observed and interviewed demonstrators on two rallies that took place during the 1984 miners' strike. On both occasions, the crowd held the same political views and was in the same town. The rallies were only two weeks apart, but one was violent while the other was not. At the second rally, the peaceful demonstration, marshalling of the protesters had been organised from within, barriers had been erected to keep the police at a discreet distance and alternative channels for arousal were provided by speakers and entertainment. Thus, the 'in group' were following their own, predetermined rules, rather than having those of the police (who were viewed at the time as allied to Margaret Thatcher's Conservative government) thrust upon them.

So, in addition to explaining riotous crowds, it is possible to see how, if alternative norms were to emerge from the behaviour of a crowd – such as in the situation described by Waddington et al, at the funeral of Princess Diana or during the Pope's visit (see page 351) – entirely different crowd behaviour could arise. If the 'in group' favoured peaceful behaviour, this would become the behavioural norm.

However, Reicher's research is not without problems. Observers who are present at the time of a riot are unlikely to be without bias. Furthermore, recollections during interviews after the event will be subject to confabulation, the changing of memories after they have been stored, as demonstrated by Loftus (see, for example, Loftus & Palmer, 1974; Loftus et al, 1978: see also Jarvis et al, 2000). In a series of studies, Loftus showed how the recall of eye witnesses was not just inaccurate but could be altered with expectations created by hearing various verbal suggestions. Such evidence indicates that interviewees who had discussed the day's events among themselves would be unlikely to have unbiased recall of the riot, and would have tended to mould their memories in line with expected behavioural norms. Since it is not ethical to perform studies of riotous crowding, researchers are faced with either the pitfalls of interviews (see, for example, Reicher & Potter, 1985; Benewick & Holton, 1987) or analyses such as that of Mullen (1986).

Not all studies of riots generate such a clear pattern as asserted by Reicher and Potter (1985) or Marsh et al (1978). Acts of destruction may spread out from the affected community and may appear in different locations at different times, as observed in the 1965 riot in the Watts district of Los Angeles. In such instances, it seems less likely that social identity and emergent norms are responsible for such forms of behaviour.

for and against

emergent norm theory

+ it can explain why some groups become riotous while others remain calm

+ it sees crowds as groups of individuals with a shared purpose, who are capable of interpreting events around them, rather than an uncontrollable mass

– it can be criticised for suggesting that individuals are unable to make appropriate judgements in a crowd situation. There is good evidence of individuals making rational choices about alternative courses of action (see, for example, Berk, 1974)

where to now?

▶ **Baron R.A. & Byrne D. (1999)** *Social psychology.* **London: Allyn & Bacon.** This text has a short but interesting section on crowding and density. It considers, for example, cultural differences perceptions of crowding and the effects of crowding in prisons.

▶ **Wren K. (1999)** *Social influences.* **London: Routledge.** This small book has a chapter on collective behaviour that covers crowd behaviour and theories of crowding.

what do you know?

1 (a) Describe **one** study of the effects of crowding on animals.

(b) Describe and assess the effects of high-density living on humans

(c) Evaluate the extent to which animals are good models of the human response to crowding.

2 Discuss **one** theory of crowding. Use research evidence in your evaluation.

3 We sometimes describe ourselves as feeling 'lost in a crowd'. Describe **two** theories of crowding and discuss the extent to which each could account for this description.

Conclusions

Living in crowded conditions has a range of detrimental effects on animals, many of which are also exhibited by humans in high-density accommodation. In animals, fecundity falls, health fails, aggression increases and some individuals become highly territorial. In response to high-density living, humans also become less socially competent; they become anxious, feel helpless, avoid social situations and grow to dislike the people they have to encounter. Furthermore, they are less inclined to seek help from others when they need it, and less likely to offer help when it is required. People also become dissatisfied with their accommodation and feel crowded, especially when they are forced into social interactions. High-density living affects health, increasing blood pressure, the incidence of illness and the risk of suicide. In crowded conditions, people may become aggressive or disruptive, and suffer reduced performance on complex mental tasks.

The behaviour of people in crowds may be explained by a number of theories. Deindividuation can explain the way in which people in crowds may cease to act rationally, as they no longer feel responsible for their own actions. Emergent norm theory can also account for differences in crowd behaviour; that is, whether they are peaceful or become riotous.

28 Changing behaviour to save the environment

what's ahead? This chapter explores an aspect of human–environment interaction in which people have an impact on their surroundings rather than simply being affected by them. Since the environment is a shared and limited resource, we have a duty to interact with it in responsible ways. We will consider the ways in which humans can affect the physical environment and consider the options available to encourage people into more environmentally friendly behaviour, including ways of changing attitudes and the use of promotional literature.

Environmental matters

The natural environment is occupied by ourselves and by non-human inhabitants. It is a scarce resource that humans are using up increasingly quickly. The human population, which already stands at 6.2 billion, is growing at a rate of 211,000 people per day. The consequence of this expansion is an increased demand on the natural environment to provide resources such as fuel, agricultural land and the space and materials required for building (stone, wood, metals and so on). These demands are compounded by the additional stress placed on the natural environment to absorb the destructive effects of modern existence; for example, the impact of advancing technology, deforestation, reduction in biodiversity and coastal land reclamation. Pollution alone has detrimental effects on landscapes, soils, rivers and the atmosphere, resulting in the greenhouse effect and destruction of the ozone layer. Humans, unlike any other occupants of the Earth, have a responsibility for the environment, because we are both the most destructive inhabitants and the only ones with the powers of reason to choose how we behave.

Environmentally friendly behaviour

Relevant factors

A number of factors dictate an individual's tendency to engage in environmentally friendly behaviour:

- their attitude to environmental issues;
- values;
- behavioural constraints;
- the effort required to engage in appropriate behaviour;
- commitment and moral responsibility;
- information and feedback.

Attitudes

Breckler and Wiggins (1989) define *attitudes* as 'enduring mental representations of various features of the social or physical world. They are acquired through experience and exert a directive influence on subsequent behavior.' Because attitudes are internal value judgements, they cannot be seen directly; they must be inferred from their effects on thoughts (as indicated by self-reports) or on behaviour (which can be observed). Thus an opinion about recycling is an attitude, and could be measured by asking people about the feelings that they have towards the issue, or by observing the frequency and diligence of their recycling activities. People may report positive, negative or neutral evaluations of the attitude object (for example, recycling) and these may differ in intensity; that is, the strength of people's judgements will vary. Differences between people's attitudes can indicate the affective component of that attitude – that is, the emotional evaluation the individual has made regarding the concept of recycling – as well as the cognitive aspects, such as their memory for relevant information, the beliefs that they hold or mental images relating to the issue. Kaiser et al (1999) view environmental attitude as the key to enabling psychology, as a discipline, to encourage people to use natural resources in a less exploitative way. In an Internet-based literature search using PsychInfo (a search facility dedicated to psychological literature) they found that almost two-thirds of all environmental–psychological publications had 'attitude' in the title.

Values

Attitudes towards the environment can be considered on a global as well as a local scale. Until recently, the dominant view of the Western world was one of human supremacy and ownership. A shift in approach to the world's resources seems now to be occurring and a new ecological paradigm is emerging. These views are summarised by Bell et al (2001).

Contrasting views of the world's resources

The dominant world view holds that:

1 Humans are unique and have dominion over all other organisms.

2 We are masters of our own destiny – we have the intellectual and technological resources to solve any problem.

3 We have access to an infinite amount of resources.

4 Human history involves infinite progress for the better.

The new ecological paradigm holds that:

1 Humans are interdependent with other organisms, such that their preservation is to our advantage.

2 Many things that we do have unintended negative consequences for the environment.

3 Some things, such as fossil fuels, are finite.

4 Ecological constraints, such as the carrying capacity of an environment, are placed upon us.

Bell et al (2001), page 479

Dunlap and Van Liere (1978) have developed the *New Environmental Paradigm* (NEP), a single measure of environmental attitude. This recognises that the relationship between people and the natural environment is changing from one of alienation and exploitation to one in which humans are an integral part of nature. Schultz and Zelezny (1999) measured environmental attitudes of students from 14 different countries using a revised version of the NEP. They found consistent patterns of environmental values across countries – for example, differences in the believed effect of destruction of the environment on the individual – that supported the use of the NEP as a tool. However, Kaiser et al (1999) argue that NEP is partly a measure of the evaluative aspects of attitudes and is not necessarily a good predictor of environmental behaviour. Their research focuses on the role of values in determining environmental attitudes. This represents a further change in approach to the study of environmental issues. They argue that values – an individual's guiding principles – are more fundamental than attitudes.

research now

ecological care counts

Kaiser F.G., Wölfing S. & Fuhrer U. (1999) Environmental attitude and ecological behaviour. *Journal of Environmental Psychology* **19: 1–19**

aim: to investigate whether environmental attitude is a reliable predictor of ecological behaviour.

procedure: questionnaires were sent to members of two different Swiss transportation associations which differed in their ideology (one aiming to promote minimal impact on humans and nature, and the other representing drivers' interests). The return rate for the former group was much higher than for the latter. The questionnaires measured social desirability, ecological behaviour and environmental attitude (including knowledge, values and behavioural intention). In addition, factors affecting the difficulties encountered in attempting to behave in ecologically sound ways were assessed as a measure of influences beyond people's actual behavioural control.

findings: it was found that environmental knowledge and environmental values explained 40 per cent of the variance in ecological behavioural intention (the extent to which people believe that they will make an effort to respond in ecological ways). In turn, behavioural intention predicted 75 per cent of the variance in ecological behaviour.

conclusion: having the intention to engage in ecological forms of behaviour is significantly related to a person's knowledge about environmental issues, and to the extent to which they have beliefs that place the environment high amongst their concerns. This intention then affects their actual performance of various kinds of ecological behaviour.

Behavioural constraints

The effort required to engage in environmentally friendly behaviour affects the extent to which people participate. Luyben and Bailey (1979) investigated the effects of rewards and the proximity of containers on newspaper recycling behaviour in four mobile home parks. In the reward condition, children earned toys for recycling: in the proximity condition, additional recycling containers were made available. Both conditions resulted in increased levels of recycling. Offering rewards increased recycling by 92 per cent over the baseline rate, while increasing the proximity of facilities increased recycling by 52 per cent. Indeed, it could be argued that both represent an increase due to reduced effort, as it was the children, rather than the adults, who generated the newpaper waste, and who were expending effort in the reward condition!

Tanner (1999) considered two specific categories of constraint that may affect pro-environmental behaviour. To investigate these, Tanner used a questionnaire with Swiss adults to determine the constraints on their environmentally friendly behaviour. She identified two factors that affected the frequency of their car use:

- subjective factors assumed to affect the preference for pro-environmental behavioural alternatives (such as a sense of responsibility or perceived behavioural barriers, such as getting wet and cold doing the recycling in the rain);
- objective conditions that inhibit the performance of pro-environmental action (socio-demographic variables, such as lack of automobile, place of residence and income).

Having a pro-environmental attitude was not sufficient to necessarily result in appropriate behaviour. The individuals also had to overcome subjective and objective barriers to pro-environmental behaviour.

Commitment and moral responsibility

The relative importance of factors other than attitude is supported by evidence that suggests that engagement in paper recycling can be induced by increasing commitment (Wang & Katzev, 1990). Using elderly residents in a retirement home and students in a dormitory, Wang and Katzev demonstrated that manipulating the commitment to recycling – for example, by asking participants to sign a pledge – is more likely to result in a sustained change in behaviour than alternative strategies (group commitment or token reinforcers). This was the case especially for individuals. Furthermore, Hormuth (1999) found that physical settings and social structures that allowed for social exchange and the establishment of social norms were better predictors of compliance with recycling rules than an individual's environmentally related attitudes. Kaiser and Shimoda (1999) found that moral responsibility predicts a considerable proportion of a person's ecological behaviour. The guilt that people feel for what they do or fail to do in respect of environmentally friendly behaviour promotes their self-ascription of responsibility and this, in turn, dictates the way in which they behave.

Information and feedback

The extent to which individuals perceive action to be necessary will depend in part on the amount of information available and whether they are aware of conflicting views about appropriate responses to a situation. For example, people may be more likely to engage in paper recycling if they are informed about the damage that virgin paper production does to the environment, but less likely to do so if they are also told that the trees grown to make paper help to combat the greenhouse effect. Conflicting information such as this may lead to cognitive dissonance – the discomfort associated with conflicting beliefs – and may disincline the public from engaging in environmentally friendly kinds of behaviour. However, an alternative response to such inconsistencies in belief may be to consolidate people's determination to behave in a particular way: having invested time and effort on recycling in the past, to abandon the habit now would suggest that their previous efforts have been wasted. Thus pro-environmental behaviour may be increased.

Brandon and Lewis (1999) investigated the effect of feedback on pro-environmental behaviour. The 120 households studied received a range of information: feedback about changes in their energy consumption, tips on energy saving either via computer or leaflets or through feedback relating to financial or environmental costs. Their energy consumption was monitored and compared to their earlier usage. Income and demographic features predicted previous usage but not changes in consumption during the study; here, environmental attitude and feedback had the most effect. The installation of computers resulted in the greatest reduction in energy consumption. People with positive environmental attitudes but who had not previously engaged in many conservation activities were most likely to change their usage following feedback. Therefore, pro-environmental attitudes are important, but without a cue such as feedback, a positive attitude alone may be insufficient to trigger environmentally friendly behaviour.

Recycling

Pro-environmental attitudes and values are important because they affect our pro-environmental behaviour. A key example of such behaviour is the reuse of materials. Recycling has two clear environmental benefits; it reduces waste and conserves resources. We will look at this example of environmentally friendly behaviour in detail. What stops people from recycling their rubbish? Inconvenience and the demands on time are frequently cited as reasons for failing to recycle (Vining & Ebreo, 1990; Gamba & Oskamp, 1994; McCarty & Shrum, 1994). As a consequence, when recycling activities are voluntary, they tend to be low priority and the behaviour reduces with time (Grogen & Bell, 1989; Werner et al, 1995). However, even mandatory requirements to recycle are not necessarily sufficient to motivate people to prepare and sort their recyclables. Unless people participate fully in recycling schemes, the output is lower in quantity and quality and so is less viable in the marketplace.

In an attempt to understand and predict people's behaviour in such situations, Sansone et al (1992) proposed a model that incorporated the factors that affect a decision to engage and persist with a task that is neither inherently rewarding nor pleasurable. They suggested that people need to redefine the task such that they transform their experience into a positive one. In the case of recycling, this may be done by:

- *changing the focus of the task*, from how time-consuming it is to how quickly recyclable material is amassed

- *adding variety to the task*, by listening to music or the radio while sorting

- *changing their definition of the task*, from an emphasis on rubbish to a means of working with a reusable resource.

Figure 28.1 What are the factors that affect your decision to recycle or not recycle waste?

research now

recycling redefined

Werner C.M. & Makela E. (1998) Motivations and behaviors that support recycling. *Journal of Environmental Psychology* **18: 373–86**

aim: to investigate factors affecting the motivation to recycle household waste as a test of Sansone *et al.*'s (1992) model of how people engage themselves in a boring but necessary task.

procedure: on two occasions, 27 months apart, participants filled in questionnaires asking about their attitudes to and satisfactions associated with recycling, and how they organised their homes to accommodate domestic recycling. They were also asked to give a self-report of their recycling behaviour.

findings: the researchers found that individuals who had strong reasons to persist with recycling (such as holding pro-recycling attitudes or having a social orientation towards recycling) tended to redefine recycling activities. They shifted their focus away from the time-consuming nature of recycling and emphasised the pleasurable aspects of the various kinds of behaviour, or the sense of satisfaction they gained from contributing to the environment. These people were also more likely to have made the task manageable, so as to ensure that recycling activities did not interfere with other aspects of their lives. Finally, they were more likely to engage in both short- and long-term recycling.

conclusion: these findings support the Sansone et al (1992) model, confirming that people who make a boring but valued task more manageable and interesting are more likely to continue with the behaviour.

The combined findings of Sansone et al (1992) and Werner and Makela (1998) thus help us to identify some factors that *stop* people from recycling. These might include being unable or unwilling to focus on the positive aspects of the task (such as fear of the noise of breaking glass at the bottle bank) or being unable to make the task manageable (such as in districts where insufficient recycling facilities exist).

interactive angles

Consider the task of recycling paper. What are the problems associated with this activity that might prevent people from engaging in the task? How could a household reduce the inconveniences associated with recycling these materials? In what ways could the task be made more interesting or pleasant? What information might enable people to redefine the task to feel more positive towards the activity?

After considering the answers to these questions, design a leaflet that could be used to encourage recycling of paper in your local area.

research now

sorted – student rubbish

Matthies E. & Krömker D. (2000) Participatory planning – a heuristic for adjusting interventions to the context. *Journal of Environmental Psychology* **20: 1–10**

aims: to investigate ways to improve the sorting of rubbish for recycling by university students.

procedure: sorting of rubbish for recycling was measured at the start of the experiment in two student residences. Participants in one residence were contacted and helped to set up an action group. This group implemented measures designed to encourage better sorting of rubbish, such as information about the sorting system, providing signs and having larger containers. They also sent all students a bogus letter threatening that their residency costs would rise unless sorting improved. Participants in the second (control) area received no additional assistance with recycling. A final measure of recycling was taken in both locations.

findings: by the end of the study the amount of unsorted rubbish had fallen from 69 per cent to 53 per cent in the experimental residence, but had risen from 64 per cent to 74 per cent in the control area.

conclusion: the involvement of students in the intervention group improved their participation in the recycling of rubbish.

Encouraging environmentally friendly behaviour

Changing attitudes towards the environment: the Yale model of persuasive communication

Hovland and his colleagues at Yale University conducted many studies that led to the development of a theory of persuasive communication, sometimes called the 'Yale model'. Whilst this laid the foundation for modern theories of attitude change, much has changed in this field since the 1950s.

Stages in persuasion

In order for a communication to be persuasive, it must first be noticed; thus *attention* is the first stage of the model. You are unlikely to be affected by a sign asking you to return your plastic cup-holder for reuse unless it is prominent. Andreoli and Worchel (1978) demonstrated the advantage of television commercials over those in print or on the radio. By using both sound and vision, the television is more likely to attract our attention. However, having attended to the message alone does not guarantee attitude change; the recipient must also be able to understand the message. *Comprehension* is required for the persuasive attempt to be successful. For example, a company may want its workers to adhere to a complex policy of sorting office waste, but if this is not clearly explained they are unlikely to follow the required procedure. Jaccoby et al (1980) found that 30–40 per cent of adults who saw a 30 second television clip misunderstood the information presented. Whilst both attention and comprehension are necessary, they are not sufficient. Finally, the message must be *accepted*. Acceptance does not necessarily demand belief, but it does require that the receiver acts on his or her understanding. Thus, if you see a notice that says *Turn taps off fully after use – or we will face another water shortage*, you may not believe that the consequences of your actions will be that significant, but because you understand the sentiment of the message that you have seen, you change your behaviour accordingly and turn off the taps.

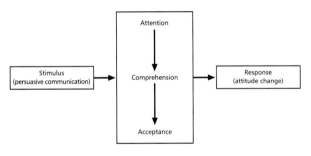

Figure 28.2 The Yale model of persuasive communication

This notion of a staged sequence in the processing of persuasive information is now referred to as *systematic processing* (McGuire, 1969), in contrast to heuristic processing (see page 364). This is believed to use a *central route to persuasion* (Petty & Cacioppo, 1986), because it requires the receiver to engage in thinking about the message, as opposed to the peripheral route to persuasion (page 364), in which the recipient is relatively passive. To account for some of the observed effects of persuasive communication, the model has been adapted to incorporate more stages. McGuire (1968) separated 'acceptance' into two stages – *yielding* and *retention* – and introduced a final stage, *action*. This version differentiates between being persuaded by the message (yielding) and retaining that changed belief (retention). You may see a poster that asks you to squash your cans for recycling so that animals can't hurt themselves on the open edges, and although you understand and accept the message you may forget why it was important after a while. Thus, initially your

behaviour changes – that is, there is action – but this may revert to inaction when retention fails.

Factors affecting persuasion

In addition to describing the process of behaviour change, the Yale model also indicates the factors that can influence the acceptance of attempted persuasive communication (Janis & Hovland, 1959). These factors are as follows:

- the *communicator* of the message – the role, affiliations and intentions of the source
- the *content* of the message – the topics, appeals, arguments and stylistic features
- the *media characteristics* of the message – whether interaction is direct or indirect and the sensory modality used
- the *situational surroundings* – such as the social setting and extraneous pleasant or unpleasant stimuli
- the *characteristics* of the recipient – such as persuasibility and self-confidence (Janis & Field, 1959).

Communicator factors

Hovland and Weiss (1951) investigated the importance of the source of the message. They found that American participants were more likely to be persuaded by a message from the American physicist Robert Oppenheimer than the Soviet newspaper *Pravda*. They concluded that the credibility of the source was a key factor affecting attitude change. Expertise also affects the likelihood of attitude change. Petty and Cacioppo (1981) showed that advice about the hours of sleep that people needed was more effective when given by a Nobel Prize-winning physiologist than by a YMCA director. Other characteristics of the source that increase the believability of the message include:

- a communicator who is arguing *against* his or her own best interests – the manager of a waste incinerator who says that the emissions are dangerous is more likely to be believed than an environmental protestor who says the same thing
- *attractiveness* of the communicator – Chaiken (1979) asked students to persuade others to sign a petition, and physically attractive individuals were more effective
- the perceived *similarity* of the communicator to the recipient – this is particularly so if the similarity is deemed to be relevant to the issue
- the *likeability* of the source – we are more readily persuaded by an individual who we find pleasant than by one we do not.

One reason why such superficial characteristics, which are unrelated to the content of the message, may be effective in attitude change is that people engage in *heuristic processing* (Chaiken, 1987); that is, they reach a decision based on simple cues, without considering the available information in any depth. Petty and Cacioppo (1986) describe this as the *peripheral route to persuasion*.

Content factors

Many characteristics of the message are also important, including:

- The *emotional content* – Is it fear-arousing?
- The *medium* – Verbal or visual?
- The *argument* – Is it presented as one-sided or a two-sided debate?

Fear-arousing arguments may be effective, although a range of factors affect the likelihood that recipients will adhere to the message. Rogers (1975) suggested that these were the unpleasantness of the fear-arousing suggestion, the probability of the event occurring if the recommendation is not followed, and the perceived effectiveness of the recommended action. Persuasive communication should therefore be most powerful if the recipient finds the suggestion relatively unpleasant, really believes it will happen and expects that the evasive action will be effective. However, it is not always the case that high levels of fear-arousal are the most effective. Janis and Feshbach (1953) found the reverse, with low levels of fear-arousal producing the most behaviour change. Thus, for environmental issues such as global warming, warnings about climate change that suggest wetter weather may be more effective than threats about rising sea levels causing mass flooding.

Some additional factors have been shown to affect attitude change. Howard (1997) found that *familiarity* had a powerful influence. Students were more likely to be persuaded by an argument couched in familiar terms, such as *Don't put all your eggs in one basket* or *Don't bury your head in the sand*, than by exposure to phrases such as *Don't pretend a problem doesn't exist*.

Media factors

We both hear and see messages geared towards encouraging our environmentally responsible behaviour. Which medium is most effective, or does the efficacy of the communication depend on the message being conveyed? The answer seems to depend on the stage at which the recipient is likely to resist the message. If difficulties are likely to arise at the comprehension stage – for instance, if you are conveying a complex message – then written communications appear to be most effective. However, where problems arise with yielding to the message, more direct media, such as face-to-face communication, are more effective (Chaiken & Eagly, 1976). So, an explanation of the impact of diesel versus unleaded fuel on the greenhouse effect would be better presented on paper, since it is a complex issue. In contrast, persuading schoolchildren to walk to separate rubbish bins with different kinds of waste (paper, cans and plastic) would be more successfully tackled face to face, as the problem is not one of difficulty with comprehension but of encouraging participation.

Situational factors

Presenting a communication as either a one- or two-sided argument can be advantageous in different situations. Where your views are likely to go unopposed, a one-sided argument is likely to achieve opinion change more quickly, if only temporarily. However, in most situations where environmental issues are at stake, one view is likely to be countered by another: the environmentalists by the industrialists, the non-smokers by the smokers, and so on. In these instances, persuasive communication is more likely to be effective if both sides of the argument are acknowledged. In these instances, primacy and recency effects come into play. If the time lag between the presentation of the two sides of the issue is small, the first message should be more effective (due to the *primacy effect*). If, however, the interval is long, the later message will be better remembered, due to the *recency effect*, so is likely to result in greater attitude change (Petty & Cacioppo, 1981). Therefore, in a heated debate in a local hall about the merits of a bypass through a local site of special scientific interest, the first speaker is advantaged, because the presentations are likely to follow one another in quick succession. However, if cases are to be presented in a local magazine in successive monthly editions, running up to a referendum on an issue, there is a distinct advantage to being the last to appear.

interactive angles

You are campaigning at your college for the provision of aluminium can recycling bins, but this is being opposed by the Estates Department. If you and the Estates Department can each design screensavers that will appear on every college computer monitor for a week, would your message be more persuasive if it appeared during the first week or during the second? If you and the Estates Manager are allocated an afternoon to give presentations to the students, would you rather speak first or last?

If your message were complex, would you opt for the verbal presentation or a written message on the computer?

One key issue in the context of a persuasive communication is the nature of the distractions with which it has to compete. It seems obvious that a message will be less effective if it is in competition with other stimuli for the recipient's attention, but this is not always the case. This is because distractions prevent us from rehearsing our argument. Whilst a viewpoint with which we agree may be disadvantaged by interruptions (as we are less able to focus on the additional supporting arguments), a contrary viewpoint may benefit from distractions. If we are attending to a message that conflicts with our own views but we are distracted, we will be unable to generate our own arguments against it, and thus it will seem more persuasive.

Recycled products and packaging

In just one hour we produce enough rubbish to fill Trafalgar Square to the height of Nelson's Column, according to statistics from the Department for Environment, Food and Rural Affairs (DEFRA).

Each tonne of paper recycled equates to around 17 trees saved, not to mention the surrounding habitat and wildlife, claim the organisation Waste Watch.

Launched in January 2002, the Christmas Card Recycling Scheme is run by the Woodland Trust in partnership with WH Smith and Tesco. People have been supporting the scheme by taking advantage of special recycling bins whilst shopping in local stores.

Tesco is just one of the supermarkets working towards recycling as much of their product packaging as possible. The store has its own recycling units, recovering virtually all paper, board and plastic that might otherwise be consigned to landfill sites or incinerated. Each year the units save over 155,000 tonnes of card – the equivalent of nearly 3 million trees.

Source: http//:www.nfucountryside.org.uk

Study this extract from the NFU countryside website. What strategies for persuasive communication have been utilised? Try to obtain some promotional literature from the sources mentioned and identify the strategies used in their production.

Personal characteristics

There is little evidence that gender or self-esteem affect the tendency for an individual to be affected by persuasive communication (Bauer, 1970; Eagly & Carli, 1981), although some results are contradictory (for example, Janis & Field, 1959). These differences might be explained using McGuire's (1968) concept of substages to the process of acceptance; people with different personalities may differ in their responses to elements of the acceptance process. For example, people with better memories, or for whom the issue is more pertinent, may find retention of information easier. Another personal characteristic, self-monitoring, may affect the likelihood that a person will be persuaded. Lavine and Snyder (1996) found that high self-monitors (people who are more sensitive to the demands of a situation and adapt accordingly) were more likely to be influenced by an imaged-focused approach that concentrated on the communicator's status, popularity and attractiveness. In contrast, messages that expressed values were more effective with low self-monitors. Therefore, high self-monitors would be more likely to be persuaded to participate in an environmentally friendly scheme if it was endorsed by a celebrity. In contrast, low self-monitors would be more likely to be influenced by messages in which the communicator described his or her personal beliefs and reasons for being environmentally friendly.

for and against

the Yale model of persuasive communication

+ there is some evidence that the process of attitude change is affected by a range of factors

+ attention and comprehension appear to be important factors in the effectiveness of persuasive communications

− there may be more factors involved in the process of attitude change than envisaged by the Yale model

− there is evidence for attitude change arising from heuristic, non-sequential processes

interactive angles

Global Warming: What's the problem?

The weather, like the times, is a-changing. In the next 100 years temperatures will rise 2 to 3 degrees and seas will rise by 1 metre, according to the Hadley Centre, the Met Office's climate research organisation. And if you think this won't affect you, Anthony Astbury at the Met Office predicts that traffic will grind to a halt and trains will be even more disrupted by global warming in the form of heavy rains, flash floods and landslides. Over the past 3 years more than 20 major extreme weather events (hurricanes etc) have cost 100,000 people their lives.

Concentrations of carbon dioxide, the main contributor to global warming, have risen from an estimated 270 parts per million in 1870 to 360 in 1990. Reasons range from deforestation (since trees absorb CO_2 and turn it into oxygen this is bad news) to the burning of fossil fuels, which release CO_2.

Carbon dioxide is a greenhouse gas: it helps to trap solar heat on earth which alters the weather and causes temperatures to rise. And it's not the only culprit: methane, water vapour, nitrous oxide from vehicle exhausts and agricultural fertilisers are also to blame.

What's the solution?

The United Nation Environment Programme's Kyoto Protocol has committed 84 countries to reducing emissions of greenhouse gases by at least 5 per cent. But some scientists claim this isn't enough. Catherine Senior of the Hadley Centre says: 'It will not really change global warming. It won't respond instantly to things we do today. It's been building up since the industrial revolution.' A spokesperson for the World Health Organisation sums up the mixture of fear and ignorance about this issue. 'No one really knows what climate change means. It could be a fairly benign process of global adaptation, or it could mean a kind of nuclear winter. We've just got to hope for the best.'

What can you do?

Future Forests, an organisation that promotes awareness about carbon management, points out that you can adopt some basic domestic practices: regularly defrost your fridge – frost build-up increases the amount of energy needed to keep the motor running – and boil water with a lid on. And instead of giving up the central heating, dishwasher and stereo, 'neutralise' them. This means paying Future Forests for a tree to be planted at one of 55 sites across the UK to offset whatever carbon dioxide you generate. For example, an average British car covering 20,000 km a year emits one tonne of carbon, so five trees would cover it. Use the calculator at http://ww.futureforests.com to work out your personal contribution to the global greenhouse (they'll make you include everything from your lawnmower to your juicer). You can make sure you buy paper and wood products from managed woodlands. These have the Forest Stewardship Council (FSC) label and you don't have to trek to some wierdy-beardy outpost to find them – Sainsbury's, Boots, Tesco, B&Q and WH Smith stock them. For the truly green, there's the carbon-neutral mortgage. Launched by Norwich and Peterborough Building Society in conjunction with Future Forests, the mortgage will offset your entire household carbon uptake for 5 years.

But will this do any good? Catherine Senior says: 'Reforestation is one way of ameliorating the problem, but it would be incredibly difficult to achieve *everything* through this.' So plant those trees and buy those managed products by all means but, overall, be energy efficient.

Source: Eve, October 2000

This example of a piece of persuasive literature uses some of the strategies discussed above. Decide how this article could be changed to make it more effective in changing people's attitudes and behaviour.

Changing behaviour towards the environment

We have considered the factors that affect people's attitudes towards the environment and control the likelihood of them acting in environmentally friendly ways. So, how could we encourage more people to engage in appropriate *behaviours* or to do so more often? We could:

- *educate people* so that they want to behave differently (change attitudes to increase intrinsic rewards)
- *make appropriate kinds of behaviour easier* (alter people's surroundings)
- *offer rewards* (employ extrinsic reinforcement)
- *penalise failure* (use punishment).

Behavioural control may be *antecedent*, measures in which the intervention occurs before the behaviour arises, or *consequent*, measures in which the intervention follows the behaviour to be changed. Antecedent procedures may include education, attitude change and inducing or preventing certain kinds of behaviour by controlling the triggers that cause them to occur. Consequent procedures can affect some forms of behaviour by using pleasant or unpleasant consequences to make their performance more or less likely, or through the use of feedback.

Antecedent control

- Notices reminding people to switch off lights on exit from a room
- The availability of a fast lane for car-pool users
- Provision of special bags or boxes for recyclables to be collected alongside domestic rubbish

Consequence control

Positive reinforcement (receiving a pleasant consequence)

- Sainsbury's penny back for a carrier bag
- Schools earning money through aluminium can recycling

Negative reinforcement (avoiding an unpleasant consequence)

- Reduced road tax for low-emissions cars
- No tariff for cars with two or more people in

Punishment

- Turning daytime heating off in halls of residence where electricity use exceeds a threshold
- Fines for littering

Antecedent control strategies

The antecedent control strategy of education suggests that the more informed people are on ecological matters, the more likely their behaviour is to be environmentally sound. Newhouse (1990) found that people who were better informed were more likely to have environmentally friendly views. Adopting a particular perspective does not necessarily result in a difference in behaviour, although there is some evidence that pro-environmental views do correspond to responsible behaviour. Kearney and De Young (1995) demonstrated the success of a knowledge-based intervention, as people who were better informed about car-pooling were more willing to participate in such schemes. Margai (1997) found that information increased recycling by over 30 per cent. Over a 1-year period, an educational programme used in East Harlem (a low-income urban area of New York) increased the daily volume of recycled material from 8.7 to 11.4 tons.

However, not all education-based interventions have been successful. Heberlein (1975) found no impact on energy consumption when people were given a booklet on electricity-saving tips, or a letter informing them about the personal and social costs of failing to conserve energy. This is in stark contrast to the more recent evidence from Brandon and Lewis (1999) (see page 369). Why might these differences arise? Perhaps it is because the information provided by Brandon and Lewis was more directly relevant than that given in the earlier study. These issues are considered in more detail under 'Attitude change'. Certainly, it would appear that education alone is insufficient as a strategy. Pardini and Katzev (1983–4) found that making a spoken or written statement of commitment to newspaper recycling resulted in a greater (and in the case of the written statement more sustained) increase in recycling than information alone.

Other antecedent strategies that have proved successful include the use of triggers or prompts to remind people of appropriate behaviours and modelling. Triggers such as signs encouraging us to save energy by turning off lights and to avoid litter are antecedent controls and can be effective. Such triggers are more effective when they are polite, when they are proximate to the site of the behaviour and when they indicate the appropriate response. Thus an anti-littering slogan will be most effective when it appears on a potential item of litter (such as a sweet wrapper), and when the instruction directs behaviour such as 'place this in a bin' rather than 'keep Britain clean'.

classic
research

copying conservation

Cook S.W. & Berrenberg J.L. (1981) Approaches to encouraging conservation behaviour: a review and conceptual framework. *Journal of Social Issues* **37: 73–107**

aim: to review the literature to search for factors affecting the tendency to engage in conservation programmes and to suggest ways to increase participation.

procedure: a literature review was conducted to assess the importance of the social embeddedness of behaviour; that is, the extent to which forms of behaviour are inherently expected by a particular social group. This included social norms (moral standards of the group), conformity (following other members of the group to avoid exclusion) and modelling (learning new forms of behaviour by observing other group members)

findings: many of the studies reviewed suggested that public scrutiny and recognition of efforts increased the effectiveness of programmes aimed at improving energy conservation.

conclusion: as people have a tendency to respond to group pressure and recognition, these techniques can be used to increase the success of conservation programmes.

Figure 28.3 An antecedent strategy: a polite, proximate trigger for conserving energy displayed in the University of Leicester's halls of residence

Proximity also matters in the location and attractiveness of waste receptacles. Finnie (1973) found that coloured dustbins resulted in a 14.9 per cent decrease in littering, against only a 3.15 per cent reduction with ordinary bins. As described on page 360, when recycling containers are nearby they tend to get more use; the same applies to littering. Finnie found that having a dustbin in sight could decrease littering by up to 30 per cent, which suggests that people will behave in environmentally friendly ways when the personal costs are low enough.

Consequent control strategies

Wolf and Feldman (1991) reported a very significant increase in recycling following the introduction of a 5 cent returnable deposit. Several US states introduced this deposit for soft drink and beer bottles in 1983. In New York alone, recycling rates rose from 1 per cent for plastics, 5 per cent for cans and 3 per cent for glass to 33 per cent for plastics, 59 per cent for cans and 77 per cent for glass over the first year after implementation. Thus a small potential positive outcome had a considerable effect on recycling behaviour. Other consequent strategies that have been shown to be effective are praise, such as litter bins that say 'thank you' (Bell et al, 2001), and feedback (Brandon & Lewis, 1999).

One problem with behavioural control, particularly legislation and fines, is the risk that, whilst performance may be altered, attitudes may remain unchanged. Thus the effect only persists while the antecedent or consequence control measures are in place. For example, some councils, such as Eastbourne Borough Council and New Forest District Council, provide facilities for mixed recyclables to be collected alongside domestic rubbish. If this provision were withdrawn, most people would be unlikely to continue to recycle so much of their waste. Such returns to baseline recycling levels following the withdrawal of reinforcement programmes have been recorded by De Young (1986) and Jacobs and Bailey (1982). A kerbside system does, however, have the advantage of not requiring the consumer to engage in much sorting of waste, a factor that increases participation in recycling.

Oskamp et al (1996) found that in a kerbside recycling scheme, 'mixed-recyclables' containers resulted in a 90 per cent participation rate amongst community residents, whereas a requirement to separate recyclables led to only 77 per cent participation.

Ophuls (1977) has described four alternative types of strategy for putting these theoretical approaches into action, to affect the behaviour of people towards the environment:

- laws and incentives to encourage prosocial behaviour;
- moral, religious or ethical appeals;
- educational and informational programmes designed to produced attitude change;
- encouraging prosocial behaviour through social groups and communities.

Each of these routes to encouraging pro-environmental behaviour can be put into practice, as indicated below:

interactive angles

The following are examples of antecedent or consequence control (the latter using either negative or positive reinforcement or punishment). Decide which of the strategies for intervention use which mechanisms for controlling behaviour:

- giving a penny back for the return of carrier bags to a supermarket;

- offering grants for loft insulation;

- having bottle banks in every car park;

- charging a toll for cars carrying only one person;

- imposing fines for dropping litter;

- reducing water rates for users who meet limited consumption targets;

- placing drinks can bins all around the edge of a school playground;

- having cheaper road tax for cars with lower emissions.

Strategy for increasing prosocial behaviour (Ophuls, 1977)	Example
Laws and incentives	Variable vehicle excise duty (road tax) according to emissions
Moral, religious or ethical appeals	Friends of the Earth have employed advertising campaigns that appeal to our moral sense (see below)
Education	Many shops inform customers about recycling through leaflets and details on packaging
Encouragement through social groups	Organisations such as the Guides and Scouts award badges for ecologically sound behaviour

wasted times

Most of the things that we throw away could be a valuable resource for someone, somewhere. That's why when we call something "waste" we are making a mistake. The problem is that we are a nation addicted to chucking stuff out. The average person in the UK throws out their own body weight in rubbish every three months.

It's not just stale food and kitchen scraps that end up in the rubbish. It's also discarded coke cans, newspapers, out-of-date clothes, broken electrical goods and old toys.

This is piling up problems for our environment and future generations worldwide. Stuff that is no longer wanted ends up in landfill or being burnt in incinerators. Both methods damage the environment.

Our endless appetite for new things is adding to these problems. When we chop down forests or dig up minerals we use huge amounts of energy. Almost all manufacturing industries also rely on using energy from fossil fuels, rather than a clean energy like solar power. But burning coal, oil and gas is causing the world's climate to change. Levels of carbon dioxide are rising at a speed that threatens catastrophic change in the future.

That's why Friends of the Earth has slammed Government plans to burn up to 10 million tonnes of household waste – in 130 new incinerators to be built by 2015 – rather than concentrate on recycling, which can save energy.

We don't have to waste our waste. This booklet highlights the ways which people have found work well at reducing the amount of waste they produce. This isn't just good for the environment; it can also be very good for people because it can improve their quality of life, save money and generate jobs.

© Friends of the Earth, 1999

Ophuls (1977) suggested that one factor that could affect ecologically sound behaviour was to appeal to people's moral beliefs. This is one way in which campaigns such as those employed by Friends of the Earth may be effective.

interactive angles

Every student room at the University of Michigan is provided with an individual blue plastic recycling box and it is the duty of the students to take their rubbish and recyclables to the appropriate collection point in or adjacent to the building. The students recycle all of the following materials: cardboard, paper, cans, glass and plastic bottles. Students are provided with both clear instructions about how to recycle and information about what happens to these materials after they are collected.

Guidelines for hall residence staff
Making the recycling programme a success:

1 *Actions speak louder than words*. Resident advisors are encouraged to serve as role models for their students; for instance, by recycling pizza boxes after end-of-session events, posting signs in the buildings and keeping the residents informed about the amount their hall recycles each month.

2 *Keeping them informed*. Offer educational programmes to students so that they can learn about the recycling process and raise their awareness about their own impact on the environment. This could also provide an opportunity for a sponsored 'fun' activity.

3 *Make your own paper*. Give students the chance to recycle their own paper, making hand-made cards from waste paper. The university can supply instructions and materials – you just need some waste paper!

4 *Promote events in a waste-free way*. Act as a role model and avoid wasting paper by putting a flyer under everyone's door. Instead, use bulletin boards or make invitations out of scrap card or soup tins!

5 *Conduct a tour of your hall of residence*. Show students where to put their recyclable waste and where it is taken to once it has been collected. Look inside recycling containers to ensure that materials have been appropriately segregated and check in waste bins for materials that should have been recycled. Discuss ideas with your students for new ways to increase participation in recycling.

6 *Sponsor a 'Recycle Night'*. Presenting this early in the term will avoid confusion. Encourage students to contribute to a discussion about the different recycling programmes in their home towns and whether they think recycling should be mandatory. Consider asking experts from the local community to speak.

Adapted from 'Residence Hall Recycling':
http://www.recycle.umich.edu/grounds/recycle/
residence_hall_recycling.html

Can you explain the reasoning behind each of these strategies?

where to now ?

The following are good sources of information about environmentally responsible behaviour:

▶ **Palmer C. (1997) *Contemporary ethics issues: environmental ethics*. Santa Barbara, CA, ABC-Clio.** This provides a thorough coverage of global environmental issues and includes many excellent reference sections for resources and organisations.

▶ **Smith E.R. & Mackie D.M. (2000) *Social psychology*. Hove, Psychology Press.** This has an excellent up-to-date chapter on attitudes and attitude change.

Conclusions

Attitude is a key issue in encouraging environmentally friendly behaviour. However, commitment, feedback, the effort required and the perceived importance of issues also play a part in determining whether people will engage in environmentally friendly behaviour. We can approach the need to change people's behaviour towards the environment either indirectly, by changing their attitudes, or directly, by changing their behaviour. There are several stages to attitude change, and the models of persuasive communication suggest that people must attend to and understand a message before they can accept it. In order for any change in attitude to be expressed as a change in behaviour, the recipient must both yield to and retain the information. Furthermore, in any communication a range of factors, including the characteristics of the communicator and the message, the context, media factors and situational factors, will influence its effectiveness. Behaviour change can be achieved through antecedent or consequent intervention strategies.

what do you know ?

1 What factors should be taken into account when preparing a piece of promotional literature that aims to encourage people to recycle their waste?

2 Describe the Yale model of persuasive communication. Evaluate the extent to which this is helpful in understanding how to motivate people into engaging in environmentally friendly behaviour.

3 How effective are rewards and punishments in encouraging environmentally friendly forms of behaviour? Use research evidence to justify your answer.

4 At Penn State University, USA, members of Eco-Action began a plan of action in conjunction with the university's officers to increase the amount of waste recycled by fellow students. The students are supposed to put plastic, newspaper and aluminium in special bins, separating these recyclables from other rubbish. They have placed more bins in some areas than others in an attempt to determine whether greater bin availability affects the incidence of recycling. If so, the university will provide more bins at all locations.

Zeiber (1999)

Are the measures described above likely to be effective? Use evidence to justify your answer. What other policies could be implemented to increase the incidence of recycling?

29 Research methods

what's ahead?

At AS you learned about research methods through each of the approaches and through your own piece of coursework. At A2 you will need to be able to recall and use all of this information to answer the examination questions on research methods in unit 5. Therefore the methods discussed are experiments, observations, questionnaires, interviews, case studies and content analysis. Other topics include sampling, hypotheses, variables, levels of measurement and descriptive statistics (averages, ranges and plotting data). So, this chapter revisits the ideas you will have already covered at AS and shows you how to apply them to A2 examination-style questions by considering examples of real research. In addition, we will explore some new issues such as subjectivity and objectivity and the role of qualitative and quantitative research in psychology. We also discuss the topic of ethical issues, in relation to research with humans and animals, which can be tested in unit 5 or unit 6 examinations.

Subjectivity and objectivity

Psychology, through its application of scientific methods, strives for *objectivity*, that is, the aim of research is to explore the mind and behaviour without reference to the (human) observer. This, however, may be an unachievable goal for psychology, which is, after all, the study of ourselves by ourselves. We are thus both the researched and the researcher so we probably cannot ever achieve absolute objectivity. We are perhaps inevitably going to place our own, subjective, interpretation on to events that we see – it would be difficult to imagine how one could avoid feeling saddened by loss or angered by injustice – our emotions would colour our ability to record information accurately. It seems that we are unable to collect data from a perspective that is not personal. However, through the prudent use of a range of techniques to minimise the effect of the researcher, psychological research is able to maintain a high degree of objectivity. The use of strategies such as double-blind procedures and standardised instructions to reduce researcher bias, and physiological measures like EEGs, mean that considerable objectivity is achieved in laboratory settings.

There are some research methods in which the degree of *subjectivity*, that is, personally biased perspective, can raise concerns. For example, in unstructured interviews, non-focused observations or case studies, the views of the researcher may affect the way they seek out or record information. This would make their data less objective than that derived from methods such as the mechanical recording of a Skinner box, a forced choice questionnaire or a rigorously controlled experiment. Nevertheless, there is still a clear role for such research in psychology. More subjective research methods offer opportunities to identify novel aspects of behaviour that may be overlooked in more objective, and therefore constrained, investigations.

Whilst the early psychological method of introspection was ousted by more scientific and objective experimental ones, psychology has seen a recent return to more subjective techniques, for example, discourse analysis. Such qualitative methods make use of subjectivity as an advantage; subjective data, such as individual experiences and opinions, are included in the research rather than being deliberately screened out. Two recent examples of the use of qualitative techniques are described below.

Murphy et al (2003) collected qualitative data to explore the sensitive issues surrounding the death of a child. They observed parents at four intervals (4, 12, 24 and 60 months) following their child's accidental death, suicide or murder. Although almost 70 per cent of the parents reported that it took three or four years to put their child's death into perspective, the nature of the violent death was not a factor in their coming to terms with their loss. Fitzsimons and Bargh (2003) investigated the effect that thinking about an individual with whom we have a relationship (such as best friend or mother) has on our goal-directed behaviour. Using qualitative methods, they found that they could manipulate representations of interpersonal goals, such as helping and understanding.

Qualitative and quantitative research

Research methods used by psychologists are, to varying degrees, qualitative or quantitative, although these terms describe the extremes of a continuum along which research may fall. Studies that focus on producing numerical results or data that can in some way be 'counted' (quantified) are described as *quantitative* research. Such studies tend to use large samples of people or animals to draw conclusions that can be extrapolated to tell us about a population in general. Such methods include experimentation, correlations and surveys. They are more likely to use data derived from a laboratory setting in which controls can be rigorously employed. The goal of such research is to develop general 'laws' of behaviour.

As an alternative to quantitative research, psychologists may investigate a limited numbers of instances studying them in much greater depth, focusing on meanings and generating context-related, detailed, descriptive data. Such approaches, focusing on the qualities of the behaviours observed, are the *qualitative* methods. They include interviews, questionnaires, observations and case studies, which are likely to be based in 'real world' settings. Each of these techniques could alternatively be used (with greater or lesser ease) to produce quantitative data, for instance by changing the phrasing or analysis of the questions asked.

As an indication of the importance of the issues surrounding the use of qualitative versus quantitative approaches, *The Psychologist* (1995) devoted a special issue to the topic. The debate that followed persisted until 1998 and was then resumed in 1999! Some of the arguments put forward are summarised below. The lively, sometimes venomous interchange makes exciting reading for those unused to the cutting edge of science.

The first article in the special issue (Henwood & Nicolson, 1995) observes that psychology uses two differing methodological standpoints, the 'scientific method' and 'constructivism' (what we have called 'constructionism'). The first requires that science research is impartial, is based on value-free observation, uses reliable and valid measurement of constructs, and controlled experiments to assess the relationship between variables. The combination of this with the empiricist tradition of collection and statistical analysis of numerical data has, according to Henwood and Nicolson, led to this model of scientific practice being described as the 'quantitative paradigm'. This can be readily contrasted with the constructionist research perspective, involving open-ended, detailed analysis of verbal, written or sometimes visual material. Such qualitative analyses are not, in general, converted into 'numbers' but used to explore the meanings the contributing participants have built up or 'constructed'.

Henwood and Pidgeon (1995) explore two further strands in the debate, described by Bryman (1988) as the 'technical' and the 'epistemological' (that is, the study of what constitutes 'knowledge') issue. The technical issue, Bryman argues, is concerned with the qualitative or quantitative methods employed. This choice, he suggests, should be governed by the needs of the research. Some questions are better answered through experiments generating numerical results, others by the analysis of unstructured, non-numerical findings, such as through discourse analysis, interviews or participant observation.

Most readers are probably more familiar with quantitative approaches to psychology than qualitative ones. In the extract below, Smith (1995) discusses an example of a qualitative study of pregnant women.

> There is not one correct method for analysing qualitative material. One has to find a way of working which is appropriate to the material and to your own personal and theoretical propensity.
>
> I began the analysis by reading the transcripts and diary entries for a single case many times until I was very familiar with the material, using one margin to note down my responses to anything in the text that struck me as interesting and significant. These comments can be in the form of, for example, preliminary interpretations and connections with things said elsewhere in the texts.
>
> I used the other margin to document emerging themes, that is using key words to capture what I thought was the essential quality of what I was finding in the text. Some of these themes, for example, ambivalent attitudes to giving up work, followed from questions on my interview schedule but others came from topics introduced by the woman herself, for example, views on the relationship with her partner. (page 123)

The value of qualitative research was defended by Griffin (1995) who explored the role of feminist-standpoint research (FSR). Key elements of FSR according to Griffin include:

● a research focus on experiences (particularly those of women);

● the responsibility of the researcher to others;

● a need for researchers to reflect on their own practice, especially to be aware of the dominance relations of gender, race, class and sexuality that pervade the structure of research.

Griffin provides a description of her qualitative research into the progression of young women from school to work. In a longitudinal study, she conducted informal semi-structured interviews and systematic observations of a group of girls in Birmingham. From a pool of 200, 25 young, white, working class women were followed for two years with 10 workplace-based case studies. This approach enabled Griffin to be 'flexible in the focus of research questions ...; to address sensitive subjects such as domestic violence and sexuality; and to set young women's experiences in a cultural context' (page 120). The aim was not to produce a generalisable analysis that could be applied to women in Britain (nor even in Birmingham), but to allow the examination of the importance of pertinent social and cultural processes such as the pressure to get a job and a man.

interactive angles

You may like to try this group exercise to demonstrate some of the differences between quantitative and qualitative approaches.

Divide your group into two, qualitative researchers and quantitative researchers. Give them both a brief to watch a James Bond film such as *The World is Not Enough* in order to investigate the way males and females are represented. The quantitative researchers may like to count instances of behaviours (such as powerful roles, use of force, having technical knowledge, being dominant or submissive) and will need to agree on operational definitions, observational techniques and establish inter-observer reliability. Their aim should be to produce numerical data that can be analysed. Qualitative researchers may want to focus on their perceptions of individuals' experiences, generate detailed descriptions of relevant situations, consider contexts, re-watch particular scenes and trace emerging themes. Ultimately they need to generate interpretations of those aspects they found significant and perhaps describe connections between ideas. Finally, they may want to reflect upon their own views and the extent to which they are important to the exercise.

Figure 29.1 The World is Not Enough

The contributions to the debate were examined by Morgan (1996), who queries the issues raised. His central tenet is that all of the research that currently falls into the domain of 'psychology' may not, in fact, belong there. First, he observes that there may indeed be instances in which research is better served by the in-depth analysis of single instances than by large numbers of more superficial observations. As he observes 'The much maligned B.F. Skinner argued that it is better to describe one rat in detail than to average over a population that may be doing different things at different times.' He cites several examples of research domains, which, like behaviourism, are predominantly experimental but still value individual analysis (such as the ethological approach to animal behaviour, and psychophysics – the study of the relationship between physical stimuli and our experience of them). Morgan's second argument is that scientific descriptions do not, necessarily, require numbers. Here too the traditionally scientific research domains demonstrate an acceptance of qualitative research as a route to the development of a theory. Darwin, for example, formulated the theory of evolution by natural selection not on quantitative data but on wide-ranging observations. In these instances, Morgan observes, the verbal, qualitative theory is gradually replaced by or develops into a quantitatively expressed idea (as evolution has done through genetics). Thus Morgan is suggesting that, whilst some approaches may necessarily study individual cases and generate qualitative data, this does not qualify them as 'science'.

A further area of doubt for Morgan (1996) is that of subjectivity. His criticism centres on whether it is appropriate for researchers following a qualitative approach to bring an overt political agenda to psychological study as, for instance, is the case in FSR. This departure from the insistence on objectivity traditional in science, raises the question of 'whether people who abandon the discipline of the objective approach are entitled to call themselves "scientists"' (page 32). Morgan believes not. One clear characteristic of science is repeatability. For those areas of psychology in which the collection of qualitative data can be reliably replicated, such as psychophysics or ethology, this condition can be satisfied. This seems not to be the case for other areas of qualitative research in which a lack of inter-observer reliability or methodological detail would prevent replication and thus verification. In these instances, while the research may be making a contribution to the understanding of human or social phenomena that cannot be investigated through an objective approach, Morgan asserts that 'science' is an inappropriate label. There are, however, further exceptions to the 'rule' that qualitative research in social domains lacks repeatability. In discourse analysis, for example, it is standard practice for researchers to independently interpret material in the same way as Morgan describes.

interactive angles

Read the section in chapter 33, on the issue of whether psychology is a science (pages 469–471). What view of science are both Morgan and Henwood & Nicolson presenting?

Cooper and Stevenson (1998) argue that the 'objectivity' of science is fundamentally flawed because researchers cannot tease out opinion and the cultural context in which those opinions are expressed, for example, the scientific search for the biological causation of sexual orientation is inextricably linked to the current cultural need to legitimise homosexuality. However, in the qualitative research methods, such as discourse analysis, meanings are explored and from these, links and structures can be built into theories.

Finally, Morgan disputes the claim that, because any data from observations are interpreted within the context of existing concepts, 'facts' cannot exist. He agrees that observation may be difficult, but not impossible, to separate from the opinions we have about the situation. If the claim were true, Morgan suggests, the need to strive for objectivity would be greater, not irrelevant.

In response to these criticisms, Sherrard (1997) argues that Morgan has ignored the social sphere, a view echoed by Cooper and Stevenson (1998). Sherrard suggests that it is precisely those aspects of the social world that reflect the experience of the observer, such as our capacity for social categorisation, which make qualitative research so fascinating. Yet it is these same aspects, for instance the judgements we make on meeting someone – of age, class or sexual orientation – that are not repeatable. However, she argues that repeatability is not entirely absent from research into social perception since responses are systematic; the processes of social inference are based on experiences that are shared within social groups but differ between them.

Sherrard refutes Morgan's claim that repeatability underpins fact. Repeatability may be achieved by members of the Flat Earth Society citing observations that support their view, but this clearly does not guarantee objectivity or, therefore, fact. Furthermore, qualitative studies may not set out to uncover facts but to seek interpretations. This does not open the door to subjectivity but demands different ways to support and test interpretations. Support, Sherrard suggests, can come from triangulation (carrying out more than one type of analysis) and collecting supplementary evidence such as documentation. Testing is achieved by looking for counter-instances, by considering alternative explanations and checking understanding with the participants themselves.

In his postscript, Morgan (1998) questions the argument put forward by Sherrard (1998) that traditional science is insufficient to explore social interactions and their accompanying mental experiences because people are different from one another (whilst the objects of study in pure science are not). He suggests that the limits of similarity and difference remain unexplained. Morgan questions the justification for dismissing the variation in, for instance, sensory systems on the grounds that we are all essentially the same yet minimising similarities in our social behaviour because we are fundamentally different. There are, for Morgan, important ways in which qualitative psychology falls short of objective science. Whilst the subjects of study in such research may often be fascinating and difficult if not impossible to investigate in any other way, this should not defend the use of 'science' to describe such work. This, according to Morgan, may mislead students and the general public by assigning undue authority to the methods in question.

The benefits of the qualitative approach are further explored by Johnson (1999). She discusses the 'horrors of science' (Woolgar, 1988) which are:

- *indexicality* – representations are inevitably linked to context so will change with time and place;

- *inconcludability* – accounts cannot ever be conclusive or complete, they can always be added to;

- *reflexivity* – a researcher's prior knowledge affects the way a phenomenon is represented and this representation inescapably influences further conceptualisation.

In quantitative research, validity, reliability and generalisibility represent attempts to overcome these 'horrors'. In qualitative research, Robson (1993) suggests that the concepts of credibility, dependability and transferability are better guides to 'trustworthiness' and are the equivalent 'horrors' in a different context. In her investigation of how mature women students cope with the transition to professional higher education, Johnson used a feminist-standpoint perspective. Her methods included semi-structured informal interviews, participant observation, and diary-keeping by the participants, which were systematically explored.

According to Johnson, reporting the context of particular instances in sufficient detail and indicating how the findings relate to a wider theoretical framework help to overcome the indexicality problem, allowing other researchers to determine whether the data can transfer to other settings. Indexicality, unlike replication, provides the achievable goal of transferability. Dependability can be attained through systematic and well-documented data collection that allows for scrutiny by other researchers. Dependability thus, in one sense, equates to replicability as a means to verify the work of others.

Johnson (1999) suggests that inconcludability can be addressed by sampling and sample sizes. In contrast to quantitative research, which aims for large, statistically viable samples (and hence loses detail about individuals), the qualitative approach aims to preserve detail in order to achieve completeness.

Rather than viewing reflexivity as a 'horror', Johnson sees benefits to the involvement of the researcher. She cites the example of having become a mother herself during her research so felt that she could empathise with women's concerns about coping with education and motherhood. Similarly, Harding (1991) suggests that feminists should make known their interpretative processes, including their own agendas and backgrounds in the interests of critical objectivity. She reports that an exploration of her own motives and interests and the practicalities of the research have led to a reduction of the 'horror' of reflexivity and thus enhanced trustworthiness.

where to now?

▶ **Banister P., Burman E., Parker I., Taylor M. & Tindall C. (1994)** *Qualitative methods in psychology: a research guide.* **Buckingham: Open University Press.** This is a relatively accessible collection of chapters on different qualitative methods including observation, interviewing, discourse analysis and feminist research.

▶ **Hayes N. (1997) (ed)** *Doing qualitative analysis in psychology.* **London: Psychology Press.** This is another collection of chapters but here each focuses on a real-life example of a qualitative approach in practice, including case studies of motherhood and interviews of people with drug problems.

Hypotheses

The outcome of research is measured against a *hypothesis*, that is, a testable statement. When we conduct a study, the results may either confirm our aims, or contradict them, so we need to have two hypotheses. The alternative (or experimental) hypothesis is accepted if the aims are supported, and the null hypotheses is accepted if the results are not what we anticipated.

Alternative and null hypotheses

The *alternative hypothesis* (H_A or H_1) proposes the expected outcome of the study. In an experiment, the H_1 says that there will be a difference in some measurable outcome (the DV) between two conditions that are controlled or observed by the experimenter (the levels of the

IV). In correlational studies the H_1 proposes a link between two variables. In any study, it must be possible for the alternative hypothesis to be contradicted by the findings. When this is the case, the H_1 is rejected but we still need a conclusion. This conclusion must be that our findings are not the consequence of the predicted effect but are instead due to chance. This is the function of the *null hypothesis* (the H_0). We can use statistical tests that employ mathematical principles to help us to decide whether a pattern we can see in our results could have arisen by chance or not (see chapter 30). In this instance, it is the null hypothesis that we are actually testing.

interactive angles

Read the research questions below, and write an alternative and null hypthesis for each situation.

1   Are younger people more likely to be helpful than older people?

2   Are scientists less likely to hold religious beliefs than non-scientists?

3   Do boys and girls differ in their ability at spatial tasks?

4   Are children more likely to imitate their parents than other adults?

5   Does emotional state affect memory?

Directional and non-directional hypotheses

Sometimes researchers can only predict that the variable(s) under investigation will **affect** the outcome rather than being able to make a more precise judgement about **how** the results will be affected. The alternative hypothesis in such instances is described as *non-directional* or two-tailed. It simply states that there will be a difference between conditions in an experiment or a link between variables in a correlation.

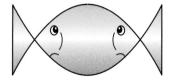

Figure 29.2 This is a two-tailed hypothofish ... can you tell in which direction it will go?

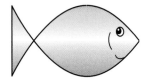

Figure 29.3 This is a one-tailed hypothofish, it has only one tail ... can you tell which way it will go?

When the H_1 predicts which of the two conditions will result in the greater or more positive change it is described as *directional* (or one-tailed). Directional hypotheses are so called because they predict that the outcome will fall in one direction. In correlational studies, a directional H_1 predicts either a positive or a negative correlation.

Methods used in psychological research

Experiment

Experimentation provides a means to investigate the effects of a single variable (or small number of variables), while controlling other factors in the situation. The findings of experiments can thus be readily replicated and validated. In an experiment one factor, the *independent variable* (IV), is systematically varied while the effect on

interactive angles

Decide whether each of the following alternative hypotheses is one- or two-tailed.

1 We can be conditioned to respond to a sound more quickly than we can to a smell.

2 Psychiatric patients are less likely to talk to themselves than psychologists.

3 Eating chocolate affects memory.

4 It is more likely that people will obey a stranger in uniform than one wearing plain clothes.

5 Performance of students who listen to music while doing their homework differs from those who work in silence.

research now

independent and dependent variables: safe sex, social skills and STDs

Metzler C.W., Biglan A., Noell J., Ary D.V. & Ochs L. (2000) A randomised controlled trial of a behavioural intervention to reduce high-risk sexual behaviour among adolescents in STD clinics. *Behavior Therapy* **31: 27–54**

aims: to investigate the effectiveness of an intervention programme on the incidence of risky sexual behaviour by adolescents.

procedure: 339 adolescents aged 15 to 19 years were recruited from sexually transmitted disease (STD) clinics and were randomly assigned to receive either the experimental intervention or usual care. The intervention programme targeted decision making about safer sex, social skills for handling difficult sexual situations and acceptance of negative thoughts and feelings about changing sexual behaviour. Participants in the intervention programme attended five weekly sessions lasting 60–90 minutes. All participants were given baseline, 6-month and 12-month follow-up assessments.

findings at the 6-month follow-up, the intervention group reported fewer sexual partners, fewer non-monogamous partners, fewer sexual contacts with strangers in the previous three months and less use of marijuana before or during sex than the control group. The intervention group also performed better on a taped situations test of skill in coping with difficult sexual situations.

conclusion: raising adolescents' awareness of the importance of monogamy and abstinence to sexual health in risky situations and providing them with the knowledge and social skills to handle such situations reduce the occurrence of high-risk sexual behaviour.

1 What is the independent variable in this study?

2 What is the dependent variable in this study?

3 Write a suitable one-tailed hypothesis.

another factor, the *dependent variable* (DV) is measured. The IV is the factor that is manipulated by the experimenter. By controlling either the nature of the participants, their experiences or the way data are selected for analysis, the experimenter generates levels of the IV. These levels or 'conditions' are used to compare the effects of the variable under investigation. For example, an experiment might be designed to test the effects of reading science fiction on the incidence of nightmares, in which case the IV would be the type of reading material and the levels would be 'science fiction' and a control such as 'historical novels'. In a study conducted by Hemmings et al (2000) the IV under investigation was sports massage, and the levels of the IV experienced by participants were either massage or rest (following a boxing exercise).

The DV is the measurable outcome in the experiment. It is called the dependent variable because we predict that any changes in this variable are caused by (ie are dependent upon) changes in the IV. So, in the science fiction example, the DV would be nightmares, which could be measured by counting the number of bad dreams occurring or by rating their unpleasantness. Hemmings et al (2000) measured the DV of the effectiveness of the massage by observing changes in the boxers' heart rate and by comparing their performance on a second set of exercises.

Other factors that might affect the dependent variable should be controlled, that is, kept constant across different conditions of the independent variable. This ensures that any difference in the dependent variable between conditions is the result of the IV and is not due to other, chance, variations.

In an experiment, the effect of the IV on the DV is a causal one; thus the hypothesis must predict a difference between the levels of the IV in terms of the outcome, that is, a change in the DV. So, if we return to the science fiction example, a hypothesis could read 'there will be a difference between the number of nightmares experienced after reading science fiction and historical novels'. This could also be expressed as a directional hypothesis: 'sleepers will have more nightmares after reading science fiction than after reading historical novels'. In each case we are suggesting that the IV of reading a particular type of book will affect the DV, namely the occurrence of nightmares. Hemmings et al (2000) investigated the effect of massage (the IV) on sports performance (the DV). They were anticipating that massage would improve performance, so a directional hypothesis would be appropriate, such as 'boxers will make a faster recovery after massage than after rest'.

interactive angles

Identifying the independent and dependent variables

In each of the situations below, identify the independent variable including each of the manipulated levels and the dependent variable, stating how this might be measured.

- Morrongiello and Dawber (2000) compared the likelihood of mothers to intervene in the play of boys and girls when there was a risk of injury.

- Low and Durkin (2000) tested children's ability to recall information from television programmes when the story was presented in either a jumbled or logical order.

- Williamon and Valentine (2000) investigated the differences between the quality and quantity of practice employed by experienced and novice musicians who were asked to learn a new piece.

- Wareing et al (2000) studied memory deficits, anxiety and arousal in current and previous users of MDMA ('Ecstasy').

interactive angles

Writing hypotheses for experiments

For each of the pairs of independent and dependent variables below, write either a directional or non-directional alternative hypothesis and a null hypothesis.

1. Research question: does watching TV during revision affect exam performance?
   IV: watching the TV
   DV: exam results

2. Research question: can a UFO researcher tell the difference between a real report of a UFO sighting and a simulated one produced under hypnosis?
   IV: hypnotically induced or genuine report of UFO sighting
   DV: apparent genuineness

3. Research question: do food additives increase aggression in children?
   IV: food additives
   DV: aggressive behaviour

Laboratory experiment

A *laboratory experiment* is conducted in a laboratory or other contrived setting away from the participants' normal environment. In this situation the researcher can manipulate the levels of the independent variable and accurately record changes in the dependent variable. In addition, considerable control can be exercised over potential confounding variables. It is this aspect that represents the most significant advantage of laboratory studies over other techniques. A researcher in a laboratory can be more confident than their counterpart in the field that any changes they observe in the DV are attributable to the IV rather than being the consequence of some uncontrolled aspect of the situation. The IV may be manipulated to create two or more experimental conditions (such as eating white, milk, plain and mint chocolate) or to compare an experimental condition with a control (chocolate and no chocolate).

Field experiment

Field experiments are studies with an experimental design (they have an IV and DV), which take place using participants in their normal surroundings. McNicholas and Collis (2000) observed the attention received from passers-by when an accomplice of the experimenter did or did not have a dog with them. The IV, the presence or absence of a dog, is manipulated by the experimenter but the setting is realistic and not in a laboratory. Field experiments such as this are described as *contrived*, since the researcher creates the levels of the IV.

research now

field experiment: dogs as social catalysts

McNicholas J. & Collis G.M. (2000) Dogs as catalysts for social interactions: robustness of the effect. *British Journal of Psychology* 91: 61–70

aim: dogs being walked by their owners are known to act as social catalysts, encouraging people to interact. This study aimed to find out whether the response of passers-by would still arise if the dog itself did not solicit attention, for instance by approaching passers-by and to test the effect across a range of situations other than dog walking.

procedure: in this study, the researchers observed the attention an individual (the handler) received from passers-by when they did or did not have a dog with them. The dog was highly trained so that it did not introduce uncontrolled variables by attracting attention. In addition, the handlers were observed in a range of daily activities, rather than only when walking their dog and when dressed in smart or scruffy clothes.

findings: the handlers were more likely to be approached by passing people when they had a dog than when they were alone in all activities, not just when walking the dog. The presence or absence of the dog had a bigger effect on the likelihood of being approached than the way the handler was dressed.

conclusion: they concluded that pet dogs can act as effective social catalysts for human interaction across a range of situations.

Field experimentation may also include *quasi-experiments* in which the experimenter does not have control over the allocation of participants to levels of the IV. Suppose a cinema was piloting an advertisement shown during the intermission. Whilst experimenters testing the effect of the advertisement on purchasing could control when it was shown, they could not dictate which participants would happen to be in the cinema at the time. Participants in the sample could not be randomly allocated to experimental groups. People who watched films on different days of the week or different times of the day might have differed from one another in some patterned way, which could affect their purchasing irrespective of their exposure to the advertisements.

research
now

field experiment: sorted – student rubbish

Matthies E. & Krömker D. (2000) Participatory planning – a heuristic for adjusting interventions to the context. *Journal of Environmental Psychology* **20: 1–10**

aims: to investigate ways to improve the sorting of rubbish for recycling by university students.

procedure: sorting of rubbish for recycling was measured at the start of the experiment in two student residences. Participants in one residence were contacted and helped to set up an action group. This group implemented measures designed to encourage better sorting of rubbish such as information about the sorting system, providing signs and having larger containers. They also sent all students a bogus letter threatening that their residency costs would rise unless sorting improved. A final measure of recycling was taken in both locations.

findings: By the end of the study the amount of unsorted rubbish had fallen from 69 per cent to 53 per cent in the experimental residence but had risen from 64 per cent to 74 per cent in the control area.

conclusion: The students' involvement with the intervention improved their participation in the recycling of rubbish.

1 Why is this a field experiment?

2 What is the IV in this study and how did the researchers create the experimental and control conditions?

3 What is the DV in this study and how was it measured?

4 Why was the second residence called the 'control area'?

Figure 29.4 What makes people recycle their rubbish? How could you investigate people's motives for recycling and use this information to test ways to improve motivation for sorting rubbish?

In one class of quasi-experiment, the *natural experiment*, the researcher cannot control the IV at all, the levels are derived from pre-existing and naturally occurring differences. For example, a study about weather and mood would require participants to be selected during sunny or cloudy conditions. Although the participants available on one occasion would not be expected to differ from those on another, they might do so. The researcher can neither control allocation of participants to conditions (sunny or cloudy) nor when or how those conditions arise.

media watch

It's the pits

Never mind letting your heart rule your head – if recent research is anything to go by, it's your nose that rules when you're out on the pull. Scientists now want us to believe the smell of male sweat is a turn on and that ugly blokes become more attractive by letting their natural body odour shine through! In tests carried out at the Northumbria University, women rated men far more attractive when secretly exposed to pheromones – the chemicals found in male sweat ... So, if you end up with a face like a monkey's bum this summer, at least you know it's only because he smells. Bonus.

Company, July 2000

How would you test the effects of human pheromones on attractiveness using a quasi-experiment?

interactive angles

Looking back at the situations and experiments described in the boxes on pages 377 and 379, try to decide which would be most effectively studied as laboratory, field or natural (quasi) experiments. Remember, it may be possible to answer some questions using several alternative methods, for others there will only be one choice.

Participant designs used in experimental studies

Experiments assess whether the IV produces a change in the DV so we must either compare the effects of the IV on participants in different conditions or observe differences in the DV for the same participants in different levels of the IV. These alternatives are essentially the different *participant designs*. It may be impossible for the same people to participate in both levels of the IV, such as in comparisons between males and females or different species of animal. On other occasions it is preferable that, while participants could participate in both conditions, they do not. In the example of the effects of bedtime reading, participation in both conditions could result in participants recalling science fiction, even when they have moved on to reading historical novels. If they had nightmares these could be mistakenly attributed to the historical novels, obscuring the experimental effect.

Repeated measures

In an experiment with a *repeated measures* (also called a within-subjects or related) *design*, each individual participates in every level of the IV, that is, the levels of the IV are compared by participants repeating their performance under different conditions. Because the participants are exposed to the experimental situation on more than one

Figure 29.5 Keeping in touch: what cost? Does your mobile fry your brain or feed it? How could you test whether it was actually an increase in frontal lobe temperature which was responsible for the improvement in cognitive function demonstrated by Koivisto et al (2000)?

occasion in repeated measures designs this repetition may affect their performance. Consider how several consecutive attempts at running a 100-metre race would affect your speed or how repeated attempts to flick a pile of beer mats would affect your ability to catch the stack effectively.

The experimental effects that arise as a result of the order in which two levels of the IV are presented to participants are called *order effects*. There are two kinds: *fatigue effects* arise when the participants become tired or bored as they repeat the task so their performance worsens in later conditions. This might occur if tests are highly repetitive or very demanding. *Practice effects* arise when the participants become more skilled in familiar tasks so their performance improves in later conditions. This might occur if a researcher uses an unfamiliar task, which, although difficult at first because of its novelty, rapidly becomes easier with practice.

research
now

repeated measures design: mobiles boost your brain power

Koivisto M., Revonsuo A., Krause C., Haarala C., Sillanmaki L., Laine M. & Hamalainen H. (2000) Effects of 902 MHz electromagnetic field emitted by cellular telephones on response times in humans. *Neuroreport* 11: 413–15

aims: to investigate whether mobile phones can enhance cognitive functioning.

procedure: participants were tested on a range of cognitive tasks including subtraction, vigilance and reaction time tasks. Their performance was compared with and without exposure to a 902-MHz electromagnetic field (as emitted by cellular phones).

findings: performance in mental arithmetic, vigilance and reaction time was significantly enhanced with exposure to the 902-MHz field, the participants were faster and no less accurate.

conclusion: the electromagnetic field emitted by mobile phones improved performance on cognitive tasks. These tasks required sustained attention and are typical of frontal lobe functions so the effect may be mediated by increasing the temperature of brain tissue in this area.

1 Why might a repeated measures design have been chosen for this study?

2 If the effects of mobile phone use are long term, why might an independent measures design have been preferable?

Male intelligence is an annual outbreak

IN SPRING, a young man's fancy turns not only to thoughts of love, but to higher things.

According to researchers, men are more intelligent in spring than autumn because seasonal changes in the production of testosterone can alter their mental performance.

Professor Doreen Kimura of the University of Western Ontario in Canada and the author of the report Sex and Cognition said: 'In Europe and North America, men have higher testosterone levels in autumn than in spring and we have found that they perform spatial tasks better in the spring. Men also do better at mathematical reasoning, and both are components of intelligence.'

Professor Kimura, who is one of the world's leading experts on sexual differences in the human brain, is currently involved in a study measuring mathematical ability and testosterone levels. She said that just why male hormone levels change seasonally is still not fully understood.

'One evolutionary reason why they may increase in the autumn is that among our early ancestors it was probably an advantage to have children conceived then and born in the summer. Most people do associate high testosterone levels with spring, but it may be that while a young man's thoughts do turn to love in the spring, they turn to sex in the autumn', she said.

Article by Roger Dobson, *The Independent*, 10 January 2000

1 How do you think the original data about spatial task performance and mathematical skill was obtained? What sort of experiment would this be?

2 Design a laboratory study using animals to test the theory that testosterone affects spatial ability. What factors would you control that cannot be controlled when studying humans?

One way in which order effects can be controlled, although not eliminated, is by the use of *counterbalancing*. This is the systematic variation of the order of presentation of the levels of the IV in a repeated measures design. For example, in an investigation of parent–child interactions, Leaper (2000) ensured that equal numbers of were observed in the order mother–father as father–mother.

Independent groups design

In an experiment with an *independent groups design*, separate groups of individuals participate in the different levels of the IV, that is, the data sets relating to each level of the IV

are independent of each other. This is also called a *between subjects*, *independent measures* or *unrelated design*. Ideally, the groups are selected from a random pool of participants but this is not always possible. For example, in natural experiments, where the IV is dictated by pre-existing groups (such as males and females), the segregation of participants is predetermined. On other occasions an independent groups design may be preferred because it avoids order effects and reduces opportunities for demand characteristics to affect performance. The less contact participants have with the experimental procedure the less chance they have of identifying (correctly or incorrectly) the aims so their behaviour is correspondingly less likely to be affected by their perceptions and anticipation.

Matched pairs design

The matched pairs design represents a compromise between repeated measures and independent groups, maintaining advantages of each. In a *matched pairs design*, scores are obtained for each level of the IV from different participants (as with independent groups). However, for each member of one group there exists in the other group an individual with certain characteristics in common. The groups are created by ensuring that every participant is part of a matched pair; two individuals who have been selected because they share features of importance to the experiment. Rosenbluth et al (2000) conducted an experiment using a matched pairs design, comparing sense of smell in blind and sighted children. Their aim in constructing experimental groups was to match each blind child to a sighted child on relevant criteria, including age, sex, grade and ethnic group and native language.

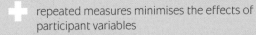

interactive angles

Working as a group, imagine you are about to conduct a study on animal phobias. You might decide to match male and female participants on criteria such as childhood pet ownership, holiday experiences on farms, in zoos and parental fears. Can you find suitable pairs?

for and against

+ repeated measures minimises the effects of participant variables

+ independent groups design reduces the impact of demand characteristics compared with repeated measures

+ matched pairs design avoids both the problems of exposure to potential demand characteristics in a repeated measures design and limits the confounding effects of participant variables between groups in an independent measures design

– appropriate criteria on which to match participants may be difficult to identify and matching participants may be hard to find

Observation

Observation may be used as a primary research method to produce detailed, descriptive, qualitative data or as a tool in experimentation to measure the dependent variable quantitatively. An observation often forms the starting point for research in psychology; we need to observe that people forget before we can study forgetting for example. Initial, casual observations such as this may lead to rigorous investigations, including structured observations that allow researchers to collect data to test hypotheses.

In *naturalistic observations* the researcher gathers data by watching participants (people or non-human animals) in their normal environment – this is not necessarily their 'natural' situation. For people, naturalistic observations may be conducted at home, work, the shops etc and for animals, in the home (for pets), parks, zoos, farms or in the wild. Such studies could also be described as field studies as they take place outside the laboratory.

The presence of observer(s) can affect the behaviour of the observed so it is necessary to control for this potential influence. *Non-participant observation* requires that the observer does not interact, so that the participant's behaviour cannot be affected by the observer's presence. This might be achieved by being a long way away, or by the observer being hidden, for example, watching children in a nursery though a one-way glass screen.

Participant observation also ensures that the participants are unaware of the presence of an observer, by disguising them as a legitimate member of the situation. This has two benefits. If permission were sought in some situations it would be denied, so the observation would be impossible. In addition, as the observer is not obvious, the participants' behaviour cannot be affected by their presence. Deception raises ethical issues so, in general, the observer's role is made clear to the participants, that is, the observations are *overt*. Nevertheless, *covert* observations in which the observer's role is not apparent to the participants may be conducted of public behaviour in some locations, such as public places.

There may be questions surrounding the physical or ethical costs to the observers and participants. Infiltration of a criminal group (such as Parker, 1974), or of a cult threatening mass suicide, may put the observer at risk. Studies using concealed observations can invade the privacy of the observed and involve unacceptable deceit, such as Humphreys's (1970) study of homosexual activity. Although Humphreys attempted to protect the unwitting participants in his study by avoiding the disclosure of the location of his research, his procedure did not respect the privacy of the people being observed (see page 418). Humphreys contrived a covert participant observation under the guise of a 'gay voyeur', someone who

research
now

observation: do we have eyes in the back of our head?

Colwell J., Schroder S. & Sladen D. (2000) The ability to detect unseen staring: a literature review and empirical tests. *British Journal of Psychology* 91: 71–85

aim: to investigate whether people are able to detect when someone they cannot see is staring at them.

procedure: the experiment compared the ability of participants to detect the presence of an unseen person. In the two conditions this person either did or did not stare at the participant.

findings: when the participants were not being stared at they were unable to detect the presence of a person behind them. In the 'staring' condition, however, participants scored better than they would have if they were just making chance guesses at detecting the observer.

conclusion: whilst this suggests that participants can detect the presence of someone they cannot see, the researchers identified some uncontrolled variables such as the effect of participants employing implicitly learned non-random response patterns which may have resulted in their apparent ability.

derives sexual pleasure from watching actual encounters between gay people. This deception was in Humphreys's view necessary because he was aware that homosexuality (then a crime in the USA) resulted in the formation of a suspicious subculture. While a small number of those being observed were aware of Humphreys's motive for watching them, the majority was unaware that their behaviour was being scrutinised for the purposes of research.

Not all observations are covert, however. In Parker's (1974) study of thieving in Liverpool, the observer's role was known to 'the Boys'; this was an overt participant observation. Similarly in Leaper (2000) (see page 386) the observers were non-participant yet the participants were aware that they were being observed.

for and against

➕ participant observation allows researchers to limit demand characteristics caused by knowledge about being observed

➕ a participant observer gains insight into the social context

➕ validity of a participant observer's records can be increased by improving integration

into the group through consideration of characteristics such as appearance, age, gender, social class and ethnic group

➖ being a participant in a social situation can colour the observer's view

➖ to be effective, participant observation may require the observers to deceive the observed

➖ as a participant, it is difficult to record observations immediately, thus introducing errors into the data

➕ participant observations tend to generate qualitative data, the participant observer being able to provide detailed accounts of their observations

➕ non-participant observations can generate quantitative data which can be analysed statistically

Non-focused observations can only generate qualitative data – descriptions of the events observed – but we may wish to generate numerical data. This is achieved using structured observations in which behaviours are categorised, selected and defined prior to observation. To

research
now

time sampling: parents and children at play

Leaper C. (2000) Gender, affiliation, assertion, and the interactive context of parent–child play. *Developmental Psychology* **36: 381–93**

aim: to search for systematic gender differences in the play of children with their parents.

procedure: 98 children (49 sons and 49 daughters) were observed during play with their mothers and fathers. The children were aged 26–65 months (mean 47.5). Other factors recorded about the families included ethnicity, siblings' ages, age of parents and parental employment and education. Families were recruited through flyers distributed at day-care centres and pre-schools and names and addresses obtained from birth announcements in local newspapers and a purchased mailing list. Letters to the families described the study as an investigation into normal children's play and lan-guage development. Each family received a children's book or a $10 gift voucher for their participation.

Observations were conducted in the family's home, typically in the living room. Mother–child and father–child interac-tions were observed on separate occasions, 1–2 weeks apart, equal numbers of visits began with mother or father observations. Three 8-minute sessions were recorded onto videotape, each with a different toy, provided by the researcher. The first toy presented was a gender-neutral Playmobil Zoo, used as a warm-up session to acclimatise the parent and child to playing together while being videotaped. The following two toys were presented in a counterbal-anced order within each family: a feminine-stereotyped Playskool kitchen toy, with food, pots and place settings, and a masculine-stereotyped Little Tikes track to be assembled with a tunnel, station and cars.

Behaviours were coded on 7-point ordinal scales for affiliation and assertion, each participant being rated on each scale every 5 seconds; thus 384 records were made in total per 8-minute session. To increase inter-observer reliability, the observers were trained for 6–8 weeks prior to the study and were retrained every 2–3 months over the two years of data collection. Spearman rank correlations between observers were $r = 0.59$ and $r = 0.66$ respectively for affiliation and assertion. These were significant at $p < 0.001$.

findings: mother–child dyads were higher in mean affiliation ratings and lower in mean assertion ratings than father–child dyads. Mothers were demonstrating higher levels of affiliation while fathers were more assertive. However, there was no significant effect of the *child's* gender on affiliation or assertive behaviour; parents were no more likely to exhibit affiliation with daughters or assertion with sons. There was, however, a difference between gender-stereotyped settings; boys were more assertive than girls in the masculine setting. The toy food situation was associated with higher rates of affiliation and assertion. Mothers, fathers and daughters, but not sons, tended to show higher affiliation in the toy food setting. No effects were found for affiliation in relation to cross-gender play.

conclusion: parental behaviour during play may reinforce stereotypes of affiliative females and assertive males. As the children were, in general, more assertive than their mothers but not their fathers, a stereotyped view that women are less powerful and can be more easily influenced may inadvertently be reinforced. The findings have implications for the equality of parents as role models.

1 Identify **two** behaviours for which the researchers would have needed opera-tional definitions.

2 What efforts were made to ensure the reliability of the recordings?

achieve this, the variables to be observed must be operationalised. Operational definitions of variables put them into operation, that is, make them usable. An *operational definition* is simply a description that identifies a variable by factors that can be manipulated or measured, for instance because they are observable. It provides a framework for improving reliability both within and between observers. An individual is more likely to be consistent if they have a clear definition of the variable being recorded. Similarly, multiple observers are more likely to record accurately if they are all working to the same definition. This is a measure of *inter-observer*, or *inter-rater*, *reliability*; the extent to which different individuals generate the same records when they observe the same sequence of behaviour. By correlating the scores of observers we can measure inter-observer reliability. Individuals (or groups) with highly correlated scores are demonstrating good inter-observer reliability.

Formalised observations generate data that are more easily interpreted than those from relatively non-focused, unstructured ones. While open-ended observations such as note-taking and diary-keeping provide rich, complete data, such observations are difficult to synthesise and analyse.

interactive angles

Watch an episode of a soap, and if possible ask other people to watch the same episode but separately. Identify each of the main individuals present. List 20 behaviours in which the individuals engage. In addition, identify and justify three states such as 'annoyed' or 'content' displayed by these characters, noting when they occurred. What differences do you find when you compare your observations? It is generally quite difficult to break the sequence of behaviour into individual events. You will probably find even greater variation in your descriptions of states. This is because you are making inferences rather than just recording direct observations.

Repeat the activity above but agree operational definitions for just five behaviours in two individuals. Your inter-observer reliability should improve.

Formal observations are therefore preferable as the losses in terms of complexity and completeness are balanced by gains in reliability, validity and ease of organising the data. Checklists, time sampling and event sampling all provide structured ways to collect observational data.

for and against

+ naturalistic observation has high ecological validity

+ compared with interviews or questionnaires, it is more difficult for participants in observations to misrepresent themselves, for instance by lying

+ participants in naturalistic observations are relatively unaffected by demand characteristics

− it is difficult to control variables in naturalistic observations

− high inter-observer reliability is hard to achieve in observations

+ naturalistic observations are an equally effective way to study both humans and non-human animals

Case study

Case studies are used in clinical settings in an attempt to understand psychopathological conditions. However, they are employed in a variety of other contexts to provide in-depth information about a family or work units as well as individuals. A family or a work unit may be analysed in depth and form a 'case study'. As with correlations, case studies are not a unique research method; they utilise other research methods (eg naturalistic observation, interviews or questionnaires). Variables are not systematically controlled or altered as in single case experimental designs. Case studies are useful tools in research because they can provide rich, complex data and may allow us to investigate single instances of interest that do not lend themselves to experimental study.

for and against

case studies

+ they are a rich source of data

– you can overlook certain factors you feel are unimportant (e.g. the relationship between two siblings), which could be causing the behaviour you are assessing

– difficult to generalise to other people

+ a good way of studying atypical behaviour

– can be time consuming

– can lose objectivity through getting to know the participant

Questionnaire

Questionnaires use a range of techniques to obtain data including Likert scales, semantic differentials, open-ended questions and closed questions. These can enable the researcher to collect data that cannot be gathered through other research methods.

Likert scales

These scales are used to measure attitudes asking participants to respond with 'strongly agree', 'agree', 'strongly disagree' etc, to a variety of statements by generating a single total 'score' for each participant. The scales can include statements that are general or specific and, within limits, more statements is better (20+ is a good benchmark), with roughly equal numbers of positive and negative statements. A positive statement is one that agrees with the attitude that a high score indicates. Positive and negative statements should be randomised through the questionnaire. This

research now

case study: feeling legless?

Halligan P.W., Athwal B.S., Oakley D.A. & Frackowiak R.S. (2000) Imaging hypnotic paralysis: implications for conversion hysteria. *The Lancet* **355, 18 March, 986–87**

aim: to investigate if hypnosis and conversion hysteria (where people claim paralysis even though there is no organic cause, eg brain damage) share common neuropsychological mechanisms.

procedure: the participant was hypnotised to believe that their left leg was paralysed. A series of trials to attempt to move the leg were performed alongside trials where the right leg had to be moved. The participant was told which trial was next (eg whether it was the turn of the left leg or the right leg to move). On some trials the leg had to move in time with a metronome, while on other trials the leg was only to be moved when tapped with a pen. Positron Emission Tomography (PET) scans were recorded for each trial to deduce which areas of the brain were activated.

findings: the left leg never moved during any of the trials (as detected by electrodes on the leg), but the *right anterior cingulate* and the *right medial orbitofrontal cortex* were activated, which probably indicates the inhibition of movement in the left leg. The brain was stopping the limb from moving!

conclusion: in comparison to brain scans of a conversion hysteric, the same brain areas were activated. Therefore, even though the research is based on the comparison of two case studies, it appears that hypnotic paralysis and conversion hysteria could share common neuropsychological mechanisms. This could help understand and treat people suffering from conversion hysteria.

1 Do you think you can generalise the results of this research to all people who have conversion hysteria?

2 How would you set up an experiment to assess the aim of this case study?

helps to reduce demand characteristics and fatigue effects. Having an odd number of choices on the scale (eg 5 or 7) enables the participant to choose 'don't know' if they have no opinion. Participants' responses are then scored ensuring that responses to negative statements are reversed compared to positive ones and added together to produce a single total.

One problem with using Likert scales is that they are subjective. The choice of items and decisions about the attitudes they represent rely on the judgement of the individual who created the scale. This problem can be overcome using a similar technique to Likert scales, the Thurstone method. This uses a panel of experts to judge the statements rather than relying on the researchers' own opinions.

Semantic differentials

This type of scale assess the respondents' feelings and thoughts about a description or a picture. These can be used to build an understanding of what a 'typical' person might be (eg pet-owner, dog-trainer). A semantic differential uses bi-polar adjectives such as strong–weak, hot–cold and introvert–extrovert. As with a a Likert scale, one 'end' of each pair indicates a particular attitude and these should be arranged to that not all of the 'good' traits are on one side and should be separated by an odd number of spaces for the participant to respond.

for and against

the Likert scale

+ ideal for measuring attitudes

+ easy to swap positive to negative statements (and vice versa)

− items analysis is rather subjective. You choose whether to accept or reject an item

− it can be difficult to create enough initial statements without repetition

− you may be left with no items after items analysis

− repetitious with the same responses for each statement

+ easy to score and add up a final total

+ a reliable measure after the items analysis

research now

semantic differentials: are alligators cute?

Baenninger R., Dengelmaier R., Navarette J. & Sezov D. (2000) What's in a name? Uncovering connotative meanings of animal names. *Anthrozoös* 13 (2): 113–17

aim: to examine whether certain animal names elicited distinct characteristics, for example, lions are perceived as being fierce.

procedure: the research team created a semantic differential questionnaire that examined each animal name on 19 criteria. A copy of part of the questionnaire is shown below:

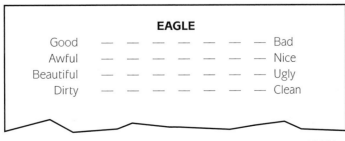

Baenniger et al 2000

Each of the 12 animals that were assessed (alligator, bullfrog, canary, deer, eagle, fox, goldfish, hamster, lion, lizard, shark and turtle) appeared at the top of the questionnaire. All 100 participants had to fill in the questionnaire for each animal. The animals were presented in a random order for each participant.

findings: there was a large consensus across the sample as to how each animal was perceived. The profiles for canary and alligator were 'mirror images' of each other. For example, the canary was seen as being beautiful, cowardly and peaceful, whereas the alligator was seen as being ugly, brave and ferocious.

conclusion: it would appear that for this sample of people, there were large similarities as to how the 12 species were perceived on the 19 chosen criteria.

for and against

semantic differentials

+ an effective technique for direct comparison between two pictures, or other stimulus material

− items analysis is subjective

− can be difficult to find two comparable pictures (eg one picture may be smiling and the other sulking!)

+ easy to calculate a total score

− cannot be sure it is just the picture or other stimulus material that is causing the responses given by the participant

− can be difficult to create enough bi-polar adjectives

+ good for assessing emotional responses in people, which can be very difficult when using the Likert scale or Thurstone method

Open and closed (fixed-choice) questions

An *open-ended question* gives us qualitative data based on the richness of the responses. Such questions ask for participants to respond using a space to answer in whatever style they choose. These assess emotions and the reasons people have for doing certain things. *Closed,* or *fixed-choice, questions* provide possible answers to the participant and they have to select the most appropriate for them. They are consequently easier than open questions to analyse quantitatively.

For example, if we are interested in why a person owns a pet we can ask them about their motives using either question form:

Open-ended: Please state your reasons for keeping a pet at present.

....

....

Fixed-choice: Please tick your main reason for owning a pet at present.

Companionship ☐

Security ☐

Stress reliever ☐

It was a stray ☐

Other (please state below)

....

interactive angles

Create a series of open-ended and fixed-choice answers as to what qualities people like to see in their friends.

Several factors may affect the success of the questionnaire method. These include:

- **making the questionnaire specific** – a single questionnaire may measure several behaviours or attitudes effectively or these may have to be tackled using different questionnaires;

- **the number of items** – long questionnaires are not necessarily the best. Angbratt and Moller (1999) showed that a short version of a questionnaire gleaned enough information to diagnose a risk of osteoporosis making the longer questionnaire comprising 52 questions unnecessary. The more specific (shorter) questionnaire reduced completion time so more people could be assessed;

- **questionnaire title** – Lund and Gram (1998) used questionnaires of varying length, with different titles. Questionnaire length had no real effect on response rates but the title of questionnaire was important. The simpler title 'Women and Cancer' resulted in the highest return regardless of questionnaire length.

for and against

questionnaires

- **+** good for research that can involve socially sensitive matters (eg sexuality, drug taking)
- **–** can be expensive to produce long questionnaires
- **–** people may give socially desirable answers
- **+** people may disclose more on a questionnaire as it does not involve talking to another person
- **–** questions have to be carefully worded to avoid bias

Interview

Many interviews utilise the questionnaire research method. The two broad categories of interview are known as structured and unstructured. *Structured interviews* are those that ask previously decided questions in a fixed order. An *unstructured interview* has a number of topic areas to be covered but it is not as prescriptive as a structured interview; it is more open-ended.

A range of factors affect the success of interviews. Breakwell (1995) identified several potential problems with the structure of the questions, including:

- *double-barrelled questions* (eg 'Do you think that cats and dogs are good pets?' A 'no' answer could mean no either to cats, or dogs, or no to both);

- *leading questions* or questions that introduce an assumption can affect the respondent's answer (eg 'Do you think Ibuprofen is more harmful than aspirin?');

- *jargon* or complicated terms (eg 'Do you agree with the neo-Freudian notion of the lesser significance of a maternal figure on cognitive-emotive development?');

- *double negatives* (eg 'Do you feel it is not true that not all children need a stable maternal figure in early years for sound development?' How would you interpret a 'yes' answer to that question?);

- *'catch-all' questions* (eg 'Tell me all you know about HIV and how it has influenced your sexual behaviour'. It would be difficult for the interviewee to continue talking without further prompts so they may omit crucial facts).

Interviews may be conducted either face-to-face or via a medium such as the telephone or computer link. Research has shown a vast difference between the techniques, even when a computer-assisted interview package is employed. For example, Hayashi et al (1999) reported a higher response rate from telephone than face-to-face interviewing when questioning a sample of Japanese people on their sexual behaviour.

Kissinger et al (1999) reported that women were more likely to give socially desirable answers in a face-to-face than a computer-assisted interview when questioned on sexual health. For instance, certain socially undesirable behaviours, such as infrequent condom usage, were less often mentioned in face-to-face interviews compared to self-administered computer interviews.

research
now

interview technique: face-to-face or on the telephone – which is best for measuring health?

Donovan R.J., Holman C.D., Corti B. & Jalleh G. (1997) Face-to-face household interviews versus telephone interviews for health surveys. *Australian and New Zealand Journal of Public Health* 21(2): 134–40

---

aim: to compare the response rates on a health survey given via face-to-face interviews or telephone interviews.

procedure: two samples of people were drawn from Perth, Australia: a face-to-face interview group (*n* = 1000) and a telephone interview group (*n* = 222). A stratified-type sample was drawn for both groups as part of a three-yearly assessment of a health foundation.

findings: there was a significantly lower reporting of smoking behaviour and unsafe alcohol consumption in the telephone interview group. There was also a significantly higher recall of 'health messages' in the telephone interview group.

conclusions: Donovan et al concluded that 'health researchers should treat comparisons between different survey modes with caution, and should be aware that campaign evaluations using telephone surveys and household surveys may yield substantially different results' (page 134).

1 What types of questions could Donovan et al have asked participants?

2 From this study, which method appears more accurate: face-to-face or the telephone?

Oh no, I don't really smoke or drink

for and
against

interviews

+ interviews can use a range of techniques including open and closed questions and may be structured or unstructured

+ data from structured interviews is quantitative and can be easily analysed

+ unstructured interviews can provide rich data that may not be obtained by any other method

+ interview techniques can be improved by avoiding double-barrelled, catch-all or leading questions and the use of double negatives or jargon

– face-to-face interviews may produce socially desirable responses

+ telephone and computer-assisted interviews may produce more reliable data than face-to-face situations

– data from unstructured interviews may be subjective and difficult to analyse

Content analysis

Content analysis is a quantitative research method in that it can be used to examine the number of certain key words or the language used in a variety of media. It can be used to explore the content of literature, speech patterns, television shows or newspaper articles or to investigate trends in presentation, tone, length of article or portrayal of characters. Conclusions are drawn from the analysis about the role of these media role in affecting our behaviour or the perception of certain activities. An example of the use of content analysis is given below.

research now

content analysis of television advertisements: watch what you eat

Lewis M.K. & Hill A.J. (1998) Food advertising on British children's television: a content analysis and experimental study with nine-year olds. *International Journal of Obesity and Related Metabolic Disorders* **22(3): 206–14**

aim: to examine the content of food advertisements shown between children's television shows.

procedure: 91 hours of children's television shown on four terrestrial channels were analysed to produce a detailed record of advertisement content and style.

findings: the following key results were reported:

● 50 per cent of advertisements were for food products;

● 60 per cent of these advertisements were for cereals or confectionery;

● food advertisements used significantly more animation to sell products than other types of advertisements;

● food advertisements also used more storytelling, humour and the promotion of fun or happiness or mood alteration to sell products compared to other types of advertisement.

conclusions: advertising time is dominated by advertisements for foods of 'dubious' nutritional value and these are designed to engage attention and produce an emotional response after watching. This may have an effect on the target audience. (It should be noted that in the experimental section of this research, Lewis and Hill found that the influence of such food-product advertisements on overweight children caused them to rate these products as more healthy.)

1 Lewis and Hill examined the content of food advertisements between children's TV shows. How do you think they categorised the advertisements?

2 How do you think you could measure the emotional response an advertisement might produce?

Robson (1993) described content analysis as a six-stage process:

- **Ask a specific research question**. In the example above the question was 'What type of advertisements are shown in between children's television shows?' Research has posed questions such as 'What do children produce when asked to draw how an alien would get to Earth?' (Roberts et al, in press) and 'Is there evidence that alcohol consumption and tobacco usage is featured in music videos?' (DuRant et al, 1997).

- **Choose the sampling strategy**. For example, a random sample of television programmes shown over one week or articles featured in a particular newspaper. The sample is usually dictated by the question posed, so for Lewis and Hill (1998), the sample was of 91 hours of terrestrially transmitted advertisements before or after children's television shows.

- **Define the recording unit**. This means identify the criteria used to record the data, the most common recording unit in content analysis of the written word being a single word. The number of occurrences of that single word is recorded, although for words with more than one meaning, for example, 'mean' or 'mode', this is problematic. Alternatively, the recording unit may be a theme, paragraph or whole item. The more precise the recording unit (such as describing the context of a word), the more reliable and valid the analysis will be.

- **Construct categories for analysis**. Mutually exclusive (non-overlapping) categories should be used as they are easier to rate. For example, in Roberts et al (in press), the researchers grouped shape of craft into categories such as 'flat bottomed disc', 'domed-disc', 'irregular curvilinear' and 'zooloid' (animal-shaped). The more specific the categories, the easier content analysis becomes. Similarly, passages could be rated on a numerical scale, for example, to say how favourable an article is towards homosexuality, where 1 = very unfavourable article, up to 10 = very favourable article.

- **Test the coding on sample material and assess reliability**. This will ensure that the categories are useable. It also enhances reliability among those doing the rating if you have a team of researchers. For example, in the research of Roberts et al (in press), 10 pictures were chosen for reliability purposes on shape and aggressive nature of picture with a concordance of 100 per cent. To keep reliability high, all three researchers rated any new shapes that featured in subsequent pictures.

- **Conduct the content analysis**. The pre-determined recording units and categories will help to avoid interpretation of material thus maintaining objectivity.

The range of research questions tackled by content analysts includes women and smoking in Hollywood movies (Escamilla et al, 2000), guidelines on handling requests for euthanasia in the Netherlands (Haverkate et al, 2000), educational media about menstruation (Havens & Swenson, 1989), and how dogs are perceived in feature films (eg *Beethoven*) and TV shows (eg *The Simpsons*) (Rajecki et al, 2000). An example of a simple content analysis with far-reaching consequences is given on the page opposite.

for and against

content analysis

- **+** it is unobtrusive. The researcher can observe things without actually using the observational research method

- **—** the material used in the analysis may not have been written for the purposes of being content-analysed. They could have been written for something completely different from what is being investigated

- **—** documentation may be limited for analysis

- **+** as the documents used are 'permanent' (eg videos, newspapers), other researchers can replicate the analysis increasing reliability

- **—** cause or effect? Are the documents a reflection of our social world or are they causing it?

- **+** as documents are archived (eg newspapers, Internet, TV shows), it is a cheap way of conducting a longitudinal study (and you do not have to wait years to conduct it)

- **—** there could be experimenter effects due to the subjective nature of the analysis, unless you conduct strict inter-rater reliability tasks

research now

content analysis of journal articles: sexuality examined by content analysis

Clark W.M. & Serovich J.M. (1997) Twenty years and still in the dark? Content analysis of articles pertaining to gay, lesbian and bisexual issues in marriage and family therapy journals. *Journal of Marriage and Family Therapy* **23(3): 239–53**

aim: to investigate the extent to which marriage and family therapy journals address gay, lesbian and bisexual issues.

procedure: the recording units were the words 'gay', 'lesbian' or 'bisexual' and the phrase 'sexual orientation'. Issues of the *Journal of Marriage and Family Therapy* were the sample strategy with the specific date range of 1975 to 1995.

findings: 13,217 articles were content-analysed and 77 contained a recording unit (this represents 0.006 per cent of all articles published).

conclusions: this research was used to fuel the debate that gay, lesbian and bisexual issues were not being tackled by marriage and family researchers.

1 Can you think of any other recording units that Clark and Serovich could have used in this research?

2 What implications do these results have for family psychologists?

Correlational design

Correlations do not constitute a separate research method because other research methods are used to gain the data. Correlational designs look for relationships between measures collected from, for example, questionnaires or observations. A *correlation* can be defined as the relationship between two measured variables.

Types of correlation

The results of correlational studies fall into three broad categories: positive, negative or no correlation. A *positive correlation* takes the form that if one measured variable increases the second measured variable also increases. For example, there may be a positive correlation between a person's height and their shoe size. That is, we expect that a taller person will have larger feet. As one variable increases, so does the other.

A *negative correlation* takes the form that if one measured variable increases, the other measured variable decreases. For example, there may be a negative correlation between the number of therapy sessions a person has and the number of depressive symptoms they exhibit. That is, we expect that people who have spent longer in therapy will have fewer depressive symptoms. As one variable increases, the other decreases.

No correlation refers to a situation in which no definite trend occurs and the two measured variables do not appear to be related to each other. For example, if we attempted to correlate head circumference and 'big-headedness' (how much a person liked to talk about themselves!) we would probably find no correlation.

interactive angles

Using your class or friends and family as participants, measure each of the following pairs of variables:

- Foot length and forearm length (from elbow to beginning of hand).

- Width of tongue and how talkative a person is on a scale from 0 to 10.

- Height and the number of strides it takes to cross the room.

What type of correlations do you think you will get for each of these?

Correlation coefficients

The 'strength' of a correlation is measured by a correlation coefficient (represented by 'r'); a numerical value generated by an inferential statistical test (see pages 437–8. These coefficients range from –1 to +1. A correlation that has a minus sign is a negative correlation (minus = '–' = negative). A correlation that has a plus sign is a positive correlation (plus = '+' = positive). A correlation with a coefficient around 0 represents no correlation. The larger the number of the coefficient, the stronger the correlation. So, a correlation that has a coefficient of +0.83 is a stronger positive correlation than one with a coefficient of +0.33. Similarly, a correlation that has a coefficient of –0.77 is a stronger negative correlation than one with a coefficient of –0.29.

Representing correlations on a graph

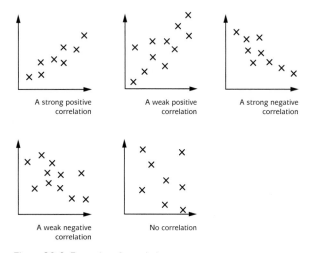

A strong positive correlation

A weak positive correlation

A strong negative correlation

A weak negative correlation

No correlation

Figure 29.6 Examples of correlations

Correlations are always represented on a *scatterplot* (sometimes called a scattergram or scattergraph), which helps to identify the type of correlation from it. Figure 29.6 gives some examples, showing different correlations and their estimated coefficient values.

for and against

correlations

+ data may already have been collected (eg archives of data such as governmental publications)

− there may be other factors that are affecting the correlation, but you are only focusing on two variables

− sometimes impossible to determine cause and effect (eg is the first measure causing the change in the second measure or vice versa)

− the correlation could be caused by a third factor that you did not measure

+ ideal for showing a link between two measures

Research methodology

In this section we consider some of the methodological issues you will have met at AS level that are common to many research methods. These include understanding the nature of the data obtained, the importance of sampling techniques and variables, and issues of validity and reliability.

Levels of measurement

The data generated by any study can be classified into one of four types: nominal, ordinal, interval or ratio; these are the *levels of measurement*. The level of measurement describes the type of scale against which a variable is being assessed. This matters as it affects the choice of descriptive and inferential statistics.

Nominal data

The simplest type of data a study can generate is *nominal data*. It takes the form of responses in discrete, named categories. Examples would be type of pet (dog, ferret, rat) or 'Did you dream last night?' (yes, no). Nominal data is the least informative type as the categories do not lie on a scale so are not related to one another, they merely provide a total or frequency.

Nominal data are often generated in studies using a questionnaire design from closed, forced choice questions to which participants might answer yes/no/sometimes/never or days of the week.

Exam tip

The mnemonic NOIR tells you the initials of the levels of measurement and the sequence from least (nominal) to most (ratio) informative. Also, if you can remember that noir is French (for black) this might also trigger the definition of nominal data, *nom* is French for *name*, nominal data refers to results in *named* categories.

research
now

correlation: extroversion, introversion – genetic?

Jang K.L., Livesely W.J. & Vernon P.A. (1999) The relationship between Eysenck's P-E-N model of personality and traits delineating personality disorder. *Personality and Individual Differences* 26: 121–8

aim: to examine whether there is a relationship between Eysenck's model of personality (psychoticism, extroversion and neuroticism: P-E-N) and personality disorders.

procedure: 200 participants completed an Eysenck personality questionnaire and the dimensional assessment of personality problems. The latter assesses personality disorders.

findings: there were many correlations between the psychoticism, extroversion and neuroticism scores with dimensions on the personality disorder questionnaire. Five of the correlations were:

Neuroticism and Identity Problems $r = +0.59$

Extroversion and Stimulus Seeking $r = +0.35$

Psychoticism and Conduct Problems $r = +0.40$

Extroversion and Social Avoidance $r = -0.41$

Neuroticism and Insecure Attachment $r = +0.47$

conclusion: the P-E-N model of personality proposed by Eysenck has some validity in predicting personality problems in the general population. In particular, the N dimension predicts general psychological distress. The E dimension is related to antisocial disorders, while the P dimension appears to be involved in conduct, drug use and violent behaviour problems.

Questions

1 Which of the above correlations is negative? What does that indicate?

2 Which of the above correlations is the strongest? What does it indicate?

interactive angles

Look at the image opposite BEFORE reading the text below.

Some people see a vase first, others the two faces in silhouette. Participants can be 'primed' to see one or the other by exposing them to images of flowers or people prior to seeing the Rubin's vase illusion. The data collected are simply in nominal categories of 'face first' or 'vase first'.

Figure 29.7 Rubin's vase

Ordinal data

Levels of measurement other than nominal are all *scales* consisting of data points that relate to each other in a linear way; scores are 'bigger' or 'smaller' relative to adjacent points. On an *ordinal scale* these points are only in rank order; they are 'smaller' or 'larger' than neighbouring

research now

nominal data: mood music

North A.C. & Hargreaves D.J. (2000) Musical preference during and after relaxation and exercise. *American Journal of Psychology* 113: 43–67

aim: to test experimentally the observation that we use music to optimise our mood.

procedure: participants either rode on an exercise bike or experienced a relaxation condition. They selected a piece of electronically generated music music to listen to, either during or after this session. The piece was either *high arousal* (faster and louder) or *low arousal* (slower and quieter). The versions were identical in other respects.

findings: during sessions participants selected the fast tempo version while exercising but the slow version while relaxing. When tested after the sessions, the choices were reversed; those who had exercised selected the slow version whereas those who had been relaxing opted for the faster version.

conclusion: music appears to be used to enhance mood during an activity but to moderate it afterwards.

1 Although North and Hargreaves used many other, more sophisticated measures, the participants' choice of music illustrates nominal data. What are the two named categories?

2 If the study were to be repeated with a condition where the participants could opt to listen to no music at all, the data generated would still be nominal. What would you call the third response?

research
now

ordinal data: measuring discrimination

Mays V. & Cochran S. (2001) Mental health correlates of perceived discrimination among lesbian, gay and bisexual adults in the United States. *American Journal of Public Health* **91: 1869–76**

aim: to assess the psychologically harmful effects of social stigma and discrimination on gay and bisexual men and women.

procedure: self-identified homosexual, bisexual and heterosexual men and women reported their experiences of discrimination (such as not being promoted at work, being prevented from purchasing a house and being hassled by the police). They were also asked about their mental health status, responding to Likert scale items asking about feeling 'so sad nothing could cheer you up', 'nervous' or 'worthless'. This generated ordinal data.

findings: homosexual and bisexual respondents reported more instances of discrimination than did heterosexuals and this was positively correlated with psychological distress.

conclusion: the experience of discrimination on the basis of sexual orientation is harmful to mental health.

1 Explain why the data collected from the Likert scales were ordinal.

2 Adding up a total of the number of instances of discrimination experienced would also generate ordinal data. Why?

points but the gaps between points may not be equal. For example, when a participant rates their experience of a horror film as (1) *mildly disturbing*, (2) *scary*, (3) *terrifying* or (4) *utterly horrific* the *order* is clear; consecutive points increase in magnitude. However, there is no assurance that the intervals between each point are equivalent; is 'utterly horrific' exactly twice as frightening as 'scary'?

Ordinal scales provide more information than nominal data because the scores are assigned *values*. We could ask 'how much' people liked dogs, ferrets or rats rather than just knowing which was their favourite. As with nominal data, questionnaires frequently generate ordinal scores, using Likert or Thurstone scales. These are discussed in more detail on pages 388–9.

Interval data

Like ordinal data, *interval data* is generated from a scale with points of increasing magnitude. In this instance the gaps between one point and the next are equivalent, hence 'interval' data. This is the case because each individual item on the scale is of *equal* value. For example, in a simple maths test a child might attempt the following sums: $23+35=\_$, $14+61=\_$, $35+42=\_$, $21+58=\_$. All of the sums are of equal difficulty: the smaller value is

first, none 'carry over' or use the 'hundreds' column and all are written in the same format. We could therefore assume that to get each sum right is 'worth the same amount' in terms of measuring a child's ability in maths. If this is so then their total out of five is an interval score. The distinguishing feature of an interval scale compared to the next category, ratio data, is that an interval scale has no real zero, it is not measured from an absolute baseline. Thinking back to the child's maths test, suppose a child scored zero on the test, could we conclude that they had no mathematical ability? No, we couldn't, perhaps they just haven't learned to use the tens column yet. If such a child were given a simpler test (such as: $2+3=\_$, $1+6=\_$, $3+4=\_$, $2+5=\_$), they may exhibit an ability that had been missed by the harder test. We therefore cannot assume that a score of zero on an interval scale really indicates an absence of that characteristic.

Ratio data

In common with interval data, *ratio data* is has linear scale with equal intervals. A ratio scale also has a real zero, that is, the measurements are made against an absolute baseline. In physics, temperature can be measured in K (Kelvin). Not only are the gaps between the

research
now

ratio data; dressed to shop

Regan P.C. & Llamas V. (2002) Customer service as a function of shopper's attire. *Psychological Reports* 90: 203–4

aim: to investigate the effect of style of dress on attention of shop assistants.

procedure: A female confederate entered women's clothing stores as if she was a shopper, dressed either informally (dressed to go to the gym) or formally (dressed for work). The time taken for an assistant to approach the confederate was observed. This was a ratio measure.

findings: shop assistants were significantly faster to approach the confederate in the 'smart attire' condition than when she was dressed casually.

conclusion: first impressions affect shop assistant behaviour.

1 Explain why time is a ratio measure.

2 What controls might have been employed in this field experiment?

points are equal (the increase in temperature from, say, 110K to 120K is the same amount as from 150K to 160K), but, in addition, the Kelvin scale has a real zero. Zero Kelvin is the lowest possible temperature.

Ratio scales are commonly used in psychology to measure physiological variables such as heart rate and blood pressure. In a ratio scale it is the measure itself that must have a baseline of zero; it does not mean that your partic-ipants have to start from a score of zero. Other more elaborate tests include the galvanic skin response (a measure of electrical resistance of the skin), which indicates perspiration and therefore fear, and the electroencephalograph (EEG), which detects brain activity. Many other psychological variables can be measured using time such as speed of performance or latency (the time to begin to respond).

interactive angles

Read the following examples of possible ways to test psychological variables. Decide which level of measurement is being used in each case and justify your answer.

1 **Drinking coffee at night affects our sleep** – participants were monitored using an electroencephalogram to measure the time spent asleep.

2 **Vocabulary size is greater in women than men** – participants selected words to complete a fill-in-the-gaps task. The list included words such as album, asymptote, back, beguile, creator, crepuscular, diameter, dorp, embarrass and embrasure.

3 **Recall differs between the senses** – participants saw, heard or smelled stimuli for three seconds and identified them two hours later answering 'yes' or 'no' to each.

4 **Jet lag is caused by crossing time zones** – biorhythm was monitored using body temperature adjustment measured in $^\circ$C.

Exam tip

You are asked to design an experiment but you don't know what the level of measurement is. Here's a rough guide.

● If you have two or more named categories and each participant selects one or more then it's probably nominal

● If your scores are rated, such as opinions, attitudes or emotions, or if you cannot be sure that every point on your scale is the same, even if you've assigned them numbers, then assume it's ordinal.

● You are relatively unlikely to have interval data. Are you sure that the points are equivalent? If so it could be interval. Does the scale get harder as you go up? If so it's probably ordinal.

● The same problems apply to ratio data; you may have a measure that is a ratio scale, such as time or weight, but do the intervals between the points really remain constant over the range you are using?

Remember to justify your explanation. Say why you think it is the scale you've stated.

interactive angles

What would the population be in these situations?

● Research into attitudes to health promotion educating people about exposure to the sun and the risk of skin cancer (Jones et al, 2000).

● A study of the relationship between first sexual encounters, safe sex, age and religious beliefs (Zaleski & Schiaffino, 2000).

● An investigation into the effects of fragrance on female arousal and mood across the menstrual cycle (Graham et al, 2000).

● An experiment that assesses the benefits of service dogs for people with ambulatory disabilities (Allen & Blascovich, 1996).

It is important to note that the population consists only of those people who could, potentially, be accessed. An advertisement posted on the Internet will only attract a population of 'people who visit the site', not 'all Internet users'. Even when a limited population is used, a range of other variables within that group is still important. Factors such as age, first language, gender, socio-economic status and many other variables may be important, and in order to obtain a diversity of participants, several recruitment routes may be used such as using flyers, sending enquiries to organisations and using newspaper advertisements. This is also likely to generate a large population ensuring that those individuals selected can be used as an indicator of the likely responses of a wider group. Sometimes, however, sample size may be minimised, such as when participation may cause distress and in experiments with animals in which they may suffer pain (see page 421).

Sampling

A *sample* of participants is drawn from the target group and studied so that the researcher can make generalisations about the whole of the original population. A sample, being smaller than the population, is easier to test but must be as similar to the parent population as possible, in order to make valid generalisations.

Random sample

A *random sample* is one in which each member of the population has an equal chance of being selected. This is a representative sampling technique as the sample should contain all the important characteristics of the parent population. Thus it is inappropriate to say that

To overview the ideas, consider a spider running across the classroom floor as you are revising levels of measurement. You could classify people into those who are frightened of spiders and those who are not; this would be a nominal categorisation. You could then ask the members of the class to rate their fear on a five-point scale. This ranking would provide an ordinal scale. Finally, you could trap the spider and leave it under a glass on the table and measure each person's pulse rate as they lifted the glass. This would give you a ratio measure. However, your teacher would stop you from doing this on the grounds that it was unethical!

Sampling techniques

Populations

Studies may test human participants or animals. The target *population* of a study consists of all the individuals falling within a particular definition, such as 'motorists' or 'inhabitants of Moscow'. Those individuals selected to participate will be drawn from this population and the results of the study will relate back to it. The target group should be relevant to the aims of the study such as identifying 'user' and 'non-user' populations to investigate the effects of drugs. In practice, however, more pragmatic factors such as availability may dictate the population.

the researcher approached random individuals in the street. To do this we would have to be equally likely to ask all individuals; this is patently not the case. We would be unlikely to invade the privacy of people in conversation or to approach someone who was apparently drunk.

research
now

representing the population: factors affecting literacy

Duncan L.G. & Seymour P.H.K. (2000) Socio-economic differences in foundation-level literacy. *British Journal of Psychology* 91: 145–66

aim: to investigate the effect of socio-economic status (SES) on the acquisition of literacy.

procedure: participants aged four to eight years were selected from two urban areas in Scotland with contrasting socio-economic profiles as indicated by 1991 census data on housing (private or public), unemployment, lone parents and car ownership. This division was reflected by the relative proportions of children in local schools in receipt of free school meals and clothing vouchers. The incidence of ethnic minorities in both areas was small and both schools adopted similar teaching strategies, introducing letter-sound correspondences concurrently with reading scheme vocabulary. At least 20 children from each area, in each school year, from nursery to primary year three were selected. They were tested seven times over a two-month period on the following scales:

- *Measures of foundation literacy*: letter and word knowledge and simple non-word reading (eg *zuf* as the name of a dinosaur).

- *Standardised assessments*: British Ability Scales Word Reading Test and a vocabulary test.

- *Metaphonological awareness*: a puppet game where the child was required to find the common sound in non-word pairs (eg what sound is the same in /tal/ and /nal/?).

findings: low SES was associated with impairments relative to chronological age with regard to letter and word knowledge, non-word reading and vocabulary. When the SES groups were equated for reading age the high and low SES performance was indistinguishable. Methodological problems arose because many of the younger low SES children had zero scores and some of the older high SES children reached the highest score, thus obscuring differences between the groups. To overcome this, zero and maximum scores were omitted from the statistical analysis.

conclusion: the delayed acquisition of literacy skills in low SES children is a consequence of delayed acquisition of letter-sound knowledge. Both groups progressed along the same pattern; the development of the low SES children was not deviant but developmentally constrained. The high SES children were achieving at approximately one academic year above their low SES peers.

1 Why was it useful to investigate the incidence of free school meals and clothing vouchers in each area?

2 Why was the incidence of ethnic minorities of importance?

3 Why was it important that the schools employed a similar approach to reading instruction?

4 If a control group of children were required for a study, would it be more important to match them for SES, age or reading ability? Why?

research
now

random sampling: healthy ageing

Perrig-Chiello P., Perrig W.J. & Stähelin H.B. (1999) Health control beliefs in old age – relationship with subjective and objective health, and health behaviour. *Psychology, Health and Medicine* 4: 83–94

aim: to examine the health control beliefs (internality, powerful others, chance) in elderly people and to explore whether these beliefs are related to actual or perceived health or to health-related behaviour.

procedure: participants were recruited for an interdisciplinary study begun in Switzerland in 1960 with 6400 healthy persons. By 1993, the pool still comprised 3768 people. A sample of 65–94-year-olds (309 males and 133 females) was selected. When the second set of tests was conducted in 1995, 332 participants remained (227 men and 105 women). On each of the two sessions, the following tests were conducted.

- *Measure of health control beliefs*: This was measured as a response to statements such as 'physical diseases are part of the destiny of old people'; 'my health depends mainly on myself'; 'health is a gift, a grace'.

- *Objective health index*: This score gave an approximate index of actual physical health which included blood pressure, blood tests (eg cholesterol, iron, blood sugar) and heart monitoring.

- *Subjective health rating*: Participants rated their health on matters such as impaired vision and headaches.

- *Health behaviour*: Participants were asked whether they performed any strenuous exercise and if so how often, and rated their use of psychiatric drugs.

findings: chance factors affecting health were believed to be more important than internality or powerful others. Objectively sick or healthy people did not differ in their health control beliefs but participants reporting the most self-appraised complaints (subjectively sick) had lower internality scores and higher chance scores than the other participants. This group also differed in their health-related behaviour; they engaged in less sport and took more psychiatric medication.

conclusion: successful ageing may depend on the acceptance of the inevitability of disease and frailty with age. Personal responsibility can allow an elderly person to actively approach these issues by seeking the assistance of powerful others if necessary, thus maintaining a belief in internal control. The findings relating to perceived health suggest that the elderly person's subjective experience of their own health may be a valuable diagnostic tool.

1 What were the attrition rates (percentage loss of participants) for males, females and overall between 1993 and 1995? What might the reasons have been?

2 Why was it better to take a random sample from the over 65s in the original group of 6400 people than to use sources such as residential care homes for the elderly?

In order to ensure that we are selecting on a random basis, we need access to the entire population being investigated. This is often problematic; lists such as birth records, school enrolments and the electoral role each have limitations. They can only provide a complete population of those registered; for instance the electoral role does not list all over 17 year olds, only those who have registered to vote. Once a source has been obtained, individuals must be chosen using a randomised system, for instance by allocating every individual a number and using a random number generator or random number tables for selection. For small groups it is possible simply to write each participant's number on a piece of paper, jumble them together and draw out the sample. If this method is to provide a truly random sample the container must be large enough to mix them effectively (hats are probably too small for this purpose!), the slips should be of equal size, should be folded in the same way and should not be visible during selection. If the condition of randomness is met and the sample is large, it should be representative of the population from which it was drawn, so generalisations can be made.

Systematic sample

In order to achieve a representative sample, a researcher may alternatively use *systematic sampling*; selecting participants across the variety of characteristics exhibited within the population. This selects every 'nth' person on a list. By dividing the total population by the size of the sample we require we obtain the basis for sampling. For example, if we have a population of 100 and wish to select a sample of 20, we would include every fifth person (100/20 = 5, hence every fifth). This technique does not result in a representative sample if individuals are arranged in a patterned way. If, they are not, however, then a systematic sample is representative so generalisations can be made.

Opportunity sample

An *opportunity sample* selects a group of participants based on the section of the population available at a given time. This is a non-representative sampling technique because there is no guarantee that the diversity existing within the population will be accessed when a sample is taken. Individuals who are unavailable may share an important criterion that will be under-represented in the sample. Conducting a survey on a cloudy day might under-represent people who dislike rain. This may not matter in an investigation of attitudes to mobile phones, but could be an important sampling error in a study about seasonal affective disorder (depression related to low light levels in winter). If the sample fails to accurately represent its parent group, then it is inappropriate to generalise from that sample.

research
now

opportunity sample: thinking of buying a car?

Williamson J., Raynard R. & Cuthbert L. (2000) A conversation-based process tracing method for use with naturalistic decisions: an evaluation study. *British Journal of Psychology* **91: 203–21**

aim: to test the Active Information Search (AIS) method used to investigate decision making. Specifically, to apply it to the naturalistic setting of consumer behaviour and to enable respondents to reply verbally, within a conversation, rather than to think into 'empty space'.

procedure: an opportunity sample of 96 paid participants was recruited through advertisements in local public places and direct face-to-face approaches. Full-time students and those with no experience of using credit were not selected since part of the study required such prior knowledge. A range of socio-economic and employment groups was represented in the sample, including manual, semi-skilled and professional occupations. There were 42 males and 54 females, in the following age categories: 18–24 years (5), 25–44 years (57), 45–64 years (32), 65+ years (2).

Respondents were briefed about the nature of the research, the task and their right to withdraw. They were assured of their anonymity, invited to ask questions and permission was sought to tape-record the protocols.

The participants' task was to make a consumer decision about the purchase of either a car or a washing machine. Interviewers were briefed to answer questions asked by the respondents in order to enable them to make decisions (orally providing facts such as the price of the item). There were several variations:

● *Conversational AIS* – interviewers prompted after 60 seconds of silence with comments such as 'Don't forget you can ask me anything you like'.

● *Conversational think aloud* – interviewers asked respondents to 'think out loud' and the interviewers responded conversationally (but without interrupting) during the respondents' monologues.

● *Post-decision interviews* were either *non-directive* cued only by the open-ended questions 'Can you say in your own words how you made each of your decisions?' and 'Anything else?' or *interactive* in which the non-directive summary was followed by questions to elicit reasons for particular decisions.

Each participant undertook both the car or washing machine task in one of these conditions. Some participants received the car task, others the washing machine task, first. After completing all the tasks, the participants were debriefed, given the opportunity to ask questions about the study and thanked for their participation.

findings: thinking aloud did not affect the number of questions asked by participants nor their post-decision summaries. One 'think aloud' protocol for the car task was recorded as follows:

> I: The Tipo is £2390 after your trade-in.
> R: £2390. And H registration is that? What year is that?
> I: 1990.
> R: 1990 and K is?
> I: 1992.
> R: Alright 1992. 34,000 miles. So that's quite low then really.
> I mean I wouldn't go for the Rover personally because they're sort of family cars.
> The old man sort of cars…I would go for the VW if I had a large disposable,
> A large disposable income? cos VWs are known for expense
> and high insurance and things like that.
> So a 1600 engine would just be more expensive basically to insure for myself.
> So Fiat Tipo is like more of a sensible choice for me.
> I: Okay.
> R: A bit small, they're pretty reliable, fairly cheap on insurance,
> and easy, cheaper to get parts for, the parts are cheaper,
> so I would probably opt for the Tipo considering the rust and all that business.

conclusion: thinking aloud did not appear to interfere with participants' decision-making processes. This suggests that when 'think aloud' is experienced in a conversational context rather than an 'empty space' it is a valuable tool in tracing the decision-making process. It enables the researcher to understand more about the thought processes without interfering with them significantly.

1 Why were full-time students excluded?

2 Why was it important to get a range of representation of different socio-economic groups and occupations?

In practice, the sample used in much psychological research consists simply of those people who are readily accessible to the researcher – commonly these are often university students. The generalisability of such a sample would be questionable in some cases (for instance in studies where the outcome being measured is dependent on age, wealth or education), but is otherwise acceptable. Many recent studies have relied wholly or partly on the student population for their participants, for example, Morrison and Ellis (2000), University of York; Deręgowski et al (2000), University of Aberdeen; Féry and Vom Hofe (2000), University René Descartes; and Rosenblum et al (2000), University of California.

Quota sample

Quota sampling is a method in which individuals are taken to represent each major strata or layer within the population. Such subdivisions might include geographical locations, ages and racial origin. Each 'quota' is selected according to the incidence of that subgroup within the population. The sample is chosen to represent each stratum of the population by questioning any available individuals. As time progresses, people are encountered who fulfil the requirements. When the target sample size for a subgroup has been met, further similar individuals are rejected. Sampling continues until sufficient numbers in each cate-gory have been obtained. The stratification of a quota sample ensures that the key variations in the population are represented therefore generalisations can be made from the sample to the population from which it was drawn.

Volunteer sampling

Much psychological research is conducted on *volunteer samples*, that is groups of participants who choose to take part. This is not a sampling technique but a description of some types of samples. Participants obtained through sampling techniques such as opportunity or random sampling may constitute a volunteer sample; this simply means that the participants are aware that they have chosen to participate and are doing so in the absence of reward (such as payment or course credits). The sample may be attracted, for example, by an advertisement or may be 'self-selected' by being present in the right place at the right time to be available to the researchers, for example, passing through a particular doorway when a survey is being conducted.

While this type of sampling has the ethical advantage of the participants having volunteered to participate there are several disadvantages. Volunteers tend to be untypical of the population in general because they are likely to be:

● better educated;

● from higher socioeconomic groups;

Snack attack

Want to slim for summer but have the willpower of Homer Simpson? Then put your hands together for those lovely scientists at University College London. They've discovered a way to trick your body into hat-ing snacks. The secret? Simply scoff some choc straight after a meal. Chocolate junkies who ate half a bar after lunch and dinner lost their cravings in just two weeks while choc-haters (?!) who indulged on an empty stomach started craving the stuff. Better pass the After Eights then…

Company magazine, April 2000

1 What is the IV in the study described in this article?

2 Psychologists have identified many variables that affect appetite, such as smell, time of day, time since last meal and social factors. How can you control for these and other factors that you suspect might affect the perception of hunger?

3 What other controls would you impose if you conducted this study?

- more sociable than non-volunteers;

- more intelligent than those individuals who do not volunteer for research in general (but not more so than those volunteering for particular types of research such as hypnosis or sex-research).

As a consequence, research based on volunteer samples may be biased so it may be inappropriate to generalise to the wider population.

Variables

A *variable* is any factor that is free to vary or can be changed, altered or examined to gauge an effect. In experiments we have two key categories of variable, the IV and the DV. In addition we must pay attention to those variables that could disrupt the effect of the IV, *confounding variables*. The control of these extraneous variables aims to limit factors that could distort the collection of valid and reliable data.

One source of uncontrolled variables is the research setting; these are *situational variables*. They are confounding effects arising from the influence of the environment on the behaviour of participants, such as lighting, noise and temperature. Within reason, the absolute conditions are less important than consistency across conditions. You cannot expect to get reliable data if you test one group of participants in a quiet place such as the canteen early in the morning and another at lunchtime when it is busy and crowded.

research
now

pouring a perfect pint

Cabe P.A. & Pittenge J.B. (2000) Human sensitivity to acoustic information from vessel filling. *Journal of Experimental Psychology: Human Perception and Performance* 26: 313–24

aims: to ascertain the extent to which people are able to use acoustic information to detect changes in the acoustic properties of a vessel as it fills with water.

method: participants were observed in situations where they detected the status of a vessel containing water. The design involved five independent variables: vision status (blind or sighted), vessel size, flow rate, sex and number of trials. The participants were tested on their ability to detect water level rising, falling or not changing and when filling a vessel to the brim or to drinking level either blindfold or sighted. Aspects of the situations that were controlled included the following:

- Participants were naïve to the purpose of the study.

- No participants had hearing problems, sighted participants had normal or corrected-to-normal vision.

These controlled for participant variables.

- All participants heard the same tape of filling, emptying, and constant level events in a vessel.

- The speed of flow into the vessel was controlled to a maximum rate.

- Tube diameter and position were the same.

- The height of the water was kept at a constant level.

These controlled for water pressure and flow rate.

- Participants listened from approximately 1 metre from the loudspeaker.

- All participants sat in the same position in relation to the apparatus.

These controlled for situational variables.

- Participants responded during 10-second intervals.

- Participants responded to multiple-choice answers.

- No feedback was given to a participant until the end of all their trials.

- Different vessels were used for demonstrations to participants than for the experiment itself.

These controlled for other aspects of the procedure.

In general it was not possible to counterbalance the order of events. When filling below the brim, participants were asked to fill to their 'preferred drinking level'.

findings: participants reliably identified water level rising, falling or not changing and were readily able to use auditory information alone to control filling (whether blind, sighted or blindfold) although where available the use of both sources of information improved accuracy. Filling to the brim was more accurate than to drinking level.

conclusion: changing acoustic information appears to afford good prospective control of vessel filling.

1 Select three controlled variables and explain why they are important.

2 Why was it important to compare blind *and* blindfold participants?

In addition to the setting, the participants themselves can be a source of uncontrolled variables. Participant variables are confounding effects that arise from the characteristics of the people performing in a study, such as their age, sex, state of hunger or level of arousal. A participant who attends an experiment asking about sources of frustration when they have just spent 40 minutes in a car getting to the laboratory is likely to answer differently from one who has arrived in 10 minutes by foot.

Demand characteristics

A well-planned experiment represents a pay-off between ethics – how much participants need to know to make

research
methods

sex hormones and smiling

Dabbs J.M. Jr, Bernieri F.J., Strong R.K., Campo R. & Milun R. (2001) Going on stage: testosterone in greetings and meetings. *Journal of Research in Personality* 35: 27–40

aim: to investigate the effect of testosterone levels on social behaviour.

procedure: 122 male and 236 female students were videotaped during social encounters (eg speaking to a video camera, meeting an experimenter, being interviewed or talking to a peer) after having testosterone levels measured from saliva samples.

findings: individuals with high-testosterone levels were less nervous and more focused. They were faster to approach, looked directly at the camera, were less nervous and were rated as more 'independent'; they were relaxed and confident in social settings. The low-testosterone individuals were attentive and friendly, but also fidgety and tense. These results were similar for males and females.

conclusion: testosterone level appears to be a significant factor in social interactions.

1 Suggest four participant variables that might have affected the results of this study (try to avoid those factors that could be attributable to the effects of differing testosterone levels).

2 Identify the independent and dependent variable in this study.

3 More than one rater was used to code the behaviours recorded in the social encounters. What would it have been important for them to do to improve validity prior to scoring, and how might they have achieved this?

informed choices, and scientific rigour – how little participants should know to ensure that this knowledge does not affect their behaviour. We must attempt to minimise the cues in an experimental setting that might enable participants to guess, correctly or incorrectly, about the purpose of the investigation. The features of an experiment that inform participants about the aim and influence their behaviour independently of the experimental objectives, thereby confounding the results, are called demand characteristics.

classic
research

demand characteristics: participants prove to be pathetic

Orne M.T. (1962) On the social psychology of the psychological experiment: with particular reference to demand characteristics and their implications. *American Psychologist* 17: 776–83

aim: to devise a task so psychologically noxious, meaningless and boring that it would counter the power of social influence, which results in participants continuing to perform in order to fulfil an experimenter's expectations even when their requests demand toleration of discomfort, boredom or pain.

procedure: participants were asked to complete 224 additions of random numbers presented to them on a sheet, to tear this into a minimum of 32 pieces, and start on the next sheet (from a stack of 2000). When the experimenter left the room saying 'Continue to work, I will return eventually' he expected the participants to give up working.

findings: after five and a half hours, it was the experimenter who gave up!

Conclusion: Orne reports that 'Thus far, we have been singularly unsuccessful in finding an experimental task which would be discontinued, or, indeed, refused by subjects in an experimental setting'. Such is the power of compliance.

1 What research method is used in this study?

2 What pressures in this situation were acting as demand characteristics?

Operationalising variables

One way to improve experimental reliability is to operationalise variables. This ensures consistency of measures and allows others to replicate the experiment. An *operational definition* is a description that identifies a variable by factors that can be measured or manipulated. Take a study investigating the effects of mobile phone use on hearing, for example. The IV of 'phone use' could be operationalised by establishing three groups: non-users, who do not have or use a mobile phone; occasional users, who use a mobile for less than ten minutes per month; and frequent users, who spend more than an hour a week calling from their mobile phone. If the outcome was hearing loss, it could be measured as the lowest audible volume (in dB), thus operationalising the DV.

Harrell et al (2000) investigated the differences in the way students assisted the way-finding of (hypothetical) visitors around their university campus. The independent variables were the sex of the participant and the nature of the visitor. Since the visitors were hypothetical (the students were given a brief description of the visitor before giving their directions) this was easy to manipulate. The experimenters controlled the following features relating to the visitors:

- *destination* (near or distant);
- *gender* (male or female);
- *age* (25 or 75 years);
- *familiarity with the campus* (unfamiliar – new to the campus and did not know his or her way around, or familiar – had formerly attended the university but had not been on campus recently).

The dependent variable was the participants' proficiency at directing the visitors, measured as the accuracy of their estimate of the time it would take the visitor to reach their destination and the completeness of a map they were asked to draw. The maps were analysed for the inclusion of the following:

- *buildings and landmarks* (one mark for each, such as university buildings, trees, doors, stairways and paths);
- *cardinal indicators* (whether north or south was marked on the map and if it was correct);
- *directional arrows* (showing the route the visitor should take);
- *supplemental directions* (additional words to guide the visitor).

Harrell et al (2000) found that male students produced more complete maps but were no more likely to include landmarks or labelled buildings. The males were also more likely to take into account the characteristics of the visitors, including more detail for older or unfamiliar visitors or those attempting to navigate complex routes.

Validity

Validity refers to whether a technique can achieve the purpose for which it was designed. A valid test should measure

interactive angles

Look at the following studies and identify how the variables have been operationalised:

North and Hargreaves (2000), page 398

Metzler et al (2000), page 377

Regan and Llamas (2002), page 400

The dependent variables in the following list are drawn from further examples in the text. Suggest how the researchers might have operationalised each of these variables:

Dabbs et al (2001), page 408; attention, nervousness, friendliness and fidgeting

Frone (2003), page 254; workplace alcohol and marijuana use

Frydenberg et al (2003), page 271; coping mechanisms of working hard and worrying

Finally, suggest how the variables in the following two studies could have been operationalised:

Gosling et al (2002) asked observers to make personality judgements of occupants on the basis of physical environments of their offices or bedrooms

Morris et al (2002) examined personality ratings of horses made by stable personnel on dimensions such as neuroticism and extroversion

what it claims to measure. For example, a test designed to gauge sexual promiscuity should successfully assess the number of partners an individual has over a fixed period of time. Metzler et al (2000) measured this variable by asking their participants to answer questions about:

- number of partners in the last three months;
- sex with non-monogamous partners;
- sex with partners not well known.

Do you think they are likely to have obtained truthful responses? If not, the test may have been measuring the participants' responsiveness to social desirability rather than their risky sexual behaviour. Validity can be described in a number of different ways (see box below). In relation to the three measures listed above, Metzler et al (2000) used an intervention aiming to reduce danger-ous sexual practices. They found that the sexual behaviour of the participants in the intervention group was much less risky than that of the usual care group so we would expect that the experimental participants would experience fewer STDs. This, however, was not the case, suggesting that the measures of behaviour change were not valid.

Three studies were reported by MacDonald et al (2000), investigating the effects of alcohol on social judgements.

Measures of internal validity: the validity of the test items themselves in relation to the objective.

- **Face validity** is whether the measure appears (at face value) to test what it claims to. It is the least sophisticated measure of validity but is more worthwhile if an expert opinion is obtained.

- **Concurrent validity** compares a new test to other tests of the same phenomenon to see if they produce similar results. If the tests agree, they have concurrent validity. For example, if a consumer organisation wishes to use a new measure of cats' preferences for different brands of tinned food it might validate this by asking cat owners which brand their cat consumes most quickly.

- **Construct validity** is demonstrated by showing that the phenomenon being measured actually exists. So, the construct validity of a test for intelligence, for example, is dependent on a model or theory for intelligence.

- **Predictive validity** indicates that the measure is valid because it can accurately forecast performance on the measure under scrutiny. If an intelligence test has predictive validity it should be able to estimate participants' future success on tasks such as examinations.

Measures of external validity
- **Ecological validity** is the extent to which a test measures a real-world phenomenon.

- **Population validity** is the extent to which a real, universal effect has been identified that is equally relevant to different populations. This has been issue because many studies are conducted on students (and, for many years, predominantly white, Western, male ones).

These differed in their ecological validity. In one test a fixed quantity of alcohol was administered in the labora-tory whereas the other studies used participants who were spending their evening at a bar, some of whom were drinking alcohol. The first study therefore had lower ecological validity than subsequent tests. This is not sim-ply because it was conducted in the field but because findings from this context are more likely to apply to other situations.

There's one diet that lets you eat what you like. If you happen to be a cat.

That diet is Whiskas and it's the perfect diet for cats. It has the taste, texture, and smell that cats prefer, and it has the ideal balance of proteins, nutrients and vitamins that every cat needs. But there's more to the Whiskas diet. With a choice of fourteen different recipes, your cats can have all the choice they like as well as the nutrition they need. So if you're looking for the perfect diet, and you happen to be a cat, then look no further than Whiskas.

whiskas
MORE CATS THAN EVER BEFORE NOW PREFER WHISKAS.

Figure 29.8 How would you measure the concurrent and predictive validity of a test that demonstrated that most cats preferred to eat Whiskas?

Reliability

Reliability is a measure of whether replications would produce similar results; if they do then the test or technique is reliable. Thinking about yourself, do you always turn up at the same time in the same place? If so, you're reliable. There are several ways to assess the reliability of a psychological test, all of which are based on the assumption that if one source of scores from the test correlates with another source then the test is reliable. The measures of reliability differ in the way they select test material to compare.

In *test–retest* assessment, participants complete the test twice, at different times. Their first and second scores are then correlated, and if the correlation coefficient is highly positive then the test is reliable. This works well if the test is not highly memorable otherwise the effect of practice may be a problem.

To overcome the effect of practice a test may be produced in *equivalent forms*, that is, different but comparable versions of the same test. This would be like IQ test books where each test claims to be of equal difficulty and is composed of identical style questions. Participants are tested twice, once with each form of the test and their results should correlate strongly if the tests are reliable.

The *split-half method* is a measure of the internal reliability of the test, that is, the extent to which the items on the test are all measuring the same phenomenon. All participants take the test only once. Their scores on one-half of the test (eg the even-numbered questions) are then correlated with their scores on the other half of the test (eg the odd-numbered questions). A high correlation indicates that the test items are 'equivalent', ie that the test has internal reliability.

classic research

issues of location: is scary sexy?

Dutton D.C. Aron A.P. (1974) Some evidence for heightened sexual attraction under conditions of high anxiety. *Journal of Personality and Social Psychology* 30: 510–17

aims: to demonstrate that a high arousal state induced by fear could be misinterpreted internally as sexual arousal.

procedure: an interviewer (either an attractive female or a male) asked male passers-by to fill out a questionnaire in which they devised a short story using an ambiguous picture of a woman as a prompt (this was from a Thematic Apperception Test, TAT). Eighty-five males aged 18–35 years and unaccompanied by a female companion were interviewed as they crossed the Capilano River. Experimental participants were interviewed on a suspension bridge only 1.75 metres wide and 160 metres long, built of wooden boards held up by wire cables spanning from one side of the canyon to the other. Hanging 70 metres above the rocky riverbed the bridge sways, tilts and wobbles precariously. Control participants were interviewed in the same way but on a solid bridge, further upstream that had higher handrails, was wider, was only 3.5 metres above a small rivulet and did not sway. Scorers working blind to the condition the participant was from later rated the story for sexual content. The inter-rater reliability was +0.87.

findings: when interviewed by a woman, the men in the high arousal condition on the suspension bridge invented stories with greater sexual imagery than those interviewed in the less arousing location. No difference was found between the conditions with a male interviewer.

conclusion: Dutton and Aron concluded that fear increased the participants' attraction to the female interviewer. Arousal level in this study was the IV (rather than a situational variable). However, it does show that the situation in which people are placed during a study can affect the results obtained.

Figure 29.9 Crossing the Capilano river

1 Which of the following terms would you use to describe this study: field experiment, natural experiment, quasi-experiment, observation, interview, survey?

2 What is the DV in this study? How was it measured?

3 What variables should have been controlled to ensure that the only difference between the two situations was the level of arousal?

4 What does an inter-rater reliability of +0.87 mean?

We discussed the need for observers to generate the same records when they are watching the same behaviours (see page 386). The extent to which they do so is their *inter-observer* or inter-rater *reliability*.

interactive angles

Are each of the measures described below valid, reliable, neither or both? Explain why.

● A student is testing whether dyslexic readers are better when the text they are reading is covered with a transparent coloured film. She times their reading speed with and without the coloured sheet in place and asks them whether they found the passages easier to read in one or the other condition. The general consensus was that the coloured sheets made reading easier but there was no difference in reading speed.

● In a study of first and third year students a psychologist measured anxiety levels using a device that recorded how tightly a participant clenched their jaw. You happen to score highly because you've just experienced an episode of road rage on the way to the laboratory. The following week you decide to walk quietly through the park instead. How will this affect your score? Another participant grinds their teeth at night. Their score is also very high.

● A group of students decides to observe affection and affiliation between couples using a field experiment. They take photos of couples in parks, restaurants, bars and the student lounge and estimate the distance between the two people.

Generalisability

Because we can only test a sample from the population we are investigating, this sample must be representative. This allows us to *generalise* from our results, that is, extrapolate the implications of the findings from the sample back to the whole population. We can justify generalisation only if the findings really do apply to the whole population. Sampling is only one factor that affects the value of the results of a study, reliability and validity of the findings are also important.

Descriptive statistics

In order to understand the results of research it is generally easier to summarise the key features of the data. This can be done numerically, by calculating measures of central tendency and spread, or pictorially, using graphs. There are three measures of *central tendency* or 'average'. These summarise data via a single index that represents a typical score from the data set. Measures of *dispersion* or 'spread' represent the way in which the data points are spread out around the average. Each technique can only be used on data of particular levels of measurement.

Measures of central tendency

The mode

The mode is the simplest measure of central tendency and can be used with any data. However, because it is the least informative measure, it is only usually used with nominal data. The *mode* is the most common score in the data set, that is, the value that occurs the greatest number of times. (Hint: think **mo**de = **mo**st.) If two scores are equally represented then the distribution of scores is *bi-modal*. If there are three 'modes' it is tri-modal and so on. The best way to calculate the mode is to draw up a frequency table and see which score has the highest frequency, for example:

Table 29.1 Shoe colour choice in males

Shoe colour choice in males	Frequency
Brown	10
Green	15
Blue	18
Black	27
White	17
Red	4

From the frequency column we can easily conclude that the modal shoe colour for this data set is black, with a frequency of 27.

The median

The *median* is the measure of central tendency indicated by the middlemost score. That is, when a data set is ranked from the smallest number to the largest number (including every repetition of a score), it is the score that lies in the middle of the data set. (Hint: think **med**ian = **mid**dle.) To calculate a median, follow these steps:

1 Rank the data from the smallest to the largest number.

2 Eliminate one score from each end of the ranked data (called a pair of scores).

3 Continue eliminating pairs of scores until either one or two scores are left. In a data set with an odd number of scores there should be left one number left (this is the median). In a data set with an even number of scores there should be two numbers left. In this case add up the two remaining numbers and divide the total by 2. This is the median.

Calculating the median

The following are questionnaire scores generated from a Likert-type scale:

11 13 13 13 15 17 17 17 18 19 19

The median is 17. Now, re-calculate with an extra score:

11 13 13 13 13 15 17 17 17 18 19 19

The two remaining numbers are 15 and 17. If we now execute step 4, we get:

15 + 17 = 32

We then divide this by 2 to get 32/2 = 16. The median score is 16.

The median can be used for any continuous data, that is, data with an ordinal, interval or ratio level of measurement. As the median is less informative than the mean (because it does not take into account the magnitude of every score), the mean is preferential for interval or ratio data. However, the median has the advantage that it is not swayed or 'skewed' by outlying scores. Very large or small scores in a data set will not affect the median at all whereas they will affect the mean.

The mean

The *mean* (or arithmetic mean) is the measure of central tendency usually called the 'average'. To calculate this complete the following procedure:

1 Add up all of the scores in the data set.

2 Divide this total by the number of scores in the data set (including zero scores).

Let's look at an example. We measured the height of 10 people and the results were as follows (in centimetres):

158 163 165 165 165 168 170 170 170 175

So, firstly we add up all of the scores:

158 + 163 + 165 + 165 + 165 + 168 + 170 + 170 + 170 + 175

Next, we divide the total score by the number of scores, which is 10:

1669/10 = 166.9

Therefore the mean height is 166.9 centimetres.

The mean should only be used with interval or ratio data because it relies on the mathematical relationship between the values of scores in the data set. Since it takes into account the magnitude of each score it is more informative than any other measure of central tendency. However, this has the disadvantage of being influenced by outlying scores, which the median and mode are not.

interactive angles

Collect the following data:

- The time it takes people to open and eat a chocolate bar.
- People's favourite type of chocolate: dark, milk, white, none.
- Get people to rate themselves on a scale of 1–10 on their current 'need for chocolate'.

From the scores, calculate an appropriate measure of average. You may wish to split it into male and female averages.

Measures of spread

The range

Measures of dispersion indicate how spread the data set is around the measure of central tendency. They show whether participants' scores cluster around the average or are spread out. It is possible to have roughly equal averages but vastly differing dispersion figures for different groups. The simplest measure of dispersion is the range. This measure of dispersion is used in conjunction with the median but can be used with any continuous data, that is, data with an ordinal, interval or ratio level of measurement. It is calculated as follows:

1 Rank the data from the smallest to the largest number (as for calculating the median).

2 Subtract the smallest number from the largest then add 1. This is the range.

Look back at the data for calculation of the mean. The smallest was 158 and the largest 175.

Largest – smallest: 175–158 = 17

Difference + 1: 17 + 1 = 18

The range = 18.

Graphical representation

There are four main ways of plotting data: bar charts, histograms, scattergraphs and frequency polygons. These are used to represent data from studies using different research designs and for data with different levels of measurement.

Bar charts

These are usually used for representing totals of nominal data or for plotting measures of central tendency derived from ordinal, interval or ratio data. The x-axis (horizontal axis) should always have the categories of data, while the y-axis (vertical axis) is used for frequency of occurrences or average values.

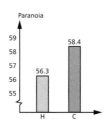

Figure 29.10 Average scores for participants recalling an alien abduction either through hypnosis (H) or consciously (C) on the personality variable of paranoia (Stone-Carmen, 1992)

Histograms

These show the distribution of scores that are measured along a continuous (numerical) scale, that is, ordinal, interval or ratio data and plotted on the x-axis (horizontal axis). The y-axis (vertical axis) should always be used for the frequency of occurrences.

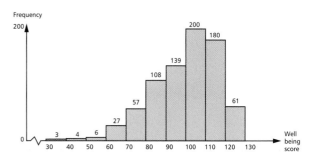

Figure 29.11 Frequency distribution of the psychological well being scores of a sample of older adults (Roberts et al, 1998)

Scattergraphs

Scattergraphs (also called scatterplots or scattergrams) are used for plotting correlations. From a scattergraph it is clear what type of correlation has been found (see pages 395–6). The x-axis (horizontal axis) should represent one of the numerical measures and the y-axis (vertical axis) the other.

Frequency polygons

Frequency polygons are also referred to as line graphs. They are used with two sets of data that can be compared on one graph. An example would be plotting the distribution of scores for males and females on a questionnaire measuring attitudes towards safe sex. The x-axis (horizontal axis) should have the scores on the task while the y-axis (vertical axis) represents the frequency of occurrences of the possible scores.

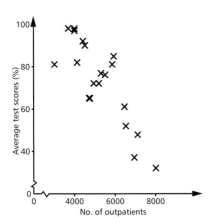

Figure 29.12 Scattergraph illustrating a negative correlation between medical students' success in their university examinations and the number of out patients they had seen. Fewer contacts with outpatients is correlated with better exam results (Neumayer et al, 1998)

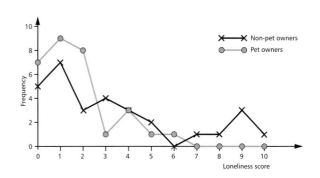

Figure 29.13 The relative distributions of loneliness score is pet owning and non-pet owning older adults showing that those indicviduals without a pet were more lonely (Roberts et al, 1996)

The golden rules of plotting data

The following are guidelines that should be applied when you plot data:

- tabulate the data either as a frequency tally chart or, for a correlation, so that each participant's score on one variable is next to their score on the other;

- choose an appropriate graph for the type of data;

- label the axes fully and clearly indicating both the measure (eg age) and the units (eg years);

- give the graph a title. Anyone should be able to read the title and know what the graph represents;

- interpret the graph as part of the data analysis.

Ethics

BPS guidelines for research with human participants

The British Psychological Society (BPS) publishes guidelines that are central to British provision against the misconduct of psychologists in research and professional

classic
research

ethics: as long as a piece of string

Asch S.E. (1955) Opinions and social pressure. *Scientific American* 193: 31–5

aim: to investigate the effect of conformity. Would participants give answers that were obviously untrue to avoid contradicting the responses or other participants?

procedure: each participant was part of a group of seven individuals each of whom was also apparently a participant but was actually a confederate of the experimenter. As a group, they were shown one large card followed by a smaller one. They were asked to match the length of the line on the second card with one of those on the first. They were arranged around a table so that the real participant always answered second to last.

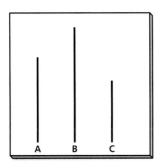 

In the experimental trials, the confederates sometimes all gave the same wrong answer. The participants were interviewed individually afterwards.

findings in 32 per cent of the experimental trials where the confederates gave the wrong answers, the real participants conformed and also answered incorrectly. Some 75 per cent of all participants conformed and gave the wrong answer at least once. When interviewed, the participants said that they knew they were giving the wrong answers but were doing so to avoid being disruptive but felt very anxious.

conclusion: the desire to avoid feeling different is sufficient to induce conformity in individuals.

1 In what ways did this experiment deceive the participants?

2 How might the participants have felt about themselves following the experiment?

interactive angles

What should a psychologist do in each of these situations?

- A researcher conducting a study on the effects of viewing text through transparent coloured acetate finds that a participant who says they are dyslexic can read more easily in this condition than with a colourless overlay. The participant asks if they should always read with a coloured sheet.

- During a consultation, a psychologist in clinical practice realises that his client would benefit more from therapy of a kind he is, as yet, unqualified to provide.

- A university student finds that in her experiment participants who are overweight are less stressed than those who are underweight. She is asked whether it is therefore better to be overweight since it protects you from the negative effects of stress.

practice. The BPS Code of Conduct, Ethical Principles and Guidelines (1998) aims to guide practising psychologists in their conduct, for instance to ensure that they value integrity, impartiality and respect for individuals. This establishes the highest possible ethical standards and to ensure that work is being carried out with the greatest possible scientific integrity. The elements of consent, confidentiality, debriefing and the right to withdraw are discussed below.

Consent

Psychologists carrying out investigations or interventions should always obtain the valid consent of the participants, ensuring that they can make an informed decision about the nature of their contribution and its potential consequences. For example, psychologists should:

- withhold information only when necessary to the objectivity of the investigation and only after consultation with experienced colleagues;

- give full information in advance to those participating in an investigation or intervention (via the brief in a study) including aspects that might affect their willingness to participate and provide full information afterwards regarding the aims, rationale and outcome as appropriate to the welfare of participants (via the debrief in a study);

- obtain consent from those persons who participate and take steps to ensure that this is valid, except where intervention is compulsory;

- seek to obtain real consent of children and adults with impairments of understanding or communication. For participants below 16 years of age, permission must additionally be obtained from parents or those in loco parentis;

- recognise and uphold the rights of those who may be unable to give valid consent such as the young, individuals with learning difficulties, the elderly and those in the care of an institution or detained by law;

- seek permission from the person(s) with legal authority to give consent for those who cannot give valid consent for themselves;

- only carry out observational research in situations where those being observed would expect to be seen by strangers unless the participants have given their consent. Researchers should take account of local cultural values and of the possibility of intruding upon the privacy of individuals who, while in a public space, may believe they are unobserved;

- not use their position of responsibility to pressurise participants to take part in or remain in the investigation;

interactive angles

In a continuation of Dutton and Aron (1974) described on page 412–3, participants were left in a laboratory with an array of electrical equipment and some copies of 'previous experiments in the area' to read, which discussed the effects of electric shocks on learning and pain in general. The experimenter went to find another participant and returned with a woman who was, in fact, a confederate. She had been told that the study involved sexual attraction but did not know the experimental hypothesis. Her actions had been rehearsed to avoid differences among conditions and she had been instructed to call either heads or tails when she flipped a coin. Eighty male students volunteered for whom the experimental protocol was as follows. The confederate took off her coat and hung it up. They were (mis)informed about the experiment and shocks and were then asked if they wanted to leave, but no one did. They were told that there were two levels of shock, quite painful or a mere tingle and a coin was tossed for allocation to conditions. (Both participants tossed the coin: in half the confederate called the same as the participant, in half the opposite.) The experimenter then said 'Today heads receives the high shock level' and explained how the shock series would take place, about the electrodes, etc. While the experimenter 'set up the equipment', the participants were taken to private cubicles to fill in a questionnaire about their feelings towards the experimental situation, including their co-participant. The questions included 'How much would you like to ask her out on a date' and 'How much would you like to kiss her' (an alternative set of questions was provided for participants who ostensibly had a male co-partner) and TAT pictures as used previously. The results showed that participants in the high anxiety (painful shock) condition demonstrated attraction to the confederate on all measures but for the TAT only when she too was in the 'painful shock' condition.

- *Were the participants able to give informed consent?*
- *Justify your answer to (1) as if you were Dutton and Aron.*
- *Why was a confederate used?*
- *What aspect of the BPS Ethical Guidelines would the use of the confederate have contravened?*
- *Did any participants ever receive electric shocks?*

- not use payment of participants to encourage them to take risks beyond that which they would experience in their normal lifestyle;
- take additional steps to obtain approval from other researchers and real consent from the participants if harm or unusual discomfort or other negative consequences for the individual might occur in the future;
- obtain consent on more than one occasion if required in longitudinal research.

For students this means providing prospective participants with a full brief of the experiment, a description of what will be expected of them during the experiment and its general purpose such that they can give their informed consent to participate.

Confidentiality

Although psychologists must maintain adequate records it is essential that the privacy of individuals and organisations, and confidentiality of any information acquired from them, is upheld. The identity of participants should not be revealed except with their express permission. Specifically psychologists should:

- communicate information without identifying individuals or organisations;

- convey personally identifiable information to others only with expressed permission except where this would either be contrary to the best interests of the individual, in contravention of the law or when information is shared within a team when this has been made clear to the participants;
- in exceptional circumstances when the safety or interests of the recipients are at risk, or when others may be at risk, inform appropriate third parties without prior consent, having first consulted an experienced and disinterested colleague unless the delay in so doing would result in a significant risk to life or health;
- maintain records, which can be personally identifiable only as long as necessary, rendering them anonymous once this is no longer essential;
- make audio, video or photographic recordings of clients or participants (except recordings of public behaviour) only with expressed agreement to the

interactive angles

- *Why are some participants, such as HM (Corkin, 1984), identified by only their initials?*
- *Explain two situations under which it would be appropriate to photograph participants.*
- *In an observation where independent raters watch video of recorded behaviour of participants, what obligations do those assistants have?*

recording and subsequent access to it;
- safeguard the security of records, including those on computer;
- take steps to ensure that other persons with whom they work also respect the need for confidentiality.

In practice, these require us to ensure that raw data from our research is kept securely, to use participant numbers rather than names and to ensure that other identifying characteristics, such as handwriting, are disguised.

Debriefing

Debriefing refers to the explanation participants receive after having participated in a study to ensure that they understand the research and their role in it. In addition, the debrief offers an opportunity to reassure them and, if necessary, to return them to the state they were in prior to participation. Psychologists should bear in mind the following.

- Following studies in which participants are aware that they have taken part, the investigator should debrief them by providing sufficient information to complete their understanding of the research. They should then discuss the participants' experience and monitor any unforeseen negative effects or misconceptions.

- Debriefing is not a justification for unethical procedures.

- Where the effects of an experiment cannot be negated by a verbal description of the research, investigators should employ active intervention before the participants leave the research setting.

interactive angles

Which aspects of the Ethical Principles would be contravened by the following procedures?

(a) A psychologist employing relaxation techniques allows participants to leave the experimental setting very sleepy to get into their cars to return home.

(b) A team of researchers studying workplace bullying describes the setting as a large manufacturing company in the south-west of England. It becomes apparent from extracts of dialogue that the company manufactures widgets. There is, however, only one widget-maker in the south-west.

(c) A psychologist using hypnosis debriefs the participants but does not tell them that they may later recall some disturbing aspects of the research.

(d) A psychology student working on stress is measuring the blood pressure of participants before and after they have attempted an insoluble logic problem as an indicator of anxiety. One participant has a very high blood pressure at the start of the experiment and the student suggests that they should cut down the amount of fat they eat and get more exercise.

How might each of the situations (a)–(d) have been adapted so that the procedures fell within the BPS guidelines?

- A student is conducting a replication of Piaget's conservation experiments at a primary school. Two children look into the room where he is working and run away. When asked to come back they say no and hide in the playhouse.

What should the student do?

- A researcher is investigating road rage by photographing drivers in a long queue of traffic to see how many of them are drumming their fingers on the steering wheel or biting their nails. She finds that in many of the photographs the drivers are engaging in behaviours we would not normally see, such as picking their nose.

Is her observational study ethical?

BPS Code of Conduct, Ethical Principles and Guidelines (1998)

Consent – ensure that you have provided sufficient information for your participants or clients to make an informed choice about their commitment:

- *deception* – do not mislead participants unless it is unavoidable, justifiable and accepted by appropriate authorities;

- *debriefing* – after completion of your study, participants must be fully informed of the purpose and expected outcomes;

- *right to withdraw* – participants must be reminded that they are free to leave a study at any time or to remove their results at the end, regardless of any payment they have received.

Confidentiality – ensure that you have disguised participants' identities and stored their data securely.

---

interactive angles

Recall Milgram's classic obedience experiment and that of Hofling et al (1966) that you studied at AS (see Angles on Psychology). *Consider the differences between the two in terms of the ethical issues they present.*

Withdrawal from the investigation

Guidelines relating to withdrawal suggest:

- participants should be made aware from the outset that they have the right to withdraw from the investigation at any time, irrespective of payment. Children may indicate their desire to withdraw by avoidance of the situation and this should be acknowledged;

- following participation or debriefing a participant may withdraw their consent retrospectively and require that their data be destroyed.

Using non-human animals in psychological research

The use of animals by psychologists is sometimes criticised. It is important, therefore, to understand the reasoning behind such research. Driscoll and Bateson (1988) suggested the following reasons for using animals in psychological investigations:

- **to understand natural principles** – because animals can provide a convenient model for a process (such as using pigeons or rats to study the general features of

---

Why might you use animals in each of the following investigations?

1 A study of overcrowding where groups are kept in closer confines than they would normally live for several months.

2 An investigation into the role of light on the early development of the retina which requires raising neonates in darkness.

3 An experiment which is investigating the way in which sexual arousal affects the release of hormones.

---

learning);

- **procedures cannot always be carried out ethically on humans** – such as developmental studies involving isolation;

- **animals may be especially good examples of particular phenomena** – such as communication in bird song or bee dances;

- **animals can be fascinating in their own right** – for example, bat sonar or whale song.

However, psychologists recognise that animals can experience pain and suffering and therefore should be protected. Protection is offered to animals by both guidelines and legislation.

Animals (Scientific Procedures) Act 1986

The Animals (Scientific Procedures) Act 1986 replaces

How are decisions about animal experiments made?

Bateson (1986) argued that when there is a conflict of interest between experimenters and their critics, this might be resolved by weighing up the degree of suffering for the animal subjects against the value of the research. This balance can be represented by the diagram below.

When a research proposal falls into the opaque region of the decision cube, the experiment should not be conducted, those falling in the clear space should proceed.

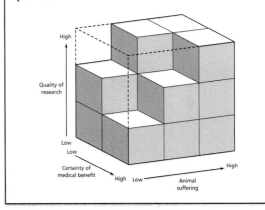

---

the Cruelty to Animals Act 1876 in the context of animal experimentation. The new legislation again depends on Home Office licences but these are issued to specific individuals for particular projects so that research on animals can be more closely monitored. A 'project licence' covers three aspects of research:

- **procedures**: the Home Secretary is required to weigh the likely adverse effects to the animals used (*animal suffering*) against the gains likely to accrue from the work (*certainty of medical benefit*);

- **animals**: their breeding and supply, daily and veterinary care;

- **premises**: which are checked by Her Majesty's Inspectorate (HMIs).

British Psychological Society Guidelines for the Use of Animals in Research (1985)

These guidelines were published to assist members of the BPS in the planning of experiments with live animals and to remind them of their general obligation to avoid, or at least to minimise, discomfort to living animals.

- **The law** – investigators must work within the laws protecting animals.

- **Ethical considerations** – if the animals are confined,

restrained, harmed or stressed in any way the investigator must consider whether the knowledge gained justifies the procedure. Options other than animal experiments should be considered.

- **Species** – animals differ in their experience of pain and discomfort and this should be considered in the choice of species.

- **Laboratory studies** – should use as few animals as possible, through the prudent choice of experimental design and statistical tests. Caging and social environment should be appropriate to the species to avoid overcrowding and response to social isolation. Experimental risks of aggression and predation should be minimised. The normal eating and drinking habits and metabolic requirements of the species and

individual should be considered when arranging schedules of deprivation.

- **Wild animals** – wild animals from endangered species should only be used in conservation attempts. In fieldwork animals should be disturbed as little as possible (as even observations may affect breeding and survival), and the stressful effects of trapping, marking and equipment should be considered.

- **Animal suppliers** – animals should only be obtained from reputable suppliers, provided with adequate food, water, ventilation and space during transit, and not unduly stressed.

- **Aversive stimulation and stressful procedures** – procedures causing pain or distress to animals are illegal in the UK unless the experimenter holds an

classic
research

ethics: monkeys' mums matter!

Harlow H.F. (1965) Love in infant monkeys. *Scientific American* **200: 68–74**

aim: to determine the role of food and comfort on attachment by rearing baby monkeys in isolation.

procedure: Rhesus monkeys (*Macaca mulatta*) were reared alone, without their mothers, in cages containing a pair of 'surrogate mothers'. One of these models provided nourishment; it was made of wire and supplied milk though a teat. The other model provided comfort; it was covered with soft terry towelling.

findings: The infant monkeys clung to the soft surrogates, ran to them if they were afraid and used them as a safe base from which to explore. If the soft surrogate was absent, the infants either froze or became highly active, apparently displaying intense fear. As adults these monkeys displayed social abnormalities; they were easily dominated, often failed to mate and were poor mothers.

Conclusion: the contact with the soft model seemed to be important in the formation of a strong bond between the infant monkey and the soft surrogate. No such bonding was demonstrated towards the wire surrogate. The formation of this bond seemed to be important to subsequent social interactions.

1 Identify the ethical issues raised by this study.

2 Why might rhesus monkeys have been chosen as the experimental species?

3 Subsequent studies have suggested that the behavioural abnormalities may have be due to the social isolation rather than absence of mothering since some of the effects could be reversed by social housing. Does this finding affect the justification for conducting this study, and if so how?

appropriate Home Office licence. Options other than aversive stimuli should be considered and where no alternative can be found the investigator must ensure that the suffering is minimised and is justified by the expected outcome.

- **Surgical and pharmacological procedures** – are illegal without an appropriate Home Office licence.

- **Anaesthesia, analgesia and euthanasia** – animals must receive adequate post-operative care to minimise suffering. If at any time an animal is suffering severe and enduring pain it must be killed in a suitable manner for the species.

- **Independent advice** – doubts about the condition of an animal should be raised with someone not directly involved in the experiment, preferably a veterinarian.

Association for the Study of Animal Behaviour Ethics in Research on Animal Behaviour (1991)

The Association for the Study of Animal Behaviour (ASAB) has played a pivotal role in the ethical treatment of animals in research. ASAB publishes guidelines for the use of animals, conducts research that justifies these recommendations and makes strategic use of the guidelines to ensure that work published in the society's journal *Animal Behaviour* is ethically sound.

The guidelines for the use of animals in research (1991) provide greater detail than the BPS guidelines, adding the following issues to those described above.

- **Choice of species** – the species chosen should be suited to answer the research question with consideration of the species' natural history and complexity, and each animal's previous experience, such as whether it has been raised in captivity.

- **Aversive stimuli and deprivation** – alternatives to deprivation could include the use of highly preferred foods and other rewards to motivate satiated animals.

- **Social deprivation, isolation and crowding** – the degree of stress experienced by a crowded or isolated animal will vary not only with species, but also with age, sex, reproductive condition, social status, biology and previous social experience.

- **Housing and animal care** – experimenters should be responsible for their animals' conditions of care. For wild animals maintenance should incorporate where possible the aspects of the natural living conditions deemed to be important such as natural materials, refuges, perches and dust and water baths. Frequency of cleaning should represent a compromise between cleanliness and the stress created by handling, and unfamiliar surroundings, odours and bedding.

- **Final disposition of animals** – where practical or feasible, researchers should distribute their animals to colleagues for further study unless this would result in their being exposed repeatedly to stressful or painful treatments. Field-trapped animals should be returned to the wild if this is feasible, legal and will not be detrimental to existing populations and when their ability to survive has not been impaired.

for and against

the use of animals in psychological research

+ the nervous system of non-human animals is similar to that of humans but is simpler, so they provide ideal models for testing hypotheses about behaviour

+ non-human animals can be used for procedures (such as isolation and surgery) that would be unethical on humans

– the similarities between non-human animals and humans may be insufficient to justify generalisation from one to the other

– procedures that are deemed to be unethical for humans may cause similar but undetectable suffering for animals

– animals cannot readily communicate their responses, they can only be observed. This may be less informative, biased by observers and excludes access to thoughts and emotions

hitch-hikers' humour

Researchers tested the effect of humour on hitch-hiking success. Hitch-hikers' success was measured when they held up signs with or without a smiley face drawn next to the destination. They compared males and females and found that, although the women were more successful at obtaining lifts overall, the smiley face reduced their chances of getting a lift but increased the rate for males.

Guegen N. (2001) Effect of humor on hitch-hiking: a field experiment. *North American Journal of Psychology* 3: 369-76 (an accessible summary can be found in **Martin N. (2002)** Hitch-hiking: a pointer. *The Psychologist* 15(4): 200)

1 Describe the research design for this study as fully as you can. [2]

2 (a) How might 'success' be measured objectively in this study? [2]

    (b) What is the level of measurement of the variable you have suggested in (a)? [1]

    (c) What measure would you use to find theaverage of the data collected to summarise the findings? [1]

3 Identify and explain three variables you would control in this study. [6]

4 Explain one ethical dilemma presented by this study and relate it to an appropriate ethical guideline. [4]

Total marks 16

get yer eyes off my pint

A group of researchers compared performance on a lexical decision tasks when their participants were either 'thirsty' (having been given three salty liquorice sweets each) or 'non-thirsty' (having been given ordinary liquorice sweets). The sweets had a letter marked on one side and each participant had one minute to decide, using their tongue, what they were. The first lexical decision task, conducted prior to eating the sweets, involved participants to decide as quickly as possible whether each of 10 'words' was real or not (five were real words, five were not). A second lexical decision task used 48 words; of these

24 were non-real and 24 were real (of these eight were related to drinking, the remainder were not). They found that thirsty participants were faster to respond to drink-related words than non-drink related ones and were faster to do so than non-thirsty participants.

Aarts H., Dijksterhuis A. & De Vries P. (2001) On the psychology of drinking: being thirsty and perceptually ready. *British Journal of Psychology* 92: 631-42 (an accessible summary can be found in Edmonds A.J. (2002) Are you looking at my pint? *The Psychologist* 15(3): 141)

1 What is the independent variable in this experiment? [1]

2 What is the dependent variable in this experiment? [1]

3 (a) Participants performed in either the 'thirsty' or the 'non-thirsty' condition. What is this design called? [1]

    (b) Outline **one** advantage and **one** disadvantage of this design [4]

4 Why did the researchers conduct the first lexical decision task? [1]

5 (a) Suggest three items for each of the three stimulus groups in the second lexical decision task. [3]

    (b) Justify your choice of non-words. [2]

Total marks 13

fast music costs lives

In an experiment studying performance on a driving simulator, students were compared while they listened to music. As they cruised the virtual streets of Chicago, the participants listened to nothing at all or to pieces of music that varied in tempo from 60 beats per minute to 140 beats per minute. Music increased the risk of the participants jumping traffic lights and, the faster the beat of the music, the greater the risk. Participants listening to the faster tempo music were also more likely to have accidents.

Brodsky W. (2001) The effect of music tempo on simulated driving performance and vehicular control. *Transportation Research* 4: 219–41 (an accessible summary can be found in **Hamer M. (2002)** Death by music. *New Scientist* 16 March 2002: 8)

1 (a) What research method was being used in this study? [1]

(b) Suggest **one** alternative method that could have been used. [1]

2 Outline **one** advantage and **one** disadvantage of the method you have suggested in 1(b). [4]

3 (a) What term would you use to describe the 'no music' condition? [1]

(b) What is the purpose of this condition in the study described? [1]

4 This study used different pieces of music for different tempo conditions. What is the disadvantage of this choice and how might it be avoided? [2]

5 (a) What is meant by the term ecological validity? [1]

(b) To what extent to you feel that this study has high ecological validity? [2]

6 (a) What ethical issues might arise in this study? [2]

(b) How might one of the ethical issues you have identified in 5(a) be tackled? [2]

Total marks 17

Frood A. (2002) Dope at the wheel. *New Scientist* 23 March 2002. Report of an unpublished report from the Transport Research Laboratory, led by B. Sexton.

1 (a) There were three groups of participants. Describe how each of the variables used to create these conditions was operationalised. [2]

(b) What participant design was being used in this experiment? [1]

2 Describe **two** participant variables that should be controlled in this study, indicating why it is important to control each of them. [4]

3 (a) What is reliability? [1]

(b) How could the reliability of the driving simulator as a test of intoxication be tested? [3]

4 (a) What is meant by the term *objectivity*? [1]

(b) Police surgeons were used to assess intoxication. Describe **one** advantage and **one** disadvantage of interviewing compared to measures such as the driving simulator. [4]

5 (a) The participants in this study were a volunteer sample. Why was this necessary? [2]

(b) Describe **one** disadvantage of this sampling method. [2]

Total marks 20

dope driving limit

There is currently no test to accurately measure the level of cannabis derivatives in the blood of drivers. However, for such a test to be useful we need to know about the impairments caused to users. To test this, researchers compared volunteers who were either given sufficient alcohol to raise their blood alcohol level to about 50 mg/100 ml (just below the drink-driving limit of 80 mg/100 ml), smoked a standard marijuana joint or received both. The participants were then given a range of psychomotor tests and were assessed on a driving simulator. The participants who had smoked cannabis had significantly impaired tracking ability, that is they found it difficult to hold a constant speed and accurately follow the road while driving around a figure-of-eight loop. Participants who had drunk the equivalent of a glass of wine were more impaired at this task and those who had been given both alcohol and cannabis even more so. However, those participants who had received cannabis, even in combination with alcohol, were more aware of their intoxication and drove more cautiously.

mood and muesli

In a study using female participants who were habitual breakfast eaters and exercisers, assessments were made of mood and motivation throughout the day. In the morning, the participants were either asked to exercise for 40 minutes or were asked not to exercise. Some participants were given a low-energy breakfast (orange juice and tea or coffee) and others a high-energy breakfast (orange juice and tea or coffee plus cereals and toast). At midday all participants received lunch. The low-energy breakfast-eaters who did not exercise reported being less content and more irritable than either those who exercised or who ate a high-energy breakfast. Eating lunch improved the mood of the low-energy breakfast-eaters. Participants who exercised felt less lethargic regardless of the breakfast they had eaten and participants who had eaten a low-energy breakfast had a greater desire to eat regardless of whether exercise was taken.

Lluch A., Hubert P., King N.A. & Blundell J.E. (2000) Selective effects of acute exercise and breakfast interventions on mood and motivation to eat. Physiology and Behaviour 68: 515–20 (an accessible summary can be found in **Martin N. (2000) Exercise – what is it good for?** *The Psychologist* 13(7): 362–3)

1 This study compares the responses of four groups of participants. List them. [1]

2 State **two** of the factors being measured as dependent variables. [1]

3 (a) Suggest how the researchers may have obtained their sample. [1]

(b) Define the term *generalisation*. [1]

(c) Identify and explain **one** reason it may not be possible to generalise from the results of this experiment. [3]

(d) Describe how you could improve the generalisability of the results by using a different sampling technique. [3]

4 (a) With respect to **either** breakfast type **or** exercise, identify the participant design. [AO3=1]

(b) With reference to the design that you identified in part (a) explain **two** advantages and **two** disadvantages of this design. [AO2=8]

Total marks 18

30 Inferential statistics

This chapter deals with parametric and non-parametric inferential statistical tests. Non-parametric statistical tests are predominantly used on data that are nominal or ordinal. Unlike parametric statistical tests they do not make assumptions about the data but can be used to examine differences, associations (links between the independent variable and dependent variable) and correlations. The non-parametric tests that you need to know about are: the sign test, the chi-squared test, the Wilcoxon test, the Mann–Whitney U test and the Spearman's rank order correlation coefficient.

In contrast, parametric statistical tests do make assumptions about the data. As a consequence of this, they enable more informative judgements to be made about patterns in the data. There are three parametric tests that you need to know about: the unrelated (or independent) t-test, the related t-test and Pearson's product moment correlation coefficient.

Introduction to inferential statistics

Inferential statistics allows us to draw firmer conclusions about a data set than descriptive statistics. They are mathematical tests that attempt to show whether there is a significant difference, association or correlation. Descriptive statistics (see page 414) compare the levels of the independent variable with a single numerical value. Analysis using inferential statistics in experiments test whether two data sets are significantly different, allowing the researcher to conclude whether the independent variable is having an effect on the dependent variable. Essentially, inferential statistics measure cause and effect against probabilities. If the IV is causing a change in the DV, then the alternative hypothesis is accepted. If the changes are attributable to chance alone the null hypothesis is accepted.

Before the tests are described we will introduce concepts that are common to all tests: the concept of p-values; levels of significance; type I and II errors; observed (calculated) values; and critical values.

P-value (probability value)

A p-value represents the probability of something happening by chance. P-values range from 0 to 1, with 0 representing no influence of chance and 1 representing a complete influence of chance. P-values are written as a proportion, that is, $p < 0.05$ represents a less than 5 in 100 probability that the results could have arisen by chance. This allows you to have confidence that the results are more likely to be due to the manipulation of the independent variable, or that the two measures are truly correlated.

Levels of significance

The level of significance refers to the p-value we set that makes us believe the results are due to the independent variable, or the relationship between two variables in a correlation, and not due to chance. How do we decide what value to use for p? We cannot expect to be 100 per cent sure because extraneous variables can affect our results, so the standard usually set for a level of significance is 5 per cent, or $p \leq 0.05$. At this level we are saying that there is less than a 5 per cent probability that this pattern of results would occur by chance or be due to other factors such as uncontrolled variables. The less likely it is that a particular difference has arisen by chance, the more confident we can be about the observed difference, association or correlation. It is possible to be more stringent with the level of significance. We could set a p-value of $p \leq 0.01$ so there is only a 1 per cent probability that the pattern of results could be due to chance. Alternatively, we can be less stringent and set a p-value of $p \leq 0.1$ so there is a 10 per cent probability that the pattern of results could occur by chance. However, if we are more stringent or less stringent with the levels of significance, we risk making either a type I or type II error.

Type I and type II errors

With less stringent levels of significance (eg $p \leqslant 0.1$ or $p \leqslant 0.2$), it is less difficult to find a significant difference, association or correlation. That is, it is easier to reject the null hypothesis (which states that the results are due to chance), but, because we are being less stringent, this rejection may be incorrect. The null hypothesis may well be correct, in which case we have made a *type I error*. For example, at a significance level of $p \leqslant 0.1$, there is still a 10 per cent probability that the particular pattern of results could occur by chance, and the results may have fallen into that 10 per cent. We could avoid type I errors by setting a more stringent level of significance, say, $p \leqslant 0.001$. However, as a result of doing this we risk making a *type II error* and accepting the null hypothesis when it should be rejected. For example, if we set a level of significance of $p \leqslant 0.01$, there is a 1 per cent probability of the pattern of results occurring by chance. We may well have a significant difference, association or correlation, but because we are being too stringent, the test may not find the difference and we incorrectly accept the null hypothesis.

Therefore, to balance the chance of committing either a type I or a type II error it is advised that the level of significance is set at $p \leqslant 0.05$.

Higher significance levels are used for replications when we want to be more confident that the result is not due to chance.

Observed values and critical values

Each of the inferential statistical tests essentially reduces the data set to one number called a calculated or *observed value*. This value is compared to a critical value, to conclude whether there is a significant difference, association or correlation. For some tests the observed value has to be greater than the critical value to show a significant result. For other tests the observed value has to be less than the critical value to indicate a significant result.

The *critical value* (that is compared to the observed value) is read from a critical value table. There is one of these for each test (see Appendix). The value is found by looking at the number of participants (N – or the degrees of freedom for the χ^2 test and parametric tests) and whether the alternative hypothesis is directional or non-directional.

The ranking of data

Two of the tests, the Mann–Whitney U test and Spearman's rank order correlation coefficient, rank the data collected. That is, each data point is assigned a rank value from 1 to N where N is the total number of data points used in the analysis. Data are ranked as follows:

1 Using all of the data, write down the scores in numerical order from the smallest to the largest value(s). For example:

12 13 15 15 17 18 18 18 20 21 21 26

2 Starting with the smallest value, assign ranks (beginning with 1) to the data points as follows. This tells you if you have written down all of the data points:

12	13	15	15	17	18	18	18	20	21	21	26
1	2	3	4	5	6	7	8	9	10	11	12

3 Some data points are represented more than once (eg 15 is represented twice, 18 three times and 21 twice) and they cannot have different rank values. This is rectified by calculating the mean of the rank values that the data points cover. You then assign that rank value to all the data points that are numerically the same.

For example, the two 15 data points cover the rank positions of **3** and **4**. The mean of these rank values is **3.5** so that is the new rank value given to both of the 15 data points. The same process is applied to points 18 and 21.

4 The correct rank values are as follows:

12	13	15	15	17	18	18	18	20	21	21	26
1	2	3.5	3.5	5	7	7	7	9	10.5	10.5	12

Although the tests can readily be worked out 'by hand' most people use computer programs to calculate the observed value. In this case the computer user is required to be able to select the appropriate test, provide the data in a suitable form and interpret the observed value that is generated. The following discussions of the tests will enable you to complete these processes. If you want to know more about how the tests work, or how to calculate the observed values yourself, details and worked examples can be found in *Angles on Psychological Research*, Russell and Roberts (2001).

The non-parametric statistical tests

The χ^2 test of association

The criteria for using this test are:

● dependent variable has *nominal* level of measurement;

● design of the research is *independent groups*;

● looking for an *association* between the independent variable and the dependent variable.

The basis for the χ^2 test of association involves comparing the data actually collected with a data set based on the null hypothesis. Therefore, any deviation from this will reveal a potential significant association. That is, the test will discover if there is a significant deviation from chance.

Using the χ^2 test of association

A *contingency table* is created showing the distribution of scores across the levels of the independent variable. These are compared mathematically to the *expected frequencies* based on the null hypothesis for each cell in the contingency table using the following equation:

$$\chi^2 = \Sigma \frac{(O - E)^2}{E}$$

This produces an observed value for the test, called χ^2. It is compared to a critical value, which is found using the following information:

- degrees of freedom;
- whether the alternative hypothesis is directional or non-directional;
- level of significance (*p*-value).

If the observed value is greater than the critical value, then the association is significant so the null hypothesis is rejected and the experimental hypothesis accepted. If the observed value is less than the critical value, then the association is not significant, so the experimental hypothesis is rejected and the null hypothesis accepted.

Using Yate's correction: if the degrees of freedom for the test equal 1, then the test calculation requires a correction factor (Yate's correction) and a slightly different formula is used:

$$\chi^2 = \Sigma \frac{(|O - E| - \frac{1}{2})^2}{E}$$

The | symbol indicates the modulus, that is, it is calculated ignoring the sign.

Now have a look at an example in 'research now'

research now

χ^2: children and UFOs – what on Earth are they drawing?

Roberts C.A., Russell J. & Chandler E. (in press) What do children produce when asked to draw how an alien would travel to Earth? Submitted to the *European Journal of UFO and Abduction Studies*

aim: children were asked to draw how they thought an alien would travel to Earth. Each drawing was classified to look for gender differences.

procedure: data collected: to assess whether boys or girls drew more aggressive pictures, each of the 321 pictures were rated as *friendly* (aliens smiling, greeting humans), *neutral* (a spacecraft, or alien not showing emotion), *moderate aggression* (some sign of armour, guns, but nothing being used against humans) or *severe aggression* (including death of humans, guns firing, attacking humans). A total of 164 boys and 157 girls drew a picture for analysis.

hypotheses: experimental – there is a significant association between sex and the aggressiveness level of UFO pictures drawn. Null – any association between sex and the aggressiveness level of UFO pictures drawn is due to chance.

findings: the data collected were *nominal* (pictures in one of the four categories above), the research design was *independent groups* (male or female), and the research team were looking for an *association* between gender and level of aggression in the pictures. The following contingency table was produced from the data collected:

Category	Male	Female	Total
Friendly	10	29	39
Neutral	98	120	218
Moderate	42	6	48
Severe	14	2	16
Total	164	157	321

A severely aggressive spaceship picture drawn in the research of Roberts, Russell and Chandler

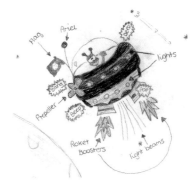

A friendly spaceship picture drawn in the research of Roberts, Russell and Chandler

In this case $\chi^2 = 47.29$.

The critical value is found from the appropriate table (Appendix, page 473) using the following information:

degrees of freedom $[(4 - 1) \, 2 \, (2 - 1) = (3) \, 2 \, (1)] =$ **3**

experimental hypothesis is **non-directional**

level of significance (p-value) $\leq$ **0.05**

The critical value for the criteria above is **7.815** and the observed value is **47.29**. As the observed value is *greater than* the critical value the *null hypothesis is rejected* and the experimental hypothesis accepted.

conclusion: there is a significant association between sex and the aggressiveness level of UFO pictures drawn.

If the data collected consist of only one row of data, for example, comparing the number of aggressive acts in four different TV programmes, a χ^2 goodness of fit test is performed. In this case the degrees of freedom are calculated by subtracting 1 from the number of categories present. So, in the TV example, the degrees of freedom would be $4 - 1 = 3$. The critical values are read from the table as for the χ^2 test of association.

The binomial sign test

The criteria for using this test are:

● dependent variable has *nominal* level of measurement;

● design of the research is *repeated measures*;

● looking for a *difference* between the effect each level of the independent variable has on the dependent variable.

The sign test examines the number of differences that occur in one direction compared with the other direction.

Therefore, if students were asked to rate two teaching methods using the descriptors Excellent (rated 1), Very Good (rated 2), Good (rated 3), Average (rated 4) or Poor (rated 5), the test would examine whether one of the teaching methods had 'better' ratings than the other. If both teaching methods were rated about the same, then the test would pick out no significant difference. However, if in a sample of 20 students, the first teaching method was rated better on 17 occasions, then it is very unlikely that we would retain the null hypothesis. Instead of examining the magnitude (size) of difference between the two teaching methods, the sign test merely looks at how many times one particular method is rated as better than the other.

Using the binomial sign test

A table of data is created with a column for scores in each level of the IV. Each participant then provides a score for each column (if a participant's score is the same for each level of the IV, they are excluded from the analysis). The columns are compared to see which scores are bigger for each participant. This produces an observed value for the test, called **s**. It is compared to a critical value, which is found using the following information:

- number of pairs of scores, N (excluding any where the participant gained the same score in both conditions, so the value of N may be less than the number of participants in the study);
- whether the experimental hypothesis is directional or non-directional;

- level of significance (p-value).

If the observed value is greater than the critical value, the test result is not significant so the null hypothesis is accepted and the experimental hypothesis rejected. If the observed value is less than the critical value, then the test result is significant so the experimental hypothesis is accepted and the null hypothesis rejected.

Now have a look at an example (Roberts, 2000):

research
now

binomial sign test: bias in investigating UFOs

Roberts C.A. (2000) UK UFO organisations: what do they have knowledge of and what do they investigate? *European Journal of UFO and Abduction Studies* 1(1): 26–32

aim: to investigate which theory is preferred as an explanation for UFO activity in the UK by UFO groups.

procedure: data collected: UFO groups were asked to rate their knowledge about different theories on the scale: *excellent knowledge* (1), *good knowledge* (2), *some knowledge* (3), *poor knowledge* (4), *heard of it but no knowledge* (5), *never heard of it* (6). Twelve groups responded.

hypotheses: experimental – there is a difference between the ratings of knowledge given to Extraterrestrial Approach and Earthlights Approach by UFO organisations. Null – any difference between the ratings of knowledge given to Extraterrestrial Approach and Earthlights Approach by UFO organisations is due to chance.

findings: the data collected were *nominal* (each UFO group rated the theory using the categories above – it should be noted that the data could also be seen as ordinal as the categories are in rank order), the research design was *repeated measures* (the independent variable was Spacecraft or Earthlights [geological phenomenon] and each group rated both levels of the independent variable). The following data were collected:

Group number	Extraterrestrial rating	Earthlights rating
1	3	2
2	1	3
3	1	2
4	1	2
5	6	6
6	1	1
7	1	3
8	1	2
9	1	3
10	1	1
11	1	2
12	3	2

The observed value of *s* is 2.

The critical value is found from the appropriate table (Appendix, page 474) using the following information:

- **number of pairs of scores** in the analysis = **9** (3 'ties' are omitted);
- experimental hypothesis is **non-directional**;
- the **level of significance** (*p*-value) ≤ **0.05**.

The critical value for the criteria above is **1** and the observed value is **2**. As the observed value is *greater* than the critical value, *the null hypothesis is accepted* and the experimental hypothesis rejected.

conclusion: any difference between the ratings of knowledge given to Extraterrestrial Approach and Earthlights Approach by UFO organisations is due to chance.

The Mann–Whitney U-test

The criteria for using this test are:

- dependent variable has *ordinal* level of measurement;
- design of the research is *independent groups*;
- looking for a *difference* between the effect each level of the independent variable has on the dependent variable.

The basis for the Mann–Whitney U-test involves ranking the entire data set (irrespective of the level of independent variable), then examining how the ranks lie per level of the independent variable. To retain the null hypothesis, which would state that a difference would be due to chance, we would expect the ranks to be randomly distributed across the two levels of independent variable. However, one level may contain more of the lower ranks for instance, and the Mann–Whitney test will examine whether the distribution of ranks is random or not. The formula for this calculation is:

$$U = N_A N_B + \frac{N_A(N_A + 1)}{2} - R_1$$

This produces two values, the smaller of which is the observed value of **U**. It is compared to a critical value, which is found using the following information:

- values for N_A and N_B (the number of scores in each of the two levels of the IV);
- whether the experimental hypothesis is directional or non-directional;
- level of significance (*p*-value).

If the observed value is greater than the critical value then the test result is not significant so the null hypothesis is accepted and the experimental hypothesis rejected. If the observed value is less than the critical value then the test result is significant so the experimental hypothesis is accepted and the null hypothesis rejected.

Now have a look at an example (Roberts et al, 1996):

research
now

Mann–Whitney U-test: loneliness, older adults and the pet owner

Roberts C.A., McBride E.A., Rosenvinge H.P., Stevenage S.V. & Bradshaw J.W.S. (1996) The pleasure of a pet: the effect of pet ownership and social support on loneliness and depression in a population of elderly people living in their own homes. *Proceedings for the Society for Companion Animal Studies Workshop September 1996,* **University of Cambridge. Nicholson J. & Podberscek A. (eds). Callender, SCAS, page 64**

aim: to examine whether older adults with pets or without pets differ in their feelings of loneliness.

procedure: data collected: participants completed the Loneliness Scale, a questionnaire of 11 items. The higher the score, the more lonely the person feels. Thirty pet owners and 30 non-pet owners completed the scale.

hypotheses: experimental – there is a difference between subjective feelings of loneliness of pet owners and non-owners. Null – any difference between the subjective feelings of loneliness of pet owners and non-owners is due to chance.

findings: the data collected were *ordinal* (the data could be ranked from most lonely to least lonely, but for instance, a participant scoring 8 points is not twice as lonely as a participant scoring 4 points), the research design was *independent groups* (pet owner or non-pet owner) and the research team were looking for a difference between the levels of loneliness reported by pet owners and non-pet owners. The following results are a portion of those collected (10 pet owners and 10 non-pet owners):

Scores for pet owners (A)	Scores for non-pet owners (B)
0	0
0	1
0	1
0	2
1	3
2	5
2	7
3	9
4	9
5	10

The observed value of U = 26.

The critical value is found from the appropriate table (see Appendix page 475–6) using the following information:

- number of scores in each group, $N_A = 10$ and $N_B = 10$;
- the experimental hypothesis is **non-directional**;
- **level of significance** (p-value) $\leqslant 0.05$.

The critical value for the criteria above is **23** and the observed value is **26**. As the observed value is *greater* than the critical value, *the null hypothesis is accepted* and the experimental hypothesis rejected.

conclusion: any difference between pet owners and non-owners on their subjective feelings of loneliness is due to chance.

The Wilcoxon signed ranks matched pairs test

The criteria for using this test are:

- dependent variable has *ordinal* level of measurement;
- design of the research is *repeated measures* or *matched pairs*;
- looking for a *difference* between the effect each level of the independent variable has on the dependent variable.

The Wilcoxon signed rank test examines the magnitude (size) of differences between two scores generated by the same participant. The test looks at how much differ-ence there is between the scores by ranking the differences and judging whether one condition consistently generates bigger (or smaller) scores for most partici-pants. If a participant has the same score on both levels of the IV, their results are omitted from the analysis. As with the sign test, if this difference is predominantly in one direction (eg participants generally score higher in condition A than condition B), the Wilcoxon test will detect a significant difference between the two condi-tions.

The number of ranks relating to the least direction of dif-ference generates an observed value for the test, called **T**. It is compared to a critical value, which is found using the following information:

- number of pairs of scores (remember to ignore those scores where the difference, *d*, was 0);
- whether the experimental hypothesis is directional or non-directional;
- level of significance (*p*-value).

If the observed value is greater than the critical value then the test result is not significant so the null hypothesis is accepted and the experimental hypothesis rejected. If the observed value is less than the critical value then the test result is significant so the experimental hypothesis is accepted and the null hypothesis rejected.

Now have a look at an example (Kirk & de Wit, 2000):

research
now

Wilcoxon test: does alcohol consumption make you want more and more?

Kirk J.M. & de Wit H. (2000) Individual differences in the priming effect of ethanol in social drinkers. *Journal for the Study of Alcohol* **61(1): 64–71**

aim: it is known that alcohol-dependent people report an increased desire for alcohol after a single drink. Is this trend replicated in non-problem social drinkers (those not classified as alcoholic)?

procedure: data collected: participants were asked to rate how much they wanted more alcohol after two drinks: one contained 0.2 g of alcohol per kilogram weight of the participant (low-alcohol drink), the other contained 0.8 g of alcohol per kilogram weight of the participant (high-alcohol drink).

hypotheses: experimental – there is a difference between how much people will want another drink after consuming a low-alcohol compared with a high-alcohol drink. Null – any difference between the amount people will want another drink after consuming a low-alcohol compared to a high-alcohol drink is due to chance.

findings: the data collected were *ordinal* (participants had to rate themselves out of 20 as to how much they desired another drink – the higher the score, the more the desire), the design was *repeated measures* (participants took part on both conditions: the low-alcohol and high-alcohol conditions) and the researchers were looking for a difference in the desire for more alcohol after drinking low-alcohol and high-alcohol drinks.

The following table presents fictitious results for this piece of research:

The observed value of T = 9.

Participant no. (A)	Low-alcohol desire score (B)	High-alcohol desire score
1	3	15
2	12	11
3	2	8
4	7	7
5	3	18
6	12	20
7	14	10
8	0	4
9	5	15
10	2	7
11	12	8
12	3	6

The critical value is found from the appropriate table (see Appendix page 477) using the following information:

● **number of pairs of scores** = **11** (1 omitted);

● experimental hypothesis is **non-directional**;

● **level of significance** (*p*-value) ≤ **0.05**.

The critical value for the criteria above is **11** and the observed value is **9**. As the observed value is *less than* the critical value, the *null hypothesis is rejected* and the experimental hypothesis accepted.

conclusion: there is a difference in how much people will want another drink after consuming a low-alcohol compared with a high-alcohol drink.

Figure 30.1 Do you feel like more after you have consumed one alcoholic drink?

Spearman's rank order correlation coefficient

The criteria using this test are:

● measured variables have *ordinal* level of measurement;

● design of the research is a *correlation*;

● looking for a relationship between the two measured variables.

The Spearman rank order correlation coefficient initially rank orders each variable separately. These ranks are compared to see whether there are any distinct similarities or differences. If the rank orders for each variable are very similar then a positive correlation is expected. If the rank orders appear to be randomly distributed and there are large differences in rank per participant's scores, then no correlation is expected. Finally, if the rank orders appear to be a mirror image of one another, then a negative correlation is expected. This expectation can be backed up by plotting a scattergraph (see page 416). It is important to be aware that the Spearman's rank order correlation coefficient does not look for the strength of a linear relationship but looks for patterns in data.

The formula for the Spearman's rank order correlation coefficient is:

$$r_s = 1 - \frac{6 \sum d^2}{N(N^2 - 1)}$$

This produces an observed value for the test, which is given the term rho or r_s. It is compared to a critical value, which is found using the following information:

● number of participants (N);

● whether the experimental hypothesis is directional or non-directional;

● level of significance (*p*-value).

If the observed value is greater than the critical value then the test result is significant so the null hypothesis is rejected and the experimental hypothesis accepted. If the observed value is less than the critical value then the test result is not significant so the experimental hypothesis is rejected and the null hypothesis accepted.

Now have a look at an example (Roberts et al, 1996):

research
now

Spearman's rank order correlation coefficient: a link between amount of social support and depression?

Roberts C.A., McBride E.A., Rosenvinge H.P., Stevenage S.V. & Bradshaw J.W.S. (1996) The pleasure of a pet: the effect of pet ownership and social support on loneliness and depression in a population of elderly people living in their own homes. *Proceedings for the Society for Companion Animal Studies Workshop September 1996,* **University of Cambridge. Nicholson J. & Podberscek A. (eds). Callender, SCAS, page 64**

---

aim: to look for a correlation between the level of social support in older adults and levels of depression.

procedure: data collected: participants completed a social support scale and the geriatric depression scale. The social support scale measured the size of the participant's social network (a high score indicated a good network). On the depression scale, a high score indicated greater depressive symptoms. We would expect that a person with a low score on the social support score will have a high score for depression scale, that is, a negative correlation is expected as a poor network (low score) should be correlated with more depression (high score).

hypotheses: alternative – there is a negative correlation between the amount of social support a person has and how depressed they feel. Null – any correlation between the amount of social support a person has and how depressed they feel is due to chance.

findings: the data collected were *ordinal* (the data could be ranked for each measure) and the research team was looking for a *correlation*. The following data are a portion of what was collected (12 pet owners and 12 non-pet owners):

Participant no.	First measure	Second measure
1	45	0.00
2	15	0.03
3	24	0.10
4	6	0.40
5	41	0.23
6	24	0.15
7	17	0.27
8	15	0.03
9	17	0.30
10	12	0.30
11	11	0.23
12	9	0.74

The observed value of $r_s = -0.60$.

The critical value is found from the appropriate table (see Appendix page 478) using the following information:

- **number of participants (N)** = 12;

- experimental hypothesis is **directional**;

- **level of significance** (*p*-value) ⩽ **0.05**.

The critical value for the criteria above is **0.5035** and the observed value is **–0.60**. As the observed value is *greater* than the critical value, the *null hypothesis is rejected* and the experimental hypothesis accepted.

conclusion: there is a negative correlation between the amount of social support a person has and how depressed they feel.

The parametric statistical tests

Parametric tests differ from non-parametric tests because the data:

- for both levels of the independent variable must have *equal variance* (the variance is the standard deviation squared – see *Angles on Psychological Research* for an explanation of this measure of spread), or both measured variables must have equal variance;

- are either *interval* or *ratio*;

- are assumed to be *normally distributed* for the population(s) used in the research from which the sample is drawn.

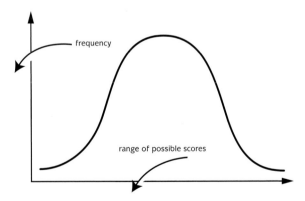

Figure 30.2 A normal distribution curve

The unrelated or independent t-test

The criteria for using this test are:

- dependent variable has *interval* or *ratio* level of measurement;

- design of the research is *independent groups*;

- looking for a *difference* between the effect each level of the independent variable has on the dependent variable;

- data are from *normally distributed* populations;

- populations for each level of the independent variable have *equal variances*.

Essentially, the unrelated t-test examines the mean and variance of each level of the independent variable to see if there is a large enough difference between them to reach significance. Scores for the two groups of participants are used in the following formula:

$$t = \frac{(\bar{x}_A - x_B)}{\sqrt{\dfrac{S_A^2 + S_B^2}{N}}}$$

(x = mean, Σ = sum of, N_A = number of participants in group A, N_B = number of participants in group B,

$$S_A^2 =$$

$$\frac{\Sigma A - \bar{x}_A}{N_A} \ , \ S_B^2 = \frac{\Sigma B - \bar{x}_A)}{N_B}$$

$$\bar{x}_A = \frac{\Sigma A}{N_A} \ , \ \bar{x}_B = \frac{\Sigma B}{N_B}$$

This generates the observed value for the test, called **t**. It is compared to a critical value, which is found using the following information:

- degrees of freedom ($N_A + N_B - 2$);

- whether the experimental hypothesis is directional or non-directional;

- level of significance (*p*-value).

If the observed value is greater than or equal to the critical value, then the test result is significant so the null hypothesis is rejected and the experimental hypothesis accepted. If the observed value is less than the critical value, the test result is not significant so the experimental hypothesis is rejected and the null hypothesis accepted.

Now have a look at an example (Grubb et al, 2000):

research
now

independent t-test: does a cardiac arrest reduce memory?

Grubb N.R., Fox K.A., Smith K., Blane A., Ebmeier K.P., Glabus M.F. & O'Carroll R.E. (2000) Memory impairment in out-of-hospital cardiac arrest survivors is associated with global reduction in brain volume, not focal hippocampal injury. *Stroke* **31(7): 1509–14**

aim: to examine whether people who have experienced a cardiac arrest have memory impairment. A region of the brain called the hippocampus (which is linked to memory) could be affected during a cardiac arrest.

procedure: data collected: 12 people who had experienced a cardiac arrest and 12 control participants with no heart condition had their amygdala-hippocampal volume in the brain measured.

hypotheses: experimental – there is a difference between amygdala-hippocampal volume in cardiac arrest victims compared to those with no heart condition. Null – any difference between the amygdala-hippocampal volume in cardiac arrest victims compared to those with no heart condition is due to chance.

findings: the data collected were *ratio* (measures of the amygdala-hippocampal volume in centimetres cubed), the participant design was *independent groups* (cardiac arrest victim or not). The following table of results shows the amygdala-hippocampal volume (in cm³) for 10 participants in each group:

Cardiac arrest group (A)	No heart problem group (B)
3.65	4.65
4.02	4.78
3.93	3.88
3.99	4.52
4.25	4.66
4.99	4.78
4.25	4.21
4.32	4.02
3.95	4.66
4.00	4.82

N, the number of participants in each group, is:

$$N_A = 10$$
$$N_B = 10$$

Part of the test requires the calculation of the mean for each group, these are:

Mean for condition A = 4.14 cm²
Mean for condition B = 4.50 cm²
The observed value of t = 2.94

The critical value is found from the appropriate table (see Appendix page 479) using the following information:

- **degrees of freedom** (using the equation $N_A + N_B - 2$) = **18**;
- alternative hypothesis is **non-directional**;
- **level of significance** (*p*-value) ≤ **0.05**.

The critical value for the criteria above is **2.101** and the observed value is **−2.94** (the minus sign indicates that condition B, the no heart problem group, scored higher on the amygdala-hippocampal volume). As the observed value is *greater* than the critical value, the *null hypothesis is rejected* and the experimental hypothesis accepted.

conclusion: there is a significant difference in amygdala-hippocampal volume in cardiac arrest victims compared to those with no heart condition.

The related t-test

The criteria for using this test are:

- dependent variable has *interval* or *ratio* level of measurement;
- design of the research is *repeated measures*;
- looking for a *difference* between the effect each level of the independent variable has on the dependent variable;
- data are from *normally distributed* populations;
- populations for each level of the independent variable have *equal variances*.

The related t-test involves assessing the magnitude of differences between the two sets of scores (remember that the sign test and Wilcoxon test do not look at the amount of difference between the scores, only the direction of difference). The related t-test examines the mean difference in scores and the deviation all scores have from this.

The related t-test uses the following formula:

$$t = \frac{\bar{d}}{sd/\sqrt{N-1}}$$

(d = the differences between scores in groups A and B (A-B), sd = standard deviation of the differences (d), Σd^2 = sum the differences squared, $\bar{d}$ = mean of the differences)

This generates an observed value for the test, called **t**. It is compared to a critical value, which is found using the following information:

- degrees of freedom (using the equation N − 1);
- whether the experimental hypothesis is directional or non-directional;
- level of significance (*p*-value).

If the observed value is greater than or equal to the critical value, then the result is significant so the null hypothesis is rejected and the experimental hypothesis is accepted. If the observed value is less than the critical value, the result is not significant so the experimental hypothesis is rejected and the null hypothesis accepted.

Now have a look at an example (Magai et al, 2000):

research
now

related t-test: depression in Alzheimer sufferers – does a drug alleviate the depression?

Magai C., Kennedy G., Cohen C.I. & Gomberg D. (2000) A controlled clinical trial of sertraline in the treatment of depression in nursing home patients with late-stage Alzheimer's disease. *American Journal of Geriatric Psychiatry* 8(1): 66–74

aim: to assess whether an antidepressant drug (sertraline) alleviated depression in late-stage Alzheimer's disease sufferers.

procedure: data collected: facial expressions of happiness (eg smiling, laughing, grinning) were scored for each patient. Twelve patients took part in the drug trial and were rated after taking the drug and when a placebo was taken.

hypotheses: experimental – there is a difference between facial expressions of happiness in Alzheimer's sufferers following sertraline compared to placebo treatment. Null – any difference in the facial expressions of happiness in Alzheimer's sufferers following sertraline compared to placebo treatment is due to chance.

findings: the data collected were *interval* (the number of facial expressions recorded) and the research design was *repeated measures* (each patient was rated after taking the drug and the placebo). The following table of results shows the facial expressions of happiness recorded for drug and no-drug observations.

Participant no.	Drug condition (A)	Placebo condition (B)
1	8	6
2	4	2
3	5	5
4	3	5
5	7	2
6	8	6
7	3	5
8	4	8
9	5	3
10	6	7
11	2	1
12	0	3

The observed value of $t = 0.24$

The critical value is found from the appropriate table (see Appendix page 479) using the following information:

- **degrees of freedom** $(N - 1) = \textbf{11}$;

- the experimental hypothesis is **non-directional**;

- **level of significance** (p-value) $\leq \textbf{0.05}$.

The critical value for the criteria above is **2.201**. The observed value is **0.24**. As the observed value is *less than* the critical value, the *experimental hypothesis is rejected* and the null hypothesis accepted.

conclusion: any difference in the facial expressions of happiness in Alzheimer's sufferers following sertraline compared to placebo treatment is due to chance.

Pearson's product moment correlation coefficient

The criteria for using this test are:

- dependent variable has *interval* or *ratio* level of measurement;

- design of the research is *correlational*;

- looking for a *linear relationship* between each of the variables that have been measured;

- data are from *normally distributed* populations;

- populations for each measured variable have *equal variances*.

In the Pearson's product moment correlation coefficient the scores generated are compared to an imaginary line through the centre of the scores (a line of best fit). Therefore, the test measures the amount of spread around the line and reports the deviation. If no deviation occurs, then we are left with an *r* value of 1, a perfect positive correlation (*r* values are interpreted in the same way as the Spearman's rho value – see page 396). A small deviation results in an *r* value close to 1, such as of +0.8 or –0.8 while a large deviation produces a small r value (close to 0), such as +0.2 or –0.2. As with the Spearman test, the higher the value, the stronger the correlation. The Pearson's test examines whether there is a *linear relationship* between the two measured variables.

The formula for the Pearson's product moment correlation coefficient is:

$$r = \frac{\Sigma XY - \dfrac{(\Sigma X)(\Sigma Y)}{N}}{\sqrt{\left(\Sigma X^2 - \dfrac{(\Sigma X)^2}{N}\right)\left(\Sigma Y^2 - \dfrac{(\Sigma Y)^2}{N}\right)}}$$

This produces an observed value, given the term **r**. It is compared to a critical value, which is found using the following information:

- df, the number of participants minus 2 (N – 2);
- whether the experimental hypothesis is directional or non-directional;
- level of significance (*p*-value).

If the observed value is greater than or equal to the critical value, then the result is significant and the null hypothesis is rejected and the experimental hypothesis accepted. If the observed value is less than the critical value, the result is non-significant so the experimental hypothesis is rejected and the null hypothesis accepted.

Now have a look at an example (Maguire et al, 2000):

research now

Pearson's product moment coefficient: clever cabbies

Maguire E.A., Gadian D.G., Johnsrude I.S., Good C.D., Ashburner J., Frackowiak R.S. & Frith C.D. (2000) Navigation-related structural changes in the hippocampi of taxi drivers. *Proceedings of the National Academy of Sciences USA* 97(8): 4398–403

aim: to examine whether taxi drivers who have spent longer in this occupation have a greater hippocampal volume (this could be linked to navigational skills as the hippocampus deals with spatial representations).

procedure: data collected: each participant had their hippocampal volume recorded via a brain scan and they were asked how long they had been a taxi driver.

hypotheses: alternative – there is a positive correlation between hippocampal volume in taxi drivers and the number of years they have been a taxi driver. Null – any correlation between hippocampal volume in taxi drivers and the number of years they have been a taxi driver is due to chance.

findings: the data collected was *ratio* (the hippocampal volume was measured in cubic centimetres and the second measure was the number of years the participant had been a taxi driver) and the research design was *correlational*

The following table shows the results for 12 of the participants:

Participant no.	Hippocampal volume (X)	Years as a taxi driver (Y)
1	2.45	12
2	2.65	15
3	1.86	5
4	2.33	12
5	2.00	9
6	2.56	15
7	2.59	18
8	1.93	6
9	2.11	8
10	2.05	7
11	2.66	22
12	2.91	25

The observed value for the Pearson test is $r = 0.95$.

The critical value is found from the appropriate table (*see* Appendix page 480) using the following information:

- **df**, the number of participants minus 2 $(N - 2) = 10$;
- the alternative hypothesis is **directional**;
- level of significance (p-value) $\leqslant$ **0.05**.

The critical value for the criteria above is **0.4973** and the observed value is **0.95**. As the observed value is *greater* than the critical value, the *null hypothesis is rejected* and the experimental hypothesis accepted.

conclusion: there is a positive correlation between hippocampal volume in taxi drivers and the number of years they have been a taxi driver.

Exam tip

Draw a table or make up a rhyme that will help you to remember the name of each test, the level of measurement it uses and whether the observed value has to be larger or smaller than the critical value for the test result to be significant. Alternatively, try to remember the pattern in the table below. For the tests in the grey shaded area the observed value has to be less than the critical value to be significant – note that the grey shape makes a backwards 'L' for 'Less than'.

Choosing a statistical test		research design		
		independent groups	repeated measures/ matched pairs	correlation
level of measurement	nominal	χ^2 test of association	Binomial sign test	X
	ordinal	Mann–Whitney U test	Wilcoxon test	Spearman's rank order correlation coefficient
	interval/ ratio	Unrelated t-test	Related t-test	Pearson's product moment correlation coefficient

The flow chart on page 482 will also help you to understand how to choose the correct test to use.

Thin slices of sexual orientation

Researchers investigated the ability of participants to judge the sexual orientation of people on silent video clips (1 or 10 seconds) and still images. Heterosexual and homosexual males and females were recruited to the study. Graduate students were asked to complete a questionnaire that included questions about their sexual orientation and were videotaped while talking and were told that the recording would be used for other participants to judge their sexual orientation. Two students then left the study and videos of the reminder were used to make the clips and stills. A further group of undergraduate students then judged the sexual orientation from these images. The gender and sexual orientation of these participants were balanced across conditions. The findings showed that sexual orientation could be detected at a significant level, more effectively so with moving images and more readily for male targets than for female ones. Gay men and lesbians were more accurate judges than heterosexual participants when information was sparse. However, no judge was always accurate and no individual target was accurately identified by all participants.

Ambady N., Hallahan M. & Conner B. (1999) Accuracy of judgements of sexual orientation from thin slices of behavior. *Journal of Personality and Social Psychology* 77: 538–47 (an accessible summary can be found in Lyddy F. (2002) Revealing yourself – briefly. *The Psychologist* 13(2): 91)

(1) (a) Identify **one** ethical issue that arose in the study and describe how it was dealt with. [2]

    (b) Identify **one other** ethical issue that could be important in this study [1]

    (c) Explain what the researchers should to act ethically with respect to the issue you have identified in part (ii) [2]

(2) (a) What is meant by the term *significance level*? [1]

    (b) What significance level would it be appropriate to use in this study? Justify your choice. [2]

(3) (a) What is meant by the term *participant variable*? [1]

    (b) Outline **one** participant variable that should be controlled in this study. [2]

(4) (a) Describe the sample used in this study. [2]

    (b) Explain **one** strength and **one** weakness of the sample taken. [4]

Total marks 17

Mobile madness

Does mobile phone use while driving have safety implications? Participants in a study designed to answer this question performed a task where they were required to track a moving target with a computer screen cursor. The target could flash red or green; if it flashed red the participants had to press a 'brake' button as quickly as possible. This simulated traffic light task occurred at 10–20-second intervals throughout two tests. First participants performed this task for 7 minutes. They then repeated the task for 15 minutes in one of the following conditions: holding a telephone conversation with a confederate using a hand held or hands-free phone or listening to the radio or to a passage from a book (that they believed would be followed by a test). Participants using phones, whether hand-held or hands-free, took more than twice as long to respond to the simulated traffic lights as participants in the other conditions. They were also significantly slower than when they had performed the task by itself. There were no significant differences between users of the two types of phone.

Stayer D.L. & Johnston W.A. (2001) Driven to distraction: dual-task studies of simulated driving and conversing on a cellular phone. *Psychological Science* 12: 462–6 (an accessible summary can be found in Edmonds A.J. (2002) On the 'ring' road. *The Psychologist* 15(1): 36)

(1) This study was a laboratory-based experiment. Outline **two** advantages and **two** disadvantages of this method. [8]

(2) (a) Write an alternative hypothesis for this study. [2]

    (b) Is the hypothesis you have written one-tailed or two-tailed? [1]

(3) (a) What is the dependent variable in this study? [1]

    (b) What is the level of measurement of the data generated? [1]

(iii) What statistical test would you use to find out whether there was a difference between the two groups of phone users on the second task? Justify your choice. [4]

(d) What was the purpose of the first, 7-minute test? [1]

Total marks 18

Lobes of love

Two experimenters found 17 participants who would describe themselves as truly in love. Using functional magnetic resonance imaging, the researchers observed the patterns of brain activation in these participants while they watched pictures of their partners and of three friends they had known for comparable lengths of time. When viewing their loved ones, activation increased in some parts of the brain and decreased in others.

Bartels A. & Zeki S. (2000) The neural basis of romantic love. *Neuroreport* 11: 3829–34 (an accessible summary can be found in Martin N. (2001) Cupid and the cortex. *The Psychologist* 14(3): 155)

1 (a) Define the term *situational variable*. [1]

(b) Identify **one** situational variable that could have affected the results of this study and outline the effect it could have on the results. [2]

2 (a) Identify **one** participant variable that has been controlled in this study. [1]

(b) Describe **one** other uncontrolled variable that may be a problem in this study and indicate how it could be controlled. [3]

3 (a) What participant design has been used in this study? [1]

(b) With reference to the design that you identified in part (a) explain **two** advantages and **two** disadvantages of this design. [8]

(c) What statistical test would you use to decide whether there is a significant difference in this experiment? Explain your answer. [3]

4 (a) What is meant by the term *significance level*? [1]

(b) What significance level would it be appropriate to use in this study? Justify your choice. [2]

Total marks 22

The language of email

It has been suggested that there are gender differences in the use of language in e-mail messages. Research on spoken and written language suggests that differences in the use of questions, compliments, apologies and intensive adverbs such as 'most' and 'very' exist between men and women.

Hartley J., Howe M. & McKeachie W. (2001) Writing through time: longitudinal studies of the effects of new technology on writing. *British Journal of Educational Technology* 32(2): 141–51

Thomson R. & Murchver T. (2001) Predicting gender from electronic discourse. *British Journal of Social Psychology* 40(2): 193–208

Thomson R., Murchver T. & Green J. (2001) Where is the gender in gendered language? *Psychological Science* 121(2): 171–5 (an accessible summary can be found in Lyddy F. & Martin N. (2001) E-male or female? *The Psychologist* 14(8): 433)

(1) Identify an appropriate research method for a study designed to look for differences in language use by males and females in electronic communication. Justify your choice. [3]

(2) Plan a study that could investigate this idea. Include a design, controls and procedure. [16]

Total marks 19

Shopping

Research has shown that shop assistants are quicker to approach a shopper who is smartly dressed than one who is casually dressed. A group of students plan to test out this idea.

Regan P.C. & Llamas V. (2002) Customer service as a function of shoppers' attire. *Psychological Reports* 90(1): 203–4 (an accessible summary can be found in **Martin N.** (2002) Clothes maketh the customer. *The Psychologist* 15(8): 424)

(1) What research method would you suggest using to test this idea? [1]

(2) Briefly describe a possible design for a study that the students could consider. [6]

(3) Discuss some of the ethical issues the students will face in attempting to conduct their investigation. [8]

Total marks 15

Coping with stress

One factor that might help people to cope with stress is social support, that is, the social network of people an individual can turn to for help. A research group is investigating this relationship.

Brissette I., Scheier M.F. & Carver C.S. (2002) The role of optimism in social network development, coping, and psychological adjustment during a life transition. *Journal of Personality and Social Psychology* 82(1): 102–11 (an accessible summary can be found in **Martin N.** (2002) Feeling optimistic? The Psychologist 15(6): 309)

(1) Name the research method they will use in this study. [1]

(2) What are the advantages and disadvantages of this research method? [8]

(3) Produce an outline design for a possible study to test this idea. Include a description of how you will operationalise the variables. [6]

Total marks 15

Eye-witness testimony

Research into eye-witness testimony has shown that people may claim to remember things that they have not seen. A study was conducted to investigate whether people might also claim to remember doing things they did not do. Participants were asked to either perform, or imagine performing, familiar tasks (such as flipping coins) and bizarre tasks (such as sitting on dice). Twenty-four hours later they imagined performing various actions (including some of those previously presented). Finally, after two weeks, they were asked to say which activities from a list they had imagined or performed.

Thomas A.K. & Loftus E.F. (2002) Creating bizarre false memories through imagination. Memory and *Cognition* 30(3): 423–31 (an accessible summary can be found in **Martin N.** (2002) Deceitful memory. *The Psychologist* 15(9): 482)

(1) What results would you expect from this study? [3]

(2) Suggest two other familiar, and two other bizarre, tasks that could be used in such an investigation. Justify your choices. [8]

(3) (a) What information would you give the participants in the brief (before the study), and why? [4]

(b) What information would you not give the participants in the brief (before the study), and why? [2]

Total marks 17

(1) Compare and contrast two different research methods, highlighting their relative advantages and disadvantages.

(2) (a) Describe how qualitative data may be gathered through observation, interview or case study.

   (b) Discuss the relative merits of qualitative methods compared to an alternative approach to research.

(3) (Briefly outline ethical guidelines that are followed by psychologists working with human participants. Use examples of research to illustrate your answer.

(4) (a) Describe the ethical guidelines that protect non-human animals used in psychological research.

   (b) Discuss the strengths and weakness of research using laboratory animals.

(5) (a) Define the terms subjectivity and objectivity.

   (b) Using named examples of approaches, discuss the importance of subjectivity and objectivity in psychological research.

(6) (a) What is meant by validity and reliability?

   (b) Discuss why validity and reliability are important in psychological research.

   (c) Use examples to describe how validity and reliability may be assessed.

31 Perspectives on psychology

what's ahead?

If you have read *Angles on psychology* (Jarvis et al, 2000) you will already have a good idea about the major theoretical approaches to psychology. The aim of this chapter is to review four approaches; behaviourism (the learning approach), the psychodynamic approach, the cognitive approach and the physiological approach, looking at how each has been applied in the real world and what each has contributed to psychology.

Behaviourism (the learning approach)

A brief recap on the approach

Behavioural psychology is based on the idea that we acquire behaviours by learning experiences, and examines the mechanisms by which this learning takes place. Research into such learning typically involves laboratory experimentation, often using animals as well as human participants. There are a number of ways in which this learning can take place, including classical conditioning, operant conditioning and social (observational) learning. Look at box 31.1 to remind yourself what these mechanisms of learning involve.

Classical conditioning: involves learning to associate two stimuli together so that we come to respond to a new stimulus as we would one we already respond to. We naturally respond in certain ways to particular stimuli and do not have to learn these responses. For example, we tend to respond to loud noises with fear or to sweet tastes with pleasure. In classical conditioning we learn to associate such an *unconditioned stimulus* (UCS) with a new stimulus, called a *neutral stimulus* (NS). When the NS is encountered with the UCS we become conditioned to respond to the NS as we already did to the UCS. The NS then becomes a CS and the response to it a conditioned stimulus (CS). For example, we can become conditioned to fear dogs if one barks at us. The bark, being a loud noise, is an unconditioned stimulus, eliciting fear. Once this loud noise becomes associated with dogs, then dogs shift from being a neutral stimulus to being a conditioned stimulus, and they elicit the conditioned response of fear.

Operant conditioning: involves learning according to the consequences of our actions. Any action that

---

leads to a positive consequence is said to be *reinforced*, and will occur more frequently in the future. By contrast, actions that lead to negative consequences occur less frequently in the future and are said to be *punished*. Both reinforcement and punishment can be positive or negative. Positive reinforcement and punishment involve introducing a new element into the situation. In the case of positive reinforcement this is a pleasant event, such as money, chocolate or a hug. In positive punishment we introduce a new unpleasant event such as a slap. Negative reinforcement and punishment involve taking something away from the situation. In the case of negative reinforcement we are taking away something unpleasant such as pain, and in negative punishment we are taking away something pleasant.

Social (observational) learning: involves learning from another individual, known as a *model*. In observational learning we imitate the actions of a model and add those actions to our own behavioural repertoire. Models are normally of the same species as the learner, and their actions are more likely to be imitated if they are of the same sex and high social status. Models are also more likely to be imitated if they are seen by the learner to be rewarded for performing the action. Social learning theory (SLT) is an approach to psychology that places particular emphasis on the importance of observational learning. According to social learning theorist Albert Bandura (1977), there are four conditions that need to be met before observational learning will occur. First, the learner needs to be paying attention to the model. Secondly, they must remember the action. Thirdly, they must reproduce it themselves following seeing it done by the model, and, fourthly, they must be reinforced (ie rewarded) for performing the action themselves.

Box 31.1 Major mechanisms of learning

interactive angles

Before going any further, test your understanding of learning mechanisms. Identify each of the following examples as classical conditioning, positive reinforcement, negative reinforcement, positive punishment, negative punishment or observational learning.

1 A football coach demonstrates how to 'bend' a ball from a free kick.

2 A student who comes in late has her *Buffy* videos confiscated.

3 An 'heretic' being tortured by the Spanish Inquisition has his torture stopped when he admits having liaised with the Devil.

4 A young man wears deodorant for the first time when clubbing and 'pulls'.

5 A paedophile is shown pictures of children and is simultaneously given painful electric shocks.

6 A playground bully picks on the wrong person and gets his butt kicked.

You will have encountered behaviourism a number of times on the A-level course. At AS level you studied the basics of the approach, including its key assumptions, research methods, the processes of conditioning and social learning and the use of behavioural methods to alter human behaviour. You should have also encountered it at A2, in particular in unit 4. Box 31.2 gives some pointers about where in units 4 and 5 you might have learnt more about the behavioural approach.

4A Clinical psychology

▶ The behavioural approach: the application of principles of conditioning to understanding the development of mental disorder, eg classical conditioning and phobias/paraphilias.

▶ One behavioural therapy: eg aversion, desensitisation, flooding or token economy.

▶ Psychological factors in specific mental disorders: eg the role of classical conditioning and social learning in the origins of phobias and the role of negative reinforcement in their maintenance.

4B Criminal psychology

▶ Effects of the media on criminal behaviour: eg the role of observational learning and vicarious reinforcement in the imitation of media violence.

▶ Controlling aggression: eg the strategies of punishment, aversion and modelling.

▶ The effect of zero tolerance: eg understanding zero tolerance in terms of learning theory, and the conditions for effective punishment.

4C Sports psychology

▶ Sport and socialisation: eg social learning and individual differences in behaviour, and the role of selective reinforcement in gender-related sporting behaviour.

5B Environmental psychology

▶ Encouraging environmentally friendly behaviour: the role of reward and punishment.

5C Health psychology

▶ Health and substance abuse: the psychological effects of abstinence, eg the role of negative punishment and negative reinforcement.

▶ Factors in addiction: learning theory, eg. positive reinforcement in initial use and negative reinforcement in maintenance.

Box 31.2 Examples of behaviourism in units 4 and 5

Contributions of behaviourism to psychology

The behavioural approach dominated academic psychology, particularly in America, from the 1920s until the 1950s/60s when the cognitive revolution saw learning theory replaced by cognitive theory as the dominant basis of academic psychology. Although relatively few psychologists would describe themselves nowadays as entirely behaviourist in their outlook, learning theory is still an important part of psychology, and it is still the subject of much current research. The following are some of the main contributions of the approach to psychology:

1 **It gave psychology credibility as a science.** In the early days of psychology, when it struggled for credibility as a science, the dominant research method of laboratory experimentation and the use of animals made psychology appear highly scientific and so

boosted its status. Behaviourism was also the first approach to psychology to generate firm rules of how the mind worked as opposed to theory. This further added to psychology's scientific credentials. Of course we now have a much broader view of science, and psychology no longer has a problem of scientific credibility. It can therefore be argued that in this sense behaviourism has outlived its usefulness to psychology.

2 **It generates simple, testable ideas.** 'Facts' are a rare commodity in psychology. What we have are a lot of theoretical explanations that can to a greater or lesser extent be investigated by psychological research and supported or disconfirmed. Because behaviourists do not indulge in complex and untestable theory, but concentrate instead on rigorously researching a limited number of principles, they have arrived at a number of reliable conclusions about human behaviour that allow us to predict and, where appropriate, control a person's behaviour in a given situation. For example, social learning theory allows us to predict that a child with lazy role models is likely to grow up lazy. It also allows us to control his development up to a point by providing better models and reinforcement.

3 **It makes us remember that human behaviour is flexible and can change for the better.** We hear a lot about advances in genetics nowadays, and the effect genes have on the characteristics and abilities of an individual. The danger in over-emphasising genes is that we can start to think of individuals as 'just made like that' and hence difficult to change. By emphasising the importance of learning in human development the behaviourists have forced us to keep in mind that behaviour is largely the result of our environment and so can be altered for the better by manipulating that environment.

Contributions to society

Behavioural techniques allow us to control people's behaviour. Although deliberately setting out to alter people's behaviour always raises ethical issues, there are a variety of situations in which altering a person's behaviour is very much for their benefit as well as for others.

1 **Behavioural therapies.** Clinicians, in particular clinical psychologists, make use of a number of behavioural techniques to tackle the symptoms of mental disorder (see page 21 for a detailed account). Classical conditioning can be applied to therapy in a number of ways. For example, in aversion therapy we can condition people to associate a stimulus with something unpleasant like an electric shock or emetic drug. This provides a way of extinguishing undesirable behaviours such as alcohol abuse and paedophilia. Operant conditioning can be used to reinforce appropriate social behaviour and so rehabilitate patients, who have, as a result of their disorder, got into bad habits.

2 **Community behaviour analysis.** Whereas behavioural therapies are conducted with individuals or small groups, we can also use behavioural techniques outside controlled environments to alter the behaviour of a whole community (see *Angles on psychology* for a fuller account). We can, for example, use token economies in institutions like schools and prisons to reward and encourage socially appropriate behaviour. Punishment, as used in criminal justice (page 156) and environmental psychology (page 367), is an example of learning theory applied in the community. Zero tolerance (page 160) is slightly more sophisticated than most punishment as it uses the principles of effective punishment – it is immediate, severe and inevitable.

3 **Understanding the importance of role models.** Social learning theory tells us that children will imitate highly visible, high-status individuals of the same sex as themselves. Thus, celebrities from the world of sport or entertainment make powerful role models, and we understand the importance of their modelling appropriate behaviour (see page 172 for a discussion in relation to sport). Our understanding of observational learning has also allowed us better to understand the debate over media violence (see page 141 for a detailed account). For example, children are more likely to imitate violence they see on television if they identify with the violent character and if they see the character rewarded for their violence.

The psychodynamic approach

A brief recap on the approach

Psychodynamic psychology is very different from behaviourism, and there is a long history of bad feeling between those favouring the two approaches. Psychodynamic approaches are concerned with the effect of early relationships and early trauma on the unconscious mind, and the impact of the unconscious on our motivation, feelings and behaviour. Research in the psychodynamic approach typically involves in-depth clinical case studies and interviews. Look at box 31.3 to remind yourself of some major psychodynamic theories (you may not have studied all of these).

Freud's theory: Freud developed the psychodynamic approach and his theory remains the best known. Freud saw the unconscious mind, comprising powerful instincts and repressed memories, as exerting a constant effect on our motivation and behaviour. Of course we are also influenced by logic and the norms and morals of society, and in his structural model of the personality Freud took account of all three of these influences, the *id* representing instinct, the *ego* our logical aspect and the *superego* our morality. The unconscious manifests itself through dreams, which represent the mind's attempts to satisfy our instinctive desires. These are presented in disguised form in order to protect the sleep of the dreamer. The unconscious also protects us from negative emotions with a set of mental strategies or *psychological defences*. Thus, we repress traumatic memories or deny unpalatable truths. Freud saw child development as comprising a sequence of stages. In the *oral* stage we are helpless and dependent, and we take pleasure largely through the mouth. In the *anal* stage we are assertive and experiencing our first conflicts with authority. Pleasure is experienced largely through releasing and withholding faeces. In the *phallic* stage we are highly curious and fully aware of gender. Pleasure is largely experienced through the genitals. We experience the *Oedipus complex* at this stage, an attraction to the opposite sex parent and the perception of the same sex parent as a rival for our affection.

Erikson's theory: Erikson developed a theory of development loosely based on Freud's but including several elements of his own. Erikson saw emotional development as a life-long process, and he proposed eight stages from birth to death. Although Erikson accepted Freud's ideas on psychosexuality, he also believed that development is *psychosocial* in nature, and each of his stages centres on a psychosocial conflict that must be overcome if future stages can be tackled effectively. Erikson's stages are shown below:

Table 3.1 Erikson's stages

Age	Psychosocial stage	Developmental task
0–1	basic trust vs mistrust	to gain a basic sense of trust in the world
1–3	autonomy vs shame and doubt	to establish an independent identity
4–6	initiative vs guilt	to feel free to explore the world
7–12	industry vs inferiority	to be busy in order to learn to achieve
12–18	identity vs identity-diffusion	to develop an adult social and sexual identity
19–25	intimacy vs self-absorbtion	to establish healthy adult relationships
26–40s	generativity vs stagnation	to surrender youth and focus on the next generation
40s+	integrity vs despair	to accept one's own life and impending death

Object relations and attachment theories: 'Object relations theory' is actually a loose collection of theories concerned with the impact of children's very earliest experiences and relationships. Object relations theory is discussed in detail in *Angles on psychology*. *Attachment theory*, which you will have studied in unit 5 if you took the child psychology option (page 200), was developed as a branch of object relations theory. It has, however, become part of mainstream child psychology and is often not thought of nowadays as a psychodynamic theory. The central assumption of object relations theories, including attachment theory, is that the quality of our first relationship with our primary carer is of enormous significance in our later development. We are born predisposed to form close emotional relationships. We carry away from the first such relationship a mental representation of what relationships with others are like, and this affects our future psychological development. Those with a good primary relationship (securely attached in terms of attachment theory) have a positive view of themselves and others. They are thus able to enjoy further relationships and are advantaged in friendship, romantic relationships, work and mental health.

You will have studied the psychodynamic approach at AS level and probably come across it again in units 4 and 5. At AS level you studied the central psychodynamic assumptions and research methods, Freud's theory and at least one other theory and the application of psychodynamic ideas to understanding and treating mental health problems. Box 31.4 shows where you may have come across psychodynamic ideas again in units 4 and 5.

Box 31.3 Some major psychodynamic theories

4A Clinical psychology

▶ The psychodynamic approach to explaining mental disorder: eg the impact of early trauma and early relationship quality on later mental health. Specific psychodynamic approaches, eg Freud's hydraulic model.

▶ One psychodynamic therapy: eg psychoanalysis, psychoanalytic therapy or brief dynamic therapy.

▶ Psychological factors in specific disorders: eg Freud's view of the role of loss experiences in depression and Bruch's view of family dynamics in the origins of eating disorders.

5A Child psychology

▶ Bowlby's attachment theory: eg the interplay between social releasers and parenting responses and internal working models.

▶ Play: the psychodynamic approach to play, eg Freud's theory and studies of the emotional significance of play. The use of play in child psychotherapy, eg the case of Dibs.

5C Health psychology

▶ Stress: the role of psychological defence mechanisms in coping with stress.

Box 31.4 Examples of psychodynamics in units 4 and 5

Contributions to psychology

Unlike behaviourism, psychodynamic approaches have often existed outside academic psychology, being more influential in psychiatry, psychotherapy and social work. However, psychologists have investigated and been influenced by psychodynamic ideas. Some commentators (eg Henry, 1994; Jarvis, 2003) have suggested that in the last 10 years psychodynamic psychology has enjoyed something of a renaissance in psychology. There are a number of reasons why this might be the case. In the postmodern era psychologists have largely ceased to look for single, 'correct' explanations for psychological phenomena and this has led to greater tolerance of non-mainstream approaches. The nature of science has also changed, becoming more theoretical and delving into areas such as quantum physics where we have to theorise on phenomena that cannot be observed directly. This has given the study of the unconscious mind, traditionally thought of as unscientific because it cannot be observed, more credibility. In addition there has been a large body of research in the last 10 years showing that psychodynamic therapies – the main application of the approach – are highly effec-

tive. The following are some of the contributions of the psychodynamic approach to psychology.

1 **It makes psychology relevant to the layperson.** Psychodynamic approaches tackle everyday aspects of human nature and experience that people want to know about. Questions such as 'Why on earth did I dream that?' and 'Why can't I hold down relationships?' are just the type of questions people regularly ask psychologists, yet they are very difficult to answer using other approaches. This is not to suggest that psychodynamic explanations are always the best, but the approach is oriented towards explaining the 'big questions' in psychology.

2 **It explains the irrational side of human nature.** Behaviourists see us as following learnt patterns of behaviour and cognitive psychologists see us as reasoning and making logical decisions based on the available information. However, more irrational human behaviour cannot easily be explained just by reference to conditioning or information processing. Why, for example, do so many of us (including heterosexual women – it's not just Sarah Michelle Gellar!) watch *Buffy the Vampire Slayer* every week? Logically, the whole premise of the programme is ridiculous and therefore it is irrational to devote so much time to watching it. However, from a psychodynamic perspective the appeal of Buffy is easy to understand. Monsters represent displaced fears, thus we can cope with our fears of death by displacing them on to vampires (the *undead*), which, unlike death, can be fought and beaten. Classic adolescent conflicts, to which we can all relate, are also played out through Buffy plot lines (Schlozman, 2000), giving the programme extra appeal.

3 **It makes us remember that we can be completely unaware of important influences on our feelings and motives.** In other words we have some form of unconscious mind. To Freud, the unconscious was driven by powerful instincts, libido and Thanatos. Although many psychologists would play down or even reject entirely the importance of sexual and aggressive drives nowadays, this does not mean that the idea of the unconscious is redundant. Attachment theory includes a more modern view of the unconscious mind in which our internal working models of our early relationships affect the way we respond to other people.

Contributions to society

Psychodynamic psychology has given us a greater understanding of human emotional needs and this understanding has a number of practical applications, most obviously in the understanding and treatment of mental disorder, but also in other areas ranging from child care to coping with life stages such as adolescence and the mid-life crisis.

1   **Psychodynamic therapies.** The first formal psychological therapy was psychodynamic, and to a greater or lesser extent, all the talking therapies we use nowadays have been developed from the psychodynamic approach, although some have diverged considerably under the influence of newer theoretical models. Much current therapeutic work is psychodynamic in orientation. In a National Health Service review of practice Parry (1996) particularly recommended psychodynamic therapies for use for depression and eating disorders. Although there have been questions asked in the past regarding the effectiveness of psychodynamic therapies (eg Eysenck, 1952), current research suggests that this remains a very effective way of tackling mental disorder and psychological distress (see page 41–2 for a review). Psychodynamic approaches may be the treatment of choice when a patient has a broad range of vague symptoms rather than a single, tightly defined symptom (Dare, 1997).

2   **Services for children.** The psychodynamic approach emphasises the importance of childhood experiences on their emotional development. This understanding has informed the way in which we treat children, in particular when they cannot be cared for by their parents. Prior to the work of John Bowlby and his colleagues (see chapters 18 and 19), hospitals separated children and their parents for extended periods when one or other required in-patient care. Thanks to the influence of psychodynamic practitioners in the 1950s and 1960s, who realised that these prolonged and unnecessary separations were highly traumatic for children, hospitals changed this policy and nowadays children are encouraged to visit sick parents and parents are often allowed to stay in hospital with their sick children. Another example of psychodynamic influence has been in nursery care. Again, prior to the work of Bowlby and his colleagues, nurseries tended to actively discourage children from forming relationships with staff. Nowadays, in line with the understanding of young children's emotional need to form relationships, emphasised in object relations and attachment theories, nurseries encourage the formation of attachments with staff, for example, by giving a child a *key worker*, who is responsible for their welfare.

The cognitive approach

A brief recap on the approach

Whereas behaviourists focused on the learning of observable behaviours and either ignored or vastly oversimplified the workings of the mind, cognitive psychologists focus instead on studying mental processes, looking in particular at the way the mind processes information. Behaviourism is sometimes said to treat the mind as a 'black box' and the aim of cognitive psychology is to fill in the black box. The difference between behaviourism and cognitive psychology is shown in figure 31.1.

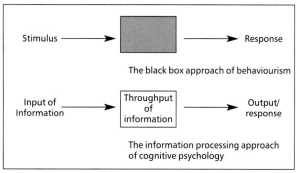

Figure 31.1 A comparison of behavioural and cognitive psychology

Pure and applied cognitive approaches

Within the cognitive approach many psychologists study 'pure' cognitive psychology, looking at the nature of mental processes in their own right. Thus psychologists have

> **Perception:** the processes of taking in and making sense of information from the environment. We use the senses of sight, hearing, touch, smell, taste and proprioception (awareness of our body position and movement) to gather this information.

> **Attention:** the processes whereby we focus on one or more pieces of information from the environment, and maintain this focus over a period.

> **Memory:** the processes of encoding and storing information, and retrieving it later when required.

> **Language:** the use of symbols to represent concepts. Language is both a tool of thought, allowing us to think more clearly about ideas, and of communication, allowing us to pass those ideas on to others.

> **Thinking and reasoning:** thinking is a broad term, covering the ways in which we mentally manipulate ideas. An important aspect of thinking is reasoning, in which we seek to understand a situation. We can also apply thinking to solving problems.

> **Metacognition:** our awareness of other cognitive processes, for example, what we are thinking about.

Box 31.5 Major cognitive processes

studied perception, attention, memory, language and thinking and reasoning, and as a result we now know quite a lot about the way the mind works. For example, at AS level you studied the processes of remembering and forgetting.

It is, however, also possible to apply the cognitive approach to other areas in psychology, enhancing, for example, our understanding of social, clinical, criminal and health psychology. Thus in social psychology we can look at how we perceive and think about other people – this is called *social cognition*. You have come across an example of social cognition if you looked at stereotyping when you studied prejudice at AS level (*Angles on psychology*). Stereotypes, the beliefs we have about particular groups, are the cognitive aspect of prejudice. We also have cognitive approaches to studying mental disorder, which emphasise abnormal mental processes, such as highly negative thinking in depression. The major cognitive processes are shown in box 31.5.

There are numerous examples where the cognitive approach has been used in applied psychology, hence it crops up many times throughout units 4 and 5. Remember that any approach that looks at how we process information is cognitive. Box 31.6 shows some examples from units 4 and 5.

4A Clinical psychology

▶ The cognitive approach: using cognitive approaches to understand mental disorder, eg negative thinking in depression.

▶ One cognitive-behavioural therapy: eg REBT (Ellis, 1962), in which the therapist argues vigorously with the patient to alter their patterns of irrational thinking.

▶ Psychological factors in specific mental disorders: eg the failure of metacognition in schizophrenia, negative thinking in depression and inaccurate perception of body shape in eating disorders.

4B Criminal psychology

▶ Eye-witness testimony: studies of the accuracy of eye-witness memory.

▶ Attribution biases: attribution is an example of social cognition. Biases in attribution reflect thinking processes, thus, for example, we have a different understanding of an event according to whether we are actor or observer

---

because we have access to different information in these two conditions.

4E Sports psychology

▶ Improving motivation: self-efficacy, ie personal beliefs about one's ability and attribution, and the cognitive processes in which athletes attribute success and failure to a range of factors.

5C Health psychology

▶ Stress: cognitive factors in stress, eg expectations, locus of control and cognitive coping strategies.

Box 31.6 Examples of cognitive approaches in units 4 and 5

Contributions of the cognitive approach to psychology

Cognitive psychology replaced behaviourism as the dominant school in academic psychology in the 1950s and 60s, a period sometimes called the 'cognitive revolution'. Psychology is still predominantly cognitive in its approach, and this has led to important developments in psychology itself and in the contribution of psychology to society.

1 **It has maintained the 'scientific' image that gave behaviourism its credibility.** Although we now have a fairly broad view of what science is and what aspects of psychology are 'scientific', there is no doubt that the extensive use of laboratory experimentation and the development of the computer, to which we compare the human mind, helped maintain the scientific credibility of psychology as it shifted away from the study of observable behaviour towards a focus on unobservable mental processes.

2 **It has taught us that cognitive processes are as important as our feelings and behaviour.** There are three domains of human experience; behaviour, emotion and cognition. Prior to the cognitive revolution, we had a reasonable understanding through psychodynamic approaches of human emotion and, through behaviourism, of behaviour. However, prior to the cognitive revolution we knew very little about the cognitive domain. Cognitive psychology has plugged this gap in our understanding of human nature. Take the field of clinical psychology. We have long known that we can understand the emotional and behavioural aspects of mental disorder. However, there are cases where an understanding of abnormal cognition is arguably the most useful way of understanding mental disorder. For example, Frith's

model of schizophrenia (pages 30 & 63–5) has arguably given us a better understanding of the experience of schizophrenia than have other psychological models.

Contributions to society

Cognitive approaches have numerous applications in the real world and, like psychodynamic and behavioural approaches, have been of great use to society. Our understanding of pure cognitive psychology has led to developments in the way we conduct education and handle situations such as eye-witness testimony, while the application of cognitive principles has given us new psychological therapies and ways to motivate sporting excellence and environmentally friendly behaviour.

1   **Eye-witness testimony.** The understanding cognitive psychology has given us of memory processes has been applied in the criminal justice system to understand the accuracy of the memory of eye witnesses to crime. For example we know that memory is a reconstructive process, and thus witnesses will piece together details of a crime using all the information available – including the questions asked in a police or courtroom interrogation. This means that we know to be careful not to include information in our questions that will suggest details of the crime that can then be built into the witness's recall of the events. We also know that the most common reason for forgetting events in cue-dependency (see *Angles on psychology*). Psychologists have made use of this in devising the cognitive interview, which works by giving the witness as many retrieval cues as possible to help them recall details of the crime.

2   **Cognitive-behavioural therapies (CBT).** The currently most popular therapies in the field of clinical psychology are based on the cognitive approach, aiming to alter maladaptive beliefs and patterns of thinking. For example, depressed patients tend to view situations negatively, but this can be identified and argued through by a therapist (see page 31 for a more detailed account). Patients with schizophrenia can similarly learn through CBT that delusions and hallucinations are not real. Cognitive therapies are applicable to a wide range of conditions and patients, and are relatively cost-effective, often reducing or eliminating symptoms in 6–12 sessions.

3   **Improving motivation.** Various approaches to improving people's motivation involve working with their cognitions. For example, we can improve their self-efficacy. Self-efficacy is the cognitive process involving our beliefs about our abilities in particular situations. It has been demonstrated that performance improves when we believe our abilities are good and declines when we believe otherwise. For example, in sport, it has been demonstrated many times that giving athletes falsely positive feedback about a performance improves their motivation and hence their subsequent performances (see page 178 for a discussion). The same principle has been applied in education and the workplace. A range of cognitive approaches has been used to motivate people to change their behaviour towards the environment (page 367) and health-related behaviour (page 289–90).

The physiological approach

A brief recap on the approach

Biological (or physiological) psychology attempts to look at psychological processes in the light of the biological processes underlying them. Biological psychologists are thus interested in the workings of the brain and nervous system, and in genes that may predispose individuals to particular psychological characteristics. Box 31.7 summarises some important biological processes.

Genetic transmission: individual differences in physiology are strongly influenced by genetic make-up. Some physiological characteristics, for example, in brain functioning, can impact on psychological functioning. This means that an individual's genetic make-up can predispose them towards particular psychological characteristics. For example, someone born with an excitable limbic system or autonomic nervous system may be more likely to display the personality characteristic of anxiety, and they may pass on this predisposition to the next generation. This means that characteristics like anxiety may run in families.

Neurophysiology: neurophysiology is the study of the structure and function of the brain and the rest of the nervous system. The closely related field of neuropsychology is concerned specifically with the relationship between brain structure and function and psychological processes. At AS level you looked at the role of brain structure and function in relation to bodily rhythms, sleep and dreams. Our understanding of neurophysiology and neuropsychology is rapidly increasing through the use of techniques like scanning, lesioning and electric monitoring. We now know, for example, that depression is associated with lower levels of electrical activity and reduced blood flow to the frontal lobes of the brain.

Neurochemistry: one of the better-understood aspects of brain function is the role of neurochemi-

---

cals in physiological and psychological functioning. Of particular interest are neurotransmitters, which pass across synapses, the gaps between one nerve cell and the next. Although the precise ways in which neurotransmitter function remain difficult to research, we do now have an idea about the effects of high and low levels of particular chemicals. For example, levels of serotonin, dopamine and norepinephrine are all associated with mood, low levels being associated with depression and high levels with happiness.

Box 31.7 Major biological processes of interest to psychologists

You will have studied some basic genetics and neurophysiology in your AS course. The extent to which you have revisited the approach at A2 depends on your options. Box 31.8 shows some examples of physiological psychology from units 4 and 5.

4A Clinical psychology

▶ The biomedical approach: the roles of genes and neurophysiology in the origins of mental disorder.

▶ One biomedical treatment: eg drugs, ECT, TMS, surgery.

▶ Biological factors in specific mental disorders: eg the dopamine hypothesis in schizophrenia or the role of low levels of serotonin in depression and eating disorders.

4E Sports psychology

▶ Trait approaches to personality: the role of genes in personality characteristics.

▶ Arousal and anxiety: the effect of arousal on performance, eg inverted U theory and drive theory.

5C Health psychology

▶ Substance abuse: physiological dependence, effects of drugs on neurotransmitters and synaptic transmission.

▶ Physiological response to stress: hypothalamic/pituitary adrenal axis and effects on the immune system. One biological factor leading to stress.

Box 31.8 Examples of physiology in units 4 and 5

Contributions of the physiological approach to psychology

Physiology was around well before psychology, and many of the pioneers of psychology came from the fields of biology and medicine. Thus Pavlov was initially interested in the digestive system when he discovered classical conditioning and Freud's interest in the unconscious mind came from his work as a neurologist with patients suffering from neurological symptoms for which no biological basis could be found. There has always been a place for a physiological approach in psychology, but, to a greater extent than other approaches, it has benefited from recent technological developments and is perhaps just coming into its own at the start of the twenty-first century. The following are some of the ways in which the physiological approach has benefited psychology.

1 **It has shown us that our psychology is influenced by the physiological processes underlying it.** We cannot really understand phenomena like sleep, jet lag or stress without reference to physiological processes. Arguments about whether these should be thought of as physiological or psychological phenomena are pointless, but there is no doubt that all have important biological as well as psychological aspects, and that our understanding would be substantially limited if we ignored these.

2 **It has taught us that we are not entirely products of our environment.** While psychodynamic and behaviourist perspectives have allowed us to understand some of the ways in which our environment and experiences affect our development, a modern understanding of the role of genes has shown that we are also influenced by our genetic make-up. This is not to say that genes are more important than environment (see page 465 for a discussion), rather that some of us are more likely than others from birth to develop particular psychological characteristics than others. This has important implications for avoiding harsh judgements of parents when the development of their children goes awry. Before the development of our modern understanding of genetics parents were sometimes held unfairly responsible for insecure attachment, criminality and mental disorder in their children.

3 **It has enhanced our understanding of other approaches to psychology.** Although we sometimes think of different theoretical approaches to psychology as rivals to one another, our increased understanding of physiology has enhanced our understanding of behavioural, psychodynamic and cognitive psychology. For example, neuropsychologists now have an idea how and where in the brain classical conditioning takes place, have isolated an area of the

brain associated with both dreaming and wishing – supporting Freud's theory, and have established some facts about the biological processes that underlie cognitive functions such as thinking and memory.

Contributions to society

The biological approach to psychology has had a number of benefits to society. These derive from our understanding of the relationship between environmental events, their physiological consequences and the resulting psychological effects, our current understanding of genetics and the use of physiological techniques such as drugs and surgery to alter psychological state.

1 **Understanding circadian rhythms.** Our understanding of the mechanisms by which we regulate our bodily rhythms have allowed us to predict when practices like shift work will cause serious disruption to rhythms, with potentially serious consequences to work performance, safety and health. This has allowed us to develop safer procedures, for example, avoiding rapidly changing shift systems that cause the most disruption to rhythms. Shift workers are also advised to use heavy curtains or blinds in order to prevent sunlight waking them and so shifting them out of the pattern they are in during a particular shift sequence. Understanding the effects of jet lag has also proved useful in sport psychology, in understanding when travelling to a match is likely to impact on sporting performance. Essentially, when we travel from west to east (against the sun), our sporting performance declines for a few days, so teams travelling east through time zones must leave themselves a few days to recover before playing.

2 **Biomedical treatments.** We now have a number of biological methods for alleviating psychological distress and other symptoms of mental disorder. Actually our discovery of some of these techniques was largely accidental rather than based on an in-depth understanding of brain function. For example, the first anti-depressant drugs were developed for treating tuberculosis, and it is thanks to observant doctors in TB wards that their anti-depressant properties were recognised. However, new drugs are designed with our current understanding of neurochemistry in mind, and this biological understanding thus contributes to the alleviation of suffering. Electroconvulsive therapy developed out of the (wrong) observation that there were no patients suffering from both epilepsy and schizophrenia. The logic went that if we could replicate the effects of epilepsy then it might be possible to eliminate the schizophrenia. Actually there are patients who suffer

both epilepsy and schizophrenia and in any case ECT is not usually effective in treating schizophrenia. However, out of this mess developed the realisation that ECT is an effective treatment for depression. Nowadays we still do not have a clear idea of how ECT works but through the use of contemporary technology – including scanning and EEG – we know that it leads very quickly to an increase in electrical activity in and blood flow to the frontal lobes of the brain.

Conclusions

We have looked at four of the major approaches to psychology and examined their different contributions to psychology and society. It should now become clear that, although each approach has its limitations, it also has a unique contribution to make to psychology. Through behaviourism we have a set of simple principles with which we can understand and control human behaviour. Psychodynamic approaches have given us an understanding of the irrational aspects of human nature and the role of the family in psychological development. It has also given us psychological therapies. Cognitive psychology has taught us about mental processes and is applied in the mental health and legal systems. Physiological psychology has informed us as to the neurological basis of the mental processes studied in the other approaches.

what do you know ?

1. (a) Discuss the contributions of the learning approach to psychology.

   (b) Discuss the contributions of the learning approach to society.

2. Some commentators have suggested that we no longer need a psychodynamic approach. Discuss this idea in the light of the contributions the approach has made to psychology and society.

3. Outline **one** application of the physiological approach, and evaluate the usefulness of the physiological approach to society.

32 Social and moral issues in psychology

what's ahead

In the first part of this chapter we look at some examples of psychological research and practice that have created controversy because of the moral and social issue they raise. We try to establish what makes a study or practice questionable on moral grounds, and look in detail at the examples of research into day care and the practice of psychiatric diagnosis. The latter part of the chapter is devoted to the related issue of how psychology has been used for social control of people's behaviour. All the major approaches to psychology can be applied to social control; we look in particular at the use of classical operant conditioning, Bernays's application of Freudian psychoanalysis and the generation of moral panics.

When does psychology raise moral and social issues?

Enshrined within the British Psychological Society code of ethics is the idea that not only do psychologists have to consider the effects their research may have on their participants, but also that we must consider the social consequences of publishing our findings. In other words if a study suggests something that is likely to have negative social consequences we should carefully consider whether this is balanced by the potential positive consequences before releasing our findings into the public domain. Such decisions can be extremely difficult as there are often two valid sides to moral debates about psychological theory and research. Before we go on to look in particular at areas of psychological research and their implications, let us consider exactly what can lay a piece of research or a practice in applied psychology open to scrutiny on moral grounds. We suggest that research and practice are most commonly questioned on moral grounds in four circumstances.

- When the topic of research is inherently sensitive because it concerns taboo topics. Taboo topics make us uncomfortable and discussion of them easily causes offence.

- When research challenges the correctness or acceptability of behaviours that are the social norm. This can be on an individual level as in the use of day care or a society wide level as in the practice of psychiatric diagnosis.

- When theory or research findings can be used by those in positions of authority or influence to restrict individual freedom of choice.

- When a piece of research or a particular practice can be used to justify discrimination against a particular group.

In addition, particular groups of psychologists are particularly concerned with particular social and moral issues. For example, social constructionists look critically at research and theory that can be seen as propping up institutions such as capitalism. Remember that raising these issues does not automatically mean throwing out the research baby with the moral bath water, just that moral issues should always be one of the things we consider when conducting research and constructing theories. Note as well that our opinions on whether a particular piece of research or theory is morally correct or incorrect will be largely personal, based on our own moral, cultural, political and perhaps religious codes.

Areas of theory and research that raise social and moral issues

There are numerous areas of psychology that you could look at in this section. Thinking back to your AS level there are important social and moral issues in several of the main approaches to psychology. Examples are shown in box 32.1.

▶ **The cognitive approach:** forgetting and the optional contemporary issue of the recovered memory debate raise social and moral issues in terms of the status of repression, and the existence of false and genuine recovered memories.

▶ **The social approach:** prejudice research raises social and moral issues because it raises taboo topics such as racism and homophobia, and challenges social norms of discrimination.

▶ **The learning approach:** the key application of behaviour change raises social and moral issues because it concerns the deliberate regulation of human behaviour and the consequent restriction of personal liberty. The optional contemporary issue of media violence is also sensitive because it can be used to justify censorship, a restriction on individual liberty.

▶ **The psychodynamic approach:** the idea of unconscious influence on behaviour raises the social and moral issue of criminal responsibility. The Oedipus complex raises further issues as it concerns the taboo topic of incest.

▶ **The physiological approach:** genetic influence on individual differences raises the social and moral issues of the potential for genetic enhancement and the extent to which it is worth providing optimum environments for children's development. The effects of shift work raise the issue of whether to legislate on shift patterns to optimise workers' health.

Box 32.1 Examples of social and moral issues at AS level

You will almost certainly have encountered additional issues at A2. Box 32.2 gives some examples of social and moral issues from units 4 and 5.

4A Clinical psychology

▶ Defining and classifying mental disorder: some definitions of abnormality, in particular deviation from social norms are open to abuse in that they allow us to put limits on acceptable behaviour and discriminate against groups more likely to deviate from norms. The decision to give a patient a diagnosis has implications for them in terms of the social stigma of mental disorder.

▶ The medical/biological approach: treatments such as drugs raise social and moral issues because they can be chosen for reasons of cost rather than effectiveness and to make patients easier to deal with rather than to make them feel better.

▶ The behavioural approach: behavioural treatments may involve anxiety and discomfort for the patient, and can be used to alter patients' behaviour against their will. For example, gay men were once 'treated' by aversion therapy – pairing images of men with painful electric shocks.

▶ The cognitive approach: cognitive-behavioural treatments (CBT) forcibly alter people's thinking. In some situations CBT techniques raise social and moral issues as they essentially remove people's right to their own opinion. Some 'stress-management training', for example, involves forcibly making workers adopt a more positive attitude towards their pay and conditions at work, and saves employers the need to improve those pay and conditions.

4B Criminal psychology

▶ The just world hypothesis: raises social issues because it challenges the social norm of attributing blame to victims of crime.

▶ Effects of media on violence: research supporting a link between media violence and criminal violence raises the social issue of censorship, which restricts personal liberty.

▶ Treating crime: controlling crime necessarily involves forcibly altering people's behaviour and taking away their freedom to behave as they would like. There is a moral issue of how and when it is acceptable to do this.

4E Sports psychology

▶ Sport as an influence on social development: there is a substantial body of research to suggest that, far from being character building, sport is associated with the development of antisocial attitudes. This raises important social issues because it challenges the cultural value we put on sport, and because of its implication that we should encourage less sport in young people, with the health implications this would bring.

5A Child psychology

▶ Criticisms of attachment research: some feminists object to attachment theory because it places so much emphasis on the maternal role, the implication being that much of what goes wrong in a person's life can be attributed to the shortcomings of their mother.

▶ Short-term deprivation: day care research raises the social and moral issue of whether to use day care. Research showing negative effects of day care suggests that mothers should not return to work soon after having a baby, restricting their liberty.

▶ Long-term deprivation: research suggests that family reordering has negative effects on children. This raises social and moral issues as it implies that families should not reorder, placing restrictions on their liberty.

5B Environmental psychology

▶ Encouraging environmentally responsible behaviour: the need to encourage people to behave more responsibly towards the environment raises issues because it challenges cultural norms of behaviour and restricts personal liberty.

Box 32.2 Examples of social and moral issues at A2

Issue 1: research into the effects of day-care

One of the most bitter and lingering controversies in psychology concerns the effects of using day-care in the form of nurseries or childminders on children's development. At issue is whether placing children in day-care has harmful, beneficial or no effects. Contemporary research into this issue is reviewed in detail on page 214, but we can sum up by saying that findings are highly mixed, although the greater volume of research has found negative as opposed to positive effects. Day-care research is inherently controversial for a number of reasons. It raises the taboo topic of how we should raise our children, offending those whose individual choices conflict with the findings of a particular piece of research. Day-care research from both sides of the argument also questions our cultural practices. Those who choose to return to work early are challenged by findings of negative effects of day-care and those who choose to remain at home are similarly undermined by studies showing positive effects for day-care.

Because both arguments suggest strongly how we should behave they can adversely affect the lives of parents, who suffer guilt and concern over whether they are a 'good parent'. Ultimately day-care research can result in restriction of our personal liberty and, of course they risk discrimination against women, to whom the bulk of child-rearing decisions fall.

Issues with particular studies

● Baydar and Brooks-Gunn (1991) surveyed 1000 mothers by telephone, asking questions about their use of day-care and their children's behaviour and academic progress. They found that children whose mothers had returned to work in their first year had a higher incidence of behaviour difficulties and poor intellectual development. This raises moral issues because it suggests that mothers who choose to return to work early are harming or at least risking harm to their children. In addition it raises the social policy question of whether mothers should be encouraged or even allowed to return to work soon after birth. Studies like this can be used to justify attempts (for example, of right-wing religious groups) to restrict the choices women have in the workplace, forcing them to take unwanted career breaks. Certainly in the past the government has found it politically convenient to pressurise mothers not to work so as to relieve male unemployment (Burman, 1994).

● Andersson (1996) followed up children who had had day-care from under one year of age in the famously good quality Swedish system to the age of 13 and found that they had better social and academic skills than a control group who had experienced full-time maternal care. This raises moral issues because it suggests that mothers who opt to retain a full-time maternal role and not use day care are not providing their children with the optimal environment. It also raises social policy issues, justifying penny-pinching by the government who currently save money by encouraging mothers to return to work rather than paying more substantial maternity benefits.

● Koren-Karie (2001) compared the attachment status of mothers who opted to remain at home with that of mothers (matched for socioeconomic factors) who chose to return to work soon after the birth of their first baby. It was found that mothers who chose to use day care were much more likely to have an insecure attachment themselves. This is interesting in its own right, as it suggests that the association between day care and developmental problems such as insecure attachment may not be a simple causal one. This has moral and social implications as it suggests that there is no problem inherent in the use of day-care and so we should be less concerned about the choice of whether to use it or to remain at home after childbirth. On this basis day-care research can be used neither by the religious right to restrict women's right to work nor by governments out to save benefits money. On the other hand it is however offensive to mothers who opt to use day-care as it implies that they made the choice because there was something wrong with them!

What can we conclude?

Day-care research presents us with a uniquely difficult moral problem, because both pro and anti arguments (at least those made by psychologists) are motivated entirely by humanitarianism – there isn't really a bad guy, although findings from both camps can be misused politically. Feminists are correct to point out that early day-care research was used as a 'rod to beat' women and drive mothers out of the workplace, and that we need to consider very carefully any contemporary research that could justify a repeat of this. However, most researchers in the field agree that long hours in day-care from a young age can be a risk factor in children's development, for example, increasing the probability of the formation of an insecure attachment. They would thus argue with equal moral authority that, far from seeking to disempower mothers, they are in fact equipping them with the knowledge to make an informed decision about childcare.

Issue 2: psychiatric diagnosis

Psychiatric diagnosis is discussed in detail in chapter 1. To briefly summarise, it is standard practice in psychiatry to diagnose patients with a particular disorder. The decision to diagnose is a pragmatic one. Although individual patients do not always fall neatly into one classification or another, we give a diagnosis based on the patient's symptoms because this allows us to target the treatments and services to a patient that are most likely to be of benefit to them. However, there are serious questions over the validity of psychiatric diagnosis; for example, it has been demonstrated that it is relatively easy to fool the diagnosing clinician. In addition, when we diagnose someone with a disorder we give that person a label that may lead them to experience social problems. The stigma attached to mental disorder may interfere with a patient's ability to lead a normal social or working life. Sociologists and psychologists influenced by social theory are also concerned that diagnosis can be used to oppress particular groups.

Issues with particular studies

- Rosenhan (1973) showed that it was relatively easy to fool doctors into diagnosing schizophrenia. Pseudopatients went to hospitals and reported hearing voices. All were admitted and diagnosed with schizophrenia. Although the pseudopatients then acted normally, in no case did doctors or nurses

recognise that there was in fact nothing wrong with them. This raises social policy issues because it challenges the validity of the medical practice of diagnosis – our social norm for thinking about mental disorder. The argument goes that if mental health professionals cannot spot in-patients with no symptoms whatever, then is there any point in their making diagnoses? The study also raises the moral issue of bringing the mental health 'establishment' into disrepute. This is risky in terms of patient welfare because it is important for patients and potential patients to trust the system; once the system has been shown up in this way such trust may be lost, and patients may choose to avoid the system altogether and so miss out on help. On the other hand, diagnostic procedures have been vastly improved in the last 30 years, in part because of studies like this. It could be argued then that the problem is not diagnosis itself, nor the Rosenhan study, but rather the continued discussion of the study in books like this!

- Philo et al (1994) investigated the role of the media in promoting unfavourable images of people with psychiatric diagnoses, and thus contributing to the social stigma of suffering a mental disorder. Only 18 per cent of cases covered in the Scottish media over a one-week period were judged to show people with mental health problems in a favourable light. Although this study is critical of the media rather than diagnosis per se, it serves to remind us of the stigma attached to mental disorder, and so can be used to challenge the practice of diagnosis. It might also discourage patients from seeking help for psychological distress for fear of stigmatisation. It also challenges the freedom of the press to cover factual stories of interest to the public and of the entertainment industry to make use of story lines of public interest. This smacks of censorship and any form of censorship restricts individual freedom of choice. On the other hand, there is no doubt that the aims of the study were entirely humanitarian – to highlight the unnecessarily negative portrayal of people with mental health problems. We could argue that the social norm of focusing on the tiny minority of people whose mental disorder makes them dangerous deserves to be challenged for the sake of the majority of patients who present no such danger and who suffer the stigma attached to mental disorder.

What can we conclude?

The practice of psychiatric diagnosis is acknowledged to be imperfect, although reliability and validity have steadily improved over the years. Pragmatically, patients probably benefit more from the use of diagnosis to target appropriate treatments and service towards them than they would from being treated as a unique case. However, a substantial minority of psychologists (particularly those influenced by social constructionism) have concerns over the historical use of psychiatric diagnosis to oppress women, gay people and minority ethnic groups, and worry that even modern diagnostic procedures can restrict individual freedom. That said, most of us would not subscribe to the view, commonly seen in sociology texts, that clinicians are motivated by anything other than humanitarianism in their dealings with patients. What does remain a genuine social and moral issue is the social stigma attached to having a psychiatric diagnosis. Rather than challenging the practice of psychiatric diagnosis, however, it may be possible to tackle the problem of stigmatisation.

interactive angles

The issues of day care research and psychiatric diagnosis are just examples of social and moral issues in psychology. It may be that you have not studied clinical or child psychology options, and that you would prefer to look at entirely different issues. Choose an issue from box 32.1 or 32.2 and analyse it using the same format as we have done; introduce the issue, look at the implications of particular studies and draw some conclusions.

Psychology and social control

There are a number of situations in which psychological knowledge and techniques are used to alter or control people's behaviour. Many of these are uncontroversial because we are pretty much all agreed that certain behaviours need controlling. Thus no one would argue with the psychiatric diagnosis of antisocial personality disorder being used to control the behaviour of psychopaths or the morality of using punishment to tackle criminal behaviour (although its effectiveness is very much open to debate). However, psychological techniques and practices are used to regulate our behaviour in many ways, some of them rather more subtle, and some of these raise trickier issues. *Social control* is term given to the regulation of people's behaviour for social purposes.

How is behaviour socially controlled?

There are several ways in which psychology can be used to control people's behaviour, taken from the major theoretical approaches to psychology. Using techniques from the learning approach we can condition people to respond in particular ways to particular stimuli or to behave in particular ways in response to a set of circumstances. From the biological approach we have developed ways to alter the functioning of the brain, for example, surgery and drugs. The psychodynamic approach gives us more subtle techniques with which to manipulate people's behaviour, appealing directly to the unconscious mind. Using our understanding of social psychology we can generate a particular discourse around a social issue in order to control what people believe in relation to that issue. Using the cognitive approach we can alter people's way of thinking about a social issue. In this chapter we consider three approaches to social control; conditioning, working with the unconscious mind and generating a biased discourse.

Who controls our behaviour?

There are a number of institutions with a vested interest in controlling how people think and behave. One obvious candidate is the government, which has the responsibility to limit criminal behaviour and to take moral stances on social issues, but which also has an obligation to respond to public opinion. The idea behind democracy is that it creates a balance between the power a government has to exert social control over people's behaviour and the power of the population to control government policy. The media are another powerful source of influence because the information the public receives concerning social issues comes through them, and can be presented in such a way as to reflect the social views of the editor. Editors thus have a degree of social control over public attitudes and behaviour. The business world has a tremendous financial interest in exerting social control over people's behaviour and attitudes – as employees we are required to be loyal and hardworking, while as customers we are required to spend our money! Thinking globally for a moment, consider as well the influence held by the world economy – in particular the multinational companies – who have a tremendous vested interest in maintaining a world view in which capitalism is seen as normal and right. Given the influence of government, media and big business we are subjected to continuous social control, and may be rather less free to choose our own attitudes and behaviour than we think.

Conditioning techniques as social control

Classical conditioning

By the systematic use of classical conditioning our responses to particular stimuli can be tightly controlled. We can, for example, condition a paedophile to respond to children with fear rather than sexual arousal by pairing images of children with painful electric shocks (an example of aversion therapy). Given social attitudes to child abuse this might seem to many of us to be perfectly reasonable, especially as the procedure is performed with the offender's consent and alongside supportive counselling. What may shock you, however, is that this painful and humiliating 'treatment' was used less than 30 years ago to 'cure' gay people, homosexuality being classed as a mental disorder under the DSM system until 1980. It is only because social attitudes towards the gay community have changed so much in recent years that we would now consider this to be barbaric, and an example of excessive social control. Clearly, then, aversion therapy is open to abuse, however, we can't now uninvent it, and it has legitimate uses. What we can do is keep in mind that it is a very powerful technique and be careful how and when we use it.

Classical conditioning can also be used to make us respond favourably towards products, and this is used to its full effect in advertising. At the start of an advertising campaign the product is a neutral stimulus but if we regularly see an advertisement in which it is paired with an unconditioned stimulus such as a sexy image it becomes a conditioned stimulus and elicits the same response. For example, a well-known bitter from the Manchester area was paired with the beautiful and scantily dressed Melanie Sykes. In classical conditioning terms she was an unconditioned stimulus and the beer became a conditioned stimulus, literally making it sexy! This is perhaps an amusing and very harmless example of classical conditioning as social control, but such is the power of conditioning in adverts that it is illegal to advertise harmful products such as tobacco.

Operant conditioning

Operant conditioning can also be used for social control. Essentially we do this as a society whenever we provide rewards for desirable behaviour and/or punishment for undesirable behaviour. One effective operant conditioning technique is the token economy system (page 24). This involves responding to desirable behaviour by recording points, which can be saved up and swapped later for a tangible reward. This is used in community settings (see *Angles on psychology*), and in prisons, schools and psychiatric hospitals. In psychiatric settings token economies can be used to rehabilitate long-term patients who need to pick up socially desirable habits again in order to fit back into society on leaving a hospital. There is a problem in this, however, in that every professional involved in recording points has a degree of power to determine what habits are 'desirable'. Patients could thus potentially be conditioned to be clean-shaven, religious etc, perhaps against their will. This illustrates the power of individuals and small institutions to exert social control over people.

There are thus social control issues to be considered when we use token economies even with entirely humanitarian aims. Much more controversial is their use to control customer behaviour for reasons of profit. This is exactly what happens to us when we use supermarket 'reward' or 'loyalty' cards. Reward cards are electronic token economies in which we receive points for spending money in a particular store. These points accumulate and allow the customer to claim a later reward. Supermarkets are keen to allow us to benefit from this because it gives them control over us – we are reinforced every time we shop there and so are more likely to do so in the future. Reward cards also allow supermarkets to push sales of particular products of which they have an excess or which attract a higher than usual profit margin by means of offering bonus points when we purchase them.

Social control using the unconscious mind

Behavioural techniques like classical and operant conditioning are powerful and overt methods for altering behaviour, and it is quite straightforward to understand how they can be applied to social control. Indeed, the aim of behaviourism was always the prediction and control of human behaviour. However, you might be surprised to know that psychodynamic psychology, which grew out of a rather different philosophy of gaining an in-depth understanding of the individual, can also be applied to effect social control.

Freud's nephew Edward Bernays devoted his career to applying Freudian ideas to the manipulation of human behaviour, and many of his techniques are used in contemporary business and politics. Importantly, they also form a large element of the theoretical underpinning to the profession of public relations (PR). The essence of Bernays's thesis is that successful politics and business are both based on satisfying fundamental human needs – the unconscious mind. The art of social control is thus to give people what they want – consciously or unconsciously. There are numerous ways in which this can be achieved. One of Bernays's greatest achievements was the marketing of cigarettes to women (Billen, 2002). This was based on Freud's idea of the penis as a symbol of social power. Although Freud himself once famously said that a cigar is sometimes just a cigar, Bernays used the image of the cigarette as a substitute for the penis as a symbol of social power. A generation of women were persuaded to smoke by the image of the cigarette as a symbol of women's increasing social power.

Focus groups

A core technique of the PR industry is the focus group. Focus groups are extensively used by both business and politicians to gain a better understanding of what customers and voters want. The use of focus groups is a psychodynamic technique, the rationale being that members of the group will free-associate and reveal unconscious wishes that can be exploited. In a group setting the desires of a number of individuals are revealed and a consensus of unconscious desire emerges. In 1999 an employee of Tesco leaked to the press that their marketing strategy for melons was based on the Freudian idea of the unconscious mind motivated by psychosexuality. Focus groups had suggested that people saw melons as breast-like and unconsciously responded to them as they would a breast. Accordingly the company bought melons whose size corresponded to the breast size of current supermodels and found that sales increased dramatically. This is not overt social control in the same way as are conditioning techniques because the aim is to give people what they really want rather than to alter their wishes, however, people's behaviour was nonetheless manipulated because they spent more money on Tesco melons.

PR consultancy and the Thatcher government

It is the business of supermarkets to sell things, and certainly no real harm has come from selling more breast-like melons. Perhaps a more serious matter is the way in which politicians and their PR 'gurus' have used an understanding of the unconscious mind to manipulate the behaviour of voters. Traditionally politics was the business of the superego, involving debates over moral issues and voting according to one's conscience. Under the influence of PR gurus, modern politics is more concerned with being able to encourage voters to indulge themselves – the province of the id. Ultimately the id represents the most fundamental and powerful part of human nature, while the superego just represents the layer of social convention that overlays our individual self. The power of the id was dramatically exploited by Margaret Thatcher in the 1980s. Thatcher famously said there was no such thing as society, just individuals. In Freudian terms this amounts to saying there is no need for a social conscience (ie a superego) and that we should simply satisfy our own desires (the id). This proved enormously popular – as we would expect, given a Freudian understanding of human nature. Under the influence of this highly individualistic political system, taxation and hence public services were cut and people were encouraged to indulge their own desires, creating huge social divisions between 'haves' and 'have-nots'.

Discourse and the manipulation of public opinion

You may recall from studying social psychology the importance of discourse. *Discourse* is the term given to the ways we use language to convey and construct ideas.

There can be different discourses around the same subject that portray it in a very different light. Burr (1995) gives the example of foxhunting. Those opposed to hunting generate and live with a discourse in which hunting is constructed as unnecessarily cruel and a pastime of the decadent rich. Pro-hunting campaigners, on the other hand, have constructed hunting within an alternative discourse as a legitimate way to control pests, as a rural tradition, which city dwellers simply do not understand, and as a mainstay of the already threatened rural economy. Because people's understanding of hunting tends to be firmly grounded within one discourse or the other there is little chance of constructive dialogue between the two sides.

A powerful way to control people's social attitudes and hence their behaviour is to generate a discourse in which a social issue becomes seen by the public in a particular light. To stick with the example of foxhunting, this is exactly what both sides have attempted to do in their campaigns. There are other examples of where two sides of a dispute have tried to construct a particular view of the situation in which their view emerges with the moral high ground. For example, Reicher and Hopkins (1996) analysed the discourses used by the Thatcher government and their opponents in the Miners' Strike of the early 1980s. They showed that while Thatcher used language that constructed the miners as a rebellious minority and the government as representing the law-abiding majority of citizens, the miners and opposition parties described events in a way that portrayed the miners as an oppressed group and the government as oppressors. The way we perceive all social issues like striking and foxhunting is profoundly affected by the discourse around the subject that we encounter.

Moral panics

A particularly potent way of manipulating public opinion on an issue is to generate a moral panic. A *moral panic* occurs when intense media coverage portrays a group of people in a negative light, leading to public outrage. Such a moral panic was generated against working mothers with young children following the first day care research in the 1950s and 1960s. In this case the government had a financial and political interest in removing as many women from the workplace as possible, so as to ease the high male unemployment that followed the Second World War. They therefore generated a discourse in which working mothers were positioned as irresponsible, risking harm to their children in their selfish desire to work.

The John Major government, backed by some elements of the tabloid press, sought to create a similar moral panic over single parenthood during the early 1990s in their 'back to basics' campaign. In this case the government had a financial interest in cutting the number of young single mothers claiming benefits and requiring council housing. Single mothers were positioned as cold and manipulative, interested only in having children in order to gain additional benefits and jump queues for council housing. In both these cases governments seeking financial gain whipped up public opinion to the extent that particular groups of women suffered persecution and hardship. Feminists have pointed out that in both these cases of moral panics, women were used as a 'soft target'. Although governments are responsible for influencing public morality, the practice of generating moral panics raises serious moral issues in itself, because they encourage people to turn against vulnerable groups such as women.

interactive angles

Look at the coverage of an issue that you might call a moral panic in two newspapers with very different views, for example, the Guardian and the Daily Mail. A suitable issue might be immigration. Look at how each paper generates a different discourse around the issue.

Conclusions

There are a number of situations where psychological research and practice raise social and moral issues, and there are numerous examples of such research and practice to draw on from your course. An example of psychological research raising complex issues lies in the field of day care. Any study showing positive or negative effects of day care on children's development is sensitive because it raises the issue of what parents should do to provide the best environment for their children. Psychiatric diagnosis is an example of a controversial practice. Studies into the reliability and validity of diagnosis, and into its negative effects such as social stigmatisation are sensitive because they challenge our cultural norm of giving people a diagnosis and bring the mental health professions into disrepute.

A particular moral issue for psychologists is the use of psychological research and techniques for social control. There are numerous ways in which social control is practised, and you may have been shocked at the extent to which powerful groups within society, such as the government, big business and the media, influence our social attitudes and behaviour. Conditioning techniques are designed to alter people's behaviour, and they are used in numerous everyday situations, for example, in supermarket reward cards. Freudian theory is used extensively in the PR industry, and moral panics, such as that concerning single parents, can be understood as discourses generated by those with a vested interest in oppressing a minority group.

what do you know ?

1 (a) Describe **one** study that raises moral/social issues.

   (b) Discuss the issues raised by this study.

2 Discuss **one** psychological practice that raises social/moral issues.

3 Discuss **one** way in which psychology has been applied to social control.

33 Debates within psychology

In this chapter we consider two debates that run through the field of psychology. The first of these is the nature-nurture debate. We examine both the debate concerning the role of genes and environment in affecting individual differences in our psychological characteristics and the 'new' nature-nurture debate concerning the relative importance of culture and evolution in determining more general psychological characteristics. Our second debate concerns the scientific status of psychology. We look at the rather different traditional and modern definitions of science and assess the extent to which psychology lives up to them.

The nature-nurture debate

The nature-nurture debate is concerned with the extent to which human psychological characteristics are the product of our genes (nature) and of our environment (nurture). In its classic form the nature-nurture debate is concerned with individual differences in our psychological characteristics, for example, our personality and intelligence and the presence of mental disorder. These influences are studied in the field of *behavioural genetics*. Behavioural geneticists investigate the role of genes and environment in the development of individual differences using a range of methods including twin studies, adoption studies and molecular studies (see *Angles on psychology* for a discussion of these methods). Running alongside the study of individual differences there is a second related debate concerning the origins of general human psychological characteristics.

How do genes affect us?

Genes do not directly affect psychological characteristics. What they do is affect the nature of physical structures including the brain and the rest of the nervous system. Thus our genetic make-up may lead us have particularly large or small, active or inactive areas of the brain, or we may produce particularly high or low levels of neurochemicals. Such subtle differences in the nervous system, in particular the brain, can *predispose* people to acquire particular psychological characteristics, ie they make people more likely to develop them. There are a few instances in which the presence of a single gene can determine a physical variation leading to a particular psychological characteristic; for example, the condition phenylketonuria (PKU) results from a genetic defect that leads the build-up of an amino acid called phenylalanine, eventu-

ally causing brain damage. However, most psychological characteristics are the product of several genes affecting the development of different physical structures, and of a number of environmental influences. Some characteristics are highly heritable, others not so at all.

How does the environment affect us?

From the moment of conception our environment impacts on our development. In fact some environmental influences may make their presence felt before fertilisation; high levels of radiation will damage the genetic material in gametes, leading to genetic abnormality in the individual embryo. There are innumerable environmental factors that have the potential to affect development. To understand how these operate we need to distinguish between the biological and psychological environments, and between the shared and non-shared environment.

Biological and psychological environments

One important distinction is between the biological environment and the psychological environment. Biological environmental factors may adversely affect development. For example, high levels of lead, gamma radiation and vitamin deficiencies can all lead to reduced intelligence. Recreational drugs, such as amphetamines, can increase the risk of mental disorder. We can sometimes intervene to counter the effects of poor biological environments. For example, vitamin supplements can be used to counter some of the adverse effects of poverty on psychological development. Because they are biological it is tempting to think of these factors as 'nature' rather than 'nurture'. However, they are very much environmental. What is more obviously 'nurture' is the psychological environment. Psychological environmental influences include socio-economic status, quality of relationship with parents, peer and sibling relationships, intellectual stimulation, abuse, neglect, bullying, education, exposure to role models, and experiences of reinforcement and punishment.

Shared and non-shared environments

Logically, we need to distinguish between two ideas about the environment; first, that growing up in the same environment will make two children develop alike, and, secondly, that raising two children in different environments will make them different. This might seem like an odd distinction but actually the two ideas are quite different. Remember, it is really a child's *experiences* that affect their development. If children grow up in quite different environments then they are very likely to have quite different experiences, and so their environment will cause them to develop differently. However, just because two children are raised in the same environment – for example, in the same home with the same family – this does not necessarily mean that they will have similar experiences. Parents may bring up a second child quite differently from the first, and two children with different interests and personalities may seek out different environments and be treated quite differently by adults.

Gene-environment interaction

Although it is convenient to think of genes and environment as separate – even rivalrous – influences on psychological development, in reality it is impossible to separate the two and they always work together. We all exist within an environment and we all bring our unique blend of genetic predispositions to that environment. Even in cases where there is a strong genetic predisposition towards a characteristic, it is often possible to manipulate the environment in such a way as to alter it. For example, in the case of PKU, although the origins of the disorder are genetic, we can prevent children developing symptoms simply by removing phenylalanine from their diet. In addition, our individual responses to an environment are influenced by our genetic make-up, meaning that a given environment will not have the same impact on different individuals. This is because we evoke different behaviour from other people and opt for different formative activities that exist within the same environment.

Theoretical approaches and the nature-nurture debate

In the above examples of environmental influences you might have recognised some that are emphasised by particular theoretical perspectives; thus quality of family relationships are emphasised within the psychodynamic tradition, whereas experiences of reinforcement and punishment are the province of behaviourism. It is perhaps worth looking at what some of the major perspectives on psychology have to say about the role of genes and environment.

- The behaviourist approach places considerable emphasis on environmental influences in the form of conditioning experiences and modelling, and plays down the role of genes. In fact the early behaviourists discounted the possibility of innate characteristics altogether, proposing that we are born a 'blank slate', which is then 'written on' by conditioning experiences. However, modern behavioural research has shown that people in general are predisposed to learning some responses rather than others (for example, we are more likely to acquire phobias to animals that posed a real danger in our recent evolutionary history). Some individuals may also be more prone to acquiring conditioned responses than others. Psychologists adopting a behavioural approach nowadays do acknowledge the influence of genetic predisposition although the emphasis of the approach remains on environmental factors.

- The psychodynamic approach also places considerable emphasis on the environment. In this case the major sources of environmental influence are the quality of early relationships. However, psychodynamic psychology also sees people as having innate emotional needs and instinctive behaviour. Early relationships are potent environmental influences because of the ways in which they interact with these instinctive tendencies. In Freudian theory, for example, we have an innate tendency to engage in a three-way family dynamic; the Oedipus complex (nature). However, it is the way that parents cope with this dynamic (nurture) that affects psychological development. In attachment theory we are seen as born with a set of instinctive behaviours that predispose us to form an attachment (nature), but it is the behaviour of the primary carer that determines the quality of this attachment (nurture).

- The physiological approach includes the study of genes, and this is the approach that places the greatest emphasis on genetic influences. Twin studies have established that identical twins are more likely than fraternal twins to share certain mental disorders, and that separated identical twins remain remarkably similar in personality. Molecular genetics studies have begun to investigate what genes might be implicated in the development of particular characteristics. For example, recent research has suggested that the TPH gene (so called because it codes for the production of an enzyme called tryptophan hydroxylase) is involved in vulnerability to schizophrenia. The physiological approach is also concerned, however, with biological aspects of the environment. For example, some studies have suggested that aspects of the biological environment including prenatal exposure to the flu virus and oxygen deprivation during birth also increase vulnerability to schizophrenia.

Culture vs evolution: the 'new' nature-nurture debate

Historically, the nature-nurture debate has been primarily concerned with explaining individual differences in psychological characteristics, although the extent to which we have innate shared psychological tendencies has also featured. In recent years, however, a further debate has gathered momentum in response to the growth of two conflicting schools of thought. Evolutionary psychologists propose that much of our social behaviour can be explained by instinct, and that such instinct has become part of human nature through the process of evolution. In direct contradiction, social constructionists have placed an increasing emphasis on the role of culture in affecting our social attitudes and behaviour. We can illustrate the conflict between evolutionary and social constructionist perspectives with the example of rape.

- **The evolutionary view:** evolutionary psychologists believe that one of the instincts guiding our behaviour is to reproduce and pass on our genes. Thornhill and Palmer (2000) have proposed that the practice of rape has evolved as a mechanism by which sexually unsuccessful men can pass on their genes to the next generation. For empirical support evolutionary psychologists draw upon examples of related behaviours in other species. In the case of rape a number of species, for example, mallards use forced sex as a reproductive strategy.

- **The social constructionist view:** Rose and Rose (2000) have challenged the evolutionary perspective, saying that rape is instead a cultural phenomenon, and that the evolutionary view contributes to the social acceptability of rape by suggesting that it is inevitable and in some ways adaptive. Social constructionists consider how cultural practices benefit those with greater social power at the expense of those with less social power. As most rape is perpetrated by men (who hold a great deal of social power) against women (who generally hold rather less power), a social constructionist view is that rape is a way for men to both practise and uphold their strong social position over women.

You can see how these approaches are radically different and very difficult to reconcile with one another. There is unsurprisingly considerable antagonism between the two factions! In defence of evolutionary psychology, the example of Thornhill and Palmer's explanation of rape – often upheld in anti-evolutionary arguments – is an extreme one, not supported by all evolutionary psychologists. Moreover it is perhaps a little arrogant to assume that of the entire animal kingdom we alone have escaped the influence of instinct on our social behaviour. On the other hand, social constructionists make an impressive case for the ways in which social behaviour is influenced by culture and the ways in which cultural practices reflect the interests of those who wield the most social power. It is clear that this new nature-nurture debate will continue for some time yet.

Examples of the nature-nurture debate

There are a number of places where you might have encountered the nature-nurture debate in psychology A level. Some examples from units 4 and 5 are shown in box 33.1.

4A Clinical psychology

▶ The medical/biological approach: the influence of genetic predisposition on the development of mental disorder.

▶ Specific mental disorders: biological factors, eg genes in the development of two disorders.

4B Criminal psychology

▶ Social and media influences on crime: self-fulfilling prophecies and media violence as environmental influences on the development of criminality.

4E Sports psychology

▶ Individual differences and sport: comparison of trait theories (including genetic basis of traits) and social learning (an environmental influence) of personality.

5A Child psychology

▶ Attachment: Bowlby's evolutionary basis for attachment (nature) and Ainsworth's maternal sensitivity (nurture). The universality of attachment (nature) vs cultural variations in attachment (nurture).

▶ Deprivation and privation: examples of influences of the psychological environment on development.

5B Environmental psychology

▶ Personal space and territoriality: instinctive territoriality (nature) and cultural differences (nurture) in personal space.

Box 33.1 Examples of the nature-nurture debate in units 4 and 5

Example: attachment

Attachment is a particularly interesting area to re-examine in terms of the nature-nurture debate as it raises several nature-nurture questions (see chapter 18 for a more detailed discussion of attachment):

1 Is the quality of attachment (largely nurture) more important than temperament (nature) in determining individual patterns of social behaviour?

2 Is quality of parenting (nurture) more important than temperament (nature) in determining the quality of attachment?

3 Is attachment an evolutionary mechanism or a product of culture?

Is attachment more important than temperament?

Attachment and temperament are the two major characteristics that can be measured in infancy and can predict later development. Temperament is believed to be a result of genetic make-up (for example, identical twins are more similar in temperament measures than fraternal twins), whereas attachment is largely (though not entirely) the product of parenting, the relative importance of temperament and attachment is an important issue in the nature-nurture debate. Actually it seems that both temperament and attachment type are important predictors of later social development.

Attachment type is highly predictive of childhood and adult relationships in a range of contexts. Securely attached infants (type Bs) typically go on to have the best friendships, romantic relationships and working relationships. Type As (avoidant) have few friends and difficulty in forming romantic relationships. They also tend to avoid work situations requiring frequent or intense social interaction. They are the most likely children and adults to suffer bullying. Type Cs (resistant) have a tendency for stormy romantic relationships and difficulty in maintaining friendships and amicable working relationships. They are the most likely to engage in bullying behaviour.

Temperament is less predictive of relationship patterns than attachment type, but it does predict more general social behaviour. For example, babies classified as irritable tend to remain irritable as adults and those classified as unsociable tend to have less interest in social interaction as adults than others. In general, then, attachment and temperament predict subtly different things and it is largely pointless to speculate on which is more important.

Is parenting more important than temperament in determining attachment type?

As well as being an influence of social development in its own right, temperament may also influence the forma-tion of attachments. Thus, although securely attached babies come from the whole range of temperament types, unsociable babies are at greater risk of developing type A attachments and irritable babies are most likely to end up type Cs. Although it is likely that temperament is an influence on attachment type, there is also a large body of research linking attachment to caring style, in particular to what Ainsworth called *sensitive responsiveness*, the skill with which a carer picks up and responds to infant signals, thus being able to satisfy their needs.

In a recent meta-analysis of studies of sensitive responsiveness Atkinson et al (2000) concluded that it is initially the most important influence on attachment type, but that this relationship becomes less pronounced with age, suggesting that either genes or different parenting skills become important later. This is consistent with behavioural genetics research showing that the influence of genes on individual differences increases with age.

Is attachment an evolutionary mechanism or the product of culture?

We can also look at attachment in the light of the 'new' nature-nurture debate concerning evolution and culture. According to John Bowlby, who first developed attachment theory, attachment is an evolutionary mechanism designed to increase the probability of infants' survival to adulthood through the maintenance of proximity to protective adults. This is a logical idea and in line with modern evolutionary psychology. Belsky (1999) has added to the evolutionary understanding of attachment by suggesting that different attachment types are adaptive in different types of environment. Thus, dangerous environments lead parents to adopt a caring style that produces type A children that are well suited to a high mortality environment in which they are likely to lose many attachment figures.

What evolutionary theory finds it harder to explain are cultural variations in attachment behaviour and the proportion of babies classified as types A, B and C. For example, Germany has a particularly high proportion of type A attachments, although it is not a high-mortality environment. Grossman and Grossman (1990) explain this in cultural terms, suggesting that type A behaviour has a different cultural meaning in Germany, being seen as independent and tough rather than avoidant and is thus more socially acceptable. It seems then that although attachment is probably the product of evolution, its nature is also affected by cultural factors.

What conclusions can we reach?

Attachment involves a complex interaction of nature and nurture. The tendency to form attachments and the existence of different attachment types are probably products of evolution, although this is difficult to directly test. However, attachment also has different meanings in different cultures and cultural norms influence caring style and hence the proportions of different attachment types. Attachment can thus also be said to be a cultural phenomenon. While caring style appears to be an important predictor of attachment type, temperament is also important and may exert an increasing influence with age. In terms of patterns of adult relationships, caring style and attachment are powerful predictors, but in terms of behavioural dimensions such as irritability, sociability etc attachment may be less important than genetically influenced temperament.

interactive angles

Choose another area you have studied involving the nature-nurture debate and draw out the evidence for the role of genes and environment.

The scientific status of psychology

A long-running debate in psychology concerns extent to which it can be called a science. As both psychology and science are very broad this is not a simple question to answer. First let us consider what science is and then look at how different theoretical approaches and research methods match up to the standards of science.

What is a science?

The word 'science' comes from the Latin word '*scire*', meaning 'to know'. Literally then science simply means knowledge. In reality we use the term a little more narrowly than that, however. We can know everything there is to know about *Buffy the Vampire Slayer* but Buffyology, valid and interesting an area of study though it is, will never be a science because it is not concerned with an aspect of the real world. Really then, a science is the study of an aspect of the world. Biology is thus the science of the living world, physics the science of the physical world and chemistry the science of the chemical world. Similarly, psychology is the 'science of mind and behaviour' (Gross, 2001), encompassing the study of, and the sum of our knowledge about, the human mind and human behaviour.

Traditional views of science

Positivism and the study of observable phenomena

All human societies have belief systems. Since the seventeenth century European society has increasingly adopted belief systems associated with the idea of discovering the *truth,* as opposed to following laid-down constructed beliefs or *dogma,* as is found, for example, in religion. This is sometimes called the modernist position. Science in the sense we traditionally understand it is a product of modernism, aiming to uncover facts about aspects of the world. The modernist view of science was crystallised in the work of a group of early twentieth-century Austrian philosophers called the *positivists*. The positivists held the view that knowledge can only be based on sensory experience and that knowledge advances only through the description of facts. Psychology that conforms to the criteria of positivism focuses on observable phenomena, and keeps theoretical speculation and interpretation of observations to a minimum. Behaviourism, which focuses on observable behaviour rather than hidden mental processes, and seeks to generate simple rules rather than speculative theories, conforms particularly closely to the positivist philosophy of science.

Falsifiability

The philosopher Popper (1969) proposed that a theory or hypothesis needs to be fully testable to be scientific. In practice this means that it must be *falsifiable*. To demonstrate that something is true is not sufficient because it may be true within a sample but not within the whole population. For example, we might hypothesise that all people are stronger and better co-ordinated in the use of their right arm (ie people are right-handed). This is a scientific hypothesis because it can be falsified by finding a single left-handed person. Some theories in psychology are much harder to falsify. Take, for example, the existence of *schemas* in cognitive and cognitive-developmental psychology. We believe that knowledge is organised into schemas and that new information is interpreted in the light of our existing schemas. However, it is impossible to design a study that, if a particular result were found, would disconfirm the existence of schemas. By Popper's standards, then, schemas are not a scientific idea.

Objectivity

Science aims for a realistic understanding of the world. One requirement for such a realistic understanding is *objectivity*. We are objective when we see things as they really are. By contrast, *subjectivity* involves seeing things from our individual perspective with our own views, biases, cultural influences etc. Of course our everyday assessment of the world involves a degree of subjectivity, but as scientists it is important to try to be as objective as possible.

The aims of science

There are three traditional aims of science; understanding, prediction and control. We understand, for example, that food decays more slowly in low temperatures because bacterial reproduction is slowed. Based on this understanding we can predict that if we lower the temperature our food will last longer. This allows us to control the rate of decay of our food by deliberately lowering temperature. Thus the concept of the fridge was born. The behaviourists in particular have always worked within this frame of reference of understanding, prediction and control. For example, our understanding of operant conditioning allows us to predict that if someone receives a punishment following an action they are less likely to repeat it. With this in mind we can then control that person's behaviour by punishing them every time they carry out that action.

A more contemporary understanding of science

The study of unobservable phenomena

If the positivist philosophy defined traditional science, it is certainly not considered sacred in the contemporary sciences. In fact, science increasingly studies phenomena that cannot be directly observed. Contemporary physics is concerned with a host of subatomic particles and phenomena that we have never directly observed, and are not likely to in the lifespan of current physicists. We can, however, say that the existence of subatomic particles would explain a number of other, observable phenomena. This is essentially what cognitive psychologists do when they talk of concepts like schemas. With current technology we will never directly observe a schema, however, we can say that the existence of schemas would neatly explain a number of research findings; therefore schemas can be said to exist. Unobservable phenomena like schemas are very difficult to falsify as well as to observe, however, most psychologists believe in schemas. Thus both falsifiability and observability may be false standards in terms of modern science.

The illusion of objectivity

Although objectivity remains an ideal in modern sciences including psychology, there is nowadays a much greater acknowledgement that true objectivity is impossible, and that all scientists are influenced by cultural norms, personal biases etc. For this we have much to thank the social constructionists. Social constructionism looks for sources of bias in supposedly objective assessments, and in particular at the social and historical context in which ideas developed. Take for example IQ tests, which were designed as a way of objectively measuring intelligence. Social constructionists see IQ tests not as such an objective way to assess intelligence, but rather as a way to strengthen the social position of the white middle classes, who generally score most highly in IQ, not because they are more intelligent but because the test questions are biased towards the skills, language and world-view of white, middle-class people.

The rejection of single truths

Modernism had at its heart the assumption that there are simple facts awaiting discovery, and that there is thus a single correct explanation for any phenomenon. If we apply this to psychology we find ourselves choosing 'correct' theories from a range of alternatives. Nowadays there is an increasing acceptance that alternative psychological theories and models can be seen, not as rivalrous, but rather as complementary, explaining different aspects of complex wholes. For example, looking back at clinical psychology we have reviewed six models of abnormality, the biomedical, behaviourist, cognitive, psychodynamic, humanistic and social approaches. Rather than choosing a single 'correct' model to explain mental disorder, a modern scientific approach would be to say that each model has made contributions to our understanding. Through the biomedical model we have gained understanding of the role of genetic predisposition and neurochemistry, from the cognitive model the role of information processing and from the social model the ways in which individual disorder can be understood within the wider social context. To adopt a *single cause explanation*, such as a biomedical approach, without awareness of cognitive and social aspects of a disorder is now widely regarded as too limiting.

Unpredictability and uncontrollability

If science has traditionally been concerned with predicting and controlling natural phenomena, a feature of at least some branches of modern science is the acknowledgement that sometimes the best we can hope for is to understand why we **cannot** predict or control a phenomenon. Thus chaos theory famously proposes that the wing movements of a butterfly might precipitate a chain of events that leads to a hurricane on the other side of the world. This gives us advanced understanding of the weather, but does not of course allow us to predict or control it. Traditionally, psychological approaches that allow us to predict and control human behaviour (like behaviourism) have been thought of as more scientific than those which do not lend themselves so easily to prediction and control (like Freudian theory). However, some contemporary psychologists argue that Freudian psychoanalysis, like chaos theory, fails to accurately predict behaviour, not because it is incorrect, but rather because it acknowledges the number of unpredictable variables in the system. It is thus in one sense more in line with modern scientific approaches like chaos theory than behaviourism, which oversimplifies human mind and behaviour in order to make it predictable and controllable.

Theoretical approaches and science

If we take a traditional view of science (and plenty of psychologists still do so), then there is a clear hierarchy of more and less scientific theoretical approaches. At one end of the spectrum behaviourism is classic science; it focuses on observable phenomena, generates falsifiable ideas, and is explicitly concerned with the prediction and control of behaviour. At the other extreme psychodynamic psychologists are concerned with unobservable aspects of human nature, generate ideas that are very difficult to investigate and are often not falsifiable, and they do not generally predict or try to control behaviour. Because of the popularity of these very traditional views of science, behaviourism is often thought of as more scientifically respectable than psychoanalysis. However, it is important to remember that a surprising number of 'respectable' ideas in modern psychology (like schemas) do not conform to the strict criteria of traditional science, and that the modern bases of science are much broader than traditionalists would have us believe. It is thus unwise to think of any theoretical approach to psychology as inherently unscientific.

Research methods and science

When we think of different research methods in psychology, it is tempting to think about how they compare to our mental image of the stereotypical scientist, who sits in a laboratory wearing a white coat and conducting experiments. According to this rather simplistic view, laboratory experiments are the most 'scientific' research method, while unstructured interviews and clinical case studies are perhaps the least scientific. However, the choices psychologists make about what research methods to use depend in reality on what it is they want to find out. It is often poor science to choose to investigate an issue by laboratory experimentation, because there is often an alternative likely to produce more valid results. Psychologists use the term 'scientistic' to describe research that fits with the popular image of science rather than being the most appropriate method to address the topic. There are in fact many highly scientific applications of case studies, for example, generating testable hypotheses and studying rare and non-replicable circumstances. The use of case studies only becomes poor scientific practice if we use them alone to try to generate universal rules or as the sole evidence to support a theory.

Conclusions

The nature-nurture debate and the scientific status of psychology are two debates that have run as long as the discipline has existed. The classic nature-nurture debate concerns the extent to which individual differences are inherited and to what extent they are products of our environment. In reality psychological characteristics are the product of the interaction of an individual with their unique genetic make-up with their environment. Nature and nurture thus do not exist as separate entities, and it is more productive to think of how genes and environment interact rather than which is the more important. A recent variation on the classic nature-nurture debate concerns the relative importance of evolution and culture on our social attitudes and behaviour. This is a particularly vigorous debate, focusing as it does on socially sensitive topics such as rape.

So, is psychology a science? If we adopt a broad, modern view of the nature and philosophy of science, then psychology in all its manifestations is unquestionably a science. However, many psychologists prefer to adhere to a more old-fashioned view of what science means, and according to this more traditionalist school of thought only some approaches to psychology can be called science.

what do you know?

1 Explain where **one** theoretical approach to psychology stands on the nature-nurture debate.

2 Taking the example of **one** psychological phenomenon compare evolutionary and cultural explanations.

3 Discuss **one** topic in psychology where the nature-nurture debate is discussed.

4 Why might some psychologists consider behaviourism to be a particularly scientific approach?

5 Is psychology science?

appendix

Statistical tables

Table 1 Percentage points of the χ^2 distribution

	Level of significance for two-tailed test				
	0.2	0.1	0.05	0.02	0.01
	Level of significance for one-tailed test				
df	0.1	0.05	0.025	0.01	0.005
1	2.706	3.841	5.024	6.635	7 879
2	4 605	5.991	7.378	9.210	10.597
3	6.251	7.815	9.348	11.345	12.838
4	7.779	9.488	11.143	13.277	14.860
5	9.236	11.070	12.833	15.086	16.750
6	10.645	12.592	14.449	16.812	18.548
7	12.017	14.067	16.013	18.475	20.278
8	13.362	15.507	17.535	20.090	21.955
9	14.684	16.919	19.023	21.666	23.589
10	15.987	18.307	20.483	23.209	25.188
11	17.275	19.675	21.920	24.725	26 757
12	18.549	21.026	23.337	26.217	28.300
13	19.812	22.362	24.736	27.688	29.819
14	21.064	23.685	26.119	29.141	31.319
15	22.307	24.996	27.488	30.578	32.801
16	23.542	26.296	28.845	32.000	34.267
17	24.769	27.587	30.191	33.409	35.718
18	25.989	28.869	31.526	34.805	37.156
19	27.204	30.144	32 852	36.191	38.582
20	28.412	31.410	34.170	37.566	39.997
21	29.615	32.671	35.479	38.932	41.401
22	30.813	33.924	36.781	40.289	42.796
23	32.007	35.172	38.076	41.638	44.181
24	33.196	36.415	39.364	42.980	45.559
25	34.382	37.652	40.646	44.314	46.928
26	35.563	38.885	41.923	45.642	48.290
27	36.741	40.113	43.195	46.963	49.645
28	37.916	41.337	44.461	48.278	50.993
29	39.087	42.557	45.722	49.588	52.336
30	40.256	43.773	46.979	50.892	53.672
31	41.422	44.985	48.232	52.191	55.003
32	42.585	46.194	49.480	53.486	56.328
33	43.745	47.400	50.725	54.776	57.648
34	44.903	48.602	51.966	56.061	58.964
35	46.059	49.802	53.203	57.342	60.275
36	47.212	50.998	54.437	58.619	61.581
37	48.363	52.192	55.668	59.892	62.883
38	49.513	53.384	56.896	61.162	64.181
39	50.660	54.572	58.120	62.428	65.476
40	51.805	55.758	59.342	63.691	66.766
45	57.505	61.656	65.410	69.957	73.166
50	63.167	67.505	71.420	76.154	79.490
55	68.796	73.311	77.380	82.292	85.749
60	74.397	79.082	83.298	88.379	91.952
65	79.973	84.821	89.177	94.422	98.105
70	85.527	90.531	95.023	100.425	104.215
75	91.061	96.217	100.839	106.393	110.286
80	96.578	101.879	106.629	112.329	116.321
85	102.079	107.522	112.393	118.236	122.325
90	107.565	113.145	118.136	124.116	128.299
95	113.038	118.752	123.858	129.973	134.247
100	118.498	124.342	129.561	135.807	140.169

Dunstan et al (1988)

Appendix

Table 2 Critical values of S for the sign test. S must be *equal to or less than* the stated value to be significant

	Level of significance for one-tailed test				
	0.05	**0.025**	**0.01**	**0.005**	**0.0005**
	Level of significance for two-tailed test				
N	**0.10**	**0.05**	**0.02**	**0.01**	**0.001**
5	0	—	—	—	—
6	0	0	—	—	—
7	0	0	0	—	—
8	1	0	0	0	—
9	1	1	0	0	—
10	1	1	0	0	—
11	2	1	1	0	0
12	2	2	1	1	0
13	3	2	1	1	0
14	3	2	2	1	0
15	3	3	2	2	1
16	4	3	2	2	1
17	4	4	3	2	1
18	5	4	3	3	1
19	5	4	4	3	2
20	5	5	4	3	2
25	7	7	6	5	4
30	10	9	8	7	5
35	12	11	10	9	7

Clegg (1982)

Table 3A Critical values of U (Mann–Whitney) for a one-tailed test at 0.005; two-tailed test at 0.01*

	n_1																			
n_2	1	2	3	4	5	6	7	8	9	10	11	12	13	14	15	16	17	18	19	20
1	–	–	–	–	–	–	–	–	–	–	–	–	–	–	–	–	–	–	–	–
2	–	–	–	–	–	–	–	–	–	–	–	–	–	–	–	–	–	–	0	0
3	–	–	–	–	–	–	–	–	0	0	0	1	1	1	2	2	2	2	3	3
4	–	–	–	–	–	0	0	1	1	2	2	3	3	4	5	5	6	6	7	8
5	–	–	–	–	0	1	1	2	3	4	5	6	7	7	8	9	10	11	12	13
6	–	–	–	0	1	2	3	4	5	6	7	9	10	11	12	13	15	16	17	18
7	–	–	–	0	1	3	4	6	7	9	10	12	13	15	16	18	19	21	22	24
8	–	–	–	1	2	4	6	7	9	11	13	15	17	18	20	22	24	26	28	30
9	–	–	0	1	3	5	7	9	11	13	16	18	20	22	24	27	29	31	33	36
10	–	–	0	2	4	6	9	11	13	16	18	21	24	26	29	31	34	37	39	42
11	–	–	0	2	5	7	10	13	16	18	21	24	27	30	33	36	39	42	45	48
12	–	–	1	3	6	9	12	15	18	21	24	27	31	34	37	41	44	47	51	54
13	–	–	1	3	7	10	13	17	20	24	27	31	34	38	42	45	49	53	56	60
14	–	–	1	4	7	11	15	18	22	26	30	34	38	42	46	50	54	58	63	67
15	–	–	2	5	8	12	16	20	24	29	33	37	42	46	51	55	60	64	69	73
16	–	–	2	5	9	13	18	22	27	31	36	41	45	50	55	60	65	70	74	79
17	–	–	2	6	10	15	19	24	29	34	39	44	49	54	60	65	70	75	81	86
18	–	–	2	6	11	16	21	26	31	37	42	47	53	58	64	70	75	81	87	92
19	–	0	3	7	12	17	22	28	33	39	45	51	56	63	69	74	81	87	93	99
20	–	0	3	8	13	18	24	30	36	42	48	54	60	67	73	79	86	92	99	105

*Dashes in the body of the table indicate that no decision is possible at the stated level of significance because the numbers of subjects are too small.

Greene and D'Oliveira (1999)

Table 3B Critical values of U (Mann–Whitney) for a one-tailed test at 0.01; two-tailed test at 0.02*

n_2 \ n_1	1	2	3	4	5	6	7	8	9	10	11	12	13	14	15	16	17	18	19	20
1	–	–	–	–	–	–	–	–	–	–	–	–	–	–	–	–	–	–	–	–
2	–	–	–	–	–	–	–	–	–	–	–	–	0	0	0	0	0	0	1	1
3	–	–	–	–	–	–	0	0	1	1	1	2	2	2	3	3	4	4	4	5
4	–	–	–	–	0	1	1	2	3	3	4	5	5	6	7	7	8	9	9	10
5	–	–	–	0	1	2	3	4	5	6	7	8	9	10	11	12	13	14	15	16
6	–	–	–	1	2	3	4	6	7	8	9	11	12	13	15	16	18	19	20	22
7	–	–	0	1	3	4	6	7	9	11	12	14	16	17	19	21	23	24	26	28
8	–	–	0	2	4	6	7	9	11	13	15	17	20	22	24	26	28	30	32	34
9	–	–	1	3	5	7	9	11	14	16	18	21	23	26	28	31	33	36	38	40
10	–	–	1	3	6	8	11	13	16	19	22	24	27	30	33	36	38	41	44	47
11	–	–	1	4	7	9	12	15	18	22	25	28	31	34	37	41	44	47	50	53
12	–	–	2	5	8	11	14	17	21	24	28	31	35	38	42	46	49	53	56	60
13	–	0	2	5	9	12	16	20	23	27	31	35	39	43	47	51	55	59	63	67
14	–	0	2	6	10	13	17	22	26	30	34	38	43	47	51	56	60	65	69	73
15	–	0	3	7	11	15	19	24	28	33	37	42	47	51	56	61	66	70	75	80
16	–	0	3	7	12	16	21	26	31	36	41	46	51	56	61	66	71	76	82	87
17	–	0	4	8	13	18	23	28	33	38	44	49	55	60	66	71	77	82	88	93
18	–	0	4	9	14	19	24	30	36	41	47	53	59	65	70	76	82	88	94	100
19	–	1	4	9	15	20	26	32	38	44	50	56	63	69	75	82	88	94	101	107
20	–	1	5	10	16	22	28	34	40	47	53	60	67	73	80	87	93	100	107	114

*Dashes in the body of the table indicate that no decision is possible at the stated level of significance because the numbers of subjects are too small.

Table 3C Critical values of U (Mann–Whitney) for a one-tailed test at 0.025; two-tailed test at 0.05*

n_2 \ n_1	1	2	3	4	5	6	7	8	9	10	11	12	13	14	15	16	17	18	19	20
1	–	–	–	–	–	–	–	–	–	–	–	–	–	–	–	–	–	–	–	–
2	–	–	–	–	–	–	–	0	0	0	0	1	1	1	1	1	2	2	2	2
3	–	–	–	–	0	1	1	2	2	3	3	4	4	5	5	6	6	7	7	8
4	–	–	–	0	1	2	3	4	4	5	6	7	8	9	10	11	11	12	13	13
5	–	–	0	1	2	3	5	6	7	8	9	11	12	13	14	15	17	18	19	20
6	–	–	1	2	3	5	6	8	10	11	13	14	16	17	19	21	22	24	25	27
7	–	–	1	3	5	6	8	10	12	14	16	18	20	22	24	26	28	30	32	34
8	–	0	2	4	6	8	10	13	15	17	19	22	24	26	29	31	34	36	38	41
9	–	0	2	4	7	10	12	15	17	20	23	26	28	31	34	37	39	42	45	48
10	–	0	3	5	8	11	14	17	20	23	26	29	33	36	39	42	45	48	52	55
11	–	0	3	6	9	13	16	19	23	26	30	33	37	40	44	47	51	55	58	62
12	–	1	4	7	11	14	18	22	26	29	33	37	41	45	49	53	57	61	65	69
13	–	1	4	8	12	16	20	24	28	33	37	41	45	50	54	59	63	67	72	76
14	–	1	5	9	13	17	22	26	31	36	40	45	50	55	59	64	67	74	78	83
15	–	1	5	10	14	19	24	29	34	39	44	49	54	59	64	70	75	80	85	90
16	–	1	6	11	15	21	26	31	37	42	47	53	59	64	70	75	81	86	92	98
17	–	2	6	11	17	22	28	34	39	45	51	57	63	67	75	81	87	93	99	105
18	–	2	7	12	18	24	30	36	42	48	55	61	67	74	80	86	93	99	106	112
19	–	2	7	13	19	25	32	38	45	52	58	65	72	78	85	92	99	106	113	119
20	–	2	8	13	20	27	34	41	48	55	62	69	76	83	90	98	105	112	119	127

*Dashes in the body of the table indicate that no decision is possible at the stated level of significance because the numbers of subjects are too small.

Greene and D'Oliveira (1999)

Appendix

Table 3D Critical values of U (Mann–Whitney) for a one-tailed test at 0.05; two-tailed test at 0.10*

n_2	|										n_1									
	1	2	3	4	5	6	7	8	9	10	11	12	13	14	15	16	17	18	19	20
1	–	–	–	–	–	–	–	–	–	–	–	–	–	–	–	–	–	–	0	0
2	–	–	–	–	0	0	0	1	1	1	1	2	2	2	3	3	3	4	4	4
3	–	–	0	0	1	2	2	3	3	4	5	5	6	7	7	8	9	9	10	11
4	–	–	0	1	2	3	4	5	6	7	8	9	10	11	12	14	15	16	17	18
5	–	0	1	2	4	5	6	8	9	11	12	13	15	16	18	19	20	22	23	25
6	–	0	2	3	5	7	8	10	12	14	16	17	19	21	23	25	26	28	30	32
7	–	0	2	4	6	8	11	13	15	17	19	21	24	26	28	30	33	35	37	39
8	–	1	3	5	8	10	13	15	18	20	23	26	28	31	33	36	39	41	44	47
9	–	1	3	6	9	12	15	18	21	24	27	30	33	36	39	42	45	48	51	54
10	–	1	4	7	11	14	17	20	24	27	31	34	37	41	44	48	51	55	58	62
11	–	1	5	8	12	16	19	23	27	31	34	38	42	46	50	54	57	61	65	69
12	–	2	5	9	13	17	21	26	30	34	38	42	47	51	55	60	64	68	72	77
13	–	2	6	10	15	19	24	28	33	37	42	47	51	56	61	65	70	75	80	84
14	–	2	7	11	16	21	26	31	36	41	46	51	56	61	66	71	77	82	87	92
15	–	3	7	12	18	23	28	33	39	44	50	55	61	66	72	77	83	88	94	100
16	–	3	8	14	19	25	30	36	42	48	54	60	65	71	77	83	89	95	101	107
17	–	3	9	15	20	26	33	39	45	51	57	64	70	77	83	89	96	102	109	115
18	–	4	9	16	22	28	35	41	48	55	61	68	75	82	88	95	102	109	116	123
19	0	4	10	17	23	30	37	44	51	58	65	72	80	87	94	101	109	116	123	130
20	0	4	11	18	25	32	39	47	54	62	69	77	84	92	100	107	115	123	130	138

*Dashes in the body of the table indicate that no decision is possible at the stated level of significance because the numbers of subjects are too small.

Table 4 Critical values of *T* at various levels of probability (Wilcoxon)

	Level of significance for one-tailed test					Level of significance for one-tailed test			
	0.05	0.025	0.01	0.005		0.05	0.025	0.01	0.005
	Level of significance for two-tailed test					Level of significance for two-tailed test			
N	*0.10*	*0.05*	*0.02*	*0.01*	*N*	*0.10*	*0.05*	*0.02*	*0.01*
5	1	–	–	–	28	130	117	102	92
6	2	1	–	–	29	141	127	111	100
7	4	2	0	–	30	152	137	120	109
8	6	4	2	0	31	163	148	130	118
9	8	6	3	2	32	175	159	141	128
10	11	8	5	3	33	188	171	151	138
11	14	11	7	5	34	201	183	162	149
12	17	14	10	7	35	214	195	174	160
13	21	17	13	10	36	228	208	186	171
14	26	21	16	13	37	242	222	198	183
15	30	25	20	16	38	256	235	211	195
16	36	30	24	19	39	271	250	224	208
17	41	35	28	23	40	287	264	238	221
18	47	40	33	28	41	303	279	252	234
19	54	46	38	32	42	319	295	267	248
20	60	52	43	37	43	336	311	281	262
21	68	59	49	43	44	353	327	297	277
22	75	66	56	49	45	371	344	313	292
23	83	73	62	55	46	389	361	329	307
24	92	81	69	61	47	408	379	345	323
25	101	90	77	68	48	427	397	362	339
26	110	98	85	76	49	446	415	380	356
27	120	107	93	84	50	466	434	398	373

*Dashes in the body of the table indicate that no decision is possible at the stated level of significance because the numbers of subjects are too small.

Greene and D'Oliveira (1999)

Table 5 Critical values of the Spearman rank correlation coefficient

One tailed Two tailed *n*	0.1 0.2	0.05 0.1	0.025 0.05	0.01 0.02	0.005 0.01
4	1.0000	1.0000	1.0000	1.0000	1.0000
5	0.7000	0.9000	0.9000	1.0000	1.0000
6	0.6571	0.7714	0.8286	0.9429	0.9429
7	0.5714	0.6786	0.7857	0.8571	0.8929
8	0.5476	0.6429	0.7381	0.8095	0.8571
9	0.4833	0.6000	0.6833	0.7667	0.8167
10	0.4424	0.5636	0.6485	0.7333	0.7818
11	0.4182	0.5273	0.6091	0.7000	0.7545
12	0.3986	0.5035	0.5874	0.6713	0.7273
13	0.3791	0.4780	0.5604	0.6484	0.6978
14	0.3670	0.4593	0.5385	0.6220	0.6747
15	0.3500	0.4429	0.5179	0.6000	0.6536
16	0.3382	0.4265	0.5029	0.5824	0.6324
17	0.3271	0.4124	0.4821	0.5577	0.6055
18	0.3170	0.4000	0.4683	0.5425	0.5897
19	0.3077	0.3887	0.4555	0.5285	0.5751
20	0.2992	0.3783	0.4438	0.5155	0.5614
21	0.2914	0.3687	0.4329	0.5034	0.5487
22	0.2841	0.3598	0.4227	0.4921	0.5368
23	0.2774	0.3515	0.4132	0.4815	0.5256
24	0.2711	0.3438	0.4044	0.4716	0.5151
25	0.2653	0.3365	0.3961	0.4622	0.5052
26	0.2598	0.3297	0.3882	0.4534	0.4958
27	0.2546	0.3233	0.3809	0.4451	0.4869
28	0.2497	0.3172	0.3739	0.4372	0.4785
29	0.2451	0.3115	0.3673	0.4297	0.4705
30	0.2407	0.3061	0.3610	0.4226	0.4629
31	0.2366	0.3009	0.3550	0.4158	0.4556
32	0.2327	0.2960	0.3494	0.4093	0.4487
33	0.2289	0.2913	0.3440	0.4032	0.4421
34	0.2254	0.2869	0.3388	0.3972	0.4357
35	0.2220	0.2826	0.3338	0.3916	0.4296
36	0.2187	0.2785	0.3291	0.3862	0.4238
37	0.2156	0.2746	0.3246	0.3810	0.4182
38	0.2126	0.2709	0.3202	0.3760	0.4128
39	0.2097	0.2673	0.3160	0.3712	0.4076
40	0.2070	0.2638	0.3120	0.3665	0.4026
41	0.2043	0.2605	0.3081	0.3621	0.3978
42	0.2018	0.2573	0.3044	0.3578	0.3932
43	0.1993	0.2542	0.3008	0.3536	0.3887
44	0.1970	0.2512	0.2973	0.3496	0.3843
45	0.1947	0.2483	0.2940	0.3457	0.3801
46	0.1925	0.2455	0.2907	0.3420	0.3761
47	0.1903	0.2429	0.2876	0.3384	0.3721
48	0.1883	0.2403	0.2845	0.3348	0.3683
49	0.1863	0.2377	0.2816	0.3314	0.3646
50	0.1843	0.2353	0.2787	0.3281	0.3610
60	0.1678	0.2144	0.2542	0.2997	0.3301
70	0.1550	0.1982	0.2352	0.2776	0.3060
80	0.1448	0.1852	0.2199	0.2597	0.2864
90	0.1364	0.1745	0.2072	0.2449	0.2702
100	0.1292	0.1654	0.1966	0.2324	0.2565

Dunstan et al (1988)

Table 6 Percentage points of Student's *t*-distribution (independent and related)

Two-tailed One-tailed	0.2 0.1	0.1 0.05	0.05 0.025	0.02 0.01	0.01 0.005	Two-tailed One-tailed	0.2 0.1	0.1 0.05	0.05 0.025	0.02 0.01	0.01 0.005
df						df					
1	3.078	6.314	12.706	31.821	63.657	29	1.311	1.699	2.045	2.462	2.756
2	1.886	2.920	4.303	6.965	9.925	30	1.310	1.697	2.042	2.457	2.750
3	1.638	2.353	3.182	4.541	5.841	31	1.309	1.696	2.040	2.453	2.744
4	1.533	2.132	2.776	3.747	4.604	32	1.309	1.694	2.037	2.449	2.738
5	1.476	2.015	2.571	3.365	4.032	33	1.308	1.692	2.035	2.445	2.733
6	1.440	1.943	2.447	3.143	3.707	34	1.307	1.691	2.032	2.441	2.728
7	1.415	1.895	2.365	2.998	3.499	35	1.306	1.690	2.030	2.438	2.724
8	1.397	1.860	2.306	2.896	3.355	36	1.306	1.688	2.028	2.434	2.719
9	1.383	1.833	2.262	2.821	3.250	37	1.305	1.687	2.026	2.431	2.715
10	1.372	1.812	2.228	2.764	3.169	38	1.304	1.686	2.024	2.429	2.712
11	1.363	1.796	2.201	2.718	3.106	39	1.304	1.685	2.023	2.426	2.708
12	1.356	1.782	2.179	2.681	3.055	40	1.303	1.684	2.021	2.423	2.704
13	1.350	1.771	2.160	2.650	3.012	45	1.301	1.679	2.014	2.412	2.690
14	1.345	1.761	2.145	2.624	2.977	50	1.299	1.676	2.009	2.403	2.678
15	1.341	1.753	2.131	2.602	2.947	55	1.297	1.673	2.004	2.396	2.668
16	1.337	1.746	2.120	2.583	2.921	60	1.296	1.671	2.000	2.390	2.660
17	1.333	1.740	2.110	2.567	2.898	65	1.295	1.669	1.997	2.385	2.654
18	1.330	1.734	2.101	2.552	2.878	70	1.294	1.667	1.994	2.381	2.648
19	1.328	1.729	2.093	2.539	2.861	75	1.293	1.665	1.992	2.377	2.643
20	1.325	1.725	2.086	2.528	2.845	80	1.292	1.664	1.990	2.374	2.639
21	1.323	1.721	2.080	2.518	2.831	85	1.292	1.663	1.988	2.371	2.635
22	1.321	1.717	2.074	2.508	2.819	90	1.291	1.662	1.987	2.368	2.632
23	1.319	1.714	2.069	2.500	2.807	95	1.291	1.661	1.985	2.366	2.629
24	1.318	1.711	2.064	2.492	2.797	100	1.290	1.660	1.984	2.364	2.626
25	1.316	1.708	2.060	2.485	2.787	125	1.288	1.657	1.979	2.357	2.616
26	1.315	1.706	2.056	2.479	2.779	150	1.287	1.655	1.976	2.351	2.609
27	1.314	1.703	2.052	2.473	2.771	200	1.286	1.653	1.972	2.345	2.601
28	1.313	1.701	2.048	2.467	2.763	∞	1.282	1.645	1.960	2.326	2.576

Dunstan et al (1988)

Table 7 Critical values of the Pearson's product moment correlation coefficient

	Level of significance for one-tailed test				
	0.1	0.05	0.025	0.01	0.005
	Level of significance for two-tailed test				
	0.2	0.1	0.05	0.02	0.01
n					
4	0.8000	0.9000	0.9500	0.9800	0.9900
5	0.6870	0.8054	0.8783	0.9343	0.9587
6	0.6084	0.7293	0.8114	0.8822	0.9172
7	0.5509	0.6694	0.7545	0.8329	0.8745
8	0.5067	0.6215	0.7067	0.7887	0.8343
9	0.4716	0.5822	0.6664	0.7498	0.7977
10	0.4428	0.5494	0.6319	0.7155	0.7646
11	0.4187	0.5214	0.6021	0.6851	0.7348
12	0.3981	0.4973	0.5760	0.6581	0.7079
13	0.3802	0.4762	0.5529	0.6339	0.6835
14	0.3646	0.4575	0.5324	0.6120	0.6614
15	0.3507	0.4409	0.5140	0.5923	0.6411
16	0.3383	0.4259	0.4973	0.5742	0.6226
17	0.3271	0.4124	0.4821	0.5577	0.6055
18	0.3170	0.4000	0.4683	0.5425	0.5897
19	0.3077	0.3887	0.4555	0.5285	0.5751
20	0.2992	0.3783	0.4438	0.5155	0.5614
21	0.2914	0.3687	0.4329	0.5034	0.5487
22	0.2841	0.3598	0.4227	0.4921	0.5368
23	0.2774	0.3515	0.4132	0.4815	0.5256
24	0.2711	0.3438	0.4044	0.4716	0.5151
25	0.2653	0.3365	0.3961	0.4622	0.5052
26	0.2598	0.3297	0.3882	0.4534	0.4958
27	0.2546	0.3233	0.3809	0.4451	0.4869
28	0.2497	0.3172	0.3739	0.4372	0.4785
29	0.2451	0.3115	0.3673	0.4297	0.4705
30	0.2407	0.3061	0.3610	0.4226	0.4629
31	0.2366	0.3009	0.3550	0.4158	0.4556
32	0.2327	0.2960	0.3494	0.4093	0.4487
33	0.2289	0.2913	0.3440	0.4032	0.4421
34	0.2254	0.2869	0.3388	0.3972	0.4357
35	0.2220	0.2826	0.3338	0.3916	0.4296
36	0.2187	0.2785	0.3291	0.3862	0.4238
37	0.2156	0.2746	0.3246	0.3810	0.4182
38	0.2126	0.2709	0.3202	0.3760	0.4128
39	0.2097	0.2673	0.3160	0.3712	0.4076
40	0.2070	0.2638	0.3120	0.3665	0.4026
41	0.2043	0.2605	0.3081	0.3621	0.3978
42	0.2018	0.2573	0.3044	0.3578	0.3932
43	0.1993	0.2542	0.3008	0.3536	0.3887
44	0.1970	0.2512	0.2973	0.3496	0.3843
45	0.1947	0.2483	0.2940	0.3457	0.3801
46	0.1925	0.2455	0.2907	0.3420	0.3761
47	0.1903	0.2429	0.2876	0.3384	0.3721
48	0.1883	0.2403	0.2845	0.3348	0.3683
49	0.1863	0.2377	0.2816	0.3314	0.3646
50	0.1843	0.2353	0.2787	0.3281	0.3610
60	0.1678	0.2144	0.2542	0.2997	0.3301
70	0.1550	0.1982	0.2352	0.2776	0.3060
80	0.1448	0.1852	0.2199	0.2597	0.2864
90	0.1364	0.1745	0.2072	0.2449	0.2702
100	0.1292	0.1654	0.1966	0.2324	0.2565

Dunstan et al (1988)

Table 8 Random digits
The table gives 2500 random digits, from 0 to 9, arranged for convenience in blocks of 5

87024	74221	69721	44518	58804	04860	18127	16855	61558	15430
04852	03436	72753	99836	37513	91341	53517	92094	54386	44563
33592	45845	52015	72030	23071	92933	84219	39455	57792	14216
68121	53688	56812	34869	28573	51079	94677	23993	88241	97735
25062	10428	43930	69033	73395	83469	25990	12971	73728	03856
78183	44396	11064	92153	96293	00825	21079	78337	19739	13684
70209	23316	32828	00927	61841	64754	91125	01206	06691	50868
94342	91040	94035	02650	36284	91162	07950	36178	42536	49869
92503	29854	24116	61149	49266	82303	54924	58251	23928	20703
71646	57503	82416	22657	72359	30085	13037	39608	77439	49318
51809	70780	41544	27828	84321	07714	25865	97896	01924	62028
88504	21620	07292	71021	80929	45042	08703	45894	24521	49942
33186	49273	87542	41086	29615	81101	43707	87031	36101	15137
40068	35043	05280	62921	30122	65119	40512	26855	40842	83244
76401	68461	20711	12007	19209	28259	49820	76415	51534	63574
47014	93729	74235	47808	52473	03145	92563	05837	70023	33169
67147	48017	90741	53647	55007	36607	29360	83163	79024	26155
86987	62924	93157	70947	07336	49541	81386	26968	38311	99885
58973	47026	78574	08804	22960	32850	67944	92303	61216	72948
71635	86749	40369	94639	40731	54012	03972	98581	45604	34885
60971	54212	32596	03052	84150	36798	62635	26210	95685	87089
06599	60910	66315	96690	19039	39878	44688	65146	02482	73130
89960	27162	66264	71024	18708	77974	40473	87155	35834	03114
03930	56898	61900	44036	90012	17673	54167	82396	39468	49566
31338	28729	02095	07429	35718	86882	37513	51560	08872	33717
29782	33287	27400	42915	49914	68221	56088	06112	95481	30094
68493	88796	94771	89418	62045	40681	15941	05962	44378	64349
42534	31925	94158	90197	62874	53659	33433	48610	14698	54761
76126	41049	43363	52461	00552	93352	58497	16347	87145	73668
80434	73037	69008	36801	25520	14161	32300	04187	80668	07499
81301	39731	53857	19690	39998	49829	12399	70867	44498	17385
54521	42350	82908	51212	70208	39891	64871	67448	42988	32600
82530	22869	87276	06678	36873	61198	87748	07531	29592	39612
81338	64309	45798	42954	95565	02789	83017	82936	67117	17709
58264	60374	32610	17879	96900	68029	06993	84288	35401	56317
77023	46829	21332	77383	15547	29332	77698	89878	20489	71800
29750	59902	78110	59018	87548	10225	15774	70778	56086	08117
08288	38411	69886	64918	29055	87607	37452	38174	31431	46173
93908	94810	22057	94240	89918	16561	92716	66461	22337	64718
06341	25883	42574	80202	57287	95120	69332	19036	43326	98697
23240	94741	55622	79479	34606	51079	09476	10695	49618	63037
96370	19171	40441	05002	33165	28693	45027	73791	23047	32976
97050	16194	61095	26533	81738	77032	60551	31605	95212	81078
40833	12169	10712	78345	48236	45086	61654	94929	69169	70561
95676	13582	25664	60838	88071	50052	63188	50346	65618	17517
28030	14185	13226	99566	45483	10079	22945	23903	11695	10694
60202	32586	87466	83357	95516	31258	66309	40615	30572	60842
46530	48755	02308	79508	53422	50805	08896	06963	93922	99423
53151	95839	01745	46462	81463	28669	60179	17880	75875	34562
80272	64398	88249	06792	98424	66842	49129	98939	34173	49883

Dunstan et al (1988)

Choosing a statistical test

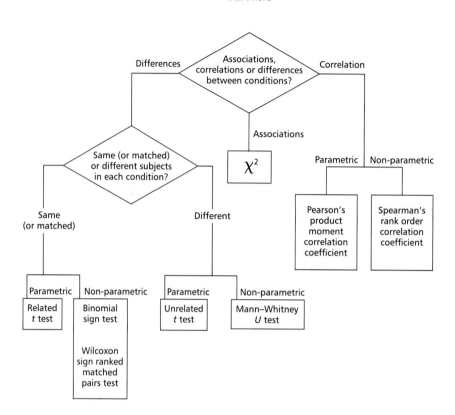

Start here

Associations, correlations or differences between conditions?

Differences

Same (or matched) or different subjects in each condition?

Same (or matched)

Parametric
Related *t* test

Non-parametric
Binomial sign test

Wilcoxon sign ranked matched pairs test

Different

Parametric
Unrelated *t* test

Non-parametric
Mann–Whitney *U* test

Associations

χ^2

Correlation

Parametric
Pearson's product moment correlation coefficient

Non-parametric
Spearman's rank order correlation coefficient

glossary

Abstinence syndrome See **withdrawal.**

Actualisation An important concept in humanistic psychology, meaning the achievement of one's potential.

Addiction Now little used term that referred to physical dependence and was associated with its negative effects, such as on social functioning.

Alcoholism Physical dependency on alcohol.

Alternative hypothesis, H_1 or H_A A testable statement that proposes the expected outcome of the study, it is a prediction based on the researcher's knowledge from observations, related studies and previous investigations.

Amplitude The aspect of a wave form that is related to the absolute size of the stimulus. For sound, this is the volume or intensity and is the magnitude of the air pressure change.

Anger management A programme designed to teach individuals how to apply self-control in order to reduce anger against others.

Anonymity A state for an individual within a crowd where each person loses their sense of individuality.

Antecedent control A behavioural measure in which the intervention occurs before the behaviour arises. Antecedent procedures include education, attitude change and inducing or preventing behaviours by controlling the triggers which cause them to occur.

Antisocial personality disorder Commonly called 'psychopathy', this condition is characterised by lack of conscience and empathy, and is associated with violent criminality.

Anxiety An unpleasant state involving high physiological arousal and fearful thoughts.

Appraisal A judgement about whether a potentially stressful situation is threatening, challenging or harmful.

Attachment A two-way bond between two individuals (humans or some other animal species), in which each individual gains a sense of security from the other.

Attachment theory A **psychodynamic** approach to developmental psychology, which places a lot of emphasis on the formation of a secure **attachment** between infant and **primary carer**(s).

Attitude An evaluation, with cognitive and affective components, that relates to a specific aspect of the world and which affects our behaviour in relation to that person, idea, object or issue.

Attribution The cognitive process in which we try to explain the causes of behaviour, our own or someone else's.

Attribution theory A theory that seeks to explain the causes of behaviour in terms of either dispositional (personality) factors or situational factors.

Attributional bias In **attribution theory**, common faults in attributing causes to behaviour such that mistakes are made and the causes of behaviour are misunderstood. An example is self-serving bias in which we attribute our own good and worthy behaviours to personality factors (I gave my mum a bunch of flowers because I am kind) and any bad or unworthy behaviours to situational factors (I shouted at mum because I've got a headache).

Auditory adaptation The tendency of repeated or continuous sounds to appear less loud over time. As we habituate to the stimulus of the sound its apparent loudness decreases.

Auditory fatigue Occurs on exposure to intense sounds which cause a persistent reduction in apparent loudness.

Autocratic Behaviour In the context of leadership or coaching, dictatorial and undemocratic behaviour.

Bar chart This is used to display nominal data and average scores in the form of a graph. There are gaps between each bar that is plotted on the graph.

Bar-and-whisker plot This is used to display the median and interquartile range in the form of a graph. The bar represents the median while the whiskers show the upper and lower quartiles.

Behaviour modification A technique based on the use of **operant conditioning** to change behaviour. The **token economy** is a form of behaviour modification sometimes used in prisons.

Behavioural psychology An approach to psychology that emphasises the learning of behaviour.

Between subjects design see **Independent groups design**.

Bi-polar adjectives These are used as part of the Semantic Differential questionnaire design. These are pairs of words with opposite meaning (eg good–bad, ugly–beautiful).

Binomial sign test A non-parametric inferential statistical test. Used when you have nominal data, the research is repeated

483

measures (or matched pairs) and you are looking for a difference in the effect each level of the independent variable has on the dependent variable.

Biomedical A way of looking at mental disorder, characterised by an emphasis on biological aspects of a condition (bio) and the processes of diagnosis and treatment (medical).

Bottom-up approach In the context of **offender profiling**, an approach that starts from the available evidence from the crimes committed by a particular offender (the 'bottom') and attempts to look for connections and links between them that will give a clue to the characteristics of the criminal.

Brief A description given to participants to indicate what will be expected of them during a study and to describe its general purpose so that they can give their informed consent to participate. It should also state their right to withdraw at any time.

British Crime Survey A regular, large, face-to-face survey of adults living in private households in England and Wales. Its main purpose is to monitor trends in crime but it also covers a range of other topics such as attitudes to crime.

Bullshit A term used in Gestalt therapy to mean the self-defensive distortions to our perception of our own behaviour.

Case study An in-depth analysis of an individual or a 'unit' of individuals (eg a family).

Castration anxiety The anxiety that boys suffer during the Oedipus complex that their rivalrous father may castrate them.

Catharsis A term used in psychodynamic psychology to mean the release of emotion. An example would be crying to release sadness.

Checklist A simple list of all the behaviours being recorded. On every occurrence of a behaviour on the list, a single tally is recorded. At the end of the observation period, the observer has a record of the number of occurrences of each of the behaviours being investigated.

Chi-squared (χ^2) test of association A non-parametric inferential statistical test. Used when you have nominal data, the research is independent groups and you are looking for an association between the independent variable and the dependent variable.

CID Criminal Investigation Department, a branch of the British police force.

Closed questions Questions that have set answers for participants to choose from.

Closure A term used in Gestalt therapy to mean the emotional experience of moving on from a past trauma.

Cognitive-behavioural programmes Programmes designed to modify behaviour by changing attitudes and thoughts.

Collectivist society A society characterised by a high level of mutual interdependence between individuals.

Comfortable Interpersonal Distance Scale A non-invasive method used to measure people's **personal space**.

Community environmental design Differs from **urban renewal** because these projects allow the current residents in the area to have an input in the redesign of the area.

Concurrent validity An indicator of **validity**, which compares measures of the same phenomenon to determine whether they produce similar results in the same circumstances.

Confounding variables Uncontrolled variables that could disrupt the effect of the phenomenon under investigation.

Consequent control A behavioural measure in which the intervention follows the behaviour to be changed. Consequent procedures can affect behaviours by using pleasant or unpleasant consequences (positive or negative reinforcement or punishment) to make their performance more or less likely or through the use of feedback.

Constant errors Uncontrolled variables that act on only one level of the **independent variable**. Their action may either be in the same direction as a predicted difference, exaggerating the apparent effect of the IV or in the opposite direction, obscuring the effect of the IV.

Construct validity An indicator of **validity**, which aims to demonstrate that the phenomenon being measured actually exists, for example, by justifying it in relation to a model or theory.

Content analysis Examination of certain types of media (e.g. books, TV, magazines, the Internet) to see what effect they may be having on our perceptions and/or behaviour. It involves the analysis of language, certain words or certain activities that appear in the chosen media.

Contextual reinstatement In the context of criminal psychology, a way of improving memory for an event by returning to the place where it happened or asking the witness to imagine themselves back in that place and in the same emotional state.

Control condition In some situations an experimenter does not want to compare two alternative levels of the IV but instead wishes to observe the effect of the presence or absence of a variable. In this instance there is an experimental condition and a *control condition*, the latter being a situation in which the variable under consideration is absent.

Controls The steps taken to limit factors that could distort the collection of valid and reliable data.

Coping A person's efforts to minimise, control or tolerate environmental demands that are judged to exceed their resources to fight or avoid.

Copycat crimes A slang term for crimes that appear to mimic another crime. Typically this refers to well-publicised crimes that are then imitated by another individual.

Correlation A relationship between two measured variables.

Counterbalancing The systematic variation of the order of presentation of the levels of the IV in a **repeated measures design**.

Counterfactual thinking Thinking about events that did not actually take place, such as winning when we in fact lost.

Critical value The value that is compared with the observed (calculated) value in an inferential statistical test. Each inferential statistical test has a table or tables of critical values. The comparison with the observed (calculated) allows you to conclude if you have found a significant result.

Cross tolerance This phenomenon arises in some drug categories, such as the opiates (heroin, morphine etc) and tryptamines (LSD, mescaline and psilocybin) when the prolonged use of one drug in the group results in the development of tolerance to the others opioids.

Cross-cultural study A study conducted across two or more cultures in order to make comparisons between them.

Crowd May refer to a large, cohesive gathering of individuals or to the act of coming together to form a tightly-spaced group. In addition, crowding is used to refer to the psychological perceptions associated with this increase in density.

Cultural relativism In the context of atypical psychology, the acknowledgement that symptoms may differ across cultures.

Culture A shared system of beliefs, values and ways of seeing the world, characterising a group of people such as a regional or ethnic group.

Culture-bound syndrome A mental disorder that appears to be confined to the members of a particular cultural group.

Day-care Any form of care of an infant or child that does not involve the **primary carer**. Ranges from care from other family members to nursery care.

Debrief A procedure that follows participation in a study. It ensures that participants are aware that they have taken part and are offered the opportunity to discuss their experience, withdraw their consent retrospectively or ask for their data to be destroyed. It also allows the researcher to ensure that the participants fully understand the purpose and expected outcome of the research and to monitor any unforeseen negative effects or misconceptions.

Decibels (dB) A measure of volume (sound intensity).

Defensible space An area that we clearly mark out as being owned by ourselves. Other people should perceive the area as being clearly owned.

Deindividuation A process through which group members cease to pay attention to individuals as individuals so losing their self-consciousness and with it the belief that they are accountable for their own actions – moral responsibility shifts from the individual to the group.

Delinquency Criminal/antisocial activity.

Delusion Characteristic of certain mental disorders. For example, schizophrenia (a delusion) is an irrational belief that one is someone else.

Demand characteristics The features of an experiment that inform participants about the aim and influence their behaviour independently of the experimental objectives and thereby confound the results.

Dependent variable (DV) The measurable outcome in an experiment. It is called the *dependent* variable because the alternative hypothesis predicts that any changes in this variable are caused by (ie dependent upon) changes in the **independent variable**.

Deprivation The separation of an infant from its **primary carer**. Can be short-term as in **daycare** or long-term as occurs in family **re-ordering**.

Design An experiment aims to investigate whether the **independent variable** produces a change in the **dependent variable**. We therefore need either to compare the effects of the independent variable for participants in different conditions or to observe differences in the dependent variable for the same participants experiencing each of the different levels of the IV. These alternatives are essentially the different formal designs used in experiments.

Diathesis-stress model An approach that explains mental disorder in terms of a combination of genetic vulnerability (diathesis) and environmental stress.

Diffusion of responsibility Occurs in groups when an individual feels less accountable because there are other people around; the responsibility is shared (ie diffused) so no particular individual feels responsible.

Directional hypotheses (one-tailed hypotheses)

These indicate the nature of an effect, for instance stating which condition in an experiment will affect the results the most or in a particular way (making them 'better' or 'worse'). In a correlation, a directional hypothesis predicts whether the relationship will be positive or negative.

Discounting principle In **attribution theory**, the tendency to discount all but the most obvious cause as a reason for behaviour. If, for example, there were black ice on the road, the cause of a car accident would be attributed to the ice rather than to carelessness.

Discourse analysis A research method associated with the social constructionist approach to psychology, discourse analysis involves 'unpacking' hidden meanings in discourse – what people say or write.

Dual bar chart Used to display nominal data where more than one category can be plotted on the same axis.

Earwitness testimony Testimony produced by a witness based on what they have heard. This may, for example, involve identifying a particular voice.

Ecological (external) validity The extent to which a test measures a real-world phenomenon.

Ego orientation A focus on winning.

Emotion-focused coping Aims to manage the negative effects of stress on the individual.

Equivalent forms May be used to establish **reliability** by using different but comparable versions of the same test. These are used with a single group of participants whose results on each version should correlate strongly if the tests are reliable.

Estimator variables In witness testimony, those variables that affect the accuracy of witness testimony but over which the police (and justice system in general) have no control. These may include variables such as the witness's eyesight, the weather and the amount of time the witness viewed the scene.

Ethnocentrism The practice of researching or theorising from the perspective of a particular ethnic or national group.

Event sampling An observational recording method in which observation, timing and recording are continuous. The onset and end of each behavioural event is recorded along a single time base.

Evolutionary psychology An approach to explaining human behaviour based on the principles of evolution, thus typical human behaviours are explained as having evolved because they convey an evolutionary advantage on that individual or others.

Experimenter expectancy effect See **investigator effect**.

Experiments These serve to investigate a causal relationship; whether one factor affects another. This is achieved by systematically varying one factor, the **independent variable**, while observing the effect of that change on another factor, the **dependent variable**. So, in an experiment, the independent variable is manipulated to create two or more levels and consequent changes in the dependent variable are measured. In addition, other factors that might affect the dependent variable should be controlled, that is kept constant across different conditions of the independent variable. This ensures that any difference in the dependent variable between conditions is the result of the IV and not due to other, chance, variations.

External validity See **ecological validity**.

Extrinsic motivation Motivation based on a tangible reward.

Eysenck Personality Inventory A personality test designed to measure the traits of extroversion and neuroticism.

Face validity An indicator of validity based on whether the measure *appears* (at *face value*) to test what it claims to.

Factor analysis A mathematical technique which shows us what types of behaviour occur in the same people and therefore make up a personality trait.

Fatigue effects Arise when participants become tired or bored if they repeat a repetitive or demanding task, so their performance worsens in later conditions.

FBI Federal Bureau of Investigation; a branch of the American police force.

Feminism A social movement united by the belief that women are socially disadvantaged as compared to men. In atypical psychology, feminists have pointed to the role of social disadvantage in the origins of disorders such as depression.

Field experiments Studies with an experimental design (they have an IV and DV) that take place using participants in their normal surroundings.

Flashbulb memory The type of memory allegedly associated with an emotionally arousing event. The name derives from the analogy that it is as if a flashbulb picture had been taken of the event causing an indelible impression in the mind.

Focused observations Direct the observers' attention to a limited number of behavioural events.

Forward-up equivalence A map orientation such that there is direct correspondence between the map and the real world – what is ahead on the road is 'up' on the map and features to the left on the map are on the left-hand side of the road.

Free association A psychodynamic technique in which a patient is encouraged to talk at will, allowing them to make their own connections between events and allowing preconscious material to come to consciousness.

Frequency polygon Used to display the distribution of scores for two groups or more on the same graph. Sometimes called a line graph.

Frequency This is the time between the peak of one wave and the next. For sound, frequency represents pitch; sound waves with a lower frequency are 'deeper'. Frequency is measured in Hertz or 'cycles per second'.

Fundamental attribution error In **attribution theory**, the tendency to overemphasise the importance of dispositional factors and underestimate the influence of situational factors as a cause of someone's behaviour. For example, if someone we do not know well speaks rather sharply to us, we are more likely to believe that they are a grumpy, bad-tempered individual than that they are very tired.

Generalisability The extent to which findings based on the investigation of a sample of participants are representative of the whole of the original population or of other populations.

Habituation The relative insensitivity to repeated stimuli such as monotonous sounds.

Health behaviours Activities that maintain or improve health.

Health habits Firmly established detrimental health related behaviours that may become so automatic that they are performed without awareness.

Health promotion Refers to strategies that aim to enable people to gain control of, and therefore enhance, their own health through lifestyle changes and preventative practices.

Hearing threshold The quietest sound that an individual can detect.

Hedonistic relevance In **attribution theory**, it applies to the fact that when the consequences of an event are serious, we are more likely to make a dispositional attribution than a situational one. It is an **attributional bias**.

Hertz A measure of frequency, cycles per second.

Histogram Used to display the distribution of scores for one set of data. The data must be numerical and there should be no gaps between the bars.

Home advantage effect The advantage teams have when playing at their home stadium.

Hypothesis A testable statement, expressing the **aims** of a study, which can be accepted or rejected to indicate the outcome of the research. It must be possible to gather evidence that will demonstrate that a hypothesis is either supported or refuted.

Iceberg profile The classic profile of an elite athlete on POMS, in which the athlete is lower than average on all measures except vigour, on which they are higher.

Identikit picture A device for building up a composite portrait from a large number of different features, such as a selection of eyes, noses, chins and so on. It is used as a means of assisting a witness to provide a likeness of someone sought by the police.

Identity parade A number of individuals (usually presented in a line – a 'line-up') from whom a witness selects the one they identify as the person sought by the police.

Impersonality A state in which individuals lose their appreciation of themselves and others as people.

Independent groups designs Used in experiments when separate groups of individuals participate in the different levels of the IV, that is the data sets relating to each level of the IV are *independent* of each other. This is also referred to as a *between subjects* or *unrelated design* since comparisons are being made *between* groups rather than within them and the data points in one level of the IV are *unrelated* in any specific way to the data points for other levels.

Independent t-test A parametric inferential statistical test. Used when you have interval or ratio data, the research is independent groups and you are looking for a difference in the effect each level of the independent variable has on the dependent variable.

Independent variable (IV) The factor that is manipulated in an experiment. By controlling either the nature of the participants, their experiences or the way data are selected for analysis, the experimenter generates levels of the IV. These levels or 'conditions' are used to compare the effects of the variable under investigation.

Individualism In the context of mental disorder, the tendency to treat mental disorder as occurring within the mind of the individual, thus disregarding the role of social processes (for example, social construction, labelling).

Individualist society A society characterised by a low level of mutual interdependence between individuals.

Insight An important concept in psychodynamic psychology; an awareness of one's own thoughts and emotions, and their origins.

Instinct A predisposition to behave in a certain way, present from birth rather than acquired by experience.

Institutionalisation In the context of atypical psychology, the tendency of patients kept in institutions for long periods to become adapted to institutional life to the extent that it becomes difficult to adjust to life outside the institution.

Inter-observer reliability A measure of the extent to which different individuals generate the same records when they observe the same sequence of behaviour. By correlating the scores of observers we can measure inter-observer reliability: individuals (or groups) with highly correlated scores are demonstrating good inter-observer reliability.

Interactional theories Approaches that see behaviour as a product of an interaction between the situation and the personality of the person in that situation.

Internal validity The validity of test items themselves in relation to the objective.

Interquartile range The spread of scores for the middle 50 per cent of scores.

Interval data Data where the gaps between one point and the next are equivalent.

Interview Usually a verbal research method where the participant answers a series of questions.

Intrinsic motivation Motivation based on taking pleasure in an activity rather than on a tangible reward.

Investigator effect (experimenter expectancy effect) A bias resulting from a prejudgement by the researcher that subsequently affects the way in which the participants behave. It is sometimes called the experimenter expectancy effect because it is the effect of the experimenter's expectations that affect the behaviour of the participants.

Items analysis A technique used to make a questionnaire more reliable. It eliminates questions or items that do not discriminate between a high and low score on your questionnaire.

Jet lag This is the fatigue experienced by air travellers as a consequence of crossing time zones, which results in their circadian rhythm becoming desynchronised from the local zeitgebers.

Just world hypothesis The assumption that the world is a fair and just place in which people get what they deserve, such that the deserving get rewarded and the undeserving get punished. In relation to criminal psychology, it is used to account for the fact that victims (especially rape victims) are often blamed for their fate.

Laboratory experiments These are conducted in a laboratory or other contrived setting away from the participants' normal environment. The experimenter is able to manipulate the levels of the independent variable and accurately record changes in the dependent variable. In addition, considerable control can be exercised over potential confounding variables.

Leading questions Questions that are liable to encourage a certain answer, for example, 'Did you see the stop sign?' which implies that a stop sign was present at the scene.

Learned helplessness A failure to exert control over one's own situation even when it becomes possible, because prior learning has taught that attempts at control are not effective.

Learning The acquisition of knowledge and skills from the environment.

Level of measurement This describes the type of scale against which a variable is being assessed. In any study it must be possible to measure the observed effect of the variable being investigated. The data collected about a variable may be used in many different ways. In any situation, the data generated by the study can be classified into one of four types: **nominal**, **ordinal**, **interval** or **ratio**.

Level of significance The probability we set (p-value) that makes us believe the results are due to the independent variable and not due to chance. This is usually $p \leqslant 0.05$.

Likert scale A common form of questionnaire design. It is a series of statements usually with a choice of answers ranging from strongly agree to strongly disagree.

Line-up See **identity parade.**

Locus of control A dimension of personality that involves the extent to which people see the results of their actions as either under their own control (referred to as having an *internal* locus of control) or as being due to circumstances outside of them (referred to as having an *external* locus of control).

Longtudinal study A research method used to investigate changes that occur as individuals age, that follows a single group of participants over time. The length of the study is dictated by the development of interest so may span many months or years. Such studies may employ questionnaires, interviews or observations and often use a battery of tests that are repeated at fixed intervals.

Loudness A measure of the perceived intensity of the sound. Loudness approximately doubles as volume increases ten-fold.

Lower quartile The data point that is at the 25 per cent point of your data set when in rank order.

Maladaptive behaviour Behaviour that is harmful to the individual, as opposed to adaptive behaviour, which benefits the individual in some way.

Mann–Whitney U-test A non-parametric inferential statistical test. Used when you have ordinal data, the research is independent groups and you are looking for a difference in the effect each level of the independent variable has on the dependent variable.

Matched pairs design In this experimental design, scores are obtained for each level of the IV from different participants (as in an independent groups design). However, for each member of one group there exists in the other group an individual with certain characteristics in common. The groups are created by ensuring that every participant is part of a *matched pair*; two individuals who have been selected because they share features of importance to the experiment.

Mean A measure of average where you add up all of the scores and divide by the number of scores you have. It is best used on data that are interval or ratio. Can be affected by extreme scores.

Median A measure of average where you rank the data from smallest to largest and find the mid-point of the ranked data. It is best used on data that are ordinal and where there are extreme scores (the median is unaffected by extreme scores).

Mental illness A term meaning mental disorder, 'mental illness' is now rarely used because it is so theoretically biased towards the biomedical model of mental disorder.

Meta-analysis A statistical technique that involves combining the results of previous studies in order to be able to analyse data from a large number of participants.

Metarepresentation The cognitive ability to be aware of one's own mental processes.

Mock juries These consist of a group of participants who are asked to behave as if they were members of a jury and make appropriate decisions about guilt/innocence and sentencing.

Mode A measure of average where you find out which is the most common category. It is best used on nominal data.

Mood disorders A category of mental disorders, characterised by their dramatic effect on the mood of sufferers. Mood may be characterised by depression or its opposite, mania.

Multiaxial diagnosis The process now employed in the DSM system whereby patients are assessed on a number of medical and social criteria, as well as their clinical condition.

Narrow-band A theory of personality that aims to identify one specific aspect of behaviour rather than to explain personality in its entirety.

Natural experiments **Quasi-experiments** in which the researcher cannot control the IV at all: the levels are derived from pre-existing and naturally occurring differences. The researcher can neither control allocation of participants to conditions nor when or how those conditions arise.

Naturalistic observation A study in which the researcher gathers data by watching participants (people or non-human animals) in their normal environment which may not, necessarily, be their 'natural' situation.

Negative correlation A relationship between two measured variables where as one measure increases the other measure decreases.

Negative reinforcer Used in **operant conditioning** programmes, it involves the removal of an unpleasant stimulus after a response as a way of increasing the strength of the response. An example is locking someone in their cell and only releasing them when they behave appropriately.

Neuroanatomy The structure of the nervous system.

Neurotic Emotionally unstable, moody and anxious.

Noise Sounds which are unpleasant. The presence of a sound is necessary but not sufficient to produce noise; a noise must in addition be 'unwanted'.

Nominal data Data that are in categories.

Non-directional hypotheses (two-tailed hypotheses) These are used when researchers can only predict that the variable(s) under investigation *will* affect the outcome rather making a more precise judgement about *how* the results will be affected. A non-directional hypothesis simply states that there will be a difference between conditions or a link between variables.

Non-parametric tests Inferential statistical tests where there is no assumption about the data collected. Usually used on data that are nominal or ordinal.

Non-participant observation This requires that the observer is unseen so that they cannot affect the behaviour of the participants. This might be achieved by being a long way away or by being hidden from the observed.

Non-representative sampling A technique for selecting participants from a population which cannot guarantee that the full range of diversity that exists within that population will be accessed when a sample is obtained. Those individuals who are unavailable may share an important criterion that will, as a consequence, be under-represented in the sample.

Normal distribution A distribution that is represented on a graph by a 'bell-shaped' curve.

Null hypothesis In any study, it must be possible for the alternative hypothesis to be contradicted by the findings. When this is the case, the H_1 is rejected but we still need a conclusion. This conclusion must be that our findings are not the consequence of the predicted effect but, instead, are due to chance. This possibility is expressed by the null hypothesis.

Object relations theory A loose collection of psychoanalytic theories characterised by their emphasis on the importance of the first relationship.

Observational learning Learning that takes place as a result of an individual observing the behaviour of another (usually referred to as a model) rather than through direct experience. This is a form of vicarious learning.

Observed (calculated) value The value that your collected data creates after an inferential statistical test. It is compared to the critical value to see if the result is significant.

Occupational noise The unpleasant sounds to which people are exposed in the workplace.

Offender profiling A technique used to provide a description of an offender based on an analysis of the crime scene and the activities involved in the crime itself. It was originally coined by the FBI.

One-tailed hypothesis See **directional hypothesis**.

Open questions Questions where there are no set answers so the participant can write an answer in or reply freely in an interview.

Operant conditioning Learning by the consequences of actions.

Operational definition A description that serves to put a variable into *operation*, that is, to make it usable. It identifies variables by factors that can be manipulated or measured, for instance because they are observable. It provides a framework for improving reliability both within and between observers.

Operationalisation The process of systematically changing a variable or making a variable measurable using an operational definition.

Opportunity sampling A technique for selecting participants based on the section of the population available at a given time. It is

non-representative because the full diversity of people within the population may not be available.

Order effects **Constant errors** that arise as a result of the order in which levels of the independent variable are presented to participants.

Ordinal data Data that can be ranked in order, but it is uncertain whether the gap between one data point and the next is equivalent (eg questionnaire scores from a Likert scale).

Ozone An oxygen molecule consisting of three, rather than two, atoms (O_3). It forms a layer high in the Earth's atmosphere that protects us from some of the harmful rays from the sun.

p-value Represents the probability of something happening by chance. *p*-values range from 0 to 1, with 0 representing no influence of chance and 1 representing a complete influence of chance. They are written as proportions, e.g. $p \leq 0.05$.

Parametric tests Inferential statistical tests that make assumptions about the data collected. These assumptions are (1) that the data are normally distributed for the population(s) used in the research from which you have drawn your sample, (2) data from both levels of the independent variable have equal variance, and (3) the data are from interval or ratio scales.

Paratelic state A motivational state in which arousal is sought.

Participant observation Ensures that the participants are unaware of the presence of an observer by their being disguised as a legitimate member of the situation.

Participant reactivity See **responder bias**.

Participant variables Confounding effects that arise from the characteristics of the people performing in a study, such as their age, gender, state of hunger or level of arousal.

Pearson's product moment correlation coefficient A parametric inferential statistical test. Used when you have interval or ratio data, the research is correlational and you are looking for a linear relationship between the two measured variables.

Personal space A 'bubble' that surrounds us that we do not like people to trespass within. The bubble changes according to the situation we find ourselves in. It helps regulate interactions we have with other people.

Personalisation The process of bringing personal belongings into work to make your work space an individual area. Items may include photographs or trinkets.

Personality profiling Measurement of an individual on several different personality traits and/or mood states.

Personality A set of characteristics, including patterns of thinking, emotion and behaviour that distinguish one individual from another.

Photospreads An array of photographs offered to a witness from which they are asked to identify the person they saw.

Physical dependence A compulsion to keep taking drugs such as alcohol, heroin, cocaine or tranquillisers that results from regular use. For a dependent user, sudden absence of the drug results in withdrawal. This term has largely replaced the term *addiction*.

Pilot study A scaled-down pre-run of an experiment used to test the method and identify any uncontrolled variables. The results obtained from these participants do not contribute to the final analysis.

Placebo An inert substance administered in place of a drug to 'blind' participants, that is, ones who are unaware that they are not receiving a real drug. A placebo can thus act as a control.

Pollution Contamination with poisonous or harmful substances.

Population (or target population) The group to which the results of the study are intended to relate and from which those individuals selected to participate in the study will be drawn. A population consists of all of the cases within a given definition from which the sample is selected and it thus includes only those individuals who it was possible to access.

Positive correlation A relationship between two measured variables where as one measure increases the other measured variable increases too.

Positive reinforcer Used in **operant conditioning** programmes, it involves offering something pleasant after a response as a way of increasing the strength of a response.

Post-event information Information given after an event has taken place (and which may influence a witness's memory for events beforehand).

Practice effects These arise if participants become more skilled in familiar tasks, so their performance improves in later conditions.

Predictive validity An indicator of **validity** based on whether a test can accurately predict future performance on the measure in question.

Predominant activity sampling (P/A) A time sampling technique in which observation is continuous and an estimate is made in relation to the activity that occupied most of the preceding time interval.

Primary appraisal An initial impression of a potentially stressful situation which generates emotions in relation to the judgement.

Primary carer The individual or individuals that take primary responsibility for the care of an infant. The primary carer is often the biological mother, but many psychologists prefer to only use the term 'mother' when referring to the biological mother.

Primary prevention Refers to strategies aimed at preventing disease in currently healthy individuals, by developing good health habits and discouraging poor ones.

Primary territory A type of **territory** where there is a high degree of occupation and perception of ownership. An example would be your house.

Privation The failure to form a normal infant-carer **attachment**.

Problem-focused coping Aims to reduce the causes of stress.

Prosocial behaviour Behaviour that is judged to be beneficial to other individuals.

Prospective study A study in which participants are followed up following a particular period or event to see whether or not that period or event appears to impact on later development. This is a superior, although more time-consuming method than the alternative **retrospective study**.

Psychiatry The branch of medicine devoted to the diagnosis, explanation and treatment of mental disorder. Note that unlike psychologists, psychiatrists are medical doctors.

Psychoanalysis A body of theory and therapeutic technique based on a **psychodynamic** understanding of human behaviour, cognition and emotion. Psychoanalysis exists mostly outside psychology, although psychoanalytic ideas are very useful in many areas of child psychology.

Psychodynamic A broad approach to explaining human behaviour, cognition and emotion based on the assumption that adults are influenced by unconscious processes that relate to childhood experience. A psychodynamic understanding of child development draws heavily on **psychoanalysis** but is not synonymous with it.

Psychological dependence Arises when a user believes that they need to keep taking the drug in order to function.

Psychosis Mental disorder, characterised by distortions of subjective reality, including delusions and hallucinations.

Psychotherapy A term meaning mental disorder or the study of mental disorder.

Public territory A type of **territory** where there is a low degree of occupation and perception of ownership. An example would be an area on the beach.

Quasi-experiment An experimental design in which control cannot be exercised over the allocation of participants to levels of the IV or over any aspect of the IV.

Questionnaire A research method that is usually written. There are many types of questionnaire design, for example the Likert scale, semantic differentials, Thurstone method and open and closed questions.

Quota sampling A technique for obtaining participants by selecting individuals from each chosen stratum of a population by questioning any available individuals. As time progresses, individuals are encountered who fulfil the requirements. When the target sample size for a subgroup has been met, further similar individuals are rejected. Sampling continues until sufficient numbers in each category have been obtained.

Random errors These are caused by uncontrolled variables which act in unsystematic ways.

Random sampling A technique for selecting participants such that each member of the population has an equal chance of being chosen.

Randomisation A technique used to minimise the effects of practice and fatigue by allocating participants to randomised orders for participation in each condition.

Range The spread of scores from the highest score to the lowest score plus one.

Ratio data Data taken from a universal scale that has a true zero point (eg Kelvin measurement for temperature).

Re-ordering Changes to structure of a family, for example divorce, separation and re-marriage.

Reappraisal This may follow the secondary appraisal of a potentially stressful situation, based on new information. This may reduce the judgement of a situation from stressful to benign or suggest that a previously innocent situation is threatening.

Recidivism Relapsing into crime (usually refers to habitual relapse).

Reductionism The tendency to focus on one aspect of a psychological phenomenon (eg observable behaviour or physiology), neglecting other aspects.

Reinforcement In learning theory, any consequence of a behaviour that increases the probability of it being repeated.

Relapse The return to drug-use by a previously recovered user.

Related design See **repeated measures design**.

Related t-test A parametric inferential statistical test. Used when you have interval or ratio data, the research is repeated measures (or matched pairs) and you are looking for a difference in the effect each level of the independent variable has on the dependent variable.

Reliability A measure of whether replications of a test or technique would produce similar results, if so then the measure is reliable.

Repeated measures design (within-subjects or related design) This is an experimental design in which each individual participates in every level of the IV, that is, the levels of the IV are compared by each participant *repeating* their performance under different conditions.

Representative sampling A method of selecting a group of participants that contains all the important characteristics of the parent population.

Research question The general question that a study intends to answer.

Researcher bias The tendency of experimenters or observers to record the response they expect from the participants in different conditions, either because of subjective observation and recording or through acting differently towards participants in different conditions causing systematic variations in their behaviour.

Resilience The capacity of the individual to withstand the effects of less than optimum environments.

Responder bias (participant reactivity) The tendency of a participant to produce responses that are socially desirable, are what the experimenter wants or are biased.

Retrospective study A study in which the impact of early experience on later development is assessed by looking back from the time of the alleged effect to the early experience.

Road-rage Occurs when aggressive behaviour towards other road users is displayed in the absence of any direct cause other than a perception of the traffic context.

Role-model A person whose behaviour is observed and imitated.

Sample The group of individuals selected from the **population** to participate in a study so that the researcher can make generalisations about the whole of the original population.

Sampling method A technique by which a sample of participants is taken from a population.

Scattergraph Used to display a correlation in the form of a graph.

Glossary

Schizophrenogenic Contributing towards the development of schizophrenia.

Scriptotherapy The therapeutic technique of writing about one's situation and feelings towards it.

Secondary appraisal This follows a primary appraisal and is the formation of an impression about one's ability to cope with the situation: a consideration of the possible options, the chances of successfully employing them and whether the action will work.

Secondary territory A type of **territory** where there is a medium degree of occupation and perception of ownership. An example would be your place in the classroom.

Seduction theory Freud's term for the explanation of mental disorder in terms of child sexual abuse.

Self efficacy An individual's belief in their own ability.

Self-esteem The emotional experience of how much an individual likes themselves.

Self-medication Using non-medicinal drugs to alter one's psychological state in response to distress, for example, using alcohol to relax in the face of stress.

Self-rating Inventories Personality tests which require that the respondent replies to a series of items or questions.

Semantic differentials A form of questionnaire design where participants rate either pictures or pieces of text on a bi-polar adjective scale.

Sensation-seeking Seeking out exciting situations.

Sensitive responsiveness (in attachment theory) The success with which a **primary carer** picks up and responds to the signals of an infant. Widely believed to be a major determinant of the quality of infant-carer **attachment**.

Shadow juries A method by which a group of participants eligible for jury service are asked to sit in the courtroom so they hear all the evidence, and then to retire to reach a verdict, much as a real jury would.

Simulated juries See **mock juries**.

Situational theories Approaches that see behaviour as purely the product of the current situation.

Situational variables Confounding effects arising from the influence of the environment on the behaviour of participants, such as lighting, noise levels and temperature.

Social comparison The tendency to judge our own behaviour against that of others.

Social constructionism An approach to psychology that emphasises the social construction of psychological ideas. Thus ideas like intelligence can be seen not so much as real things but more as ideas that have served the interests of society or groups within society.

Social constructivism A collection of approaches to psychology linked by the belief that there is no single universal truth, and that we construct meaning through our use of language.

Social contagion A theory suggesting that when individuals within a crowd become aroused and respond to one another they amplifying the intensity of their interactions.

Social density Refers to the density of the population as controlled by varying the number of individuals per unit area.

Social learning theory A version of learning theory that emphasises the influence of observation and the imitating of behaviour that is observed in others.

Social loafing The phenomenon in which people working together on a task tend to contribute less individual effort than they would if working alone.

Social norms Conventional standards of behaviour for a particular society.

Social skills training A programme designed to teach people how to improve skills such as making eye contact, holding reasoned discussions and dealing with confrontation without using aggression.

Sociofugal designs Designs that are used to keep people apart.

Sociometry The study of the interactions between a group of children.

Sociopetal designs Designs that are used to promote interaction between people.

Sound The vibration of air. Sound intensity (**volume**) increases in volume as the **amplitude** of the waves increases.

Spatial density Refers to the density of the population as controlled by varying the available space.

Spatial zones Different zones of **personal space**. They include an intimate zone, a personal zone, a social zone and a public zone.

Spearman's rank order correlation coefficient A non-parametric inferential statistical test. Used when you have ordinal data, the research is correlational and you are looking for a relationship between the two measured variables.

Spirituality Important in humanistic psychology, the subjective experience of one's relationship with the universe.

Split-half reliability A measure of the internal reliability of the test. It indicates whether all the items on the test are measuring the same phenomenon by correlating participants' scores on one half of the test with their scores on the other half. These should correlate highly if the test is internally reliable.

Standard deviation A measure of dispersion (spread) based around the mean score of your results.

Standard error bar This is used to display the mean and standard deviation in the form of a graph. The bar represents the mean and the whisker shows the standard deviation.

Standardised instructions Guidance given to participants in a study to ensure that each one receives the same information about the requirements of the task to minimise variation between their experiences.

Stigmatisation The consequence of having a socially unacceptable characteristic such as mental disorder, characterised by isolation and discrimination.

Structured observation A systematic approach to recording behaviours in which target actions are categorised, selected and defined prior to observation.

Subsonic jet An aircraft with cannot travel faster than the speed of sound but may still be very loud on take-off.

Suggestibility The tendency of individuals to become more responsive to the ideas of others, especially when these are proposed in an authoritative manner.

Supersonic jet An aircraft capable of flying faster than the speed of sound, such as Concorde. As a consequence of their design they are both loud on take-off and generate a sonic boom as the aircraft breaks the sound barrier. This is very loud on the ground but cannot be heard from within the aircraft.

Syndrome A collection of symptoms that tend to be found together. Unlike the terms 'condition' or 'disorder', 'syndrome' does not imply a single cause or set of causes for those symptoms.

System variables In witness testimony, those variables that affect the accuracy of witness testimony and over which the police (and justice system in general) have some influence. These may include the interviewing techniques and the way an identity parade is conducted.

Systematic sample This is a technique for obtaining participants which generates a sample that is representative of the population variety of characteristics exhibited within the population. The basis of systematic sampling is very simple: we select every nth person on a list. By dividing the total population by the size of the sample we require we find the basis for sampling. For example, if we have a population of 100 and wish to select a sample of 20, we would include every fifth person (100/20 = 5, hence every fifth). However, this technique does not necessarily result in a representative sample.

Task orientation A focus on perfecting skills.

Telic dominance The extent to which an individual is in telic or paratelic states.

Telic state A motivational state in which arousal is avoided.

Temperament The aspects of a child's personality that are present at birth and generally believed to be genetic in origin.

Territory An area that you perceive you have ownership over.

Test-retest reliability A measure of the consistency of measurement exhibited by a psychological test. The respondent takes the test on two occasions and a correlation is produced between the answers given on the two occasions.

Theory of mind The child's understanding of the emotions and motives of other people.

Therapeutic Having a positive effect on mental health.

Thurstone method A questionnaire design where an 'expert panel' rate each question before participants fill the questionnaire in. Each item is weighted depending on what the judges believe.

Time sampling A technique that enables the observer to record some information about *when* behaviours occur. There are three recording schedules each providing only an indication of the frequency and duration of behaviours rather than the sequential relationship between behaviours. The observation period is divided into predetermined intervals and records of behaviours are related to these.

Token economy A behaviour modification technique in which secondary reinforcers called tokens, which can be collected and exchanged for primary reinforcers (for example, desirable substances such as confectionery), are used to encourage certain behaviour.

Tolerance The development of a need for greater amounts of a drug with repeated use, in order to achieve the same effect.

Top-down approach In the context of **offender profiling**, an approach that starts from a classification of serious crimes (the 'top') and appraises which category a particular crime fits into, based on the evidence at the crime scene.

Trait theories Theories which see personality as made up of genetically determined and measurable aspects called traits.

Transportation noise The unpleasant sounds generated by motor vehicles, trains, aeroplanes and other means of transport.

Two-tailed hypothesis See **non-directional hypotheses**.

Type I error Rejecting the null hypothesis when in fact we should accept it. If we set our level of significance less stringently, eg $p \leqslant 0.1$, it is easier to reject the null hypothesis and we may commit a Type I error as the null hypothesis may well be correct.

Type II error Accepting the null hypothesis when in fact we should reject it in favour of the alternative/experimental hypothesis. If we set our level of significance too stringently, eg $p \leqslant 0.001$, it is easier to accept the null hypothesis and we may commit a Type II error as the experimental/alternative hypothesis may well be correct.

Unconscious Mental processes of which we are not aware. In psychodynamic theory, the unconscious mind has a powerful effect on our behaviour, thinking and emotional states.

Upper quartile The data point that is at the 75 per cent point of your data set when the data is ranked in order.

Urban renewal Using the principles of Environmental Psychology (e.g. **defensible space**) to aid the development of run down areas in cities, usually in an attempt to reduce crime and vandalism.

Validity The extent to which a technique achieves the purpose for which it was designed. A valid test would measure what it claims to measure.

Variance A measure of spread based around the mean. It is the square of the standard deviation.

Variation ratio A measure of spread that is the proportion (usually a percentage) of scores that are not the mode.

Vicarious reinforcement Learning behaviour by witnessing others being rewarded for doing behaviour in a particular way.

Voir dire A pre-trial interview of potential jurors during which the judge or opposing lawyers (those for the prosecution and the defence) can apply for the dismissal of anyone they consider not to be impartial.

Volume An increase in magnitude of vibration in the air (measured in decibels). Sounds increase in **volume** as the **amplitude** of the waves increases.

Volunteer sample In most cases, those individuals who participate in a study do so voluntarily, so they thus constitute a *volunteer sample*.

Weapon focus effect The tendency for witnesses to a crime involving a weapon to remember details of the weapon, but to be less accurate on other details such as the perpetrator's face (as compared to witnessing events not involving a weapon).

White noise Sound of a wide range of frequencies generated in an unpatterned way like the 'static' of an out-of-tune radio or television.

Wide band (broad band) noise Unwanted sound that is composed of a range of frequencies.

Wilcoxon's signed rank matched pairs test A non-parametric inferential statistical test. Used when you have ordinal data, the research is repeated measures (or matched pairs) and you are looking for a difference in the effect each level of the independent variable has on the dependent variable.

Withdrawal (or the abstinence syndrome) The experience of physically painful and unpleasant symptoms (such as vomiting, shaking, headaches and convulsions) suffered by a physically dependent user as the effects of the drug wears off. A physically dependent user needs to continue to take the drug to avoid feeling ill.

Within subjects design See **repeated measures design**.

Yerkes-Dodson law This law states that performance will first improve as a person's arousal level increases but then reach a point at which further arousal (possibly in the form of stress) will result in a decrease in performance. In terms of witnessing a crime, if the situation causes great stress, the ability of witnesses to recall events accurately will be adversely affected.

Zero tolerance An umbrella term for any regime in which certain behaviours, however mildly exhibited, are not tolerated. In terms of crime control, it usually refers to the apprehension of people performing any crime however small, such as begging or throwing litter.

references

Clinical psychology

Abrams M. & Ellis A. (1996) Rational emotive behaviour therapy in the treatment of stress. In Palmer S. & Dryden W. (eds) *Stress management and counselling*. London: Cassell.

Abramson L.Y., Alloy L.B. & Metalsky G.I. (1989) Hopelessness depression: a theory based subtype of depression. *Psychological Review* 96: 358–72.

Alanen, Y. (1994) An attempt to integrate the individual-psychological and interactive concepts of the origin of schizophrenia. *British Journal of Psychiatry* 164: 56–61.

Angrist B., Sathananthan G., Wilk S. & Gershon S. (1974) Amphetamine psychosis: behavioural and biochemical aspects. *Journal of Psychiatric Research* 11: 13–23.

Allyon T. & Azrin N.H. (1968) *The token economy: a motivational system for therapy and rehabiliation*. New York: Appleton-Century-Crofts.

Barlow D.H. & Durand V.M. (1999) *Abnormal psychology*. Pacific Grove: Brooks/Cole.

Bateman A. & Holmes J. (1995) *Introduction to psychoanalysis*. London: Routledge.

Baxter L., Schwartz J. & Bergman K. (1992) Caudate glucose metabolic rate changes with both drug and behaviour therapy for obsessive compulsive disorder. *Archives of General Psychiatry* 49: 681–9.

Beck A.T. (1976) *Cognitive therapy and the emotional disorders*. New York: International Universities Press.

Bentall R., Baker G.A. & Havers S. (1991) Reality monitoring and psychotic hallucinations. *British Journal of Clinical Psychology* 30: 213–22.

Bergin A.E. & Garfield S. (1978) *Handbook of psychotherapy and behaviour change*. New York: Wiley.

Beutler L.E. (1991) Have all won and must all have prizes: revisiting Luborsky et al's verdict. *Journal of Consulting Clinical Psychology* 59: 226–32.

Bion W.R. (1967) *Second thoughts: selected papers on psychoanalysis*. London: Heinemann.

Black D., Noyes R., Goldstein R. & Blum N. (1992) A family history of obsessive compulsive disorder. *Archives of General Psychiatry* 49: 362–8.

Blakemore C. (1988) *The mind machine*. London: BBC Publications.

Borkovec T.D. & Mathews A. (1988) Treatment of nonphobic anxiety disorders: a comparison of non-directive, cognitive and coping desensitisation therapy. *Journal of Consulting and Clinical Psychology* 56: 877–84.

Botella C., Villa H., Banos R., Perpina C. & Garicia-Palacios A. (1999) The treatment of claustrophobia with virtual reality: changes in other phobic behaviours not specifically treated. *CyberPsychology and Behaviour* 2(2): 135–41.

Bradley B.P., Mogg K., White J., Groom C. & de Bono J. (1999) Attentional bias for emotional faces in generalised anxiety disorder. *British Journal of Clinical Psychology* 38: 267–78.

Breslau N., Davis G. & Andreski P. (1991) Traumatic events and post-traumatic stress disorder in an urban population of young adults. *Archives of General Psychiatry* 48: 216–21.

Breuer J. & Freud S. (1896) *Studies on hysteria. The complete works of Sigmund Freud*, Vol II. London: Hogarth.

Brewin C.R., Dalgeish T. & Joseph P.H. (1996) A dual representation theory of post-traumatic stress disorder. *Psychological Review* 103: 670–86.

Brown D. & Pedder J. (1991) *Introduction to psychotherapy*. London: Routledge.

Brown G.W. (1972) Influence of family life on the course of schizophrenic disorders: a replication. *British Journal of Psychiatry* 121: 241–8.

Brown G.W. & Harris T.O. (1978) *The social origins of depression: a study of psychiatric disorder in women*. London: Tavistock.

Brown R. (1996) Life events, loss and depressive disorders. In Heller T. et al (eds) *Mental health matters*. Basingstoke: Macmillan.

Bruch H. (1982) Anorexia nervosa: therapy and theory. *American Journal of Psychiatry* 132: 1531–8.

Burnett P.C. (1999) Children's self-talk and academic self-concepts. *Educational Psychology in Practice* 15: 195–200.

Burstow B. (1992) *Radical feminist therapy*. New York: Sage.

Callanan M. (2000) Anxiety. In Champion L. & Power M. (eds) *Adult psychological problems*. Hove: Taylor & Francis.

Carson R.C. & Butcher J.N. (1992) *Abnormal psychology and modern life*, 9th edn. New York: HarperCollins.

Castle D., Scott K., Wessley S. & Murray R.M. (1993) Does social deprivation during gestation and early life predispose to schizophrenia? *Social Psychiatry and Psychiatric Epidemiology* 25: 210–15.

Chadwick P., Sambrooke S., Rasch S. & Davies E. (2000) Challenging the omnipotence of voices: group cognitive behaviour therapy for voices. *Behaviour Research and Therapy* 38: 993–1003.

Champion L. & Power M. (2000) *Adult psychological problems*. Hove: Psychology Press.

Chartier M.J., Walker J.R. & Stein M.B. (2001) Social phobias and potential childhood risk factors in a community sample. *Psychological Medicine* 31: 307–15.

Chowdhury U. & Lask B. (2001) Clincial implications of brain imaging in eating disorders. *Psychiatric Clinics of North America* 24: 222–34.

Christo G. (1997) Child sexual abuse: psychological consequences. *The Psychologist* 10: 205–9.

Cinnerella M. & Loewenthal K.M. (1999) Religious and ethnic group influences on beliefs about mental illness: a qualitative interview study. *British Journal of Medical Psychology* 72: 505–25.

Colman C.E. (1993) *Facts, fallacies and frauds in psychoogy*, 2nd edn. London: Routledge.

Comer R. J. (1992) *Abnormal psychology*, 2nd edn. New York: W.H. Freeman.

Comer R.J. (1995) *Abnormal psychology*. New York: Freeman.

Cooper M. & Turner H. (2000) Underlying assumptions in anorexia nervosa and dieting. *British Journal of Clinical Psychology* 39: 215–18.

Coopersmith S. (1967) *The antecedents of self-esteem*. San Francisco, CA: Freeman.

Costello T.W., Costello J.T. & Holmes D. (1995) *Abnormal psychology*, international edn. New York: HarperCollins.

Crisp A.H. & Kalucy R.S. (1974) Aspects of perceptual disorder in anorexia nervosa. *British Journal of Medical Psychology* 47: 349–61.

Crisp A.H., Palmer R.L. & Kalucy R.S. (1976) How common is anorexia nervosa? A prevalence study. *British Journal of Psychiatry* 128: 549–54.

Critchley E.R.M., Denmark J.C., Warren F. & Wilson K.A. (1981) Hallucinatory experiences in prelingually profoundly deaf schizophrenics. *British Journal of Psychiatry* 138: 30–2.

Crits-Christoph P. (1992) The efficacy of brief dynamic psychotherapy: a meta-analysis. *American Journal of Psychiatry* 149: 151–8.

Crowe M.J. (1997) Sexual disorders. In Murray R., Hill P. & McGuffin P. (eds) *The essentials of postgraduate psychiatry*. Cambridge: Cambridge University Press.

Crowe T.J. (1980) Molecular pathology of schizophrenia: more than one disese process? *British Medical Journal* 280: 66–88.

Crow T.J., Ball J., Bollm S.R., Brown R., Bruton C.J., Colter N., Frith C.D., Johnstone E.C., Ownes D.G.C. & Roberts G.W. (1989) Schizophrenia as an anomaly of development of cerebral asymmetry. *Archives of General Psychiatry* 46: 1145–50.

Culbertson F.M. (1997) Depression and gender: an international review. *American Psychologist* 52: 25–31.

Dare L. & Eisher I. (1997) Family therapy for anorexia nervosa. In Garner D.M. & Garfinkel P.E. (eds) *Handbook of treatment for eating disorders*. New York: Guilford.

Davidson J., Hughes D., Blazer D. & George L. (1991) Post-traumatic stress disorder in the community: an epidemiological study. *Psychological Medicine* 21: 713–21.

Davison G.C & Neale J.M. (1994) *Abnormal psychology*. New York: Wiley.

Davison G.C. & Neale J.M. (2001) *Abnormal psychology*, 8th edn. New York: Wiley.

Davey G.C.L. (ed) (1997) *Phobias: a handbook of therapy research treatment*. Chichester: Wiley.

de Jonghe F., Kool S., van Alkst G., Dekker J. & Peen, J. (2001) Combining psychotherapy and antidepressants iin the treatment of depression. *Journal of Affective Disorders* 64: 217–29.

Department of Health (1997) *The Spectrum of Care: Local Services for People with Mental Health Problems*. London: HMSO.

Depatie L. & Lal S. (2001) Apomorphine and dopamine hypothesis of schizophrenia: a dilemma? *Journal of Psychiatry and Neuroscience* 26: 203–20.

De Rubies et al (1998).

Donnelly C.L., McEvoy J.P., Wilson W.H. & Narasibacharic N. (1996) A study of the potential confounding effects of diet, caffeine, nicotine and lorazepam on the stability of plasma and urinary homovanillic acid levels in patients with schizophrenia. *Biological Psychiatry* 40: 1218–21.

Dwyer D. & Scampion J. (1996) *Mastering A-level psychology*. Basingstoke: Macmillan.

Eley T.C. & Stevenson J. (2000) Specific life-events and chronic experiences differentially associated with depression and anxiety in young twins. *Journal of Abnormal Child Psychology* 28: 383–94.

Ellis A. (1962) *Reason and emotion in psychotherapy*. New York: Life Stuart.

Ellis A. (1991) The revised ABCs of rational emotive therapy (RET) *Journal of Abnormal Child Psychology* 28: 383–94.

Engles G.I., Garnekski N. & Diekstra R.R.W. (1993) Efficacy of rational-emotive therapy: a quantitative analysis. *Journal of Consulting and Clinical Psychology* 61: 1083–90.

Eysenck H.J. (1952) The effects of psychotherapy: an evaluation. *Journal of Consulting Psychology* 16: 319–24.

Eysenck H.J. (1967) *The biological basis of personality*. Springfield, IL: Charles C. Thomas.

Eysenck H.J. (1992) The tyranny of psychotherapy. In Dryden W. and Feltham C. (eds) *Psychotherapy and its discontents*. Milton Keynes: Open University Press.

Eysenck H.J. (1997) *Anxiety and emotion: a unified theory*. Hove: Psychology Press.

Eysenck M.J. & Keane M.T. (2000) *Cognitive psychology: a student's handbook*, 3rd edn. London: Psychology Press.

Fairburn C.G. (1982) *Binge eating and bulimia nervosa*, vol 1(4). Welwyn Garden City: Smith Kline & French.

Fancher R.T. (1995) *Cultures of healing*. New York: Freeman.

Ferguson E. & Cassaday J.J. (1999) The Gulf War and illness by association. *British Journal of Psychology* 90: 459–75.

Fernandez A.F., Dahme B. & Meerman R. (1999) Body image in eating disorders: a preliminary study. *Journal of Psychosomatic Research* 47: 419–28.

Fichter M.M. & Pirke K. M. (1986) Effects of experimental and pathological weight loss on the hypothalomo-pituitary-adrenal axis. *Psychonuroendocrinology* 11: 295–305.

Fichter M.M. & Pirke K.M. (1995) Starvation models and eating disorders. In Szmukler G., Dare C. & Treasure J. (eds) (1995) *Handbook of eating disorders*. Chichester: Wiley.

Finkelhor D. (1994) The international epidemiology of child sexual abuse. *Child Abuse and Neglect* 18: 409–17.

Foa E. & Tillmanas A. (1980) The treatment of obsessive-compulsive neurosis. In Goldstein A. & Foa E. (eds) *Handbook of behavioural interventions*. New York: Wiley.

Fonagy P. (1996) *What works with whom? A critical reveiw of psychotherapy research*. London: Guilford Press.

Freeman H.L. (1984) The scientific background. In Freeman H.L. (ed) *Mental health and the environment*. London: Churchill Livingstone. .

Freeman H.L. (1994) Schizophrenia and city residence. *British Journal of Psychiatry* 164: 39–50.

Freud S. (1896) *The aetiology of hysteria*. Collected Papers, vol 1. London: Hogarth.

Freud S. (1909) *Analysis of a phobia in a five-year-old boy*. Collected Papers, vol III. pages 149–295. London: Hogarth.

Freud S. (1912) *The dynamics of transference*. Completed Works of Sigmund Freud, vol 12. London: Hogarth.

Freud, S. (1917) *Mourning and melancholia*. Collected Works of Sigmund Freud, vol 14. London: Hogarth.

Freud S (1926) *Inhibitions, symptoms and anxiety*. London: Hogarth.

Friedman B.H. and Thayer J.F. (1998) Anxiety and autonomic flexibility: a cardiovascular approach. *Biological Psychology* 49: 303–23.

Friedman B.H., Thayer J.F. & Borkovec T.D. (2000) Explicit memory bias for threat words in generalised anxiety disorder. *Behaviour Therapy* 31: 745–56.

Frith C.D. (1987) The positive and negative symptoms of schizophrenia reflect impairments in the perception and initiation of action. *Psychological Medicine* 17: 631–48.

Frith C.D. (1992) *The cognitive neuropsychology of schizophrenia*. Hove: Psychology Press.

Frith C.D. & Done D.J. (1983) Routes to action in reaction time tasks. *Psychological Medicine* 13: 779–86.

Frith C.D. & Done D.J. (1986) Steroetyped responding by schizophrenics on a two-choice guessing task. *Psychological Research* 48: 169–77.

Frith C.D. & Done D.J. (1989) Experiences of alien control in schizophrenia reflect a disorder in the central monitoring of action. *Psychological Medicine* 19: 359–63.

Fromm-Reichmann F. (1948) Notes on the development of treatment of schizophrenics by psychoanalytic psychotherapy. *Psychiatry* 11: 263–73.

Gagne G.G., Furman M.J., Carpenter L.L. & Price L.H. (2000) Efficacy of continuation ECT and antidepressant drugs compared to long-term antidepressants alone in depressed patients. *American Journal of Psychiatry* 157: 1960–5.

Garcia-Pelacios A., Hoffman H.G., See S.K., Tsai A. & Botella C. (2001) Redefining therapeutic successes with virtual reality exposure therapy. *CyberPsychology and Behaviour. Special Issue* 4(3): 341–8.

Garner D.M., Garfinkel P.E., Schwartz D. & Thompson M. (1980) Cultural expectation of thinness in women. *Psychological Reports* 47: 483–91.

Geller J.L. (1992) A historical perspective on the role of state hospitals viewed from the era of the 'revolving door'. *American Journal of Psychiatry* 149: 1526–33.

George M.S., Wasserman E.M. & Williams W.A. (1995) Daily repetitive transcranial magnetic stimulation improves mood in depression. *Neuroreport* 6: 1853–6.

Gergen K.J. (1985) The social constuctionist movement in modern psychology. *American Psychologist* 40: 266–75.

Gilroy L.J., Kirkby K.C., Daniels B.A., Menzies R.G. & Montgomery I.M. (2000) Controlled comparison of computer-aided vicarious exposure versus live exposure in the treatment of spider phobia. *Behaviour Therapy Special Issue* 31(4): 733–44.

Glenmullen J. (2001) *Prozac backlash*. California: Touchstone Books.

Goldfried M.R. & Davison G.C. (1994) *Clinical behaviour therapy*. New York: Holt, Rinehart & Winston.

Goldstein J.M. et al (1999) Cortical abnormalities in schizophrenia identified by structural magnetic resonance imaging. *Archives of General Psychiatry* 56: 537–47.

Gomm R. (1996) Mental health and inequality. In Heller T., Reynolds J., Gomm R., Muston R. & Pattison S. (eds) *Mental health matters*. Basingstoke: Macmillan.

Goodwin F.K. & Jamison K.R. (1990) *Manic depressive illness*. New York: Oxford University Press.

Gottesman I. I. (1991) *Schizophrenia genesis: the origins of madness*. New York: Freeman.

Grazioli R. & Terry D.J. (2000) The role of cognitive vulnerability and stress in the prediction of postpartum depressive symptomatology. *British Journal of Clinical Psychology* 39: 329–47.

Greenberg L.S., Elliott R.K. & Lieater G.

(1994) Research on experiential psychotherapies. In Bergin A.E. & Garfield S. (eds) *Handbook of psychotherapy and behaviour change*. New York: Wiley.

Gross R., McIlveen R., Coolican H., Clamp A. & Russell J. (2000) *Psychology: a new introduction*. London: Hodder & Stoughton.

Guthrie E. (2000) Psychotherapy for patients with complex disorders and chronic symptoms: The need for a new research paradigm. *British Journal of Psychiatry* 177: 131–7.

Guthrie E., Kapur N., Mackway-Jones K., Chew-Graham C., Moorey J., Mendel E., Marino-Francis F., Sanderson S., Turpin C., Boddy G. & Tomenson B. (2001) Randomised control trial of brief psychological intervention after deliberate self-poisoning. *British Medical Journal* 323: 7305.

Hammen C. (1997) *Depression*. Hove: Psychology Press.

Harriman E. (2001) The missing warning on a drug for desperate people: users of an antidepressant are not yet alerted to a possible suicide risk. *Guardian*, 17 May 2001.

Healy D. (1993) *Psychiatric drugs explained*. Kings Lynn: Mosby.

Heenan C. (1996a) Women, food and fat: too many cooks in the kitchen? In Burman E., Alldred P., Bewley C., Goldberg B., Heenan C., Marks D., Marshall J., Taylor K. & Ullah S. (eds) *Warner challenging women: psychology's exclusions, feminist possiblities*. Buckingham: Open University Press.

Heenan, C. (1996b) Feminist therapy and its discontents. In Burman E., Aitken G., Alldred P., Allwood P., Billington T., Goldberg B., Godo-Lopez A.J., Heenan C., Marks D., & Warner S. (eds) *Psychology discourse practice: from regulation to practice*. London: Taylor and Francis.

Henry W.P. (1994) Psychodynamic approaches. In Bergin A.E. & Garfield S. (eds) *Handbook of psychotherapy & behaviour change*. New York: Wiley.

Hepworth J. (1999) *The social construction of anorexia nervosa*. London: Sage.

Herpertz-Dahlmann B., Hebebrand J., Muller B., Herpertz S., Heussen N. & Remschmidt H. (2001) Prospective 10 year follow-up in adolescent anorexia nervosa: course, outcome, psychiatric comorbidity and psychosocial adaptation. *Journal of Child Psychology and Psychiatry* 42: 603–12.

Heston L.L. (1966) Psychiatric disorders in foster home reared children of schizophrenic mothers. *British Journal of Psychiatry* 112: 819–25.

Hetterna J.M., Neale M.C. & Kenler K.S. (2001) A review and meta-analysis of the genetic epidemiology of anxiety disorders. *American Journal of Psychiatry* 158: 1568–78.

Hodgson R.J. & Rachman S.J. (1972) The effects of contamination and washing on obsessional patients. *Behaviour Research and Therapy* 10: 111–17.

Hollander E., Decaria C. & Nitescu A. (1992) Serotonergic function in obsessive compulsive disorder: behavioural and neuroendocrine responses to oral-M-chlorophenylpiperazine and fenfluramine in patients and healthy volunteers. *Archives of General Psychiatry* 49: 21–8.

Hong C.J., Du Y.W.Y. & Lin C.H. (2001) Association analysis for NMDA receptor subunit 2B (GRIN2B) genetic variants and psychopathology and dozapine response in schizophrenia. *Psychiatric Genetics* 11: 219–22.

Horowitz M.J. (1990) Psychotherapy. In Bellack A.S. & Hersen M. (eds) *Handbook of comparative treatments for adult disorders*. New York: Wiley.

Hsu L.K.G. (1990) *Eating disorders*. New York: Guilford.

Humphrey L.L. (1989) Observed family interactions among subtypes of eating disorders using structured analysis of social behaviour. *Journal of Counselling and Clinical Psychology* 57: 206–14.

Hunt L. (1997) *Trauma in older adults*. London: Jessica Kingsley.

Jablensky A. (1988) Schizophrenia and environment. In Henderson A.S. & Burrows G.D. (eds) *Handbook of social psychiatry*. Amsterdam: Elsevier.

Jarvis M. (2001) *Angles on child psychology*. Cheltenham: Nelson Thornes.

Jarvis M., Russell J., Flanagan C. & Dolan L. (2000) *Angles on psychology*. Cheltenham: Nelson Thornes.

Jarvis M. & Russell J. (2002) *Key ideas in psychology*. Cheltenham: Nelson Thornes.

Jarvis M. (2003) *Psychodynamic psychology: classical theory and contemporary research*. London: Thomson Learning.

Jimerson D.C., Lesem M.D., Kaye W.H. & Brewerton T.D. (1992) Low serotonin and dopamine metabolite concentrations in cerebrospinal fluid from bulimic patients with frequent binge episodes. *Archives of General Psychiatry* 49: 132–8.

Johanson A., Gustafson L., Passant U., Risberg J., Smith G., Warkentin S. & Tucker D. (1998) Brain function in spider phobia. *Psychiatry Research: Neuroimaging* 84: 101–11.

Johnstone E.C., Crow T.J., Frith C.D., Carney M.W.P. & Price J.S. (1978) Mechanism of the antipsychotic effects in the treatment of acute schizophrenia. *Lancet*, i, 848–51.

Joiner T.E. (2000) A test of the hopelessness theory of depression in youth psychiatric patients. *Journal of Clinical Child Psychology* 29: 167–76. .

Jones M.C. (1924) The elimination of children's fears. *Journal of Experimental Psychology* 7: 383–90.

Kane G.C., Leone F.T. & Rowane J. (1998)

Guidelines for depot anti-psychotic treatment in schizophrenia. *European Psychopharmacology* 8: 55–6.

Kapci E.G. (1998) Test of the hopelessness theory of depression: drawing negative inference from negative life events. *Psychological Reports* 82: 355–63.

Kazdin A.E. & Weisz J. R. (1998) Identifying and developing empirically supported child and adolescent treatments. *Journal of Consulting and Clinical Psychology* 66: 19–36.

Kelly J. & Murray R.M. (2000) What risk factors tell us about the causes of schizophrenia and related psychoses. *Current Psychiatry Reports* 2: 378–85.

Kendler K.S., Neale M.C., Kessler R.C., Heath A.C. & Eaves L.J. (1992) Major depression and generalised anxiety disorder: same genes (partly) different environments? *Archives of General Psychiatry* 49: 716–22.

Kim Y. & Berrios Ge.E. (2001) Impact of the term schizophrenia on the culture of ideograph: the Japanese experience. *Schizophrenia Bulletin* 27: 181–5.

Kindt M. & Brosschot J.F. (1997) Phobia-related cognitive bias for pictorial and linguistic stimuli. *Journal of Abnormal Psychology* 106: 644–8.

Kippin T.E. (2000) Olfactory-conditioned ejaculatory prefences in the male rat: implications for the role of learning in sexual partner preferences. *Dissertation Abstracts International* 61: 1678.

Kivlighan D.M., Multon K.D. & Patton M.J. (2000) Insight and symptom reduction time-limited psychoanalytic counselling. *Journal of Counselling Psychology* 47: 50–8.

Klein D.N., Rison L.P., Donaldson S.K., Schwartz J.E., Anderson R.L., Ouimette P.C., Lizardi H. & Aronson T.A. (1995) Family study of early-onset dysthymia. *Archives of General Psychiatry* 52: 487–96.

Klein E. (2000) Magnetic brain stimulation – a new therapeutic tool in psychiatry. *Israel Journal of Psychiatry and Related Sciences* 37(1): 1–2.

Klein M. (1946) Notes on some schizoid mechanisms. *International Journal of Psychoanalysis* 27: 99–110.

Klimek V., Stockmeir C., Overholser J., Meltzer H.Y., Kalka S., Dilley G. & Ordway G.A. (1997) Reduced levels of norepinephrine transporters in the locus coeruleus in major depression. *Journal of Neuroscience* 17: 8451–8.

Kluft R.P. (1993) *Clinical perspectives on multiple personality disorder.* Washington DC: American Psychiatric Press.

Kortegaard L.S., Hoerder K., Joergensen J., Gillberg C. & Kuvik K.O. (2001) A preliminary population-based twin study of self-reported eating disorder. *Psychological Medicine* 31: 361–5. .

Koss M.P., Goodman L.A. & Browne A. (1994) *No safe haven: male violence against women at home, at work and in the community.*

Washington DC: American Psychological Association.

Kraepelin E. (1896) Dementia praecox (trans). In Cutting J. & Shepherd M. (eds) (1987) *The clinical routes of the schizophrenic concept.* Cambridge: Cambridge University Press.

Kramer P. (1997) *Listening to Prozac.* London: Penguin.

Krystal J.H., KostenT.R., Southwick S., Mason J.W., Perry B.D. & Giller E.L. (1989) Neurobiological aspects of PTSD: review of clinical and preclinical studies. *Behaviour Therapy* 20: 177–98.

Lai K.Y.C. (2000) Anorexia nervosa in Chinese adolescents. Does culture make a difference? *Journal of Adolescence* 23: 561–8.

Laing R.D. (1965) *The divided self: an existential study into sanity and madness.* Harmondsworth: Penguin.

Laing R.D. (1967) *The politics of experience and the bird of paradise.* Harmondsworth: Penguin.

Laing R.D. & Esterson A. (1964) *Sanity, madness and the family: families of schizophrenics.* London: Tavistock.

Lang P.J. & Lazovik D.A. (1963) Experimental desensitisation of a phobia. *Journal of Abnormal and Social Psychology* 66: 519–25.

Lau S. & Pun K. (1999) Parental evaluations and their agreement: relationship with children's self-concepts. *Social Behaviour and Personality* 27: 639–50.

Lavender T. (2000) Schizophrenia. In Champion L. & Power M. (eds) *Adult psychological problems.* Hove: Psychology Press.

Leff J. (1997) *Care in the community – illusion or reality?* Chichester: Wiley.

Lemieux G., Davignon A. & Genest J. (1965) Depressive states during rauwolfia therapy for arterial hypertension. *Canadian Medical Association Journal* 74: 522–6.

Lemma-Wright A. (1995) *Invitation to psychodynamic psychology.* London: Whurr. .

Lemma-Wright A. (1996) *Introduction to psychopathology.* London: Sage.

Leon G., Fulkerson J.A., Perry C.L. & Cudeck R. (1993) Personality and behavioural vulnerabilities associated with risk status for eating disorders in adolescent girls. *Journal of Abnormal Psychology* 102: 438–44.

Leshner A.I. (1992) *Outcasts on Main Street: Report of the Federal Taskforce on Homelessness and Severe Mental Illness.* Washington, DC: Interagency Council on the Homeless.

Levav I., Kohn R., Golding J.M. & Weissman M.M. (1997) Vulnerability of Jews to affective disorders. *American Journal of Psychiatry* 154: 1703–10.

Lidz T., Flec S. & Cornelison A. (1965) *Schizophrenia and the family.* New York: International Universities Press.

Lindstroem L.H., Gefvert O., Hagberg G.,

Lundberg T., Bergstroem M., Hartvig P. & Langstroem B. (1999) Increased dopamine synthesis rate in medial profrontal cortex and striatum in schizophrenia indivated by L (beta-sup-l-sup-lc) DOPA and PET. *Biological Psychiatry* 46: 681–8.

Littlewood R. & Lipsedge M. (1997) *Aliens and alienists: ethnic minorities and psychiatry.* London: Routledge.

Lohr J.M., Tolin D.F. & Lilienfled S.O. (1998) Efficacy of eye movement desensitisation and reprocession: implications for behaviour therapy *Behaviour Therapy* 29: 123–56.

Lovibond P.F. (2001) The 'near miss' as a fourth pathway to anxiety. *Behavioural and Cognitive Psychotherapy* 29: 123–56.

Lukoff (1998).

Lupien S.J., King S., Meaney M.J. & McEwen B.S. (2000) Children's stress hormone levels correlate with mothers' socioeconomic status and depressive state. *Biological Psychiatry* 48: 976–80.

MacDonald J. & Morley I. (2000) Shame and non-disclosure: a study of the emotional isolation of people referred for psychotherapy. *British Journal of Psychotherapy* 74: 1–22.

Magee W.J. (1999) Effects of negative life experiences on phobia onset. *Social Psychiatry and Psychiatric Epidemiology* 34: 343–51.

Mahon L. & Kempler B. (1995) Perceived effectiveness of therapeutic factors for ACOAs and non-ACOAs in heterogeneous psychotherapy groups. *Alcoholism Treatment Quarterly* 13: 1–11.

Maier E.H. & Lachman M.E. (2000) Consequences of early parental loss and separation for health and well-being in mid-life. *International Journal of Behavioural Development* 24: 183–9.

Malan D. (1995) *Individual psychotherapy and science of psychodynamics.* London: Butterworth-Heinemann.

Marks I. (1987) *Fears, phobias and rituals.* New York: Oxford University Press.

Marks I.M. (1976) The current status of behavioural psychotherapy: theory and practice. *American Journal of Psychiatry* 133: 253–61.

Masling J.M. & Bornstein R.F. (1996) *Psychoanalytic perspectives on developmental psychology.* Washington DC: American Psychologyical Association.

Masson J. (1984) *The assault on truth.* New York: HarperCollins.

Masson J (1992) The tyranny of psychotherapy: In Dryden W. & Feltham C. (eds) *Psychotherapy and its discontents.* Milton Keynes: Open University Press.

Mayhew J. (1996) *Psychological change: a practical introduction.* Basingstoke: Macmillan.

McGuffin & Sturt ((1986).

McGuffin P., Katz R., Watkins S. & Ruther-

References

ford J. (1996) A hospital-based twin register of the heritability of DSM-IV unipolar depression. *Archives of General Psychiatry* 53: 129–36.

McKeon P. & Murray R. (1987) Familial aspects of obsessive-compulsive neurosis. *British Journal of Psychiatry* 151: 528–34.

McLeod J. (1996) The humanistic paradigm. In Woolfe R. & Dryden W. (eds) *Handbook of counselling psychology*. London: Sage.

McNeal E.T. & Cimbolic P. (1986) Antidepressants and biochemical theories of depression. *Psychological Bulletin* 99: 361–74.

Mearns D. & Thorne B. (1988) *Person-centred counselling in action*. London: Sage.

Menditto A.A., Vales L.A. & Beck N.C. (1994) Implementing a comprehensive social-learning program within the forensic psychiatric service of Fulton State Hospital. In Corrigan P.W. & Liberman R.P. (eds) *Behaviour therapy in psychiatric hospitals*, pages 61–78. New York: Springer.

Menzies R.G. (1996) The origins of specific phobias in a mixed clinical sample: classificatory differences between two origins instruments. *Journal of Anxiety Disorders* 10: 347–54.

Merry T. (1995) *Invitation to person-centred psychology*. London: Whurr.

Meyer V. & Chesser E.S. (1970) *Behaviour therapy in clinical psychology*. Baltimore, IL: Penguin.

Miller E. (1999) Conversion hysteria: is it a viable concept? *Cognitive Neuropsychiatry* 4: 181–92.

Mineka S., Davidson M., Cook M. & Keir R. (1984) Observational conditioning of snake fear in rhesus monkeys. *Journal of Abnormal Psychology* 93: 355–72.

Moffaert M.V. & Dierick M. (1999) Noradrenaline and depression: role in aetilogy and therapeutic implications. *CNS Drugs* 12: 293–305.

Molnos A. (1995) *A question of time*. London: Karnac.

Mullan B. (1995) *Mad to be normal: conversations with R.D. Laing*. London: Free Association Books.

Mumford D. B. (1996) The 'Dhat syndrome': a culturally determined symptom of depression? *Acta Psychiatrica Scandinavica* 94: 163–7.

Mumford D.B., Whitehouse A.M. & Platts M. (1991) Sociocultural correlates of eating disorders among Asian schoolgirls in Bradford. *British Journal of Psychiatry* 158: 222–8.

Muraoka M.Y., Carlson J.G. & Chemtob C.M. (1998) Twenty-four hour ambulatory blood pressure and heart rate monitoring in combat-related post-traumatic strees disorder. *Journal of Traumatic Stress* 11: 473–84.

Murray R., Hill P. & McGuffin P. (eds) *The essentials of postgraduate psychiatry*. Cambridge: Cambridge University Press.

Myers S. (2000) Empathic listening: reports on the experience of being heard. *Journal of Humanistic Psychology* 40: 148–73.

Newman L., Waller G. & Thomas G. (2000) Outcome of group cognitive-behaviour therapy for bulimia nervosa: the role of core beliefs. *Behaviour Research and Therapy* 38: 145–56.

Ng C., Schweitzer I., Alexopoulous P., Celi E., Wong L., Tuckwell V., Sergejew A. & Tiller J. (2000) Efficacy and cognitive effects of right unilateral electro-convulsive therapy. *Journal of ECT* 16: 370–9.

Nicholls D., Chater R. & Lask B. (2000) Children into DSM don't go: a comparison of classification systems for eating disorders in childhood and adolescence. *International Journal of Eating Disorders* 28: 317–24. .

O'Callaghan E., Gibson T. & Colohan H. (1991) Season of birth in schizophrenia: evidnece for confinement of an excess of winter births, to patients, without a family history of mental disorder. *British Journal of Psychiatry* 158: 764–9.

Oie T.P.S. & Free M.L. (1995) Do cognitive behaviour therapies validate cognitive models of mood disorders? A review of the empirical evidence. *International Journal of Psychology* 30: 145–80.

Opler L.A., Caton C.L.M., Shrout P., Dominguz B. & Kass F.I. (1994) Symptom profiles and homelessness in schizophrenia. *Journal of Nervous and Mental Disorders* 182: 174–8.

Orbach S. (1986) *Hunger strike*. London: Faber & Faber.

Owen P.R. & Laurel-Seller E. (2000) Weight and shape ideals: thin is dangerously in. *Journal of Applied Social Psychology* 30: 979–90.

Palmer S. & Dryden W. (1995) *Counselling for stress problems*. London: Sage.

Papolos D. (1997) *Overcoming depression*. New York: HarperCollins.

Parker G., Mitchell P. & Wilhelm K. (2000) Twelve-month episodes of non-melancholic depressive subjects: refinements of subgroups by examination of trajectories. *Annals of Clinical Psychiatry* 12: 219–25.

Parker I., Georgaca E., Harper D., McLaughlin T. & Stowell-Smith M. (1995) *Deconstructing psychopathology*. London: Sage.

Paul G.L. & Menditto A.A. (1992) Effectiveness of inpatient treatment programs for mentally ill adults in public facilities. *Applied and Preventative Psychology, Current Scientific Perspectives* 1: 41–63.

Perez M.G., Rivera R.M., Banos F. & Amparo B. (1999) Attentional bias and vulnerability to depression. *Spanish Journal of Psychology* 2: 11–19.

Petkova B. (1997) Understanding eating disorders: a perspective from feminist psychology. *Psychology Review* 4(l): 2–7.

Petry N.M., Martin B., Cooney J.L. & Kranzler H.R. (2000) Give them prizes, and they will come: contingency management for treatment of alcohol dependence. *Journal of Counselling and Clinical Psychology* 68(5): 250–7.

Philo G., Secker J., Platt S., Henderson L., McLaughlin G. & Burnside J. (1994) The impact of mass media on public images of mental illness: media content and audience belief. *Health Education Journal* 53: 271–81.

Pigott T., Pato M.T. & Bernstein S.E. (1990) Controlled comparisons of clomipramine and fluoetine in the treatment of obsessive-compulsive disorder: behavioural and biological results. *Archives of General Psychiatry* 47: 926–32.

Plomin R. et al (1997) *Behavioural genetics*. New York: Freeman.

Pridmore S., Bruno R., Turnier-Shea Y., Reid P. & Rybak M. (2000) Comparison of unlimited numbers of rapid transcranial magnetic stimulation (rTMS) and ECT treatment sessions in major depressive episode. *International Journal of Neuropsychopharmacology* 3(2): 129–34.

Purdon S.E., Woodward N.D. & Flor-Henry P. (2001) Asymmetrical hand force persistence and neuroleptic treatment in schizophrenia. *Journal of the International Neuropsychological Society* 7: 606–14.

Putwain D.W. (2000) Living with schizophrenia: family, communication and expressed emotions. *Psychology Review* 6(4): 15–18.

Putwain D.W., Gray M. & Emiljanowicz C.M. (2000) Psychopathology: the social approach. *Psychology Review* 7(2): 8–11.

Pynoos R., Goenjian A. & Tashjian M. (1993) Post-traumatic stress reaction in children following the 1988 Armenian earthquake. *British Journal of Psychiatry* 163: 239–47.

Radziszewska B., Richardson J.L., Dent C.W. & Flay B.R. (1996) Parenting style and adolescent depressive symptoms, smoking and academic achievement: ethnic, gender and SES differences. *Journal of Behavioural Medicine* 19: 289–305.

Renfrey G. & Spates C.R (1994) Eye movement desensitisation: a partial dismantling study. *Journal of Behaviour Therapy and Experimental Psychiatry* 25: 231–9.

Richards, G. (1996) *Putting psychology in its place*. London: Routledge.

Rimland B. (1964) *Infantile autism*. New York: Appleton-Century-Crofts.

Ritsher J.E.B., Warner V., Johnson J.G. & Dohrenwend B.P. (2001) Intergenerational longitudinal study of social class and depression: a test of social causation and social selection models. *British Journal of Psychiatry* 178: 84–90.

Rizzo A.A., Buckwalter J.G., Neumann U., Kesselman C. & Thieaux M. (1998). Basic issues in the application of virtual reality for the assessment and rehabilitation of cognitive impairments and functional disabilities. *Cyberpsychology and Behaviour* 1: 59–78.

Rogers A. & Pilgrim D. (1996) *Mental health policy in Britain: a critical introduction*. Basingstoke: Macmillan.

Rogers C. (1959) A theory of therapy, personality and interpersonal relationships, as developed in the client-centred framework. In Koch S. (ed) *Psychology: a study of a science*, vol 3. New York: McGraw-Hill.

Rogers C. (1961) *On becoming a person: a therapist's view of psychotherapy*. Boston, MA: Houghton-Mifflin.

Romano S.J. & Quinn L. (1995) Binge eating disorder: description and proposed treatment. *European Eating Disorders Review* 3: 67–9.

Rose D.T., Abramson L.Y., Hodulik C.J., Halberstadt L. & Leff G. (1994) Heterogeneity of cognitive style among depressed inpatients. *Journal of Abnormal Psychology* 103: 419–29.

Rosenhack R., Cramer J. & Allan E. (1999) Cost effectiveness of clozapine in patients with high and low levels of hospital use. *Archives of General Psychiatry* 56: 565–72.

Rosenhan D.L. (1973) On being sane in insane places. *Science* 179: 250–8.

Roth A., Fonagy P., Parry G. & Target M. (1996) *What works for whom: a critical review of psychotherapy resarch*. New York: Guilford Press.

Rothbaum B.O., Hodges L., Kooper R., Opdyke D., Williford J. & North M.M. (1995) Effectiveness of virtual reality graded exposure in the treatment of acrophobia. *American Journal of Psychiatry* 152: 626–8.

Rothbaum B.O., Hodges L., Smith S., Lee J.H. & Price L. (2000) A controlled study of virtual reality exposure therapy for fear of flying. *Journal of Counselling and Clinical Psychology* 68: 1020–6.

Salzman L. (1995) *Treatment of obsessive and compulsive behaviours*. Northvale: Aronson.

Sandahl C., Herlitz K. & Ahlin G. (1998) Time-limited group psychotherapy for moderately alcohol dependent patients: a randomised controlled clinical trial. *Psychotherapy Research* 8: 361–78.

Sandell R., Blomberg J., Lazar A., Schubert J., Carlson J. & Broberg J. (1999) As time goes by: long-term outcomes of psychoanalysis and long-term psychotherapy. *Forum der Psychoanalyse* 15: 327–47.

Schmidt U., Humfress H. & Treasure J. (1997) The role of family environment and sexual and physical abuse in the origins of eating disorders. *European Eating Disorders Review* 5: 184–207.

Schofield W. & Balian L. (1959) A comparative study of the personal histories of schizophrenic and non-psychiatric patients. *Journal of Abnormal and Social Psychology* 59: 216–25.

Scott M.J. & Stradling S.G. (2001) *Counselling for post-traumatic stress disorder*. London: Sage.

Senior J. (2001) Eye movement desensitisation and reprocessing: a matter for serious consideration? *The Psychologist* 14(7): 360–3.

Shallice T. (1988) *From neuropsychology to mental structure*. Cambridge: Cambridge University Press.

Shapiro F. (1989) Efficacy of eye movement desensitisation procedure in the treatment of traumatic memories. *Journal of Traumatic Stress* 2: 199–223.

Shepherd G. (1998) Models of community care. *Journal of Mental Health* 7: 165–77.

Shepherd G., Muijen M., Dean R. & Cooney M. (1996) Residential care in hospital and the community – quality of care and quality of life. *British Journal of Psychiatry* 168: 448–56.

Siebert A. (2000) How non-diagnostic listening led to a rapid recovery from paranoid schizophrenia: what is wrong with psychiatry? *Journal of Humanistic Psychology* 40: 34–58.

Silberg J. et al (1999) The influence of genetic factors and life stress on depression among adolescent girls. *Archives of General Psychiatry* 56: 225–32.

Silverman M.S., McCarthy M. & McGovern T. (1992) A review of outcome studies of rational-emotive therapy from 1982 to 1989. *Journal of Rational-Emotive and Cognitive-Behaviour Therapy* 10: 111–75.

Skre I., Onstad S., Torgersen S. & Kringlen E. (2000) The heritability of common phobic fear: a twin study of a clinical sample. *Journal of Anxiety Disorders* 14: 549–62.

Slade D.D. & Russell G.F.M. (1973) Awareness of body dimensions in anorexia nervosa: cross sectional and longitudinal studies. *Psychological Medicine* 3: 188–99.

Smith M.L., Glass G.V. & Miller T.I. (1980) *The benefits of psychotherapy*. Baltimore, MD: Johns Hopkins University Press.

Smyth J.M. & Greenberg M.A. (2000) Scriptotherapy: the effects of writing about traumatic events. In Duberstein P.R. & Masling J.M. (eds) *Psychodynamic Perspectives on Sickness and Health*. Washington DC: American Psychological Association.

Solomon A. & Haaga D.A.F. (1995) Rational emotive behaviour therapy research: what we know and what we need to know. *Journal of Rational-Emotive and Cognitive-Behaviour Therapy* 13: 179–91.

Spitzer R.L., Yanovski S.Z. & Wadden T. (1993) Binge eating disorder: its further validation in a multisite study. *International Journal of Eating Disorders* 13: 137–53.

Steiner et al (1991).

Stoppard J.M. (2000) *Understanding depression: feminist social constructionist approaches*. London: Routledge.

Stowell-Smith M. & McKeown M. (1999) Race, psychotherapy and the self: a discourse analytic study. *British Journal of Medical Psychology* 72: 459–70.

Swaffer T. & Hollin C. (2001) Anger and general health in young offenders. *Journal of Forensic Psychiatry* 12: 90–102.

Sweet R.A., Mulsant B.H. & Gupta B. (1995) Duration of neuroleptic treatment and prevalence of tardive dyskinesia in late life. *Archives of General Psychiatry* 52: 478–86.

Szmukler G., Dare C. & Treasure J. (1995) *Handbook of eating disorders*. Chichester: Wiley.

Thorne B. (1992) *Carl Rogers*. London: Sage.

Thornicroft G. & Sartorius N. (1993) The course and outcome of depression in different cultures: a 10 year follow-up of the WHO collaborative study on the assessment of depressive disorders. *Psychological Medicine* 23: 1023–32.

Tienari P. (1992) Implications of adoption studies on schizophrenia. *British Journal of Psychiatry* 161: 52–8.

Trauer T., Farhall J., Newton R. & Cheung P. (2001) From long-stay psychiatric hospital to Community Care Unit: evaluation at 1 year. *Social Psychiatry and Psychiatric Epidemiology* 36: 416–19.

True W., Rice J. & Eisen S. (1993) A twin study of genetic and environmental contributions to liability for post-traumatic stress symptoms. *Archives of General Psychiatry* 50: 257–64.

Venable V.L., Carlson C.R. & Wilson J. (2001) The role of anger and depression in recurrent headache. *Headache* 41: 21–30.

Vitousek K. & Manke F. (1994) Personality variables and disorders in anorexia nervosa and bulimia nervosa. *Journal of Abnormal Psychology* 103: 137–47.

Wahlberg K.E., Wynne L.C., Oja H.l., Kekitalo P., Pykalainen L., Lahti I., Moring J., Naarala A., Sorin S., Seitamaa M., Laksy K., Kolassa J. & Tienari P. (1997) Gene-environment interaction in vulnerability to schizophrenia: findings from the Finnish Adoptive Family Study of schizophrenia. *American Journal of Psychiatry* 154: 355–62.

Watson J.B. & Rayner R. (1920) Conditioned emotional responses. *Journal of Experimental Psychology* 3: 1–14.

Weiderhold B.K. & Weiderhold M.D. (1999) Clinical observations during virtual reality therapy for specific phobias. *CyberPsychology and Behaviour* 2(2): 161–8.

Weinberger D.R. (1988) Premorbid neuropathology in schizophrenia. *Lancet* ii: 959–60.

Weissman M.M. (1984) Depression and anxiety disorders in parents and children: results from the Yale family study. *Archives of General Psychiatry* 41: 845–52.

Weissman M.M. & Olfson M. (1995) Depression in women: implications for health care research. *Science* 269: 799–801.

Wilson D.L., Silver S.M., Covi W.G. & Foster, S. (1996) Eye movement desensitisation and reprocessing: effectiveness and automatic correlates. *Journal of Behaviour Therapy and Experimental Psychiatry* 27: 219–29.

Wolpe J. (1958) *Psychotherapy by reciprocal inhibition.* Stanford CA: Stanford University Press.

Wolpe J. (1973) My philosophy of psychotherapy. *Journal of Contemporary Psychotherapy* 6: 59–62.

Youssef H.A. & Youssef F.A. (1999) Time to abandon electroconvulsion as a treatment in modern psychiatry. *Advances in Therapy* 16(1).

Criminal psychology

Abwender D.A. & Hough K. (2001) Interactive effects of characteristics of defendant and mock juror on U.S. participants' judgement and sentencing recommendations. *Journal of Social Psychology* 141: 603–15.

Ainsworth P.B. & Pease K. (1987) *Police work.* London & New York: Methuen.

American Medical Association (1986) Council Report: scientific status of refreshing recollection by the use of hypnosis. *International Journal of Clinical and Experimental Hypnosis* 34: 1–12.

Anderson C.A. & Dill K.E. (2000) Video games and aggressive thoughts, feelings and behaviour in the laboratory and in life. *Journal of Personality and Social Psychology* 78(4): 772–90.

Asch S.E. (1955) Opinions and Social Pressure. *Scientific American* 193(5): 31–5.

Ayllon T. & Mullan M.A. (1979) *Correctional rehabilitation and management: a psychological approach.* New York: Wiley.

Bandura A. (1965) Influence of Models' Reinforcement Contingencies on the Acquisition of Imitative Responses. *Journal of Personality and Social Psychology* 1(6): 589–95.

Bell S.T., Kuriloff P.J. & Lottes I. (1994) Understanding attribution of blame in stranger rape and date rape situations: an examination of gender, race, identification, and students' social perceptions of rape victims. *Journal of Applied Social Psychology* 24: 1719–34.

Berry D. & McArthur L. (1985) Some components and consequences of a babyface. *Journal of Personality and Social Psychology* 48: 312–23.

Blackburn R. (1993) *The psychology of criminal conduct: theory, research and practice.* England: Wiley.

Boon J. & Davies G. (1992) Fact and fiction in offender profiling. *Issues in Legal and Criminological Psychology* 32: 3–9.

Brehm S.S. & Kassim S.M. (1996) *Social psychology,* 3rd edn. Boston and Toronto: Houghton Mifflin Company.

Briton P. (1992) Home Office/ACPO Review of offender profiling: unpublished. Reported in Copson (1996).

Brown R. & Kulik J. (1977) Flashbulb memories. *Cognition* 5: 73–99.

Bruce V., Henderson Z., Newman C. & Burton A.M. (2001) Matching identities of familiar and unfamiliar faces caught on CCTV images. *Journal of Experimental Psychology: Applied* 7: 207–18.

Bull R. & McAlpine S. (1998) Facial appearance and criminality. In Memon A., Vrij A. & Bull R., (eds), *Psychology and Law: Truthfulness, Accuracy and Credibility.* New York: McGraw-Hill.

Burton S., Kitzinger J., with Kelly L. & Regan L. (1998) *Young people's attitudes towards violence, sex and relationships.* Zero Tolerance Charitable Trust: Edinburgh.

Bushman B.J. (1995) Moderating role of trait aggressiveness in the effects of violent media on aggression. *Journal of Personality and Social Psychology* 69: 950–60.

Campbell C. (1976) Portrait of a mass killer. *Psychology Today* 9: 110–19.

Canter D. (1989) Offender profiles. *Psychologist* 2(1): 12–16.

Canter D. (1994) *Criminal shadows.* London: Harper.

Charlton T., Gunter B. & Hannan A. (eds) (2000) *Broadcast television effects in a remote community.* Mahway, NJ: Lawrence Erlbaum Associates.

Coleman B.L., Stevens M.J. & Reeder G.D. (2001). What makes recovered-memory testimony compelling to jurors? *Law and Human Behavior* 25(4): 317–38.

Commission for Racial Equality (2002) *Discrimination in the criminal justice system.* London: The Stationery Office.

Copson G. (1996) At last some facts about offender profiling in Britain. *Forensic Update* 46: 4–10.

Crombag H.F.M., Wagenaar W.A. & VanKoppen P.J. (1996) Crashing memories and the problem of source monitoring. *Applied Cognitive Psychology* 10: 93–104.

Cumberbatch G. (1997) Media violence: sense and common sense. *Psychology Review* 3(4): 2–7.

Davies G. (1997) in Jackson J.L. & Bekerian D.B. (eds), *Offender Profiling. Theory, Research and Practice.* Chichester: Wiley.

Dennis N. (ed.) (1998) *Zero tolerance. Policing a free society.* IEA Health and Welfare Unit. Lancing: Hartington Fine Arts Ltd.

DeRidder R., Schruijer S.G.L. & Rijsman J.B. (1999) Retaliation to personalistic attack. *Aggressive Behaviour* 25(2): 91–6.

Diamond B.L. (1980) Inherent problems in the use of pretrial hypnosis on a prospective witness. *California Law Review* 68: 313–49.

Dietz T.L. (1998) An examination of violence and gender role portrayals in video games: implications for gender socialisation and aggressive behaviour. *Sex Roles* 38: 425–42.

Dion K.K., Bershield, E. & Hatfield (Walster E. (1972) What is beautiful is good. *Journal of Personality and Social Psychology* 24: 285–290.

Dixon J.A., Mahoney B. & Cocks R. (2002) Accents of guilt? Effects of regional accent, race, and crime type on attributions of guilt. *Journal of Language and Social Psychology* 21(2): 162–8.

Dominick J.R. (1984) Videogames, TV violence and aggression in teenagers. *Journal of Communication* 34: 134–44.

Douglas J.E. (1981) Evaluation of the (FBI) psychological profiling programme: unpublished. Reported in Pinizzotto (1984) and Copson (1996).

Downs A.C. & Lyons P.M. (1991) Natural observations of the links between attractiveness and initial legal judgements. *Personality and Social Psychology Bulletin* 17: 541–7.

Duncan B.L. (1976) Differential social perception and attribution of intergroup violence: testing the lower limits of stereotyping of Blacks. *Journal of Personality and Social Psychology* 34(4): 590–8.

Dwyman J. & Bowers K. (1983) The use of hypnosis to enhance recall. *Science* 222: 184–5.

Emes C.E. (1997) Is Mr Pacman eating our children? A review of the effect of video games on children. *Canadian Journal of Psychiatry* 42: 409–14.

Eron L.D. (1995) Media violence: how it affects kids and what can be done about it. Invited address presented at the annual meeting of the American Psychological Association. New York.

Eron L.D. & Huesmann L.R. (1986) The role of television in the development of antisocial and prosocial behaviour. In Olweus D., Block J. & Radke-Yarrom M. (eds), *Development of Antisocial and Prosocial Behaviour, Theories and Issues.* New York: Academic Press.

Eron L.D., Huesmann L.R., Leftowitz M.M. & Walder L.O. (1972) Does television violence cause aggression? *American Psychologist* 27: 253–63.

Fernandez Y.M. & Marshall W.L. (2003) Victim empathy, social self-esteem and psychopathy in rapists. *Sexual Abuse: Journal of Research and Treatment* 15(1): 11–26.

Fling S., Smithe L., Rodriguez T., Thornton D., Atkins E. & Nixon K. (1992) Videogames, aggression and self-esteem: a survey. *Social Behaviour and Personality* 20: 39–46.

Gendron M.J. (2001) The effects of arousal on memorial accuracy: a comparison of arousal as part of content material and as part of contextual environment. *Dissertation Abstracts International, Section B: The Sciences and Engineering* 61(12–B): 6728.

Gibson H.B. (1982) The use of hypnosis in police investigations. *Bulletin of the British Psychological Society* 34: 138–41.

Gibson H.B. (1989) The Home Office attitude to forensic hypnosis: a victory for scientific evidence or medical conservatism? *British Journal of Experimental and Clinical Hypnosis* 6: 25–7.

Glaser B.A., Calhoun G.B., Bradshaw C.P., Bates J.M. & Socherman R.E. (2001) Multi-observer assessment of problem behaviour in adjudicated youths: Patterns of discrepancies. *Child and Family Behaviour Therapy* 23(2): 33–45.

Goldstein J.H. (1986) *Aggression and crimes of violence*, 2nd edn. Oxford: Oxford University Press.

Goldstein A.P., Glick B., Irwin M.J., Pask-McCartney C. & Rubama I. (1989) *Reducing delinquency: Intervention in the community*. Elmsford, NY, US: Pergamon Press.

Griffiths M.D. (2000) Video game violence and aggression. *British Journal of Social Psychology* 39: 147–9.

Gunter B. & McAleer J. (1997) *Children and television*. London: Routledge. .

Hagell A. & Newbury T. (1994) *Young offenders and the media*. London: Policy Studies Institute.

Hastie R., Penrod S.D. & Pennington N. (1983) *Inside the Jury*, Cambridge, MA: Harvard University Press.

Heider F. (1958) *The psychology of interpersonal relations*. New York: Wiley.

Henderson Z., Bruce V. & Burton A.M. (2001) Matching the faces of robbers captured on video. *Applied Cognitive Psychology* 15: 445–64.

Hinz V.B. & Davis J.H (1984) Persuasive argument theory, group polarization, and choice shifts. *Personality and Social Psychology Bulletin* 10: 260–8.

Hobbs T.R. & Holt M.M. (1976) The effects of token reinforcement on the behaviour of delinquents in cottage settings. *Journal of Applied Behaviour Analysis* 9: 189–98.

Holbrook M.I. (1997) Anger management training in prison inmates. *Psychological Reports* 81(2): 623–6.

Hollin C.R. (1990) *Cognitive-behavioural interentions with young offenders*. New York: Pergamon.

Hollin C.R., Huff G.J., Clarkson F. & Edmondson A.C. (1986) Social skills training with young offenders in a borstal: an evaluative study. *Journal of Community Psychology* 14: 289–99.

Holmes R. (1989) *Profiling violent crimes*. Newbury Park: Sage.

Holmes R.M. & Holmes S.T. (1996) *Profiling violent crimes: an investigative tool*, 2nd edn. California: Sage Publications.

Huesmann L.R. & Malamuth N.M. (1986) Media violence and antisocial behaviour: an overview. *Journal of Social Issues* 42(3): 1–6.

Hunter D. (1993) Anger management in the prison. An evaluaton. *Research on Offender Programming Issues* 5(1): 3–15.

Hunter J.A., Figueredo A.J., Malamuth N.M. & Becker J.V. (2003) Juvenile sex offenders: toward the development of a typology. *Sexual Abuse: Journal of Research and Treatment* 15(1): 27–48.

Jackson J.L., van Koppen P.J, & Herbrink J.C.M. (1993) Does the service meet the needs? *Report NSCR 93–05*. Netherlands Institute for the Study of Criminality and Law Enforcement.

Jackson J.L. & Bekerian D.B. (1997) *Offender Profiling. Theory, Research and Practice*. Chichester: Wiley.

Jahoda G. (1954) A note on Ashanti names and their relationship to personality. *British Journal of Psychology* 45: 192–5.

Johnson J.D., Simmons C.H., Jordan A., MacLean L., Taddei J., Thomas D., Dovidio J.F. & Reed W. (2002) Rodney King and O.J. Simpson revisited: the impact of race and defendant empathy induction on judicial decisions. *Journal of Applied Social Psychology* 32(6): 1208–23.

Jones E.E. & Harris V.A. (1967) The attribution of attitudes. *Journal of Experimental Social Psychology* 3: 1–24.

Kalat J.W. (1993) *Introduction to psychology*, 3rd edn. Belmont, CA: Wadsworth.

Kerr N.L., Harmon D.L. & Graves J.K. (1982) Independence of multiple verdicts by jurors and juries. *Journal of Applied Social Psychology* 12: 12–29.

Kostinsky S., Bixler E.O. & Kettl P.A. (2001) Threats of school violence in Pennsylvania after media coverage of the Columbine High School massacre: examining the role of imitation. *Archives of Pediatric and Adolescent Medicine* 155(9): 994–1001.

Kramer T.H., Buckhout R. & Eugenio P. (1990) Weapon focus, arousal and eyewitness memory. Attention must be pai. *Law and Human Behaviour* 14: 167–84.

Law K. (1997) Further evaluation of anger-management courses at HMP Wakefield: An examination of behavioural change. *Inside Psychology: The Journal of Prison Service Psychology* 3(1): 91–5.

Lennings C.J. (2000) Harm minimization or abstinence: an evaluation of current policies and practices in the treatment and control of intravenous drug using groups in Australia. *Disability and Rehabilitation: An International Multidisciplinary Journal* 22(1–2): 57–64.

Lerner M.J. (1980) *The belief in a just world: a fundamental delusion*. New York: Plenum.

Leyens J.P., Camino L. Parke R.D. & Berkowitz L. (1972) Effects of movie violence on aggression in a field setting as a function of group dynamics and cohesiveness. *Journal of Personality and Social Psychology* 32: 346–60.

Lin S. & Lepper M.R. (1987) Correlates of children's usage of video bgames and computers. *Journal of Applied Social Psychology* 17: 72–93.

Livingstone S. (2001) Media effects research. *Psychology Review* 7(3): 29–31.

Lloyd-Bostock S. (1983) Attributions of cause and responsibility as social phenomena. In Jaspers J.M.F., Fincham F.D. & Hewstone M. (eds), *Attribution theory and research: conceptual, developmental and social dimensions*. London: Academic Press.

Lock T.G. (2000) Implanting or unplanting memories? The role of recall enhancement, anxiety, and psychological symptom interpretation in the creation of false memories. *Dissertation Abstracts International: Section B: The Sciences and Engineering* 61(5B): 2769.

Loftus E.F. & Zanni G. (1975) Eyewitness testimony: the influence of working of a question. *Bulletin of the Psychonomic Society* 5: 86–8.

Loftus E.F. (1986) Experimental psychologyist as advocate or impartial educator. *Law and Human Behaviour* 10: 63–78.

Loftus E.F., Loftus G. & Messo J. (1987) Some facts about 'weapon focus'. *Law and Human Behaviour* 11: 55–62.

Loftus E.F., Miller D.G. & Burns H.J. (1978) Semantic integration of verbal information into a visual memory. *Journal of Experimental Psychology: Human Learning and Memory* 4(1): 19–31.

Loza W. & Loza-Fanous A. (1999) The fallacy of reducing rape and violent recidivism by treating anger. *International Journal of Offender Therapy and Comparative Criminology* 43(4): 492–502.

MacLeod C. & Shepherd J.W. (1986) Sex differences in eyewitness reports of criminal assaults. *Medicine Science and Law* 26: 311–18.

MacLin Q.H., MacLin M.K. & Malpass R.S. (2001) Race, arousal, attention, exposure and delay: An examination of factors moderating face recognition. *Psychology, Public Policy and Law* 7(1): 1324–52.

Mazzella R. & Feingold A. (1994) The effects of physical attractiveness, race, socioeconomic status, and gender of defendants and victims on judgments of mock jurors: a meta-analysis. *Journal of Applied Social Psychology* 24: 1315–44.

McKelvie S.J. & Coley J. (1993) Effects of crime seriousness and offender facial attractiveness on recommended treatment. *Social Behaviour and Personality* 21: 265–77.

McLaughlan A. (1986) The effects of two forms of decision reappraisal on the perception of pertinent arguments. *British Journal of Social Psychology* 25: 129–38.

Milavsky J.R., Kessler R.C., Stipp H. & Rubens W.S. (1982) *Television aggression: a panel study*. New York: Academic Press.

References

Milgram S. (1963) Behavioural study of obedience. *Journal of Abnormal and Social Psychology* 67: 371–8.

Moscovici S. (1980) Towards a theory of conversion behaviour. In Berkowitz L. (ed.) *Advances in Experimental Social Psychology*, vol 13, pages 208–39. New York: Academic Press.

Moyes T., Tennent T.G. & Bedford A.P. (1985) Long-term follow-up study of a ward-based behaviour modification programme for adolescents with acting-out and conduct problems. *British Journal of Psychiatry* 147: 300–5.

Muirhead J. (1997) Assessment of anger and negative affect as they relate to the prediction of criminal violence in a federal inmate population: a retrospective study. Unpublished doctoral dissertation. Carleton University, Ottawa, Canada.

Myers D.G. & Kaplan M.F. (1976) Group-induced polarization in simulated juries. *Personality and Social Psychology Bulletin* 2(1): 63–6.

Neisser U. & Harsch N. (1992) Phantom flashbulbs: false recollections of hearing the news about Challenger. In Winograd E. & Neisser U. (eds) *Affect and accuracy in recall: studies of 'flashbulb' memories*, pages 9–31. Cambridge: Cambridge University Press.

Nemeth C. (1977) Interactions between jurors as a function of majority vs. unanimity decision rules. *Journal of Applied Social Psychology* 7: 38–56.

Oleson J.C. (1996) Psychological profiling: does it actually work? *Forensic Update* 46, July, 11–14.

Orne M.T. (1979) The use and misuse of hypnosis in court. *International Journal of Clinical and Experimental Hypnosis* 27: 311–41.

Parke R., Berkowitz L., Leyens J., West S. & Sebastian R. (1977) Some effects of violent and non-violent movies on the behaviour of juvenile delinquents. In Berkowitz L. (ed) *Advances in experimental psychology*, vol 10. New York: Academic Press.

Pfeifer J.E. & Ogloff J.R. (1991) Ambiguity and guilt determinations: a modern racism perspective. *Journal of Applied Social Psychology* 21: 1713–25.

Phillips D.P. (1983) The impact of mass media on homicide. *American Sociological Review* 48: 560–8.

Phillips D.P. (1986) Natural experiments on the effects of media violence on fatal aggression: Strengths and weaknesses of a new approach. In Berkowitz L. (ed.) *Advances in experimental social psychology*, vol 19, pages 207–50. New York: Academic Press.

Piaget J. (1932) *The moral development of the child*. Harmondsworth: Penguin.

Pickel K.L. (1998) Unusualness and threat as possible cause of 'weapon focus'. *Memory* 6: 277–95.

Pickel K.L. (1999) The influence of context on the 'weapon focus' effect. *Law and Human Behaviour* 23(3): 299–311.

Piliavin I. & Briar S. (1964) Police encounters with juveniles. *American Journal of Sociology* 70: 206–14.

Pinizzotto A.J. (1984) Forensic psychology: criminal personality profiling. *Journal of Police Science and Administration* 12: 32–40.

Pinizzotto A.J. & Finkel N.J. (1990) Criminal personality profiling: an outcome and process study. *Law and Human Behaviour* 14(3): 215–33.

Pollard C. (1998) Zero tolerance: short-term fix, long-term liability? In Dennis N. (ed) *Zero tolerance. Policing a free society*. IEA Health and Welfare Unit. Lancing: Hartington Fine Arts Ltd.

Pollard P. (1992) Judgements about victims and attackers in depicted rapes: a review. *British Journal of Social Psychology* 31: 307–26.

Provenzo E.F. (1991) *Video kids – making sense of Nintendo*. Harvard: Harvard University Press.

Quigley B.M., Johnson A.B., & Byrne D. (1995, June) Mock jury sentencing decisions: A meta-analysis of the attractiveness-leniency effect. Paper presented at the meeting of the American Psychological Society. New York.

Rice M.E., Quinsey V.L. & Houghton R. (1990) Predicting treatment outcoume and recidivism among patients in a maximum security token economy. *Behavioural Sciences and the Law* 8: 313–26.

Ross L.D. (1977) The intuitive psychologist and his shortcomings: distortions in the attribution process. In Berkowitz L. (ed) *Advances in experimental social psychology*, vol 10, pages 173–220. New York: Academic Press.

Ross R.R. & Mackay H.B. (1976) A study of institutional treatment programs. *International Journal of Offender Therapy and Comparative Criminology* 20: 165–73.

Saladin M., Saper Z. & Breen L. (1988) Perceived attractiveness and attributions of criminality: what is beautiful is not criminal. *Canadian Journal of Criminology* 30: 251–59.

Saks M.J. (1974) Ignorance of science is no excuse. *Trial* 10: 18–20.

Saks M.J. (1977) *Jury verdicts: The role of group size and social decision rule*. Lexington, MA: Lexington Books.

Shaw J.I. & Skolnick, P. (1999) Weapon focus and gender differences in eyewitness accuracy: arousal versus salience. *Journal of Applied Social Psychology* 29(11): 2328–41.

Skiba R.J. & Peterson R.L. (2000) School discipline at a crossroads: From zero tolerance to early response. *Exceptional children* 66(3) 335–46.

Skolnick P. & Shaw J.I. (1997) The O.J. Simpson criminal trial verdict: racism or status shield? *Journal of Social Issues* 53(3): 503–16.

Smith E.R. & Mackie D.M. (1995) *Social psychology*. New York: Worth Publishers, Inc.

Smith M.C. (1983) Hypnotic memory enhancement of witnesses: does it work? *Psychological Bulletin* 94: 87–94.

Smith E.R. & Mackie D.M (2000).

Spence S.H. & Marziller J.S. (1981) Social skills training with adolescent male offenders: 2. Short-term, long-term and generalisation effects. *Behaviour Research and Therapy* 19: 349–68.

Stalnaker J.M. & Riddle E.E. (1932) The effect of hypnosis on long-delayed recall. *Journal of General Psychology* 6: 429–40.

Stanny C.J. & Johnson T.C. (2000) Effects of stress induced by a simulated shooting on recall by police and citizen witnesses. *American Journal of Psychology* 113(3): 359–86.

Stasser G. & Stewart D. (1992) Discovery of hidden profiles by decision-making groups: Solving and problem versus making a judgement. *Journal of Personality and Social Psychology* 63: 426–34.

Stewart J.E. (1980) Defendant's attractiveness as a factor in the outcome of criminal trials: an observational study. *Journal of Applied Social Psychology* 10(4): 348–61.

Strodtbeck F.L. & Hook L. (1961) The social dimensions of a twelve man jury. *Sociometry* 24: 397–415.

Towl G.J. (1993) Anger control groupwork in practice. *Issues in Criminological and Legal Psychology* 23: 31–5.

Towl G.J (1995) Anger management groupwork. *Issues in Criminological and Legal Psychology* 23: 117–23.

Troseth G.L. (2003) Two-year-old children learn to use video as a source of information. *Developmental Psychology* 39(1): 140–50.

Ulmer R.G., Preusser D.F., Williams A.F., Ferguson S.A. & Farmer C.M. (2000) Effect of Florida's graduated licensing program on the crash rate of teenage drivers. *Accident Analysis and Prevention* 32(4): 527–32.

Vidal-Vazquez M.A. & Clemente-Diaz M. (2000) The attraction of media violence. *PSICO* 31(2): 49–80.

Vingoe F.J. (1991) The truth and nothing but the truth about forensic hypnosis. *The Psychologist* 14(9): 395–7.

Wells G.L. (1978) Applied eyewitness-testimony research; system variables and estimator variables. *Journal of Personality and Social Psychology* 36: 1546–57.

Wells G.L. & Bradfield A.L. (1998) 'Good, you identified the suspect': feedback to eyewitness distorts their reports of the witnesing experience. *Journal of Applied Psychology* 83(3): 360–76.

Wells G.L., Wright E.F. & Bradfield A.L. (1999) Witness to crime: social and cognitive factors governing the validity of people's reports. In Roesch R., Hart S.D. & Ogloff J.R.P. (eds) *Psychology and law: the state of the discipline.* New York: Kluwer Academic/Plenum Publishers.

Wiegman O. & van Schie E.G.M. (1998) Video game playing and its relation with aggressive and prosocial behaviour. *British Journal of Social Psychology* 37: 367–78.

Wood W., Wong F.Y. & Chachere J.G. (1991) Effects of media violence on viewers' aggression in unconstrained social interaction. *Psychological Bulletin* 109: 371–83.

Wuensch K.L., Campbell M.W., Kesler F.C. & Moore C.H. (2002) Racial bias in decisions made by mock jurors evaluating a case of sexual harassment. *Journal of Social Psychology* 142(5): 587–600.

Yuille J.C. & Cutshall J.L. (1986) A case study of eyewitness memory of a crime. *Journal of Applied Psychology* 71: 291–301.

Yukawa S., Endo K. & Yoshida F. (2001) The effects of media violence on aggression: focus on the role of anger evoked by provocation. *Japanese Journal of Psychology* 72(1): 1–9.

Zamble E. & Quinsey V.L. (1997) *The criminal recidivism process.* Cambridge: Cambridge University Press.

Zeisel H. (1971) And then there were none. the diminuition of the federal jury. *University of Chicago Law Review* 38: 710–24.

Zillman D. (1993) Mental control of angry aggression. In Wegner D. & Pennebaker J. (eds) *Handbook of mental control,* vol 5, pages 370–92. Englewood Cliffs, NJ: Prentice Hall.

Sports psychology

Amorose A.J. & Horn T.S. (2001) Pre to post-season changes in the intrinsic motivation of first-year college athletes: relationships with coaching behaviour and scholarship status. *Journal of Applied Sport Psychology* 13: 355–73.

Apter M.J. (1993) Phenomenological frames and the paradoxes of experiences. In Kerr J.H., Murgatroyd S. & Apter M.J. (eds) *Advances in reversal theory.* Amsterdam: Swets & Zeitlinger.

Ashford B., Biddle S. & Goudas M. (1993) Participation in community sport centres: motives and predictors of enjoyment. *Journal of Sport Sciences* 11: 249–56.

Bandura A. (1977) *Social learning theory.* Englewood Cliffs: Prentice Hall.

Bandura A. (1982) Self-efficacy mechanisms in human agency. *American Psychologist* 37: 122–47.

Beal B. (1996) Alternative masculinity and its effects on gender relations in the subculture of skateboarding. *Journal of Sport Behaviour* 19: 204–20.

Biddle S. & Hill A.B. (1992) Relationships between attributions and emotions in a laboratory-based sporting contest. *Journal of Sport Sciences* 10: 65–75.

Caron S.L., Halteman W.A. & Stacy C. (1997) Athletes and rape: is there a connection? *Perceptual and Motor Skills* 85: 1379–93.

Carron A.V., Widmeyer W.N. & Brawley L.R. (1985) The development of an instrument to assess cohesion in sport teams: the group environment questionnaire. *Journal of Sport Psychology* 7: 244–66.

Cattell R.B. (1965) *The scientific analysis of personality.* Harmondsworth: Penguin.

Chase M. (1998) Sources of self-efficacy in physical education and sport. *Journal of Teaching in Physical Education* 18: 76–89.

Chirivella E.C. & Martinez L.M. (1994) The sensation of risk and motivational tendencies in sports: an empirical study. *Personality and Individual Differences* 16: 777–86.

Cockerill I. (ed) (2002) *Solutions in sport psychology.* London: Thomson Learning.

Costa P.T. & McCrae R.R. (1985) *The NEO Personality Inventory manual.* Odessa: Psychology Assessment Resources.

Cottrell N.B. (1968) Performance in the presence of other human beings: mere presence, audience and affiliation effects. In Simmel E.C. et al (ed) *Social facilitation and imitative behaviour.* Boston: Allyn & Bacon.

Cox R. (1998) *Sport psychology.* New York: McGraw-Hill.

Craig K.M. (2000) Defeated athletes, abusive mates? Examining perceptions of professional athletes who batter. *Journal of Interpersonal Violence* 15: 1224–32.

Deci E.L. (1972) The effects of contingent and noncontingent rewards and controls on intrinsic motivation. *Organisational Behaviour & Human Decision Processes* 8: 217–29.

Drewe S.B. (1998) Competing conceptions of competition: implications for physical education. *European Physical Education Review* 4: 5–20.

Duck J.M. (1990) Children's ideals: the role of real life versus media figures. *Australian Journal of Psychology* 42: 19–29.

Duda J. & Pensgaard A.M. (2002) Enhancing the quantity and quality of motivation: the promotion of task involvement in a junior football team. In Cockerill I.(ed) *Solutions in sport psychology.* London: Thomson Learning.

Egloff B. & Gruhn A.J. (1996) Personality and endurance sports. *Personality & Individual Differences* 21: 223–9.

Engler B. (1999) *Personality theory and research.* Boston: Houghton-Mifflin.

European Federation of Sport Psychology (1996) Position statement of the EFPSC: definition of sport psychology. *Sport Psychologist* 10: 221–3.

Eysenck H.J. (1952) *The scientific study of personality.* London: Routledge & Kegan Paul.

Eysenck H.J. (1967) *The biological basis of personality.* Springfield: Charles Thomas.

Eysenck H.J. (1975) *The inequality of man.* San Diego: Edits.

Eysenck H.J., Nias K.D.B. & Cox D.N. (1982) Sport and psychology. *Advances in Behavioural Research and Therapy* 4, 1: 1–56.

Fazey J. & Hardy L. (1988) The inverted U hypothesis: a catastrophe for sport psychology? *British Association of Sport Sciences Monograph 1,* Leeds: National Coaching Foundation.

Feher P., Meyers M.C. & Skelly W.A. (1998) Psychological profiles of rock climbers: state and trait attributes. *Journal of Sport Behaviour* 21: 167–80.

Ferraro T. (1999) A psychoanalytic perspective on anxiety in athletes. *Athletic Insight* 1: np.

Fortier M.S., Vallerand R.J., Briere N.M. & Provencher P.J. (1995) Competitive and recreational sport structures and gender: a test of their relationship with sport motivation. *International Journal of Sport Psychology* 26: 24–39.

Francis L.J., Kelly P. & Jones S.J. (1998) The personality profile of female students who play hockey. *Irish Journal of Psychology* 19: 394–9.

Garland D.J. & Barry J.R. (1990) Personality and leader behaviors in collegiate football: a multidimensional approach to performance. *Journal of Research in Personality* 24: 355–70.

Geisler G.W.W. & Leith L.M. (1997) The effects of self-esteem, self-efficacy and audience presence on soccer penalty shot performance. *Journal of Sport Behaviour* 20: 322–37.

Gervis M. (1991) Children in sport. In Bull S. (ed) *Sport psychology: a self help guide.* Marlborough: Crowood.

Gill D. (1992) Gender and sport behaviour. In Horn T.S. (ed) *Advances in sport psychology.* Champaign: Human Kinetics.

Gill D. (2000) *Psychological dynamics of sport.* Champaign: Human Kinetics.

Gould D., Guinan D., Greenleaf K., Medbery R. & Peterson K. (1999) Factors affecting Olympic performance: perceptions of athletes and coaches in more and less successful teams. *Sport Psychologist* 13: 371–94.

Grieve F.G., Whelan J.P. & Meyers A.W. (2000) An experimental examination of the cohesion-performance relationship in an interactive sport. *Journal of Applied Sport Psychology* 12: 219–35.

Guillet E., Sarrazin P. & Fontayne P. (2000) 'If it contradicts my gender role I'll stop': introducing survival analysis to study the effects of gender typing on the time of withdrawal from sport practice: a 3-year study. *European Review of Applied Psychology,* 50: 417–21.

Hagger M. (1997) Children's physical activity levels and attitudes towards physical activity. *European Physical Education Review* 3, 2: 144–64.

Hanin Y. (1986) State-trait anxiety research on sports in the USSR. In Spielberger C. & Dias-Guerrero R. (eds) *Cross-cultural anxiety*. Washington, Hemisphere.

Hardy L., Parfitt G. & Pates J. (1994) Performance catastrophes in sport: a test of the hysteresis hypothesis. *Journal of Sport Sciences* 12: 327–34.

Hardy L. (1996) Testing the predictions of the cusp catastrophe model of anxiety and performance. *Sport Psychologist*, 10: 140–56.

Harry J. (1995) Sports ideology, attitudes toward women and anti-homosexual attitudes. *Sex Roles* 32: 109–16.

Hastie P.A. & Sharpe T. (1999) Effects of a sport education curriculum on the positive social behaviour of at-risk rural adolescent boys. *Journal of Education for Students Placed at Risk* 4: 417–30.

Hills P. & Argyle M. (1998) Positive moods derived from leisure and their relationship to happiness and personality. *Personality & Individual Differences* 25: 523–35.

Holt N.L. & Sparkes A.C. (2001) An ethnographic study of cohesiveness in a college soccer team over a season. *Sport Psychologist* 15: 237–59.

Hull C.L. (1943) *Principles of behaviour*. New York: Appleton-Century-Crofts.

Inlay G.J., Carda R.G., Stanborough M.E., Dreiling A.M. & O'Connor P.J. (1995) Anxiety & performance: a test of zone of optimal functioning theory. *International Journal of Sport Psychology* 26: 295–306.

Jambor E.A. (1999) Parents as children's socialising agents in youth soccer. *Journal of Sport Behaviour* 22: 350–9.

John O.P. (1990) The 'Big Five' factor taxonomy: dimensions of personality in natural language and in questionnaires. In Pervin L.A. (ed) (1990) *Handbook of personality: theory and research*. New York: Guildford Press.

Jones G. (1991) Recent developments and current issues in competitive state anxiety research. *The Psychologist* 4: 152–5.

Kerr J.H. (1997) *Motivation and emotion in sport*. Hove: Taylor & Francis.

Kozub S.A. & Button C. (2000) The influence of competitive outcome on perceptions of cohesion in rugby and swimming teams. *International Journal of Sport Psychology* 31: 82–95.

Krane V. (1998) Lesbians in sport. *Proceedings of the 1998 BPS annual conference* 6: 2, 109.

Kremer J. & Scully D. (1994) *Psychology in sport*. London: Taylor & Francis.

Landers D.M. & Boutcher S.H. (1993) Arousal-performance relationships. In Williams J.M. (1993) *Applied sport psychology*. Mountain View: Mayfield.

Lantz C.D. & Schroeder P.J. (1999) Endorsement of masculine and feminine gender roles: differences between participation in and identification with the athletic role. *Journal of Sport Behaviour* 22: 545–57.

Martens R., Burton D., Vealey R.S., Bump L.A. & Smith D. (1990) Development and validation of the competitive state anxiety inventory – 2. In Martens R. et al (ed) *Competitive anxiety in sport*. Champaign: Human Kinetics.

Martin K.A., Sinden A.R. & Fleming J.C. (2000) Inactivity may be hazardous to your image: the effects of exercise participation on impression formation. *Journal of Sport & Exercise Psychology* 22: 283–91.

McClelland D.C., Atkinson J.W., Clark R.W. & Lowell E.J. (1961) *The achievement motive*. New York: Appleton Century Crofts.

Medvec V.H., Madey S.F. & Gilovich T. (1995) When less is more: counterfactual thinking and satisfaction among Olympic medallists. *Journal of Personality & Social Psychology* 69: 603–10.

Michaels J.W., Blommel J.M., Brocato R.M., Linkous R.A. & Rowe J.S. (1982) Social facilitation and inhibition in a natural setting. *Replications in Social Psychology* 2: 21–4.

Miller J.L. & Levy G.D. (1996) Gender role conflict, gender-typed characteristics, self-concept and sports socialisation in female athletes and non-athletes. *Sex Roles* 35: 111–12.

Mischell W. (1973) Towards a cognitive social learning conception of personality. *Psychological Review* 80: 252–83.

Morgan L.K., Griggin J. & Heywood V.H. (1996) Ethnicity, gender and experience effects on attributional dimensions. *Sport Psychologist* 10: 4–16.

Murgatroyd S., Rushton C., Apter M. & Ray C. (1978) The development of the telic dominance scale. *Journal of Personality Assessment* 12: 519–28.

Nevill A.M. & Cann G.J. (1998) Does home advantage peak with crowd sizes? *Proceedings of the 1998 BPS annual conference* 6: 2, 112.

Nicholls J. (1984) Concepts of ability and achievement motivation. In Ames R. & Ames C. (eds) *Research on motivation in education: student motivation* vol 1 (pages 39–73). New York: Academic Press.

Norman W.T. (1963) Towards an adequate taxonomy of personality attributes. *Journal of Abnormal and Social Psychology* 66: 574–83.

Orbach I., Singer R. & Price S. (1999) An attribution programme and achievement in sport. *Sport Psychologist* 13: 69–82.

Pervin L. (1993) *Personality*. New York: Wiley.

Piedmont R.L., Hill D.C. & Blanco S. (1999) Predicting athletic performance using the five-factor model of personality. *Personality & Individual Differences* 27: 769–77.

Randle S. & Weinberg R. (1997) Multidimensional anxiety and performance: an exploratory examination of the Zone of Optimal Functioning Hypothesis. *The Sport Psychologist* 11: 160–74.

Roese N.J. (1997) Counterfactual thinking. *Psychological Bulletin* 121: 133–48.

Russell W.D. & Cox R.H. (2000) A laboratory investigation of positive and negative affect within individual zones of optimal functioning theory. *Journal of Sport Behaviour* 23: 164–80.

Schurr K.T., Ashley M.A. & Joy K.L. (1977). A multivariate analysis of male athlete personality characteristics; sport type and success. *Multivariate Experimental Clinical Psychology* 3: 53–68.

Scully D. (2002) 'The team just hasn't gelled.' In Cockerill I.(ed) *Solutions in sport psychology*. London: Thomson Learning.

Sevcikova L., Ruzanza S. & Sablova M. (2000) Neuroticism, physical activity and nutritional habits in school children. *Homeostasis in Health & Disease* 40: 143–4.

Shields E.W. (1999) Intimidation and violence by males in high school athletics. *Adolescence* 34: 503–21.

Slater M.R. & Sewell D.F. (1994) An examination of the cohesion-performance relationship in university hockey teams. *Journal of Sport Sciences* 12: 423–31.

Steinberg G.M., Singer R. & Murphy M. (2001) The benefits to sport achievement when a multiple goal orientation is emphasised. *Journal of Sport Behaviour* 23: 407–22.

Sturman T.S. & Thibodeau R. (2001) Performance-undermining effects of baseball free-agent contracts. *Journal of Sport & Exercise Psychology* 23: 23–36.

Swain A. (1996) Social loafing and identifiability: the mediating role of achievement goal orientations. *Research Quarterly for Exercise & Sport* 67: np.

Thelwell R.C. & Maynard I.W. (2000) Professional cricketers' perceptions of the importance of antecedents influencing repeatable good performance. *Perceptual & Motor Skills* 90: 649–58.

Triplett N. (1898) The dynamogenic factors in pacemaking and competition. *American Journal of Psychology* 9: 507–53.

Tutko T.A. & Ogilvie B.C. (1966) *Athletic motivation inventory*. San Jose: Institute for the Study of Athletic Motivation.

Waxmonsky J. & Beresin E.V. (2001) Taking professional wrestling to the mat: a look at the appeal and potential effects of professional wrestling on children. *Academic Psychiatry* 25: 125–31.

Weiner B. (1974) *Achievement motivation and attribution theory*. Morristown: General Learning Press.

Wells C.M., Collins D. & Hale B.D. (1993) The self-efficacy-performance link in maximum strength performance, *Journal of Sport Sciences* 11: 167–75.

Woolfson S. (2002) Reflections on past events: the role of social cognition in sport. In Cockerill I.(ed) *Solutions in sport psychology*. London: ITP.

Wright E.F., Voyer D. & Wright R.D. (1995) Supporting audiences and performance under pressure: the home-ice disadvantage in hockey championships. *Journal of Sport Behaviour* 18: 21–8.

Yerkes R.M. & Dodson J.D. (1908) The relation to stimulus to rapidity of habit formation. *Nature* 84: 459–82.

Zahariadis P.N. & Biddle S.J.H. (2000) Goal orientations and participation motives in physical education and sport: their relationships in English schoolchildren. *Athletic Insight* 2: np.

Zajonc R.B. (1965) Social facilitation. *Science* 149: 269–74.

Child psychology

Ainsworth M.D.S. (1967) *Infancy in Uganda: infant care and the growth of love*. Baltimore: Johns Hopkins University Press.

Ainsworth M.D.S. (1985) Patterns of infant-mother attachments: antecedents and effects on development. *Bulletin of the New York Academy of Medicine* 61: 771–91.

Ainsworth M.D.S. & Wittig B.A. (1969) Attachment theory and the exploratory behaviour of one-year-olds in a strange situation. Foss B.M. (ed) *Determinants of Infant Behaviour, vol. 4*. London: Methuen.

Ainsworth M.D.S., Blehar M.C., Waters E. & Wall E. (1978) *Patterns of attachment*. Hillsdale: Erlbaum.

Andersson B.E. (1996) Children's development related to day care, type of family and other home factors. *European Child and Adolescent Psychiatry* 5: 73–6.

Asher S.R., Parkhurst J.T., Hymel S. & Williams G.A. (1990) Peer rejection and loneliness in childhood. In Asher S.R. and Coie J.D. (eds) *Peer rejection in childhood*. Cambridge: Cambridge University Press.

Axline V.M. (1947) *Dibs in search of self*. London: Penguin.

Barnett M.A. (1984) Similarity of experience and empathy in preschoolers. *Journal of Genetic Psychology* 145: 241–50.

Baydar N. & Brooks-Gunn J. (1991) Effects of Maternal employment and child care arrangements on pre-schoolers' cognitive and behavioural outcomes. *Development Psychology* 27:932–45.

Bifulco A., Brown G.W. & Alder Z. (1991) Early sexual abuse and clinical depression in later life. *British Journal of Psychiatry* 159: 115–22.

Bjorkland D.F. & Brown R.D. (1998) Physical play and cognitive development: integrating activity, cognition and education. *Child Development* 69: 604–6.

Bowlby J. (1946) *Forty four juvenile thieves*. London: Balliere, Tindall & Cox.

Bowlby J. (1951) *Maternal care and mental health*. Geneva: World Health Organisation.

Bowlby J. (1957) Symposium on the contribution of current theories to an understanding of child development *British Journal of Medical Psychology* 30: 230–40.

Bowlby J. (1958) The nature of the child's tie to his mother. *International Journal of Psychoanalysis* 39: 350–73.

Bowlby J. (1969) *Attachment and loss, vol I*. London: Pimlico.

Bowlby J. (1988) *A secure base*. London: Routledge.

Brazleton T.B. (1979) Behavioural competence in the newborn infant. *Seminars in Perinatology* 3: 35–44.

Burman E. (1994) *Deconstructing developmental psychology*. London: Routledge.

Carlson V., Cicchetti D., Barnett D. & Braunwald K. (1989) Disorganised/disoriented attachment relationships in maltreated infants. *Developmental Psychology* 25: 525–31.

Cash T.F. (1995) Developmental teasing about physical appearance: retrospective descriptions and relationships with body image. *Social Behaviour and Personality* 23: 123–9.

Clarke A.M. & Clarke A.D.B. (1992) How modifiable is the human life path? *International Review of Research in Mental Retardation* 18: 137–57.

Clarke A.D.B. & Clarke A.M. (1998) Early experience and the life path. *The Psychologist* 11: 433–6.

Cockett M. & Tripp J. (1994) Children living in re-ordered families. *Social Policy Research Findings* 45, Joseph Rowntree Foundation.

Coie J.D. & Dodge K.A. (1983) continuities and changes in children's social status: a five-year longitudinal study. *Merrill-Palmer Quarterly* 29: 261–82.

Coie J.D. & Dodge K.A. (1988) Multiple sources of data on social behaviour and social status in the school: a cross-age comparison. *Child Development* 59: 815–29.

Connolly J.A. & Doyle A. (1984) Relation of social fantasy play to social competence in preschoolers. *Developmental Psychology* 20: 797–806.

Cowie H. (1995) Child care and attachment. In Barnes P. (ed) *Personal, social and emotional development of children*. Oxford: Blackwell.

Cross T.L. (1998) Understanding family resiliency from a relational world view. In McCubbin H.I. (ed) *Resiliency in Native American and Immigrant Families. Vol. 2*. Thousand Oaks: Sage Publications.

Curry N.E. & Arnaud S.H. (1984) Play in developmental preschool settings. In Yawkey T.D. & Pellegrini A. (eds) *Child's play: devel-*

opmental and applied. Hillsdale: Lawrence Erlbaum.

Curtiss S. (1977) *Genie: a psycholinguistic study of a modern day 'wild child'*. London: Academic Press.

Das Gupta P. (1995) Growing up in families. In Barnes P. (ed) *Personal, social and emotional development of children*. Milton Keynes: Open University Press.

Dunn J. (1988) *The beginnings of social understanding*. Oxford: Blackwell.

Dunn J. & Munn P. (1985) Becoming a family member: family conflict and the development of social understanding in the first year. *Child Development* 50: 306–18.

Dunn J., Hughes C. & Omotoso S.G.D.P. (1999) Violent fantasies and anti-social behaviour in hard to manage preschoolers' dyadic peer play. *Proceedings of the British Psychological Society* 7: 97.

Erwin P. (1998) *Friendships in childhood and adolescence*. London: Routledge.

Faulkner D. (1995) Play, self and the social world. In Barnes P. (ed) *Personal, social and emotional development of children*. Oxford: Blackwell.

Fein D. (1975) A transformational analysis of pretending. *Developmental Psychology* 11: 291–6.

Fergusson D.N., Horwood L.J. & Lynskey M.T. (1992) Family change, discord and early offending. *Journal of Child Psychology and Psychiatry* 33: 1059–75.

First E. (1994) The leaving game, or I'll play you and you play me: the emergence of dramatic role play in 2 year-olds. In Slade A. & Wolf D.P. (eds) *Children at play*. Oxford: Oxford University Press.

Flanagan C. (1999) *Early socialisation*. London: Routledge.

Flanagan C. (1999) Early privation and developmental catch-up. *Psychology Review* 6(1): 24–5.

Fonagy P. & Targe M. (1994) The efficacy of psychoanalysis for children with disruptive disorders. *Journal of the American Academy of Child & Adolescent Psychiatry* 33(1).

Fonagy P., Steele M., Moran G., Steele H. & Higgitt A. (1993) Measuring the ghost in the nursery: an empirical study of the relation between parents' mental representations of childhood experiences and their infants' security of attachment. *Journal of the American Psychoanalytic Association* 41: 957–89.

Fonagy P., Steele H., Steele M. & Holder J. (1997) Attachment and theory of mind: overlapping constructs? In Forrest G. (ed) *Bonding and attachment: current issues in research and attachment*. Occasional Papers 14. London: Association for Child Psychology and Psychiatry.

Fox N.J., Joesbury H. & Hannay D.R. (1991) Family attachments and medical sociology: a valuable partnership for student learning.

References

Medical Education 25(2): 155–9.

Frankel K.A. & Bates J.E. (1990) Mother-toddler problem solving: antecedents in attachment, home behaviour and temperament. *Child Development* 61, 810–19.

Freud S. (1922) Author's abstract of a congress address. *International Journal of Psychoanalysis* 8: 486.

Goldsmith H.H. & Alansky J. (1987) Maternal and infant temperamental predictors of attachment: a meta-analytic review. *Journal of Consulting and Clinical Psychology* 55: 805–16.

Goossens L., Marcoen A., van Hees S. & van de Woestijne O. (1999) Attachment style and loneliness in adolescence. *European Journal of Psychology of Education* 13: 529–42.

Gross R. (1997) Attachment theory; extensions and applications. *Psychology Review* 4: 10–13.

Grossman K.E. & Grossman K. (1990) The wider concept of attachment in cross-cultural research. *Human Development* 33: 31–47.

Haight W.L. & Miller P.J. (1993) *Pretending at home: early development in a socio-cultural context.* Albany: SUNY Press.

Harr G.A.R. (1999) The impact of maternal employment on the academic attainment and social adjustment of school-age children. *Dissertation Abstracts International* 60: 0333.

Harrison A.O., Stewart R.B., Myambo K. & Teveraische C. (1995) Perceptions of social networks among adolescents from Zimbabwe and the United States. *Journal of Black Psychology*, 21: 382–407.

Hayes N. (1998) *Foundations of psychology.* London: Nelson.

Hazan C. & Shaver P. (1987) Romantic love conceptualised as an attachment process. *Journal of Personality and Social Psychology* 52: 511–24.

Hinde R.A., Titmus G., Easton D, & Tamplin A. (1985) Incidence of friendship and behaviour toward strong associates versus nonassociates in preschoolers. *Child Development* 68: 234–45.

Hobson R. (1985) *Forms of feeling.* London: Routledge.

Hodges J. (1996) The natural history of non attachment. In Bernstein B. & Branner J. (eds) *Children, research and policy.* London: Taylor & Francis.

Hodges J. & Tizard B. (1989a) IQ and behavioural adjustment of ex-institutional adolescents. *Journal of Child Psychology and Psychiatry* 30: 53–76.

Hodges J. & Tizard B. (1989b) Social and family relationships of ex-institutional adolescents. *Journal of Child Psychology and Psychiatry* 30: 77–98.

Holmes J. (1993) *John Bowlby and attachment theory.* London: Routledge.

Isaacs S. (1929) *The nursery years.* London: Routledge & Kegan Paul.

Jarvis M. (2003) *Psychodynamic psychology: classic theory and contemporary research.* London: Thomson Learning.

Jekielek S.M. (1998) Parental conflict, marital disruption and children's emotional well-being. *Social Forces* 76: 905–36.

Jones W.H., Hobbs S.A. & Hockenbury D. (1982) Loneliness and social skills deficits. *Journal of Personality and Social Psychology* 42: 682–9.

Juffer F., Hoksbergen R.A.C., Rene A.C., Riksen-Walraven J.M. & Kohnstamm G.A. (1997) Early intervention in adoptive families: supporting maternal sensitive responsiveness, infant-mother attachment and infant competence. *Journal of Child Psychology and Psychiatry and Allied Disciplines* 38 1039–50.

Kerns K.A. (1994) A longitudinal examination of links between mother-infant attachment and children's friendships. *Journal of Personality and Social Relationships*, 11: 379–81.

Kerns K.A. & Stevens A.C. (1996) Parent-child attachment in late adolescence. *Journal of Youth and Adolescence* 25, 323–42.

Kirkby R.J. & Whelan R.J. (1996) The effects of hospitalisation and medical procedures on children and their families. *Journal of Family Studies* 2: 56–77.

Koluchova J. (1972) Severe deprivation in twins: a case study. *Journal of Child Psychology and Psychiatry* 13: 23–8.

Koluchova J. (1991) Severely deprived twins after 22 years observation. *Studia Psycholgica* 33: 23–8.

Koren-Karie N. (2001) Mothers' attachment representations and choice of infant care: centre care vs home. *Infant & Child Development* 10: 117–27.

Ladd G.W. & Golter B.S. (1988) Parents' management of preschoolers' peer relations: is it related to children's social competence? *Developmental Psychology* 24: 109–17.

LaFreniere P.J. & Sroufe L.A. (1985) Profiles of peer competence in the preschool: interrelations between measures, influence of social ecology and relation to attachment theory. *Developmental Psychology* 21: 56–69.

Langlois J.H., Ritter J.M., Casey R.J. & Sawin D.B. (1995) Infant attractiveness predicts maternal behaviours and attitudes. *Developmental Psychology* 31: 464–72.

Lanyado M. & Horne A. (1999) *The handbook of child and adolescent psychotherapy.* London: Routledge.

LeBlanc M. & Ritchie M. (1999) Predictors of play therapy outcomes. *International Journal of Play Therapy* 9(2): 19–34.

Levanean M. & Silven M. (2000) Does the mother's quality of attachment predict maternal sensitivity? *Psykologia* 35: 58–70.

Levinger G. & Levinger A.C. (1986) The temporal course of close relationships: some thoughts about the development of children's personalities. In Hartup, W.W. and Rubin, Z. (eds) *Relationships and development.* Hillsdale: Erlbaum.

Lewis M., Young G., Brooks J. & Michalson L. (1975) The beginnings of friendship. In Lewis M. & Rosenblum L. (eds) *Friendship and peer relations.* New York: Wiley.

Lyons-Ruth K., Bronfman E. & Parsons E. (1999) Maternal frightened, frightening or atypical behaviour and disorganised infant attachment patterns. In Vondra J.I. & Barnett D. *Atypical attachment in infancy and early childhood among children at developmental risk.* Monographs of the Society for Research into Child Development.

Main M. & Solomon J. (1986) Discovery of a disorganised disorientated attachment pattern. In *Affective development in infancy.* Norwood, Ablex.

McCarthy G. (1999) Attachment style and adult love relationships and friendships: a study of a group of women at risk of experiencing relationship difficulties. *British Journal of Medical Psychology* 72, 305–21.

Meins E. (1997) *Security of attachment and the development of social cognition.* Hove: Psychology Press.

Melzak S. (1999) Psychotherapeutic work with child and adolescent refugees from political violence. In Lanyardo M. (ed.) et al *The handbook of child and psychotherapy: psychoanalytic approaches.* New York: Routledge.

Montmayer R. & Van Komen R. (1985) The development of sex differences in friendship patterns and peer group structure during adolescence. *Journal of Early Adolescence* 5: 285–94.

Myron-Wilson P. & Smith P.K. (1998) Attachment relationships and influences on bullying. *Proceedings of the British Psychological Society* 6(2): 89–90.

Nair H. (1999) A study of the effects of divorce on maternal parenting and attachment security in preschool-aged children. *Dissertation Abstracts International* 59: 5617.

Newcomb A.F. & Bagwell C.L. (1995) Children's friendship relations: a meta-analytic review. *Psychological Bullentin* 117(2): 306–47.

Nowak-Fabrykowski K. (1995) Can symbolic play prepare children for their future? *Early Child Development and Care* 102: 63–9.

O'Brien S.F. & Bierman K.L. (1988) Conceptions and perceived influence of peer groups: Interviews with preadolescents and adolescents. *Child Development* 59(5): 1360–5.

Parker J.G. & Asher S.R. (1987) Peer relations and later personal adjustment: are low-accepted children at risk? *Psychological Bulletin* 102:357–89.

Parsons M. (1999) The logic of play in psychoanalysis. *International Journal of Psychoanalysis* 80, 871–84.

Parten M. (1932) Social participation among pre-school children. *Journal of Abnormal and Social Psychology* 27: 243–60.

Pellegrini A.D. (1994) The rough play of boys of different sociometric status. *International Journal of Behavioural Development* 17: 525–40.

Pellegrini A.D. & Melhuish E.C. (1998) Friendship, individual differences and children's literacy. *Proceedings of the British Psychological Society* 6: 90.

Pellegrini A.D. & Smith P.K. (1998) Physical activity play: the nature and function of a neglected aspect of play. *Child Development* 69: 577–98.

Radke-Yarrow M., McCann K., DeMulder E., Belmont B., Martinez P. & Richardson D.T. (1995) Attachment in the context of high risk conditions. *Development and Psychopathology* 7, 247–65.

Richards M.H., Boxer A.M., Peterson A.C. & Albrecht, R. (1990) Relation of weight to body image in pubertal girls and boys from two communities. *Developmental Psychology* 26: 313–21.

Robertson J. & Bowlby J. (1952) Responses of young children to separation from their mothers. *Courier Centre International d'Enfance* 2: 131–42.

Rubin K.H., Fein G. & Vandenberg B. (1983) Play: In Hetherington, E.M. (ed) *Handbook of child psychology*, vol 4. New York: Wiley.

Russell C.M. (1999) A meta-analysis of published research on the effects of nonmaternal care on child development. *Dissertation Abstracts International, A (Humanities and Social Sciences)* 59(9–A) 3362.

Rutter M. (1979) *Changing youth in a changing society*. London: Nuffield Provincial Hospitals Trust.

Rutter, M. (1981) *Maternal deprivation reassessed*. Harmondworth: Penguin.

Rutter M. & the English and Romanian Adoptees Study Team (1998) Developmental catch up and deficit after sever global early privation. *Journal of Child Psychology and Psychiatry* 39: 465–76.

Schafer M. & Smith P.K. (1996) Teachers' perceptions of play fighting and real fighting in a primary school. *Educational Research* 38: 173–81.

Schaffer, H.R. (1996) *Social development*. Oxford: Blackwell..

Shaffer, D.R. (1999) *Developmental psychology: childhood and adolescence*. Pacific Grove: Brooks/Cole.

Shultz N.R. & Moore D. (1989) Further reflections on loneliness research. In Hojat, M. & Crandall R. (eds) *Loneliness: theory, research and applications*. Newbury Park: Sage.

Skuse D.H. (1993) Extreme deprivation in early childhood. In Messer D. & Dockerell J. (1999) (eds) *Developmental psychology, a reader*. London: Arnold.

Slade A. & Wolf D.P. (eds) (1994) *Children at play: clinical and developmental approaches to meaning and representation*. Oxford: Oxford University Press.

Sloan S.A. (1999) Effects of aggressive therapeutic play: does it increase or diminish spontaneous aggression? *Dissertation Abstracts International* 59: 3677.

Smith P. (1998) Social development. In Eysenck M. (ed) *Psychology, an integrated approach*. Harlow: Longman.

Smith P.K., Cowie H. & Blades M. (1998) *Understanding children's development*. Oxford: Blackwell.

Sroufe L.A. (1985) Attachment classification from the perspective of infant-caregiver relationships and infant temperament. *Child Development* 56: 1–14.

Stone G.P. (1981) The play of little children. In Stone, G.P. & Faberman H.A. (eds) *Social psychology through symbolic interaction*. New York: Wiley.

Sylva K. (1994) The therapeutic value of play. *Psychology Review* 1.

Takahashi K. (1990) Affective relationships and their lifelong development. In Baltes P.B. (ed) et al *Life-span development and behaviour*, vol. 10. Hillsdale: Lawrence Erlbaum Associates, Inc.

Tarullo L.B. (1994) Windows on social worlds: gender differences in children's play narratives. In Slade A. & Wolf D.P. (eds) *Children at play*. Oxford: Oxford University Press.

Tizard B. & Hodges J. (1978) The effect of early institutional care on eight year old children. *Journal of Psychology and Psychiatry* 19, 99–118.

Tizard B. & Rees J. (1974) A comparison of the effects of adoption, restoration to the natural mother and continued institutionalisation on the cognitive development of four-year old children. *Child Development* 45: 92–9.

Tobin J.J., Wu D.Y.H. & Davidson D.H. (1989) *Preschool in three cultures: Japan, China and the United States*. New Haven: Yale University Press.

Tracy R. & Ainsworth M.D.S. (1981) Maternal affectionate behaviour and infant-mother attachment patterns. *Child Development* 52: 1341–3.

Tremblay-Leveau H. & Nadel J. (1996) Exclusion in triads: can it serve metacommunicative knowledge in 11 and 13 year-old children? *British Journal of Developmental Psychology* 14: 145–58.

Troy M. & Sroufe L.A. (1987) Victimisation among preschoolers: role of attachment relationship history. *Journal of the Academy of Child and Adolescent Psychiatry* 26: 166–72.

Vandell D.L. (1980) Sociablity with peer and mother during the first year. *Developmental Psychology* 16: 355–61.

Van den Boom D.C. (1994) The influence of temperamnet and mothering on attachment and exploration: an experimental manipulation of sensitive responsiveness among lower-class mothers with irritable babies. *Child Development* 65: 1457–77.

Van Ijzendoorn M.H. (1997) Attachment, emergent morality and aggression: toward a developmental socioemotional model of antisocial behaviour. *International Journal of Behavioural Development* 21: 703–27.

Vondra J.I. & Barnett D. (1999) Atypical attachments in infancy an dearly childhood among children at developmental risk. *Monographs of the Society for Research in Child Development*. Oxford: Blackwell.

Vygotsky L.S. (1967) Play and its role in mental development of the child. *Soviet Psychology* 12: 62–76.

Warren S.L., Emde R.N. & Sroufe L.A. (2000) Internal representations: predicting anxiety from children's play narratives. *Journal of the Academy of Child and Adolescent Psychiatry* 39: 100–7.

Watson M.W. (1994) The relation between anxiety and pretend play. In Slade A. & Wolf D.P. (eds) *Children at play*. Oxford: Oxford University Press.

Whiting B.B. & Edwards C.P. (1988) *Children of different worlds: the formation of social behaviour*. Cambridge: Harvard University Press.

Health psychology

Abraham C. & Sheeran P. (1993) In search of a psychology of safer-sex promotion: beyond beliefs and text. *Health Education Research: Theory and Practice*, 8: 245–54.

Abraham C. & Sheeran P. (1994) Modelling and modifying young heterosexuals' HIV-preventative behaviour: a review of theories, findings and educational implications. *Patient Education and Counseling* 23: 173–86.

Abraham S.C.S., Sheeran P., Spears R. & Abrams D. (1992) Health beliefs and the promotion of HIV-preventative infections among teenagers: a Scottish perspective. *Health Psychology*, 11: 363–70.

Ajzen I. & Fishbein M. (1980) *Understanding attitudes and predicting social behavior*. Englewood Cliffs, NJ: Prentice-Hall.

Ajzen I. (1985) From intentions to actions: A theory of planned behavior. In Kuhl J. & Beckman J. (eds), *Action-control: from cognition to behavior*, pages 11–39. Heidelberg: Springer.

Ajzen I. (1991) The theory of planned behavior. *Organizational Behavior and Human Decision Processes* 50: 179–211.

Ames S.L., Zogg J.B. & Stacy A.W. (2002) Implicit cognition, sensation seeking, marijuana use and driving behavior among drug offenders. *Personality and Individual Differences*, 33(7): 1055–72.

Anderson B., Erwin N., Flynn D., Lewis L. & Erwin J. (1977) Effects of short-term crowding on aggression in captive groups of pigtail monkeys. *Aggressive Behavior* 3: 33–46.

Armitage C.J. & Conner M. (1998) Efficacy of the theory of planned behaviour: a meta-analytic review. Unpublished manuscript, University of Leeds.

Aspinwall L.G., Kemeny M.E., Taylor S.E., Schneider S.G. & Dudley J.P. (1991) Psychosocial predictors of gay men's AIDS risk-reduction behavior. *Health Psychology*, 10: 432–44.

Bachman J.G., Johnson L.D., O'Malley P.M. & Humphreys H. (1988) Explaining the recent decline in marijuana use: differentiating the effects of perceived risk, disapproval, and general life-style factors. *Journal of Health and Social Behaviour* 29: 92–112.

Bandura A. (1992) Exercise of personal agency through the self-efficacy mechanism. In Schwarzer R. (ed) *Self-efficacy: thought control and action*. Washington: Hemisphere.

Baron R.M., Mandel D.R., Adams C.A. & Griffen L.M. (1976) Effects of social density in university residential environments. *Journal of Personality and Social Psychology* 34: 434–46.

Barrera Jr M., Sandler I.N. & Ramsey T.B. (1981) Preliminary development of a scale of social support: studies on college students. *American Journal of Community Psychology* 9: 435–47.

Bartone P.T. (2000) Hardiness as a resiliency factor for United States forces in the Gulf War. In Volanti J.M. & Paton D. (2000) *Post-traumatic stress intervention: challenges, issues, and perspectives*. Springfield, Il: Charles C. Thomas.

Baum A. & Valins S. (1977) *Architecture and social behavior: psychological studies of social density*. Hilldale, NJ: Erlbaum.

Becker M.H. & Rosenstock I.M. (1987) Comparing social learning theory and the health belief model. In Ward W.B. (ed) *Advances in health education and promotion*, pages 245–9. Greenwich, CT: JAI Press. .

Belloc N.B. & Breslow L. (1972) Relationship of physical health status and health practices. *Preventative Medicine* 1: 409–21.

Ben-Eliyahu S., Yirmiya R., Liebeskind J.C., Taylor A.N. & Gale R.P. (1991) Stress increases metastatic spread of mammary tumor in rats: evidence for mediation by the immune system. *Brain, Behavior and Immunity* 5: 193–205.

Berkman L.F. & Syme S.L. (1979) Social networks, host resistance, and mortality: a nine-year follow-up of Almeda County residents. *American Journal of Epidemiology* 109: 186–204.

Bernstein Hyman R., Baker S., Ephrain R., Mondel A. & Philip J. (1994) Health Belief Model variables as predictors of screening mammography utilization. *Journal of Behavioural Medicine* 17: 391–406.

Bishop G.D. (1994) *Health psychology: integrating mind and body*. London: Allyn & Bacon.

Blakey V. & Frankland J. (1995) Evaluating HIV prevention for women prostitutes in Cardiff. *Health Education Journal* 54: 131–42.

Bohman M., Sigvardsson S. & Cloninger C.R. (1981) Maternal inheritance of alcohol abuse. *Archives of General Psychiatry* 38: 965–9.

Botvin G.J., Eng A. & Williams C.L. (1980) Preventing the onset of cigarette smoking through life skills training. *Preventative Medicine* 9: 135–43.

Bouchard C., Temblay A., Depres J.P., Nadeau A., Lupien P.J., Theriault G., Dussault .J, Moorjani S., Pinault S. & Fournier G. (1990) The response to long-term overfeeding in identical twins. *New England Journal of Medicine* 322: 1477–87.

Brannon L. & Feist J. (2000) *Health psychology: an introduction to behavior and health*. London: Wadsworth, Thomson Learning.

Breslow L. & Enstrom J. (1980) Persistence of medical conditions habits and their relation to mortality. *Preventive Medicine* 9: 469–83.

Brooner R.K., King V.L., Kindorf M. (1997) Psychiatric and substance abuse comorbidity among treatment-seeking opioid abusers. *Archives of General Psychiatry* 54: 71–80.

Brownell K.D. & Wadden T.A. (1992) Etiology and treatment of obesity: Understanding a serious, prevalent and refractory disorder. *Journal of Consulting and Clinical Psychology* 60: 505–17.

Brubaker C. & Wickersham D. (1990) Encouraging the practice of testicular self examination: a field application of the theory of reasoned action. *Health Psychology* 9: 154–63.

Calhoun J.B. (1962) Population density and social pathology. *Scientific American* 206: 139–48.

Calhoun J.B. (1971) Space and the strategy of life. In Esser A.H. (ed) *Behavior and environment: the use of space by Animals*. Bloomington, IN: University of Indiana Press.

Carlson N.R. (1998) *Physiology of behavior*. London: Allyn & Bacon.

Cassidy T. (1999) *Stress, cognition and health*. London: Routledge.

Champion V.L. (1990) Breast self-examination in women 35 and older: a prospective study. *Journal of Behavioral Medicine* 13: 523–38.

Channing C.E., Hughes B.O. & Walker A.W. (2001) Spatial distributions and behaviour of laying hems housed in an alternative system, *Applied Animal Behaviour Science* 72: 335–45.

Cho K., Ennaceur A., Cole J.C. & Kook-Suh, C. (2000) Chronic jet lag produces cognitive deficits. *Journal of Neuroscience* 20: RC 66.

Christian J.J. (1955) The effects of populations size on the adrenal glands od male mice in populations of fixed size. *American Journal of Physiology* 185: 292–300.

Cloninger C.R., Bohman M. & Sigvardsson S. (1981) Inheritance of alcohol abuse. *Archives of General Psychiatry* 38: 861–8.

Cohen S. & Wills T.A. (1985) Stress, social support, and the buffering hypothesis. *Psychological Bulletin* 98: 310–57.

Cohen S., Frank E., Doyle W.J. (1998) Types of stressors that increase susceptibility to the common cold in healthy adults. *Health Psychology* 17: 214–23.

Cohen S., Mermelstein R., Kamarck T. & Hoberman H.N. (1985) Measuring the functional components of social support. In Sarason I.G. & Sarason B.R. (eds) *Social support: theory, research, and applications*, pages 73–94. Dordrecht: Martinus Nijhoff.

Cohen S., Tyrell D. & Smith. A (1993) Negative life events, perceived stress, negative affect, and susceptibility to the common cold. *Journal of Personality and Social Psychology* 64: 131–40.

Collins D.L., Baum A. & Singer J. (1983) Coping with chronic stress at Three Mile Island; psychological and biochemical evidence. *Health Psychology* 2: 149–66.

Condon L. (2001) Cruising for safer sex. *The Advocate* 13 March 2001. .

Cooper C.L., Cooper R.D. & Eaker L.H. (1988) *Living with Stress*. London: Penguin.

Cornwell A. & Cornwell V. (1993) *Drugs, alcohol and mental health*. Cambridge: University of Cambridge Press.

CREDES (1994) In Patel T. (1995) Thank heaven for little pills. *New Scientist*, 1 April 1995: 14–15.

Crowcroft P. & Rowe F.P. (1958) The growth of confined colonies of the wild housemouse (*Mus musculus* L.): the effect of dispersal on female fecundity. *Proceedings of the Zoological Society of London* 131: 357–65.

Curran J.W., Morgan W.M., Hardy A.M. (1985) The epidemiology of AIDS: Current status and future prospects, *Science* 229: 1352–7.

de Groot J., Boersma W.J.A., Scholten J.W. & Koolhaas J.M. (2002) Social stress in male mice impairs long-term antiviral immunity selectivity in wounded subjects. *Physiology & Behavior* 75: 277–85.

de Wit J.B.F., Kok G.J., Timmermans C.A.M. & Wijnsma P. (1990) Determinanten van veilig en condoomgerbruik bij jongeren. *Gedrag en Gezondheid* 18: 121–33.

DeLongis A., Folkman S. & Lazarus R.S. (1988) The impact of daily stresses on health and mood: Psychological and social resources as mediators. *Journal of Personality and Social Psychology* 54: 486–95.

Department of Health and Social Security (1998) *Our healthier nation: a contract for health*. London: The Stationery Office.

Devane W.A., Dysarz F.A. III, Johnson M.R., Melvin L.S. & Howlett A.C. (1988) Determination and characterisation of a cannabinoid receptor in rat brain. *Molecular Pharmacology* 34: 605–13.

Di Marzo V., Fontana A., Cadas H., Schinelli S., Cimino G, Schwartz J.-C. & Piomelli D. (1994) Formation and inactivation of endogenous cannabinoid anandamide in central neurons. *Nature* 372: 686–91. .

Di Marzo V., Sepe N., De Petrocellis L., Berger A., Crozier G., Fride E. & Mechoulam R. (1998) Trick or treat from food endocannabinoids? *Nature* 396 (6712): 636.

Diamond E.G., Kittle C.F. & Crockett J.F. (1960) Comparison of internal mammary artery ligation and sham operation for angina pectoris. *American Journal of Cardiology* 5: 483–6.

Dohrenwend B.P. (1973) Social status and stressful life events. *Journal of Personality and Social Psychology* 28: 225–35.

Dunkel-Schetter C. & Bennett T.L. (1990) Differentiating the cognitive and behavioral aspects of social support. In Sarason B.R., Sarason I.G. and Pierce G.R. (eds) *Social support: an international view*, pages 267–96. New York: Wiley.

Dyson M. & Passmore N.I. (1992) Inter-male spacing and aggression in African painted reed frogs, *Hyperolius marmoratus*. *Ethology* 91: 237–47.

Eagly A.H. & Chaiken S. (1993) *The psychology of attitudes*. Fort Worth: Harcourt Brace Jovanovich.

Elder J.P., Sallis J.F., Woodruff S.I. & Widley M.B. (1993) Tobacco-refusal skills and tobacco use among high-risk adolescents. *Journal of Behavioral Medicine* 16(6): 629–42.

Epping-Jordan J.E., Compas B.E. & Howell D.C. (1994) Predictors of cancer progression in young adult men and women: avoidance, intrusive thoughts, and psychological symptoms. *Health Psychology* 13: 539–47.

Evans G.W. (1979) Behavioral and physiological consequences of crowding in humans. *Journal of Applied Social Psychology* 9: 27–46.

Evans P. (1998) Stress and coping. In Pitts M. & Phillips K. (1998) *The psychology of health: an introduction*, pages 47–67. London: Routledge.

Evans R.I. (1976) Smoking in children: developing a social-psychological strategy of deterrence. *Journal of Preventative Medicine* 5: 122–7.

Evans R.I., Dratt L.M., Raines B.E. & Rosenberg S.S. (1988) Social influences on smoking initiation: importance of distinguishing descriptive versus mediating process variables. *Journal of Applied Social Psychology* 18: 925–43.

Eysenck, H.J. (1988) Personality, stress and cancer: prediction and prophylaxis. *British Journal of Medical Psychology* 61: 57–75.

Fan P. (1995) Cannabinoid agonists inhibit the activation of 5-HT3 receptors in rat nodose ganglion neurons. *Journal of Neurophysiology* 73: 907–10.

Farley C., Haddad S. & Brown B. (1996) The effects of a 4-year program promoting bicycle helmet use among children in Quebec. *American Journal of Public Health* 86: 46–51.

Fenwick R. & Tausig M. (2000) Scheduling stress: family and health outcomes of shift work and schedule control. *American Behavioral Scientist* 44: 1179–98.

Fils-Aime M.-L., Eckhardt M.J., George D.T., Brown G.L., Meford I. & Linnoila M. (1996) Early-onset alcoholics have lower cerebrospinal fluid 5-hydroxyindoleacetic acid levels than late-onset alcoholics. *Archives of General Psychiatry* 53: 211–16.

Flay B.R., Ockene J.K. & Tager I.B. (1992) Smoking: epidemiology, cesstion and prevention. *Chest* 102: 277S–301S.

Fleming R., Baum A., Davidson L.M., Rectanus E. & McArdle S. (1987) Chronic stress as a factor in physiologic reactivity to change. *Health Psychology* 6: 221–37.

Fleming I., Baum A., Grisriel M.M. & Gatchel R.J. (1982) Mediation of stress at Three Mile Island by social support. *Journal of Human Stress*, 8: 14–22.

Fletcher J.M., Page J.B., Francis D.J., Copeland K., Naus M.J., Davis C.M., Morris R., Krauskopf D. & Satz P. (1996) Cognitive correlates of long-term cannabis use in Costa Rican men. *Archives of General Psychiatry* 53: 1051–7.

Folkman S., Larazus R.S., Gruen R.J. & DeLongis A. (1986) Appraisal, coping, health status and psychological symptoms. *Journal of Personality and Social Psychology* 50: 571–9.

Forgays D.K., Ottaway S.A., Guarino A. & D'Alessio M. (2001) Parenting stress in employed and at-home mothers in Italy. *Journal of Family and Economic Issues* 22: 327–51.

Freeman R., Lindner R.L., Rooney J. & Narendran S. (2000) Dental students in Northern Ireland in 1992 and 1995: changing trends in psychological stress. *Stress Medicine* 16: 233–8.

Friedman M. & Rosenman R.H. (1974) *Type A behavior and your heart*. New York: Knopf.

Fromme K., Katz E.C. & Rivet K. (1997) Outcome expectancies and risk-taking behavior. *Cognitive Therapy and Research* 21(4): 421–42.

Frone M.R. (2003) Predictors of overall and on-the-job substance use among young workers. *Journal of Occupational Health Psychology* 8(1): 39–54.

Frydenberg E., Lewis R., Kennedy G., Ardila R., Frindte W. & Hannoun R. (2003) Coping with concerns: an exploratory comparison of Australian, Colombian, German and Palestinian adolescents. *Journal of Youth and Adolescence* 32(1): 59–66.

Fuller T.D., Edwards J.N., Semsri S. & Vorakitphokatorn S. (1993) Housing, stress and physical well-being: evidence from Thailand. *Social Science and Medicine* 36: 1417–28.

Garner D.M., Garfinkel P.E., Schwartz D. & Thompson M. (1980) Cultural expectations of thinness in women. *Psychological Reports* 47: 483–91.

Gibson D.R. (2001) Effectiveness of syringe exchange programs in reducing HIV risk behavior and HIV seroconversion among injecting drug users. *AIDS* 15(11): 1329–41.

Gruzelier J., Levy J., Williams J. & Henderson D. (2001) Self-hypnosis and exam stress: Comparing immune and relaxation-related imagery for influences on immunity, health, and mood. *Contemporary Hypnosis* 18: 73–86.

Haas H., Fink H. & Hartfelder G. (1959) Das placeboproblem. *Fortschritte der Arzneimittelforschung* 1: 279–354.

Haefner D. & Kirscht J. (1970) Motivational and behavioral effects of modifying beliefs. *Public Health Reports* 58: 478–84.

Haller J., Fuchs E., Halasz J. & Makara G.B. (1999) Defeat is a major stressor in males while social instability is stressful mainly in females. Towards the development of a social stress model in female rats. *Brain Research Bulletin* 50: 33–9.

Harlan L.C., Bernstein A.M. & Kesler L.G. (1991) Cervical cancer screening: who is not screened and why? *American Journal of Public Health* 81: 885–90.

Haynes R.B., Taylor D.W., Sackett D.L., Gibson E.S., Bernholz C.D. & Mukherjee J. (1980) Can simple clinical measurements detect non-compliance? *Hypertension* 2: 757–64.

Helman C.G. (1994) *Culture, health and illness: an introduction for health professionals*. Oxford: Butterworth-Heinemann. .

Herbert T.B. & Cohen S. (1993) Stress and immunity in humans: a meta-analytic review. *Psychonomic Medicine* 55: 364–79.

Hochbaum G.M. (1958) *Public participation in medical screening programmes: a sociopsychological study* (Public Health Service Publication 572). US Government Washington DC: Printing Office.

Hodgson C.J.R. (2001) Health locus of control, perception of risk and risk-taking behaviour in older adolescents. *Dissertation Abstracts International: Section B* 61(9–B): 4650.

Holmes T.H. & Rahe R.H. (1967) The social readjustment rating scale. *Journal of Psychosomatic Research* 11: 213 –18.

Horner B.R. & Scheibe K.E. (1997) Prevalence and implications of attention deficit hyperactivity disorder among adolescents in treatment for substance abuse. *Journal of the American Academy of Child and Adolescent Pscyhiatry* 36: 30–6.

House J.S., Robbins C. & Metzner H.L. (1982) The association of social relationships and activities with mortality: prospective evidence from the Tecumseh Community Health Study. *Americal Journal of Epidemiology* 116: 123–40.

Iljas J.M. (2001) Effects of Chinese scalp acupuncture and basic qi gung exercises on the experiences of multiple sclerosis: three case studies. *Dissertation Abstracts International; Section B (The Sciences & Engineering)* 62(6–B): 2987.

Jaffe J.H. (1993) Opiates: clinical aspects. In Lowinson J.H., Ruiz P., Millman R.B. & Langrod J.G. (eds), *Substance abuse: a comprehensive textbook*, pages 186–94. Baltimore: Williams & Wilkins.

Janis I.L. & Feshbach S. (1953) Effects of fear-arousing communications. *Journal of Abnormal and Social Psychology* 48: 78–92.

Janz N.K. & Becker M.H. (1984) The Health Belief Model: a decade later. *Health Education Quarterly* 11: 1–47.

Jarvis M., Russell J., Flanagan C. & Dolan L. (2000) *Angles on psychology*. Cheltenham: Nelson Thornes.

Johanson C.E. & Fischman M.W. (1989) The pharmacology of cocaine related to its abuse. *Pharmacological Reviews* 41: 35. .

Julien R.M. (1998) *A primer of drug action*. New York: WH Freeman.

Kalat J.W. (1998) *Biological psychology*. London: Brooks/Cole.

Kann L., Kinchen S.A., Williams B.I., Ross J.G., Lowry R., Hill C.V., Grunbaum J.A., Blumson P.S., Collins J.L. & Kolbe L.J. (1998) Youth risk behavior surveillance – United States, 1997. *Morbidity and Mortality Weekly Report* 47: No SS-3.

Keilcot-Glaser J.K. & Glaser R. (1986) Psychological influences on immunity, *Psychosomatics* 27: 621–4.

Keilcot-Glaser J.K., Malarkey W.B., Cacioppo J.T. & Glaser R. (1994) Stressful personal relationships: immune and endocrine function. In Glaser R. & Keilcot-Glaser J.K. (eds), *Handbook of human stress and immunity*, pages 321–39. San Diego, CA: Academic Press.

Keller S.E., Shifflett S.C., Schleifer S.J. & Bartlett J.A. (1994) Stress, immunity, and health. In Glaser R. & Keilcot-Glaser J.K. (eds), *Handbook of human stress and immunity*, pages 217–44. San Diego, CA: Academic Press.

Kelley A.J. (1979) A media role for public health compliance? In Hayes R.B., Taylor D.W. & Sackett D.L. (eds) *Compliance in health care*. Baltimore, ML: Johns Hopkins University Press.

Kelly J.A., St Lawrence J.S., Brasfield T.L. & Hood H.V. (1989) Behavioral intervention to reduce AIDS risk activities. *Journal of Counseling and Clinical Psychology* 57: 60–7.

Kelly J.A., St Lawrence J.S., Brasfield T.L., Lemke A., Amideé T., Roffman R.E., Hood H.V., Smith J.E., Kilgore H. & McNeill C. Jr (1990) Psychological factors that predict AIDS high-risk versus AIDS precautionary behavior. *Journal of Consulting and Clinical Psychology* 58: 117–20.

Keys A., Brozek J., Henschel A., Mickelsen O. & Taylor H.L. (1950) *The biology of human starvation*. 2 vols. Minneapolis: University of Minnesota Press.

Kirscht J.P., Becker M., Haefner D. & Maiman L. (1978) Effects of threatening communications and mothers' health beliefs on weight change in obese children. *Journal of Behavioral Medicine* 1: 147–57.

Klesges R.C., Vasey B.S. & Glasgow R.E. (1986) A worksite smoking modification competition: potential for public health impact. *American Journal of Public Health* 76: 198–200.

Kobasa S.C. (1979) Stressful life events and health: an enquiry into hardiness. *Journal of Personality and Social Psychology* 37: 1–11.

Lambert N. (1998) In Motluk A. (1998) Calm before the storm. *New Scientist*, 2130: 18–19.

Langer E.J. & Rodin J. (1976) The effects of choice and enhances personal responsibility for the aged: a field experiment in an institutional setting. *Journal of Personality and Social Psychology* 34: 191–8.

Langlie J.K. (1977) Social networks, health beliefs, and preventative health behaviour. *Journal of Health and Social Behaviour* 18: 244–60.

Lepore S.J., Evans G.W. & Schneider M.L. (1991) Dynamic role of social support in the link between chronic stress and psychological distress. *Journal of Personality and Social Psychology* 61: 899–909.

Leventhal H. & Cleary P.D. (1980) The smoking problem: a review of the research and theory in behavioural risk moderation. *Psychological Bulletin* 88: 370–405.

Levine J.D., Gordon N.C. & Fields H.L. (1979) The role of endorphins in placebo analgesia. In Bonica J.J., Liebeskind J.C. & Albe-Fessard D. *Advances in pain research and therapy*, vol. 3. New York: Raven Press.

Lewis T., Osborn L.M., Lewis K., Broackert J., Jacosen J. & Cherry J.D. (1988) Influence of parental knowledge and opinions on 12-month diphtheria, tetanus, and pertussis vaccination rates. *American Journal of Diptheria C* 142: 283–6.

Lin N., Simeone R.S., Ensel W.M. & Kuo W. (1979) Social support, stressful life events, and illness: a model and an empirical test. *Journal of Health and Social Behaviour* 20: 108–19.

Longshore D., Bluthenthal R.N. & Stein M.D. (2001) Needle exchange program attendance and injection risk in Providence, Rhode Island. *AIDS Education and Prevention* 13(1): 78–90.

Lundqvist T. (1995) Chronic cannabis use and the sense of coherence. *Life Sciences* 56: 2145–50.

MacAndrew C. & Edgerton R.B. (1970) *Drunken Comportment: A social explanation.* London: Nelson.

MacAndrew C. (1989) Factors associated with the problem-engendering use of substances by young men. *Journal of Studies on Alcohol* 50: 552–6.

Manstead A.S.R., Proffitt C. & Smart J.L. (1983) Predicting and understanding mothers' infant-feeding intentions and behavior: testing the theory of reasoned action. *Journal of Personality and Social Psychology* 44: 657–71.

Marks D.F., Murray M., Evans B. & Willig C. (2000) *Health psychology: theory, research and practice*. London: Sage.

Marucha P.T., Keilcot-Glaser J.K. & Favagehi M. (1998) Mucosal wound healing is impaired by examination stress. *Psychosomatic Medicine* 60: 362–5.

Mason E. (1970) Obesity in pet dogs. *Veterinary Record* 86: 612–16.

McAlister A.L., Perry C., Killen J., Slinkard L.A. & Maccoby N. (1980) Pilot study of smoking, alcohol, and drug abuse prevention. *American Journal of Public Health* 70: 719–21.

McCann U. & Ricaurte G. (1993) In Miller S.K., How ecstasy blows your mind. *New Scientist* 20 November 1993: 4.

McCaul K.D., Dyche Bransetter A., Schroder D.M. & Glasgow R.M. (1996) What is the relationship between breast cancer risk and mammography screening? A meta-analytic review. *Health Psychology* 15: 423–9. .

Mendelson J.H. & Mello N.K. (1996) Management of cocaine abuse and dependence. *New England Journal of Medicine* 334: 965–72.

Meszaros J.R., Asch D.A., Baron J., Hershey J.C., Kunreuther H. & Schwartz-Buzaglo J. (1996) Cognitive processes and the decisions of some parents to forgo petussis vaccination for their children. *Journal of Clinical Epidemiology* 59: 697–703.

Michie S., Marteau T.M. & Kidd J. (1992) Predicting antenatal class attendance: attitudes of self and others. *Psychology and Health* 7: 225–34.

Miller M., Eskild A., Mella I., Moi H. & Magnus P. (2001) Gender differences in syringe exchange program use in Oslo, Norway. *Addiction* 96(11): 1639–51.

Montano D.E. & Taplin S.H. (1991) A test of an expanded theory of reasoned action to predict mammography participation. *Social Science and Medicine* 32: 733–41.

Morgan M. & Grube J.W. (1991) Closeness and peer group influence. *British Journal of Social Psychology* 30(2): 159–69.

Morrison A.F., Kline F.G. & Miller P. (1976) Aspects of adolescent information acquisition about drugs and alcohol topics. In Ortman R. (ed) *Communication research and drug education*. Beverly Hills, CA: Sage.

Mosbach P. & Leventhal H. (1988) Peer group identification and smoking: Implications for intervention. *Journal of Abnormal Psychology* 97: 238–45.

Murray M. & McMillan C. (1993) Health beliefs, locus of control, emotional control and women's cancer screening behaviour. *British Journal of Clinical Psychology* 32: 87–100.

Musty R.E. & Kaback L. (1995) Relationships between motivation and depression in chronic marijuana users. *Life Sciences* 56: 2151–8.

New S.J. & Senior M. (1991) 'I don't believe in needles': qualitative aspects of study into the uptake of infant immunisation in two English health authorities. *Social Science and Medicine* 33: 509–18.

Newmeyer J.A., Feldman H.W., Biernacki P. & Watters J.K. (1989) Preventing Aids contagion among intravenous drug users. In Bolton R. (ed) *The AIDS Pandemic: A Global Emergency*. New York: Gordon & Breach, pages 75–83.

Nolen-Hoeksema S. & Larson J. (1999) *Coping with loss*. Mahwah, NJ: Lawrence-Earlbum.

Norman N.M. & Tedeschi J.T. (1989) Self-presentation, reasoned action, and adolescents' decisions to smoke cigarettes. *Journal of Applied Social Psychology* 19: 543–58.

Norman P., Bennett P., Smith C. & Murphy S. (1998) Health locus of control and health behaviour. *Journal of Health Psychology* 3: 171–80.

North R.A. (1992) Cellular actions of opiates and cocaine. *Annals of the New York Academy of Sciences* 654: 1–6.

Nutbeam D., Macaskill P., Smith C., Simpson J.M. & Catford J. (1993) Evaluation of two school smoking education programmes under normal classroom conditions. *British Medical Journal* 306: 102–7.

Nutbeam D., Smith C. & Catford J. (1990) Evaluation on health education: a review of progress, possibilities and problems. *Journal of Epidemiology and Community Health* 44: 83–9.

O'Brien S. & Lee L. (1990) Effects of videotape intervention on Pap smear knowledge, attitudes and behavior. Special Issue: Behavioural research in cancer. *Behaviour Changes* 7: 143–50.

O'Carroll R.E., Smith K.B., Grubb N.R., Fox K.A.A. & Masterton G. (2001) Psychological factors associated with delay in attending hospital following a myocardial infarction. *Journal of Psychosomatic Research* 51: 611–14.

Page B., Chitwood D.D., Prince P.C., Kane N. & McBride D.C. (1990) Intraveous drug use and HIV infection in Miami. *Medical Anthropology Quarterly* (New Series) 4: 56–71.

Parry O., Platt S. & Thomson C. (2000) Out of sight, out of mind: workplace smoking bans and the relocation of smoking at work.

Health Promotion International 15(2): 125–33.

Pearce G.P. & Patterson A.M. (1993) The effect of apace restriction and provision of toys during rearing on behavior, productivity and physiology of male pigs. *Applied Behaviour Science* 36: 11–28.

Perry A.R. & Baldwin D.A. (2000) Further evidence of associations of type A personality scores and driving-related attitudes and behaviors. *Perceptual and Motor Skills* 91(1): 147–54.

Pert C.B. & Snyder S.H. (1973) The opiate receptor: Demonstration in nervous tissue. *Science* 179: 1011–14.

Pettingale K.W., Morris T., Greer S. & Haybittle J.L. (1985) Mental attitudes to cancer: an additional prognostic factor. *The Lancet* 1: 750.

Pinel J.P.J. (1997) *Biopsychology*. London: Allyn & Bacon.

Pinfold J.V. (1999) Analysis of different communication channels for promoting hygiene behaviour. *Health Education Research* 14(5): 629–39.

Pitts M. & Phillips K. (1998) *The psychology of health: an introduction*. London: Routledge.

Plant M. (1987) *Drugs in perspective*. London: Hodder & Stoughton.

Plummer K. (1988) Organizing AIDS. In Aggleton P. & Homans H. (eds) *Social aspects of AIDS*. Lewes: Falmer Press, pages 22–51.

Pope (1998) In Acheson D. & Mullin T. (1998) Marijuana: special report, *New Scientist* 2122: 24–34.

Povey R., Conner M., Sparks P., James R. & Shepherd
R. (2000) Application of the theory of planned behaviour to two dietary behaviours: role of perceived control and efficacy. *British Journal of Health Psychology* 5: 121–39. .

Quirk M., Godkin M. & Schwenzfeier E. (1993) Evaluation of two AIDS prevention interventions for inner-city adolescents and young adult women. *American Journal of Preventive Medicine* 9: 21–6.

Rajaratnam S.M.W. & Arendt J. (2001) Health in a 24-h society. *The Lancet*, 358: 999–1005.

Reddy C.V. (1989) Parents' beliefs about vaccination. *British Medical Journal* 299: 739.

Reneman L., Majoie C.B.L.M., Schmand B., van den Brink W. & den Heeten G.J. (2001) Prefrontal N-acetylaspartate is strongly associated with memory performance in (abstinent) ecstasy users: Preliminary report. *Biological Psychiatry* 50(7): 550–4.

Rhodewalt F. & Zone J.B. (1989) Appraisal of life change, depression and illness in hardy and non-hardy women. *Journal of Personality and Social Psychology* 56: 81–8.

Rimer B.K., Trock B., Lermon C. & King E.

(1991) Why do some women get regular mammograms? *American Journal of Preventative Medicine* 7: 69–74.

Roberts C. & Russell J. (2002) *Angles on environmental psychology*. Cheltenham: Nelson Thornes.

Robinson L.A., Klesges R.C., Zbikowski S. & Galser R. (1997) Predictors of risk for different stages of adolescent smoking in a biracial sample. *Journal of Consultative Clinical Psychology* 65: 653–62.

Ronis D.L. (1992) Conditional health threats: health beliefs, decisions and behaviors among adults. *Health Psychology* 11: 127–34.

Rosenman R.H., Brand R.J., Jenkins C.D., Freidman M., Straus R. & Wurm M. (1975) Coronary heart disease in the Western collaborative group study: final follow-up experience of eight and a half years. *Journal of the American Medical Association* 223: 872–7. .

Rosenstock I.M. (1966) Why people use health services. *Millbank Memorial Fund Quarterly* 44: 94–124.

Rotter J.B. (1954) *Social learning and clinical psychology*. New York: Prentice Hall.

Rotter J.B. (1966) Generalised expectancies for internal versus external control of reinforcement. *Psychological Monographs* 80 (1, No 609).

Rounsaville B.J., Anton S.F., Carroll K., Budde D., Prusoff B.A. & Gawin F. (1991) Psychiatric diagnosis of treatment-seeking cocaine abusers. *Archives of General Psychiatry* 48(1): 43–51.

Rushton C. (1997) Recreational drug use. *The Psychologist* 10(8): 345.

Rutter D.R. (2000) Attendance and reattendance for breast cancer screening: a prospective 3-year test of the theory of planned behaviour. *British Journal of Health Psychology* 5: 1–13.

Sacks J.J., Holingreen P., Smith S.M. & Sosin D.M. (1991) Bicycle-associated head injuries and deaths in the United States from 1984 through 1988. *Journal of the American Medical Association* 266: 3016–18.

Salmon P. (2000) *Psychology of medicine and surgery*. Chichester: John Wiley.

Sapolsky R.M. (1994) *Why zebras don't get ulcers*. New York: Freeman.

Sayette M.A. & Hufford M.R. (1997) Alcohol abuse/alcoholism. In Baum A., Newman S., Weinman J., West R. & McManus C. (eds) *Cambridge handbook of psychology, health and medicine*. Cambridge: Cambridge University Press.

Schenk S. (1998) In Motluk A. (1998) Calm before the storm. *New Scientist* 2130: 18–19.

Schifter D.E. & Ajzen I. (1985) Intention, perceived control, and weight loss: an application of the theory of planned behavior. *Journal of Personality and Social Psychology* 49: 843–51.

Schleifer S.J., Keller S.E., Camerino M.,

Thornton J.C. & Stein M. (1983) Suppression of lymphocyte stimulation following bereavement. *Journal of the American Medical Association* 250: 374–7.

Schwarz M., Chiang S., Mueller N. & Ackenheil M. (2001) T-helper-1 and T-helper-2 responses in psychiatric disorders. *Brain, Behavior and Immunity* 15: 340–70.

Schwarzer R. (1992) Self-efficacy in the adoption and maintenance of health behaviors: theoretical approaches and a new model. In Schwarzer R. (ed) *Self-efficacy: taught control of action*, pages 217–43. Washington, DC: Hemisphere.

Sciacchitano M., Goldstien M.B. & DiPlacido J. (2001) Stress, burnout and hardiness in RTs. *Radiology Technology* 72(4): 321–8.

Sclafani A. & Springer D. (1976) Dietary obesity in adult rats: similarities to hypothalamic and human obesity. *Physiology and Behavior* 17: 461–71.

Seidell J.C. & Rissenen A.M. (1998) Time trends in world-wide prevalence of obesity. In Bray G.A., Bouchard C. & James W.P.T. (eds), *Handbook of obesity*. New York: Marcel Dekker.

Seligman M.E.P. & Visintainer M.A. (1985) Turnout rejection and early experience of uncontrollable shock in the rat. In Brush F.R. & Overmier J.B. (eds) *Affect conditioning and cognition: essays on the determinants of behavior*. Hillstate, NJ: Erlbaum.

Selye H. (1947) *Textbook of endocrinology*. Montréal: University of Montréal.

Serdula M.K., Collins M.E., Williamson D.F., Anda R.F., Pamuk E. & Byers T.E. (1993) Weight control practices of US adolescents and adults. *Annals of Internal Medicine* 119: 667–71.

Sher K.J., Gershuny B.S. & Raskin G. (1997) The role of childhood stressors in the intergenerational transmission of alcohol use disorders. *Journal of Studies on Alcohol* 58: 414–27.

Simkins L. & Ebenhage M. (1984) Attitudes towards AIDS, herpes II and toxic shock syndrome, *Psychological Reports* 55: 779–86.

Sims E.A.H. & Horton E.S. (1968) Endocrine and metabolic adaptation to obesity and starvation. *American Journal of Clinical Nutrition* 21: 1455–70.

Six B. (1996) Attitude-behavior relations: a comprehensive meta-analysis of 887 studies published behtween 1927 and 1993. Paper presented at the XXVI International Congress of Psychology, Montréal, Canada.

Slenker S.E. & Grant M.C. (1989) Attitudes, beliefs and knowledge about mammography among women over forty years of age. *Journal of Cancer Education* 4: 61–5.

Smeldslund G (2000) A pragmatic basis for judging models and theories in health psychology: the axiomatic method. *Journal of Health Psychology*, 5(2): 133–49.

Smetana J.G. & Alder N.E. (1980) Fishbein's Value x Expectancy Model: an examination of some assumptions. *Personality and Social Psychology Bulletin* 6: 89–96.

Soendergaard H.P. & Theorell T. (2003) A longitudinal study of hormonal reactions accompanying life events in recently resettled refugees. *Psychotherapy and Psychosomatics* 72(1): 49–58.

Solowij N. (1995) Do cognitive impairments recover following cessation of cannabis use? *Life Sciences* 56: 2119–26.

Stacy A.W., Newcomb M.D. & Bentler P.M. (1993) Cognitive motivations and sensation seeking as long-term predictors of drinking problems. *Journal of Social and Clinical Psychology* 12(1): 1–24.

Steptoe A. & Wardle J. (2001) Locus of control and health behaviour revisited: a multivariate analysis of young adults from 18 countries. *British Journal of Psychology* 92: 659–72.

Strecher V.J. & Rosenstock I.M. (1997) The health belief model. In Baum A., Newman S., Weinman J., West R. & McManus C. (eds) *Cambridge handbook of psychology, health and medicine*. Cambridge: Cambridge University Press, pages 113–16.

Strecher V.J., Champion V.L. & Rosenstock I.M. (1997) The health belief model and health behavior. In Gochman D.S. (ed) *Handbook of health behavior research I: personal and social determinants*. New York: Plenum Press, pages 71–91.

Stevenson T. & Lennie J. (1992) Empowering school children in developing strategies to increase bicycle wearing. *Health Education Research* 7(4): 555–66.

Strickland B.R. (1978) Internal-external expectancies and health-related behaviors. *Journal of Consulting and Clinical Psychology* 46: 1192–211.

Stroebe W. (2000) *Social psychology and health*. Buckingham: Open University Press.

Stroebe N. & Stroebe M. (1987) *Bereavement and health*. New York: Cambridge University Press.

Stunkard A.J. (1988) Some perspectives on human obesity: its causes. *Bulletin of the New York Academy of Medicine* 64: 902–23.

Stunkard A.J., Sørensen T.I.A., Hanis C., Teasdale T.W., Charkaborty R., Scull W.J. & Schulsinger F. (1986) An adoption study of human obesity. *New England Journal of Medicine* 314: 193–8.

Sussman S. & Ames S.L. (2001) *The social psychology of drug abuse*. Buckingham: Open University Press.

Sussman S., Dent C.W. & Stacy A.W. (1996) The relations of pro-drug myths with self-reported drug use among youth at continuation high schools. *Journal of Applied Social Psychology* 26: 2014–37.

Swerdlow N.R., Geyer M.A., Vale W.W. & Koob G.F. (1986) Corticotropin releasing factor potentiates acoustic startle in rats: blockade by chlordiazepoxide. *Psychopharmacology* 88: 147–52.

Taffinder N.J., McManus I.C., Gul Y., Russell R.C.G. & Darzi A. (1998) Effect of sleep deprivation on surgeons' dexterity on laparoscopy simulator. *The Lancet* 352: 1191.

Taylor S.E. (1995) *Health psychology*. London: McGraw-Hill.

Temoshok L., Sweet D.M. & Zich J.A. (1987) A three city comparison of the public's knowledge and attitudes about AIDS, *Psychology and Health* 1: 43–60.

Townsend J. (1993) Policies to halve smoking deaths. *Addiction* 88: 43–52.

US Department of Health and Human Services (USDHHS) (1989) *Reducing the health consequences of smoking: 25 years of progress. A report of the Surgeon General* (DHSS Publication No CDC 89–8411). Rockville, MD: US Government Printing Office.

Van den Putte B. (1991) 20 years of the theory of reasoned action of Fishbein & Ajzen: a meta-analysis. Unpublished manuscript, University of Amsterdam.

Vertefeuille J., Marx M.A., Tun W., Huettner S., Strathdee S.A. & Vlahov D. (2000) Decline in self-reported high-risk injection-rellated behaviors among HIV-seropositive participants in the Baltimore needle exchange program. *AIDS and Behavior* 4(4): 381–8.

Vines G. (1994) I'm relaxed, you're drunk. *New Scientist*, 10 December 1994: 35–8.

Wadden T.A. & Brownell K.D. (1984) The development and modification of dietary practices in individuals. In Matarazzo J.D., Weiss S.M., Herd J.A., Miller N.E. & Weiss S.M. (eds), *Behavioral health: a handbook of health enhancement and disease prevention*. New York: Wiley.

Walker J. (2001) *Control and the psychology of health*. Buckingham: Open University Press.

Wallston K.A., Walston B.S. & DeVellis R. (1978) Development of the Multidimensional Health Locus of Control (MHLC) Scale. *Health Education Monographs*, 6: 5–25.

Wareing M., Fisk J.E. & Murphy P.N. (2000) Working memory deficits in current and previous users of MDMA ('Ecstasy'). *British Journal of Psychology* 91: 181–8.

Warner K.E. & Murt H.A. (1982) Impact of the anti-smoking campaign on smoking prevalence: a cohort analysis. *Journal of Public Health Policy* 3: 374–90. .

Warner K.E. (1977) The effects of the anti-smoking campaign on cigarette consumption. *American Journal of Public Health* 67: 645–50.

Waterhouse J., Edwards B., Nevill A., Atkinson G., Reilly T., Davies P. & Godfrey R. (2000) Do subjective symptoms predict our perception of jet lag? *Ergonomics* 43: 1514–27.

Weinstein N.D. (1987) Unrealistic optimism about susceptibility to health problems: conclusions from a community-wide sample. *Journal of Behavioral Medicine* 10: 481–500.

Wellbrock K.D. (2000) Stress, hardiness, social support network orientation, and trauma-related symptoms in police officers. *Dissertation Abstracts International: Section B* 61(3–B): 1687.

WHO (1995) In Patel T. (1995) Thank heaven for little pills. *New Scientist* 1 April 1995: 14–15.

Wills T.A., Pierce J.P. & Evans R.I. (1996) Large-scale environmental risk factors for substance use. *American Behavioral Scientist* 39: 808–22.

Wiseman C.V., Gray J.J., Moismann J.E. & Ahrens A.H. (1992) Cultural expectations of thinness in women: an update. *International Journal of Eating Disorders* 11: 85–9.

Woodcock A., Stenner K. & Ingram R. (1992) Young people talking about HIV and AIDS: interpretations of personal risk of infection. *Health Education Research: Theory and Practice* 7: 229–47.

Yeoman M. (1995) In Parrot A. & Yoeman M., Wobble, rave, inhale or crave? *The Psychologist* 8(7): 305.

Yoast R., Williams M.A., Deitchman S.D. & Champion H.C. (2001) Report of the Council on Scientific Affairs: Methadone maintenance and needle-exchange programs to reduce the medical and public health consequences of drug abuse. *Journal of Addictive Diseases* 20(2): 15–40.

Zautra A.J. (1998) Arthritis: behavioral and psychosocial aspects. In Blechman E.A. & Brownell K.D. (eds) *Behavioral medicine and women: a comprehensive handbook*, pages 554–8. New York: Guilford.

Zuckerman M. (1987) Biological connection between sensation seeking and drug abuse. In Engel J. & Oreland L. (eds) *Brain reward systems and abuse*. New York: Raven Press.

Zuckerman M. (1994) *Behavioral expressions and biosocial bases of sensation seeking*. New York: Cambridge University Press.

Zuckerman M., Ball S. & Black J. (1990) Influences of sensation seeking, gender, risk appraisal, and situational motivation on smoking. *Addictive Behaviors* 15: 209–20.

Environmental psychology

Acton W.I. (1970) Speech intelligibility in a background noise and noise-induced hearing loss. *Ergonomics* 13: 546–54.

Aiello J.R., Epstein Y.M. & Karlin R.A. (1975) Field experimental research in human crowding. Paper presented at the Eastern Psychological Association.

Ajzen I. (1985) From intentions to actions: a theory of planned behaviour. In Kuhl J. & Beckmann J. (eds) *Action control: from cognition to behavior* (pages 11–39). Berlin: Springer-Verlag.

Altman I. (1975) *The environment and social behaviour*. Monterey, CA: Brooks/Cole.

Andersen P.A. & Leibowitz K. (1978) The development and nature of construct touch avoidance. *Environmental Psychology and Non-verbal Behaviour* 1: 18–32.

Anderson B., Erwin N., Flynn D., Lewis L. & Erwin J. (1977) Effects of short-term crowding on aggression in captive groups of pigtail monkey. *Aggressive Behaviour* 3: 33–46.

Andreoli V. & Worcehl S. (1978) Effects of media, communicator, and message position on attitude change. *Public Opinion Quarterly* 42: 59–70.

Asmus C.L. & Bell P.A. (1999) Effects of environmental odour and coping style on negative affect, anger, arousal and escape. *Journal of Applied Social Psychology* 29: 245–60.

Banbury S. & Berry D.C. (1988) Disruption of office-related tasks by speech and office noise. *British Journal of Psychology* 89: 499–517.

Baron R.A. & Byrne D. (1999) *Social psychology*. London: Allyn & Bacon.

Baron R.M., Mandel D.R., Adams C.A. & Griffen L.M. (1976) Effects of social density in university residential environments. *Journal of Personality and Social Psychology* 34: 434–46.

Bauer R.A. (1970) Self-confidence and persuasibility: one more time. *Journal of Marketing Research* 7: 256–8.

Baum A. & Valins S. (1977) *Architecture and social behavior: psychological studies of social density*. Hilldale, NJ: Erlbaum.

Beard R.R. & Wertheim G.A. (1967) Behavioural impairment associated with small doses of carbon monoxide. *American Journal of Public Health* 57: 2012–22.

Bell P.A., Greene T.C., Fisher J.D. & Baum A. (1996) *Environmental psychology*, 4th edn. Fort Worth, TX: Harcourt College Publishers.

Bell P.A., Greene T.C., Fisher J.D. & Baum A. (2001) *Environmental psychology*, 5th edn. Orlando, FL: Harcourt College Publishers.

Belojevic G., Slepcevic V. & Jakovljevic B. (2001) Mental performance in noise: the role of introversion. *Journal of Environmental Psychology* 21: 209–13.

Benewick R. & Holton R. (1987) The peaceful crowd: crowd solidarity and the Pope's visit to Britain. In Gaskill G. & Benewick R. (eds) *The crowd in contemporary Britain*. London: Sage.

Bickman L., Teger A., Gabiele T., McLaughin C., Berger M. & Sunaday E. (1973) Dormitory density and helping behaviour. *Environment and Behaviour* 5: 465–90.

Bleda P. & Bleda E. (1978) Effects of sex and smoking on reactions to spatial invasion at a shopping mall. *Journal of Social Psychology* 104: 311–12.

Blossom N. (2000) Connections and collaborations to sustain the environment. Proceedings of the 16th IAPS Conference, Paris, France (4–7 July), page 62.

Brandon G. & Lewis A. (1999) Reducing household energy consumption: a qualitative and quantitative field study. *Journal of Environmental Psychology* 19: 75–85.

Breckler S.J. & Wiggins E.C. (1989) On defining attitude and attitude theory: once more with feeling. In Pratkanis A.R., Breckler S.J. and Greenwald A.G. (eds) *Attitude structure and function*. Hillsdale, NJ: Erlbaum.

Breisacher P. (1971) Neuropsychological effects of air pollution. *American Behavioral Scientist* 14: 837–64.

Borksy P.N. (1969) Effects of noise on community behaviour. In Ward W.D. & Fricke J.E. (eds) *Noise as a public health hazard*. Washington, DC: American Speech and Hearing Association.

Brodsky S.L., Hooper N.E., Tipper D.G. & Yates S.B. (1999) Attorney invasion of witness space. *Law and Psychology Review* 23: 49–68.

Bronzaft A.L. & McCarthy D.P. (1975) The effects of elevated train noise on reading ability. *Environment and Behaviour* 7: 517–27.

Brower S., Dockett K. & Taylor R.B. (1983) Residents' perceptions of territorial features and perceived local threat. *Environment and Behaviour* 15(4): 419–37.

Bruins J. & Barber A. (2000) Crowding, performance and effect: a field experiment investigating mediating processes. *Journal of Applied Social Psychology* 30: 1268–80.

Brunson L.N. (2000) Resident appropriation of defensible space in public housing: implications for safety and community. *Dissertation Abstracts International: Section B: The Sciences and Engineering* 60(11-B): 5831.

Calhoun J.B. (1962) Population density and social pathology. *Scientific American* 206: 139–48.

Calhoun J.B. (1971) Space and the strategy of life. In Esseer A.H. (ed) *Behavior and the environment: the use of space by animals*. Bloomington, IN: University of Indiana Press.

Cassidy T. (1992) Commuting-related stress: consequences and implications. *Employee Counselling Today* 4(2): 15–21.

Cassidy T. (1997) *Environmental psychology: behaviour and experience in context*. Hove: Psychology Press.

Chaiken S. (1987) The heuristic model of persuasion. In Zanna M.P., Olson J.M. & Herman C.P. (eds) *Social influence: the Ontario Symposium* (vol 5) pages 3–40). Hillsdale, NJ: Erlbaum.

Chaiken S. & Eagly A.H. (1976) Communication modality as a determinant of message persuasiveness and message comprehensibility. *Journal of Personality and Social Psychology* 34: 605–14.

References

Chan Y.K. (1999) Density, crowding and factors intervening in their relationship: evidence from a hyper-dense metropolis. *Social Indicators Research* 48: 103–24.

Channing C.E., Hughes B.O. & Walker A.W. (2001) Spatial distribution and behaviour of laying hens housed in an alternative system. *Applied Animal Behaviour Science* 72: 335–45.

Chapko M.K. & Solomon M. (1976) Air pollution and recreation behaviour. *Journal of Social Psychology* 100: 149–50.

Christian J.J. (1955) The effects of population size on the adrenal glands of male mice in populations of fixed size. *American Journal of Physiology* 182: 292–300.

Cohen S., Glass D.C. & Singer J.E. (1973) Apartment noise, auditory discrimination and reading ability in children. *Journal of Experimental Social Psychology* 9: 407–22.

Cook S.W. & Berrenberg J.L. (1981) Approaches to encouraging conservation behaviour: a review and conceptual framework. *Journal of Social Issues* 37: 73–107.

Corah W.L. & Boffa J. (1970) Perceived control, self-observation and responses to aversive stimulation. *Journal of Personality and Social Psychology* 16: 1–4.

Costa G., Pickup L. & Di-Martino V. (1988) A further stress factor for working people: evidence from the European Community. 1. A review. *International Archives of Occupational and Environmental Health* 60: 371–6.

Cox V.C., Paulus P.B. & McCain G. (1984) Prison crowding research: the relevance for prison housing standards and a general approach regarding crowding phenomena. *American Psychologist* 39: 1148–69.

Crowcroft P. & Rowe F.P. (1958) The growth of confined colonies of the wild housemouse (*Mus musculus L.*): the effect of dispersal on female fecundity. *Proceedings of the Zoological Society of London* 131: 357–65.

Cunningham M.R. (1979) Weather, mood, and helping behaviour: quasi experiments with the sunshine Samaritan. *Journal of Personality and Social Psychology* 37: 1947–56.

De Young R. (1986) Some psychological aspects of recycling: the structure of conservation satisfactions. *Environment and Behaviour* 18: 435–49.

Deaux K.K. & LaFrance M. (1998) Gender. In Gilbert D.T., Fiske S. & Lindzey G. (eds) *The handbook of social psychology*, 4th edn (vol 1, pages 788–827). New York: McGraw-Hill.

Demirbas O.O. & Demirkan H. (2000) Privacy dimensions: a case study in the interior architecture design studio. *Journal of Experimental Psychology* 20: 53–64.

Diener E. (1979) Deindividuation, self-awareness and disinhibition. *Journal of Personality and Social Psychology* 37: 1160–71.

Dohrenwend B.P. (1973) Social status and stressful life events. *Journal of Personality and Social Psychology* 28:225–35.

dos Santos A.L.V. & Duarte C.R. (2000) The absent home. *Proceedings of the 16th IAPS Conference, Paris, France (4–7 July)*, page 117.

Duke M.P. & Nowicki S. (1972) Diagramming the shape of personal space: a new measure and social learning model for interpersonal distance. *Journal of Experimental Research in Personality* 6: 119–32.

Dunlap R.E. & Van Liere K.D. (1978) The 'new environmental paradigm': a proposed instrument and preliminary results. *Journal of Environmental Education* 9: 10–19.

Durkheim E. (1898) Representations individuelles et representations collectives. *Revue de Metaphysique et de Morale* 6: 273–302.

Dwyer D. (2001) *Angles on criminal psychology*. Cheltenham: Nelson Thornes.

Dyson M.L. & Passmore N.I. (1992) Intermale spacing and aggression in African painted reed frogs, *Hyperolius marmoratus*. *Ethology* 91: 237–47.

Eagly A.H, & Carli L. (1981) Sex of researchers and sex-typed communications as determinants of sex differences in influence-ability. A meta-analysis of social influence studies. *Psychological Bulletin* 90: 1–20.

Ellison-Potter P.A., Bell P.A. & Deffenbacher J.L. (2001) The effects of anonymity, aggressive stimuli, and trait anger on aggressive driving behaviour: a laboratory simulation. *Journal of Applied Social Psychology* 31(2): 431–43.

Epping-Jordan J.E., Compas B.E. & Howell D.C. (1994) Predictors of cancer progression in young adult men and women: avoidance, intrusive thoughts and psychological symptoms. *Health Psychology* 13: 539–47.

Evans G.W. (1979) Behavioural and physiological consequences of crowding in humans. *Journal of Applied Social Psychology* 9: 27–46.

Evans G.W. (2000) Motivational consequences of environmental stress. *Proceedings of the 16th IAPS Conference, Paris, France (4–7 July)*.

Evans G.W., Hygge S. & Bullinger M M. (1995) Chronic noise and psychological stress. *Psychological Science* 6: 333–8.

Evans G.W., Jacobs S.V., Dooley D. & Catlano R. (1987) The interaction of stressful life events and chronic strains on community mental health. *American Journal of Community Psychology* 15: 23–34.

Feroleto J.A. & Gounard B.R. (1975) The effects of subjects' age and expectations regarding an interviewer on personal space. *Experiments and Ageing Research* 1(1): 57–61.

Festinger L., Pepitone A. & Newcomb T. (1952) Some consequences of deindividuation in a group. *Journal of Abnormal and Social Psychology* 47: 382–9.

Fidell S. & Silvati L. (1991) An assessment of the effect of residential acoustic insulation on prevalence of annoyance in an airport community. *Journal of the Acoustical Society of America* 89: 244–7.

Finnie W.C. (1973) Field experiments in litter control. *Environment and Behaviour* 5: 123–44.

Fisher J.D. & Byrne D. (1975) Too close for comfort: sex differences in response to invasions of personal space. *Journal of Personality and Social Psychology* 32(1): 15–21.

Fleming R., Baum A., Davidson L.M., Rectanus E. & McArdle S. (1987) Chronic stress as a factor in physiologic reactivity to challenge. *Health Psychology* 6: 221–37.

Folkman S., Larazus R.S., Gruen R.J. & DeLongis X. (1986) Appraisal, coping, health status and psychological symptoms. *Journal of Personality and Social Psychology* 50: 571–9.

Freedman J.L., Klevansky X. & Ehrlich P.I. (1971) The effect of crowding on human task performance. *Journal of Applied Social Psychology* 1: 7–26.

Freedman J.L., Levy A.S., Buchanan R.W. & Price J. (1972) Crowding and human aggressiveness. *Journal of Experimental and Social Psychology* 8: 528–48.

Fuller T.D., Edwards J.N., Semsri S. & Vorakitphokatorn S. (1993) Housing, stress and physical well-being: evidence from Thailand. *Social Science and Medicine* 36: 1417–28.

Gale A., Spratt G., Chapman A.J. & Smallbone A. (1975) EEG correlates of eye contact and interpersonal distance. *Biological Psychology* 3(4): 237–45.

Gamba R.J. & Oskamp S. (1994) Factors influencing community residents' participation in commingled curbside recycling programs. *Environment and Behaviour* 26: 587–612.

Gaulin S.J.C. & Fitzgerald R.W. (1989) Sexual selection for spatial learning ability. *Animal Behaviour* 322–31.

Glass D.C. & Singer J.E. (1972) *Urban stress*. New York: Academic Press.

Green D.M & Fidell S. (1991) Variability in the criterion for reporting annoyance in community noise surveys. *Journal of the Acoustical Society of America* 89: 234–43.

Greenbaum P.E. & Rosenfeld H.M. (1980) Varieties of touching in greetings: sequential structure and sex-related differences. *Journal of Nonverbal Behaviour* 5: 13–25.

Grogen P. & Bell R. (1989) Local impact of state recycling laws. *Biocycle* 30(5): 50-5.

Hall E.T. (1963) A system for the notation of proxemic behaviour. *American Anthropologist* 65: 1003–26.

Haller J., Fuchs E., Halasz J. & Makara G.B. (1999) Defeat is a major stressor in males while social instability is stressful mainly in females. Towards the development of a social stress model in female rats. *Brain Research Bulletin* 50: 33–9.

Ham-Rowbottom K.A., Gifford R. & Shaw K.T. (1999) Defensible space theory and the police: assessing the vulnerability of residences to burglary. *Journal of Environmental Psychology* 19: 117–29.

Hanazato T. (2000) Pencil-houses or apartments: alternatives of urban dwelling in Hanoi. *Proceedings of the 16th IAPS Conference, Paris, France (4–7 July)*, page 78.

Harris L. & Associates (1980) *The Steelcase National Study of Office Environments, II: Comfort and Productivity in the Office of the 80s.* Grand Rapids, MI: Steelcase Inc.

Health & Safety Executive (1995) Noise. Circular AS8 (rev.): http://www.hse.gov.uk/pubns/as8.htm.

Heberlein T.A. (1975) Conservation information: the energy crisis and electricity consumption in an apartment complex. *Energy Systems and Policy* 1: 105–17.

Henley N.M. (1973) Status and sex: some touching observations. *Bulletin of the Psychonomic Society* 2: 91–3.

Hormuth S.E. (1999) Social meaning and social context of environmentally relevant behaviour: shopping, wrapping and disposing. *Journal of Environmental Psychology* 19: 277–86.

Hoogland, J.L. (1979) Aggression, ectoparasitism and other possible costs of prairie dog (*Sciuridae: Cynomys spp.*) coloniality. *Behaviour* 69-1-35.

Horton P.B. & Hunt C.L. (1976) *Sociology.* New York: McGraw-Hill.

Hovland C.I. & Weiss W. (1951) The influence of source credibility of communication effectiveness. *Public Opinion Quarterly* 15: 635–50.

Howard D.J. (1997) Familiar phrases as peripheral persuasion cue. *Journal of Experimental Social Psychology* 33: 231–43.

Jaccoby J., Hoyer W.D. & Sheluga D.A. (1980) *Miscomprehension of Televised Communications.* New York: American Association of Advertising Agencies.

Janis I.L. & Feshbach S. (1953) Effects of fear-arousing communications. *Journal of Abnormal and Social Psychology* 48: 78–92.

Janis I.L. & Field P.B. (1959) A behavioural assessment of persuasiblity: consistency of individual differences. In Hovland C.I. & Janis I.L. (eds) *Personality and persuasability* (pages 29–54) New Haven, CN: Yale University Press.

Janis I.L. & Hovland C.I. (1959) An overview of persuasibility research. In Hovland C.I. & Janis I.L. (eds) *Personality and persuasability* (pages 1–26). New Haven, CN: Yale University Press.

Jarvis M., Russell J., Flanagan C. & Dolan L. (2000) *Angles on psychology.* Cheltenham: Nelson Thornes.

Johnson R.D. & Downing L.L. (1979) Deindividuation and valence of cues: effects on prosocial and antisocial behaviour. *Journal of Personality and Social Psychology* 37: 1532–8.

Jones J.W. & Bogat A. (1978) Air pollution and human aggression. *Psychological Reports* 43: 721–2.

Kaiser F.G. & Shimoda T.A. (1999) Responsibility as a predictor of ecological behaviour. *Journal of Environmental Psychology* 19: 243–53.

Kaiser F.G., Wolfing S. & Fuhrer U. (1999) Environmental attitude and ecological behaviour. *Journal of Environmental Psychology* 19: 1–19.

Karlin R.A., Rosen L. & Epstein Y. (1979) Three into two doesn't go: a follow-up of the effects of overcrowded dormitory rooms. *Personality and Social Psychology Bulletin* 5: 391–5.

Katz P. (1937) *Animals and men.* New York: Longmans Green.

Kaya N. & Erkip F. (1999) Invasion of personal space under the condition of short-term crowding: a case study on an automatic teller machine. *Journal of Environmental Psychology* 19: 183–9.

Kaya N. & Erkip E. (2001) Satisfaction in a dormitory building: the effects of floor height on the perception of room size and crowding. *Environment and Behavior* 33: 35–53.

Kearney A.R. & De Young R. (1995) A knowledge-based intervention for promoting carpooling. *Environment and Behaviour* 27: 650–78.

Larsen K.S. & LeRoux J. (1984) A study of same sex touch attitudes: scale development and personality predictors. *Journal of Sex Research* 20: 264–78.

Lavine H. & Snyder M. (1996) Cognitive processing and the functional matching effect in persuasion: the mediating role of subjective perceptions of message quality. *Journal of Experimental Social Psychology* 32: 580–604.

Lawton C.A. (1996) Strategies for indoor way-finding: the role of orientation. *Journal of Environmental Psychology* 16: 137–45.

Lawton M.P., Nahemow L. and Teaff J. (1975) Housing characteristics and the well-being of elderly tenants in federally assisted housing. *Journal of Gerontology* 30(5): 601–7.

Le Bon G. (1879) *The crowd: a study of the popular mind.* London: Unwin.

Lepore S.J., Evans G.W. & Schneider M.L. (1991) Dynamic role of social support in the link between chronic stress and psychological distress. *Journal of Personality and Social Psychology* 61: 899–909.

Lewis J., Baddeley A.D., Bonham K.G. & Lovett D. (1970) Traffic pollution and mental efficiency. *Nature* 225: 95–7. .

Little K.B. (1968) Cultural variations in social schemata. *Journal of Personality and Social Psychology* 10(1): 1–7.

Loftus E.F & Palmer J.C. (1974) Reconstruction of automobile destruction: an example of the interaction between language and memory. *Journal of Verbal Learning and Verbal Behaviour* 13: 585–9.

Loftus E.F., Miller D.G. & Burns H.J (1978) Semantic integration of verbal information into a visual image, *Journal of Experimental Psychology: Human Learning and Memory* 4: 19–31.

Luyben P.D. and Bailey J.S. (1979) Newspaper recycling: the effects of rewards and proximity of containers. *Environment and Behaviour* 11: 539–57.

MacDonald J.E. & Gifford R. (198) Territorial cues and defensible space theory: the burglar's point of view. *Journal of Environmental Psychology* 9(3): 193–205.

Machleit K., Eroglu S. & Mantel S.P. (2000) Perceived retail crowding and shopping satisfaction: what modifies the relationship? *Journal of Consumer Psychology* 9: 29–42.

Maier R.A. & Ernest R.C. (1978) Sex differences in the perception of touching. *Perceptual and Motor Skills* 46: 577–8.

Major B. (1981) Gender patterns in touching behaviour. In Mayo C. & Henley N.M. (eds) *Gender and nonverbal behaviour* (pages 15–37). New York: Springer-Verlag.

Mann L., Newton J.W. & Innes J.M. (1982) A test between deindividuation and emergent norm theories of crowd aggression. *Journal of Personality and Social Psychology* 42: 260–72.

Margai F.L. (1997) Analyzing changes in waste reduction behaviour in a low income urban commmunity following a public outreach program. *Environment and Behaviour* 29: 769–92.

Marsh P, Rosser E. & Harre R. (1978) *The rules of disorder.* London: Routledge & Kegan Paul.

Matthews K.E. & Canon L.K. (1975) Environmental noise as a determinant of helping behaviour. *Journal of Personality and Social Psychology* 32: 571–7.

Matthies E. & Kromker D. (2000) Participatory planning – a heuristic for adjusting interventions to the context. *Journal of Environmental Psychology* 20: 1–10.

McCarty J.A. & Shrum L.J. (1994) The recycling of solid wastes: personal values, value orientations, and attitudes about recycling as antecedents of recycling behaviour. *Journal of Business Research* 30:53–62.

McFarland D. (1999) *Animal behaviour.* Harlow: Longman.

McGuire W.J. (1968) Personality and attitude change: a theoretical housing. In Greenwald A.G., Brock T.C. andostrom T.M. (eds) *Psychological foundations of attitudes.* New York: Academic Press.

McGuire W.J. (1969) The nature of attitudes and attitude change. In Lindzey G. & Aronson E. (eds) *Handbook of Social Psychology*, 2nd edn (vol 2, pages 136–314). Reading, MA: Addison-Wesley.

Medalia N.Z. (1964) Air pollution as a

References

socio-envirnmental health problem: a survey report. *Journal of Health and Human Behaviour* 5: 154–65.

Meijanders A.L., Slangen-de Kort Y.A.W & Dinnissen L.A.J. (2000) Privacy and identity in non-territorial office environments. *Proceedings of the 16th IAPS Conference, Paris, France (4–7 July)*, page 90.

Menezes P.R., Scazufca M., Rodrigues L.C. & Mann A.H. (2000) Household crowding and compliance with outpatient treatment in patients with non-affective functional psychoses in Sao Paulo, Brazil. *Social Psychiatry and Psychiatric Epidemiology* 3: 116–20.

Milgram S. & Toch H. (1969) Collective behaviour: crowds and social movements. In Lindzey G. & Aronson E. (eds) *Handbook of social psychology*, vol 4. Reading, MA: Addison-Wesley.

Morgan D.G. & Stewart N.J. (1998) High versus low density special care units: impact on the behaviour of elderly residents with dementia. *Canadian Journal on Ageing* 17: 143–65.

Mullen B. (1986) Atrocity as a function of lynch mob composition: a self-attention perspective. *Personality and Social Psychology Bulletin* 12: 187–97.

Navarro P.L., Simpson-Housely P. & DeMan A.F. (1987) Anxiety, locus of control and appraisal of air pollution. *Perceptual and Motor Skills* 64: 811–14.

Newhouse N. (1990) Implications of attitude and behaviour research for environmental conservation. *The Journal of Environmental Education* 22: 1.

Newman O. (1972) *Defensible space*. New York: Macmillan.

Newman O. & Franck K.A. (1982) The effects of building size on personal crime and fear of crime. *Population and Environment: Behavioural and Social Issues* 5(4): 203–20.

Ng B., Kumar S., Ranclaud M. & Robinson E. (2001) Ward crowding and incidents of violence on an acute psychiatric inpatient unit. *Pyschiatric Services* 52: 521–5.

Ng C.F. (2000) Effects of building construction noise on residents: a quasi experiment. *Journal of Environmental Psychology* 20: 375–85.

Nijman H.L. & Rector G. (1999) Crowding and aggression on inpatient psychiatric wards. *Psychiatric Services* 50: 830–1.

Nivision M.E. & Endresen I.M. (1993) An analysis of relationships among environmental noise, annoyance and sensitivity to noise and the consequences for health and sleep. *Journal of Behaviour Medicine* 16: 257–76.

Nolen-Hoeksema S. & Larson J. (1999) *Coping with loss*. Mahway, NJ: Lawrence Erlbaum.

Olsen M.E. (1981) Consumers' attitudes toward energy conservation. *Journal of Social Issues* 37: 108–31.

Ophuls W. (1977) *Ecology and the politics of scarcity*. San Francisco: Freeman.

Oskamp S., Zelezney L., Schultz P.W., Hurin S. & Burhardt R. (1996) Commingled versus separated curbside recycling: Does sorting matter? *Environment and Behaviour* 28: 73–91.

Page R. (1977) Noise and helping behaviour. *Environment and Behaviour* 9: 311–14.

Pandey S. (1999) Role of perceived control in coping with crowding. *Psychological Studies* 44: 86–9.

Pardini A.U. & Katzev R.D. (1983–1984) The effets of strenth of commitment on neyspaper recycling. *Journal of Environmental Systems* 13: 245–54.

Parkinson B. (2001) Anger on and off the road. *British Journal of Psychology* 92: 507–26.

Paulus P.B. (1988) *Prison crowding: a psychological perspective*. New York: Springer-Verlag.

Paulus P.B, McCain G. & Cox V. (1978) Death rates, psychiatric commitments, blood pressure and perceived crowding as a function of institutional crowding. *Environmental Psychology and Nonverbal Behaviour* 3: 107–16.

Pearce G.P. & Patterson A.M. (1993) The effect of space restriction and provision of toys during rearing on behaviour, productivity and physiology of male pigs. *Applied Behaviour Science* 36: 11–28.

Peluso M.L. (2000) Comfort, intimacy and privacy among the poor in Brasilia/Brazil. *Proceedings of the 16th IAPS Conference, Paris, France (4–7 July)*, page 98.

Petty R.E. & Cacioppo J.T. (1981) *Attitudes and persuasion: classic and contemporary cpproaches*. Dubuque, IO: William C.Brown.

Petty R.E. & Cacioppo J.T. (1986) *Communication and persuasion: central and peripheral routes to attitude change*. New York: Springer-Verlag.

Postman L. & Egan J.P. (1949) *Experimental psychology*, New York: Harper.

Postmes T. & Spears R. (1998) Deindividuation and antinormative behaviour: a meta-analysis. *Psychological Bulletin* 123: 1–22.

Prentice-Dunn S. & Rogers R.W. (1982) Effects of public and private self-awareness on deindividuation and aggression. *Journal of Personality and Social Psychology* 43: 503–13.

Raloff J. (1982) Occupational noise – the subtle pollutant. *Science News* 121: 347–50.

Rankin R. (1969) Air pollution control and public apathy. *Journal of the Air Pollution Control Association* 19: 565–9.

Rathbone D.B. & Huckabee J.C. (1999) Controlling road rage: a literature review and pilot study. Prepared for the AAA Foundation for Traffic Safety. Accessed electronically at: *http://www.aaafts.org/Text/research/RoadRageFinal.htm*.

Reicher S.D (1984) The St Paul's riot: an explanation of the limits of crowd action in terms of a social identity model. *European Journal of Social Psychology* 14: 1–21.

Reicher S.D. & Potter J. (1985) Psychological theory as inter-group perspective: a comparative analysis of 'scientific' and 'lay' accounts of crowd events. *Human Relations* 38: 167–89.

Rishi P., Sinha S.P. & Dubey R. (2000) A correlational study of workplace characteristics and work satisfaction among Indian bank employees. *Psychologia: an International Journal of Psychology in the Orient* 43: 155–64.

Rogers R.W. (1975) A protection motivation theory of fear appeals and attitude change. *Journal of Psychology* 91: 93–114.

Rotton J. & Frey J. (1985) Air pollution, weather, and violent crimes: concomitant time-series analysis of archival data. *Journal of Personality and Social Psychology* 49: 1207–20.

Rotton J., Yoshikawa J. & Kaplan F. (1979) Perceived control, malodorous air pollution and behavioural after effects. Paper presented at the annual meeting of the Southeastern Psychological Association, New Orleans.

Sansone C., Weir C., Harpster L. & Morgan, C. (1992) Once a boring task always a boring task? Interest as a self-regulatory mechanism. *Journal of Personality and Social Psychology* 63: 379–90.

Saegert S. (1975) Effects of spacial and social density on arousal, mood, and social orientation. *Dissertation Abstracts International* January, 35(7-B), 3649.

Sanders J.L. (1978) Relation of a personal space to the human menstrual cycle. *Journal of Psychology* 100(2d), 275–8.

Sauser W.L., Arauz C.G. & Chambers R.M. (1978) Exploring the relationship between level of office noise and salary recommendations: a preliminary research note. *Journal of Management* 4: 57–63.

Schneider H.A. (1946) On breeding 'wild' house mice in the laboratory. *Proceedings of the Society for Experimental Biology New York* 63: 1615.

Schultz P.W. & Zelezny L. (1999) Values as predictors of environmental attitudes: evidence for consistency across 14 countries. *Journal of Environmental Psychology* 19: 255–65.

Sherman P.W., Jarvis J.U.M. & Braude S.H. (1992) Naked mole rats. *Scientific American* 245: 102–10.

Shon S.K. & Kim S.H. (2000) The perspective on housing policy of Korea: a transition from housing supply to stock housing management. *Proceedings of the 16th IAPS Conference, Paris, France (4–7 July)*, page 107.

Sinha S.P. & Sinha S.P. (1991) Personal space and density as factors in task performance and feeling of crowding. *Journal of Social Psychology* 131(6): 831–7.

Skorjanc A.D. (1991) Differences in interpersonal distance among non-offenders as a function of perceived violence of offenders. *Perceptual and Motor Skills* 73(2): 659–62.

Sommer R. (1987) Crime and vandalism in univeristy residence halls: a confirmation of defensible space theory. *Journal of Environmental Psychology* 7(1): 1–12.

Staples S.L., Cornelius R.R. & Gibbs M.S. (1999) Disturbance from a developing airport: Perceived risk or general annoyance? *Environment and Behaviour* 31: 692–710.

Stevens S.S. (1956) The direct estimation of sensory magnitudes – loudness. *American Journal of Psychology* 69: 1–25.

Stewart W.P. & Cole D.N. (2001) Number of encounters and experience quality in Grand Canyon backcountry: consistently negative and weak relationships. *Journal of Leisure Research* 33: 106–20.

Stroebe N. & Stroebe M. (1987) *Bereavement and Health.* New York: Cambridge University Press.

Tanner C. (1999) Constraints on environmental behaviour. *Journal of Environmental Psychology* 19: 145–57.

Taylor R.B. (1978) Human territoriality: a review and a model for future research. *Cornell Journal of Social Relations* 13: 125–51.

Taylor R.B., Gottfredson S.D. & Brower S. (1984) Understanding block crime and fear. *Journal of Research in Crime and Delinquency* 21: 303–31.

Taylor S.M. (1984) A path model of aircraft noise annoyance. *Journal of Sound and Vibration* 96: 243–60.

Taylor S. & Todd P. (1995) An integrated model of waste management behaviour: a test of household recycling and composting intentions. *Environment and Behaviour* 27: 603–30.

Teare J.F., Smith G.L., Osgood D.W., Peterson R.W., Authrier K. & Daly D.L. (1995) Ecological influences in youth crisis shelters: effects of social density and length of stay on youth problem behaviours. *Journal of Child and Family Studies* 4: 89–101.

Turner R.H. & Killian L.M. (1972) *Collective behaviour.* Englewood Cliffs, NJ: Prentice-Hall.

Verhallen T.M.M. & Van Raaji W.F. (1981) Household behaviour and the use of natural gas for home heating. *Journal of Consumer Research* 8: 253–7.

Vining J. & Ebreo A. (1990) What makes a recycler? A comparison of recyclers and nonrecyclers. *Environment and Behaviour* 22: 55–73.

Waddington D., Jones K. & Critcher C. (1987) Flashpoints of public disorder. In Gaskill G. & Benewick R. (eds) *The crowd in contemporary Britain.* London: Sage.

Wang T.H. & Katzev R.D. (1990) Group commitment and resource conservation: two field experiments on promoting recy-

cling. *Journal of Applied Social Psychology* 20: 265–75.

Wells M.M. (2000) Office clutter or meaningful personal displays: the role of office personalisation in employee and organizational well-being. *Journal of Environmental Psychology* 11: 373–86.

Werner C.M. & Makela E. (1998) Motivations and behaviours that support recycling. *Journal of Environmental Psychology* 18: 373–86.

Werner C.M., Turner J., Shipman K., Twitchell F.S., Dickson B.R., Bruschke G.V. & von Bismarck W.B. (1995) Commitment, behaviour, and attitude change: an analysis of voluntary recycling. *Journal of Environmental Psychology* 15: 197–208.

Willis F.N. & Rawdon V.A. (1994) Gender and national differences in attitudes to same-gender touch. *Perceptual and Motor Skills* 78(Pt 1): 1027–34.

Willis F.N., Rinck C.M. & Dean L.M. (1978) Interpersonal touch among adults in cafeteria lines. *Perceptual and Motor Skills* 47: 1147–52.

Winneke G. & Kastka J. (1987) Comparison of odour-annoyance data from different industrial sources: problems and implications. In Koelega H.S. (ed) *Environmental annoyance: characterization, measurement and control* (pages 129–38). Amsterdam: Elsevier Science.

Wolf N. & Feldman E. (1991) *Plastics: America's packaging dilemma.* Washington, DC: Island Press.

Wren K. (1999) *Social influences.* London, Routledge. .

Yildirim A. & Kulodlu N. (2000) The planning criterias of decreasing of vandalism in urban open space. *Proceedings of the 16th IAPS Conference, Paris, France (4–7 July)*, page 120.

Yinon Y. & Bizman A. (1980) Noise, success and failure as determinants of helping behaviour. *Personality and Social Psychology Bulletin* 6: 125–30.

Zimbardo P.G. (1970) The human choice: individuation, reason, and order versus deindividuation, impulse and chaos. In Arnold W.J. & Levine D. (eds) *Nebraska Symposium on Motivation* 1969(17): 237–307. Lincoln: University of Nebraska Press.

Zimmer K. & Ellermeier W. (1999) Psychometric properties of four measures of noise sensitivity: a comparison. *Journal of Environmental Psychology* 19: 295–302.

Methodology in psychology

Aarts H., Dijksterhuis A. & De Vries P. (2001) On the psychology of drinking: being thirsty and perceptually ready. *British Journal of Psychology* 92: 631–42.

Ambady N., Hallahan M. & Conner B.

(1999) Accuracy of judgements of sexual orientation from thin slices of behavior. *Journal of Personality and Social Psychology* 77: 538–47.

Angbratt M. & Moller M. (1999) Questionnaire about calcium intake: can we trust the answers? *Osteoporosis International* 9(3): 220–5.

Banister P., Burman E., Parker I., Taylor M. & Tindall C. (1994) *Qualitative methods in psychology: a research guide.* Buckingham: Open University Press.

Bartels A. & Zeki S. (2000) The neural basis of romantic love. *Neuroreport* 11: 3829–34.

Breakwell G.M. (1995) Interviewing. In Breakwell G.M., Hammond S. & Fife-Shaw C. (eds) *Research methods in psychology*, chapter 15, pages 230–42. London: Sage Publications.

Brissette I., Scheier M.F. & Carver C.S. (2002) The role of optimism in social network development, coping, and psychological adjustment during a life transition. *Journal of Personality and Social Psychology* 82(1): 102–11.

British Psychological Society (1985) *Guidelines for the use of animals in research.* Leicester: British Psychological Society.

British Psychological Society (1998) *Code of conduct, ethical principles and guidelines.* Leicester: British Psychological Society.

Brodsky W. (2001) The effect of music tempo on simulated driving performance and vehicular control. *Transportation Research* 4: 219–41.

Bryman A. (1988) *Quality and quantity in social research.* London: Unwin Hyman.

Clark W.M. & Serovich J.M. (1997) Twenty years and still in the dark? Content analysis of articles pertaining to gay, lesbian and bisexual issues in marriage and family therapy journals. *Journal of Marriage and Family Therapy* 23(3): 239–53.

Cooper N. & Stevenson C. (1998) 'New science' and psychology. *The Psychologist* 11(10): 484–5.

Dabbs J.M. Jr, Bernieri F.J., Strong R.K., Campo R. & Milun R. (2001) Going on stage: testosterone in greetings and meetings. *Journal of Research in Personality* 35: 27–40.

Deręgowski J.B., McGeorge P. & Wynn V. (2000) The role of left–right symmetry in the encodement of spatial orientations. *British Journal of Psychology* 91: 241–57.

Driscoll J.W. & Bateson P. (1988) Animals in behavioural research. *Animal Behaviour* 36: 1569–74.

DuRant R.H., Rome E.S., Rich M., Allred E., Emans S.J. & Woods E.R. (1997) Tobacco and alcohol use behaviors portrayed in music videos: a content analysis. *American Journal of Public Health* 87(7): 1131–5.

Edmonds A.J. (2002) Are you looking at my pint? *The Psychologist* 15(3): 141.

Edmonds A.J. (2002) On the 'ring' road. *The Psychologist* 15(1): 36.

Escamilla G., Cradock A.L. & Kawachi I. (2000) Women and smoking in Hollywood movies: a content analysis. *American Journal of Public Health* 90(3): 412–14.

Féry Y.-A. & Vom Hofe A. (2000) When will the ball rebound? Evidence for the usefulness of mental analogues in appraising the duration of motions. *British Journal of Psychology* 91: 259–73.

Fitzsimons G.M. & Bargh J.A. (2003) Thinking of you: nonconscious pursuit of interpersonal goals associated with relationship partners. *Journal of Personality and Social Psychology* 84(1): 148–63.

Frone M.R. (2003) Predictors of overall and on-the-job substance use among young workers. *Journal of Occupational Health Psychology* 8(1): 39–54.

Frood A. (2002) Dope at the wheel. *New Scientist* 23 March 2002. Report of an unpublished report from the Transport Research Laboratory, led by B. Sexton.

Frydenberg E., Lewis R., Kennedy G., Ardila R., Frindte W. & Hannoun R. (2003) Coping with concerns: an exploratory comparison of Australian, Colombian, German and Palestinian adolescents. *Journal of Youth and Adolescence* 32(1): 59–66.

Gillett G. (1995) The philosophical foundations of qualitative psychology. *The Psychologist* 8(3): 111–14.

Gosling S.D., Ko S.J., Mannarelli T. & Morris M.E. (2002) A room with a cue: Personality judgements based on offices and bedrooms. *Journal of Personality and Social Psychology* 82(3): 379–98.

Griffin A. (1995) Verbal protocol analysis. *The Psychologist* 8(3): 126–9.

Grubb N.R., Fox K.A., Smith K., Blane A., Ebmeier K.P. Glabus, M.F. & O'Carroll R.E. (2000) Memory impairment in out-of-hospital cardiac arrest survivors is associated with global reduction in brain volume, not focal hippocampal injury. *Stroke* 31(7): 1509–14.

Guegen N. (2001) Effect of humor on hitchhiking: a field experiment. *North American Journal of Psychology* 3: 369–76.

Hamer M. (2002) Death by music. *New Scientist* 16 March 2002: 8.

Harding S. (1991) *Whose science? Whose knowledge? Thinking women's lives.* Milton Keynes: Open University Press.

Harrell A.W., Bowlby J.W. & Hall-Hoffarth D. (2000) Directing wayfinders with maps: the effects of age, route complexity and familiarity with the environment. *The Journal of Social Psychology* 140: 169–78.

Hartley J., Howe M. & McKeachie W. (2001) Writing through time: longitudinal studies of the effects of new technology on writing. *British Journal of Educational Technology* 32(2): 141–51.

Haverkate I., Muller M.T., Cappetti M., Jonkers F.J. & van der Wal G. (2000) Prevalence and content analysis of guidelines on handling requests for euthanasia or assisted suicide in Dutch nursing homes. *Archives of International Medicine* 160(3): 317–22.

Hayashi M., Iwanaga T., Mitoku K. & Minowa M. (1999) Getting a high response rate of sexual behaviour survey among the general population in Japan: three different methods of survey on sexual behaviour. *Journal of Epidemiology* 9(2): 107–13.

Hayes N. (ed) (1997) *Doing qualitative analysis in psychology.* London: Psychology Press.

Hemmings B., Smith M., Graydon J. & Dyson R. (2000) Effect of massage on physiological restoration, perceived recovery and repeated sports performance. *British Journal of Sports Medicine* 34: 109–15.

Henwood K. & Nicolson P. (1995) Qualitative research. *The Psychologist* 8(3): 109–10.

Henwood K. & Pidgeon N. (1995) Grounded theory and psychological research. *The Psychologist* 8(3): 115–18.

Hofling K.C., Brotzman E., Dalrymple S., Graves N. & Pierce C.M. (1966) An experimental study in the nurse–physician relationship. *Journal of Nervous and Mental Disorders* 143: 171–80.

Humphreys L. (1970) *Tearoom trade.* London: Gerald Duckworth & Co.

Jang K.L., Livesely W.J. & Vernon P.A. (1999) The relationship between Eysenck's P-E-N model of personality and traits delineating personality disorder. *Personality and Individual Differences* 26: 121–8.

Johnson S. (1999) The 'horrors' of scientific research. *The Psychologist* 12(4): 186–9.

Kirk J.M. & de Wit H. (2000) Individual differences in the priming effect of ethanol in social drinkers. *Journal for the Study of Alcohol* 61(1): 64–71.

Kissinger P., Rice J., Farley T., Trim S., Jewitt K., Margavio V. & Martin D.H. (1999) Application of computer-assisted interviews to sexual behaviour research. *American Journal of Epidemiology* 149(10): 950–4.

Leaper C. (2000) Gender, affiliation, assertion, and the interactive context of parent–child play. *Developmental Psychology* 36: 381–93.

Lewis M.K. & Hill A.J. (1998) Food advertising on British children's television: a content analysis and experimental study with nine-year olds. *International Journal of Obesity and Related Metabolic Disorders* 22(3): 206–14.

Lluch A., Hubert P., King N.A. & Blundell J.E. (2000) Selective effects of acute exercise and breakfast interventions on mood and motivation to eat. *Physiology and Behaviour* 68: 515–20

Lund E. & Gram I.T. (1998) Response rate according to title and length of questionnaire. *Scandinavian Journal of Social Medicine* 26(2): 154–60.

Lyddy F. & Martin N. (2001) E-male or female? *The Psychologist* 14(8): 433.

Lyddy F. (2002) Revealing yourself – briefly. *The Psychologist* 13(2): 91.

MacDonald T.K., Fong G.T., Zanna M.P. & Martineau A.M. (2000) Alcohol myopia and condom use: can alcohol intoxication be associated with more prudent behaviour? *Journal of Personality and Social Psychology* 78: 605–19.

Magai C., Kennedy G., Cohen C.I. & Gomberg D. (2000) A controlled clinical trial of sertraline in the treatment of depression in nursing home patients with late-stage Alzheimer's disease. *American Journal of Geriatric Psychiatry* 8(1): 66–74.

Maguire E.A., Gadian D.G., Johnsrude I.S., Good C.D., Ashburner J., Frackowiak R.S. & Frith C.D. (2000) Navigation-related structural changes in the hippocampi of taxi drivers. *Proceedings of the National Academy of Sciences USA* 97(8): 4398–403.

Martin N. (2000) Exercise – what is it good for? *The Psychologist* 13(7): 362–3.

Martin N. (2001) Cupid and the cortex. *The Psychologist* 14(3): 155.

Martin N. (2002) Clothes maketh the customer. *The Psychologist* 15(8): 424.

Martin N. (2002) Deceitful memory. *The Psychologist* 15(9): 482.

Martin N. (2002) Feeling optimistic? *The Psychologist* 15(6): 309.

Martin N. (2002) Hitch-hiking: a pointer. *The Psychologist* 15(4): 200.

Mays V. & Cochran S. (2001) Mental health correlates of perceived discrimination among lesbian, gay and bisexual adults in the United States. *American Journal of Public Health* 91: 1869–76.

McNicholas J. & Collis G.M. (2000) Dogs as catalysts for social interactions: robustness of the effect. *British Journal of Psychology* 91: 61–70.

Metzler C.W., Biglan A., Noell J., Ary D.V. & Ochs L. (2000) A randomised controlled trial of a behavioural intervention to reduce high-risk sexual behaviour among adolescents in STD clinics. *Behavior Therapy* 31: 27–54.

Morgan M. (1996) Qualitative research: a package death. *The Psychologist* 9(1): 31–2.

Morgan M. (1998) Postscript. *The Psychologist* 8(3): 488.

Morris P.H., Gale A. & Duffy K. (2002) Can judges agree on the personality of horses? *Personality and Individual Differences* 33(1): 67–81.

Morrison C.M. & Ellis A.W. (2000) Real age of acquisition of effects in word naming and lexical decision. *British Journal of Psychology* 91: 167–80.

Murphy S.A., Johnson L.C., Wu L., Fan J.J. & Lohan J. (2003) Bereaved parents' outcomes 4 to 60 months after their children's death by accident, suicide or homicide: A comparative study demonstrating differences. *Death Studies* 27(1): 39–61.

Neumayer L., McNamara R.M., Dayton M. & Kim B. (1998) Does volume of patients seen in an outpatient setting impact test scores? *American Journal of Surgery* 175(6): 511–14.

North A.C. & Hargreaves D.J. (2000) Musical preference during and after relaxation exercise. *American Journal of Psychology* 113: 43–67.

North A.C. & Hargreaves D.J. (2000) Musical preference during and after relaxation and exercise. *American Journal of Psychology* 113: 43–67.

Parker H.J. (1974) *View from the boys.* Newton Abbott: David & Charles.

Rajecki D.W., Rasmussen J.L. & Conner T.J. (2000) Relinquish the dog? Movie messages about misbehaviour. *Antrozoös* 13(3): 140–9.

Regan P.C. & Llamas V. (2002) Customer service as a function of shoppers' attire. *Psychological Reports* 90(1): 203–4.

Roberts C.A. (2000) UK UFO organisations: what do they have knowledge of and what do they investigate? *European Journal of UFO and Abduction Studies* 1(1): 26–32.

Roberts C.A., McBride E.A., Rosenvinge H.P., Stevenage S.V. & Bradshaw J.W.S. (1996) The pleasure of a pet: the effect of pet ownership and social support on loneliness and depression in a population of elderly people living in their own homes. *Proceedings for the Society for Companion Animal Studies Workshop September 1996*, University of Cambridge. Nicholson J. & Podberscek A. (eds). Callender: SCAS.

Roberts C.A., McBride E.A., Horn S., Rosenvinge H. & Bradshaw J.W.S. (1998) Pet ownership, social support and psychological health in community older adults. *Proceedings of the 8th International Conference on Human–Animal Interactions: the changing roles of animals in society*, 77. Praha: Ceska Republika.

Roberts C.A., Russell J. & Chandler E. (in press) What do children produce when asked to draw how an alien would travel to Earth? *European Journal of UFO and Abduction Studies.*

Robson C. (1993) *Real world research.* Oxford: Blackwell.

Rosenblum L.D., Yahal D.A. & Green K.P. (2000) Face and mouth inversion effects and audiovisual speech perception. *Journal of Experimental Psychology: Human Perception and Performance* 26: 809–19.

Rosenbluth R., Grossman E.S. & Kaitz M. (2000) Performance of early-blind and sighted children on olfactory tasks. *Perception* 29: 101–10.

Sherrard C. (1997) Qualitative research. *The Psychologist* 10(4): 161–2.

Sherrard C. (1998) Social dimensions of research. *The Psychologist* 11(10): 486–7.

Smith J.A. (1995) Qualitative methods, identity and transition to motherhood. *The Psychologist* 8(3): 122–5.

Stayer D.L. & Johnston W.A. (2001) Driven to distraction: dual-task studies of simulated driving and conversing on a cellular phone. *Psychological Science* 12: 462–6.

Stone-Carmen J. (1992) Personality characteristics and self-identified experiences of individuals reporting possible abduction by unidentified flying objects (UFOs). Dissertation as part fulfilment of a Doctorate in Philosophy and Psychology, San Diego, USA, 10–59.

Thomas A.K. & Loftus E.F. (2002) Creating bizarre false memories through imagination. *Memory and Cognition* 30(3): 423–31.

Thomson R. & Murchver T. (2001) Predicting gender from electronic discourse. *British Journal of Social Psychology* 40(2): 193–208.

Thomson R., Murchver T. & Green J. (2001) Where is the gender in gendered language? *Psychological Science* 121(2): 171–5.

Woolgar S. (1988) *Science: the very idea.* London: Tavistock.

Issues, perspectives and debates

Andersson B.E. (1996) Children's development related to day care, type of family and other home factors. *European Child and Adolescent Psychiatry* 5: 73-5.

Atkinson L., Niccols A., Paglia A. Cool bear J., Parker K.C.H. Poulton L., Guger S. & Sitarenios G. (2000) A meta-analysis of time between maternal sensitivity and attachment assessments: implications for internal working models in infancy/toddlerhood. *Journal of Social and Personal Relationships* 17: 791-810

Bandura A. (1977) *Social learning theory.* Engelwood Cliffs: Prentice Hall.

Baydar N. & Brooks-Gunn J. (1991) Effects of maternal employment and child-care arrangements on preschoolers' cognitive and behavioral outcomes: evidence from the children of the National Longitudinal Survey of Youth. *Developmental Psychology* 27: 932–45.

Belsky J., Steinberg L. & Draper P. (1991) Childhood experience, interpersonal development and reproductive strategy: an evolutionary theory of socialisation. *Child Development* 62: 647-70

Billen A. (2002) Full of their selves. *The New Statesman* March, 3–25.

Burman E. (1994) *Deconstructing developmental psychology.* London: Routledge.

Burr V. (1995) *An introduction to social construction.* London: Routledge.

Dare L. & Eisher I. (1997) Family therapy for anorexia nervosa. In: Garner D.M. & Garfinkel, P.E. (eds) *Handbook of treatment for eating disorders.* New York: Guilford.

Ellis A. (1962) *Reason and emotion in psychotherapy.* New York: Life Stuart.

Eysenck H.J. (1952) The effects of psychotherapy: an evaluation. *Journal of Consulting Psychology* 16: 319–24.

Gross R. (2001) *Psychology, the science of mind and behaviour.* London: Hodder & Stoughton.

Grossman K.E. & Grossman K. (1990) The wider concept of attachment in cross-cultural research. *Human Development* 33: 31–47.

Henry W.P. (1994) Psychodynamic approaches. In Bergin A.E. & Garfield S. (eds) *Handbook of psychotherapy and behaviour change.* New York: Wiley.

Jarvis M., Russell J., Flanagan C. & Dolan L. (2000) *Angles on psychology.* Cheltenham: Nelson Thornes.

Jarvis M. (2003) *Psychodynamic psychology: classical theory and contemporary research.* London: Thomson Learning.

Koren-Karie N. (2001) Mothers' attachment representations and choice of infant care; centre care vs home. *Infant and Child Development* 10: 117–27.

Parry G. (1996) *NHS psychotherapy services in England.* Wetherby: National Health Service Executive.

Philo G., Secker J., Platt S., Henderson L., McLaughlinG. & Burnside J. (1994) The impact of mass media on public images of mental illness: media content and audience belief. *Health Education Journal* 53: 271-281.

Popper K.R. (1969) *Conjectures and refutations.* London: Routledge.

Reicher S. & Hopkins N. (1996) Self category constructions on political rhetoric: an analysis of Thatcher's and Kinnock's speeches concerning the British miner's strike (1984-5). *European Journal of Social Psychology* 26: 353-71.

Rose H. & Rose S. (2000) *Alas poor Darwin.* London: Vintage.

Rosenhan D.L. (1973) On being sane in insane places. *Science* 179: 250-8, 365-9

Schlozman S. (2000) Vampires and those who slay them: using *Buffy the Vampire Slayer* in adolescent therapy and psychodynamic education. *Academic Psychiatry* 24: 49–54.

Thornhill R. & Palmer C. (2000). *A natural history of rape.* Cambridge: MIT Press.

index

Terms defined in the text are indicated by page numbers in **bold**. Figures or research boxes are shown by page numbers in *italics*.